COMMUNICAT
CANADIAN SOCIETY

FIFTH EDITION

RELATED TITLES FROM
THOMPSON EDUCATIONAL PUBLISHING
~ ~ ~

MEDIA AND MINORITIES
Representing Diversity in a Multicultural Canada
Augie Fleras and Jean Lock Kunz
ISBN 1-55077-123-X

CANADIAN SOCIAL TRENDS
Volumes 1, 2 and 3
Statistics Canada
ISBNs 1-55077-010-1 (Vol 1:), 1-55077-062-4 (Vol. 2), 1-55077-105-1 (Vol. 3)

For information on these and other titles:
www.thompsonbooks.com

Website for *Communications in Canadian Society*

One of the editors of this volume maintains an interesting list of website
links pertaining to communications in Canadian society.
You may go to this site from the book's main website at:
www.thompsonbooks.com/communications

Reader's Comments

If you have suggestions or information that might improve future editions of
this book, the editors and publisher would be pleased to hear from you.
Please send your comments to: author@thompsonbooks.com

COMMUNICATIONS IN CANADIAN SOCIETY

FIFTH EDITION

Edited by

CRAIG MCKIE

Carleton University

BENJAMIN D. SINGER

University of Western Ontario

THOMPSON EDUCATIONAL PUBLISHING, INC.

TORONTO

Information on how to obtain copies of this book may be obtained from:
  Web site: www.thompsonbooks.com
  E-mail: publisher@thompsonbooks.com
  Telephone: (416) 766-2763
  Fax: (416) 766-0398

National Library of Canada Cataloguing in Publication Data

Main entry under title:

Communications in Canadian society
5th ed.

ISBN 1-55077-118-3

1. Mass media - Social aspects - Canada. 2. Mass media - Canada - Influence. I. McKie, C. (Craig), 1944-   . II. Singer, Benjamin D., 1931-   .

HM1013.C65S55 2001   302.23'0971   C00-933246-4

Cover Design: Elan Designs

Every reasonable effort has been made to acquire permission for copyright materials used in this book and to acknowledge such permissions accurately. Any errors or omissions called to the publisher's attention will be corrected in future printings.

We acknowledge the support of the Government of Canada through the Book Publishing Industry Development Program for our publishing activities.

Printed in Canada.
1 2 3 4 5   06 05 04 03 02 01

Table of Contents

Preface

This fifth edition of *Communications in Canadian Society* marks its passage into the new millennium with a new editorial team headed by Professor Craig McKie, a new publisher, Thompson Educational Publishing, Inc., and several new authors who will be expanding the range of topics covered. The majority of the remaining essays have been updated.

Communications in Canadian Society has now been in print for a third of a century, marking a record for this field. During that time it has served as a multidisciplinary source, publishing essays by leading Canadian authorities in social scientific and applied areas of communication drawn from the fields of communication studies, journalism, political science, psychology, and sociology.

The goal of the text remains the same: to continue to function as a standard resource in providing the foremost analyses of Canadian communication processes and institutions. It is intended for use in classroom instruction at universities and other post-secondary institutions but has been helpful as a reference tool for research organizations and educational institutions.

The basic structure of the book has been retained. Part 1 comprises an overview of important Canadian media organizations and processes. Part 2 examines our transition as a society to the Information Age and the consequences of our transformation. Part 3 examines the processes and impact of communications media. The essays of Part 4 analyze problems of national control and policy. Part 5 is concerned with some of the most controversial social problems linked to communications media.

The rate of change in communications technology, technique, substance, and stylistics continues at an impressively high level. From one year to the next, many new services and much new content appears while some old forms fail. We could never hope to remain fully current in our content and approach given this state of affairs. Nevertheless, we continue to try to capture the essential core of Canadian communications institutions and behaviour as they exist and thrive in the new millennium.

CRAIG MCKIE
BENJAMIN D. SINGER

List of Contributors

Jody Berland teaches cultural studies in the Department of Humanities, Atkinson College, York University. She has published extensively on music, media, and social space, and on Canadian perspectives in cultural theory. She is co-editor of *Theory Rules: Art and Theory/ Theory as Art* (1996) and *Capital Culture: A Reader on State Institutions, Modernist Legacies and the Value(s) of Art* (2000). She is editor of *Topia: Canadian Journal of Cultural Studies*.

Roger Bird is an associate professor in the School of Journalism and Communications at Carleton University, where he has taught journalism history, the history of ideas, reporting, and the history of broadcasting. He is editor of *Documents of Canadian Broadcasting*. In his non-academic persona, Professor Bird has worked as an editor for various Canadian newspapers and news organizations such as Southam News and *The Ottawa Citizen*. He is a member of the Editorial Advisory Committee of *Canadian Geographic* and is a fellow of the Royal Canadian Geographical Society.

Augustine Brannigan is professor of Sociology at the University of Calgary. He has written widely on the sociology of science and the sociology of law. He is the author of *The Social Basis of Scientific Discoveries, Crimes, Courts and Corrections,* and numerous scholarly articles.

Robert S. Brown has been a research consultant and media analyst since 1983, and was with TVOntario's Evaluation and Project Research Department from 1984 to 1990. He is currently a project co-ordinator in the Academic Accountability Department of the Toronto District School Board. He studied Canadian history at the University of Western Ontario, holds an M.A. in Communication Studies from the University of Windsor and a doctorate in education from OISE/UT.

Peter Desbarats retired as dean of the Graduate School of Journalism at the University of Western Ontario. He has published widely on the Canadian media and is a renowned journalist, television commentator, and editor. He is also known as the author of the book *Guide to Canadian News Media*. He held the Maclean Hunter Chair of Communication Ethics in 2000-2001 at Ryerson Polytechnic University and is a director and research chair of the Canadian Journalism Foundation.

Philip Evans, co-author of *Blown to Bits*, is a senior vice-president in The Boston Consulting Group's Boston office and co-leader of BCG's Media and Convergence practice group. He is the co-author of three articles published in the *Harvard Business Review* and a frequent speaker on the new economics of information.

Prior to joining BCG, he obtained the top double first-class honours degree from Cambridge University in economics. He was subsequently a Harkness Fellow in the economics department at Harvard University and obtained an M.B.A. from the Harvard Business School.

Robert Everett lectures on politics and the mass media in the Department of Political Science at York University. He has written on media and elections, government-information services, and media coverage of public policy.

Augie Fleras teaches in the Department of Sociology at the University of Waterloo. He has published extensively in the areas of race and ethnic relations. His most recent publications include *Media and Minorities: Representing Diversity in a Multicultural Canada; Multiculturalism in Canada: The Challenge of Diversity; The Nations Within: Comparative Perspectives in Aboriginal-Government Relations* (both with Jean Leonard Elliot); *Diversity in Change: An Introduction to Sociology for Canadians,* and *Social Problems in Canada*.

Frederick J. Fletcher is professor of Political Science and in Environmental Studies at York University and Director of the Ryerson/York Joint Graduate Programme in Communication and Culture. He is co-author and editor of *Media, Elections and Democracy* and has written extensively on media and elections, communication policy, campaign advertising, and, most recently, on the media and national identity. He served as research co-ordinator, Media and Elections, for the Royal Commission on Electoral Reform and Party Financing.

Shari Graydon served for eight years as the national president of MediaWatch and has taught media analysis and women's studies at Simon Fraser University. Prior to becoming press secretary to the premier of British Columbia, she wrote a regular column for *The Vancouver Sun*, produced a 13-part TV series about women and the media for WTN, and provided media analysis commentary to CBC radio and television. Alison Jacques assisted her in assembling research for this chapter.

David R. Hall is an assistant professor of Sociology at Nipissing University. Prior to this, he was employed in market research at TVOntario. He has previously published on Canadian media and on family demography.

John A. Hannigan is professor of Sociology at the University of Toronto. He attended the University of Western Ontario and Ohio State University, where he received his Ph.D. in 1976. He is author of two books,

Environmental Sociology: A Social Constructionist Perspective (1995) *and Fantasy City* (1998), both published by Routledge. *Fantasy City* was nominated for the 1999/2000 John Porter Award. He is currently working on a book about the branding of the urban landscape. He recently began a three-year term as secretary of the Canadian Sociology and Anthropology Association.

Kelly Hardwick is a doctoral candidate in the Department of Sociology at the University of Calgary. He is currently doing research and teaching in criminology. Other research and academic interests include theories of action, criminological theory, ethnicity, immigration, and inequality.

John D. Jackson is a retired professor of sociology. He was a co-founder and past director of the Concordia University Centre for Broadcast Studies. He is author of *Community & Conflict*, as well as articles on cultural and community studies, and is co-editor of several books on radio drama.

Kathleen McConnell is a doctoral candidate in Culture, Communications and Society at the Institute of Education, University of London. She is researching how the media influence children's conceptions of peace. From 1990-92, she worked in Japan for Mombusho and from 1992-95 she taught sociology and communications for the European Division of the University of Maryland. She lives in London and Northern Italy.

Tannis MacBeth is in the Department of Psychology at the University of British Columbia, where she has contributed to the development of both an undergraduate major in women's studies and the university's Centre for Research in Women's Studies and Gender Relations. She has done media content analysis and has conducted research into the effects of television on behaviour. She is also well known for her feminist research and publications in other aspects of developmental psychology.

Craig McKie teaches sociology at Carleton University when not living in British Columbia. He recently published a Canadian edition of Shirley Biagi's textbook *Media Impact* and prior to that published two books on using the Web in the social sciences. Previously, he was for six years editor-in-chief of *Canadian Social Trends*, Statistics Canada's social statistical quarterly.

John Meisel retired as the Sir Edward Peacock Professor of Political Science at Queen's University and president of the Royal Society of Canada. In the early 1980s he served for almost four years as the chair of the Canadian Radio-television and Telecommunications Commission.

Andrew M. Osler, until his recent untimely death, taught courses in communications theory, policy, and media ethics in the Graduate School of Journalism at the University of Western Ontario. He worked as a reporter for the *Toronto Star* and *The Globe and Mail* before shifting to an academic career. He served as a researcher and consultant for a number of media research inquiries, and his book, *News, the Evolution of Journalism in Canada*, was published in 1993.

Robert M. Pike is professor of Sociology at Queen's University. He divides his research between the fields of education and sociohistorical research on the diffusion of new communications systems and technologies. He has published a number of articles on the social consequences of the development of postal and telephone services in Canada.

Jonathan Rose teaches and researches Canadian politics and political communications in the Department of Political Studies at Queen's University. He is the author of *Making Pictures in Our Heads: Government Advertising in Canada.*

Benjamin D. Singer is emeritus professor of Sociology at the University of Western Ontario. He is author of *Advertising and Society,* as well as books and articles on such subjects as mass communication, collective behaviour, and the sociology of standards.

David R. Spencer is former president of the American Journalism Historians Association and is an associate professor in the Faculty of Information and Media Studies at the University of Western Ontario.

Will Straw is an associate professor of Communications within the Department of Art History and Communications Studies at McGill University in Montreal. He has published in the areas of culture and media studies and has served as president of the Canadian Communications Association.

Eugene D. Tate is emeritus professor of Sociology at University of Saskatchewan, Saskatoon. He taught communication studies from 1970 to 1992 in the Department of Sociology, St. Thomas More College. He was the second editor of the *Canadian Journal of Communication* from 1982 to 1986. From 1992 to 1996 he taught communication and social psychology for the European Division of the University of Maryland. He has published articles in communication and religious studies. He edited the volume on Media and Violence published in *Peace Research Reviews* (15, Nos. 4, 5 [2000]).

Edward J. (Ted) Withers worked at TVOntario in a variety of research positions from 1982 to 1995, serving as manager of audience research, 1989-95. Since 1995, he has worked at ICOM Information and Communications, and maintains an abiding interest in media and audience measurement. He holds a Ph.D. in Sociology from McGill University, an M.A. from the University of New Orleans, and a B.Sc. from Florida State University.

Thomas S. Wurster, co-author of *Blown to Bits*, is a vice-president with The Boston Consulting Group and leads the Los Angeles office. He is also co-leader of BCG's Media and Convergence practice group. He writes on media and strategy and received his Ph.D. in Economics from Yale University.

PART 1

CANADIAN MEDIA INSTITUTIONS AND AUDIENCES

For most of the twentieth century, the traditional mass media–newspapers, magazines, and broadcasting–were the principal means by which Canadians received news, information, and entertainment. Although they are called "media," suggesting that they are simply carriers of data, the organs of mass communication are themselves social institutions–organizations whose structures and dynamics must be examined prior to any analysis of their content and impact. Thus, in this introductory section, the authors provide a critical overview of the structure, the underlying business infrastructure, and the audiences of the institutions of mass communication in Canada. While one focus is upon structure–that which endures–yet another is upon the dynamics of change and the interplay of forces that produce change.

David R. Hall provides an introduction to the larger picture by presenting and analyzing recent trends in Canada in the growth of mass media, ranging from daily newspapers to radio, television, cable, and videocassette recorders, and the more recent advent of individualized media such as is delivered on the Internet.

In what might be described as an "ecology of media" approach, he links the changes in the media to changes in economic and social structure and developments in technology. For example, sociological forces such as population growth and urban development, as well as changes in working hours, helped shape the differential growth of mass media. The population shift to cities in the 1920s helped to provide the urban population base needed for the introduction and growth of such forms of communication as newspapers, motion pictures, radio, and, eventually, television. Moreover, the shift from agricultural to industrial work made possible more time for leisure, thus creating more potential for use of mass media.

Hall also anticipates fuller treatments later in the text by taking account of the role of new technology and its effect on the survival of specific forms of media. As he reveals, competition from TV and videocassette recorders has changed our definition of "movies"; per-capita attendance in theatres has plummeted by more than two-thirds in a few decades, while "home attendance" through cable and videotape has increased. Simultaneously, newspaper circulation, also a victim of electronic media, has been declining. Yet radio–once considered the major victim of the new media–continues to prosper by changing its format and content.

Roger Bird details five stages through which the Canadian press has evolved, from the first press period of small populations, high illiteracy, and a single editor who did most of the work on a newspaper, through to the present fifth-press period, in which the newspaper enters the Information Age. If the prerequisites for the viability of early newspapers were an adequate population base, a healthy socioeconomic climate, and good physical conditions, then technology has come to play an increasingly important role, with the emergence of new media that has threatened to usurp the news function of the press.

As population growth levelled off, at a time when technology helped generate threats from new media, newspapers began the process of rationalization, during the fifth press period, by developing cheaper electronic typesetting, and by initiating the movement towards concentration. The newspaper survived its entry into the information age, but witnessed the demise of the evening edition due to competition from television news and its virtual replacement by the morning paper. Nearly as many new newspapers were born as died during the crucial years of 1964-90. Competition from other media in the 1960s made it possible for news consumers to "pick from a plethora of sources." Yet the newspaper adapted to the very electronics that made possible its competition, for satellites and computers cut costs and increased the velocity of the news process for newspapers, and the adoption of computer-generated informational news graphics satisfied the reader who grew up watching television.

The message of the history of the Canadian press is *struggle, adaptation, and survival.* The newspaper's adaptability—through population changes, economic turmoil, and technology-driven competition—saw it enter the new Internet-based environment still a vital institution.

The history of Canadian broadcasting comprises two "waves" of development in Robert Pike's essay, the earlier roughly corresponding to radio broadcasting and its technological infrastructure, and the latter, television, based on "visual technology." Within either wave, the key variables in the Canadian broadcasting environment may be seen as dichotomies of choice: public versus private, American versus Canadian, monolingualism versus bilingualism, national interest or centralization versus local interest. The power of communications media to aid in building a distinct Canadian identity, once considered the most compelling argument for substantial government funding of public broadcasting, is questioned, notwithstanding the present need to provide increased financial support to the Canadian Broadcasting Corporation (CBC). It should be noted, as Pike makes clear, that the freedom to make such choices is limited by the increasing power of technological innovation to influence or determine them.

Peter Desbarats traces the history of Canadian magazines from the first magazine in 1789 to the contemporary "reinvention" of themselves as media that fill selective audience niches. Their history is a struggle that seems to mirror the Canadian experience, for as Desbarats says, "the Canadian magazine industry has been torn between the desire for independence and the need for protection." Desbarats's historical analysis demonstrates that, more than any other medium, the Canadian magazine has suffered from the competition of U.S. publications. As he points out, there have been times in this century when as many as eight U.S. magazines were sold for one Canadian magazine sold. To assuage this problem, the Canadian government, through a series of ambivalent laws, applied tariffs to the sales price of U.S. magazines, and in more recent years has taxed Canadian advertising in them in order to encourage support for Canadian magazines. Paradoxically, the problems that afflicted magazines universally in the 1990s may be increasing the capability of Canadian magazines to withstand the assault from without.

In David Spencer's article on political cartooning in early Canada, we get a glimpse of the power once wielded by printed political commentary and in particular the focussed power of the acid political cartoon in bringing down governments and punishing offending politicians through public ridicule. While political satire today is most often found in television programs, its origins in Canada can be traced back to the earliest days of political journalism.

If any expression truly fits a society, certainly "ratings society" characterizes ours. People (often referred to as "markets") are constantly probed for their attitudes, likes, desires, and potential behaviours with respect to household products, cars, politics, and television programs. Given the emphasis of a society on collective measures of potential behaviour, institutions specializing in such measurement, known as "criterial industries," have emerged and have acquired enormous power to guide our standards.[1] Of these, some of the most venerable serve broadcasting firms, and their findings with respect to audience behaviour and attitudes guide the producers of TV programs and radio stations. Today's ratings determine tomorrow's content. Hence it is important for an industry that accounts for so much of our time to understand the mechanisms by which such decisions are made. Given that, we may ask not only what such measurement reveals about broadcast audiences, but about the very accuracy of their portraits of audiences.

Tomorrow's TV content may be a function not only of audience choice but also of the idiosyncracies of the tools of measurement. The diary method of former times, which told us that adult women watched more than 26 hours of television per week, that viewing drops in the month of June, or that Canadians spend twice as much time watching news and public-affairs programs as variety and game shows, may be in error. The traditional measurements of audiences, which have been primary determinants of future content and advertising expenditures, are being replaced by new technologies of assessment, "people meters," which sharply reduce turn-around time for the data and, more importantly, may be a more accurate tool of the ratings society.

John D. Jackson contributes an entirely new dimension to the analysis of the relationship of mass media to identity. If others are concerned with cross-national media flows and their effects on national identity, Jackson, employing content analysis, examines the historical role of one Canadian medium, radio broadcasting, in helping to fortify Canadian identities.

Jackson argues that "Canadianness" and identity must be fashioned from materials of the culture. It is an active process in which institutions may consciously work at generating a specific identity—national, regional, linguistic, or other. "The authority conferred to central institutions allows them to capture the means of communication." Radio and, later, TV have been given a mandate for the promotion of national identity.

Yet the process is not an easy one, for identity-building inevitably generates a conflict over limited resources. There is a kind of dynamic equilibrium of opposing forces that is brought into play when there is an imbalance—a movement towards continentalism prompting reactive nationalism; the latter, if stressed too strongly, functions as a regional reaction.

With great skill, Jackson analyzes the content of broadcasting media historically and he is able to show its nationalist motives in opposition to continentalism (or American culture), as well as to illuminate the dynamics of the nexus between communication systems and identity. Promotion of public broadcasting is the most likely way to promote nationalist motives. This may then bring into play opposition from private groups. However, as Jackson points out, broadcasting in the service of nationalism (as opposed to continentalism) tends to subordinate regional interests. In this he agrees with the Canadian economist Harold Innis, who described radio's sociological impact as facilitating centralization.

Thus, we see that communications media are not only tools of a nation's identity but also mirror the conflicts and struggles of the different interests that seek to determine that identity. Those interests are represented by political institutions.

Note

[1] See Benjamin D. Singer, "Dependence on ratings services impairs critical judgment," *The Globe and Mail* (30 December 1993), p.A22.

1

The Growth of the Mass Media in Canada

David R. Hall[1]

The examination of the growth of mass communication within societies is attracting increasing attention from social historians and sociologists, as well as other social scientists. There are a number of reasons for this, not the least of which is the controversy over the exact nature of the relationship between the extent of mass communication and the level of economic and social development within a country.[2] Although controversy continues over the direction of this relationship–whether mass media *cause* cultural, political, or economic changes, or whether such changes are normally accompanied by accelerated growth of the mass media–there is agreement that all developed societies have an extensive mass communication infrastructure.

The purpose of this essay is to examine the growth trends of the various forms of mass communication in Canada during the last century. Such an examination will serve primarily to indicate the extent of the pervasiveness of Canadian mass media penetration, and will provide the initial data and impetus for those wishing to explore further the role of mass communication as a possible agent for social change in Canadian society. Before examining these trends, it would be useful to place them in a broader context, namely the development of the concept of "mass society" during the nineteenth and twentieth centuries.[3]

The Development of Mass Society

Although the model of society implied in the terms industrialization and mass society is still debated, much of the world experienced dramatic shifts in economic, political, and social structures in the twentieth century. These shifts were marked by sustained and often rapid increases in economic output, increases in capital-intensive production, and a decline in the percentage of the labour force engaged in agriculture, primary industry, and, more recently, manufacturing. There was a corresponding rise in the percentage of the population working in the service and information or "knowledge" sectors of the economy.[4] These economic changes were accompanied by an expansion in transportation and communications infrastructures. As well, literacy increased rapidly in most developed and developing societies because of advances in systems of formal education. The mass media have also shown enormous growth and pervasiveness in developed nations. Admittedly, there are many theoretical difficulties and uncertainties regarding the part played by communications media in the modernization process, but it is widely accepted that a country's level of mass communication sophistication is a valid indicator of social, political, and economic development.[5]

Although these are all quantifiable changes, industrialization has also brought about corresponding shifts in social structures, beliefs, values, and expectations. The middle class holds a dominant position of authority in most industrial societies, while the population as a whole has been afforded increasing opportunities for democratic political participation. It is worth noting, however, that the organizational and technological changes accompanying the transition to "post-industrial" could materially undermine the position of the middle class.[6]

Many social theorists have discussed the emergence of mass society, although there is no consensus on the defining characteristics of such, and whether it is a positive or negative phenomenon.[7] Nevertheless, the development of modern society has been crucially determined by the growth and proliferation of various forms of mass communication (usually identified with mass society) and their ability to reduce the perceived distance between individuals and groups. According to some observers, this has encouraged greater empathy or "psychological openness" among the population, as well as a wider recognition of the common needs and values of society. Hence, as the mass media become a more powerful social force, geographic and social distance become less salient, and the end results are tendencies towards unity, centralization, and integration.[8]

Some theorists have suggested that such tendencies are potentially dangerous and could produce "rule by the mob," "tribalism," or totalitarian political states. Others argue that the "global village"

TABLE 1: Population of Canada: Urban vs. Rural, 1901-1996

Year	Total Population	Urban (%)	Rural (%)
1901	5,371,315	37.0	63.0
1911	7,206,643	43.7	56.3
1921	8,787,949	48.4	51.6
1931	10,376,786	53.7	46.3
1941	11,506,605	56.9	43.1
1951	14,009,429	62.9	37.1
1956	16,080,791	66.6	33.4
1971	20,014,880	73.6	26.4
1981	24,343,181	75.7	23.7
1991	27,296,860	76.5	23.5
1996	28,847,761	77.9	22.1

Sources: For 1901-56, Census Bulletin; for 1971, Statistics Canada; for 1981, Census of Canada; for 1991, Census Profile Bulletin No. 94-129; for 1996, Census Profile Bulletin No. 93-357.

engendered by the expansion of the mass media has decisively contributed to market integration among leading industrialized countries. Within this emerging global economy, concerns have been raised about cultural independence, social fragmentation, regional inequality, and the shift of political power away from democratic institutions and towards great corporations. In this regard, the concentration of mass media ownership in the hands of relatively few private corporations, combined with the convergence of various mass media, is cause for concern.[9] Of course, the development of mass society, especially on a global scale, is likely to have negative effects, but it would be difficult to deny that societies have benefitted from improved mass communication systems.

The Historical Examination of Mass Media Growth

An examination of the historical growth pattern of the mass media in society can also add to an understanding of how these same media function today. First, it allows us to infer the impact of the society on the development of various forms of mass communication, and the political, economic, or cultural conditions that have shaped the media into their present form. Second, it provides clues as to how the media function in that society: What is the process of mass communications, and how does it differ from the more direct (personal) forms of communication it often replaces? Third, and perhaps more important, it outlines the impact that mass communications have had on the society: How have they reshaped

the beliefs, values, and behaviour of the population?[10]

In the past, historians and sociologists have neglected the mass media as major elements in the processes of social change. Fortunately, the work of Harold A. Innis, Lawrence W. Stone, Marshall McLuhan, and the recent work of Alvin Toffler and Neil Postman, has created greater awareness of the importance of communication systems as historical and sociological determinants.[11]

The Growth of the Mass Media in Canada

The growth and development of the mass media in Canada should be examined in the context of the shift in demographic patterns during the last 100 years. As Table 1 indicates, it was not until the early 1930s that Canada became a predominately urban-based society, about a decade later than the United States. This population shift to the cities had a profound effect on the development of the mass media since it provided the broad population base necessary for the successful introduction of commercially based forms of communication, such as newspapers, motion pictures, radio, and television. Without a strong urban concentration of population, mass communication delivery costs would have become prohibitive, but with a guaranteed audience in close geographic proximity, delivery costs to a wider area could be subsidized.

As the Canadian population moved into cities, people left behind traditional, rural forms of recreation. In order to fill this cultural vacuum, new urban-based recreational and leisure pursuits were

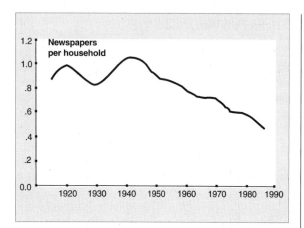

FIGURE 1: Daily Newspaper Circulation in Canada, 1920-1987

created; foremost among these were various forms of mass communication. Also, with the shift from agriculture to manufacturing and services, most workers in urban areas found relatively more time for recreational activity.

The Growth of Newspapers

The first major form of mass communication in Canada was the daily newspaper.[12] Table 2 shows the readership of daily newspapers in Canada per household from 1921 to 1997. Figure 1 plots the diffusion curve for daily newspapers in the same period. Newspaper readership per household reached its peak in the 1950s, although the total daily circulation has continued to rise. The curve of diffusion shows characteristics of the "S" shape, which is more or less typical of the acceptance pattern for innovations by a given population.[13]

It is interesting to compare the differences between the patterns of acceptance of the mass media in the U.S. and Canada, since it is generally assumed that the two countries constitute one giant "media monolith." This is not in fact an accurate assumption, as each society has been subjected to different pressures at different times in its history, and this is reflected in the differences in media growth patterns. For example, in the U.S. newspaper readership reached its peak in the 1920s, 30 years earlier than in Canada. Several factors account for this: first, the move to a predominantly urban society came later in Canada; second, there was a fairly dramatic population growth in Canada after 1945, due mainly to immigration from Europe, and most of this additional population moved into urban areas; third, because of this new population, the other competing forms of

mass communication, such as radio and news magazines, do not serve as functional alternatives in the same way as they did in the U.S.[14] However, with the introduction of television into Canada in the early 1950s there has been a gradual shift away from newspapers as the primary source of news. Notwithstanding the recent launch of a new Canadian daily in the *National Post*, the decline in newspaper readership has continued throughout the 1990s with uncertain implications for the future of print newspapers in Canada. Of course, most major newspapers in Canada now publish electronic editions of their papers on the Internet, and these "virtual papers" are to some extent countering the decline in print readership.

Despite the decline in readership per household, newspapers continue to play an important role in the social fabric of Canada. However, Canada suffers from the problem that has plagued all industrialized countries, as the ownership of daily newspapers becomes concentrated in the hands of a few major newspaper chains.[15] Before the First World War, there were 138 daily newspapers in Canada, each with its own publisher. Despite a sixfold increase in Canada's population since 1901, the number of dailies actually declined to 105 in 1996. More important, over one-half of these newspapers are now being produced by only two publishing companies (Southam and Thomson), with nearly three-quarters of Canada's total newspaper circulation controlled by the four largest publishing companies–Southam, Thomson, Sun Media, and Hollinger.[16] This growing concentration of corporate control has raised a number of concerns with respect to the current and future role of newspapers in Canada.[17]

The question of technological innovations, and their impact on the structure of the newspaper industry, is one that has received a great deal of attention. For example, the use of satellites for transmitting "computerized" newspaper copy to printing facilities across the country could exacerbate concentration of ownership. On the other hand, the development of "e-newspapers," with print and pictures electronically available to readers through the Internet, will give readers greater choice and control over the content of their newspapers. Given the sharp increase in the percentage of Canadian households with computers and Internet access, Internet publishing will become an even more salient medium of newspaper distribution within the next few years. By changing the structure of newspapers, such technological

TABLE 2: Growth of Canadian Daily Newspapers (English and French), 1921-1997

Year	Total Circulation of Dailies (000s)	Estimated Households (000s)	Circulation per Household
1921	1,716	1,897	.905
1923	1,732	2,002	.865
1925	1,783	2,065	.863
1927	2,001	2,141	.935
1929	2,197	2,229	.986
1931	2,233	2,275	.982
1933	2,052	2,473	.830
1935	2,230	2,522	.884
1937	2,357	2,569	.918
1939	2,129	2,620	.813
1941	2,250	2,706	.832
1943	2,442	2,877	.849
1945	2,742	2,944	.931
1947	3,069	3,061	1.003
1949	3,453	3,280	1.053
1951	3,556	3,409	1.043
1953	3,656	3,641	1.004
1955	3,876	3,872	1.001
1957	4,003	4,053	.988
1959	3,876	4,303	.899
1961	4,064	4,509	.901
1963	4,213	4,744	.888
1965	4,272	5,000	.854
1969	4,549	5,616	.810
1971	4,692	5,933	.791
1973	4,803	6,301	.762
1975	4,880	6,721	.726
1977	5,180	7,157	.723
1979	5,354	7,572	.707
1981	5,730	8,026	.714
1983	5,544	8,460	.655
1985	5,640	9,079	.621
1986	5,720	9,331	.613
1989	5,993	9,477	.632
1991	5,815	9,873	.588
1997	5,525	11,580	.478

Source: For 1921-91, *Canada Year Book;* for 1997, *Canadian Newspaper Association Newsletter,* July 1998.

innovations will also modify the social function and meaning of newspapers in Canada.

The Rise of the Motion Picture

The motion picture became a major entertainment form in Canada just after the turn of the twentieth century. Motion pictures were originally shown as special features in vaudeville theatres, but by 1903 they were seen in specialized "picture palaces" in all major urban areas. The public immediately embraced this new entertainment, and in a very short time the movies were the largest paid-amusement attraction Canada had ever known. The medium was readily accepted at this time of increasing immigration and urbanization, because it did not require a knowledge of the English language; it was easily accessible, especially for those living in cities; and it was cheap—an entire family could attend for less than 50 cents.[18]

Although we have no reliable statistics on movie attendance in Canada prior to 1934, the percentage of the population going to the movies was lower than in the more urbanized United States. Thus, in 1934 the Canadian population of 10.7 million averaged approximately 2 million admissions per week, while the American population of 126 million averaged over 70 million admissions per week. (In 1934, Canadian per-household movie attendance was 0.83 per week, compared with 2.24 in the U.S.)

Except for the wildly fluctuating attendances during the Great Depression years, Canadian movie audiences grew steadily and peaked in 1952, when weekly attendance averaged over 4.76 million. Here again we have an interesting comparison with the U.S., where peak attendance was achieved six years earlier in 1946, with a weekly average of over 90 million. The difference is largely attributable to the introduction of TV in the U.S. in 1948, which attracted a large audience away from the movie theatres. Television did not appear in major Canadian cities until 1952. It is significant to note, however, that in Canada the peak attendance per capita was also achieved in 1946 (Table 3, Figure 2).

Since 1952, the movie audience has plummeted to less than one-third its former size, and the number of movie theatres has declined by over 60 percent. Moreover, while the number of screens in Canadian movie theatres climbed to over 1,500 by 1995, average capacity utilization was less than 30 percent. Most important, per-capita attendance is only about one-fifth of what it was in the mid-1950s. Although these long-term trends stabilized during the 1970s,

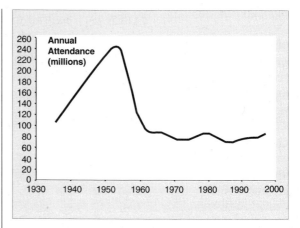

FIGURE 2: Motion Picture Attendance in Canada, 1930-2000

the decline in motion picture attendance resumed during the 1980s. After nearly four decades of decline, however, the 1990s saw a modest recovery in motion picture attendance as the growing number of large, multi-screen movie theatres allowed for more variety and flexibility in movie screening. These findings suggest that the introduction of TV and videocassette recorders (VCRs) is the major reason for the relative decline of movies as the main form of mass entertainment.[19] However, in the period after 1945, Canadians were provided with a much wider choice of recreational opportunities, and increasing interest in theatre, professional sports, and outdoor recreation have all diminished the audience for movies. Nevertheless, motion pictures continue to attract a significant audience, particularly those in the younger age groups.[20]

Despite the decline in motion picture attendance in the last 50 years, the medium itself continues to play a significant role in our culture. One motion picture can have a much greater influence over a longer period of time than can most television shows. One only has to consider the enormous appeal of films such as *The Godfather, Star Wars, E.T., Platoon, Jurassic Park, Schindler's List* and *Titanic* to see the depth of the impact of specific films on mass culture. The stunning box office success of such films is one reason that attendance rates fluctuate from year to year.

The development and growth of new communication technologies such as pay TV, pay-per-view TV, videotape, and DVD will clearly affect the structure of the motion picture industry. Indeed, during the 1980s home video emerged as the fastest-growing market for film distributors. By the early 1990s,

TABLE 3: Motion Picture Attendance in Canada, 1934-1997

Year	Movie Theatres	Paid Admissions (000s)	Population (000s)	Attendance per Capita
1934	796	107,355	10,741	9.99
1936	956	126,914	10,950	11.59
1938	1,130	137,381	11,152	12.31
1940	1,229	151,591	11,381	13.31
1942	1,247	182,846	11,654	15.68
1944	1,298	208,167	11,946	17.42
1946	1,477	227,539	12,292	18.51
1948	1,604	219,289	12,823	17.10
1950	1,801	231,747	13,712	16.90
1952	1,843	247,733	14,459	17.13
1954	1,938	218,509	15,287	14.29
1956	1,849	162,859	16,081	10.12
1958	1,622	136,335	17,080	7.98
1960	1,427	107,705	17,870	6.02
1962	1,278	91,258	18,583	4.92
1964	1,209	90,913	19,290	4.71
1966	1,149	87,694	20,015	4.38
1968	1,148	84,937	20,701	4.10
1970	1,157	78,918	21,001	3.75
1972	1,128	81,241	21,830	3.72
1974	1,116	79,020	22,364	3.53
1976	1,129	82,328	22,992	3.58
1978	1,079	81,597	23,533	3.46
1980	1,037	88,980	24,057	3.69
1982	983	87,602	24,656	3.55
1984	860	73,515	25,150	2.92
1986	788	74,942	25,446	2.94
1988	675	81,489	25,802	3.15
1990	650	78,942	26,218	3.01
1991	633	76,275	27,951	2.72
1992	620	69,195	28,317	2.44
1993	598	71,678	28,740	2.49
1994	581	76,510	28,865	2.65
1995	582	81,090	29,191	2.77
1996	590	84,997	29,509	2.88
1997	587	89,406	29,835	2.99

Source: Adapted from Statistics Canada, Bulletin No. 63-207; Statistics Canada, Bulletin No. 87-204; Statistics Canada, Catalogue 87-004XPE; Statistics Canada, *Report on the Demographic Situation in Canada*, 1999.

Canadians were spending over $1 billion on pre-recorded videocassettes and renting over 300 million videotapes annually.[21] Reflecting the growing importance of the home video audience, a small but growing number of films are bypassing movie screens entirely, and are being distributed directly to the home video market. Clearly, video and DVD rentals and sales, pay-TV, and pay-per-view TV will account for a growing portion of the motion picture audience and revenue. Although these new communication technologies ensure that movies will remain important to Canadian society, the fierce competition for the shrinking movie-theatre audience could have major effects on the motion picture industry. To begin with, theatre ownership is likely to continue to become concentrated in the hands of a few large corporate chains.[22] Today over 80 percent of movie attendance in Canada is at movie theatres controlled by the two largest chains, Cineplex Odeon and Famous Players. As well, feature films that are widely distributed and extensively promoted in theatres may reflect the interests of a core or "target" market of regular moviegoers. Alternatively, the growing number of small screens in theatres could enable theatres to provide greater choice in films and to attract more heterogeneous audiences. Finally, the boundaries between motion pictures and TV may become increasingly blurred should movies be distributed simultaneously in theatres and on pay-per-view TV.

The Development of Radio

Before the development of radio, a means of instantaneous communication that could leap oceans and span continents had been long sought. Canada, with its immense geographic expanse and far-flung settlements, quickly realized the benefits of the development of wireless telegraphy, and the subsequent refinement of radiotelephone technology. This dramatic innovation was a result of the efforts of several inventors, such as Faraday, Maxwell, and Hertz, all of whom made important contributions to the apparatus eventually perfected by Guglielmo Marconi at the turn of the century.[23]

Canada and Canadians have played an important role in the development of radio. It was in Newfoundland in December 1901 that Marconi received his first transatlantic radiotelegraph message, and the Canadian government later gave the Italian inventor an $80,000 subsidy to continue his experimental work. Further, the development of voice transmission was made possible by the work of two men—a Canadian, Reginald A. Fessenden, and an American, Dr. Lee de Forest.

Regular radio broadcasting began in Canada in December 1920; a month after similar broadcasts had been inaugurated by station KDKA in Pittsburgh. The 20-year period between Marconi's initial experience and the first public broadcasts was taken up by the slow perfection of voice-transmission technology and in increasing the public awareness of the possibilities of the new communications medium. By 1920 the North American public was anxious to try this exciting new development, and once freed from wartime restrictions on the use of radio, manufacturers quickly began producing the necessary equipment for public consumption. The Marconi Company of Canada had received a broadcast licence in Montreal in 1919 for station XWA, and it was this station that went on the air in late 1920 with regular programs for gramophone records, news items, and weather reports. Station XWA later became Montreal's CFCF and still broadcasts under these call letters.

It is significant to note that this station was established by a manufacturer of radio equipment as an inducement to potential buyers of domestic radio receivers. In fact, almost all of the early radio stations in Canada, as in the U.S., were owned and operated either by a radio manufacturer or by a newspaper using the medium for self-promotional activities. By March 1923, the Canadian government had issued broadcasting licences to 62 private, commercial broadcasting stations and 8 amateur groups. However, it is estimated that only about 34 of these stations were in actual operation. By comparison, in the United States there were 556 radio-station licences issued by March 1923, although some of these were not operational.[24]

Professor Frank W. Peers, in his admirable history of Canadian broadcasting, has shown that until 1928, public authorities paid little attention to the state of radio, unlike the intense activity that took place in both Great Britain and the U.S.[25] However, the Canadian government had been involved in discussions with the United States regarding the problems of channel interference, and had imposed an annual licence fee on all owners of radio sets. Even at this early stage there were numerous complaints that stations carried too many commercials and that station operators ignored Canadian talent in favour of recorded American material. Another concern was the apparent reluctance of broadcasters to transmit to less-populated areas of the country because of their

TABLE 4: Private Radio Licences* Issued in Canada, 1923-1940

Year	Licences
1923	9,956
1925	91,996
1927	215,650
1929	297,398
1931	523,100
1933	761,288
1935	812,335
1937	1,038,500
1939	1,223,502

Source: Statistics Canada, *Canada Year Book*. Reproduced by authority of the Minister of Industry, 1994.
* Required for legal posession and operation of radios by private citizens.

TABLE 5: Estimated Number of Canadian Households with Radios, 1941-1997

Year	Estimated Households (000s)	Households with Radios (000s)	Percentage with Radios
1941	2,706	2,003	74
1947	3,136	2,818	90
1949	3,504	3,247	93
1954	3,734	3,598	96
1956	3,974	3,817	96
1958	4,173	4,003	96
1960	4,404	4,236	96
1962	4,625	4,445	96
1964	4,872	4,675	96
1966	5,126	4,944	96
1968	5,458	5,284	97
1970	5,784	5,623	97
1972	6,111	5,965	98
1973	6,301	6,158	98
1975	6,721	6,606	98
1977	7,157	7,014	98
1979	7,572	7,451	98
1981	8,026	7,898	98
1983	8,460	8,355	99
1985	9,079	8,961	99
1987	9,556	9,444	99
1989	9,477	9,377	99
1991	9,873	9,762	99
1992	10,056	9,935	99
1993	10,247	10,134	99
1994	10,387	10,270	99
1995	11,243	11,114	99
1996	11,412	11,258	99
1997	11,580	11,425	99

Source: Adapted from Statistics Canada, *Household Facilities and Equipment Survey*, Bulletin No. 64-202.

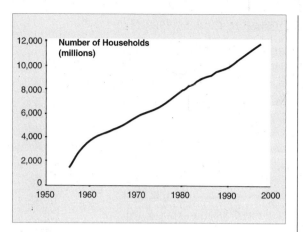

FIGURE 3: Canadian Households with Radios, 1940-1997

dependence upon the large audience base necessary to attract advertisers. Although there was a duplication of service in the urban areas, many rural areas either received no radio or were forced to rely on powerful American stations.

After publication of the Aird Commission report on broadcasting (1929), the Canadian government was forced to agree with the commission's observation that "public service" should be the basis of all broadcasting and that it should be provided by one national system. At hearings conducted in 1932 to consider the report, evidence was given that outside of Toronto and Montreal, only about two-fifths of the population could regularly pick up Canadian programs, and even these consisted largely of imported recordings. Organizations such as the newly formed Canadian Radio League argued vigorously for public ownership of radio stations, contending that the radio spectrum was, in fact, part of the public domain. Proponents of public ownership won, and on May 26, 1932, Parliament unanimously passed the *Canadian Radio Broadcasting Act*, providing for the creation of the Canadian Radio Broadcasting Commission (CRBC), forerunner of the present Canadian Broadcasting Corporation (CBC).

During its first year, the CRBC established stations in Vancouver, Montreal, Toronto, Ottawa, and Chicoutimi, and, using these stations as a base, began a regular schedule of network programs in May 1933. By 1935, the network had expanded to include another 43 private stations and by 1936 was broadcasting six hours of programs per day, confined to the evening hours. There were still many serious deficiencies in this system of national broadcasting,

and, as a result, a new committee recommended the complete recasting of the national radio organization. On November 2, 1936, Parliament passed a law establishing the CBC. By 1941, there were nine CBC transmitters covering almost the entire country, and a separate, more effective French-language network had also been established. After the war, the CBC expanded its facilities, adding stations in the Prairie region, the Maritimes, and in 1958 in the extreme northern part of the country.

The CBC, quite rightly, has emphasized its role as provider of an essential service to all Canadians and its function in maintaining the vital links of communication in this vast nation. However, private radio stations have also been a vital factor in Canadian broadcasting and attract a much larger share of the radio audience than CBC stations in the same markets. While most of these private stations do not have the same news facilities as the national network, the vast majority of Canadians rely on them for their entertainment and information needs. In the early years of radio in Canada, it was the private stations that provided broadcasting service for most of the country, and they have continued to do so.

Unfortunately, the statistics on the growth of radio listenership are not complete for the earliest period, but we do have rough measures obtained by using the figures on the number of receiving licences issued in the period prior to 1940 (Table 4). No valid data are available on the number of households with radios. We do know that, while radio had a rapid diffusion in Canada, geography presented a formidable obstacle to complete coverage, and therefore, such diffusion was not as extensive as in the U.S. The period during the Second World War witnessed a rapid increase in the number of households with radios, no doubt spurred by the desire to hear the latest war news (see Table 5, Figure 3). Since the 1950s, at least 95 percent of all Canadian households have had access to radio broadcast. Indeed, by 1997 over one-third of all households had at least four radios available for listening (Table 6).

Radio has shown a remarkable resilience in the face of heavy competition from TV. Ironically, when the introduction of television became inevitable, it was radio that appeared to be doomed, not the movies. However, radio was able to readjust its content sufficiently to provide a clear alternative to the medium, while the movies were not.[26] Now radio has secured a place for itself in the media mix of Canadian society by providing music, news, sports, and syndicated programming geared mainly to regional and

TABLE 6: Households with Multiple Radio Sets, 1962-1997

Year	Estimated Households (000s)	Households with Radios by Number of Radios (000s)			
		One	Two	Three	Four +
1962	4,625	2,814	1,087	344	199
1964	4,872	2,770	1,201	429	274
1966	5,126	2,345	1,419	663	517
1968	5,458	2,309	1,559	769	647
1970	5,784	2,210	1,677	918	818
1972	6,111	2,135	1,833	1,044	953
1974	6,513	2,000	1,985	1,220	1,189
1976	6,949	2,007	2,185	1,322	1,336
1978	7,357	1,867	2,417	1,503	1,457
1980	7,787	2,135	2,541	1,554	1,452
1984	8,857	2,069	2,732	1,860	2,096
1986	9,331	2,339	2,833	1,931	2,141
1988	9,244	1,965	2,620	1,939	2,600
1990	9,624	1,800	2,653	2,160	2,919
1992	10,156	2,194	2,822	2,180	2,739
1993	10,247	2,218	2,872	2,171	2,873
1994	10,387	2,298	3,013	2,244	2,715
1995	11,243	2,011	2,875	2,331	3,903
1996	11,412	2,093	2,850	2,371	3,943
1997	11,580	2,034	2,918	2,360	4,112

Source: Adapted from Statistics Canada, *Household Facilities and Equipment Survey*, Bulletin No. 64-202.

local "target" audiences. CBC radio generally provides more "serious" programming designed for both national "mass" audiences as well as minority interests. The continued popularity of phone-in and talk radio shows confirms the valuable feedback function inherent in this medium.[27] Further, since the 1960s, there has been a trend towards increasing amounts of FM listening and less AM listening. Recent Canadian Radio-television and Telecommuni cations Commission (CRTC) proposals could make FM radio even more competitive by allowing much more flexibility in FM programming. The move towards FM listening (as well as AM stereo broadcasting) has in itself shifted the emphasis of radio away from speech and dramatic presentations towards music as the staple ingredient.

Although radio has reached a saturation point and several stations—especially AM broadcasters—are experiencing serious declines in advertising revenue, there is little indication that listenership has declined. A typical Canadian listens to the radio 19 hours per week. Of all the older mass media forms, radio has best weathered the storm caused by the introduction of TV. This may change, however, with the arrival of pay-audio programming in the next few years. The CRTC has approved Canada's first pay-audio services that offer cable-TV subscribers between 30 and 40 commercial-free 24-hour audio channels dedicated to specialized music formats and tastes. The pay-audio "narrowcast" service will utilize digital technology to provide compact disc-quality sound to listeners.[28] While pay-audio and "RealAudio" on the Internet will force radio to carve out new niches, the eventual adoption of digital radio transmission should enable radio to remain an integral part of modern life by offering "free" compact-disc quality entertainment, and timely information to a mobile society. There are few places one cannot find or take a radio.

The Emergence of Television

Although Canadians began to experiment with television during the early 1930s, it was not until after the Second World War that the government seriously considered the introduction of the visual medium. In 1951, the Royal Commission on National Development in the Arts, Letters and Sciences proposed the development of a national system of TV. In September 1952, the CBC started minor television operations in Toronto and Montreal, and by November 1955, new stations were on the air in Vancouver, Winnipeg, and Halifax. These stations formed the base of what was to become the national CBC Television Network. In 1960, the Board of Broadcast Governors authorized the establishment of a privately owned network–the Canadian Television Network (CTV)–which began operation in October of that year. This new network provided an alternative service for the large majority of the Canadian audience.

Prior to the introduction of Canadian TV programming, many viewers in Toronto, Vancouver, and Montreal had been watching TV from American border stations. Out of habit, and because of the greater diversity of programming, Canadians continued to spend a significant portion of their viewing hours watching American channels. Only in recent years has the Canadian TV audience begun to spend a more significant amount of their time viewing Canadian programming. By 1988, Canadian programming accounted for nearly two-thirds of the total viewing time of Francophones and over one-quarter of the total viewing time of Anglophones. Moreover, the viewing share of American network stations dropped to 20 percent in the 1990s.[29]

After the introduction of TV in Canada in 1952-55, there was a rapid increase in the number of households with TV sets (see Table 7, Figure 4). By 1963, over 90 percent of Canadian households had television, and by the 1980s virtually every household in Canada had a TV set. Recent advances in communications technology have made possible television transmission to remote areas in the North.

In recent years, the overwhelming majority of Canadians have obtained colour TV sets. By 1997, around 50 percent of all households reported one colour set in the home, while nearly 60 percent indicated that they had two colour sets in the household (see Table 8). As well, there has been a steady rise in the number of household with multiple TV sets. Between 1962 and 1997, the percentage of homes with two or more TVs skyrocketed from 6% to 56%. Yet

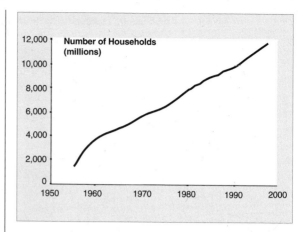

FIGURE 4: Canadian Households with Televisions, 1950-1997

during this same period, the average amount of time Canadians spent viewing television has remained fairly constant at around 23 hours per week.[30] These data are consistent with the suggestion of some that individual members of households are becoming more selective and perhaps less compromising in their TV viewing.

Furthermore, the continued growth of newer communication technologies, such as pay-per-view TV, direct-broadcast satellite service (DBS), direct-to-home satellite service (DTS), pay TV, and video-cassettes/DVD, may not only accelerate current trends but drastically alter the social uses and impact of television. Regarding satellite TV, the number of Canadian households with direct-to-home satellite service (DTH) has more than doubled since 1986, with as many as 500,000 homes receiving up to 100 channels from orbiting direct-broadcast satellites. These households have direct access to a variety of specialized viewing options ranging from dedicated religious, sports, movies, and news networks to "adult" movie channels. Additionally, Canadian-based DBS satellite services using the latest digital compression technologies plan to increase their DTH satellite offerings to over 200 channels in the near future. These include multi-channel pay-per-view as well as a plethora of speciality or "niche" TV services.[31] Continued improvements in satellite technology and reductions in dish size and cost could have a material impact on cable TV in Canada. Indeed, growth in the DTH market has likely contributed to the recent stagnation in the percentage of Canadian households subscribing to cable television, and modest growth in cable-delivered pay-TV since its inception in 1983.

TABLE 7: Estimated Number of Canadian Households with Television, 1953-1997

Year	Estimated Households (000s)	Households with Television (000s)	Percentage with Television
1953	3,641	373	10
1955	3,872	1,496	39
1957	4,053	2,545	63
1959	4,303	3,206	75
1961	4,509	3,797	84
1963	4,744	4,260	90
1965	5,000	4,631	93
1967	5,293	5,006	95
1969	5,616	5,391	96
1971	5,933	5,703	96
1973	6,301	6,051	96
1975	6,721	6,506	97
1977	7,157	6,954	97
1979	7,572	7,402	98
1981	8,026	7,850	98
1983	8,460	8,286	98
1985	9,079	8,930	98
1987	9,556	9,410	98
1989	9,477	9,355	99
1991	9,873	9,756	99
1992	10,056	9,933	97.5
1993	10,247	10,147	97.7
1994	10,387	10,286	98.2
1995	11,243	11,143	98.5
1996	11,412	11,305	98.5
1997	11,580	11,482	99.1
1995	11,243	11,114	99
1996	11,412	11,258	99
1997	11,580	11,425	99

Source: Adapted from Statistics Canada, *Household Facilities and Equipment Survey*, Bulletin No. 64-202.

In contrast, the percentage of households with VCRs has leaped from 6 percent in 1983 to 85 percent in 1997. Such spectacular growth clearly marks this comparatively new communication technology as pivotal to changes in the nature of TV. The use of VCRs to record TV programs transforms these from one-time to repeatable experiences and collectable objects. As well, the high degree of viewer discretion concerning which programs to tape, and when or how often to view them, amounts to a fundamental shift in the locus of communication control away from the broadcaster towards the viewer.[32] Combined with the channel selections offered by cable, DBS, and the burgeoning specialty services available through pay TV, pay-per-view TV and direct-to-home satellites (DTS), the heightened viewer control of television-based information realized through VCR and Camcorder technology will contribute to fundamental changes in the structure of TV in the next decade. Of special interest to Canada will be the impact of these new technologies on the ability of state agencies such as the CRTC to protect and promote national culture through regulation of Canadian broadcasters, cable TV, and satellite television.

TABLE 8: Households with Multiple Television Sets, 1962-1997

Year	Estimated Households (000s)	Households with All Kinds (000s)		Households with Colour Sets (000s)	
		One Set	Two Sets	One Set	Two Sets
1962	4,625	3,749	259	–	–
1964	4,872	3,997	435	–	–
1966	5,126	4,115	698	–	–
1968	5,458	4,232	964	229	–
1970	5,784	4,282	1,270	682	19
1972	6,111	4,407	1,447	1,444	35
1974	6,513	4,295	1,981	2,777	122
1976	6,949	4,432	2,281	3,958	254
1978	7,357	4,654	2,503	4,837	485
1980	7,787	4,627	2,982	5,585	734
1982	8,254	4,886	3,215	5,999	1,014
1984	8,857	4,728	3,953	6,258	1,574
1986	9,331	4,829	4,375	6,478	2,221
1988	9,244	4,470	4,643	5,777	3,016
1990	9,624	4,381	5,149	5,537	3,791
1992	10,156	4,631	5,303	5,513	4,295
1992	10,056	4,631	5,303	5,513	4,295
1993	10,247	4,562	5,585	5,293	4,722
1994	10,387	4,512	5,773	5,169	5,034
1995	11,243	4,841	6,302	5,483	5,593
1996	11,412	4,834	6,472	5,373	5,873
1997	11,580	4,920	6,562	5,424	6,010

Source: Adapted from Statistics Canada, *Household Facilities and Equipment Survey*, Bulletin No. 64-202.

TABLE 9: Households with Videocassette Recorders, Pay TV, Camcorders, and Home Computers, 1983-1997

Year	Estimated Households (000s)	Percentage of Households with			
		VCRs	Pay TV	Computers	Camcorders
1983	8,460	6	–	–	–
1984	8,857	12	5	–	–
1985	9,079	23	–	–	–
1986	9,331	35	10	10	–
1987	9,556	44	–	–	–
1988	9,244	52	10	12	3
1989	9,477	59	–	–	–
1990	9,624	66	12	16	6
1991	9,873	68	–	18	–
1992	10,056	74	–	20	10
1993	10,247	77	–	23	12
1994	10,387	79	–	25	14
1995	11,243	82	–	29	15
1996	11,412	84	–	32	16
1997	11,580	85	–	36	18

Source: Adapted from Statistics Canada, *Household Facilities and Equipment Survey*, Bulletin No. 64-202.

TABLE 10: Households with Cable Television, 1972-1996

Year	Estimated Households (000s)	Households in Licenced Areas(000s)	Households Subscribing (000s)	Percentage Subscribing
1967	5,293	1,225	517	42.2
1968	5,458	1,607	710	44.2
1969	5,616	1,700	924	54.3
1970	5,784	2,392	1,164	48.7
1971	5,933	2,681	1,398	52.1
1972	6,111	3,561	1,620	45.5
1973	6,301	3,967	2,062	52.0
1974	6,513	4,267	2,508	58.8
1975	6,721	4,500	2,805	62.3
1976	6,949	4,883	3,086	63.2
1977	7,157	5,218	3,367	64.5
1978	7,357	5,792	3,727	64.3
1979	7,572	6,143	4,039	65.7
1980	7,787	6,312	4,293	68.0
1981	8,026	6,585	4,654	70.7
1982	8,254	6,827	4,885	71.5
1983	8,460	7,027	5,086	72.3
1984	8,857	7,261	5,311	73.1
1985	9,079	7,600	5,602	73.7
1986	9,331	7,842	5,921	75.5
1987	9,556	7,928	6,033	76.0
1988	9,224	8,234	6,283	76.3
1989	8,477	8,642	6,560	76.0
1990	9,624	8,773	6,864	78.2
1991	9,873	8,945	7,050	78.8
1992	10,056	9,499	7,274	76.7
1993	10,247	9,718	7,465	76.8
1994	10,387	9,922	7,665	77.3
1995	11,243	10,274	7,791	75.6
1996	11,412	10,547	7,866	74.5

Source: Adapted from Statistics Canada, Cable Television Bulletin No. 56-205.

The Promise of Cable Television

Canada is one of the world's foremost cable users, with fully 75 percent of all households attached to a cable-TV system. In some provinces, such as British Columbia, the percentage of all households that subscribe to cable TV is approaching 90 percent, while in Ontario at least 80 percent of all households purchase cable-TV service. Cable TV penetration is lowest in Quebec, P.E.I., and Saskatchewan.[33] Table 10 documents the rapid development of cable TV throughout the late 1960s and early 1970s. While a tenfold rise in the number of subscribers has occurred since 1968, the increase in the percentage of viewers taking advantage of a potential cable hook-up has been slower. Currently, 95 percent of Canadian households are serviced by cable TV, with 70 percent of these electing to purchase this service (see Table 10).

Of all the mass media, cable TV currently has the greatest potential for offering the range of specialty services and niche programming necessary in our increasingly multicultural country. Since the licensing

TABLE 11: Households with Modems and Internet, 1994-1997

		Percentage of Households with	
Year	Estimated Households (000s)	Modems	Internet
1994	10,387	8	–
1995	11,243	12	–
1996	11,412	16	7
1997	11,580	21	13

Source: Adapted from Statistics Canada, *Household Facilities and Equipment Survey*, Bulletin No. 64-202.

of the nation's first multilingual TV station, CFMT-TV, in 1979, several additional services for various minority groups have become available through basic cable, speciality cable, or pay-TV services.[34]

While the rising number of cultural, religious, and other specialty channels provided through cable TV will play an important role in a multicultural Canada, new cable-distributed services could have an even greater social impact. Specifically, the adoption of digital-video compression (DVC) and addressability technology by the nation's cable systems will increasingly enable cable households to be served on an individual and interactive basis. On the one hand, these technologies will allow for much greater choice and flexibility in programming and open up a myriad of possibilities for customized cable service including Internet access. On the other hand, these same technologies have the potential for extensive "electronic surveillance" of cable subscribers.[35] As well, a pay-per-view mass media environment could produce an "information underclass" of citizens who cannot afford to access new cable services. Although most of these new technologies and services are still being developed, their full implementation will radically alter the way in which we utilize the mass media. At a minimum, the future broadcast environment in Canada will encourage us to become active media consumers and selective information users rather than passive viewers.[36] Indeed, cable-TV systems could provide much of the basic infrastructure for the rapidly emerging information and knowledge-based economy.

If the diffusion curves for all mass media are standardized (Figure 5), based on the year of peak audience or participation, it is clear that newspapers are gradually declining while motion pictures have stabilized. Interestingly, radio and television have yet to reach their zenith.[37] It is particularly interesting to note the relationship between the growth of TV and the decline of the movies.

Future Mass Media Trends in Canada

It is virtually certain that in Canada the broadcast media—especially cable TV, direct broadcast satellite service, and direct-to-home satellite service—will continue to become more powerful at the expense of print media and the motion picture. With the growth in digital compression technology, addressability technologies, and Internet access, existing mass media boundaries could rapidly erode as Internet editions of newspapers and magazines, digital radio and "RealAudio," and new movies become available on an individual basis through cable TV. The remarkable growth in households using the Internet in Canada, which skyrocketed from only 2 percent of households in 1990 to over 40 percent in 1999, clearly point to a central role for this new medium in the near future. Similarly, the disturbing trend towards concentration of corporate ownership of the mass media is likely to continue, despite measures to counter mergers, such as the 1986 federal *Competition Act* and recent court challenges by concerned groups such as the Council of Canadians. There are, however, important developments currently taking place with respect to increasing the amount of indigenous content in all segments of the mass media, particularly broadcasting. Content regulations introduced by the CRTC over the years have ensured that broadcasters and cable/satellite service providers make more Canadian programming available, and public response has been generally favourable to this policy. Yet, because of its relatively small population base, Canada is unable to produce a sufficient amount and variety of TV programming to meet the public's needs. Since this problem will worsen as the broadcast environment expands to include hundreds of channels, the CRTC has responded with recent

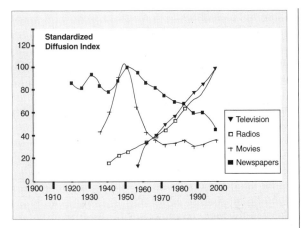

FIGURE 5: Standardized Diffusion Curves, All Media

initiatives to improve the funding available for Canadian programming.[38] However, as long as Canadians exhibit a strong interest in American TV content, Canadian programming will face rapidly growing competition in the emerging multi-channel, global milieu.

Canada's societal evolution will continue to be heavily influenced by a relatively strong mass media, as well as the presence of various minority ethnic and cultural groups. The mosaic quality attributed to Canadian society will ensure a different type of mass society from that found in the melting pot of the U.S. The existence of a large French-Canadian population and the enormous changes in post-war immigration patterns will guarantee a heterogeneous society, with a wide variety of cultural expressions and values. The key question is whether the mass media can cater to this diversity of cultural needs, while continuing to play a pivotal role as a national social bond. Put differently, will the convergence and digitization of the mass media of the future promote cultural pluralism and unity or social fragmentation? The answer will depend in part on how Canada deals with problems arising from the concentration of corporate control of media, and on maintaining a relevant Canadian presence in the emerging "borderless" world of global mass media.

Historically, mass communications have played a major role in the creation of a national consciousness in Canada, but now the mass media are being relied upon to an ever-greater extent to act as a force for economic growth and competitiveness. As Canadian links to the global economy and communication system increase, it remains to be seen how much the mass media can contribute to Canada's social bond.

Notes

1. In previous editions, Garth S. Jowett was an active contributor to authorship.

2. For a representative view of the various theories of the role of mass communication and development, see Lucien Pye, ed., *Communications and Political Development* (Princeton University Press, 1963); Frederick W. Frey, "Communications and Development," Ithiel de Sola Pool et al., eds., *The Handbook of Communications* (Rand McNally, 1973); Everett M. Rogers, "Communications and Development: The Passing of the Dominant Paradigm," *Communication Research 3*, no. 2 (1976). Recent discussions of this subject include Melvin L. DeFleur and Sandra Ball-Rokeach, *Theories of Mass Communication* (Longman, 1988); L. John Martin et al., *Current Issues in International Communication* (Longman, 1990); and Robert Babe, *Information, Communication and Economics* (Kluwer, 1994).

3. A detailed discussion of the concept of "mass society" can be found in William Kornhauser, "Mass Society," *The Encyclopedia of Social Sciences* (Macmillan, 1968); Salvador Giner, *Mass Society* (Academic Press, Inc., 1976); and James R. Beniger, "Toward an Old New Paradigm: The Half-Century Flirtation with Mass Society," *Public Opinion Quarterly* 51 (1987, supplement): S46-66. For an argument on how globalization is producing a mass society rather than a "global village" see Richard Barnet and John Cavanaugh, *Global Dreams: Imperial Corporations and the New World Order* (Simon and Schuster, 1994); and James Lull, *Media, Communication, Culture: A Global Approach* (Columbia University Press, 1995).

4. Frey, "Communications and Development," pp.338-40. See also Alvin Toffler, *The Third Wave* (William Morrow, 1980) and Angus Reid, *Shakedown: How the New Economy Is Changing our Lives* (Doubleday, 1996).

5. UNESCO has published several studies examining the relative size of the communications infrastructure of countries and their socioeconomic development. See "Mass Media in the Developing Countries," *Reports and Papers on Mass Communication*, no. 33 (Paris: UNESCO, 1961). The relationship between the communications infrastructure and socioeconomic development is explored by Alvin Toffler in *Powershift* (Bantam, 1990), and by Robert Stevenson in *Communication, Development and the Third World* (University Press of America, 1993).

6. The theory of greater participation is discussed in Edward Shils, "Mass Society and Its Culture," Bernard Rosenberg and David Manning White, eds., *Mass Culture Revisited* (Van Nostrand Reinhold, 1971), and in John Naisbitt, *Megatrends* (Warner Books, 1983). An optimistic examination of the social, political, and economic implications of changes in communications and information technology can be found in Alvin and Heidi Toffler, *Creating a New Civilization: The Politics of the Third Wave* (Turner Publishing, 1994). For a contrary analysis see Heather Menzies, *Whose Brave New World? The Information Highway & the New Economy* (Between the Lines, 1996), or Robert McChesney's *Rich Media, Poor Democracy: Communication Politics in Dubious Times* (University of Illinois Press, 1999).

7. Kornhauser, "Mass Society"; also see W. Russell Neuman, *The Future of the Mass Audience* (Cambridge University Press, 1991), for a balanced look at mass society and its relationship to changes in mass communications.

8. The role of communications in altering the spatial dimensions of society is discussed in Richard L. Meier, *A Communications Theory of Urban Growth* (MIT Press, 1965); Alan R. Pred, *The Spatial Dynamics of U.S. Urban-Industrial Growth and the Circulation of Information* (Harvard University Press, 1973). Kenneth J. Gergen highlights the social and psychological implications of the altering of spatial dimensions by the growth of mass communications in *The Saturated Self* (Basic Books, 1991).

9. The classic theoretical statements on the "rule of mob" are found in Gustave Le Bon, *The Crowd* (Viking Press, 1960); and Jose Ortega Gasset, *The Revolt of the Masses* (W.W. Norton, 1932). Toffler explores recent tendencies towards "tribalism" in *Powershift*, pp.382-87. Recent critical works exploring the relationship between the growth of the mass media, corporate domination, and post-industrial society are Herbert I. Schiller, *Culture Inc: The Corporate Takeover of Public Expression* (Oxford University Press, 1989); Neil Postman, *Technopoly* (Alfred A. Knopf, 1992), and Heather Menzies, *Whose Brave New World? The Information Highway & the New Economy* (Between The Lines, 1996).

10. The ideas in this section are based upon similar concepts expressed in Melvin DeFleur, *Theories of Mass Communication* (David McKay, 1970), Three studies that focus on the impact of mass media on socialization and beliefs, values, and behaviours are Neil Postman, *Amusing Ourselves to Death* (Penguin Books, 1985), Bill McKibben, *The Age of Missing Information* (Penguin Books, 1993), and David Buckingham, *After the*

Death of Childhood: Growing Up in The Age of Electronic Media (Polity Press, 2000).

11. There is a great deal of important work to be done in this area, and most social scientists are only now beginning to realize the need to take into account the development of mass communications as important factors in social change. In terms of sociological theory, Jeffrey Alexander, Noam Chomsky, Jurgen Habermas, and Jean Baudrillard are among those who have made notable contributions to understanding mass communications in modern (and postmodern) social change.

12. The best account of the growth of journalism in Canada is found in Wilfred Kesterton, *A History of Journalism in Canada* (McClelland & Steward, 1967); other historical analyses of early journalism include Paul Rutherford, *A Victorian Authority: The Daily Press in Late Nineteenth-Century Canada* (University of Toronto Press, 1982), and Minko Sotiron, *From Politics to Profit: The Commercialization of Canadian Daily Newspapers* (McGill-Queens University Press, 1997).

13. For a detailed examination of the literature regarding the process of innovation diffusion, see Everett M. Rogers and F. Floyd Shoemaker, *Communication of Innovation: A Cross-Cultural Approach* (The Free Press, 1971).

14. A "functional alternative" is a social or technical innovation that fulfils the same function as an existing arrangement or mode of action. This makes existing arrangements or actions obsolete or forces changes in their current function.

15. For an extensive examination of the problems of media ownership in Canada see the Special Committee on Mass Media, *Report* (Queen's Printer, 1970), and the Royal Commission on Newspapers, *Kent Report* (Supply and Services, 1981). This issue is updated in Peter Desbarats, *Guide to Canadian News Media* (Harcourt Brace Jovanovich, 1990).

16. *Canadian Newspaper Association Newsletter 1*, no. 1 (Nov. 1996).

17. An excellent analysis of political issues and cultural concerns regarding the concentration of corporate ownership of newspapers can be found in Arthur Siegel, *Politics and the Media in Canada* (McGraw-Hill Ryerson, 1983). Other works that highlight the political and cultural implications of corporate concentration in various mass media are Maude Barlow and James Winter, *The Big Black Book: The Essential Views of Conrad Black and Barbara Amiel Black* (Stoddart, 1997); David Taras, *Power & Betrayal in the Canadian Media* (Broadview Press, 1999); and Rowland Lorimer and Michael Gasher, *Mass Communication in Canada* (Oxford University Press, 2000)

18. The reasons for the popularity of the movies during this early period are examined in depth in Garth Jowett, *Film: The Democratic Art* (Little, Brown, 1976).

19. The relationship between the growth of TV and the decline of the motion-picture audience is examined in depth by Fredric Stuart, *The Effects of Television on the Motion Picture and Radio Industries* (Arno Press, 1975). The recent boom in movie theatre attendance is detailed in Statistics Canada Catalogue 87-004-XPB, 10,4.

20. The age variation regarding the motion-picture audience in Canada is discussed in Carol Kirsh et al., *A Leisure Study–Canada 1972* (Culturcan Publications, 1973), and in *Canadian Arts Consumer Profile 1990-91* (Supply and Services, 1992).

21. *Canada Year Book* 1995 (Supply and Services, 1994); also see NGL Consulting Ltd., *Home Video in Canada* (Ottawa, 1989), for detailed data on the videocassette market.

22. See Vipond, *The Mass Media*, pp.78-79.

23. See DeFleur, *Theories*, pp.49-55.

24. Frank W. Peers, *The Politics of Canadian Broadcasting 1920-1951* (University of Toronto Press, 1969), p.6. Also see Mary Vipond, *Listening In: The First Decade of Canadian Broadcasting, 1922-1932* (McGill-Queen's University Press, 1992), for a comprehensive look at the early years of radio in Canada.

25. Peers, *Politics*, p.12.

26. See Stuart, *The Effects of Television*, on how radio was able to survive while the movies continued to decline.

27. For a detailed discussion of radio phone-in shows, see Benjamin D. Singer, *Feedback and Society* (Heath Lexington Books, 1973).

28. Additional information on regulatory proposals for FM radio can be found in CRTC News release (Nov. 2, 1992). CRTC Decision 93-235, CRTC Decision 93-236, and CRTC Public Notice 1993-94 deal with pay-audio programming services in Canada.

29. Statistics Canada, *Television Viewing in Canada* (Supply and Services, 1990).

30. Ibid.; CRTC *Annual Report, 1991* (Supply and Services, 1991); Statistics Canada Catalogue 87-004-XPB vol. 11, no. 4 has recent data on television viewing among Canadians. For data suggesting a decline in average time watching television to less than 20 hours per week, see the 1998 Canadian General Social Survey.

31. A detailed discussion of direct broadcast satellites and satellite TV can be found in *The Role of Satellites in the Canadian Broadcast System: A Study Prepared for the Task Force on Broadcasting Policy* (Via World Inc., 1986); Task Force on Broadcasting Policy, *Report* (Supply and Services, 1986); Vipond, *The Mass Media*, pp.140-48; *Canada Year Book* (Statistics Canada, 1997).

32. The ideas in this section build on insights developed in Gary Gumpert, *Talking Tombstones and Other Tales of the Media Age* (Oxford University Press, 1996), pp.26-37.

33. An extensive assessment of cable-TV penetration of the telecommunications infrastructure in Canada is found in *Convergence, Competition and Cooperation: Policy and Regulation Affecting Local Telephone and Cable Networks* (Supply and Services, 1992).

34. Task Force on Broadcasting Policy, *Report*, contains a useful summary of data on cable TV, pay TV, and the growth of TV services for various cultural minorities.

35. David H. Flaherty explores the surveillance and privacy implications of advanced digital communications technologies in his *Telecommunications Privacy: A Report to the Canadian Radio-television and Telecommunications Commission* (Flaherty Inc., 1992). Although Flaherty's work focusses on telecommunications, his work is also relevant to cable TV as it moves towards universal addressability using advanced digital technology. A novel "social science fiction" on the surveillance and privacy issues involved with the digital revolution in mass communications can be found in William Bogard, *The Simulation of Surveillance: Hypercontrol in Telematic Societies* (Cambridge University Press, 1996).

36. Discussions of the political possibilities and impact of cable TV and other media can be found in Ithiel de Sola Pool, ed., *Talking Back: Feedback and Cable Technology* (Cambridge: MIT Press, 1973); Wilson P. Dizzard, *The Coming Information Society* (Longman, 1983); W. Russell Neuman, *The Future of the Mass Audience* (Cambridge University Press, 1991); Ithiel de Sola Pool and Lloyd Etheridge, ed., *Politics in Wired Nations* (Transaction, 1998). CRTC Public Notice 1993-75 and the CRTC report *Competition and Culture on Canada's Information Highway* (Government Services Canada, 1995) summarize recent public hearings and policy on the future of cable, satellite TV and the Internet in Canada. For a critical examination of this issue see Andrew Reddick, *Sharing the Road: Convergence and the Information Highway* (Public Interest Advocacy Centre, 1995).

37. To arrive at a standardized diffusion chart, each medium was indexed at 100 for the year of peak audience, and the other years calculated accordingly. This allows the diffusion curves to be compared on a single scale.

38. *Household Internet Use Survey* (Statistics Canada, 1999); CRTC Public Notice 1993-75; *Competition and Culture on Canada's Information Highway* (Ottawa: Government Services Canada, 1995). The broader issue of how government should regulate communication standards and technology is the focus of W. Russell Neuman, *The Gordian Knot: Political Gridlock on the Information Highway* (MIT Press, 1997).

2

The Press in Canada: An Historical Overview

Roger Bird

For decades, the newspaper was unchallenged as a purveyor of news to a devoted and wide readership. Then, after the 1920s, the communications landscape changed, and the newspaper's future existence became, for a time, doubtful because of the development of other media–first radio, then television, and more recently, the Internet–that threatened to make it obsolete. Despite the power of these newer media, by the turn of the twenty-first century, the Canadian daily or weekly newspaper remained a vital medium of news, entertainment, and advertising and continued to enjoy massive public influence and to attract significant spending by advertisers.

After developing through five historically visible "press periods"[1] characterized by great shifts in population and technological changes, newspapers have co-opted some aspects of the later-arriving electronic media, revisited and revised what they have always provided–a wide spectrum of the news of the day for the general reader–and bolstered that basic coverage with analysis and commentary. They continue to be a major part of Canada's media industries despite a fragmenting marketplace since mid-century and, more recently, a decade of drastic changes in ownership.

Newspaper life in Canada, or anywhere, begins with certain social and physical preconditions. There must first and most basically be enough people with the wherewithal for an interest in public affairs, a conducive social and economic climate, and the material ingredients that go into the making of a printed news organ: printing press, type, ink, and paper. But during the early years of British North American history, neither social nor physical conditions were enough for the development of the institution known as the press. Long after New England had produced its first newspaper (in Boston, in 1690), the colonies that were to become Canada were enduring conditions of war, near-war, and physical privation that delayed the birth of the newspaper until the second half of the eighteenth century–Canada's first press period.

First Press Period: 1752-1807

The first serious attempt at colonization in what is now Canada came in 1749 when Edward Cornwallis, a retired British army officer recently appointed governor of Nova Scotia, brought 2,576 immigrants to the Nova Scotia coast from England. Many of the newcomers were so discouraged by hardships, the threat of the French at Louisbourg, and conflict with the original Mi'kmaq people, that they soon left for New York and Boston. The dreaded typhus, carried by lice and fleas and invincible to available medical treatment, killed many more. But immigrants from New England were lured by the government aid that the original settlers seemed only too ready to relinquish to their more enterprising replacements. As a result, conditions became suitable for the establishment of an English-language journal. When John Bushell of Boston founded the *Halifax Gazette* on March 23, 1752, he became the business colleague and equal of the joiner, the linen draper, the distiller, the blacksmith, the lawyer, the cabinetmaker, the tallow chandler, and the soap maker.

Pioneer journalism spread out as European settlers extended their territory. The papers were small and often failed, but as a group they were a tenacious element in colonial life. Today's newspaper reader would find these early prototypes alien creations. In contrast to the news media of today, this was a time of newspaper penury. The papers were financially dependent on and politically deferential towards the colonial government. And most basically there was little news in the four-page, one-folded-sheet newspaper. Story headings were one column wide, and there were no illustrations and no attempts at visual appeal. Columns of type were filled from top-left to bottom-right as material became available over a week or two, leaving no scope for "design" even if anyone had the urge. It was the revenue earned as a minor government appointee–King's Printer–that nurtured the printer-editor's modest newspaper sideline during its first years. The money received was not much, but when a handful of lead type and a wooden, flatbed hand press were sufficient to start a newspaper, it was enough. The pioneer printer-editor served as King's Printer, sometimes without carrying the title of his or her office, but getting government money nonetheless. Frequently newspaper contemporaries and competitors shared it. Often the King's Printer for a province was also its postmaster, making the financial position of the news organ more secure.

With its 72 subscribers (there were no street sales or home delivery), the fortnightly *Halifax Gazette* typified pioneer newspapers. Its content was government announcements, items clipped from foreign papers long after their original publication, and local advertisements. There was little local news–in a town as small as Halifax there was no need for it, since local news circulated effectively by word of mouth. This colonial press provided no platform for liberty of expression and served no function as a critic of government. The prevailing political philosophy was authoritarian, the notion that "wisdom, including political wisdom, is the special prerogative of the chosen few ... to fulfill their role as governors, those in authority are entitled to decide what is true and to decide what the people are entitled to know. To this end those who rule must control the press."[2] The editor usually carried out all the tasks connected with the newssheet, either unaided or with the help of one apprentice, but he or she met the needs of the community in a day when populations were small and illiteracy high. Thus, the *Royal American Gazette* of Charlottetown at first served about 50 subscribers, the *Quebec Gazette*, 143. Even in 1800, towards the end of the first pioneering press period, three Halifax newspapers had a combined circulation of only 2,000.

After the Peace of Paris in 1763, English-speaking immigrants, notably those from the colonies to the south, brought journalism to Lower Canada, today's Quebec. No religious or political authoritarianism discouraged these press ventures as it had during the French regime–not a single printing press was established in Quebec before the defeat of the French by the British in 1763. Moreover, the birth of the newspaper was hastened by the establishment of a government that needed a gazette to give currency to its records, enactments, and pronouncements. Under British rule, the capital of the province of Quebec was a stable middle-class community that provided a suitable climate and market for the *Quebec Gazette*, established by William Brown and Thomas Gilmore in 1764.

The County of Sunbury, later New Brunswick, was the next colony to acquire a newspaper. When the American Revolution caused Loyalists to stream northward, many came to a large, uninhabited area across the Bay of Fundy from peninsular Nova Scotia. On an apparently unpromising part of the Saint John River they started the only important city owing its origin to United Empire Loyalists. It was first called Carleton, later Parrtown, and finally Saint John. A total of 3,000 refugees from New York arrived there in May 1783; 2,000 more arrived in late June, and 3,000 in September. However, after this initial unstable boom, the population dropped to 2,000. With less fluctuating numbers, the centre began a sound development. The citizens were politically alert and proud of their county's progress; from Saint John's very beginning, the *Royal Gazette* and *Nova Scotia Intelligencer*, issued first on December 18, 1783, by John Ryan and William Lewis, reflected the life of the town.

Eight months later, the County of Sunbury became New Brunswick when it was separated from the rest of Nova Scotia. This separation, carried out because England preferred small colonies and because the settlers disliked being so far from the capital at Halifax, meant more government patronage for New Brunswick journalists. Christopher Sower III became the first King's Printer for New Brunswick and began the *Royal Gazette* and *New Brunswick Advertiser* in 1785.

Prince Edward Island was called Saint-Jean Island in 1713 when the Treaty of Utrecht left it in the possession of France. It came under British rule in 1763 and was granted to about a dozen wealthy proprietors who paid a "quit-rent" to the Crown, a method dating from feudal times, which allowed them to treat the island as their private domain. Most never set foot on the island and they were able to block any attempts to open up land for farming by ordinary immigrants who had no influence with the government in London. After a series of corrupt land dealings, the island's economy was strangled and its cultural development stifled. Under such unfavourable conditions, a newspaper finally appeared only with the artificial stimulus of government commissions. Arriving in the colony of Prince Edward Island in 1787, Lieutenant-Governor Edmund Fanning found that the settlement had no printed laws, no printed assembly records, and no newspaper to give notice of legal business. He saw the immediate need for a printer, and brought in James Robertson, who, before the year was out, had begun to print the laws and to edit the *Royal American Gazette and Weekly Intelligencer* in Charlottetown. It lasted only two years.

Upper Canada, which was to become today's Ontario, was an untouched wilderness when the *Halifax Gazette* reached its 30th birthday. The first appreciable development of the western area began when the United Empire Loyalists started to arrive in large numbers in 1783-84. At first the Loyalists were so busy overcoming hardships that they had little time to think about newspapers; but by 1789 transportation and communications had developed. The change brought the first urgent need for a newspaper, and the new lieutenant-governor, John Graves Simcoe, brought Louis Roy from Quebec City as his printer. It was in the new capital of Newark, today's Niagara-on-the-Lake, that Roy began to publish the *Upper Canada Gazette* or *American Oracle*, first issued on April 18, 1793.

Although newspapers appeared in Upper Canada several years later than in today's Maritime Provinces, the *Upper Canada Gazette* predated any journalism in Newfoundland. There were many reasons why Newfoundland was slow to receive and develop journalism. For more than two centuries it was little more than a fishing station in the North Atlantic. Each year fishermen would come in the spring, set up temporary quarters on the coast, gather as large a catch as possible, and then return to Europe for the winter. Geography and climate discouraged settlement, and the rocky soil hampered agriculture, and there was no hope for a newspaper—just as today's small-town newspapers have found that journalistic quality cannot overcome social and economic limitations.

In addition to these factors, the impermanence and uncertainty of Newfoundland governments contrived by naval officers who policed the fishing fleet discouraged such social institutions as newspapers. However, between 1764 and 1774, residents began to outnumber visitors to the island, and the population rose to 12,000, helping to generate the preconditions necessary for a newspaper. Thereafter the population reached 17,000 in 1793, 20,000 in 1804, and 52,000 in 1822. The greatest concentration of people was in St. John's, and it was here that the first stirrings of civic growth took place. Around the year 1800, the city's inhabitants established schools, a sanitation system, a fire brigade, a post office, and a newspaper. St. John's was the most important settlement and the home of the governor. The other coastline communities remained mere outports of the government seat. Therefore, St. John's was the logical site for a

government printing business. Here the New Brunswick journalist John Ryan first published the *Royal Gazette and Newfoundland Advertiser* on August 27, 1807.

Second Press Period: 1807-1858

After the first transplants from New England, British American (the adjective "Canadian" still lay in the future) newspapers proliferated. As communities multiplied, so did the newspapers; as communities grew, so did newspaper circulation. The growth of population and wealth, along with healthy new industries, provided the economic basis for a non-government press financed by subscriptions and advertising. With this economic change came a change in the political philosophy and function of the press, which assumed an active partisan political role in the life of the colonies.

The War of 1812 over, a wave of immigration in the 1820s raised the population of Upper Canada from 213,000 to 430,000.[3] In the decade of the 1840s, when the Canadas made a combined gain of 677,000, Canada West (the name changed from Upper Canada in 1841) more than doubled its population. More significant than numerical increase as a factor in press growth, however, was the rise of towns. This development was aided by the specialization of primitive manufacturing. It was a modest change, merely involving a transfer of work from the home to the local shop, but it encouraged pioneer artisans to come together.

An April 1853 newspaper listing records 44 cities, towns, and villages in Canada West being served by newspapers.[4] By 1857, Canada East and Canada West were served by 213 weekly journals.[5] The story told by the numbers is not just one of rapid growth. What they show is that settlements, which would barely make it onto a modern map, often supported two or more newspapers, a reflection of both the public hunger for news and the publisher's desire for both political influence and profit.

In Newfoundland there were 27 newspaper registrations between 1807 and 1860.[6] In 1855 there were 22 newspapers published in New Brunswick, 21 in Nova Scotia, and 5 in Prince Edward Island. It has been estimated that in 1857 a total of 291 papers were published in the provinces then constituting British North America.[7]

These newspapers, all of them weeklies, were gaining legitimacy as a necessary part of public life: the public, the legislature, and the press had evolved an interdependent relationship as the Canadian colonies groped towards democracy and, by 1867, nationhood. British North Americans of all political persuasions were debating the merits of "responsible" government, a form of limited democracy, and the notion that the governors of the colonies, who had been appointed by London, should be "responsible" or answerable to the elected legislatures. Should the legislature disapprove of a governor's action, he (it was always a he) should resign. Editors such as William Lyon Mackenzie in York (now Toronto) and Joseph Howe in Halifax famously attacked the authoritarian system. Mackenzie lost his battle—his printing presses and type were thrown into the harbour by a Tory gang—but won his war for responsible government in Upper Canada. Howe attacked the Halifax establishment basically for stealing public funds, and won the consequent trial for seditious libel by defending himself in court; he was carried through the streets by a triumphant crowd and toasted at a public banquet. These men illustrate that to be a newspaper editor-publisher during the second press period was to be a prominent political figure. Not all were on the winning side—other editor-publishers vigorously supported the traditional forms of privilege and authority.

Third Press Period: 1858-1900

In 1858, the development of journalism entered a phase similar to the first press period. Similar social, political, and economic factors were again at work as European settlement moved west. In the John Bushell tradition, the later pioneer editor followed the settler to the Pacific coast, the migrating farmer to the prairies, and the prospector to the river valleys of interior British Columbia. Everywhere, tiny villages and hamlets sprang up. And almost immediately newspapers appeared to serve these communities.

The discovery of gold attracted an influx of European immigrants and created conditions favourable to press development. In 1856, substantial gold discoveries were made on the Fraser and Thompson rivers in what is now British Columbia, and by 1858 migration was at the flood. In May of that year, 1,262 people set out from San Francisco for the Fraser; 7,149 departed in June, and 6,278 in July. Others came from Oregon, Washington, Minnesota, Utah, other western states, Hawaii, and Central and South America, for an estimated total of 25,000. This number included merchants, traders, and adventurers. The people were funneled through Esquimalt, Victoria, and Puget Sound, and many remained in Victoria. Victoria became the stopping place for ships and

a supply point for prospectors; population increased, warehouses, shops, and houses sprang up, and business flourished. On June 25, 1858, the *Victoria Gazette and Anglo American* became its first newspaper.

On the mainland, wherever settlement became permanent, the newspapers' hold became secure. Elsewhere, where towns mushroomed, flourished, and died, the careers of both newspapers and towns were meteoric. Short-lived gold rushes meant short-lived mining centres and short-lived journals. As gold-seekers pushed upstream, the centre of population moved deeper into the interior and the press followed.

Manitoba's pioneer newspaper had to wait until the Red River settlement from which the province grew ended its isolation from the rest of British North America. Established in 1812 as a private venture by a Scot, Thomas Douglas, the earl of Selkirk, the colony was a Selkirk family affair linked to one private enterprise, the Hudson's Bay Company, and faced the hostility of its rival, the North West Company, until 1821. In 1836 the Hudson's Bay Company bought the whole settlement outright, increasing the resentment of completely disenfranchised residents. Frosts, high winds, hail, plagues of grasshoppers, floods, government mismanagement, and attacks by the Sioux kept the colony weak. However, after 1846, several factors caused the colonists to seek defensive bonds with fellow British subjects in the east. In that year, the Oregon Treaty was signed and the American mid-west began to fill up. In 1857, when an American army detachment arrived in Pembina on the Manitoba-North Dakota border, petitions were circulated in the settlement asking for annexation to the province of Canada. The Palliser, Ross, and Hind expeditions and the writings of George Brown and William McDougall aroused eastern interest in the western colony. The *Anson Northrup*, the first of many steamers, navigated the Red River from Minnesota to Fort Garry in 1859, and a railway was built to St. Paul. The isolation thus ended, the future province of Manitoba received its first newspaper, the *Nor'Wester*, in 1859 at Fort Garry. After 10 years it was seized and suppressed by Louis Riel. Today's *Winnipeg* (then *Manitoba*) *Free Press* was set up in 1872.

The newspaper did not come to the Northwest Territories until two decades later. When Manitoba became a province and the rest of Rupert's Land was transferred to Dominion jurisdiction in 1870, the fur trader was the unchallenged king in the non-provincial territories. Settlements were weak, isolated communities in the shadow of the

TABLE 1: Newspapers and Periodicals in British North America and Canada, 1857-1900

Year	Number
1857	291
1864	298
1874	470
1881	579
1891	837
1895	919
1900	1,227

fur-trading posts. However, in what was to become Saskatchewan, homesteaders and farmers, as well as shopkeepers and artisans, were beginning to flock to little towns where newspapers appeared. The first of these was the *Saskatchewan Herald,* established in Battleford in 1878. As territorial capital and North-West Mounted Police station, the centre needed and gave highly prized governmental revenue to the press.

In what is today Alberta, railway and settlement also brought newspapers. In Edmonton, established early as a trading post, a method of instantaneous long-distance communication that almost everywhere accompanied the railway brought news. The extension of the telegraph from the east to Hay Lakes provided the needed impetus to journalism. To disseminate a weekly budget of news from the east through the Hay Lakes telegraph operator, the *Edmonton Bulletin* was first issued on December 6, 1880. This service soon developed fuller coverage.

In Canada's north, press developments were similar to those in the interior of British Columbia 40 years earlier. After gold discoveries in 1896, experienced prospectors and ill-prepared amateurs flocked into the Klondike from 1897 to 1905. During the 18 months before 1900, some 40,000 people entered the area, and on January 10, 1899, police estimated the population of the Klondike region to be 28,018.[8] The largest centre was Dawson City, the supply point and jumping-off place for every new find. Journalism was part of Dawson City life, with the *Yukon Sun* and *Klondike Nugget* established there as pioneer papers in June 1898.

While the population of the territory making up modern-day Canada was rising from 3,300,000 in 1861 to 5,592,299 in 1901, newspaper numbers were increasing as well.[9] Table 1 shows this increase.

Fourth Press Period: 1900-1952

In the twentieth century, Canadian journalism, originally a transplant from New England or Britain, became firmly rooted and spread to areas of the country previously unoccupied by immigrants from overseas or the United States. The development resembled that of Canada's second press period but, whereas the earlier change had been achieved by proliferation of papers across the geographical expanse of the country, twentieth-century growth was of a different nature—big circulation. The daily replaced the weekly as the most prominent and important kind of paper. Its soaring circulation gave it social influence and great wealth and it emerged as a giant enterprise driven more by profit than politics. The new, heavily capitalized newspaper was always ready to pre-empt competition by driving it out of business or linking it to itself in a chain of ownership.

Modern newspaper journalism became an industry requiring great resources of capital, equipment, and personnel. To direct it, the quasi civil-servant printer-editor of the eighteenth century and the political editor of the nineteenth century gave way to the publisher-capitalist of the twentieth. John Bushell would have been impressed, even awed, by the large 1950 metropolitan dailies with their thundering presses. The booming population, a widespread growth of literacy, and faster production methods meant a huge increase in total daily newspaper circulation and the circulation of individual dailies. The newspaper became, for a time, what one historian has called "a Victorian authority,"[10] the predominant social, political, and economic force in Canadian life, replacing the sermon, the school, the circulating library, and the political speech as a guide to private thought and social attitudes.

Changing economic conditions caused irregular population growth. The first boom days lasted from 1901 to 1913 when, in percentage terms, what was then called the Dominion of Canada grew at its highest rate in history. Then the First World War virtually cut off immigration and the population boom collapsed in 1914. A depression began and ended the 1921-31 period. After economic hardship lasting from late 1920 until 1923, economic expansion was resumed, but when the stock market crashed in October 1929, the most serious economic depression in recent history began. Its harsh effect was felt during the following decade.

Between 1931 and 1941 the government passed legislation to keep out immigrants so as to keep relief payments as low as possible. For similar reasons, other countries made Canadians unwelcome and the number of emigrants also dwindled. Most population gains came from natural increase, although the birth rate was low. World War II wiped out the dying depression but did not stimulate population growth. When war ended in 1945, refugees from Europe (they were called "displaced persons" or DPs in the jargon of the time) and other immigrants flooded into a prosperous Canada. The development of Canada's largely untapped resources and an active arms industry fostered by the Cold War created a buoyant economy, and the birth rate increased. As a result, in the years 1941-51, Canada enjoyed the greatest absolute growth in population for any decade in its history.

Table 2 outlines the percentage of the total population that was urban at each chronological stage; the rise of urban population has been more important than total population increase to the development of daily newspapers, because it is in the cities and larger towns that dailies flourish. Conditions a half century later reflect this truth. The owners of Canada's small-town dailies have put them up for sale. The Thomson chain sold most of its small dailies to Hollinger in 1998, and Hollinger decided in early 2000 to get rid of them. The population numbers behind these decisions are stark: by 1996, only 22 percent of Canadians were considered rural residents by Statistics Canada. These figures exclude the population of Newfoundland, which joined Canada in 1949.

A revolution in newspaper technology interacted with Canada's population increase to transform the Canadian daily in the fourth press period. Electrically driven rotary presses replaced the old one-sheet-at-a-time technology; whole pages could be cast in metal stereotypes. Instead of patiently putting letter type into the page form by hand, operators of massive Linotype ("line of type") machines could keyboard a story from paper copy directly into metal. Illustrations got a boost from half-tone engraving, which allowed shaded nuance into photographic reproduction, replacing the line "cut" descended from a wooden, carved ancestor. These seeming antiquities were pre-1900 inventions, brought to full development in the twentieth century, and now completely replaced by the computer technology of the second half of the century. Technological advances illustrate the industry's ruthless attitude to its machinery. Newspaper owners have been quick to abandon expensive physical plant and reinvest in the newest machinery in order to remain competitive, fast, and flashy.

An example is the Teletype, which came to Canadian dailies in the 1920s. News copy punched in by a keyboard operator in one city was converted into perforated paper tape at the other end of the line. The tape instructed a Linotype machine that converted the perforated instructions into slugs of lead type. This made the offerings of the Associated Press and the Canadian Press technically easy, and cheap to handle—an incentive to widen the horizons of sometimes parochial papers just in time to handle the birth of broadcast news in the 1930s.

The growth in circulation and technology sometimes demonstrates a vicious circle. To serve vastly increased readership, newspapers require costly equipment; to pay for elaborate and costly equipment, publishers must secure vastly enlarged readership. Under such conditions, entrepreneurs in the fourth press period were caught up in a situation in which they had to gain all or nearly all the potential subscribers in the region if the newspaper were to survive. Thus, in many communities there was no longer room for competing newspapers as there had been in the days of Mackenzie and Howe. Rival journals have given no quarter in publishing battles that have ended only when all but one contestant have been driven from the field.[11]

Big money meant less competition. In 1900 most cities, even small ones, had competing newspapers. By 1950, only a few big cities had competing dailies. The number of daily newspapers dropped from 121 in 1900 to 94 at the end of the fourth press period in 1951. During the period total circulation increased about six times from about 600,000 to 3.5 million. In 1900, 18 communities published two or more dailies, for a total of 66 daily newspapers in direct competition. In 1951, 11 cities supported two or more dailies each, for a total of 34 competitive dailies.[12] While

TABLE 2: Canadian Population Changes During the First Half of the 20th Century

Year	Population	Increase over Previous Census	Urban	Urban Percentage
1901	5,371,315	-	2,014,222	38%
1911	7,206,654	34%	3,272,947	45%
1921	8,787,949	22%	4,352,122	50%
1931	10,376,786	18%	5,572,058	54%
1941	11,506,655	11%	6,252,416	54%
1951	14,009,655	22%	8,628,253	62%

circulation increased, there was a marked concentration of control in the hands of fewer and fewer publishers and owners. The trend is indicated by the fact that in 1930, 99 publishers controlled 116 dailies; by 1953, 11 publishers accounted for 42 dailies or about half the total.[13]

The Fifth Press Period: 1952 Onward

The fifth press period, beginning at mid-century, is distinguished from the fourth not so much by the number and circulation of newspapers in Canada, as by revolutionary changes in the communications environment in which newspapers operated. These changes influenced the nature, appearance, and profitability of newspapers.

The number of individual newspaper titles—94 at mid-century and 114 in 2000—increased, and their circulation relative to population remained healthy. There were 3.5 million copies published daily in 1951 in a pre-television, pre-Internet country with 14 million people, and about 5.5 million in 1999[14] in a country with about 30 million people. This means a newspaper industry that once provided one paper a day for every four people now provides a paper a day for every 5 ½ people. This shows considerable tenacity by newspapers in the face of a wide array of other news sources. In the year 2000, about three-quarters of all Canadians were urban, thus forming a convenient market for the daily newspaper—at least in larger centres.

Newspapers made technological changes in the 1950s and 1960s in order to compete better with television, specifically in the direction of faster typesetting and improved picture reproduction. After Canadian television broadcasting began in 1952, newspapers risked simply reproducing a richer and more voluminous version of the previous evening's nightly television news by dinnertime the next day. First came teletypesetting to extend the technological reach of the telegraph and speed up production of the old hot type—helping to overcome the handicap of presenting yesterday's TV news. The next challenge was visual. Television is pictures, in colour by the late 1960s, and newspaper pictures were black and white and fuzzy, produced on metal plates. The solution was the photo-offset press in which an image is transferred from a printing plate to a rubber blanket to paper, thus "offset." These presses were cheaper and easier to operate, weighed less, and, most importantly, provided sharper photographic reproduction. This innovation at first could handle only the limited press runs of small newspapers in small towns, because the image faded after a few thousand impressions. But improvements soon made them practical for dailies with the largest circulations. Offset-process colour then brought a new visual appeal to the daily. The colour, though startling to a readership accustomed to unrelieved grey, was murky through the 1970s, until computerized photoprocessing and printing techniques brought almost magazine-quality colour to newsprint pages. The stage was set for the computer revolution.

Starting in the 1970s, typewriters and teleprinters were replaced by video display terminals where editors could manipulate the functions of a central, main frame computer. Copy paper disappeared as did the smell of hot metal Linotype machines. Composing room workers took up magic markers and Exacto knives and learned to paste up laser-printed type. Gone was the stereo department that cast the heavy plates for the rotary presses; in came computers, almost everywhere by the mid-1980s, which churned out "cold type" paper strips, to be pasted on photo-ready paper dummies. Then proto-pages of wafer-thin plates engraved photographically were placed on sophisticated presses, ready to roll. By the mid-1990s many newspapers invested in desktop publishing software and designed the entire edition on computers. The technologies of satellites and computers made it faster and cheaper to move news into the newspaper. By the 1980s, reporters in the field could write stories on a laptop computer, link up with the home paper's computer by means of a modem in a hotel room or phone booth, and transmit their story directly. Along the way home, the telephone company often bounced their information off a satellite.

Having invested heavily in computer technology inside, newspapers were well positioned to make themselves available to PC users off the premises. Online versions of newspapers–after unsuccessful attempts at audio services, videotext and fax newspapers–had almost universally supplemented, though certainly not replaced, the paper parent by the year 2000.

But beyond making these improvements on earlier technologies, the papers had to contend with a communications revolution that brought other forms of news, and sharp competition for the advertising dollar. The newspaper was no longer the major news medium. Television broadcasting and television news came to Canada in 1952. In less than 10 years, more people got their news from television and, because of the personality and personalities of the medium, found television news more convincing, effortless, and easier to understand. Television also meant that newspapers had to compete vigorously against a new, attractive advertising medium. The pre-war challenge mounted against the newspaper by radio was multiplied tenfold by television:

> By the end of 1955, [Canada] was to become in many respects the world's second television country–in terms of programs, number of stations, network service, extent of coverage, and per capita ownership of sets. Montreal became the fourth and Toronto the fifth largest world TV production centre. The [CBC] gave the world's largest French television service in terms of sets-in-use and production of programs.[15]

One of the most immediate effects of television–which dominated the evening hours–was that it began to kill off evening newspapers and encourage the growth of morning editions.

> Between 1970 and 1980 morning newspaper circulation increased by 66%, while evening newspaper circulation declined by 2%.... There are several reasons ... besides competition from the electronic media. Distribution costs, particularly for metropolitan dailies, are less. Production costs are lower because fewer editions and page changes are necessary. More important, research has demonstrated that morning papers attract more readers per copy than evening papers do. Several people may read or look through one copy of a newspaper during the course of a day at work, or

traveling to or from work. Readership, measured by the total number of adults reading a paper during a day, is becoming a key factor in obtaining advertising.[16]

In the 1960s, the accessibility and volume of news were multiplied as the transmission of data was speeded up and made more economical with, first, microwave relay towers and later, in the 1970s, with the positioning of satellites above the equator that could be used to reflect streams of data from one point to another in the country.

Thus the news readers of the first half of the twentieth century were replaced by news consumers who could pick from a plethora of sources. There were local and national radio and television news–including all-news channels–over the airwaves, on cable, and on the Internet. In print, specialty magazines and weekly news magazines looked for a narrower market on paper or online. There were "community" or weekly newspapers with flavours ranging from sober local coverage to rank boosterism to entertainment hype. The local daily was available in a sidewalk newsbox, on the computer screen, or home delivered by car or truck in the early morning. (The "paper boy," or girl, disappeared as a delivery mechanism in the mid-1990s when papers shifted to morning editions, which would have required schoolchildren to get up at 3 a.m. to deliver the paper.)

The computer-communications revolution offered more than journalistically oriented Web sites. With this technology arose the possibility of a redefinition of the news itself: people began to use the Internet to filter their chosen reality through the computer, and to let the rest of the world go by. The born-again religious devotee may choose to access only those sources of information that meet the dictates of that religion and block out the rest. The same holds true for the stock market junkie, the environmental activist, the gun collector, the pedophile, and the anarchist. But what these users choose is a long way from news as it has traditionally been selected by what communications scholars have called the "gatekeepers" on the news desk. Given this technology choice, some computer network users will never encounter another story about dinosaurs, about famine in Africa, about fashion, or about city council because they have no interest in those topics. Old-fashioned news willy-nilly put such topics in front of the reader, viewer, or listener if only for a moment.

Self-selected news is a reversal of an earlier trend made possible by the same computer technology. It made available an instantaneous flow of digitalized news stories and features from a wide variety of syndicates. In 1951, an average daily was linked only to the Canadian Press, which also carried Associated Press and Reuters copy. Some papers carried the British United Press, amalgamated into United Press International in 1958. This short menu was a reflection of the costs and difficulty of moving news around the world or around the country by surface mail, telegraph wire, or undersea cable.

By 1970 a few larger Canadian papers offered copy from the New York Times service or the Washington Post-Los Angeles Times service. Southam newspapers had the small Southam News service. A few British news services could be found in Canadian papers–those of the Economist and Observer, and the Gemini service–though their stories came in the mail, not over the increasingly misnamed "wire."

But by the 1990s, as an example, the *Ottawa Citizen* was using these resources: CP-AP-Reuters as the main news wire; from Europe, The Independent, Gemini, the Guardian-Observer news services, and Deutchepresse; in Canada, the Southam News service and *Toronto Star* copy, distributed on the Southam-Toronto Star satellite; from the United States, the New York Times service, some Hearst newspapers, the Cox news service, L.A. Times-Washington Post and Knight-Ridder. Also available on a pay-per-use basis was copy from the *Moscow News* and the *Jerusalem Post.*

In addition to news stories, there were new "informational news graphics." The Canadian Press graphics network began operations in 1989 and the Southam News service started a similar operation for client papers in 1990. Both offered maps, graphs, charts, and illustrations, in black and white and in colour. Such services would have been impossible before the satellite era with its ease of transmission. The graphics themselves were pioneered by the Apple computer company, largely through the widespread adoption of the Macintosh computer for graphics applications, and were first thrust vividly before the world in 1982 by *USA Today.*

This revolution was an attempt by the newspaper industry to capture the younger, visually literate customer, raised on "Sesame Street," who was unimpressed by the old-fashioned, grey newspaper with its orderly columns of type and reluctant use of illustration. Their innovators saw informational news graphics as an easy point of entry into the story for the hurried customer of the television age. As well as the visual, many papers in the fifth press period

began offering audiotex services that allowed the "reader" to touch-tone his or her way into hourly updated information via the telephone, hours before the appearance of the paper on the streets. This service was popular before the dawn of the Internet and free for the mass of the population. A pricier and short-lived effort to reach the reader before the normal delivery was the fax paper: "In January 1990, the *Globe and Mail* introduced FAXsummary, a four-page fax edition that [gave] two pages of general news and two pages of business news" aimed mainly at Canadians overseas at a cost of $175 a month.[17] The Internet rendered this service obsolete.

All these efforts to stay on top of the information revolution began with the electronic movement of copy into newspapers. Canadian Press inaugurated computer data transfer for the country's newspaper industry in July 1972 when it installed a DEC PDP8/I message-switching computer for its universal desk in Toronto, at a cost of about $200,000. The investment would in the end save money, because a whole stage in the conversion of a reporter's story into a printed page disappeared. The Teletype operators who keypunched stories to be set in type were out of a job. Canadian Press followed up with its first installation of four video display terminals (VDTs, then called cathode ray tubes, or CRTs) in its Halifax newsroom in September 1973. The huge Hendrix 5200s were cumbersome and alien but there was no looking back. The Toronto universal desk was equipped in time for Christmas that year, and the whole news service was converted to VDTs during 1974 and 1975.[18]

With computerized information waiting at the "front door" of the newspaper, the pressure was on to use computers inside, because of their labour- and money-saving potential. The labour force, which would lose its pay cheques in this revolution, was understandably resistant to the idea. In Toronto in 1964, the International Typographical Union struck all three dailies, but ultimately lost its jurisdiction over the computers that took over the type-composition previously performed by its members. The union later (1986) affiliated with the broader-based Communications Workers of America. Publishers and unions generally worked hard to avoid this kind of disruption and employees were pacified by guarantees of job protection for those employed at the time the computers were brought on line. At most papers–with the notable exception of a 1976-77 lockout at the now-defunct *Ottawa Journal*–labour and management were successful in bringing computers on board without strikes, lock-outs, or severe job dislocations.

The usual sequence was the installation of computer technology to hyphenate and justify lines of type (which means to make the right-hand margin of a column of type even, just like the left-hand margin), then to photocompose the entire text, which would be printed by the offset method. This first stage occurred from 1964 to the late 1970s. Thomson Newspapers, then the major chain in the country, began in 1968 to convert its letter press newspapers to computer-controlled photo-composition and offset printing, and by late 1977, all Thomson papers had this technology.[19] Typically during this stage of the computer revolution, reporters continued to write their stories on typewriters. Their "hard copy"–typed on paper–was edited with the time-honoured technology of heavy black pencil, scissors, and glue pot. Special operators converted the edited copy into punched tape, which, fed into the computer, was converted to photo-ready "cold type." Papers later bought main-frame computers that were linked to VDTs throughout the newsroom for editing and writing. A reporter finished a story on the VDT screen and copied it electronically over to the desk for editing. Once finished, the editor hyphenated and justified the copy, measured it electronically to the millimetre and converted it into type.

With pagination, the creation of the physical newspaper page moved from the control of technical staff in the composing room to journalistic staff on the copy desk. Pagination means the copy editor not only edits the copy, but also designs and controls the contents of the news space. The copy editor lays out the page, writes the heads and cutlines, electronically selects typefaces, puts boxes around stories, selects and places pictures, spaces the type–technical tasks formerly done by typesetters and compositors–as well as staying alert to the journalistic values of the stories on the page. The complexity of these tasks has, in the view of some in the industry, meant a shift in copy desk personality from that of the wordsmith to a more computer-friendly and visually oriented individual. This shift was welcomed by some as adaptation to the readership of a video age, and detracted by others as a capitulation to the demands of image over content.[20]

One area that benefitted indisputably from the resources of the Information Age was what used to be called the morgue, or library, of the newspaper. In the pre-computer age of paper, backgrounding a story meant going to the morgue to extract a file folder of news clippings on the subject at hand, ranging from the prime minister of the day to the price of wheat. In the 1980s, major newspapers began to provide electronic databanks and trained staff to call up computerized information on the VDT screen from a growing variety of sources. In 1979, *InfoGlobe,* with stories from the *Globe and Mail* dating from November 1977, became available to its own newsroom and outside customers. In 1986, InfoMart began offering the contents of the *Ottawa Citizen, Montreal Gazette, Financial Times of Canada,* and the *Toronto Star.* Since then it has expanded to include the Canadian Press and a wealth of other resources from Canada and the U.S.[21]

In the 1990s this process continued to develop. Newspaper reporters, as well as journalists in other media, began to explore the possibilities of what they called computer-assisted reporting–the purchase or creation of relational databanks, which the journalist could manipulate for the sake of a story he or she defined. The impetus for this kind of journalism came mostly from the United States, because governments there were initially more willing than those in Canada to provide information in electronic form. Canada started to get on side after a group headed by the Social Science Federation of Canada proposed a new project called the Data Liberation Initiative. In a nutshell, it makes all Statistics Canada's publicly available databases, datasets, and geographic files available to universities for a set, annual fee. With this example before them, journalists have found ways to get at government data in convenient electronic form. Despite this slow start, the Canadian Association of Journalists has formed a caucus to pursue the possibilities of this powerful form of information processing.

Communications technology also brought the country its first national edition of a daily newspaper. The *Globe and Mail* was the Canadian pioneer in satellite transmission of a whole edition, page by page, to other newspaper presses across the country for local production and sale. The huge satellite transmission dish was installed in the *Globe's* backyard parking lot after years of frantic attempts to get the Report on Business delivered by air in time for it to be of use to the business world in Calgary, say, or Halifax. The satellite operation began in September 1980, transmitting the whole national edition to printing presses in Calgary and Montreal. Vancouver was added the next year, then Moncton in 1982 and Brandon in 1983. A fire at La Presse in 1981 forced the *Globe's* operation there to move, lock, stock, and satellite, to the printing presses of Le Droit in Ottawa.[22] There have been other moves since, and the paper is now being printed in Vancouver, Calgary, Brandon, Boucherville, and Halifax, as well as the Toronto edition in Mississauga.

The ever-rising costs of newspaper technology and competition from television for the advertiser's dollar made daily newspaper operation difficult, but not impossible. In 1998 (the latest year for which figures are available), newspapers were still in front with 25.7 percent of the country's net advertising revenues. Television took 24.2 percent of the market, catalogues and direct mail took 13.1 percent, the Yellow Pages, 9.8 percent, radio, 9.7 percent, community newspapers, 8 percent, magazines, 6.9 percent, and a combination of billboards, posters on buses or in subway stations, and the Internet together had just over 3 percent.[23]

The economics of newspaper publication meant that fewer and fewer publishers owned more and more newspapers. In 2000, only 12 of 114 dailies were independents.[24] Concentration of ownership was intensified first by interdependent ownership among groups, then by acquisitions as different chains bought up their rivals. Late in 1992, the Hollinger group bought 22.6 percent of the stock of Southam Inc. from the *Toronto Star*. This set off a spate of the buying and selling of newspapers from one massive corporation to another as the venerable Southam chain fell under the control of Conrad Black's Hollinger Newspaper Division. With the Southam big-city dailies now part of its holdings, Hollinger launched the country's second national paper, the *National Post*, in 1998, taking on the *Globe and Mail* across the country and in the crucial Toronto market, but the costs were high. In 1999, Quebecor bought the *Toronto Sun* chain, which itself had fought off a takeover bid by the *Toronto Star*. For a while, it seemed everyone but Thomson was interested in buying more newspapers.

In February 2000, the Thomson organization announced it was selling all its remaining newspapers worldwide except for the *Globe and Mail* in Toronto. Hollinger had already bought many of Thomson's Canadian dailies. But in April 2000, Hollinger too decided to sell all its titles except for its biggest dailies: "Mr. Black said the *National Post, The Gazette* in Montreal, the *Ottawa Citizen, The Vancouver Sun*, the *Edmonton Journal*, the *Calgary Herald* and *The Province* in Vancouver are the only Canadian newspapers not being offered for sale."[25] Critics of the Canadian newspaper industry had long scorned the quality of

the typical Thomson small-town paper, with a circulation anywhere from 15,000 to 50,000. When Thomson put them up for sale, most became Hollinger papers, owned by a company that was throwing vast resources at the new *National Post*. And suddenly, for whatever reason, the Hollinger group in turn was selling them all. Government and critics alike wondered where the buyers would come from.

They did not have long to wait. In early August of this momentous year, the television giant, CanWest Global, bought about half the Hollinger dailies, including the "not for sale" papers in the big cities, making the Winnipeg company the leading newspaper chain in terms of circulation. Part of the deal was a half-interest in Hollinger's *National Post* itself, making it a substantial force in the highly competitive Toronto market. The price was $3.5 billion, the largest media deal in Canadian history. Another buyer appeared in November 2000, when Hollinger sold three French-language dailies—*Quebec Le Soleil, Ottawa-Hill Le Droit* and *Chicoutimi Le Quodien*—to Power Corp., the owner of Montreal's *La Presse*, the country's largest-circulation French-language newspaper.

Although the transfer of ownership included many papers in small towns (for example, the *Welland Tribune* and the *Port Alberni Valley Times*), many dailies in small communities were still looking for buyers. An example of the plight of such papers was the *Lloydminster Times*, circulation 13,500. Founded as a weekly in 1903, it became a daily newspaper in 1979 and ceased publication in January 1987. It was revived as a daily by Sterling Newspapers, owned by Hollinger, in May 1997. Hollinger sold it to Bowes Publishing, owned by Quebecor, in December 1999. Quebecor folded the paper in April 2000, leaving the town of 20,000 people on the Alberta-Saskatchewan border with a lively community newspaper but one that had no national or international news, and which published only twice a week. To say the newspaper industry in Canada is getting by in the face of the new media is accurate if we restrict that statement to say the *big city* newspaper industry. The same forces that have deprived smaller communities of other forms of communication and commerce—banks, post offices, railroad stations, and grain elevators—are threatening the existence of their newspapers.

In mid-2000, the country's newspapers were almost all owned by chains, with two companies, CanWest Global and Quebecor, holding about 50 percent of the circulation. Other major players were the *Toronto Star* company called Torstar, Power Corp., and the Irving group in New Brunswick. Thomson, once the owner of scores of smaller papers as well as the *Globe and Mail*, had opted for the electronic information industry and intended to sell all its papers except the *Globe and Mail*. The briefly dominant Hollinger group was reduced to half ownership of the *National Post*, and small dailies in Quebec, Ontario, and British Columbia. The ownership picture looked like this:

Ownership of Daily Newspapers, 2001

Hollinger (26 ½)

- *Barrie Examiner*
- *Belleville Intelligencer*
- *Chicoutimi Le Quotidien*
- *Cobourg Daily Star*
- *Cornwall Standard-Freeholder*
- *Cranbrook Daily Townsman*
- *Fort St. John Alaska Highway News*
- *Kamloops Daily News*
- *Kimberly Daily Bulletin*
- *Kingston Whig-Standard*
- *Kirkland Lake Northern News*
- *Lennoxville Record*
- *Lindsay Daily Post*
- *National Post (half ownership)*
- *Nelson Daily News*
- *North Bay Nugget*
- *Orillia Packet and Times*
- *Owen Sound Sun Times*
- *Peace River Block News (Dawson Creek, B.C.)*
- *Pembroke Observer*
- *Peterborough Examiner*
- *Port Hope Evening Guide*
- *Prince George Citizen*
- *Prince Rupert Daily News*
- *Sault Ste. Marie Star*
- *Sudbury Star Timmins Daily Press*
- *Trail Times*

CanWest Global (28 ½)

- *Alberni Valley Times (Port Alberni)*
- *Brantford Expositor*
- *Calgary Herald*
- *Cape Breton Post*
- *Charlottetown Guardian*
- *Chatham Daily News*
- *Corner Brook Western Star*
- *Edmonton Journal*
- *Halifax Daily News*
- *Moose Jaw Times-Herald*
- *Nanaimo Daily News*
- *National Post (half ownership)*
- *New Glasgow Evening News*
- *Niagara Falls Review*
- *Ottawa Citizen*
- *Prince Albert Daily Herald*
- *Regina Leader-Post*
- *Sarnia Observer*
- *Saskatoon StarPhoenix*
- *St. Catharines Standard*
- *St. John's Telegram*
- *Summerside Journal-Pioneer*
- *Truro Daily News*
- *Vancouver Province*
- *Vancouver Sun*
- *Victoria Times Colonist*
- *Welland Tribune*
- *Windsor Star*

Quebecor Inc. (15)

- *Brockville Recorder and Times*
- *Calgary Sun*
- *Edmonton Sun*
- *Fort McMurray Today*
- *Grande Prairie Herald-Tribune*
- *Kenora Miner*
- *London Free Press*
- *Le Journal de Montreal*
- *Ottawa Sun*
- *Portage La Prairie Daily Graphic*
- *Le Journal de Quebec*
- *St. Thomas Times-Journal*
- *Stratford Beacon Herald*
- *Toronto Sun*
- *Winnipeg Sun*

Torstar Corp (9)

- *Burlington News*
- *Calgary Sing Tao*
- *Cambridge Reporter*
- *Guelph Mercury*
- *Kitchener-Waterloo Record*
- *Hamilton Spectator*
- *Toronto Star*
- *Toronto Sing Tao*
- *Vancouver Sing Tao*

Thomson Newspapers Canada (6)

- *Brandon Sun*
- *Globe and Mail*
- *Lethbridge Herald*
- *Medicine Hat News*
- *Thunder Bay Chronicle-Journal*
- *Winnipeg Free Press*

Power Corp (7)

- *Chicoutimi Le Quotidien*
- *Granby La Voix de l'Est*
- *Montreal La Presse*
- *Ottawa Le Droit*
- *Quebec Le Soleil*
- *Sherbrooke La Tribune*
- *Trois Rivieres Le Nouvelliste*

NB Publishing (Irving) (4)

- *Fredericton Gleaner*
- *Saint John Telegraph-Journal*
- *Saint John Times Globe*
- *Moncton Times-Transcript*
- *Horizon Operation BC Ltd.*
- *Kelowna Courier*
- *Penticton Herald*

Annex Publishing

- *Woodstock Sentinel-Review*
- *Simcoe Reformer*
- *United Daily News*
- *Toronto World Journal*
- *Vancouver World Journal*

Independents (10)

- *Amherst News*
- *Caraquet L'Acadie Nouvelle*
- *Flin Flon Reminder*
- *Fort Frances Bulletin*
- *Halifax Mail-Star/Chronicle-Herald*
- *Montreal Le Devoir*
- *Red Deer Advocate*
- *Toronto Corriere Canadese*
- *Toronto Ming Pao Daily News*
- *Whitehorse Star*

Though these numbers are subject to rapid change since both Hollinger and Thomson are still seeking buyers, they provoke anyone who cares about newspapers to wonder whether there will ever again be channels for a diversity of editorial opinion within Canada. During the twentieth century, the characteristic daily captured all or nearly all of its community's readership. It tended to reflect majority opinion and refused to offend minority opinion. Some argue that this condition, coupled with ownership by a big chain or international media tycoon, means the newspaper will reflect the views of those with wealth and power, attacking corruption when it manifests itself in government, but paying less attention when abuse of power occurs, as it inevitably does in all human affairs, in the world of business.

In tune with these worries, and reflecting a long-standing tradition of official attention to communications media, there have been major media studies by federal authorities since the mid-twentieth century. Newspaper concentration and centralization of control was one theme in 1970 when the Special Senate Committee on the Mass Media (known by the name of its chair, Senator Keith Davey) recommended the setting up of a press ownership review board to represent public interest in future mergers and takeovers; a publications development loan fund; a study of advertising in the media; provision of postgraduate scholarships for media specialists; prohibition of increases in second-class mailing rates; and the setting up of a Press Council. Except that the Quebec, Ontario, Alberta, and Windsor press councils were formed, none of Davey's newspaper-related recommendations were implemented.

When, in 1980, Southam Inc. closed the *Winnipeg Tribune* at the same time as Thomson Newspapers closed the *Ottawa Journal*, the government responded by setting up a Royal Commission on Newspapers, known as the Kent Commission after its chairperson, Tom Kent. It reported in 1981.

The commission proposed a federal *Newspaper Act*. By that Act government would put a stop to further chain growth. It would enforce divestment to weaken newspaper monopolies. It would use subsidies and tax exemption to reward newspaper excellence and impose surtaxes to punish journalistic failings. It would establish, within the Human Rights Commission, a Press Rights panel to monitor Kent Commission proposals and to act as ombudsman. It would institute a system whereby an editor-in-chief, except in the case of an "individual" newspaper, would be appointed under contract so as to shield him [sic] from proprietor control of editorial matter and make him answerable to an advisory council to whom the editor-in-chief would report annually on his stewardship; the council would report in turn to the government-appointed Press Rights panel.

None of the commission's proposals came to pass. There is no *Newspaper Act*, only a section of the *Income Tax Act* that effectively limits foreign ownership of a Canadian newspaper to 25 percent. Once foreign ownership goes over that threshold, advertisers who buy space can no longer deduct the costs as a business expense. Prosecutions against newspaper monopoly under the *Combines Investigation Act* and its successor, the *Competition Act*, have proved ineffective in checking the trends that Davey and Kent examined. When Hollinger announced it was putting

TABLE 3: Percentage of National Circulation Controlled by Major Groups, Mid-2000

	Number of Papers	Average Daily Circulation	Percentage of National Circulation
CanWest Global	28½ dailies	1,640,066	29.4
Quebecor Inc.	15 dailies	1,116,145	20.0
Torstar Corporation	9 dailies	831,239	15.1
Hollinger	26½ dailies	455,582	8.2
Thomson	6 dailies	560,645	10.1
Power Corp.	9 dailies	496,657	9.0
Irving	4 dailies	142,847	2.6
Others	16 dailies	302,992	5.4

up for sale all but a handful of its larger holdings ("buy three, get one free," one editor quipped at a newspaper awards ceremony in Windsor), the Heritage Minister Sheila Copps reacted: "The federal government will launch a full review of newspaper-ownership and concentration regulations, a step that could lead to Ottawa relaxing the rules that limit foreign ownership of Canadian newspapers."[26]

The evidence regarding Canadian media giants until recently is that they have rarely exercised overt control over editorial content. One of the rare examples of chain ownership dictating editorial policy occurred in 1965 when Richard Malone, head of Free Press Publications, directed all his newspapers to attack the new *Income Tax Act*, which disallowed tax deductions for advertising aimed at the Canadian market but placed in a non-Canadian publication. More typical was the appearance of Southam newspaper editorials on both sides of that argument, and the replication of this diversity of opinion on the matter of free trade with the United States during the 1988 federal election, and the arguments leading up to the referendum on the Charlottetown constitutional accord in 1992.

After the major increase in ownership by Hollinger during the 1990s, a lot of former Southam employees would argue that there was a return to centralized control. When the fourth edition of this book was published in 1995, Hollinger owned nine small-town Canadian dailies. Since that time it acquired the mass-circulation Southam chain and many other papers. Hollinger's owner, Conrad Black, was quite clear during the manoeuvring for acquisition of Southam that he regarded those papers as being poorly managed and providing news that was "soft, left, bland, envious, mediocre pap." Whatever their views, editors quit or were fired when the

takeover was complete, most notably Jim Travers at the *Ottawa Citizen* and Joan (now Senator) Fraser at the *Montreal Gazette*. The nineteenth-century, hands-on, highly political, highly vocal publisher had returned. Now with many major newspapers in the hands of CanWest Global, employees must wonder what the future holds.

The computer revolution and the rigorous centralized management by growing newspaper chains have had at least one significant economic by-product: labour costs for newspaper production have dropped dramatically. This has allowed money to be diverted to profits at a higher rate, greater expenditures on the editorial product, or both. Newspaper profits remain healthy: in 1992, for example, *The Globe and Mail* reported that "Thomson Corp., which owns The Globe and Mail, reported a nine-month operating profit in its newspaper division of $128-million (U.S.), a notch lower than the $153-million earned last year but still a handsome return on revenue of $838-million."[27] The same report goes on to record respectable profits for Southam, Toronto Sun Publishing, and Hollinger. By the end of the decade the picture was about the same, with a dip in profits for the big companies as they slugged it out in the wake of the aggressive entry of the *National Post* into the market: At Torstar, "profit for [1998] rose to $81.9 million from $80.0 million in 1997. However the company's flagship paper, the Toronto Star, saw its profits decline to $40 million, from $52.1 million in 1997 [because of] heavy spending on promotions prompted by new competition from [the] National Post."[28] Another measure of potential profitability is the willingness of entrepreneurs to risk the enormous start-up costs, and try for a share of the $2.4 billion[29] that individuals, corporations, and governments spend annually on the 40 percent or more of a newspaper that is allocated to advertising.

From the year of the first computer-generated newspaper strike in Canada, 1964, many businesses have been willing to risk starting a new newspaper even though old ones continued to fold. Not all the newcomers were successful. The list of successes and failures looks like this:

The Rise and Fall of Canadian Newspapers, 1964-2000

- *Le Journal de Montréal*, born 1964
- *Le Journal de Québec*, born 1967
- *Alberni Valley Times*, Port Alberni, goes daily 1967
- *Daily Townsman*, Cranbrook, goes daily 1969
- *Corriere Canadese*, Toronto, goes daily 1969
- *The Telegram*, Toronto, died 1971
- *The Toronto Sun*, born 1971
- *Quebec Chronicle-Telegraph*, goes weekly 1971
- *L'Action*, Quebec, died 1973
- *Le Quotidien du Saguenay-Lac-St-Jean*, Chicoutimi, born 1973
- *Fort McMurray Today*, born 1974
- *Le Jour*, Montreal, born 1974, died 1976
- *The Daily News*, Halifax, born 1974
- *Alaska Highway News*, Fort St. John, goes daily 1976
- *World Journal*, Toronto (Chinese), born 1976
- *Ottawa Today*, born 1977, died 1978
- *Matin*, Montréal, died 1978
- *The Edmonton Sun*, born 1978
- *Peace River Block News*, Dawson Creek, goes daily 1979
- *The Montreal Star*, died 1979
- *Sing Tao Chinese Daily*, Toronto, born 1980
- *The Albertan*, Calgary, died 1980
- *The Winnipeg Sun*, born 1980
- *The Victoria Times* and *The Daily Colonist*, merged 1980
- *Tribune*, Winnipeg, died 1980
- *The Journal*, Ottawa, died 1980
- *The Calgary Sun*, born 1981
- *L'Evangeline*, Moncton, died 1982
- *Kamloops Daily News*, goes daily 1982
- *Sing Tao Chinese Daily*, Vancouver, born 1983
- *The Times-Transcript*, Moncton, born 1983
- *Daily Sentinel*, Kamloops, died 1983
- *The Columbian*, New Westminster, died 1983
- *The Daily News*, St. John's, died 1983
- *Terrace-Kitimat Daily Herald*, died 1983
- *Citizen*, Thompson, died 1983
- *L'Acadie Nouvelle*, Caraquet, born 1984
- *Whitehorse Star*, goes daily 1985
- *The News*, Roblin, died 1985
- *Daily Bulletin*, Sioux Lookout, died 1985

- *Le Matin*, Moncton, born 1986, died 1987
- *Le Matin*, Montreal, born and died 1987
- *Report*, Swan River, died 1987
- *Daily Bulletin*, Dauphin, died 1988
- *The Financial Post*, Toronto, goes daily 1988
- *The Ottawa Sun*, born 1988
- *Sing Tao Chinese Daily*, Calgary, born 1988
- *The Daily Times*, Brampton, died 1989
- *Daily News*, Montreal, born 1988, died 1990
- *Ming Pao Daily News*, Scarborough, born 1993
- *World Journal*, Vancouver (Chinese), born 1993
- *The National Post*, Toronto, born 1998
- *The Financial Post*, Toronto, incorporated in *National Post*, 1998
- *Lloydminster Times*, died 2000

Counting shifts from weekly to daily as a success and the reverse situation as a failure, and counting a merger as the failure of one of the partners, there have been 30 daily newspapers born since the computer age began and 28 that have failed. As well, in 2000, there were nine cities or towns with competing daily newspapers, up from the eight reported by the Kent Commission in 1981.

Though chain ownership has been heavily criticized, it often means more resources for papers with the potential for big profits. Two indicators of how much money is being spent on the editorial product are the number of reporters and editors in the newsroom and their salaries, and the number of outside news sources routinely used in the paper. As indicated above, the use of outside news sources has proliferated. A large (but by no means the largest) chain-owned Canadian daily in the 1990s was spending about $1 million a month on its newsroom. The Southern Ontario Newspaper Guild reported in February 2000 that the "top minimum" wage for a reporter (someone with four to six years' experience) in a unionized newsroom at a medium-sized daily was around $56,000 a year, somewhat higher for a copy editor. At the bigger papers, a six-year reporter was making $65,000.[30] This is a wage well above the poverty line, and though it illustrates the folly of going into newspaper journalism just for the money, it allows the journalists of the fifth press period considerably more self-respect than was possible for all but the elite in earlier times.

As more and more Canadians found themselves living in larger cities in the fifth press period, one consequence was the growth of "community" (usually weekly) newspapers. The notion of community could be defined in two ways, one geographical, and one social. The geographical community newspaper served a local region of a large urban conglomeration, or a smaller town outside the major urban centre. So an English-speaking reader working in Ottawa, for example, might read either the *Citizen* or the *Sun*, but also return home to the *Kanata Courier*, the *Arnprior Chronicle*, or the *West Quebec Gazette*.

The socially defined community newspaper is often an energetic tabloid aimed at a young, urban, sophisticated readership. These papers, typified by Toronto's *Now* or Vancouver's *Georgia Straight*, have a full measure of cultural and entertainment news but also contain lengthy in-depth stories slightly off the beaten track of the big-city dailies. In some ways these papers are descendants of the "underground" press that disappeared with the fading of the counter-culture of the 1960s. But they are managed in a professional, profit-conscious manner, have survived a blizzard of social changes, attitudes and cultural trends (from rock to hip hop, from pot to ecstasy), and have shown substantial growth.

The geographically defined papers are represented in part by The Canadian Community Newspapers Association, which reported in 2000 that there were 1,141 such papers in English and French Canada; the 678 who were members of the association had a weekly circulation of almost 6.9 million, compared to about 2.5 million in 1980. The attractiveness of the weekly newspaper business could be measured by the phenomenon of large corporations buying up whole groups of weeklies. One example is Metrospan, a group of weeklies around Toronto, owned by Torstar, the parent company of the *Toronto Star*.

Canada has seen many changes in population, economic growth, and technological advancement that have transformed the financial bases, social organization, and patterns of ownership of Canadian newspapers. They have adapted to these changes and to the increased competition from the new media. A 250-year history is continuing despite premature predictions of the demise of the newspaper. While there will undoubtedly be in the future even greater integration between such media as newspapers, computers, and video, the newspaper has survived its entry into the Information Age. The biggest question facing the industry is its viability outside the larger centres. As the opening paragraphs of this essay should make clear, demography and economics are central to a newspaper's success. There seems no uncertainty about the continued commercial and cultural success of the big-city—Quebec, Edmonton, Toronto—daily. But whether citizens in smaller centres will continue to have access to a locally edited and produced newspaper is in question.

Notes

1. The phrase and concept come from Wilfred Kesterton, *A History of Journalism in Canada* (Toronto: MacLellan and Stewart, 1967).
2. Kesterton, *A History of Journalism in Canada*, p.8.
3. A.W. Currie, *Canadian Economic Development* (Toronto: Nelson, 1942), p.65.
4. Robert W. Stuart Mackay, *A Supplement to the Canada Directory ... Brought Down to April, 1853* (Montreal: J. Lovell, 1853), pp.360-61.
5. From a table in *The Canada Directory for 1857-58*, pp.1140-45.
6. *The Daily News*, St. John's, Dec. 20, 1927.
7. *Canadian Newspaper Directory*, 1892, p.58.
8. S.D. Clark, *The Social Development of Canada* (Toronto: University of Toronto Press, 1942), p.320.
9. Kesterton, *A History of Journalism in Canada*, p.39.
10. Paul Rutherford, *A Victorian Authority: the Daily Press in Late Nineteenth-Century Canada* (Toronto: University of Toronto Press, 1982).
11. W.H. Kesterton, "A History of Canadian Journalism (circa) 1900 to 1958," *Canada Year Book, 1959* (Ottawa: Queen's Printer, 1959), p.883.
12. *Canada Year Book* for appropriate years and Kesterton, *A History of Journalism*, p.214.
13. *Canada Year Book, 1959*, p.887.
14. *Matthews Media Directory*, September 1999. The total is 5,575,522.
15. Kesterton, *A History of Journalism*, p.214.
16. Leonard Kubas, "Newspapers and Their Readers," in *Royal Commission on Newspapers,* Research Publications (Ottawa: Supply and Services, 1981), Vol. 1, p.5.
17. *Content*, May-June 1991, p.7.
18. Interview with Keith Kincaid, general manager of the Canadian Press, May 1990.
19. Interview with Daryll Johnstone, production director, Thomson Newspapers, May 1990.
20. Catherine McKercher, "The Push to Pagination: The Impact of a New Technology on Canadian Daily Newspapers," *Canadian Journal of Communication*, Vol. 16 (1991), pp.110-117.
21. Interview with Pat Teall-Trudeau of InfoMart, May 1990.
22. Interview with Tom Hogan, director of production, *Globe and Mail*, May 1990.
23. Television Bureau of Canada, "Net Advertising Volume," 1999.
24. *Matthews Media Directory*, September 1999; *Canadian Advertising Rates and Data*, January 2000.
25. *National Post*, 26 April 2000, p. A1.
26. *Globe and Mail*, 2 May 2000, p. A1.
27. Harvey Enchin, "Industry pessimism no more than a paper tiger," *Globe and Mail*, 23 November 1992, p. A-1.
28. *Canadian Press*, 25 February 1999.
29. Television Bureau of Canada, "Net Advertising Volume," 1998.
30. Southern Ontario Newspaper Guild, *News Release*, February 2000.

3

Uncertainties and Paradoxes in Public Policies for Canadian Television

Robert M. Pike[1]

In a 1992 address, the former chairman of Ontario's public television network, Bernard Ostry, noted that while the original aim of Canadian broadcasting had been to ensure a strong Canadian presence on radio, and later television, in the pursuit of indigenous cultural goals, this aim has since been defeated by the process of "Canadianization." This was the name given by other nations, suffering from a similar problem, to "the flood of slick American programming overwhelming home-grown production" and to the willingness to build "a gleaming delivery system for American culture and entertainment."[2] While we should be cautious here (French-language TV, especially in Quebec, offers considerable home-grown entertainment), the term does point to the extreme difficulty of maintaining an indigenous Canadian presence in television broadcasting in the context of a shared 5,000-mile-long border with the world's biggest producer, and most aggressive distributor, of popular cultural commodities. The main aim of this chapter is to review how Canadian policy-makers have recently grappled with this issue in the context of powerful countervailing pressures for ever-increased consumer access to U.S. broadcasting signals. The review is particularly apropos as other countries, notably those of the European Union, continue to debate the possibility of instituting quotas on American television and film productions.

Within the above review, we explore an apparent paradox: the undermining by successive federal governments of the economic viability, and hence, the social and cultural role, of Canada's main producer of indigenous television programming, the Canadian Broadcasting Corporation (CBC). The CBC was formed in 1936 as a public corporation with the mandate to provide radio services throughout Canada's huge geographical expanse. Its formation came after a decade of intense lobbying by powerful competing groups favouring alternatively the U.S. model of private (commercial) broadcasting or some variant of the publicly funded British Broadcasting Corporation that was established in 1926. The latter–non-profit public broadcasting–won the day mainly because the previously dominant private radio sector had no economic incentive to produce expensive domestic programming or ensure its universal distribution. The small size of the Canadian market (especially in the context of geographical scale) and the tempting availability of a huge volume of cheap programming generated in the United States dictated otherwise. Consequently, as the first of many Royal Commissions on broadcasting (the Aird Commission, 1929) noted, "the majority of programs heard (on radio) are from sources outside Canada."[3]

Ironically, these two fundamental economic problems of the Canadian broadcasting industry–U.S. "overrun" programming and the small domestic market–are still with us, only now transferred to television, as is the competition between a predominantly market-driven vision of broadcasting and one in which the state should continue to act as a major regulatory and funding agent. This time around though, in the light of major public funding cuts to the CBC, it appears that the former vision might prevail. However, not all of the economic difficulties of the CBC are directly attributable to its public status and mandate. Some of them are linked to the fragmented market and poor economic resources of the entire Canadian conventional television system, and will be examined as such.

We commence with an overview of the main characteristics of Canadian broadcasting structures and policies. This is followed by a discussion of TV viewing patterns and content, and of the economic status of conventional television at this time. Recent shifts in public broadcasting policies in the light of the impending multi-channel universe are then examined, followed by a review of the current problems of the CBC and of alternative visions for its financial future. Since public broadcasting is everywhere under attack, and since Canada has long faced the problem of the mass inflow of foreign cultural products that is now part of the broader theme of cultural globalization, it is hoped that this chapter has a relevance that extends beyond the particularities of Canadian society.

A Brief Perspective on the Structure and Goals of Canadian Broadcasting

Broadcasting in Canada consists of two sectors, public and private. The first comprises the radio and television services of the CBC and of provincial educational-TV broadcasters. The second consists of four main elements: over-the-air private radio and TV stations and networks, satellite-TV networks, cable-TV distributors and direct-to-home (DTH) satellite companies. Though intensive corporate competition for advertising and audiences would suggest otherwise, the whole broadcasting system has been considered for the past 65 years to be a single entity pursuing the same broad objectives, and subject to the same federal public regulator.[4] Currently that is the Canadian Radio-television and Telecommunications Commission (CRTC), a formally independent federal agency responsible, as its name suggests, for the regulation of both broadcasting and telecommunications. The mandate of the CRTC under the 1991 *Broadcasting Act* extends beyond licensing into programming, including the supervision of complex regulations pertaining to Canadian content.

Revealing a mix of European and North American traditions, it has always been a fundamental policy principle since the establishment of the CBC that the funding of broadcasting should be drawn from a blend of public and private sources. Thus, although the CBC's publicly owned and operated radio stations now rely entirely on annual federal government grants for their financial support, CBC television derives the major part of its revenues from such grants and much of the rest from commercial advertising.[5] The private radio and TV stations and networks are overwhelmingly dependent upon such advertising revenues, while the cable and satellite companies charge subscribers for their basic packages of TV channels as well as for discretionary and pay-TV services. The most manifest weakness of this public/private funding mix, in the eyes of those who support national public broadcasting, lies in the lack of a stable and clearly designated public-funding base for the CBC. Canadians do not have to purchase annual licences for radio and TV sets, which, as utilized in such countries as Britain and Japan,

provide a stable and secure mode of financing public broadcasting.[6] Consequently, the CBC's reliance on fickle parliamentary grants, combined with advertising revenues in the television sector, offers little scope or hope for long-term corporate planning.

As already noted, the public and private broadcasting sectors in Canada (albeit the former was long dominant)[7] are conceived as a single broadcasting entity working in the national interest. In its most recent manifestation, the *Broadcasting Act* of 1991, this unitary principle is embodied in a series of objectives assigned to both sectors, of which the most general is "to safeguard, enrich and strengthen the cultural, political, social and economic fabric of Canada."[8] However, as the national public broadcaster, the duties of the CBC are more stringent than those of the private sector, formally mandating the Corporation to act as a powerful agency of cultural production, expression, and influence in support of Canadian cultural identity and the social and political fabric of the nation. To this end, the CBC runs distinctive radio and television services in both of Canada's official languages, English and French, as well as two cable news channels, one domestic and one for international satellite viewers. However, since program cross-over between the two official language groups is rare, the CBC may be more successful in supporting the discrete identities of English Canada and French Canada rather than the admittedly amorphous concept of national cultural identity.[9] Even if this were not so, the federal government's treatment of the CBC during recent decades makes the *Broadcasting Act* a triumph of rhetoric.

Technological Nationalism and the American Trojan Horse

The view of broadcasting, and especially the CBC, as a key element in maintaining national identity, has a wider historical tradition in Canada. Communications scholar Robert Babe refers to this tradition as the myth of "technological nationalism"; the view that Canada's nationhood has always been heavily dependent upon effective systems of east-west communication, from the trans-Canada railroad of the late nineteenth century to television and satellite communications today.[10] It is summed up in the statement of a distinguished Canadian public servant: "Broadcasting has become a sort of railway of the imagination,"[11] and indeed is given credence by the importance to social science research in communications of such eminent Canadian scholars as Harold Innis and Marshall McLuhan.[12] However,

Babe's opinion—not unlike that of Ostry mentioned earlier—is that the tradition is a myth because, with rare exceptions, communications media have consistently been deployed in support of continental integration, not national identity. Conventional television arrived in Canada in 1952, followed during the next two decades by cable systems, pay-TV, satellite-to-cable and the VCR. While regulatory policy certainly focussed upon mechanisms for using these visual technologies in the national interest, one of their major outcomes was to give consumers an internationally unrivalled choice of channel, program, and video options, including a vast media spillover from the United States. The latter is what American author Barry Berlin refers to as the "American Trojan Horse."[13]

In a nutshell, although Anglophone Canadians have a manifestly wider choice of visual media than unilingual Francophones, one may suggest that, in a "chicken and egg" fashion, the range of TV offerings placed before the citizenry has encouraged an avid acquisition of the new technologies and, in turn, the new technologies have enhanced the offerings. Thus, in 1996, household ownership of at least one TV was almost universal, almost 84 percent of households owned a VCR and 74 percent subscribed to cable.[14] The latter figure, supplemented by an estimated 8 percent of households with satellite dishes, makes Canada one of the most "TV connected" of all Western nations.[15] Typically, the household with a discretionary cable package can access around 50-75 channels including a substantial number of both Canadian and American specialty channels. Satellite TV distributors currently offer up to 200 visual channels, and numerous music audio-channels.

In this context, in the fall of 1997, Anglophone Canadians spent about 70 percent of their average of 23 hours per week of TV viewing tuned into foreign programs on all available stations. For news and public affairs, as well as sports, they were more likely to look at Canadian rather than foreign programs. But in the area of entertainment programming other than sports (drama, variety, comedy, and so on), a negligible 6 percent of total viewing time, including VCR use, was devoted to Canadian programming compared with 53 percent to foreign (and overwhelmingly U.S.) programs. For Francophone viewers, the insulation of language resulted in far more indigenous TV viewing patterns—just 35 percent of total viewing time was devoted to foreign programming, although such programming, including productions from France, still loomed large in drama and comedy.[16] Most viewing time for both language groups was actually devoted to Canadian stations and channels (72 percent for Anglophones and 94 percent for Francophones in 1993), but ironically almost two-thirds of Anglophone viewing on these stations and channels was, nonetheless, devoted to foreign programs.

Audiences can only watch Canadian programs if they are aired. Thus, even given the existence of Canadian content regulations, a major reason why Anglophones do not spend much time viewing indigenous drama and variety programming is that little of it is available on their TV screens. For example, the production of original drama by all English-language networks amounts to only about 145 hours per year. This output, on a per-capita basis, falls badly behind the 1,300 hours of domestic drama produced for television in England. French-language drama output, at roughly 370 hours per year, is considerably better and, on a per capita basis, compares favourably with France.[17] Overall, while the CBC endeavours within the framework of its budget to produce a modest amount of English-language drama, the private, conventional English TV networks rely almost exclusively on U.S. sitcoms and dramas for prime-time content.

In sum, Anglophone Canadians are offered plenty of scope for watching their own news, public affairs, and sports programs on TV—and indeed do so—but are limited in the amount of indigenous variety and drama programming to which they have access. Indeed, much to the concern of cultural nationalists, like audiences in many other countries they appear to be strongly attracted to the rich production values of many U.S. shows in comparison with similar Canadian offerings, and certainly would resent attempts to restrict seriously their wide freedom of choice.[18] By contrast, Francophone Canadians have considerably more choice of indigenous variety and drama programming, and viewer surveys indicate they show an evident preference for it.[19] We need to explore, therefore, the kinds of structural and economic constraints that have so limited quality indigenous variety and drama output, especially for private, conventional English-language TV networks. The issue of the public funding of the CBC, and also the economics of the cable industry, will be considered later.

The Economics of Conventional Canadian Television Broadcasting

Air-time sales to sponsors are the financial life-blood of commercial radio and television, and

TABLE 1: TV Viewers–Breakdown of Viewing Hours by Program Source, 1983, 1993, 1998 (%)

Program Source	1983 (%)[a]	1993 (%)	1998 (%)[c]
Canadian conventional stations	75	66.3	56.4
Foreign conventional stations	23	17.5	13.1
Canadian pay and specialty services	2	6.9	15.8
Foreign pay and specialty services	-	3.4	7.1
VCR[b]	-	5.1	5.4
Unknown source	-	0.8	2.2
Totals	100	100.00	100.00

[a] Percentages approximate; derived from bar graph. [b] Viewing hours of pre-recorded programs. [c] For Fall 1998.

increasingly of CBC TV. In 1998, net advertising volume for all Canadian TV outlets amounted to $2.31 billion, or approximately $76.00 per capita. Radio air time earned another $921 million.[20] By way of comparison, U.S. television air-time sales were $US47.9 billion in 1998, or approximately $US177.00 per capita.[21] Even without taking into account the Canadian dollar exchange rate at 68 cents U.S., it is evident that advertising dollars are much harder to come by for Canadian broadcasting. Indeed, a federal task force report on the economic status of the television industry noted in 1991 that, in comparison to similar markets in the United States, Australia, and the United Kingdom, Canadian TV advertising was "underdeveloped" by up to $1 billion. Factors deemed to be involved at the time included high advertising rates (which reduced the proportion of total advertising outlays devoted to TV far below comparable countries), cross-border advertising from U.S. border stations and a 30 percent market reduction loss because of Anglophone audiences tuning to U.S. stations.[22] At the time, the above task force noted that TV advertising sales, though underdeveloped, had shown a strong growth trend of 8.6 percent per annum between 1985-89.[23] Between 1989 and 1998, that growth trend was a little more modest, at 6 percent per annum, and proportionately the largest revenue increase was in advertising on the growing host of specialty channels.[24] Commercial TV and radio have turned a limited profit in recent years, following a net loss for TV of $65 million in 1991.[25] However, this profit has clearly come from cautious budgeting and staff reduction since, like television networks everywhere, the Canadian industry has been facing growing production expenses and rental charges as the result of increasing competition in the so-called global TV marketplace.[26] In his review of the conditions of this new marketplace, Jay Blumler writes of "a chaos of competitors,"[27] and

certainly competition for programs and audiences has become severe in Canada as cable, pay TV, and satellite transmissions have been added to the conventional networks. Consequently, a major concern of the industry in the context of rising costs and limited advertising revenues has been audience fragmentation resulting from greater viewer choice. Audience fragmentation dilutes advertising revenues by reducing the audience market share of individual networks and channels.

As shown in Table 1, when average hours of TV viewing are broken down by program source, the main change between 1983 and 1998 was the growth of VCR use and of Canadian and foreign (U.S.) pay television and specialty services at the major expense of both Canadian and American conventional stations. As a still more recent indication of the decline of the conventional TV market, viewer data suggests that, among cabled households, Canadian conventional broadcasters will capture only 35.1 percent of the Anglophone market and 67.6 percent of the Francophone market in 2000, compared with 54.8 percent and 95.7 percent respectively in 1989.[28]

Add the fragmentation phenomenon to the other economic pressures on the industry, and one can understand why, especially in the Anglophone commercial TV market, logic dictates a search for cheap ways to fill air time commensurate with maintenance of market share. The answer patently is to acquire U.S. entertainment programs that, mainly as the result of their low incremental cost of international distribution, can still be acquired in a competitive market at about one-tenth of the cost of producing comparable programs in-house and will usually yield a similar audience rating.[29] Tellingly, some years ago, the private CTV network informed the Task Force on the Economic Status of Canadian Television that each hour of Canadian entertainment represented over $5 million in lost annual profit margin because

U.S. programming could be acquired so much more cheaply.[30] Nothing much apparently has changed in this area since the time of the Aird Commission in 1929.

Thus, marketplace logic indicates that English-language conventional TV will continue to be dominated by U.S. entertainment programs, as indeed is TV in Latin America and in many countries elsewhere. The alternative is to reduce the "opportunity cost"—the profit margin differential between an hour of Canadian programming and an hour of a similar rated U.S. show—by increasing audiences for Canadian entertainment programs and/or by developing policies to promote and protect Canadian visual broadcasting. Some of these policies are reviewed in the next section, although the most important of them historically—the maintenance of public broadcasting—will receive separate consideration.

State Policies in Support of Canadian Television Broadcasting

For many decades, the federal government as well as some provincial governments have endeavoured to foster Canada's cultural industries through a variety of policy strategies. Some strategies are primarily promotional such as the maintenance of public broadcasting and public financial assistance for the production of Canadian movies and TV drama through a major cultural agency, Telefilm Canada (without which, incidentally, the production of indigenous TV drama would amount to even less than it currently is).[31] Others are primarily protectionist, including the requirement of majority Canadian ownership for broadcasting companies, Canadian content regulations, and various measures intended to increase the flow of advertising dollars to the broadcasting sector. Even a sharp critic of such strategies, English sociologist Richard Collins, agrees that they have helped to establish financially viable cable and broadcasting industries, kept wealth and jobs in Canada, and allowed—especially through CBC Radio-Canada—a wide diversity of programs, and especially news programs, with substantial audiences.[32] However, since the early 1980s, major policy shifts have been occurring in which the fate of indigenous TV programming has been increasingly taken out of the hands of the conventional broadcasters and placed in those of the cable-TV industry.

The logic behind the new policies has been mandated partly by the seemingly inexorable advance of technology. Media, as observed in a 1992 report from the federal Department of Communications (now Department of Canadian Heritage), are becoming increasingly consumer-driven. If we miss a movie at the theatre, we can pick it up later on a specialty TV channel or rent it on video. "During the last decade we have grown accustomed to an abundance of media products and services" and "we insist that media providers adjust to our schedules and willingness to pay."[33] Thus, competition in the media market is fierce as well as increasingly globalized. For Canadian television, this was brought home when, in recent years, some Canadian consumers began to subscribe to U.S. direct-to-home (DTH—the so-called Deathstar) satellites that transmit directly into Canadian homes, by-passing domestic regulatory policies. The official answer in this new environment has been to take a more competitive and "pro-active" stance—that is, allowing the liberal distribution of U.S. programming but making sure that there are windows for Canadian programming, side-by-side with foreign programs.[34] In practice, this has meant a major growth in the number of cable specialty channels available, for a fee, to the increasingly selective consumer. It has also stimulated the development and growth of home-grown DTH satellite services, notably ExpressVu and StarChoice. Both delivery modes of cable and satellite are competing for the consumer with costly advertising campaigns.

With the wide diffusion of cable, the original policy of expanding the choice of specialty channels makes some sense in Canada, although it would be less appropriate in many other Western countries where cable is less developed. Between 1987 and 1998, the CRTC licensed 37 specialty services in Canada, of which 11 are in French and the remainder, though predominantly in English, include services broadcasting in Chinese, Italian, and Spanish.[35] In general, the bidders for these new channels have come from among the top corporate names in Canadian broadcasting and the chance to gain a licence for one of them is highly coveted.[36] This is nowhere more evident than in the 452 applications recently submitted in response to the CRTC's call for applications for digital TV channels. Currently, companies like Alliance Atlantis and CanWest Global are "angling for spots on the dial with channels dedicated to auctions, comedy for kids, Celtic music, gambling, and the National Hockey League's Maple Leaf Toronto franchise, among others."[37]

Clearly, specialty and pay-TV services are seen as both profitable and patriotic, and, as shown in Table 1, they are attracting an ever-increasing audience.

This growing viewer popularity, in turn, yields these services increasing revenues from three main sources—subscribers, advertisers, and funds provided by the cable companies—which for both Canadian pay-TV and specialty channels amounted to over $880 million in 1999 compared with just $353 million in 1994.[38] For their part, the cable companies themselves glean an increasing proportion of their revenues from "non basic services" (that is, optional add-on packages for which subscribers pay additional charges) in which many of the specialty and pay channels are located.[39] Overall, therefore, it would seem that the CRTC is having some success in offering viewers the sort of program fare, but with a Canadian twist, that they are likely to find on U.S. specialty or DTH satellite channels. However, one should not be too optimistic here. The cable industry contributes about $50 million a year to the Canadian Television Production Fund that helps to fund television programs in such crucial areas as drama and children's TV, but otherwise spends little of its net income (some 4-5 percent) in initiating Canadian programming.[40] Not unexpectedly, in 1998, only 40 percent of all programs viewed on Canadian specialty and pay-TV channels actually originated in Canada, and the percentage for English-language viewing alone would undoubtedly be much lower.[41] Indeed, some years ago, a federal policy review report on DTH satellites stated categorically that the cable-led policy has resulted in increased penetration by American programs and new Canadian specialty channels have actually been created to be linked with the distribution of U.S. channels.[42] The latter is done to meet CRTC regulations that necessitate that cable companies provide a mix of both countries' channels to their customers, but in this instance the driving force is clearly consumer access to a popular U.S. service such as The Discovery Channel.

Thus, it is an irony that cable technology has been seen as something of a saviour for Canadian television in the multi-channel universe, since (aside from the Television Fund) its impact on Canadian viewers, following Babe's argument noted earlier, has always been to increase their access to American programs rather than to promote Canadian ones. However, aside from the technological imperative, there are a couple of other important reasons for the recent dominance of cable in CRTC policy. First, diplomatically the specialty channel policy is relatively, if not entirely, uncontroversial in the context of the North American Free Trade Agreement (NAFTA), since a liberal interpretation of NAFTA would seem to open many of Canada's traditional cultural policies to a hostile U.S. reaction as being "unfair subsidies" or in restraint of trade.[43] Secondly, as we have suggested, the policy combines profit with patriotism and is actually a classic example of the mutual back-stroking that has taken place between the Canadian state and private interests in the sphere of communications. The cable industry is dominated by a number of major conglomerates that have legal monopoly control over cable in their own market regions.[44] In the view of many critics, past CRTC policies, which continued to hand over more power and resources to the cable industry, suggested that "the broadcast regulator ... is behaving as a captive of the very monopoly that Parliament asked it to regulate."[45]

However, as a textual footnote to the above, one must observe that technologically "times are a-changing." As already noted, the advent of Canadian DTH satellite TV has brought the satellite and cable companies into competition for the TV market. In addition, with the growing convergence of communications technologies on the so-called information highway, Canadians have the prospect of accessing, for a price, a potentially vast array of entertainment and leisure services, as well as such standard on-line services as the Internet, either through their computers or their TV sets. Since the delivery of such services could occur through cable, wireless telephone, or the telephone lines (just as access to Internet does now), the cable companies face competition for such potentially rich terrain from the major telephone companies (this competition extends into DTH satellite, since Bell Telephone Enterprises controls ExpressVu). From this perspective, therefore, their traditional monopoly is under siege but some of the cable giants are girding for the battle by pursuing the worldwide trend of corporate mergers and acquisitions in the communications field. While the desire for industrial diversification plays a part in this trend, so does the wish to acquire more ready access to the great quantities of visual content that will be needed to fuel the insatiable demand of the information highway.[46]

But What Happened to the Canadian Broadcasting Corporation?

Since the 1980s, the ideological environment within which public communications policy is formulated has not been favourable to the promotion of national public broadcasting as a first-line player in the maintenance of a Canadian presence on television. Indeed, as is the case in many other countries, public broadcasting in Canada, in the shape of the CBC, is under constant assault.[47] This assault rests on the supposed virtues of private sector efficiency and corporate competition, the desirability for less regulation in the communications sphere, the perceived need for massive deficit-reduction in public sector spending, and the view that a national broadcaster has become increasingly irrelevant in the multi-channel universe. It is led by a variety of forces–the country's most prestigious newspaper, the *Globe and Mail* with its strong corporate agenda,[48] right-wing think-tanks such as Vancouver's Fraser Institute and the "free-market" economists whom it sponsors, and privatization-minded politicians, including the current premier of Ontario. As noted in the introduction, these forces are clearly in the ascendant, although public opinion polls and a plethora of federal government reports on broadcasting are usually very favourable to the CBC, and support its adequate financing.[49] The contradiction here, indeed, is sufficiently sharp to lead one CBC supporter to state that "everybody is against the CBC–except the Canadian people."[50]

There follows below a brief case study of what might be described as "a national institution in decline." It focusses on a series of areas of concern, many of which were well documented in a 1996 federal report on Canadian broadcasting and film, the Juneau Committee report. While substantial use has been made of this report, it is supplemented by more recent sources of information that indicate that the CBC's problems have gone from bad to worse since the mid-1990s.

Declining Public Financial Support

Although the CBC faced initial budget cuts as early as 1975, its public financial base began to erode seriously after the mid-1980s, mostly during the jurisdiction of a privatization-minded Conservative government. Thus, between 1986 and 1996, total parliamentary grants to the Corporation fell 23 percent in terms of their purchasing power.[51] From 1996 through 1998, federal financial support dropped another 29 percent, while, by contrast, most of the other major countries in the Organization for Economic Co-operation and Development increased their support for public service broadcasting during this period.[52] To put this funding cut into perspective, note that, in 1996, Canada already spent less per capita on public broadcasting than any other Western country except the United States.[53] The outcome of such drastic financial paring for the CBC has been a long-term corporate downsizing (often euphemistically referred to in such terms as *restructuring, corporate efficiency, accountability*) including a major reduction in employees.[54] Currently–and although the structural and programming commitments of the CBC are patently far greater in terms of Canada's geographical size, bilingual, northern services, and regional needs than are the commitments of many European public service broadcasters with far greater financial resources–there is no evidence that any federal government likely to be elected or re-elected in the foreseeable future is soon going to reverse this downward financial trend.

Increasing Commercialization

CBC television has responded to past financial cuts by increasing its network television competition with other media for scarce advertising revenues. Such revenues have increased gradually until they now constitute about 33 percent of net income, a trend which, as the CBC notes in its annual report, makes the "level of operations ... now more dependent on the economic and other fluctuations in the marketplace ... and places the Corporation in a more volatile position than in the past."[55] The result for CBC TV has been the creation of a hybrid functioning "unsteadily in a grey zone between the public and private sectors."[56] By contrast, CBC radio, which is totally non-commercial, was considered by the Juneau Committee to embody the principles that should govern the CBC generally. Its programming, so noted the Committee, "is informative, intelligent, diversified, culturally-oriented and overwhelmingly Canadian."[57] CBC radio, unlike CBC television, is rarely subjected to major external criticism. It remains quite distinctive in programming from the private radio stations.

Audience Loss

Audience fragmentation has reduced the size of CBC TV audiences, especially in English Canada. Between 1992 and 1997-98, the overall audience share of the English network for the whole program schedule fell from 16.1 percent to 9.6 percent, though the CBC cable news channel added another 1.3 percent in the latter year. Prime-time CBC English TV audience share stood at 9.4 percent in 1999 compared with 11.3 percent two years earlier.[58] This audience loss has been proportionally somewhat greater than that of the English Canadian and U.S. commercial networks, and it has led many critics–including the commercial networks that must compete with the

CBC for advertising—to claim that federal government expenditures on the CBC are both a poor use of scarce public money and a form of unfair competition. However, such arguments depend upon the business assumption that the only basis for judging the CBC is market share, an argument that would not, for example, go down well in Japan where the public broadcaster is considered an essential cultural service and is well funded despite low audience ratings.[59] But, even if the argument is accepted at face value, it should be pointed out that CBC French-language TV services still captured 25 percent of the prime-time market in 1998-99, and the top-ranking French-language entertainment program, *La Petite Vie*, attracts three million viewers. The highest ranking show on CBC English TV is *The Royal Canadian Air Farce* with 1.5 million viewers.[60] Thus, despite fragmentation, the CBC Radio-Canada service continues to play a vital broadcasting role in Francophone communities.

Programming Changes

In the 1993 comparative study of public broadcasting commissioned for the BBC, the effects of government funding cuts to both the CBC and the Australian Broadcasting Commission are neatly summed in the following comment: "Both ABC and CBC are trapped in a vicious circle that prevents them from building up their market share: cuts in funds lead to compromises in program quality that create a disillusioned audience. Consequently, the public purse strings are further tightened in the next funding round."[61] In this equation, the effect on quality of programming plays a vital part, and indeed, in 1996, the Juneau Committee noted a long-term drop in time devoted to variety programming in the CBC English-language prime-time schedule, replaced mainly by Canadian sports and news.[62] The Committee also noted other changes—increased American programming in the day-time schedule on the English network; less emphasis on children's programming on that network; a general reluctance to take risks with minority programs of any kind.[63] And since 1996, CBC has witnessed a continuation of its drastic restructuring which, among other impacts, is shown, in a recent survey, to have led to a major reduction in locally produced CBC TV programs in regions outside the Toronto-Montreal axis.[64] At the time of writing (May 2000) the recently appointed president of the CBC, Robert Rabinovitch, has proposed the termination of many regionally produced supper-hour news programs (at the cost of over 600 jobs) in favour of a Canada-wide show produced in Toronto. Given the popularity of such news programs, especially in the Atlantic region, the proposal has finally tweaked a nerve among members of the federal government who fear an upswell of public opposition.[65]

Is there any light in this dark scene? Affirmatively, one can point to the quality of CBC radio; to the continued importance of Francophone services; to the fact that the Corporation certainly has a better reputation for producing and distributing original entertainment programming than the private TV networks (in 1999, it still provided 42 percent of the audience to English-language Canadian programming in peak periods); and finally to CBC endeavours to make substantial use of the new media (for example, its Galaxie digital audio music services are offered in DTH satellite TV packages).[66] Yet, inevitably the viability of the CBC's mandate as a broadcaster is being brought into question.

Changing Conceptions of the CBC Mandate

Because of greater reliance on advertising revenues, and the related search for audiences, the CBC faces the inevitable criticism that the public purse is now subsidizing a television service that overlaps significantly in TV program scheduling with the private sector. Since official review committees on Canadian broadcasting (of which there have been many) usually recommend that CBC television should be "distinctively and almost totally Canadian ... a clear and intelligent alternative to commercial television,"[67] this overlap has raised a fundamental debate on the relative roles of the public and private broadcasting sectors. Traditionally, private radio and television was seen to *complement* the work of the dominant public sector. Now, however—and irrespective of the centrality of the CBC's mandate in successive broadcasting acts—this relationship is being reversed, not least in the recommendations of "free market" policy analysts (see below) who suggest that CBC television should become essentially an appendage to the private sector. In sum, the CBC is clearly in a financial and structural crisis that can only deepen without some rational resolution. The most obvious solution, as often proposed by the lobby-group "Friends of Canadian Broadcasting," is for the federal government to recognize the centrality of the CBC to Canadian cultural identity, and reverse its deficit-cutting strategy. Another very different solution is that the CBC should cope with revenue reduction in a multi-channel universe by accepting a much narrower interpretation of its mandate. For example, two scholars at the University of Alberta have published a series of articles[68] in which they recommend that CBC television could cope with a much-reduced parliamentary grant, and end reliance on advertising revenue, by selling off many of its assets and limiting itself to broadcasting only during the evening hours as a specialized network offering distinctive (culture-specific) programming.[69] Such programming would consist mainly of material that was not readily accessible through other media, or that was not financially attractive to private broadcasters. Defined this way, sports, foreign shows, and local and regional TV programming would fall–with the resulting revenue gains–to the private sector.[70]

Manifestly, however, if this narrowing of the mandate is not seen to be an acceptable solution, then the only alternative is to find some major source of non-governmental revenue to support the Corporation. Generally speaking, this is the solution proposed by recent review bodies including the Federal Standing Committee on the Canadian Heritage,[71] and the Juneau Committee. The latter, obviously in general support of the current mandate, recommended that the CBC be provided with "stable, predictable, long-term funding" through a Communications Distribution Tax that would be levied on cable, satellite, and some telephone services supplied to consumers.[72] Such a tax would be an alternative to the licence fees charged in many other countries, and would replace both advertising revenue and the annual parliamentary grant. While this proposal made a lot of sense if the main aim was to support and strengthen the CBC, it was never seriously considered. A consumer tax is not likely to sell well during a period when tax reductions are a policy anchor for many Canadian jurisdictions, especially after it was originally condemned by one *Globe and Mail* columnist as "Pay-or Else-TV" and the proposal attributed to "Canada's cultural imperialists."[73]

It is our purpose here to note the existence of these alternative solutions, not to explore their relative merits. Typically, however, the federal government is unlikely to pay much attention to any of them, since, if implemented, each would cause offence to some major and influential segment of the community. Thus, we face the seeming paradox that, at the very time when Canada is facing ever-greater pressures for enhanced cultural integration into the U.S. television market, the federal government–and other influential agencies–are acquiescing in the gradual demise of the one national institution that has offered, even if imperfectly, some creative alternative to this

trend. But, as our concluding remarks will suggest, once the main motivation for recent public broadcasting initiatives is carefully scrutinized, the paradox becomes more apparent than real.

Conclusion

The 1995 report of the policy review panel on DTH satellite broadcasting includes a valuable statement on the reasons for Canadian cultural support strategies, as well as the American response to them:

> Canadians insist on being able to hear uniquely Canadian voices that resonate with their own distinct national experience. Canadians have shown over the years that they are prepared to accept some restrictions on imports of foreign cultural products, in whatever form, in order to protect Canadian creators and producers. Canadians also accept that government intervention may be necessary to ensure the viability of Canada's cultural industries. The American "entertainment industry", which seeks only to remove barriers to market entry for its products, often has misunderstood and misrepresented this Canadian desire for balanced choice of both foreign and indigenous products.[74]

A 1996 dispute over the CRTC replacement of a U.S. cable channel on Canadian cable by a competing Canadian channel demonstrates the veracity of the review panel's observations on U.S. reactions. Echoing the concerns of the evicted American channel, an acting U.S. trade representative reportedly described CRTC action as "an egregious form of protectionism" and continued, "This administration will not tolerate discrimination against any U.S. industry. It is of special concern when it involves Canada, one of our largest export markets (actually the largest) and our free trade partner."[75] Given this kind of response, and in view of a high level of economic dependence upon the United States, it is not surprising that Canadian cultural policies have generally been extremely, perhaps excessively, cautious.[76] Indeed, a report from the federal Department of Communications notes that other Western countries with greater "natural" barriers–larger domestic market, smaller geographical size and the barrier of the national language–do much more to protect their cultural industries than does Canada.[77]

But there are other important factors influencing the nature of Canadian cultural strategies. The massive influence of American culture is evident in all sectors of Canadian society, although the term "Canadianization" as defined in the introduction to this chapter applies most aptly to English-language television. Indeed Anglo-Canadian viewers' long-acquired taste for U.S. entertainment programming, linked to its ready availability as an inexpensive import, led the above policy review panel to state that the perceived threat from American satellite TV, although couched in the discourse of cultural nationalism, is based as much on economic as cultural considerations. Thus the panel noted that Canadians themselves "have not felt threatened by the penetration of foreign TV signals. On the contrary [they] ... appear to be in favour of DTH satellite signals, whatever their origin, as an attractive alternative to cable TV."[78] This observation, based on 468 submissions received by the panel, is significant for the implicit acceptance of the viewpoint that "Canadians clearly do not believe in erecting electronic barriers to cultural influences from beyond their borders ... they want access to the best the world has to offer."[79] This is a viewpoint that, subject to the presence of windows for Canadian TV programming, provides the internal rationale for de-emphasizing strong protectionist measures.

However, the policy review panel's view that the perceived threat of American DTH satellite is as much economic as cultural adds a further dimension to the broadcasting policy equation. By "cultural," they mean presumably the continued desire of Canadians to hear and see programs that "resonate with their own distinct national experience."[80] By "economic" is evidently implied the economic dimension of regulations that require broadcasting entities to be owned and effectively controlled by Canadians; regulations that all too often have allowed Canadian communications firms to reap rich economic rewards from state-sponsored monopoly control. But, as been suggested in the case of cable TV, the distinctively cultural benefits arising from these policy initiatives are less evident. Increasingly, it seems, this is the way of Canadian broadcasting policies—their rhetoric, still linked to the myth of technological nationalism, stresses the support of national culture and the public interest, but their reality is more and more that of "the bottom line."

If correct, the above observations may help to explain the seeming paradox associated with the financial decimation of the CBC. The Corporation costs a lot of money to run, and its capacity to fulfil its formal mandate is limited by economic, linguistic, and technological realities. Nonetheless, as political scientist David Taras has argued, the view that national public broadcasting is much less essential in the multi-channel universe takes no account of the possibility that this universe may prove a mirage; many viewers may simply not want a plethora of channels and satellite services.[81] Even if it is not a mirage, there is still a need, in Taras' view, for a strong national

broadcaster that can set journalistic standards, probe deeply into vital social issues, offer quality entertainment, and offer some competition to the private corporate empires that increasingly dominate the press and airwaves. However, these solid arguments in favour of public broadcasting are based on social and cultural benefits that, we have suggested, now exert less influence on public policy than the prospect of cutting the public deficit by encouraging private sector initiatives. So the CBC as a contributor to the deficit is drastically down-sized, even though past experience yields little hope that the private sector will be able, or willing, to compensate culturally for its diminution.

In the last resort, we agree with American media analyst Les Brown's plea for public broadcasting: "somewhere in the frantic scramble for even larger profits on the television superhighway there must be a service that represents the mainstream of national life."[82] If this paper has but one dominant message for readers, it is that such a service can only be maintained if the state has fully committed itself economically and ideologically to the support of indigenous cultural goals. If this commitment is diluted by economic and political counter-pressures, backed as these are by the rationalizations of technological inevitability and consumer freedom of choice, then the game is lost—and in Canada, despite the variety of alternative methods suggested for financing the CBC, it probably is.

Notes

1. This is a revised and updated version of an article originally published in the *International Journal of Social Economics* (25, no. 6/7/8: 1998), pp.1279-1299. Permission to republish is gratefully acknowledged.

2. Bernard Ostry, "The Survival of Canada through Broadcasting," *Canadian Speeches* (17, no 3: 1992), notably p.12.

3. Canada, *Report of the Royal Commission on Radio Broadcasting* (Aird Commission) (Ottawa: Minister of Supply and Services, 1929), p.6.

4. Broadcasting and telecommunications in Canada are a responsibility of the federal government. Publicly supported provincial television networks are permitted insofar as they are designated as "educational" since education is a provincial government responsibility. In practice, the designation is applied very loosely indeed.

5. The provincial educational TV broadcasters, like the Public Broadcasting Service in the United States, rely heavily on corporate sponsorship, public donations, and public funding from their respective governments.

6. For a comparative discussion of financing public service broadcasting, see British Broadcasting Corporation, *Public Service Broadcasters around the World: a McKinsey Report for the BBC* (London, 1993).

7. The CBC was responsible for licensing and regulating the private radio and, later, television stations until 1958, when this task was taken over by another agency.

8. Canada, *The Broadcasting Act of 1991* (Ottawa: Minister of Supply and Services), Section 3, clause 1.

9. The Broadcasting Act says that, among other goals, the CBC's programming should be "predominantly and distinctively Canadian,"

"contribute to shared national consciousness and identity," "strive to be of equivalent quality in English and in French," and "reflect the multicultural and multiracial nature of Canada" (Canada, 1991), Section 3 (1)(m). However, a notable exclusion from the 1991 Act in contrast to its predecessor formulated in 1968, is the expectation that the CBC should promote Canadian unity. This was seen to be too politically sensitive to include (and an impossible task in practice) in the context of nationalist sentiments in Quebec.

10. Robert Babe, *Telecommunications in Canada* (Toronto: University of Toronto Press, 1990), pp.5-8.

11. InterMedia News Analysis, "Canada, Communications and Culture: an Interview with Alain Gourd," *InterMedia* (20, no.4-5:1992), pp.4-6.

12. In an article in *InterMedia,* Mark Alleyne writes of the impressive list of Canadians in communications research, both in the social sciences and in computing and electronics. For example, Canada was a pioneer in satellite technology. See Mark Alleyne, "Why Canada? The Dominance of Canadian Communications Research," *InterMedia* (18, no.1: 1990), *passim.*

13. Barry Berlin, *The American Trojan Horse: U.S. Television Confronts Canadian Economic and Cultural Nationalism* (New York: Greenwood Press, 1990), p.8.

14. Data from Canada, *Information and Communication Technologies: Economic and Statistical Information* (Ottawa: Industry Canada, March 1998), p.11.

15. In 1988-89, the household cable penetration rate was given as 79% in Canada, 55% in the United States, 32% in West Germany, 2.8% in the United Kingdom and 1.5% in France. The reason for the difference between the 1997 penetration rate of 74% and the earlier higher rate is not known. See Canada, *New Media ... New Choices* (Ottawa: Communications Canada, 1992), pp.24-25. The household penetration rate for satellite TV is based on approximately 800,000 subscribers to the two main companies in May of 2000 (unpublished data from the companies).

16. The viewing data include Canadian and U.S. over-the-air broadcasters, satellite delivery signals, and signals available only via cable distribution systems. The 1997 data on Canadian and foreign programming for both official language groups also includes viewing time devoted to the VCR, but this is excluded from the 1993 data. Source for all data: Statistics Canada, *Culture and Leisure Statistics: Television Viewing Time, fall 1997* (Catalogue no. 870086XPB) <http://www.statcan.ca/english/pgdb/People/Culture/arts22a.htm>.

17. Drama production figures are for the mid-1990s. It is probable that international comparisons might now be still less favourable; especially in the light of continued budget cuts at the CBC. See Canada, *Making Our Voices Heard: Canadian Broadcasting and Film for the 21st Century,* Report of the Mandate Review Committee (hereafter Juneau Committee) (Ottawa: Ministry of Supply and Services,1996), p.76.

18. In 1996, the Juneau Committee suggested that anglophone viewers will watch good quality drama series if offered them and cited such internationally successful CBC series as "Road to Avonlea" and "North of 60" which attracted large audiences (Juneau Committee, 1996, p.76). This is undoubtedly true, but much of the evidence suggests that, in general, Anglophone viewers may actually spend less of their time viewing Canadian variety and drama programs than the total air-time devoted to such programs. As a case in point, see C. Hoskins and S. McFadyen, "The Mandate, Structure and Financing of the CBC" in H. Holmes and D. Taras (eds.), *Seeing Ourselves: Media Power and Policy in Canada* (2nd ed), (Toronto: Harcourt Brace, 1996), p.291, table 4.

19. For example, a survey carried out in 1994 showed that 10% of French-language TV broadcast time consisted of Canadian drama, and Francophones spent about 20% of their total viewing time watching it. This compared with 2% of both broadcast and viewing time for Anglophones. This data covered all available TV stations and networks, including U.S. stations and networks available in Canada. See Canada, *Report of the Task Force on Broadcasting Policy* (Ottawa: Minister of Supply and Services, 1986), p.95.

20. Advertising volume data received from Television Bureau of Canada, May 2000. All amounts are given in Canadian dollars unless otherwise stated.

21. U.S. Bureau of the Census, *Statistical Abstract of the United States 1998* (Washington: Bureau of Census, 1999), p.592, table 947.

22. Canada, *The Economic Status of Canadian Television,* Report of the Task Force (Ottawa: Ministry of Supply and Services, 1991), notably pp.74-83. The task force noted that television gross advertising revenues per capita in 1989 were $65 in Canada, $116 in the United States, $94 in Australia, and $86 in the United Kingdom. All revenues are expressed in Canadian dollars. TV's share of total gross advertising outlays was 19% in Canada, 26% in the U.S., 33% in Australia, and 31% in the United Kingdom in the same year. In 1998, television's share of all Canadian advertising revenues was slightly higher, at 24.2%.

23. *The Economic Status of Canadian Television, op cit.,* 39.

24. The increase in advertising on specialty TV channels rose from $30 million in 1989 to $241 million in 1998 (Television Bureau of Canada, private communication).

25. Commercial (private) television made a net profit before taxes of $82 million in 1994 and $112 million in 1998. Net revenue after taxes in 1994 was $38.4 million. Commercial radio had a $28 million deficit before taxes in 1994, but has since shown some profitability. See Statistics Canada, *Radio and Television Statistics, 1998,* Service Bulletin, Communications (28, no. 1: July 1999; Catalogue no. 56-001-XIB).

26. Employment in the commercial (private) TV industry fell 6.1% between 1994-1998, from 8,273 to 7,761 employees. In commercial radio, the drop was 6.4%, from 9,251 to 8,650 employees. By comparison, employment in the cable TV industry dropped only 1.6%, from 9,432 to 9,272 over the period. Source: Statistics Canada, *Radio and Television* Statistics, 1998, *op. cit.*

27. J. Blumler, "The New Television Market: Imperatives, Implications, Issues" in J. Curran and M. Gurevitch (eds). *Mass Media and Society* (London: Edward Arnold, 1992), p.196.

28. Data from Canadian Cable Television Association, *Annual Report, 1999-2000,* p.23.

29. See C. Hoskins et al., "U.S. Television in the International Market: Unfair Pricing?", *Journal of Communication* (39 no. 2: 1989), pp.55-75.

30. Task Force Report, *op. cit.,* p.39.

31. TeleFilm Canada was originally created as the Canadian Film Development Corporation in 1968 with the role of fostering a feature film industry in Canada. In 1983 its mandate was broadened to include support for broadcasting through the Broadcast Fund. In November 1994, 84% of anglophone viewers and 94% of francophone viewers watched at least one program that resulted from TeleFilm support. A federal government report in 1996 called it "Canada's second largest cultural institution" (Juneau Committee, 1996, *op. cit.,* p.194). Later developments include the creation of the Canada Television Fund in 1996 which helps finance Canadian programs with money provided both by TeleFilm Canada and the cable industry.

32. R. Collins, *Culture, Communication and National Identity: The Case of Canadian Television* (Toronto: University of Toronto Press, 1991), pp.336-337. In particular, there is no doubt that Canadian content regulations helped to revive the once moribund Canadian recording industry.

33. Canada, *New Media ... New Choices op. cit.,* pp.27-28.

34. *InterMedia News/ Analysis* (1992) , *op. cit.*

35. Data from Fiona Downey, "CRTC looks into French Specialty Channels."http//.www.infoculture.cbc.ca/archives/cultpol/cultpol_120719 98-crtc.html.

36. H. Enchin, "TV Treasure Hunt Begins," *The Globe and Mail* (May 6,1996), pp.B1 and B3.

37. D. Walton, "Hundreds of New Specialty Channels Pitched to CRTC," *The Globe and Mail* (April 12, 2000), pp.B1 and B10.

38. Canadian Cable Television Association, *Annual Report 1999-2000,* p.19.

39. For example, in 1998, cable industry revenues from such services amounted to 31.1% of total revenues, or over $1 billion, compared with 29.3% just a year earlier. This trend can be expected to continue. See Statistics Canada, *Cable Television, 1998,* Service Bulletin, Communications (Feb. 2000; Catalogue no. 56-001-XIB).

40. See I. Morrison, " How Cable TV Picks its Consumers' Pockets," *The Globe and Mail* (July 1, 1993), p.A15.

41. Data calculated from unpublished Statistics Canada summary table: "TV Viewing in Canada by Signal Source and Canadian Content of Program, Fall 1998" available from Statistics Canada, Culture Statistics Program-87F0006XPB.

42. Canada, *Direct-To-Home Satellite Broadcasting,* Report of the Policy Review Panel (Ottawa: Department of Heritage and Department of Industry, 1995), p.12.

43. The cultural industries were not included in the terms of NAFTA, but certain clauses allow either country to respond "with equivalent commercial effect" to new measures affecting trade related to these industries. The past few years have indeed seen a series of threats and actions launched by the U.S. government, not least through the World

Trade Organization, against various Canadian cultural measures deemed as protectionist. Attempts to protect the Canadian magazine industry against "split-run" U.S. publications have been a particular target of late.

44. Although there are a large number of small cable companies, the industry is dominated by four of them–Vidéotron in Quebec, Rogers Communications and Shaw Communications in English Canada, and Cogeco Communications in both markets.

45. L. Morrison, *op. cit.,* p.15.

46. As a case in point, Rogers Communications acquired the large multi-media corporation MacLean Hunter some years ago, and has since bought the CTV network. It is now in the bidding to buy cable giant Vidéotron which has itself multi-media interests. And, in case one should assume that competition between satellite and cable companies is inevitable, it is well to note that DTH satellite company StarChoice is a subsidiary of Cancom in which Rogers has a 20% financial stake.

47. The attack on public broadcasting extends to the provincial public networks. Public funding for them has been substantially cut in Ontario and Quebec, and the network in Alberta has been privatized. For a recent strong condemnation of Canadian communications policies, see D. Taras, *Power and Betrayal in the Canadian Media* (Broadview Press: Peterborough, 1999). For a useful international study of the "decline" of public service broadcasting see M. Tracey, *The Decline and Fall of Public Service Broadcasting* (Oxford University Press, 1998).

48. A review of *The Globe and Mail's* editorials on broadcasting and telecommunications over the past few years shows strong opposition to the regulatory policies of the CRTC, frequent criticisms of the CBC and, overall, strong support for the principles of deregulation and open competition. To be fair, however, it does not go so far as to advocate the privatization of the CBC, and recently some of its editorials on the Corporation have actually been sympathetic.

49. According to an independent poll conducted by the pro-CBC lobby group "Friends of Canadian Broadcasting" in 1999, 62% of Canadians believed that the federal government was more committed to cutting down the CBC than to preserving and rebuilding it, and 80% claimed that they would prefer the government to preserve and rebuild. See Friends of Canadian Broadcasting web-site <http://www.friendsco.org/pressreleases/CBC/pollmay1999.htm>.

50. C. Harris, "Majority Supports CBC, Survey Suggests," *The Globe and Mail* (June 26, 1996), p.C1.

51. Juneau Committee, p.36.

52. For Canadian data, see *Globe and Mail* editorial "A Sense of Purpose in Public Broadcasting" (Aug. 11, 1999), p.A10; For international funding of public media, see Organization for Economic Co-operation and Development, *Communications Outlook, 1999* (Paris, 1999) p.121, table 6.6.

53. David Taras, 1999, *op. cit.,* p.179, gives per capita expenditures on public broadcasting in 1996 as Sweden $116, United Kingdom $60, France $40, Australia $33, Canada $19. All figures are quoted in Canadian dollars.

54. Thus, in its 1997-98 annual report, the CBC notes "to say the least, 1997-1998 has been a painful year for the Corporation; a year marked by the completion of the restructuring plan, painful job losses and downsizing." See CBC, *Annual Report for 1997-1998,* p.49.

55. "Management Discussion and Analysis" in CBC *Annual Report 1997-98* at <http://cbc.src.ca/CBC/htmen/6_1_4_1b.htm>.

56. J. Geddes in *The Financial Post* (Nov. 17, 1995).

57. Juneau Committee, *op. cit.,* p.47.

58. Data on changes in proportions of overall CBC viewing audiences taken from CBC *Annual Reports for 1995-96, 1997-98* and for viewing in prime time from CBC, *Annual Reports, 1997-98, 1998-99.*

59. See BBC, *Public Service Broadcasters Around the World, op. cit.,* p.19.

60. CBC *Annual Report, 1998-99,* notably p.29 and p.34.

61. *Public Broadcasters around the World,* p.17.

62. Juneau Committee, notably pp.64-68.

63. Juneau Committee, p.37.

64. Arlan Gates, *Leaving Town: an Analysis of Availability and Audience for Locally-Produced Programming on CBC TV and Private Broadcasters in Winnipeg and Five Other Canadian Markets in Fall 1999* (Friends of Public Broadcasting, April 2000). The survey shows, for example, that total average weekly hours of locally produced programming on CBC TV in Winnipeg fell between the sample weeks of 1986-87 and 1999 from 26.6 to 8.4 hours. Generally, the record of the private broadcasters in this respect was found to be better (Gates, 2000), notably p.7.

65. For commentary on this issue, see H. Windsor, "CBC Plans to Attract Liberals' Interest," *The Globe and Mail* (May 10, 2000), p.A4. The CBC announced subsequently that the plan to end the news programs had been abandoned.

66. CBC, *Annual Report, 1998-99,* p.41.

67. Juneau Committee, p.100.

68. C. Hoskins and S. McFadyen, "The Role of the CBC in the Canadian Broadcasting System: Revisited, *Canadian Public Policy* (10, no. 3: 1994) pp.352-358; and "The Mandate, Structure and Financing of the CBC" (1996), *op. cit.*

69. Hoskins and McFadyen (1996), notably p.293.

70. Hoskins and McFadyen define culture-specific programming in terms of information, drama, children's, and variety shows that are all sorely limited in Canadian television schedules. It is interesting that their proposals for a dramatically restructured CBC television service have some similarities to recent proposals of the CBC president which would de-commercialize news programming and sell off many of CBC's buildings and transmission towers (see "Remaking the CBC," *MacLeans,* May 8, 2000, p.21).

71. One recommendation of the federal Standing Committee on the Canadian Heritage, in 1995, was that the CBC should receive 50% of a fund derived from a mandatory financial contribution levied on all present and future private distributors of broadcasting services. Typically, nothing came of this recommendation. Canada, *The Future of the CBC in the Multi-Channel Universe,* Report of the Standing Committee on Canadian Heritage (Ottawa: 1995), notably p.58.

72. Juneau Committee, p.149 and chap.6, *passim.*

73. T. Corcoran, "Cultural Imperialists Trick Ottawa to Save CBC," *The Globe and Mail* (Feb.3, 1996), p.B2.

74. *Direct-to-Home-Satellite Broadcasting* (1995), *op. cit.,* p.11.

75. D. Fagan, "Country Music TV Station Pact Set," *The Globe and Mail* (Aug.9, 1996), p.B3.

76. The Canadian theatre movie and video rental markets are major cases in point. Lack of regulation in these industries, notably the absence of a quota system for Canadian productions, has almost entirely excluded domestic movies from Canadian theatre screens and video stores. Furthermore, as Carr notes, the pressure from the U.S. that the cultural industries not be exempted from the North American Free Trade Agreement has been relentless, but based on the false premise that the Canadian state intervenes in culture while the American state does not. In fact, U.S. governments intervene to promote and protect culture in ways that parallel Canadian practices. G. Carr, *Trade Liberalization and the Political Economy of Culture: An International Perspective on FTA* (University of Maine: Orono, 1991), pp.2-3.

77. Canada, *Vital Links-Canadian Cultural Industries* (Ottawa: Department of Communications, 1987), p.67 and p.71.

78. *Direct-to-Home-Satellite Broadcasting, op. cit.,* p.12.

79. *Op. cit.,* p.10.

80. Ibid.

81. D. Taras, "We Need the CBC," *Policy Options* (16, no.7: 1995), pp.44-45.

82. L. Brown, "The Seven Deadly Sins of the Digital Age," *InterMedia* (22, no.3: 1994), p.37.

4

The Special Role of Magazines in the History of Canadian Mass Media and National Development

Peter Desbarats

"Magazines are special," the 1970 report of the Special Senate Committee on the Mass Media states. "Magazines constitute the only national press we possess in Canada," the report continues. "Magazines, in a different way from any other medium, can help foster in Canadians a sense of themselves. In terms of cultural survival, magazines could potentially be as important as railroads, airlines, national broadcasting networks, and national hockey leagues."[1] (This litany of national icons reads strangely now when transcontinental passenger-rail service has disappeared, the publicly owned airline has been privatized, public broadcasting services are under attack, and the National Hockey League is resident primarily in the U.S.) The report adds, with absolute predictability, "But Canadian magazines are in trouble."

Canadian magazines have always been in trouble, it seems, ever since John Howe, father of the more famous Joseph, began to publish *The Nova-Scotia Magazine and Comprehensive Review of Literature, Politics and News* in 1789 for 200 subscribers. British North America's first magazine lasted less than three years.[2] In other English-speaking parts of the world, particularly the U.S. and the U.K. as being most relevant to the Canadian experience, magazines also routinely appeared and disappeared. A high mortality rate was in the nature of the business. But only in Canada would the fate of magazines, from pre-Confederation to the present day, be linked so closely to the question of national survival.

A proclaimed connection with the fate of the nation is characteristic of Canadian media in general, to some extent, and much has been written about this over the years. But in this ongoing discussion, perhaps not enough attention has been paid to the special role of Canadian magazines, situated as they are in a curious halfway house between newspapers and the electronic media of radio and TV. In this perspective, Canadian magazines are seen to be indeed special; a study of the magazine industry in Canada can thus reveal a great deal about our distinctive system of mass media, its peculiar problems, and its special contribution to our struggle for cultural survival. It might even throw some optimistic light on our prospects for cultural development.

Newspapers, Electronic Media, and Magazines: Different Approaches to Government

Major Canadian newspapers, like their counterparts in the U.S. and England, have always been the product of private enterprise. They have been independent, in theory and most of the time in practice, of direct government support. Tax breaks and postal subsidies aside, and overlooking the almost total dependence of colonial newspapers on government advertising and patronage, newspaper publishers as a group have seldom linked the question of their survival to public subsidies, tariff protection, or the fate of the nation. This spirit of independence was based in part on a traditional view of the role of the press in a free-enterprise democratic society and in part on the fact that newspapers, because of their local and national subject matter, and because of the time and cost involved in shipping them over long distances, have always enjoyed a strong degree of natural protection from foreign competition.

Canadian radio, by contrast, was vulnerable to competition from the U.S. from the very beginning because radio frequencies ignored national boundaries and because much of radio's program content was popular entertainment that was North American in character and almost universal in appeal. From the start of radio broadcasting to the public in Canada in 1919, the federal government was involved in allocating frequencies to Canadian radio stations and trying to protect them from powerful U.S. stations.

Publicly owned radio began in 1923 when the newly formed Canadian National Railways established a radio department to provide broadcasts for passengers. By 1936, when the Canadian

Broadcasting Corporation (CBC) was created, Canada had combined the principles of public ownership of radio and protection from U.S. programming into a nationalist doctrine. Its essential elements had been described in 1932 by the late Graham Spry, a lobbyist for public broadcasting, when he instructed a parliamentary committee: "The question is the State or the United States?"[3] It hasn't altered at all since then. The dominance of the CBC in Canadian broadcasting, as the operator of the largest radio and TV networks in either language, is a characteristic feature of Canadian media and cultural life that distinguishes this country from the U.S. Pleas for support of public broadcasting are always based on cultural nationalism, although the regulatory instruments that can effectively protect Canadian broadcasting from American competition are increasingly hard to define in the current period of multiplying TV channels and with the prospect of unlimited digital radio channels.

In this context, magazines exist somewhere between the print world of newspapers and the electronic world of radio and TV. Almost invariably they are, like newspapers, privately owned, but the subject matter of magazines is often more like that of radio and TV. Apart from a few specialized publications, few magazines are devoted to local or national news. Most contain information rather than news, and many provide as much entertainment as information. For this reason, and because magazines have a long "shelf life" and can be shipped over long distances without losing timeliness, Canadian magazines have always suffered from competition by imported periodicals.

Paradoxically, the larger a Canadian magazine is, the more vulnerable it is to foreign competition, as a general rule. This has been true throughout our history, although there are a few more exceptions to this rule today than there were almost 25 years ago when the Special Senate Committee on the Mass Media published its report. In general, smaller and more specialized Canadian magazines have had greater success in Canada, sharing something of the natural market protection enjoyed by newspapers. It is larger Canadian magazines that appealed to a broader range of general interests, and that purveyed entertainment as well as information of a general character, that suffered from the kind of competition familiar to owners of Canadian TV stations. In this respect, the current direction of the entire North American magazine market towards more

specialized publications may promise a more level playing field for Canadian magazines in future.

Because of the free-enterprise nature of their industry, Canadian magazine publishers have never supported the principle of public ownership of national print media, or regulation of national print media in the public interest. On the other hand, the struggle to survive against strong foreign competition has driven them time and again to seek protective measures from the federal government. From its earliest decades, the Canadian magazine industry has been torn between the desire for independence and the need for protection. Much of its history can be described in terms of the conflict between these two forces and, in this sense, the magazine industry is perhaps more characteristic of Canada's national situation than either its newspapers or electronic media.

Energetic and Optimistic Pioneer Magazine Publishers

A survey of the history of Canadian magazines of the nineteenth century, littered with false starts, dashed expectations, and expensive disasters, creates an impression not of failure but of incredible energy and optimism. Our ancestral publishers, editors, and writers, confronting odds that would discourage most of our contemporaries, never seemed to lose hope that the next *Gazette* or *Miscellany* or *Repository* would be the one to bring them fame and fortune.

Among writers and journalists of various sorts, magazine editors and contributors have always been a somewhat special breed. Compared with a newspaper, particularly a modern giant with hundreds of editorial workers, a magazine is usually a more personal creation that carries the stamp of an editor's opinions and personality. Even *Time*, with its committees of editors and rewrite staff in New York and its formulas for processing information, has always been seen as the creation of its founder, Henry Luce, even years after his death. Most magazines approach the reader in a more leisurely, cultivated manner than do newspapers, in the style of the raconteur rather than the tipster.

"A magazine appeals to the miscellaneous imagination," according to Fraser Sutherland's 1989 history of Canadian magazines. "From the beginning, magazines were that way."[4]

Although the British are inveterate publishers and readers of magazines, it was the French who invented the format. The first periodical other than a newspaper is generally considered to be the *Journal des Scavans* launched in Paris in 1665, 209 years after

Gutenberg's Bible began the era of print.[5] It was a monthly review of new books, interested particularly in the natural sciences, and was the inspiration for the *Philosophical Transactions of the Royal Society* published in London the same year. Within a few decades, periodicals of such sober character were joined by more popular journals such as the *Weekly Memorials for the Ingenious,*[6] followed by question-and-answer magazines that were like catechisms on current events and general knowledge. This form remained popular into the early years of this century when Sir George Newnes was publishing his hugely successful *Tit-Bits* for British readers, the first periodical in Britain and probably in the world to sell a million copies of each issue.[7]

Among its definitions of the word "magazine," the *Oxford English Dictionary* includes "a portable receptacle for articles of value,"[8] a description that Fraser Sutherland found suggestive of "the printed magazine's essential qualities."[9] The container or cover of the magazine, whether garish or restrained in style, is designed to reflect its contents and attract a certain kind of reader. Opening the magazine should create the same sense of anticipation as unlocking a treasure chest. Each article in the magazine aims at being a small work of art. Canada's first magazine, mentioned earlier, advertised itself on the title page as "being a collection of the most valuable articles that appear in the periodical publications of Great-Britain, Ireland and America with various pieces in verse and prose never before published,"[10] a kind of *Reader's Digest* of old-world journalism with a dash of the new.

In the 50 years after the appearance of *The Nova-Scotia Magazine and Comprehensive Review,* Canadian magazines made what historian Wilfrid Kesterton describes as a "token beginning."[11] Most magazines of the period lasted for only a few years at most, often for only a few months, although there were exceptions such as *La Bibliothèque Canadienne* published from 1825 to 1830 by the journalist, historian, and poet Michel Bibaud, and John Lovell's *Literary Garland,* which lasted from 1838 to 1851 and first published Susanna Moodie's classic description of life in the bush of Upper Canada.[12]

The pace of publishing activity of all kinds accelerated in the second half of the century. By 1865, there were almost 400 newspapers publishing in British North America, including 35 dailies.[13] In retrospect, knowing what we do about the trials of Canadian publishing in the following century, the ambition of Canadian magazine publishers of the period was breathtaking. When George Desbarats[14] launched his 16-page *Canadian Illustrated News* in 1869, and followed it with a French-language edition, the population of Montreal was about 130,000. There were only 3,300,000 people in the entire country. The *Canadian Illustrated News* survived until 1883, by which time Desbarats had also launched the *Daily Graphic* in New York, the first newspaper in the world to use photographic illustrations, the product of advanced Canadian technology.

Like other Canadian publishers of his time, Desbarats closely identified the *Canadian Illustrated News* and his other magazines with an emerging sense of Canadian nationalism. In his prospectus for the new magazine, he promised that, "by picturing to our own people the broad dominion they possess," the illustrated periodical would help its readers "to feel still prouder of the proud Canadian name."[15]

During this period, Canadian magazines multiplied in number and showed more durability. One of the most popular and longest-lived was *Grip,* an illustrated satirical weekly established in 1872 by John W. Bengough, the most prolific and influential political cartoonist of his day. It survived for more than 20 years, all the more surprising in light of the failure of humorous magazines in recent times to attract and hold a large Canadian audience, at least in English-speaking Canada.

In our own day, satirical magazines have flourished in French-speaking Quebec, where *Croc* celebrated its 14th anniversary in 1993 with a monthly circulation of 45,000.[16] In the early years of this century, humorous publications such as Bob Edwards's *Calgary Eye-Opener,* a newspaper, and *The Goblin,* a magazine launched by University of Toronto students after the First World War, were immensely popular. *The Goblin* claimed to have a circulation of more than 10,500 copies and the biggest newsstand sale in Canada after its first year of publication,[17] but English-speaking Canadians seemed to lose their sense of humour after that. One of *The Goblin's* best cartoonists, Richard Taylor, subsequently moved to the U.S. and became a regular contributor to *The New Yorker;*[18] about 60 years later, Graydon Carter abandoned a failing magazine in Ottawa to achieve a huge success in New York, where in 1985, he co-founded the monthly satirical scandal magazine *Spy.*[19] (*Spy* ceased publication in 1994.) More recently, *Frank* magazine, launched in Halifax in 1987 by David Bentley and associates, has proved to be exceptionally popular and durable. While the Halifax edition continued to publish, Bentley moved to

Ottawa to start a national edition of *Frank* in 1989.[20] The magazine published its first hardcover anthology in 1993, *The Best of Frank,* and claimed a national circulation of 18,000.[21]

Magazine editors of a century ago were often as colourful and grandiloquent as their Victorian prose. Edmund Sheppard, a flamboyant journalist from St. Thomas, Ontario, who spent a short time as an American cowboy and subsequently adopted boots, chewing tobacco, and the pen name "Don" as his trademarks, started *Saturday Night* in 1887, the only magazine of that period which still publishes.[22] Goldwyn Smith, the expatriate British author and academic who married a widowed heiress and adopted Toronto as his home, not without some condescension, edited *The Week* from 1883 to 1896 and helped to make it the most influential periodical of its time.[23]

The Struggle for Survival against U.S. Competition

Goldwyn Smith produced his magazine towards the end of a period when Canadian magazine publishers had managed to co-exist with foreign periodicals and even, in the earlier days, to benefit from them. Distance and lax copyright regulations enabled Canadian publishers of the nineteenth century, before the overseas telegraph brought instant communication with Europe, to scalp stories from British and French periodicals. Reprints from U.S. periodicals were also available to Canadian magazines at little or no cost. At a time when magazines were relatively expensive and provided an elite readership with political, business, and cultural information, Canadian magazines had enjoyed something of the natural monopoly that protected Canadian newspapers from American competition. This began to change towards the end of the nineteenth century, as Goldwyn Smith noted in his own magazine in 1894. "In the field of periodical literature," he wrote, "what chance can our Canadian publishers have against an American magazine with a circulation of a hundred and fifty thousand, and a splendour of illustration such as only a profuse expenditure can support?"[24]

Goldwyn Smith and his contemporaries in the fledgling Canadian magazine industry were beginning to feel the effects of a shift in North American magazine publishing from class to mass. In the years just before and after the turn of the century, the success of the 10-cent magazine created a revolution in the industry. The decision of *McClure's* magazine to go to 10 cents in 1893 forced most of its chief competitors to follow suit—*Munsey's, Peterson's, Godey's,* and *Cosmopolitan.* By 1903, the publisher Frank Munsey estimated that 10-cent periodicals comprised about 85 percent of the total circulation of magazines in the U.S. Some magazines, such as the *Saturday Evening Post,* dropped to 5 cents per copy, and a few publishers even experimented with magazines selling for 1 cent or 2 cents.[25]

As prices dropped and readership increased dramatically, the largest and most profitable magazines were those that carried entertainment in the form of fiction and light features, or service information such as recipes and other types of household intelligence. Unlike political or cultural information, this type of content carried little national bias. Deprived of the protection from competition that their distinctive content had provided in the days of elitist magazine publishing, and dependent on a relatively small readership and advertising base, it was almost impossible for Canadian magazines to compete with a growing number of American publications coming across the border. The best-selling U.S. periodicals in Canada in the 1920s were *Saturday Evening Post, Pictorial Review,* and *McCall's Magazine.*[26]

By 1925 it was estimated that for every domestic magazine sold in Canada eight were imported from the U.S. In total, about 50,000,000 copies of U.S. magazines were sold in Canada annually.[27] Among the imports were the first issues of Benarr Macfadden's *True Detective,* launched in 1924, the precursor of a flood of sensational pulp magazines and tabloid newspapers that continues in our own day with the strong presence of the *Star* and the *National Enquirer* on supermarket newsstands.

Canadian publishers were running into exactly the same type of competition from the U.S. that the owners of the first commercial Canadian TV stations were to experience about 40 years later. By that time, however, the TV industry had a history of regulation and public ownership that made protective legislation an instinctive response to U.S. competition. Canadian magazine publishers in the early decades of this century had no such tradition, but that didn't restrain them for a moment from turning to the government for protection.

Government Protection for Canadian Magazines

Rationale and Contradictions

As an editorial in *Saturday Night* declared in 1924: "The Government must get behind the product to the extent of giving publishers some degree of protection against the dumping process which is now going on and which over the space of ten years has increased the sale of United States periodicals in the Canadian market by upward of three hundred percent."[28]

Mary Vipond states in her 1989 history of the mass media in Canada that there was nothing unusual about this in the world of business. Some Canadian industries had relied on tariff protection long before Confederation; the introduction of the Conservatives' national policy in 1879 "suited manufacturers perfectly, for while aiding them by reducing competition, it preserved the free-enterprise system.... Thus it is not surprising that the magazine publishers, also facing American competition rooted in economies of scale and prior establishment in the market, turned to the tariff as a remedy."[29]

The publishers made three arguments, which Vipond summarizes as "the puritanical, the economic and the nationalist." The first claimed that many U.S. magazines were salacious and immoral, ostensibly unlike those produced by Canadian or British publishers. The economic argument was the same as that used by any other threatened industry: thousands of Canadians would be thrown out of work if the Americans' low-cost "overflow" production was allowed to enter Canada unimpeded. To this argument was added what Vipond calls "a unique twist ... if Canada lacked its own magazines, it lacked a vital agency of national communication."[30] She quotes Frederick Paul, the editor of *Saturday Night*, writing in 1926: "Without the slightest notion of flag-waving or sloppy patriotism, it must be apparent that if we depend on these United States centers for our reading matter we might as well move our government to Washington, for under such conditions it will go there in the end."[31]

The publishers' case, however, contained the seeds of its own rebuttal. In assigning a national role for their magazines—"a stronger cohesive agent than Parliament," in the words of Frederick Paul[32]—the publishers opened their argument to discussion of the character of a free press in a democratic society. An essential attribute of this press is freedom from government influence; the separation of press and state is an article of faith for journalists, as is a belief in the free flow of information. Asking the government to exert its influence on behalf of the magazine industry appeared, at least to some, to create the possibility of the government asking for something in return or, at the very least, of publishers and journalists being less critical towards a protective government.

Suggesting that the government should exert this influence to interfere with the flow of publications across the border appeared to be even more dangerous, particularly to journalists who opposed censorship on principle.

A History of Half-Hearted Protection

These contradictions partly explained why successive Canadian governments hesitated to protect this particular industry, especially when the affected industry in the U.S. was one of the most vocal and politically influential. From the 1920s until 1975, every economic crisis in the Canadian magazine industry brought forward the same arguments with the same internal contradictions and, as a consequence, the same half-hearted responses from the government in Ottawa.

The pattern was set in the 1920s when the Liberals, traditionally the party of low tariffs, rejected a request for protection from the newly formed Magazine Publishers Association. Two groups that supported this decision, for entirely different reasons, were the Consumers' League of Canada, whose members were concerned that a duty on U.S. magazines would make them more expensive in Canada, and the American News Company, which since the 1880s had monopolized a large segment of the newsstand distribution business in both the U.S. and Canada.[33] Having refused to impose a tariff, the Liberal government then, in another prototypal decision, slightly reduced postal rates for Canadian magazines, imposed a duty on a few U.S. pulp magazines such as *Argosy* and *Real Romance,* and gave Canadian publishers some relief from customs duties on imported paper and printing materials.[34] This policy of combining a refusal to offer significant help, particularly if it threatened to annoy the United States, with minor concessions designed to alleviate the industry's most pressing problems became familiar to Canadian magazine publishers in the following decades as they followed a well-worn path to and from Ottawa.

The publishers glimpsed utopia briefly in 1930 when the unsympathetic Liberals were replaced by a Conservative government that imposed a tariff on U.S. magazines based on their ratio of advertising to editorial matter. The freedom-of-the-press argument was made on that occasion by Mackenzie King, former and future prime minister, who stated from the opposition benches in Parliament, in defence of the rights of U.S. magazines, that "thought is cosmopolitan,"[35] presumably unaware of the pun. Between

1931 and 1935, the circulation of U.S. periodicals in Canada decreased by 62 percent while Canadian magazines, even in the face of depressed economic conditions, increased their circulation by almost the same proportion: 64 percent. About 50 U.S. periodicals began printing in Canada. As Mary Vipond wrote, "The imposition of tariffs against imported magazines was an unprecedented act.... Yet, it did not prove to be the beginning of a whole new approach to fostering the Canadian media."[36] In 1935, King and the Liberals, back in power again, signed a three-year Canada–U.S. Trade Agreement that included removal of tariffs on magazines. Once again, the Liberals attempted to sweeten this bitter pill for Canadian magazine publishers by adopting measures to cushion the effects of duties on imported paper, ink, and other publishing materials. Within three years of the removal of tariffs, American magazines tripled their total Canadian circulation.[37]

The next significant development occurred in 1943 when wartime paper shortages persuaded both *Time* and *Reader's Digest* to set up shop in Canada to obtain Canadian paper rations. After the war, they began to enlarge the distinctive editorial content of these Canadian editions and to aggressively sell advertising in them.

Competition from U.S. periodicals and the initial effects of TV endangered the few established Canadian periodicals of general interest that had survived the Depression of the 1930s and the war years. *New World Illustrated,* a major periodical, disappeared in 1948, *National Home Monthly,* in 1950, and the *Canadian Home Journal,* in 1958. *Saturday Night* led a precarious existence. *Maclean's* survived only because its publisher, Maclean Hunter, owned a profitable stable of business magazines. Like Canadian newspapers, specialized magazines provided distinctive types of service information to their readers and consequently were immune to some extent from the kind of U.S. competition that made life abnormally difficult for Canadian consumer magazines of general interest.

By 1954, U.S. magazines were occupying 80 percent of the Canadian market compared with 67 percent in 1948. By 1955, the Canadian editions of *Time* and *Reader's Digest* were accounting for 37 percent of the total advertising revenues of general-interest magazines in Canada; they had doubled their share of the advertising market since 1948.[38]

The last half of the 1950s saw another example of stop-and-go protectionism when a tax on advertising in Canadian editions of U.S. periodicals, imposed by the Liberals in 1956, was removed by the Conservatives in 1958. By 1960, the state of Canada's magazine industry was so precarious that the Conservative government of Prime Minister John Diefenbaker appointed a Royal Commission on Publications under Senator Grattan O'Leary, a former Ottawa newspaper editor.[39]

The O'Leary Commission: Freedom and Competition

Freedom of the press once again became a major issue as U.S. magazines resisted any suggestion, during public hearings of the commission, that their right to do business in Canada be curtailed in any way. But from the outset, Grattan O'Leary indicated that he would resist an interpretation of press freedom that would allow unrestricted foreign competition in Canada. Freedom of the press is not an absolute freedom, he would often say; his favourite analogy was that freedom of expression did not give anyone the right to stand up in a crowded theatre and shout, "Fire!"[40]

O'Leary's definition of press freedom prevailed in the commission's report. It stated as a principle that "a nation's domestic advertising expenditures should be devoted to the support of its own media of communications,"[41] and it recommended that Canadian firms advertising in foreign magazines or Canadian editions of foreign magazines should not be allowed to deduct the cost of this advertising as a business expense for tax purposes. This would have the effect of doubling the cost of advertising placed in foreign publications or diverting it, as the Royal Commission hoped, to Canadian periodicals. O'Leary's controversial recommendations, juggled indecisively by the Diefenbaker government until it was defeated in 1963, and finally adopted with qualifications by the Liberals in 1965, stirred up what an inside observer later described as "several nests of hornets of great ferocity."[42] One was located in Washington where the U.S. State Department warned that action against *Time* and *Reader's Digest* might jeopardize the future of U.S. defence contracts offered to Canadian firms and congressional approval of the Canada-U.S. Autopact.[43] Then Finance Minister Walter Gordon recalled later that "pressure was brought to bear on the prime minister not to do anything that would interfere with *Time* or upset its proprietor."[44]

The other hornet's nest of opposition was among the ranks of the Canadian Daily Newspaper Publishers Association, split by conflicting reactions to the Liberals' decision to extend provisions of the legislation to newspaper advertising, thus preventing foreign ownership of Canadian newspapers. At the time, there were rumours that European interests intended to make an offer for *La Presse* and that *The Globe and Mail* might be sold to a U.S. publisher.[45] Some Canadian publishers, fearing that prohibiting foreign takeovers might diminish the value of their properties, and perhaps interfere eventually with their own ability to purchase foreign publishing companies if other governments retaliated, opposed the legislation as a dangerous infringement by the state on their rights as free-enterprise publishers.[46]

Bill C-58 and the Renaissance of Canadian Magazine Publishing

Despite this opposition, the Pearson government in 1965 enacted legislation based on the O'Leary Report. Because of opposition from Washington, the legislation contained a grandfather clause that exempted *Time* and *Reader's Digest* from its provisions. The ineffectiveness of this half-measure was evident five years later to the Senate Committee on the Mass Media, which "deeply regretted that *Time* and *Reader's Digest* were exempted from the O'Leary legislation" and said that this had been "a bad decision."[47] After five more years, the Liberal government of Prime Minister Pierre Trudeau introduced Bill C-58, which finally completed the legislation proposed by the O'Leary Commission almost 15 years earlier by including *Time* and *Reader's Digest* in its provisions. A few weeks after the legislation was passed in 1976, *Time* abandoned its Canadian edition, although the U.S. edition with some Canadian advertising (not eligible as a business expense for tax purposes) is still available in Canada. *Reader's Digest* created a Canadian foundation to publish its Canadian edition, which remains eligible for tax deductibility, while ownership of its book- and record-distribution activities and other profitable enterprises remained in the U.S.

Bill C-58 coincided with, and was partly responsible for, the dawn of a renaissance period in Canadian magazine publishing that bore a closer resemblance to the creative optimism of the nineteenth century than to the depressed conditions and mentality of the first half of the twentieth century. Although there is disagreement about the precise effects of the legislation, most authorities would agree with Fraser Sutherland's assessment that "there is no doubt that Bill C-58 had given an important psychological boost to many smaller magazines. ... Certainly it was difficult to see that anyone lost from it."[48]

Although the Canadianized *Reader's Digest* remained the magazine with the largest circulation in Canada, and the American edition of *Time* continued to sell here in substantial if reduced numbers, other magazines signified a growing Canadian presence. The U.S.-owned *TV Guide*, by then one of the most popular magazines, was taken over by Télémedia, a Montreal-based company. Maclean Hunter, one of the main beneficiaries of Bill C-58, was able in 1978 to fulfil its ambition to make *Maclean's* a weekly news magazine. Specialty magazines such as *Harrowsmith*, a periodical about country living that appealed strongly to affluent city dwellers and was successful almost from its first issue in 1976, demolished the notion that it was impossible for new Canadian magazines to achieve national renown and financial stability in their first few years. Publishing out of a village near Kingston, Ontario, *Harrowsmith* achieved both in its first few issues and continues to be successful under its current owner, Télémedia. Controlled-circulation magazines, paid for by advertisers and distributed without charge to selected groups of readers, multiplied so rapidly after 1975 that the whole concept of paying for a magazine was thrown into question for a time. Among the giveaways were dozens of city magazines that attempted to repeat the success of *Toronto Life*, one of the most prosperous city magazines in North America.

In the decade after 1975, the number of city and entertainment-oriented magazines published in Canada increased from 17 to 56.[49] From 1971 to 1986, the share of the national magazine market occupied by Canadian publications increased from 30 percent to 40 percent.[50] Despite several sharp increases in postal rates, subscription sales jumped from 37 percent to 60 percent of the market in the same period.[51] In the 12 years following the adoption of Bill C-58, the annual revenues from circulation of Maclean Hunter Publications rose from about $5 million to about $50 million.[52]

Not all of the new magazines prospered. The supernova of the new generation of Canadian periodicals was a glossy, controlled-circulation magazine called *Quest*, which appeared in 1972, reached 700,000 Canadian households by 1978, and went out of business in 1984. One of the most expensive failures was *Vista*, launched with a reported $10-million investment by automotive-parts manufacturer Frank Stronach in 1988, and killed two years later. This generally expansive period for the magazine industry also saw the demise, at the beginning of the 1980s, of such national weekly-newspaper supplements as

Weekend and *The Canadian,* among the most profitable Canadian magazines of the early 1970s. Despite this experience, *The Globe and Mail* entered the magazine field in 1984 with its monthly *Report on Business Magazine,* adding city magazines and others devoted to travel, fashion, and health to its stable by the end of the decade, all delivered to *Globe* subscribers at no extra cost. These ventures symbolized the expansionist spirit that still pervaded the Canadian magazine industry at the end of the 1980s after 15 years of unprecedented activity and prosperity, although the recession in the first half of the following decade curbed this trend. By 1994, for instance, *The Globe and Mail* had ceased publishing all its magazines except for the original *Report on Business.* Statistics Canada data indicates that total revenues of Canadian magazines hit a peak of $903 million in 1989-90 and subsequently declined to $846.4 million in 1991-92.[53]

The most recent cycle of the enduring efforts of Canadian magazine publishers to protect their industry from uninhibited American competition began in April 1993, when *Time* magazine launched a Canadian edition of its *Sports Illustrated.* Pointing out that 43 U.S. magazines have circulations of more than 50,000 in Canada, the industry feared that the *Sports Illustrated* initiative might encourage other American publishers to attempt to create similar Canadian editions supported by Canadian advertising.[54] The federal government responded by creating the latest in an apparently endless series of task forces that have studied the magazine industry.

In the 1990s Canadian magazine publishers also lobbied for exemption from the Goods and Services Tax (GST), joining book publishers in criticizing the "tax on reading" imposed by the Conservative government of Prime Minister Mulroney. The federal Liberals promised to abolish the GST during their successful 1993 election campaign, but rejected a plea for special exemption from publishers early in 1994 while the government reviewed the entire tax system.[55]

Problems and Portents

It is significant that the problems encountered by Canadian magazines in the past 15 years, since the enactment of Bill C-58, were variants of problems common to magazines in the U.S. and other Western countries, rather than being peculiar to Canada. This seems to indicate a normalization of the industry under conditions that approached those experienced by magazine publishers in other countries.

Competition by imported periodicals will always be a major factor, at least in English-speaking Canada. But it is noteworthy that, by 1987, only one of the 12 largest magazines sold in Canada (*National Geographic*) was U.S.-owned, and that the circulation of *Maclean's* was about double that of *Time* in Canada.[56] Imported periodicals, primarily from the U.S., still accounted for 65 percent of the consumer magazines sold in Canada, but it is also true that Canadians were reading more copies of more Canadian magazines than ever before. It is now difficult to imagine this trend being reversed, particularly in view of the protection afforded to Canadian cultural industries under the Canada-U.S. Free Trade Agreement, the specific protection for the provisions of Bill C-58 under the agreement,[57] and similar protection included in the 1993 North American Free Trade Agreement (NAFTA). In fact, the problems now faced by magazines everywhere may increase the competitiveness of Canadian magazines. This is because the magazines that appear to be facing the most severe problems in the 1990s are those general-interest magazines that traditionally have been the most troublesome competitors for Canadian magazines.

This is an unexpected and perhaps positive result, for Canadian magazine publishers, of international trends that have changed the industry over the past few decades, largely in response to TV.

It was the initial impact of TV that destroyed such landmarks of U.S. magazine publishing as *The Saturday Evening Post, Life, Collier's,* and, in Canada, *Canadian Home Journal, Mayfair, Liberty,* and the glossy weekend newspaper supplements. Once the initial impact of TV had been absorbed, however, magazines showed great resilience in developing new formats and styles to reach new audiences. In this, they were more successful than newspapers, particularly those that responded to TV by trying to imitate its visual impact and becoming, in the process, a kind of "frozen television."[58] Controlled-circulation magazines liberated publishers to some extent from their dependence on subscribers, although "readership" as defined by surveys remained important. Magazines became more specialized, tailoring themselves to specific audiences and interests. Both established and new magazines reflected to some degree a style that was sometimes referred to as the New Journalism, "in which authors expressed feelings and opinions and told about first-hand experiences."[59] By reinventing themselves, magazines not only remained relevant to a growing number of readers, while newspapers reached fewer and fewer of their potential readers, but also prepared themselves for survival in a media market of accelerating fragmentation.

Even the giant TV networks are now being affected by the erosion of their huge audiences under the impact of cable TV and satellites, specialty TV channels, VCRs, and changing lifestyles. In the 1980s, for the first time in the history of TV, network audiences began to shrink appreciably while ratings for local TV newscasts increased.[60] Similar trends in print journalism have created speculation that national news magazines in the U.S. may be in trouble. Total newsstand sales of *Time, Newsweek,* and *U.S. News & World Report* have decreased by 25 percent since 1968, largely because of competition from newspapers that have become more magazine-like in their approach to news, from specialized magazines, and from a multitude of specialized information programs now available on TV.[61] The most important trade journal of the U.S. magazine industry, *Folio,* published a forecast for the decade in 1990 predicting that "mass market magazines will find it more and more difficult to increase their circulation at all" because of slow population growth in the U.S. and increased competition from specialized magazines.[62]

If the mass audiences for traditional national and international print and electronic media are truly fragmenting, magazines, books, TV programs, and other cultural "products" created for the "regional" North American markets represented by English-speaking and French-speaking Canada will have better opportunities to communicate with their special audiences. Canadians, reflecting this larger trend, presumably will be more receptive to magazines and other cultural works produced specifically for them. The experience of Canada's magazine industry in recent years, not to mention theatre, cinema, book publishing, and other cultural activities, seems to indicate that this is what has begun to happen.

Charting the progress of Canada's magazine industry, and its distinctive ongoing relationship to government, may give us a clearer idea of future patterns of Canadian cultural development than we would gain by monitoring the progress of newspapers or TV, as we have tended to do in the past.[63]

Notes

1. Special Senate Committee on the Mass Media, *Report* (Ottawa: Queen's Printer, 1970), vol. I, p.153.

2. Fraser Sutherland, *The Monthly Epic—A History of Canadian Magazines* (Toronto: Fitzhenry & Whiteside, 1989), p.18.

3. Quoted in Michael Nolan, *Foundations: Alan Plaunt and the Early Days of CBC Radio* (Toronto: CBC Enterprises, 1986), p.31.

4. Sutherland, *The Monthly Epic,* p.1.

5. John Feather, *A History of British Publishing* (London: Routledge, 1988), p.106.

6. Feather, *A History,* p.107.

7. Anthony Davis, *Magazine Journalism Today* (London: Heinemann, 1988), p.8.

8. *The Shorter Oxford English Dictionary* (London: Clarendon Press, 1973), p.1256.

9. Sutherland, *The Monthly Epic,* p.2.

10. Ibid., p.7.

11. W.H. Kesterton, *A History of Journalism in Canada* (Toronto: McClelland & Stewart, 1967), p.9.

12. Peter Desbarats, *Guide to Canadian News Media* (Toronto: Harcourt Brace Jovanovich, 1990), p.11.

13. Desbarats, *Guide,* p.10.

14. The great-grandfather of the author, elected to the Canadian News Hall of Fame in Toronto in 1987, an admitted example of posthumous or reverse nepotism. The author was on the selection committee.

15. Peter Desbarats, *The Canadian Illustrated News 1869–1883* (Toronto: McClelland & Stewart, 1970), p.4.

16. Interview with *Croc Magazine* editor Jacques Hurtubise, January 10, 1994.

17. Peter Desbarats and Terry Mosher, *The Hecklers* (Toronto: McClelland & Stewart, 1979), p.83.

18. Desbarats and Mosher, *The Hecklers,* p.83.

19. Sutherland, *The Monthly Epic,* p.304.

20. Howard Akler, "Aiming to Displease," *Ryerson Review of Journalism* (March 1991), pp.34–39.

21. Information provided to the author by the Toronto bureau of *Frank,* January 6, 1994.

22. Sutherland, *The Monthly Epic,* p.81.

23. Desbarats, *Guide,* p.12.

24. Sutherland, *The Monthly Epic,* p.32.

25. John Tebbel, *The Media in America* (New York: Crowell, 1974), p.279.

26. Sutherland, *The Monthly Epic,* p.114.

27. Mary Vipond, *The Mass Media in Canada* (Toronto: James Lorimer, 1989), p.24.

28. Quoted in Sutherland, *The Monthly Epic,* p.114.

29. Vipond, *The Mass Media,* p.25.

30. Ibid., p.26.

31. Ibid., p.27.

32. Ibid.

33. Ibid., pp.21, 27.

34. Sutherland, *The Monthly Epic,* p.115.

35. Vipond, *The Mass Media,* p.28.

36. Ibid., p.29.

37. Sutherland, *The Monthly Epic,* p.116.

38. Vipond, *The Mass Media,* p.61.

39. The author of this paper, a reporter for *The Montreal Star* in the 1960s, was the only Canadian journalist to cover every public hearing of the Royal Commission on Periodicals and vividly recalls the confrontation between Grattan O'Leary, the crusty Ottawa editor from the Gaspé region of Quebec, and Henry Luce, the legendary Chinese-born founder of *Time.* O'Leary won part of the debate when Luce finally agreed, under pressure, that the Canadian edition of *Time* was not really a Canadian magazine, but a discussion of journalistic objectivity and its role at *Time* ended when Luce said, "That is a philosophical question which I would be very glad to discuss on a philosophical basis. As you know very well, it is impossible to discuss." The quotation is taken from an article that I wrote for the February-March 1962 issue of *Exchange,* another short-lived and long-defunct Canadian magazine.

40. Author's recollection.

41. Sutherland, *The Monthly Epic,* p.186.

[42.] Tom Kent, *A Public Purpose* (Montreal/Kingston: McGill-Queen's University Press, 1988), p.317.

[43.] Sutherland, *The Monthly Epic*, p.187.

[44.] Walter Gordon, *A Political Memoir* (Toronto: McClelland & Stewart, 1977), p.205.

[45.] Gordon, *A Political Memoir*, p.207.

[46.] Kent, *A Public Purpose*, pp.321-22.

[47.] Special Senate Committee on Mass Media, *Report*, vol. I, p.164.

[48.] Sutherland, *The Monthly Epic*, , p.260.

[49.] Ibid., p.262.

[50.] Ibid., p.263.

[51.] Ibid.

[52.] Desbarats, *Guide*, p.12.

[53.] "Circulation up, revenue down," *Masthead* 6, no. 10 (September 1993): 8.

[54.] "Heading for a showdown," *Masthead* 6, no. 4 (February 1993): 6-7.

[55.] "Government won't drop GST on reading materials for now," *London Free Press* (7 January 1994), p.A5.

[56.] *Canadian Magazine Publishing* (Cultural Industries and Agencies Branch, Government of Ontario, May 23, 1989). By the end of 1992 *Time* magazine had narrowed the gap somewhat, reporting an average weekly circulation of 333,815, compared with 559,716 for *Maclean's*, according to statistics published in *Masthead* 6, no. 5 (March 1993): 7.

[57.] Stan Sutter, "Free Trade Presents No Direct Threat to Health of Canada's Business Press," *Marketing* 93, no. 21 (23 May 1988), pp.26-27.

[58.] David Taras, *The Newsmakers* (Toronto: Nelson, 1990), p.58. Taras attributed the phrase "frozen television" to Professor Fred Fletcher of York University in "The Prime Minister as Persuader," Thomas Hockin, ed., *Apex of Power*, 2nd ed. (Scarborough, Ont.: Prentice-Hall, 1977), p.11.

[59.] Taras, *The Newsmakers*, p.58.

[60.] Desbarats, *Guide*, pp.46-47.

[61.] Bruce Porter, "The Newsweeklies: Is the Species Doomed?" *Columbia Journalism Review* 27, no. 6 (March/April 1989): 23-29.

[62.] Doris Walsh, "Who Will Your Readers Be in the Next Decade?" *Folio* 19, no. 1 (January 1990): 84-89.

[63.] Another sign of change in 1990 was the federal government's response to the magazine industry's complaints about the imminent Goods and Services Tax (GST) and steep increases in postal rates for magazines. Despite the ritual claim by the Canadian Magazine Publishers Association that "magazines are a vital medium in the definition and dissemination of the essence of what makes Canada," the relative health of the industry since 1975 made it difficult to create the kind of political pressure that historically had forced governments to introduce protective measures. In announcing a system of subsidies for magazines to compensate for higher postal rates starting in 1993 (Communications Canada press release, June 27, 1990), the government indicated a desire to normalize its relationship with the magazine industry by treating it as one of many cultural industries requiring subsidies. The industry itself generally supported this; see Tony Van Alpen, "Mail Rate Up for Foreign Books," *Toronto Star* (28 June 1990), p.C1. This was a considerable advance over similar situations prior to 1975 when the industry would always present itself as a "basket case" urgently requiring special protective measures if it were to survive at all.

Bringing Down Giants: Thomas Nast, John Wilson Bengough, and the Maturing of Political Cartooning

David R. Spencer

[This article originally appeared in American Journalism *15, no. 3 (summer 1998): 61-88.] Reprinted by permission.*

Thomas Nast and John Wilson Bengough had a lot in common. Both came from immigrant families. Both crafted careers on the antics of corrupt political figures and both prospered at least intellectually because of their art and their wit. Early in their careers both were single crusaders who were major actors in bringing down political dynasties with the power of their pictures and words. Both had the good fortune to become journalists when a new type of magazine was emerging, one devoted to investigating the less desirable aspects of political and social life that accompanied the Gilded Age of trade, urbanization, and industrialization following the Civil War in the United States and the articles of Confederation in Canada. In the two decades between 1865 and 1885, the number of politically oriented periodicals grew from 700 to 3,300 in the United States alone.[1]

There were fortunes to be made in the second half of the nineteenth century. Empires were being forged by Britain, France, Germany, Spain, and Portugal. Emergent industrialization in North America was a key player in what was becoming a global economic community stretching across all the world's oceans. The interdependency of homeland and colony was responsible for an economic culture that operated with few rules and regulations. Clever entrepreneurs stood side by side with robber barons as symbols of wealth and power. To get rich one had to take risks, but these risks were not necessarily destined to be legal. Both Boss Bill Tweed in New York and Sir John A. Macdonald in Canada refused to let minor matters such as law and ethics stand in their way. It took the genius of Nast in New York and the probing satire of Bengough in Toronto to prove to these two titans of politics that Lord Acton was right when he observed that absolute power corrupts absolutely.

Both Thomas Nast and John Wilson Bengough began their journalistic careers against a background of conflict between industrialization on one hand and labour activism on the other. In Canada, the year before Bengough launched *Grip*, the nation was gripped by a landmark labour dispute that turned the tide on labour-management relations in the country. The politician upon whom Bengough built his career, Canada's first prime minister Sir John A. Macdonald, was front and centre in the events.

The Toronto Typographers Union had struck the Toronto newspaper *The Globe* in 1872, demanding an eight-hour day. The owner of the *Globe* was George Brown, a father of the Canadian Confederation and a founder of the federal Liberal Party that sat in opposition to Macdonald's governing Conservatives. Brown, not one to be intimidated by unionists, retaliated by swearing out sedition charges against the union leadership. Macdonald, a long-time foe of the Toronto publisher, reacted in two ways. He passed the country's first legislation that legalized labour organizations and funded one of the country's first trade-union newspapers, the *Ontario Workman* if only to cause discomfort to Brown. As much as Nast was prepared to take on the New York city political elite, Bengough, who was born into a decidedly political and Liberal family, was handed a ready-made target in Macdonald, who had inherited a political stripe with a strong Tory past. Bengough was unable to attack the prime minister in his defence of the working class. But, as the Pacific Scandal of 1873 would prove, the prime minister had skeletons in his closet, skeletons with a strong connection to the nation's elites.[2]

Although neither was born into an affluent family, neither suffered the pains of deprivation and starvation that was so common throughout the world prior to the mid-point of the nineteenth century. The

FIGURE 1: John Wilson Benough

ALL ABOARD FOR THE ELYSIAN FIELDS! AT THE CHRISTOPHER STREET FERRY

FIGURE 2: All Aboard for the Elysian Fields! At the Christopher Street Ferry

young Nast grew up in a culture dominated by music and performance. As a young man in Landau, Germany, where he was born on September 27, 1840, Thomas Nast travelled with his father, sometimes carrying the musician's trombone when he played with the local regimental band in Landau or as a pit player for local theatrical presentations, most of which had a military theme.[3]

Similarly, there is no indication that John Wilson Bengough's life-long love affair with sketching and cartooning evolved as an influence in his family. He was the son of a Scottish immigrant, Captain John Bengough, who was born in St. Andrew's, Fifeshire, Scotland, in 1819. The elder Bengough showed no signs of artistic passion, save his career as a cabinet-maker and staircase builder. His major contribution to his son's life was a political agenda that remained with the younger Bengough throughout his career as an artist, journalist, and travelling lecturer. The elder Bengough was deeply involved in Canadian politics prior to the formation of Canada in the Confederation articles of 1867. He chose to shape the fortunes of one Oliver Mowat, a leading intellectual in the Reform movement of journalist George Brown, a movement that gave birth to the modern Canadian Liberal Party. Captain John helped launch Mowat's career, hoping that his friend, a rising political star in the mid-Victorian period, would adopt the single-tax principles of Henry George to which he and his son were both devoted.[4]

Thomas Nast arrived at journalism through art. John Wilson Bengough arrived in art through journalism. In spite of his father's urging to either study music or learn a trade, the young Thomas Nast was only interested in becoming an artist. After moving to New York, he registered in a drawing class conducted by a German émigré named Theodore Kaufman. When Kaufman's studio burned to the ground, destroying everything in it, Nast no longer had an artistic home until he registered in the New York Academy of Design. He drew and painted, and at the tender age of 15, decided he was ready to enter the commercial world.

He approached Frank Leslie, founder and editor of *The Weekly*. Leslie, impressed by his sketches, commissioned the young artist to draw a crowd of revellers travelling to the Elysian fields on the New Jersey side of the river. He spent the day creating the scene, a feat that launched his career with the legendary New York publisher.[5] For the remainder of his working days, Thomas Nast was primarily in the service of others.

John Wilson Bengough grew up in the town of Whitby, now a suburb on the eastern borders of Toronto. It was there in his spare time that he made a regular trip downtown to read the latest copy of *Harper's Weekly*. Bengough, nine years junior to Thomas Nast, had become fascinated with the influence that Nast was exercising in New York politics.

> My interest in cartooning was first awakened by the work of Thomas Nast in Harper's Weekly. I was amongst the devoted admirers of his elaborate and slashing full page attacks in that "journal of civilization" on Boss Tweed and the Tammany Ring, as the paper reached our town each week through the local bookstore. Nast had the field of political cartooning practically to himself for years, and must have inspired thousands of boys as he did me.[6]

After leaving school, Bengough tried his hand at photography and clerking in a law office. He was happy with neither. He then sought employment with the local newspaper, the *Whitby Gazette*, where he began his journey into journalism as a printer's devil. It was here that he made his first contact with Thomas Nast. In 1870, he wrote to his hero at *Harper's*, enclosing one of his own sketches, a picture of Boss Tweed cowering in front of the cartoonist Nast. It had been sketched in the Nast style. The gracious Nast responded to the correspondence, commending the young Bengough for the accuracy of his imitation of the well-known U.S. figure. More than ever, Bengough was determined to follow his idol's pathway in life.

Looking for a more challenging career, Bengough moved to Toronto to take a reporter's position with the *Toronto Globe*. A man with Bengough's spirit could not thrive under the tight reign that Brown held at the *Globe*. In spite of the fact that editorially driven cartoons had appeared as early as the mid-1840s in magazines such as *Punch In Canada*, the newspaper industry saw itself as something distinct from commentary magazines. Although cheeky upstarts such as *Diogenes*, *Grinchuckle*, and *Canadian Illustrated News* actively competed with daily newspapers in the area of political news, Brown and his colleagues in the daily press had neither the inspiration or technology to add illustrations to their newspapers. While specialty journals, both political and non-political, were adding more and more visual effects to their publications, newspaper owners and publishers decided to leave the field to them. It was not until Hugh Graham of the *Montreal Star* hired illustrator Henri Julien in 1888 that the first editorial cartoons appeared regularly in Canadian dailies.[8] However, the impact and importance of the politically charged drawing did not escape the attention of John Wilson Bengough. In New York, the persistent Nast was becoming an irritant to some powerful people, particularly the Tammany Hall leader Boss Tweed. Tweed was so vexed by the attention he received from Nast in *Harper's Weekly* that he considered banning textbooks published by the Harper Brothers from city schools.[9]

The Nast legend has merited no less than twenty-seven entries in John A. Lent's *International Biography of Animation, Caricature and Gag and Political Cartoons in the United States and Canada*.[10] Until Carmen Cumming's "Sketches of a Young Nation," Bengough had been the subject of only two master's theses and one journal article.[11] There is no need to repeat much of what has been written about Nast in

THE DEMOCRATIC SCAPEGOAT

FIGURE 3: The democratic scapegoat

this discourse. Yet it is important to recognize that Nast, working with the sole support of his publishers the Harper Brothers, staked his career and reputation on his visual dissection of the Tammany Ring in cartoons such as this. Although Tweed was a very large man at six feet tall and nearly three hundred pounds, he was not the lead-footed, grotesquely fat drunk that Nast pictured him to be.[12] The long, lean, and devious Macdonald, a far more accurate caricature, would become Bengough's trade mark.

The Nast style, with its exaggerated figures and enclosed dialogues to explain the motives behind the cartoon, would characterize Bengough's work throughout his life. Yet, as we shall see, much of Bengough's work lacked the bite and wit of Nast. Unlike Nast, he at least had the support of the opposition members of the Canadian Parliament upon whom he could depend.

While lingering at the *Globe* with dreams of becoming Canada's Thomas Nast, Bengough realized that he had to improve his artistic skills. He enrolled at the Toronto school The Society of Artists. During his one term, he was exposed to a traditional artistic curriculum. He saw little value in spending time carving imitations of classic sculptures and decided to leave.[13] Fortune was on his side. The new technology of lithography had reached the Toronto media and Bengough learned to use it well enough to sell his sketches on the city's street corners. It was at this time he decided to launch the satirical magazine *Grip*.

The first edition of *Grip* appeared in Toronto on May 24, 1873. *Grip* was named in honour of the raven in the Charles Dickens' novel *Barnaby Rudge*.

FIGURE 4: GRIP's front page

Dickens' was Bengough's second literary passion. In the first issue, Bengough noted that

> Dickens had not amongst his various and inimitable literary progeny a more original or entertaining creation than "Barnaby Rudge's protege, the well-known and beloved raven GRIP. Though the raven race have no enviable reputation, being traditionally stigmatized as bearers of ill-omen only, there is no reader but likes GRIP's company, for he is in all points an exceptional bird: there is for instance, such a wholesome contrast between his glad and frequent "Never Say Die!" and the croaker that perched upon Mr. Edgar Poe's bust of PALLAS, and according to the latest account, "still is sitting, still is sitting there." Well, having assumed his name, we will emulate GRIP's virtue, and look for the same respect abroad.[14]

From that point to the end of the journal in 1892, Bengough never spoke unless it was through the character GRIP. In the first issue, he stated the journal's editorial perspective: GRIP will be entirely independent and impartial, always and on all subjects. Nothing unworthy of good breeding will be admitted to his columns, though it will be his to offer timely admonitions to all who may need them; and lastly, his literary character will be jealously guarded by all the clever people in the land. And now, as GRIP's prologue is spoke, he bows and backs to his post, and the curtain, rolling gracefully down, shuts out for a little his generous patron–she knows they'll be so–the grave but sympathetic public.[15]

Almost as a side issue, Bengough announced that "a cartoon on a popular subject will occupy the third page of each issue. Political and Social Affairs will always be treated with independence."[16]

The success of a journal based on political commentary must have some political controversy upon which to comment. Nast had his Tweed and the Tammany Ring to gorge on in the pages of *Harper's Weekly.* Although we do not know whether or not John Wilson Bengough was gifted with great insight or happened to be in the right place at the right time, he launched *Grip* at the height of rumours that something was rotten in the government of Sir John A. Macdonald. Macdonald's Conservative Party had been elected as the country's first federal administration following Confederation in 1867 with a majority of seventy-five members in the House of Commons.[17] Macdonald presided over the four original provinces of Ontario, Quebec, New Brunswick, and Nova Scotia, the latter forced into Confederation against its will by the British Government.

Macdonald, like his arch enemy George Brown, was of Scottish heritage. He came to the national capital as a young lawyer from the Lake Ontario town of Kingston with the reputation of being a ribald drinker and carouser. In spite of the frailties of the flesh, Macdonald had a vision of a great new nation stretching from coast to coast based on British Imperial principles that he believed would help curtail what he regarded as the excesses of American liberal democracy in North America. And, like many of his contemporaries in Canada, he feared the possibility that the small nation forming north of the forty-ninth parallel would be swallowed up by the giant to the south.

Annexationist sentiment was alive and well in the Canada of the second half of the nineteenth century. It was supported by some of the country's leading intellectual lights such as psychiatrist Richard Maurice Bucke who yearned for a reunification of North American Anglo-Saxonism with his idol Walt Whitman as "the prophet of world empire and imperialism."[18] The question came to a head, at least in intellectual circles, when Toronto academic Goldwyn Smith published his treatise "Canada and The Canadian Question" in 1891 when he urged Canadians to abandon the dream of nationhood and submit to the pull of the south to create a strong North American economic and political union.[19]

To be labelled an annexationist in Victoria Canada was roughly parallel to being called a misogynist in modern parlance. When Macdonald became prime minister in 1867, he was determined to defeat what he considered to be a noisy, misguided minority anchored largely in intellectual circles. The first step in his dream was to bring British Columbia, Canada's most western territory, into Confederation as the nation's fifth province. Macdonald was convinced that if he successfully convinced west coasters that their collective future lay within the Canadian union, it would be only a matter of time before new provinces would be carved out of the vast aboriginal lands lying between the Great Lakes and the Rocky Mountains. His vision would prove to be prophetic.

In 1871, the federal government signed the accord of union with the territorial government of British Columbia. It came with an extremely high price. Macdonald promised to build a railway connecting the new province to the rail system that was starting to appear in the country's two most populous provinces, Ontario and Quebec. As well, Macdonald agreed that eventually the railway system should be extended to Atlantic Canada. The railway, from ocean to ocean, was to be the steel spine upon which the nation would be built. As a man of his word, the prime minister introduced the *Canadian Pacific Railway Act* into the House of Commons in 1872. Following passage, construction was to begin immediately to take place over a ten-year period.[20]

The government decreed that the railway should be built only on Canadian territory. A line through Michigan and the U.S. Midwest would have been much shorter. As well, construction workers would not have had to face the landscape of the Laurentian shield north of Lake Superior that would prove to be both treacherous and expensive. Future governments were not so nationalistically inclined. Faced with the history of the construction of the westward links, they decided that eastern links could pass through Maine and terminate in Halifax, Nova Scotia. Following passage of the legislation, the government set out to award contracts. The incentives were massive. The government set aside a fund of $30,000,000 and 50,000,000 acres of land as its contribution to the scheme. As Edward Blake, a Liberal member from Ontario, noted, "it is difficult for the mind to apprehend the magnitude of these figures. $30,000,000 is a national treasure; from 50,000,000 acres you can carve several independent states."[21]

Rumours persisted in Ottawa that Macdonald's government was prepared to award the contract to a Montreal consortium headed by Sir Hugh Allan. Like Macdonald and Liberal leader Alexander

Mackenzie, Allan was Scottish, hailing from a poor area of Glasgow. Determined to escape the poverty of the old country, he speculated what little income he earned in marine stocks. By the time that he contended for the Canadian Pacific contract, Allan had made a vast fortune in transatlantic shipping. His entrepreneurial spirit had attracted two influential Canadian investors, George Stephen and Donald Smith. Smith eventually assumed the noble title Lord Strathcona. He was the man who drove the last spike for the Canadian Pacific at Craigellachie, British Columbia. Allan and his partners had been advocating the construction of a transcontinental railway since 1870, when the British government ceded the Hudson's Bay Company lands to Canada, thus making a transcontinental line feasible.

In spite of the nationalist fervour that coloured Macdonald's rhetoric in the campaign to sell the project to Canadian voters, Allan lined up a consortium of backers who would not share in the enthusiasm unless the venture could prove to be highly profitable. In fact, most of the major players were Americans. Allan's backers included George McMullen who had been born in Canada but had emigrated to the United States where he set up a number of businesses in Chicago. McMullen persuaded other American investors to join the scheme, including William Butler Ogden and General George Cass, both major figures in the Northern Pacific Railway. The most controversial acquisition was a Philadelphia banker named Jay Cooke. Cooke had been most vocal about his support for annexationists in Canada. He joined the scheme with the primary mission of ensuring that the Canadian Pacific would become part of the U.S. rail system in the north-west.[22]

On the second of April 1873, Lucius Huntington, a Liberal member of the House of Commons rose in the chamber and made the following motion:

That Mr. Huntington, a member of this House, having stated in his place, that he is credibly informed and believes that he can establish by satisfactory evidence, That in anticipation of the Legislation of last Session, as to the Pacific Railway, an agreement was made between Sir Hugh Allan, acting for himself, and certain other Canadian promoters, and G. W. McMullen, acting for certain United States capitalists, whereby the latter agreed to furnish all the funds necessary for the construction of the contemplated railway, and to give the former a certain percentage of interest in consideration of their interest and position, the scheme agreed on being ostensibly that of a Canadian Company with Sir Hugh Allan at its head. That the Government were aware that negotiations were pending between these parties, That subsequently, an understanding was come to between the Government and Sir Hugh Allan and Mr. Abott, M.P., – that Sir Hugh Allan and his friends should advance a large sum of money for the

FIGURE 5: After the session; or the situation
J.A. M-cd-n-ld: *"Come On Old Fellow, It's all Right,*
You Know; It's My Turn to Treat."
A. M-k-nz-e: *"Ou, Aye, Joney; But Y'Maun Recollect*
I'm Teetotal –More Especially Till August"

purpose of aiding the Elections of Ministers and their supporters at the ensuring General Election, – and that he and
his friends should receive the contract for the construction of
the Railway, – That accordingly Sir Hugh Allan did advance
a large sum of money for the purpose mentioned, and at the
solicitation and under the pressing instances of Ministers.[23]

Huntington fueled the fire of corruption by further
announcing that the money came from American
sources, specifically the Chicago businessman
McMullen and his cronies. Parliament came to a
halt. Finally, by the end of May, it was apparent that
the nation's business could no longer be conducted
in the legislature and Macdonald prorogued the session, which inspired the following poem and cartoon
from Bengough.

PROROGATION
by a conscientious M.P.

The boys are all dismissed again;
The sweep has locked the doors and gone;
Mid pastures green now rusticate
In peace, brave ALECK and Sir JOHN

What have we done, constituents dear?
What have I of results to show?
Let's see; - you mean by way of work?
I've got -why-hang me if I know![24]

Bengough's sketch of May 31 (Figure 5) shows the
prime minister with his hand on the shoulders of Alexander MacKenzie of the Liberal Party, trying to
convince the opposition leader that the closing of
Parliament was in effect "his turn to treat." It would
not be the last time that the two Scots immigrants, the
pillars of Canadian politics, would be sketched as a
team by Bengough.

At the centre of Huntington's accusation was concrete evidence. He had acquired a letter written from
Montreal by Sir Hugh Allan to his partner in Chicago complaining about the tardiness of the negotiations that would award him the Canadian Pacific
contract. As always, Sir Hugh remained optimistic
about the final outcome, which was being delayed by
Macdonald's concerns about the upcoming federal
elections due in 1873. Allan advised the prime minister that his backers had to be assured that Sir Hugh
was satisfied with any agreement. Macdonald conceded and Allan reported to his partners that an
agreement had been finally reached. As his words
demonstrate, this in itself was not particularly
damaging.

> Yesterday we entered into an agreement by which the Gov-
> ernment bound itself to form a company of Canadians only,
> according to my wishes, that this Company will make me
> President, and that I and my friends will get a majority of the
> stock, and that the contract for building the road will be
> given to this Company in terms of the Act of Parliament.

Then Sir Hugh began to drift into the more controversial aspects of his deal.

> Americans are to be carefully excluded in the fear that they
> will sell it to the Northern Pacific. But I fancy we can get over
> that some way or other.

He continued with the most damaging confession in
the correspondence.

> This position has not been attained without large payments
> of money. I have already paid over $200,000, and I will have
> at least $100,000 more to pay. I must now soon know what
> our New York friends are going to do. They did not answer
> my last letter.[25]

Allan revealed that he had funded, almost single
handedly, Macdonald's bid for re-election. And, in
spite of loose laws concerning the behaviour of political parties in Canada, this was illegal.

With the Houses of Parliament closed indefinitely,
Macdonald felt that he could diffuse the growing
storm surrounding the scandal. Although opposition
members of the House of Commons did not have direct access to the prime minister in the daily debates,
they did have access to sympathetic newspapers. On
July 4 and on July 18 respectively, the *Montreal Herald*

FIGURE 6: Canada's laocoon or virgil on the political situation

and the *Toronto Globe* published additional letters from Sir Hugh Allan that confirmed Huntington's position that the contract had been awarded in exchange for financial assistance for the ruling Conservative Party. The intricate knot that tied Macdonald (seen on the left in Figure 6) and his finance minister Sir Francis Hincks (seen on the right) to Sir Hugh Allan (seen here in the centre) was the subject of Bengough's view of the matter in the July 19 issue of *Grip*.

The artist was inspired by the story of Laocoon and his war with serpents, which Bengough adapted for his own purposes. Bengough also toyed with developing a new language to describe the major players in the Pacific Scandal. For Macdonald, he created the new word "Jonatiate," which he announced meant "to wriggle-prevaricate-recriminate- procrastinate." For Sir Hugh, the word "Allanise" meant "to scheme-to subsidize-to affidavitise." George Brown did not escape the wrath of the cartoonist. He was pilloried for his coverage of the Pacific Scandal, which Bengough felt was far too politically driven. Brown's new word was "Brownoric" meaning "ambiguous-muddy-in fact brown." The ocean to which the railway was to stretch was "boisterous-ill-omened-suggestive of sinking." The politician who

broke the Pacific Scandal, Lucius Huntington, was one of the few who received favourable treatment. His word "Huntingtonic" meant "inquisitive-prying-impertinent." However, Sir Francis Hincks word "Hinksize" was used to describe "a stick in the mud; that's the size of that," said Benough. For his readers who were getting nightmares thinking about the Pacific Scandal, Bengough advised them that the situation could be resolved by staying awake.[26]

As July rolled into August, even Macdonald realized that the accusations of corruption and bribery would have to be aired in the House. He announced that Parliament would re-convene on the thirteenth of August. Bengough was certain that the prime minister and the Conservative Party would not be able to survive the session. In his August 9 issue, he mused on Macdonald's fate. Looking a decade into the future in the town of Kingston, Ontario, he saw

> a melancholy individual clothed in sackcloth seated on a fragment of granite. We were told his name was Macdonald, and that he had been a minister of something. He was singing a mournful ditty, the words of which we had the curiosity to preserve.
>
> Harken to me, Christian people;
>   while my sorrows I disclose,
>
> While I sing in doleful numbers,
>   all the story of my woes;
>
> I, who once so gaily rolled up every large majority—alas! am
>   now no longer, leader Parliamentary.
>
> Carelessly, ah! Sir Hugh Allan!
>   didst thou both of us betray;
>
> Why concealed'st thou not those letters from the
>   fatal eye of day?
> Happy were those dark-age statesmen,
>   who did never use to write,
> Thou hads't roads built—I still governed—had we kept from
>   black and white
>
> All the country to the canines, now in rapid progress goes,
> Brown has grabbed his final dollar
>   and in Scotland seeks repose;
>
> I in grief all unavailing, sing my sorrows far and near,
>   Give one obolus of pity to old Belisarius here.[27]

In what eventually proved to be Bengough's most memorable cartoon, he sketched what he felt would be the dominant theme to be laid before the members.

In the cartoon (Figure 7), Bengough takes liberty with the old nursery rhyme "Four and Twenty Blackbirds." Presenting the dainty dish to the Speaker of the House are Alexander Mackenzie on the right, leader of the Liberal Party, and Edward Blake, who joined the Mackenzie cabinet after the fall of

FIGURE 7: Isn't that a dainty dish to set before a king? (nursery rhyme)

FIGURE 8: Wither are we drifting

Macdonald. Macdonald is just below the speaker's scepter. To his right is Uncle Sam, representing the American involvement in the scandal. Just below Uncle Sam is Sir Francis Hincks. To his right is T.C. Patterson, owner of the *Toronto Mail*, one of Macdonald's staunchest supporters. Immediately to the left of Hincks is James Beaty, owner of the *Toronto Leader*, another Toronto journalist and Macdonald supporter. To his left is Sir Hugh Allan, and finally, just across from Blake's elbow, is the Honourable M. Langevin, who was accused by the Liberal Party of stealing over two million dollars in graft money.[28] The two journalists were included because both had what one observer noted as a "natural instinct to protect the government."[29]

The Parliament of Canada began sitting once again on August 13. Members had only one thing on their minds: the Pacific Scandal. The government was totally unable to conduct any business as accusations blew across the floor faster than a hurricane travelling up the Caribbean Sea. Once again, Macdonald pulled the plug before the day was out. Bengough was deeply disturbed by the events. In his August 16 issue, he commented on the ways of politics with both verse and sketch. The Clear Grit, an

old term for Reform Liberals, is a reference to opposition leader Alexander MacKenzie.

> "The Clear Grit Chief, and ninety of his men,
> To Ottawa went, and then back again."

He recalled a humourous, at least for the time, children's hymn that went as follows:

> If I were a cassowary,
> On the Plains of Timbuctoo,
> I'd devour the missionary,
> Hat and boots, and hymn-book too.

The Macdonald version read as follows:

> If I were a cuss-so-wary,
> On the Plains of Ottawa,
> I'd appoint Commission nary
> Till I'd papers got away.[30]

His cartoon was not nearly as humourous as his verse. The anxiety that Bengough demonstrated throughout his life for what he felt was the decaying state of democracy is clearly stated in this drawing of Macdonald stomping on the prostrate form of Miss Canada (Figure 8). Note the liquor bottle protruding from his jacket pocket.

Macdonald made one major concession to the opposition. He appointed a three-person Royal Commission to investigate the charges. The three investigators, James Cowan, Antoine Polette, and Charles

THE BEAUTIES OF A ROYAL COMMISSION.
"WHEN SHALL WE THREE MEET AGAIN?"

FIGURE 9: The beauties of a royal commission

Day, were all members of the judiciary and known supporters of the government. The commissioners stated:

> Coinciding with Your Excellency (Macdonald) in the view that the terms of the Commission do not require them to pronounce judicially on the evidence, consider that their duty will have been fully discharged when they shall have forwarded to the Secretary of State the accompanying depositions and documents with this Report, in triplicate, as required by their instructions-unless a report of their opinion on the result of the evidence should be specially required.[31]

In essence, the Commission was only empowered to call witnesses and transcribe their testimonies. It had no powers to subpoena or punish those who refused to testify. One of the reluctant witnesses was none other than Lucius Huntington, who felt that the Commission was nothing more than a process through which the government could cover up all its sins. He had a point. The Commission sat from September 4 to October 1, taking depositions from 36 witnesses. All were known government supporters or hangers-on. The Commission, in keeping with its mandate, refused to lay blame. In fact, the entire report consists of no more than a few introductory pages followed by transcripts of the evidence and copies of correspondence between the principle players.[32]

In the August 23 issue of *Grip*, Bengough showed his disgust for the procedure by drawing a picture of Macdonald standing in the witness box in front of his appointees (Figure 9). A closer look reveals that judge, witness, and attorney are all Macdonald –Bengough is accusing the prime minister of trying himself.

Also note that the two prominent Toronto journalists who supported Macdonald without question are enshrined under the titles of the *Mail* and *Leader* to the left and right of the bench. However, not all journalists were fooled by the antics of the government. In Macdonald's hometown of Kingston, Ontario, the *British Whig* declared that

> Public Opinion has for years been demoralised by the corrupt rule of Sir John A. Macdonald, a man whose abilities fitted him to play a distinguished part in the government of the country, but whose insatiable lust of office and unconquerable love of corruption have not only ruined any enviable reputation he might otherwise have earned, but have, to a lamentable extent, saturated the public mind with his noxious influence and lowered standard of public morals.[33]

While the Commission sat, the House of Commons did not. However, opposition members took the road and returned to their respective home territories to pillory the government every chance they had. Speaking in London, Ontario, just before the first Royal Commission hearings, Edward Blake charged that the government was well aware of the implications of Sir Hugh Allan's correspondence. He charged that a faithful Conservative had been told to keep the letters secret until the next federal election had been completed. Blake pointed his finger directly at Macdonald and announced to his audience that he knew the prime minister was guilty of immoral acts of the highest order.[34]

The Honourable David Mills, an Ontario Liberal M.P. speaking to an audience in Aylmer, Ontario, noted that it was impossible for any member of the House of Commons to vote on legislation in which that member stood to gain financially. But, as Mills pointed out, the legislation that granted the Canadian Pacific franchise not only condoned such behaviour, but promoted it. He concluded his address by accusing Macdonald of accepting $45,000 from Sir Hugh Allan to influence the outcome of elections in Ontario. This, noted Mills, was a direct contravention of electoral law.[35]

Bengough came to the defense of Huntington, whose refusal to testify in front of the Royal Commission resulted in several vicious attacks in the Tory press. Macdonald's journalistic friends declared that

FIGURE 10: Waiting for Huntington

Huntington was afraid to face the prime minister, lest his accusations be exposed for the lies they were. Macdonald, in this unflattering caricature (Figure 10), awaits his prey while Mackenzie and the *Globe* refuse to remain at the potential scene of battle.

Editorial writers at Kingston's *British Whig* were particularly incensed, but not because Macdonald was a native of the city. For them, the question of Canada's British purity and morality had been severely undermined by the government's behaviour. To the disgust of the editorial staff, Canada was starting to behave like America where corruption and immorality typified by the Tweed scandals in New York were characteristic and thought to be normal in U.S. political life. In a reference to Canadians, the journal on July 22, 1873, noted that

> people have long thought that they were exempt from the corruption with which they were fond of taunting their American neighbours but they were furnished with proofs of greater political rascality in their public men than the other country was ever cursed with.[36]

Meanwhile back in Toronto, home of *Grip*, business matters involved some major changes. When the journal was founded, its first editor was Charles P. Hall. Some believed this was a pseudonym for Bengough, who was still employed on a full-time basis by the *Globe*. "Hall" was succeeded on July 26

FIGURE 11: Blackwash or whitewash

by Jimuel Briggs, D.B. (Dead Beat) a.k.a. Phillips Thompson, a lawyer who had become a journalist associated with dozens of radical and esoteric ideologies through the Victorian period. Thompson made the mistake of printing an editorial sympathetic to liquor interests, forgetting, or ignoring, that his boss was a dedicated teetotaler and prohibitionist. He departed after the September 6 issue at the height of interest in the Pacific Scandal. It was at this point that "Barnaby Rudge" and "Demos Mudge" a.k.a. R.H. Larminie of the *Globe* became joint editors of the paper. It wasn't until March 29, 1879, that it was published for the first time that Rudge was in effect J.W. Bengough.[37]

Under the Demos and Rudge mandate, Macdonald and his government came under close scrutiny in both verse and sketch. Free of Thompson and his flirtation with anti-capitalist attitudes and pro-socialist commentaries, Bengough brought a Victorian liberal and moral approach to his pillory of Macdonald. Although closely allied with the federal Liberal Party, Bengough refused to allow partisanship to influence his disgust at the government's behaviour in the Pacific affair. He was an editor and a humourist driven by a need for morality in politics, a morality governed by the firm belief that there were right and wrong approaches to public decision making.[38] As the accompanying cartoon demonstrates (Figure 11), Bengough feared that Macdonald would escape justice. While Mackenzie and his cohorts on the left continued to paint the prime minister with the tar of corruption, Macdonald's friends on the Royal Commission are covering him with the bath of whitewash.

Bengough was encouraged when the *Mail*, one of Macdonald's most fervent supporters, wrote in its

FIGURE 12: We in Canada seem to have lost all idea of justice, honor and integrity

FIGURE 13: Miss Canada's school—dedicated to the new premier

September 26 issue that "We in Canada seem To Have Lost All Idea Of Justice, Honor and Integrity." The defection of the *Mail* did more than inspire the accompanying cartoon by Bengough (Figure 12), it signalled the beginning of a number of defections by prominent Conservatives that would bring about the end of Macdonald's government before the year was out. Here Macdonald is seen confessing to his old adversary and eventual successor, Alexander Mackenzie, that he did indeed accept money to award a railway contract to Sir Hugh Allan. But in typical Bengough fashion, it becomes not a question of expediency and foolhardiness, but one of morals and politics.

Macdonald called Parliament back into session on October 23, 1873. He was facing a divided House, with many of his own loyal members questioning whether or not the government should be allowed to continue. The Report of the Royal Commission was presented to the members along with several dispatches by the governor-general. The battling went on for over a week. Alexander MacKenzie presented a motion of non-confidence in the government, a motion that, had it succeeded, would have forced the government to resign. The Conservatives retaliated with motions of confidence. Although no vote was

taken, Macdonald became convinced that he could not survive. The prime minister offered his resignation and that of his government to Lord Dufferin, the governor-general, on November 5. It was accepted and Mackenzie was asked to form a new administration. He did, and immediately called for new elections.[39] On November 8, Bengough took what he must have felt at the time was his final salvo against Macdonald. He could not have predicted that the old warrior would once again be prime minister after defeating Mackenzie in 1878.

In the first issue of Volume 2 of *Grip*, Bengough paid a "tribute" to the man whom he considered as the reason for his journalist and artistic success. Like many of his tales, the story is told as a parable.

It was a midnight dreary. A spare-built Knight Companion of the Bath, with kinky hair, one lock of which fell over his pale brow, reclined dreamily upon a rich couch in his chamber, gazing at the ghosts wrought upon the floor by the flames dying in the fireplace, and reading in their mystic movements the story of a political chieftain's career. While he was still looking, he beheld a brave spirit driven to earth, and as he fell the light danced readily o'er the battle-field a moment, and then the embers expired. Suddenly, there was a silken and sad rustling at the window curtain, and when the Knight rose and opened the window a lordly Raven strutted in and perched himself over the door, upon a marble bust whose features closely resembled one ALEXANDER MACKENZIE. There he continued to sit in solemn silence (not deeming it polite to be the first to speak). The Knight on his part, was lost in awe at the strange visitor, and it was quite a long time before he demanded, in a frenzy of fear, "Whence Comest thou?" To this the Raven replied, "Don't be afraid, Sir John, I'm only your friend GRIP. I just dropped in to pay you my respects, and to present you with my FIRST VOLUME, whose extraordinary success has been due in no small measure to yourself.[40]

FIGURE 14: An irresponsible infant

At the height of the Pacific Scandal, the journal sold more than two thousand copies a week to subscribers and more on newsstands. Bengough's brother Thomas who was also involved in the Grip Publishing Company reported that weekly bundles of the magazine were shipped to the national capital in Ottawa to an awaiting market of members of the House of Commons. To keep up with demand, Bengough redrew many of his memorable cartoons of Macdonald, which were lithographed and sold in book form. By 1886, Bengough boasted that *Grip* was read by 50,000 persons weekly.[41]

Bengough continued to edit copy and draw for *Grip* until he was removed as editor and cartoonist by Frank Wilson, who had taken over management of the printing side of the business in 1883. The journal remained in existence with a number of freelance cartoonists who were unable to attract the loyal following of Bengough. In October 1892, Bengough joined the *Montreal Star* as a cartoonist, but by January 1894, he was once again running *Grip*. However, the man who had made the magazine, Sir John A. Macdonald, had been dead since 1891. Bengough, who confessed to meeting Macdonald only once in his long career,[42] had lost the "raison d'être" for his journal. In December 1894, *Grip* closed its doors forever.[43]

Although his magazine was gone, the cartoonist did not suffer for lack of demand for his talents. He travelled across Canada and throughout the world, in particular to the United States, Australia, and New Zealand, giving humourous talks in which he would sketch characters while chatting with his audience. With the death of *Grip*, he sketched for the *Globe*, the aforementioned *Montreal Star*, the British-based *Morning Chronicle* (London), the *Single Tax Review*, the labour newspaper *The Industrial Banner*, the *Canadian Graphic*, the *Christian Endeavor World*, the Toronto *Evening Telegram* and eventually from 1906 to 1907 for the Chicago-based liberal political journal, *The Public*, predecessor to the modern day *New Republic*.[44] On August 18, 1897, Bengough paid tribute to a rising young cartoonist in New York with a sketch in the *Toronto Globe*.

On October 23, 1923, while sketching a cartoon on the evils of tobacco, he died of a heart attack at his easel.

In the many instances in which journalists have been involved in bringing down governments, there remains considerable controversy as to just how effective the fourth estate really is. Had Boss Tweed, Sir John A. Macdonald, Jimmy Walker, and Richard Nixon not participated in events that were clearly beyond the point of tolerance in their respective societies, it is questionable whether the journalistic knife could have been driven to a fatal contact with the political infrastructure. Many others have survived where these aforementioned four did not. One can certainly speculate that most citizens will tolerate some indiscretion in their political leaders, but there is clearly a boundary that cannot be exceeded.

It is a tribute to both Thomas Nast and John Wilson Bengough, ordinary people with ordinary lives, that they understood and successfully exploited violations of standards of behaviour expected of those holding elected office. Yet, there is no indication that they themselves were desirous of power or fame and fortune. They were not of the political or social class in the societies in which they lived and worked. They were journalists in every meaning of the word, and to the last, they remained what they always were, workers in a world dominated by the rich and powerful. Nast died as an impoverished consul for the American government in Ecuador. Bengough ran for and was elected to Toronto City Council in 1907. At his death he left a modest but hardly extravagant estate to his second wife.

With Nast and Bengough, political cartooning came of age in both the United States and Canada. It is easy to speculate that someone, somewhere, would have taken up the mantle of satire that these two artists and commentators perfected and that may be very well true. But, they were at the right place at the right time, proving, perhaps, that once and for all, without a good scandal to caricature, the craft and art in political cartooning would be missing one of its core ingredients.

Notes

1. Sidney Kobre, *The Yellow Press and Gilded Age of Journalism* (Tallahasee, Florida: The Florida State University Press, 1952) pp.314-15.

2. David R. Spencer, "Alternative Visions: The Intellectual Heritage of Nonconformist Journalism in Canada," in Hanno Hardt and Bonnie Brennan (eds.) *Newsworkers: Toward a History of the Rank and File* (Minneapolis, London: University of Minnesota Press, 1995), p.160.

3. Albert Bigelow Paine, *Thomas Nast. His Period and His Pictures* (New York and London: Harper & Brothers Publishers, 1904), pp.5,6.

4. Whitby, Ontario *The Whitby Chronicle*, 3 November 1899 (copied from clippings on the J.E. Farewell Scrapbooks, McLaughlin Public Library, Oshawa, Ontario.

5. Paine, *Thomas Nast*, pp.16-20.

6. J.W. Bengough, *Bengough's Chalk-Talks* (Toronto, Ontario: The Musson Book Company, 1922), p.5.

7. J.M.S. Careless, *Brown of the Globe (Vol.2)*, (Toronto, Ontario: The University of Toronto Press, 1963), p.290.

8. Toronto, Ontario, "J.W. Bengough: Pioneer Cartoonist," *Saturday Night Magazine*, 13 October 1923.

9. Oliver E. Allen, *The Tiger: The Rise and Fall of Tammany Hall* (New York, N.Y.: Addison-Wesley Publishing Company, 1993), p.121.

10. John A. Lent, *Animation, Caricature, and Gag and Political Cartoons in The United States and Canada: An International Bibliography* (Westport, Connecticut, and London, England: The Greenwood Press, 1994), pp.339-341.

11. See Stanley Paul Kutcher, *John Wilson Bengough: Artist of Righteousness* (Hamilton, Ontario: Unpublished M.A. Thesis, 1975); and Dennis Edward Blake, *J. W. Bengough and Grip: The Canadian Cartoon Comes of Age* (Waterloo, Ontario: Unpublished M.A. Thesis, 1985). Kutcher published part of his dissertation in *Urban History*, 1976 76(2), pp.3-49.

12. Allen, *The Tiger*, p.81.

13. Blake, *J.W. Bengough*, pp.16-17.

14. Toronto, Ontario, *Grip*, Volume 1, No. 1, 24 May 1873.

15. Ibid.

16. Ibid.

17. Address by Edward Blake, federal Liberal member at Bowmanville, Ontario, 26 May 1873, CIHM, No. 23820.

18. Ramsay Cook, *The Regenerators: Social Criticism in Victorian English Canada* (Toronto, Ontario: The University of Toronto Press, 1985), p.28.

19. Ibid., p.101.

20. James Beaty, *The History of the Lake Superior Ring* (Toronto, Ontario: The Leader and The Patriot, 1874) p.1. It should be noted here that Beaty was an active Conservative. This pamphlet was composed in defence of Macdonald and the actions of his government following the collapse of the Conservative administration. It was directed at Alexander Mackenzie and the Browns in Toronto (i.e. George Brown) whom Beaty charged sold their interests in the railway construction to well-known American annexationist Jay Cooke of Philadelphia. Ironically, Cooke had been included in the original consortium.

21. Blake, Address, 26 May 1973.

22. Donna McDonald, *Lord Strathcona: A Biography of Donald Alexander Smith* (Toronto, Ontario: The Dundurn Press, 1996), pp.211-212.

23. CIHM, No. 23823, Comments on the Proceedings and Evidence of Charges Preferred by Mr. Huntington, M.P., Against the Government of Canada.

24. Toronto, Ontario, *Grip*, Volume 1, No.2, 31 May 1873.

25. CIHM, No. 16495, Edmund Burke Wood, Speech of the Hon. E. B. Wood in the House of Commons on the Pacific Scandal. Reading of letter from Sir Hugh Allan.

26. Toronto, Ontario, *Grip*, Volume 1, No.7, 12 July 1873.

27. Toronto, Ontario, *Grip*, Volume 1, No.11, 9 August 1873.

28. CIHM, No. 09047, "Liberal Party Canada: Wholesale plunder: The McGeevy Langevin Scandal at Quebec. Nearly Two Million Stolen."

29. David Hugh Russell, *The Ontario Press And The Pacific Scandal of 1873* (Kingston, Ontario: Unpublished M.A. Thesis, Queen's University, 1970), p.10.

30. Toronto, Ontario, *Grip*, Volume 1, No.12, 16 August 1873.

31. CIHM, No. 15566, Report of the Royal Commissioners, Appointed by the Government, addressed to them, under the Great Seal of Canada, bearing the date fourteenth of August A.D., 1873.

32. Russell, *The Ontario Press*, pp.6-7.

33. Ibid., pp.39-40.

34. CIHM, No. 23822, Edward Blake Speaking at London on Thursday, 28 August 1873.

35. CIHM, No. 15648, Condensed Report of An Address by Mr. Mills, M.P., at Aylmer, Ontario.

36. Russell, *The Ontario Press*, p.48.

37. Carl Spadoni, "*Grip* and The Bengoughs as Publishers and Printers," Papers of The Bibliographic Society of Canada, XXXVII, p.16.

38. Kutcher, *John Wilson Bengough*, p.16.

39. Russell, *The Ontario Press*, p.7.

40. Toronto, Ontario, *Grip*, Volume 2, No.1, 29 November 1873.

41. Spadoni, "*Grip*," pp.24-25.

42. Bengough, *Bengough's Chalk-Talks*, p.31.

43. Spadoni, "*Grip*," pp.12, 24-25.

44. The William Ready Division, Archives and Research Collections, the J. W. Bengough Papers, Box 2, File 8.

6

Broadcasting: Centralization, Regionalization, and Canadian Identity

John D. Jackson[1]

anada first, my province second" (and, at times, the reverse) was a frequently expressed sentiment in English Canada, by whatever side and however phrased, during the Meech Lake and Charlottetown constitutional debates of 1990-92. Though an apparently simple and straightforward expression of nation over region, the underlying meanings were exceedingly complex—because the whole process put the question of Canada and "Canadianness" into relief. Is Canada a federation of 10 provinces and two territories, a federation of two nations—Quebec and English Canada—a coalition of no less than 32 ethnic groups and four or more aboriginal groupings, or something different? The multiplicity of national visions was quite apparent in the debate.

The term *Canadianness* refers to identity, i.e., to the way in which a people collectively and individually define themselves—their answer and yours to the questions "Who are we?" and "Who am I?" Identities—one's conception of oneself and a group's conception of itself as a collectivity—are constructed in time and place. People actively create their identities, but to do so—to create a self-concept—requires materials. The materials out of which identities are created are inevitably social. Identity is constructed in interaction with others and with the institutional order of the society in which one lives.

One's identity as a man or woman, teacher or bricklayer, Québécois or English-Canadian, Amerindian or Italian-Canadian, Canadian or American, is constructed from the patterned responses of others in face-to-face interaction, participation in large-scale organizations such as schools and churches, reading newspapers and novels, and watching TV. We may, as does Shibutani, think of a "social matrix of identification."[2] If we are to follow Mead, the matrix out of which identities are constructed includes the institutionalized media of communication.[3] It includes broadcasting (radio and TV in all forms), the

regulations governing broadcasting, and the various interests involved in shaping policies.

The objective of this chapter is to explore the interaction between identity construction and broadcasting as cultural practices. I begin with a brief discussion of "identity" as a concept used, in part, to express the ways in which people think of themselves. I then consider the development of broadcasting in Canada, with an emphasis on policy and programming for radio as part of the social matrix of identity formation.

To consider identification places us in the domain of culture. The concept of "culture" is problematic, no less so than that of "society" or "structure." As one writer expressed the problem:

> All that we can observe is an infinite number of concrete, individual actions and the products thereof. As such, these phenomena are neither social nor cultural. Only by selecting and ordering them do we fashion both concepts, "culture" and "society," which subsequently condition even our perception and apprehension.[4]

The point is, "culture" and "society" are analytical distinctions: one is no more or less real than the other. I say this in order to caution against the common tendency to reify society and social structure while allocating culture to the "unreal." Culture is meaning and perception and, as such, penetrates all human actions and the products of these actions. People act by virtue of their unique capacity to confront reality by meaningful action.[5] Analytically the distinction between the two concepts is useful, if not necessary, but keep in mind that each penetrates the other in the course of human interaction. My use of "culture" here is a consequence of selection and emphasis: I wish to emphasize the creation of identities as significations in interaction with those institutions that produce and reproduce meaning.

Identity Formation

The key to the concept of "identity" as it is used in sociology lies in the phrase "to identify with." The individual identifies or does not identify with his or her occupation, ethnic background, first language learned, nation, or any combination of these or other social categories. Layers of identifications circle around the core of an individual's self-concept.[6] Just which layer takes priority or is closest to the core of the self at any one time depends on historical circumstances and the creative capacity of the individual. For example, national and/or linguistic identification may take priority over occupational or gender identification during periods of open linguistic or national conflicts. This was indeed the case for many in Canada and Quebec during the constitutional debates of the early 1990s.[7]

Clearly an identity is fashioned in response to others. It is a dialogue with others in the context of patterned ideas, concepts, linguistic and social categories, and the like, which predate the individual. In this sense, the focus for any discussion of identification must be on relationships and communication, not on static objects. Nevertheless, there is a tendency to view people as passive recipients of pre-existing institutions through a process of socialization. The tendency was present in Durkheim's work[8] and in Mead's social philosophy, though Mead allowed for uniqueness, in the sense that each individual uniquely selects from the organized structures of societies in constructing a self.[9]

Obviously, pre-organized and defined (i.e., carrying meaning) structures set the agenda for the thinking and actions of a people at any one point in time. The responses of Newfoundlanders and aboriginal peoples to constitutional questions in the 1990s were constructed, in part, from pre-existing definitions of the situation. It would be more useful and accurate, however, to view these responses as having taken place within a set of constraints than as having been caused, in a physical and mechanical sense, by responses internalized through socialization.

A constraint is neither a cause, like a physical force, nor a positive control, like steering, that makes something happen. Constraints are limits, like grammar, conscious or not, that define the conditions of what is allowed or what is not supposed to happen.[10]

Humans are goal-seeking creatures. Goals are defined before they happen and an individual or a people moves within given constraints to reach a pre-defined goal. In this sense, cause and effect are reversed: the goal "causes" a certain complex path of pre-existing organized and meaningful structures to be activated.

Wilden's position is several steps ahead of Mead's functionalism. The problem with Mead's conception of self-development is that in empirical studies it was easily translated into a mechanical cause-effect paradigm.[11] The process of identification is one of creating and re-creating meaning in the sense of marking boundaries between "we" and "they," self and other. As noted by Anthony Cohen, "boundary encapsulates the identity of the community and, like the identity of an individual, is called into being by the exigencies of social interaction."[12]

It is in response to the demands of everyday social interaction that people perceive, interpret, and create meaning. "Behaviour does not 'contain' meaning intrinsically; rather, it is found to be meaningful by an act of interpretation; we 'make sense' out of what we observe."[13]

Identification is one of the tools of interpretation. To return to the preceding problem, are acts of interpretation "caused" or determined by Mead's pre-existing social matrix, Durkheim's social facts, or Marx's superstructure, or do they occur anew in the course of interaction? Neither option offers an acceptable proposition. Though the creation and recreation of meaning is continuously in process, the act of interpretation is not random. Interpretation occurs within the constraints of given languages, ideologies, and beliefs, or, in a word, institutions. Constraints, however compelling at any one point in time, are not absolute. On the contrary, the constraints bearing on any variety of potential behaviours are in flux—simultaneously instituted as a consequence of past actions and in the process of being instituted. The process of instituting is as important in a consideration of identification as is the instituted.[14] Ethnic, national, and regional identifications are first experienced as givens, as the instituted, but they are not mere labels with objective reference points. True, particular regional designations (Maritimers or western Canadians, for example) denote sets of people in recognizable territories with political, economic, and geographic boundaries. But at the same time they connote a complex of qualities rooted in the social imagination. From time to time one hears such statements as, "Maritimers live at a slower, more 'laid-back' pace than do 'Upper Canadians,'" or "Westerners place a priority on equality, participation, and social programs." These are qualities attributed to identifications, qualities taken on as a way of defining self by "self and others." These become part of one's identity and enter into the collective rhetoric of definitions of self and others. Though imaginary, their impact is very real.[15]

Self and other–"Canadianness" (however constructed) and its necessary other–are imagined socially. As noted by Anderson in his discussion of the imagined community, "nation-ness, as well as nationalism, are cultural artifacts of a particular kind."[16] The social imagination, the central component of identification constructed in interaction, in both its radical and actual modes, is inherent in institutional practices.[17] Instituted or official culture (the policies and programming practices of broadcasting institutions, for example) arise as people representing particular interests act to formulate a social imagination–a set of symbols confirmed by the power of those interests. The symbols may be identifications such as Canadian, Amerindian, or Québécois (which include both administrative designations regarding location, economy, status, and so on, and sets of imaginary qualities), or flags, or captured in the thematic structures of TV or radio programs. The connotations, rather than the administrative denotations, are the principal materials of identifications and are incorporated into the consciousness of individuals and collectivities. However, the presence of the capacity to imagine that which has not taken place or which is not supposed to happen provides emancipatory capabilities to create counter-identifications: i.e., to institute as opposed to receiving the instituted. Identities are given but they are also changed.

As pointed out by Bleicher in his discussion of the quality of Scottishness, the construction of "a group's self-understanding," once it is brought from the pre-reflexive attitude of everyday life into the sphere of conscious formulation and dissemination, requires the mediatory or interpretive efforts of interested sections, which I want to refer to as "cultural producers."[18]

He goes on to describe the role of the Scottish literati in the articulation of a social identity.[19] Likewise have Canadian writers, broadcasters, politicians, and so on played a role in the articulation of Canadian social identities. Our interest is in the role played by the Canadian Broadcasting Corporation (CBC) as an agency of the state in attempting to articulate a particular Canadian identity. If our notions regarding identity formation hold, we would expect to find a general tendency towards an official definition of "Canadianness" combined with conflicting and opposing definitions.

Identity and Broadcasting

Broadcasting is a complex cultural industry. A complete analysis would, at a minimum, include policy as formulated by the Canadian Radio-television and Telecommunications Commission (CRTC) and implemented by the federal government, the political, cultural, and economic foundations of such policy, the complex of broadcasting organizations in the public (CBC, provincial units, community and ethnic units) and private sectors, the output of radio, TV, and cable media, and the networks of writers, performers, producers, and so on. Our objective is to capture some of this complex and to show how it articulates a Canadian social imagination. Certain decisions of scope and depth are necessary in order to reduce the magnitude of a complete undertaking while maintaining the objective. We will concentrate on public broadcasting, especially the development of the CBC, and radio drama as a particular domain of production.

As a way of further unravelling this complex, I would like to suggest the following continua common to Canadian political discourse and the discourse of cultural agencies: a nationalist/continentalist continuum, a centralist/regionalist continuum, and a public/private enterprise continuum. All three revolve around a central point, clockwise and counter-clockwise, with practices and discourse moving, sometimes in tandem, sometimes independently, along each continuum from pole to pole. Theoretically, a move towards the nationalist pole on one continuum tends to trigger a move towards the centralist and public-enterprise poles on the other two. A move towards the continentalist pole will tend to trigger a move towards the regionalist and private-enterprise poles on the other two. The poles form a matrix in which political and cultural practices are born and nurtured or aborted. In this matrix, national institutions in combination with other factors depress local institutions. It is specifically this process I wish to examine.

In the complex of Canadian identities two visions dominate: the dual-nation vision of French (Quebec) and English Canada; and the single-nation vision, which views Canada as a centralized nation-state composed of regions ultimately subordinated to the central authority.[20] It should be obvious to anyone who has experienced the Canadian political scene over the last five years that the former vision rests mainly in Quebec, the latter in English Canada, revealing two collective identities, two definitions of

"Canadianness." The centralized vision and its corresponding identification is invoked by English Canada in relation to Quebec (defined as a region in English Canadian terms) or to the U.S. as significant others. Assuming the dual-nation vision, the Quebec population has shifted from identification of self as Canadien(ne) to Québécois(e), translating Canadien to Canadian and reserving this term for English Canadians.

It is within English Canada that regional identifications (as opposed to national in Quebec) remain and may become dominant when invoked in relation to perceived or real central domination over westerners, Maritimers, Newfoundlanders, and the like. The intersection of these two continua—regionalization/centralization and nationalism/continentalism—contributes to considerable ambiguity. According to the time and circumstance, one identifies with one's region against Ottawa or Quebec, or with Ottawa (i.e., the nation-state) against Quebec or the U.S. If you add identities tied to aboriginal status or ethnicity, the ambiguities become more profound.

Public Broadcasting and Nationalism

The story of public broadcasting began at the regional level with such stations as CKUA (Edmonton) operated by the Alberta Telephone Company, and CKY (Winnipeg) and CKX (Brandon), operated by the Manitoba Telephone Company. These stations were closely tied to local theatrical, musical, and educational groups as well as agricultural co-operatives. They broadcast in a regional voice, creating and reinforcing regional identities. At the same time, during the early 1920s, the Canadian National Railways (CNR) established a radio network. Using its telegraph facilities, the CNR was broadcasting news, music, and drama from all major cities. CNR units like CNRV (Vancouver) and CNRM (Moncton) also maintained close ties with local entertainment talent, but the seeds of centralization had already been sown.

The move to establish CNR radio and, later, the Canadian Radio Broadcasting Commission (CRBC) as national cultural institutions had its roots in the beginnings of English-Canadian nationalism in the mid-nineteenth century. The call for a Canadian culture began in Upper Canada some years prior to Confederation. At this point, roughly between 1833 and 1864, while anxiety over the dominance of the "old country" remained, the imperial centre shifted to the United States. D'Arcy McGee's urging of

tariffs on imported material in print, and other demands for a national literature as an "essential element in the formation of national character," were registered with an eye on the U.S. By 1868 the Canada First Movement was in full swing, arguing against any form of continentalism.[21] Indeed, it was the early representations on behalf of Canadian publishing by the Canada Firsters that set the connection between nationalism and state control of media.[22] This position set in place the elements that were to structure cultural policy through to the present and from which emerged the CBC's mandate to advance the cause of national unity, a cause clearly located at the nationalist pole on the nationalist/continentalist continuum.

The first of these elements of relevance to this discussion and present before Confederation was to place an emphasis on the institution as a protective device, presumably on the assumption that the cultural base for a new centre and identity would emerge only under the protection of central institutions. If we combine this thrust with the marketplace interests of Canada's "merchant princes," the inauguration of CNR broadcasting was less than altruistic in motive. Sir Henry Thornton, the president of the CNR, was well aware of the advantages of linking cultural institutions moulded in a national vision with western economic expansion. The *Romance of Canada* drama series, a set of radio plays that re-created epic moments in Canadian history, was designed to encourage a sense of national identity over and against local identities.[23] In Thornton's words, "We hope to kindle in Canadians generally a deeper interest in the romantic history of their country."[24] This sentiment was extended through to the formation of the Canadian Radio Broadcasting Commission a year later. Consider the following statement by R.B. Bennett, then prime minister:

> This country must be assured of complete Canadian control of broadcasting from Canadian sources. Without such control, broadcasting can never be the agency by which national consciousness may be fostered and sustained and national unity still further strengthened.[25]

Herein lay the base for the mandate to promote national unity, a mandate that was explicitly stated in the *Broadcasting Acts* of March 1968 and February 1991.[26] The following appears in the 1991 Act: "The Canadian broadcasting system … provides, through its programming, a public service essential to the maintenance of national identity and cultural sovereignty."[27] With respect to the CBC, the following is of interest:

The programming provided by the Corporation should be (1) predominantly and distinctively Canadian; (2) reflect Canada and its regions to national and regional audiences, while serving the special needs of those regions; and (3) contribute to shared national consciousness and identity.[28]

The creating and sustaining of a "national consciousness" through a broadcasting agency may be understood as a move towards nationalism along the nationalist/continentalist continuum, notwithstanding references to regional and minority interests in the Act. Evidence suggests that the adoption of this position rested firmly on opposition to a perceived encroachment of American culture via private broadcasting. Furthermore, as mentioned earlier, a move along one of the continua usually activates motion on the remaining two. This was indeed the case. Defining the "other" as American culture tended to push regional identities to the periphery of the collective consciousness, directing resources towards the formation of a centralist national identity. In addition, the instruments of the federal state in the form of public broadcasting were utilized to oppose the growth of private enterprise in the field.

Largely under the leadership of Graham Spry and Alan Plaunt, a coalition of regionally based agricultural groups, co-operatives, local public broadcasters, churches, educational groups, intellectuals, and artists were brought together under the Canadian Radio League to lobby for the nationalization of broadcasting. They were opposed by private broadcasters, newspaper publishers, manufacturers of electrical and radio equipment, and other related interests. The Canadian Association of Broadcasters (CAB) became their principal representative. On the side of public broadcasting was a vision of Canada emphasizing the elements of centrality, public enterprise, and nationalism. The opposing vision emphasized private enterprise, continentalism, and, following the logic of the corporate world, centrality.

Though it did not appear to be part of the original concept of the Canadian Radio League, regional voices were subordinated in the process. Initially, the Royal Commission on Radio Broadcasting (the Aird Commission, which reported in 1929) recommended that a broadcasting director be appointed to have full control over broadcasting within each province, and that provincial advisory councils be appointed to act through provincial authority.[29] However, the *Broadcasting Act* of 1932 placed the control of technical, administrative, and program activity in the hands of federal authority.[30] The government's apparent unwillingness to negotiate with the

provinces was indicated in its neglecting to arrange for assistant commissioners appointed by the provinces, and provincial advisory committees, as called for in the Act. Between 1932 and the 1970s, regional advisory committees were to come and go as the political sector pressed for regional representation and the CBC resisted. From the Massey-Lévesque report in the early 1950s to the *Broadcasting Act* of 1991, increases in regional participation were called for, though the long-range trend towards centralization continued.

The struggle for regional control and the maintenance of regional voices in Canada has continued to this day. In the first instance it was a case of the CRBC/CBC quietly taking over local units and centralizing program control. Such was the case with CKUA in Alberta.[31] In other centres the process unfolded somewhat differently. In Montreal, for example, the CNR station was absorbed by the CRBC as a regional unit with, in the drama department, scripts vetted in Toronto.[32] To illustrate, let us follow the process more closely in Winnipeg.

CKY: The Termination of a Regional Voice

Owned and operated by the Manitoba Telephone System since 1923, CKY was the first high-powered station in Canada. Under an early agreement giving it veto power over the establishment of any other stations in Manitoba, it was the keystone to prairie regional broadcasting. Aside from a subsidiary station in Brandon (CKX) and the CNR phantom station (CNRW), which used CKY's transmitter, CKY had a monopoly on broadcasting in Manitoba until the late 1920s. (CNRW began broadcasting part of one evening per week from its own studios in the Fort Garry Hotel in early 1924.) CKY was also the key station in a prairie network linking stations in all three provinces (including CKUA) via telephone lines.[33]

With the establishment of the CRBC in 1932, CKY became a major affiliate. By 1933, the CRBC was leasing three hours per evening from CKY, with the latter producing some material for the CRBC, especially in the area of drama. The push towards nationalism and centralization was signalled by the CRBC's decision to transfer broadcasts from the Manitoba telephone wires to the CN/CP telegraph system. A memo (unsigned) to W.J. Major, minister of Telephones for Manitoba, noted that the province had agreed to assist the CRBC "on the understanding that this station [CKY] would maintain its identity with the province ... since then a number of things have been done that are not to the best

TABLE 1: Major Production Centres by Percentage of Plays Broadcast during Four Phases

Centres	1st	2nd	3rd	4th
Vancouver	26.25	25.10	21.98	20.09
Winnipeg	16.75	16.42	13.21	4.72
Toronto	37.94	44.24	47.88	53.59
Montreal	18.88	7.64	8.63	9.00
Halifax	.17	6.60	8.30	11.6
Total	**1,737**	**1,833**	**3,626**	**3,732**

advantage of Manitoba."[34] In 1936 the minister pointed out that CKY then averaged only 4 hours per month in sponsored regional network programs compared with 27 hours per month in 1931.[35] The period up to 1945 was a time of rapid centralization, limited only by the resources available to the CBC and the influence of the war years on centralized broadcasting. By 1947 CKY had received notification of its takeover.

In the early summer of 1947, Stewart Garson, premier of Manitoba, announced the termination of the two stations operated by the Manitoba Telephone Company (CKY and CKX). In his words:

In the exercise of the authority over radio which the Privy Council had held to be possessed by the Dominion Parliament, not the provinces, the CBC had been developing a national policy. Under this policy all of the 50,000 watt stations in Canada were to be owned by the CBC. In the meanwhile, efforts had been made by at least three other provincial governments, Alberta, Saskatchewan and Québec, to get licenses to operate provincial broadcasting stations and their applications had been refused.[36]

CBW (Winnipeg), the new CBC station, went on air during the summer of 1948. CKY was purchased by the CBC for $200,000; its call letters were adopted by a private station in 1950. CKX (Brandon) was sold to the private sector. Since 1970 four provinces have returned to the air: TVOntario; Access Alberta (a continuation of CKUA); Radio-Québec; and British Columbia's Knowledge Network of the West. Ontario made an application for a licence in 1966, but it was refused under the same policy that had led to the end of CKY in 1948. The federal government then attempted to set up an educational broadcasting authority, a move that was met with considerable hostility by the provinces, led by Ontario and Quebec.[37]

With respect to radio drama in Winnipeg, as one among many areas of production, the story up to the mid-1980s may be divided into four phases:

- The period up to 1945, when the CRBC/CBC was founded and consolidated;

- The period from 1945 to 1951, when CKY was sold to the CBC, the so-called "golden age of radio drama" came into being, and English-language radio production was centralized in Toronto;

- The period from 1951 to 1961, which saw a continuation of the centralizing process, modified in radio drama by one national producer's (Esse W. Ljungh) policy to encourage regional production, and the struggle to maintain radio drama in the new world of TV;

- The period up to 1985, which included the 1968 *Broadcasting Act*, the closing of one of the CBC's radio networks, budget cuts, a new look at regional demands, and the regionalization of prairie broadcasting resulting in the loss of Winnipeg's position as prairie regional headquarters.

The various events that occurred during each phase were reflected in the frequency of drama production in Winnipeg. Table 1 presents the distribution of plays according to selected CBC production centres. The total number of plays—10,928—from all five centres through all four phases represents those plays for which a record existed at the time of the compilation of the radio drama bibliographies and where the centre from which the plays were broadcast (not necessarily produced) was noted.[38]

The expected pattern emerges. The proportion broadcast from Toronto increases through time to over one-half of those broadcast during the fourth phase. Only one-twentieth of the plays were broadcast from Winnipeg during this last phase. In part this would be accounted for by Winnipeg's demise as a regional centre and the increase in drama broadcasts from Calgary and Regina. The long-range trend is clear enough—a weakening of the regional voice.

Creative Formations

Creative formations (or social networks) are crucial to successful political activity and creative work in the arts. The collective nature of production in theatre and radio drama is perhaps more obvious than in other art forms. Writers, performers, musicians, and technicians must communicate directly or indirectly in the course of producing a sound drama. High-density formations can and do develop as the amount of interactional time, and therefore the intensity of communication, increase among a particular group creating radio drama. Such formations often come close to creating "schools" of radio drama, as was the case with Andrew Allan's team in Toronto and Rupert Caplan's team in Montreal.[39] Perhaps even more obvious to the casual observer is that political work—the marshalling of forces to achieve some political objective—requires the ability to tap various social networks.

It was this ability that enabled Graham Spry and Alan Plaunt to develop the Canadian Radio League into an effective political instrument for achieving the nationalization of broadcasting in the 1930s. Under the threat of the link between private enterprise and U.S. domination of the airwaves, they were able to forge a coalition of people from farm co-operatives, women's groups, churches, prairie wheat pools, and adult education groups to demand public control of broadcasting. Two points are of note in passing: first, though the vision of many was not that of the highly centralized state, they did not realize that their particular local interests would suffer under a move towards the nationalist pole; and second, the coalition carried a political ideology that was strongly left- to left-liberal oriented and rooted in the academic, journalism, and arts communities.[40]

A decade later the young men and women who were to become part of radio drama production in Toronto, principally under Andrew Allan, either had direct connections with the earlier political formation or were connected ideologically. Though they were mainly from western Canada and their ideology was most certainly that of the periphery, they defined the new centralized and national vision in their particular domain of broadcasting. From the perspective of the regions they became "the controlling clique in Toronto."

The appropriation of regional artists from western Canada—such as Tommy Tweed, Jean Tweed, and

Esse W. Ljungh, to name but three previously associated with Winnipeg—meant that a strong and persistent formation did not develop in Winnipeg. Further contributing to this problem was that Winnipeg had at least 10 different drama producers (with minimal overlap), combined with periods of time without a producer from the 1940s to the early 1980s. Loose formations of performers and writers did develop around certain producers—formations that reached into the Winnipeg theatre community. Indeed, when commercial theatre in Winnipeg failed during the late 1930s, radio drama continued and managed to provide a new base for theatre during the 1950s.[41] The ability to sustain such locally based networks diminished considerably as Winnipeg producers became "subcontractors" for scripts sent from Toronto. Technology, too, had its effects: no longer did "the team" have to be on hand for live performances; a producer could have lines read by performers in Toronto, Vancouver, or elsewhere, and then splice and edit a tape for broadcasting. The mode of creation itself had shifted in response to the demands of centralization.

Creative formations in the arts interact with bureaucracies in the "cultural industries" and with the canons of their particular art form. But they are also composed of individuals who bring with them their own particular identities and, in this case, their particular visions of Canada or sense of "Canadianness." Any one source of their work may be found to be complementary, contradictory, or ambiguous in relation to any other. The canons of their discipline (what we write and how we write or perform) may clash with the economic, political, and cultural definitions of the situation by their employers, sponsors, or patrons. It is out of such contradictions and ambiguities that the imaginary, that capacity to dream the impossible as the possible, is activated.

Radio has played a peculiar role in this respect. In its early days, from the 1920s through the 1940s, it was a new form of communication. In the field of drama it presented a space in which artists could leap over the canons of their disciplines—in writing and theatre, for example. Artists involved in theatre and writing used radio as a testing ground for ideas and forms through a medium that spoke more directly to audiences than either the book or conventional theatre. Also, radio began at the local level involving people who were simply captivated with the new possibilities. Strong regional voices developed in this context.

Centralization and technological change in public and private broadcasting contributed to the demise of locally based formations. With respect to Winnipeg, centralization proceeded on two fronts. First, the nationalization of broadcasting shifted control to Toronto and Ottawa; centrality is a feature of administrative bureaucracy. Production followed, though the CBC and the CRTC continued to exhibit ambivalence on the region/centre issue. This fact, combined with the migration of cultural industries in general to Toronto, drew local artists eastward. The location of cultural activities in Toronto was, in turn, related to general cultural policies at the federal level, represented, for example, in the Canada Council. In sum, the national project marginalized regional production and its accompanying visions of Canada. A final irony was the reduction of Winnipeg, which had held the status of prairie regional headquarters, to a local production centre in the name of regionalization.

Second, Winnipeg as the "gateway city" to the west was gradually losing its economic centrality as a consequence of changing markets, technology, and corporate centralization. Thus, economically, politically, and culturally, regional identities retreated to the periphery of English Canadian life, to be redefined and reactivated in crises. In such times regional voices gain centrality, articulating opposition and alternatives to the official definition of "Canadianness."

Conclusion

Institutions, by definition, are patterns of beliefs, values, goals, ways of doing and seeing things. The CBC, as a large-scale organization, incorporates a particular institutional set, and though the "Canada" which it has articulated in its formation and broadcasting is restricted, it has been presented as universal. To the extent that the idea of region is incorporated, it is not as a living community, as lived culture, but as a parochialism tied to the centre through a bureaucratic hierarchy.

The political will to establish an official culture (or *the meaning*) is not only effected through institutions, but in the process, creates institutions. These in turn produce and reproduce official culture. The latter, so constituted, enters into and increases its domain of influence in the social matrix of identification. Another way of expressing this process is that the priority of official definitions of the situation increases relative to competing definitions in the matrix. The authority conferred to central institutions allows them to capture the means of communication, thereby increasing not only the diffusion of official culture, but also the very legitimacy of the process itself. In this sense institutions do not reflect reality but create reality.

In the process of identity formation and revision, individuals and groups will tend to give priority to official meanings, given their legitimacy and their linkage with institutions of socialization. One might add that positive and negative sanctions accompany official culture. An outright rejection of official meanings and the proclamation of competing meanings can bring sanctions ranging all the way from ridicule to the use of armed forces. Lived culture over and against official culture is local rather than cosmopolitan and tends to generate and reinforce competing meanings.

The function of central institutions is to incorporate, depress, or eliminate competing meanings. This chapter revealed a facet of this more general process, focussing on the formation of the CBC as a meaning-producing institutional complex specifically mandated to promulgate a particular vision of Canada–Canada as a centralized nation-state. Early CNR broadcasting, the first to receive the mandate, carried the seeds of centralization–seeds that would germinate in the CRBC and grow in the CBC. Using Winnipeg broadcasting as an example, we were able to examine the centralization process that led to the demise of Manitoba's CKY and CKX in the name of technically better broadcasting and superior programming. Whatever the rationale, Manitoba (not the first, as we saw) lost the authority of its regional voice–the voice of lived culture.

A closer look at drama, as one among many areas of production, revealed the details of the process at the production level. Not only did the CBC buy out CKY/CKX through the enforcement of federal broadcasting policy, but Winnipeg's relation to its own hinterland was reduced, local production was reduced, artists were appropriated, and production was increasingly brought under central control. It was noted that locally based producers now tend to see themselves as subcontractors, and regional production and its characteristically local voice were marginalized. The marginalization of lived culture shifts legitimacy to official culture, giving it a priority position in the social matrix from which identities are constructed.

The struggle between identities and the identity is neverending. Canada, envisioned as a centralized nation-state, is a product of the institution–the officially sanctioned matrix of identification. The story of public broadcasting in English Canada is the story of one such set of institutional patterns bearing on the question "Who am I?"

Notes

1. The author wishes to acknowledge the contributions of Prof. Mary Vipond, Concordia University, for her assistance on the Winnipeg project, Susan Adams for the analysis of Winnipeg data, and the Social Sciences and Humanities Research Council of Canada for its support on the Winnipeg project.

2. Tamotsu Shibutani, *Society and Personality: An Interactionist Approach to Social Psychology* (Englewood Cliffs, N.J.: Prentice-Hall, 1961), pp.239–48.

3. George H. Mead, *Mind, Self, Society* (Chicago: University of Chicago Press, 1934), p.257.

4. Friedrich H. Tenbruck, "The Cultural Foundations of Society," Hans Haferkamp, ed., *Social Structure and Culture* (New York: Walter de Gruyter, 1989), p.20.

5. Tenbruck, "Cultural Foundations." See also Raymond Williams, *Culture* (London: Fontana Paperbacks, 1981), p.13.

6. Milton M. Gordon, *Assimilation in American Life* (New York: Oxford University Press, 1964), pp.25–28.

7. On the other hand, there were positions taken on the proposed constitutional accords rooted in other than national or linguistic identities. Note, for example, the strongly argued position presented on behalf of women by the National Action Committee on the Status of Women.

8. Emile Durkheim, *The Rules of Sociological Method* (Chicago: University of Chicago Press, 1938), pp.1–13.

9. Mead, *Mind, Self, Society,* p.202.

10. Anthony Wilden, *The Rules Are No Game: The Strategy of Communication* (London: Routledge & Kegan Paul, 1987), p.77.

11. For examples of this type of research, see Theodore R. Sarbin, "Role Theory," Gardiner Lindzey, ed., *Handbook of Social Psychology,* vol. I (Reading, Mass.: Addison-Wesley, 1954), pp.238–55.

12. Anthony P. Cohen, *The Symbolic Construction of Community* (London: Tavistock Publications, 1985), p.12.

13. Cohen, *Symbolic Construction,* p.17.

14. Marcel Rioux, "Remarks on Emancipatory Practices and Industrial Societies in Crisis," *The Canadian Journal of Sociology and Anthropology* 21, no. 1 (1984). See also Margaret S. Archer, *Culture and Agency: The Place of Culture in Social Theory* (Cambridge: Cambridge University Press, 1988), p.xxii. With respect to identity formation one might assume a cultural conditioning extant at one point in time and providing the constraints (the instituted) within which interaction takes place. In turn, within this interactive setting elaboration and invention (instituting) occurs, yielding new configurations of thought and behaviour.

15. Cornelius Castoriadis, *The Imaginary Institution of Society* (Cambridge, Mass.: MIT Press, 1987), pp.147–49.

16. Benedict Anderson, *Imagined Communities: Reflections on the Origin and Spread of Nationalism* (London: Verson, revised 1991), p.4.

17. In his *The Imaginary Institution of Society,* p.388ff. Castoriadis refers to: "The ultimate or radical imaginary, that is the capacity to make arise as an image something which does not exist and has never existed, and the *product* of this imaginary, which could be designated as the *imagined* ... [or actual imaginary]."

18. Josef Bleicher, "The Cultural Construction of Social Identity: The Case of Scotland," Hans Haferkamp, ed., *Social Structure and Culture* (New York: Walter De Gruyter, 1989), p.229.

19. Bleicher, "Cultural Construction," p.233.

20. There are other visions; the sense of a Canadian nation within or side by side with nations of aboriginal peoples may be slowly gaining credence in the Canadian imagination.

21. See Carl Berger, *The Sense of Power: Studies in Ideas of Canadian Imperialism, 1867– 1914* (Toronto: University of Toronto Press, 1970), pp.49–66. See also George Woodcock, *Northern Spring: The Flowering of Canadian Literature* (Vancouver: Douglas & McIntyre, 1987), p.10.

22. As suggested by Sylvia Bashevkin, *True Patriot Love: The Politics of Canadian Nationalism* (Toronto: Oxford University Press, 1991), p.8.

23. Trevor Grigg, "Text and Context: 'The Romance of Canada' and the Construction of a National Imagination" (M.A. thesis, Concordia University, Department of Sociology and Anthropology, Montreal, 1988).

24. E.A. Weir, *The Struggle for National Broadcasting in Canada* (Toronto: McClelland & Stewart, 1965), p.53.

25. Task Force on Broadcasting Policy, *Report* (Ottawa: Supply and Services, 1986), p.6.

26. Roger Bird, ed., *Documents of Canadian Broadcasting* (Ottawa: Carleton University Press, 1988), p.375; and *Statutes of Canada,* Chapters 1–44, 1991, vol. 1, chapter 11, "Broadcasting Policy for Canada" (Ottawa: Queen's Printer, 1992).

27. *Statutes of Canada,* Chapter 1–44, 1991, vol. 1, chapter 11, p.3.

28. Ibid., p.5.

29. Bird, *Documents,* p.52.

30. F.W. Peers, *The Politics of Canadian Broadcasting, 1920-1951* (Toronto: University of Toronto Press, 1968), p.106.

31. Howard Fink, "CKUA: Radio Drama and Regional Theatre," *Theatre History in Canada* 8, no. 2 (1987).

32. John D. Jackson and Paul Millen, "English-Language Radio Drama: A Comparison of Regional and Central Production Units," *Canadian Journal of Communication* 15, no. 1 (1990).

33. C.E. L'Ami, "History of Radio in Winnipeg," *Winnipeg Tribune* (3 February 1934). See also Mary Vipond, "CKY Winnipeg in the 1920s: Canada's Only Experiment in Monopoly Broadcasting," *Manitoba History* 12, no. 1 (1986).

34. Concordia University, Centre for Broadcasting Studies Archives, File: Winnipeg #1.

35. Manitoba, Manitoba Provincial Archives, Major, 444ff.

36. The Honourable Stewart Garson, excerpt from a tape of a broadcast over Station CKY Winnipeg, c. June 1947, "Hon. Stewart Garson, Premier of Manitoba, CKY to CBC," Concordia Centre for Broadcasting Studies Archives.

37. Task Force on Broadcasting, *Report,* pp.337–39.

38. Howard Fink with Brian Morrison, *Canadian National Theatre on the Air, 1925-1961: A Descriptive Bibliography* (Toronto: University of Toronto Press, 1983); and Howard Fink et al., *Canadian National Theatre on the Air II: 1962 to 1985: A Descriptive Bibliography* (Kingston: Quarry Press, 1993).

39. Howard Fink and John Jackson, eds., *All the Bright Company: Radio Drama Produced by Andrew Allan* (Toronto/Kingston: CBC Enterprises/Quarry Press, 1987), pp.ix–xvi. See also Jackson and Millen, "English-Language Radio Drama," pp.6-10.

40. Bashevkin, *True Patriot Love,* pp.8, 28.

41. Reg Skene, "C.P. Walker and the Business of Theatre: Merchandizing Entertainment in a Continental Context," Jim Silver and Jeremy Hull, eds., *The Political Economy of Manitoba* (Regina: Canadian Plains Research Centre, 1990).

PART 2

CANADA AND THE NEW MEDIA

If when you try to predict what may happen in ten years, your predictions sound like science fiction, you may well be wrong. But if your predictions ten years out don't sound like science fiction, you are certain to be wrong.–David R. Henderson[1]

More than two decades ago, pioneering studies were being done in eastern Canada on the use of communications technology to give new voice to citizens in isolated areas. Through the use of motion pictures, previously "voiceless" citizens were able to communicate effectively with politicians and officials. In the 1970s as well, mass-media channels for participation and interaction reached their peak as newspaper ombudspersons and radio call-in shows boomed. Today, there are fewer of both; most newspapers have discontinued their action lines, and many of the radio phone-in programs do not have the star status they once had. They have been left behind by the surge in development of the "new media." It was during the apex of the citizens' communication movement in 1970 that a prescient essay in a special edition of the U.S. publication *The Nation* anticipated what is now taking place. In "The Wired Nation," Ralph Lee Smith forecast that cable TV was about to launch a revolution in communications.[2] Apart from predicting correctly the immense power that cable networks would soon wield, he also pointed out their tremendous potential to contribute to what is now called "the information society" and popularized the metaphor "electronic highway."

By 1994, the wired nation had expanded to become the "Wired World."[3] Today, there is optimism that "new media"–networking through all manner of electronic devices including computers, fax machines, mobile phones, on-line shopping–will provide the kind of interaction and participation heralded in the 1970s. Perhaps that optimism is realistic and warranted, and perhaps not. These are the kinds of issues examined critically by the authors in this section.

Craig McKie provides further support for the concept of the "wired world" by linking the new media to an infrastructure of communications technology.

The telephone line has become, at least for the time being, the key channel through which most of the new media provide services. Massive numbers of new nexuses have become available through telephone lines and other media that exponentially increase the accessibility of people to others, and services to people in an increasingly borderless world.

McKie provides census data on Canadian households with such communications technology as telephones, TVs, VCRs, cable TV, and computers, showing their dramatic increase in recent years, and draws out some of their potential social impacts. The number of households with an active Internet user is growing rapidly, perhaps at a greater rate than televisions appeared in Canadian households in the 1950s. The computer is the core of the "electronic cottage" concept, and is already impacting individuals and families in ways previously unimagined; for example, computer-telephone connections are helping workers reduce the "dead time" of commuting in major urban centres of the world. But telephone-line-based devices will result in more than shifting the time and location of work. It is expected that rewiring the world will result in a reorientation of social time, as modems operating through telephone lines or cable TV make possible information acquisition, services, and personal contacts to and from around the world at all hours, leading to what McKie calls "the 24-hour world."

On the other hand, Singer's conjectural chapter suggests that our entry into the Information Age may not result only in that which technological optimists have predicted, particularly where the properties of existing institutions are concerned. He argues that new communication technology that promotes the opening of borders that formerly separated organizations from one another (and one arm of an organization from other arms), and mass media from other kinds of media and from non-media organizations, will lead to changes in social institutions that are not precisely as foreseen by proponents of "electronic cottage" theories. The opening of "communications borders" can create new kinds of social disorganization in part because of the erosion of some forms of social authority, linked to traditional interpersonal communication, that have fulfilled important social functions. The sharp reduction in courtesy among network communicators is one indicator, among others, of changes that may herald a new kind of mass society rather than, as some commentators have suggested, one of small, highly socially integrated electronic peer groups.

Some of these evolving changes to existing institutions are discussed in the excerpt by Philip Evans and Thomas Wurster. They show how the realities of the new information economy destroy critical elements of venerable business institutions such as newspapers and create havoc with companies' ability to make a profit where it was once easy, and ultimately threaten their very existence as it is presently understood.

Each contribution reflects, in its own way, the fact of the heavy impact of the new media on existing ways of doing things in Canadian society. In fairly rapid order, the institutions with which we have become familiar, both public and private, are being subjected to extreme pressures to adapt to the new information realities. Inevitably, ordinary Canadians who work in these institutions, or who rely on their services, see the social impact first hand. Canadians' responses to these "new information economy" pressures are bound to create broad social and cultural change. As Michael Adams, pollster, founder and president of Environics, and erstwhile young Red Tory has observed:

> Canadians are now forming new attachments with a diversity of communities, within *and* without Canada. These include the new on-line communities that disregard national borders and individual stereotypes. Canadians' enthusiasm for these new technologies, and their growing ability to form their own networks rather than rely on historical institutions, is contributing to the "values tribalization" of the country. Once defined by our race, religion or region, now we define ourselves by our values, by our personal priorities and by our life choices.[4]

Notes

[1] David R. Henderson, "Information Technology as a Universal Solvent for Removing State Stains," *The Independent Review* IV, no.4, Summer 2000, p.523 <http://www.independent.org/tii/lighthouse/LHLink 2-30-8.html>.

[2] Ralph Lee Smith, "The Wired Nation," *The Nation* 210 (18 May 1970), pp.587-606.

[3] *Maclean's*, 17 January 1994, pp.40-47.

[4] Michael Adams, *Sex in the Snow* (Toronto: Penguin Books, 1998) pp.18-19.

7: AT HOME IN CYBERSPACE: CITIZENS OF A NEW WORLD   93

devices, such as telephone books and Yellow Pages, can help one cope with this problem in terms of traditional voice telephone. But with information sources that change by the minute, it is often impossible to construct a "menu" general enough to allow serendipitous conjunctions and at the same time specific enough to avoid an unmanageably large product of a search.

We must then distinguish between the machines and the uses to which they can be put. It is not possible to anticipate how services will be used. For example, tone generators designed for other purposes, such as interacting with phone-answering boxes, can be used by the knowledgeable to trick phone exchanges into awarding free long-distance calls. Personal computers can be used in combination with modems to gain illegal entry into private databases, then to alter or destroy valuable records, and of course computer viruses or "Trojan horse" programs can be used to damage, destroy, and extort if deposited unwittingly on a host machine.

Technology and Social Change

In the late Middle Ages, material social change of vast importance has been traced to the introduction of a few relatively simple devices: the wheeled plough and horse harness,[5] and the letterpress. In the present era we are faced with the rapid introduction of a flood of communications and personal-computing technology. It is not simply one item but a family of devices. A prime example is the fax machine, unsuccessfully introduced by the Xerox Corporation but later wedded to computer technology by Japanese technologists, which rendered irrelevant the physical constraints of paper carried over a distance.[6]

The availability of cheap microprocessor-controlled electronic devices is now so pervasive that for most purposes they form a distinct class of products and services. They have quietly become indispensable elements of modern life in a short period of time. A categorization of their functions must of necessity be arbitrary, but one distinction is between those that have the ability to communicate machine-to-machine using some form of telecommunications link, and those that are isolated in their function (such as the computers that control combustion in modern automobiles). Indeed, telecommunications equipment is now, almost by definition, computer-based.

Working documents now pass between individuals across time zones and between offices, houses, cars, or indeed anywhere a phone and receiving device is available—even by mobile phone or graphics-capable pager connection in the street if necessary. Here, the user is capitalizing on the proliferating network of telephone services throughout the world. It is now easy to direct-dial a number halfway round the world and is not exceedingly expensive to do so. Once the connection is established, it is quite simple to pass images and text via fax, "encrypted" text (computer-to-computer via modem), TV images of a sort, and of course voice traffic. One of the sociological consequences of such new media technology is that it makes it possible to take advantage of time-zone differences for international shift work. It also does away with the necessity for humans to physically group together for the purposes of non-manufacturing work, thus challenging the existing patterns of commuting to office and factory space.

Telework from the home is not yet prevalent enough to be the subject of much analysis. There are methodological problems, such as identifying informants to volunteer information, and definitional problems as well. In September 1992, the Treasury Board of the Canadian government introduced a pilot program to allow government employees to work at home. Among the advantages for employees cited were suitability for balancing the demands of work and home and reduced costs of transportation. On the employer side, improvements in morale and productivity and reduced office-space costs were cited.[7] This program continues to grow into a normal feature of the work world.

Hypothetically, though, it is possible to imagine several concrete and mutually beneficial outcomes. Consider, for example, three academics working on a paper with an eight-hour time difference between each. Person 1 works a normal day on a manuscript, and at the end of the day sends the work on to Person 2, who receives it at the beginning of his work day. At the end of his day, he sends it on to Person 3. In this fashion, it is possible to carry out continuous work on a manuscript by taking advantage of the solar cycle, something that was once an impediment. All that is required is a time-insensitive text-transmission facility that stores incoming messages temporarily until the recipient picks them up. Such a system already exists as an integral part of Internet e-mail. Employed for less glorious purposes, the commercial data networks apply the same principles to ensure that your American Express bill is always up to date and your credit limit promptly enforced, and that you have the opportunity to pay your almost over-due bill at 2 a.m. on the corporate website of your bank. Increasingly, it is difficult to distinguish be-tween discrete networks, be they commercial or edu-cational in nature ("ports" connect them), or between the various types of activities that users do during the day and the night. Work has spread from normal business hours into evening at-home times, and like-wise play has spread to the workplace in the form of personal surfing and buying episodes in the work day.

Telephone Use in Canada

Telephone use continues to increase in Canadian society. The telephone has become a central tool of Canadian households and businesses. It has eased the demographic transition away from large and close extended families towards a more insular "resi-dent expatriate" existence by allowing dispersed members of much smaller families to remain in con-tact. At the same time, it has allowed greater (and at the same time safer and more impersonal) contact with a much wider range of service providers.

While a direct measure of toll calls made is avail-able only for public statistical purposes for the years 1971 through 1992 in Canada—at which time this measure was discontinued—the pattern of use is one of explosive growth. The number of toll calls in-creased from 386,522,000 to 3,293,540,000 during that period.[8]

This represents a nearly ten-fold increase in the number of toll calls between 1971 and 1992. There is no reason to think that this figure has not continued to rise further in the years since. We can see the in-crease indirectly in the toll call revenues that have been measured continuously to the present time. Note that during the period, the tolls themselves have fallen dramatically. In many cases, such as in the cost of international calls, the per minute charge has fallen to 10 percent or less of their cost prior to long distance deregulation, which began in the early 1990s. Deregulation brought with it the entry of new long-distance competitors, aggressive, well-publicized price wars, and promotion of long-distance calling itself into the Canadian telephone service world. The decline in overall toll revenue (see Table 1) has been offset by sharp increases in the cost of local service lines, which had previously been cross-subsidized by high long-distance charges. Ca-nadian local service usage is still not metred and paid for by the minute and the call as it is in Western Eu-rope. This represents a tremendous competitive

TABLE 1: Telephone Toll Service Revenue, 1971-1998

Year	Thousand $
1971	567,375
1972	844,425
1973	994,712
1974	1,172,034
1975	1,407,088
1976	1,663,708
1977	1,892,426
1978	2,238,721
1979	2,636,005
1980	3,052,850
1981	3,624,973
1982	4,058,185
1983	4,404,299
1984	4,842,474
1985	5,332,875
1986	5,816,737
1987	6,054,806
1988	6,318,774
1989	6,791,380
1990	7,142,721
1991	7,005,601
1992	6,915,401
1993	6,794,544
1994	6,475,449
1995	5,982,718
1996	5,483,297
1997	5,391,087
1998	4,792,919

Source: Statistics Canada, CANSIM, Series D462090.

advantage for Canadians and their enterprises vis-à-vis Western Europe.

Certainly, the presence in Canada of large num-bers of recent immigrants, for whom the telephone has become the primary means of staying in touch with relatives overseas, has played a part, and with-out question, fax-machine-generated long-distance calls have been an important factor in the increase, to some extent supplanting letter mail over long distances.

Many statistical series that once had pertinence have been made the better part of irrelevant by the national wiring project that has taken place over the last 20 years. Single-copper-pair wiring, the basic unit of telephony for instance, can be made to carry multiple conversations and data connections now.

TABLE 2: Cellular Telephone Services–Selected Historical Statistics

	Cellular Service Revenue ($ Thousands)	Subscribers as of Dec 31 (Number)	Capital Expenditures ($ Thousands)
1987	117,611	98,364	158,928
1988	226,006	202,633	253,131
1989	361,871	345,178	422,010
1990	619,230	583,766	627,356
1991	762,799	775,831	361,654
1992	932,178	1,026,611	422,659
1993	1,173,471	1,332,982	456,460
1994	1,508,546	1,865,779	416,837
1995	1,921,812	2,589,780	618,267
1996	2,440,841	3,420,318	1,099,580

Source: Statistics Canada, *The Daily*, Cellular telephone service industry: Historical statistics 1987 to 1996, Wednesday, April 1, 1998.

This makes the traditional measure of telephone service lines no longer of great interest. We do know that virtually all of Canada's approximately 10 million households have telephone service. As to the total of business service, private and carrier-provided service line totals can only be estimated. One telephone number per employee would be a good place to start. Recently, large corporations have begun to use their own dedicated trunk data lines to carry internal phone calls as well, further blurring the circuit/toll call/total call statistical mixture. Big employers have tended to switch their operations to privately owned local exchanges, which they control themselves and which are capable of supporting many extensions with fewer service lines. These internal exchanges also support additional and advantageous internal services such as intercom facilities. This now applies also to householders, who now may purchase and connect various devices within their own homes, as well as using the copper-pair and electrical-service wiring for such unrelated purposes as printer sharing and central lighting control in the household.

The number of domestic and business service lines in operation began to accelerate upward in 1988 and 1989, largely on the strength of new domestic installations but coincident with the widespread appearance of modem and fax machines in the Canadian household. The observed social trends towards living alone and a high level of marital separations have decreased average household size and artificially increased the number of households—a phenomenon of considerable sociodemographic interest. Both would have an upward effect on the number of private service lines required. Large blocks of increasingly scarce telephone numbers are also allocated to the burgeoning mobile telephone system, though these are not "lines" connected directly to the system. Shortages of allocation blocks of 10,000 telephone numbers (released from the regulator to the local telephone companies as required) has led to the adoption of more numerous area codes and new superimposition schemes for area codes in which their geographic mappings are no longer distinct.[9] For whatever reason, more and more devices are being connected to the networks all the time. Each must remain uniquely addressable to be of use. The same is incidentally true of each computer connected to the Internet by whatever physical means.

Mobile telephones (cellular, PCS and dual or tri-mode models that are designed to work worldwide) have become prevalent very rapidly. In 1985, there were only 12,000 cellular telephones in Canada;[10] by 1990, there were more than 500,000, and by 1992, the total had risen to more than 1 million, according to Statistics Canada (see Table 2). In the meantime, the devices have grown smaller, cheaper, and more reliable. Full portability, city-to-city and along the corridors of the densest population, become a necessary feature necessitating huge investment in service towers and carrying capacity. Though improved in a technical sense, the devices had by 1993 become giveaway items for the providing companies trying to attract new customers.

Within this context, the number of telephones or even the number of service lines in use no longer conveys the extent or meaning of the full load of telephone use, or the dependence on the telephone as an essential tool for personal and professional life in the 1990s.

Telecommunications-Based Devices

Telecommunications-based devices move information, digital or voice and sometimes both together, from one place to another. In action, they appear in the hand of the user to be one end of a direct link between themselves and the source or recipient of information. While the technology of coding and switching is important, if it works well it should be transparent to the user. The world's current state of "wiredness" is such that one can, without assistance, direct-dial a link to most places in the world. Systems work independently of solar day and night and preferential charging rates work to even out the flow over a 24-hour cycle and seven-day week. The actual links may be formed by copper wire, fibre-optics cable, terrestrial-microwave transmission, satellite-microwave transmission, or any combination of these.

Links follow network rules and not shortest-link rules, so that transmission across town might in fact be routed by load-managing computers through spare capacity in another city or, exceptionally, through international links. Since parallel networks exist in jurisdictions that have abolished telecommunications monopolies, sometimes the actual routing is not knowable in its complexity, but this indeterminacy is irrelevant for the user, since distance travelled by the signal is not considered in the cost formula per se. Only slight delays in transmission or voice dropouts in a phone call, or noise introduced into a fax or data transmission, may betray the physical nature of the connection that a network arranges, independent of human intervention.

Some of the many devices in this class are:
- Computers, ranging from the familiar desktop model to tiny handheld portable versions designed to be used anywhere;
- Phone answering boxes;
- Imaging devices such as fax machines;
- Public Internet terminals, which are appearing in public places such as airports;
- Communicating personal, pocket-sized agenda organizers;
- Devices that produce real-time images from space for such purposes as crop surveillance, weather forecasting, traffic monitoring, Global Positioning Satellite (GPS) mapping and direction-giving to travellers and motorists by means of highly accurate location determination. Devices for remote-broadcasting feeds with satellite uplink from remote locations, useful in disasters or area surveillance, or locations of more than average interest, such as sporting events and battlefields;
- Phone-in local information (such as highly localized bus-schedule information with electronic voice, available by telephone in Ottawa);
- Household surveillance devices that dial civic authorities in case of break-in or fire;
- Health-crisis autodialers that call an ambulance at the touch of a button;
- Autodialers used by telephone-survey takers and used on occasion for annoying recorded sales pitches;
- Slow-scan television linked to a central location by telephone line for the surveillance of public spaces;
- Short-range domestic portable phones;
- Long-range mobile phones including satellite phones usable anywhere on earth;
- Telephones in the seats of airliners;
- Stream-separation devices that channel voice, modem, fax connections to appropriate machines in home or office from a single service line or trunk data line;
- Local exchanges (multi-line) with conferencing, scrambling, auto-redial, diversion, pooling, call-forwarding, and so on. Personal voice mail and third-party voice mail through public phones;
- Beepers, pagers, voice and data pagers;
- Toll free 800 and 888 numbers for information, such as those offered by the Statistics Canada regional office system; 900 numbers for a multitude of commercial services such as chatlines.

Needless to say, this plethora of communication devices has created special technical problems for those whose business it is to covertly monitor telecommunications content for purposes of national security or the investigation of criminal offences. While little has been written on the subject, it is a useful assumption that the content of most, if not all, telecommunication is potentially subject to monitoring if not actually monitored, again by machine, in some sets of circumstances. James Bamford has described the technical means by which this can be accomplished in considerable detail.[11] The degree of exposure to eavesdropping became clear with the publication of audiotape transcripts of the cellular-telephone conversations of then B.C. Attorney-General Bud Smith in 1990. A similar disclosure of a "private" conversation between public servants in Quebec had a significant impact on the public debate surrounding the ultimate defeat of the Constitutional referendum in 1992.

Thus telecommunication is a public affair unless specific encryption measures are taken. Certainly with respect to the voice telephone specifically, the ubiquity of the telephone has been matched by the technical ability to tap, intercept, and otherwise monitor conversations and data transmissions. The introduction of fibre-optic transmission is said to have made the process of interception much easier, since it is no longer necessary to interfere physically with the connection to effect monitoring. While no reliable estimates of telephone interceptions exist for Canada, more detail is available for Britain. *The Manchester Guardian* reported in the summer of 1990 that 30,000 lines in Britain were officially tapped in 1988 and that the number of British Telecom tapping engineers had increased by 50 percent in the preceding decade.[12] More recent figures from the United States suggest that at least 2,450,000 telephone conversations were legally intercepted there in 1999.[13] In addition, there were 1,350 authorized wiretaps on cellphones, pagers, fax machines and e-mail.[14]

Services Based on Telecommunication

While the telecommunications-based devices themselves are of undoubted importance, so too are the service industries that have grown up around them, since they provide added value through the new media. Some of these services are:

- Dialog and Lexis-Nexis (literature-search services) and data-archive sources dispensing catalogues and actual data, either through the Internet or similar private services. Since archives are accessible from anywhere, there is the need for only one "data vault" in the world, though in practice there will probably be regional "mirrors" of major holdings such as ICPSR in Ann Arbor, Michigan. By utilizing the time zones, the workload can be spread evenly across the regional "mirrors";

- On-line newspapers;

- E-books (which first gained public prominence with the publication of Stephen King's short novel *Riding the Bullet* in March 2000);

- Chat lines, including phone-sex services, which charge a fee for use;

- For those truly addicted to news, access to the Associated Press, Reuters, the Press Association of Britain, Agence France Press, and many other newswires via the Web;

- Archives of the periodical press including most major magazines and a growing proportion of serious commentary publications.

In addition, a growing number of scientific journals are published in purely electronic form (e.g., *Transplant News, Drug Detection Report*). The full text of an issue is either posted on the Web or is delivered to the reader's e-mail account, where it can be scanned, stored, or deleted.

The Use of Personal Computers in Canada

Nowhere is the inequality-augmenting aspect of the new media more evident than with respect to personal-computer installations and use. Introduced to well-off children in their tender years by solicitous parents in hopes of securing advantage in school later, they have become, in some respects, the amulets of success. Universal e-mail access has begun to loom on the horizon of possibility. Home computers are also very useful to adults for keeping accounts of investment income, carrying out investment analysis, calculating tax returns, and preparing mortgage-amortization schedules–tasks that do not, as a rule, trouble welfare recipients.

The adoption of Internet use and the computer equipment and services necessary to use it has been extremely swift in Canadian society, approaching the rate of adoption of television by Canadian households in the 1950s. By the time of the Statistics Canada 1999 Household Internet Use Survey, about 42 percent of Canadian households had at least one regular Internet user and more than a quarter of Canadian households had at least one person using the Internet from home. By way of comparison, a National Science Foundation survey in early 2000 found that 54 percent of Americans had access to a computer at home. This figure was 11 percent above the comparable proportion in 1997 (and up from 8 percent in 1983). Forty-six percent of homes had computers with modems (up from 21 percent in 1995). Hours of use have increased considerably as well.[15] Elsewhere, Japanese personal computer shipments exceeded those of televisions for the first time in 1999 as almost 10 million units were shipped to Japanese domestic distributors.[16]

There is really no way of knowing for sure what the nature of that use is, whether for work, education, entertainment or other pursuits, but it is clear that Web resources are at the disposal of a rapidly increasing number of Canadian households. The regional patterns are not homogenous however. Conspicuous are the lower rates of adoption in Quebec and the very high rates of adoption in Alberta and British Columbia. Among urban areas, Calgary had the highest percentage of households in 1999 with a regular Internet user (60.1 percent), virtually identical to the proportion for Ottawa (59.9 percent) and Victoria (56.4 percent). Corresponding low proportions were recorded in Windsor (33.6 percent) and Quebec City (33.9 percent) and Montreal (39.1 percent). These proportions fall far short of comparable American figures. The highest U.S. rate was found in Salt Lake City (73 percent), San Francisco (72 percent) and Washington D.C. (71 percent). Even the rust-belt American cities compared favourably (lowest of all, Charleton W.Va., at 46 percent).[17]

Computer-Linked Devices: Breaking the Interdevice Barriers

Even the most modest personal computer can now be equipped with a modem and/or fax board for less than $40, and thus become capable of "conversing" with other computers and fax machines through the phone system, directly through wired or fibre local-area networks or, in the most esoteric of cases, through a remote satellite transmitting and/or receiving station. Access to the Internet is available free of charge through an ordinary telephone line in most of urban Canada (if one accepts the presence of advertising banners through such services as NetZero) or for a modest monthly charge if one is not interesting in the advertising banner or if one insists on connecting on the first try every time. Cable TV Internet access and DSL service from the telephone company and wireless Internet service are all higher priced, higher speed alternatives. The penetration of Cable TV Internet access in Canada is much higher than it is in the United States with approximately 10 percent of households so equipped, according to a survey carried out by ACNielson/DJC Research in March 1999.[18] The fibre-optic backbone that has been installed by a combination of public and private investments has made possible message systems of incredible complexity based on packet-switching techniques; and they have delivered these services directly to the home computer, to the office desktop, and to laptop computers connected to cellular telephones literally anywhere on the globe, in many cases free of any usage charge at all.

Anyone with access to such services through a personal computer or other type of terminal gains immensely; a new mode of information exchange and synthesis and dissemination has been created. Many new occupations and whole enterprises have this activity at their core. The arrival of the free Internet Service Provider in both North America and parts of Europe now confers unimpeded access on anyone and everyone in the local calling area regardless of age, institutional affiliation, or financial resources; all one needs is a personal computer or a terminal and a telephone service line, something that many public libraries now provide if one does not have a personal telephone, a state of affairs that has become uncommon in Canadian society. Some have styled this unconditional access the beginnings of "electronic democracy," though having the tools and using them in an effective manner are two different things.

One of the initial problems with fax machines and computers *qua* fax machines was the format barrier between the digital image and the text file, and the consequent inability to convert an incoming fax into a text file for subsequent revision. This barrier was effectively broken with the introduction of computer software for fax modems with embedded text scanning potential in 1993, software that allows the computer user to capture an incoming fax as a digital-image file and scan it internally with a built-in software optical-character reader, thence creating a text file. The software also allows the user to overlay the arriving fax image with marginal notes and re-transmit it back to the point of origin with comments added without ever having to resort to paper. Such programs effectively break through the previously impermeable text-digitized image barrier. Subsequently, with the collapse in price of flatbed scanners for personal computers (often falling below $100 per unit), most users gained the ability to scan text documents and convert them to text files (not to mention being able to scan photographs as images and send them around the world as e-mail attachments).

Because of the cost of phone calls associated with long-distance fax transmission, considerable effort has been expended on creating a system that allows faxes to be sent as digital files, via the Internet, to an Internet address in the local calling area of the recipient, where the fax image could then be sent at no

TABLE 3: Canadian Households with at least One Regular Internet User by Point of Use, 1999

	% of Households			
	From any Location		From Home	
	1997	1999	1997	1999
Canada	**29.4**	**41.8**	**16.0**	**28.7**
Newfoundland	26.6	35.2	12.4	18.1
Prince Edward Island	26.0	40.5	10.5	20.1
Nova Scotia	32.2	41.1	14.3	26.7
New Brunswick	29.1	38.0	12.1	23.6
Quebec	20.1	33.1	10.2	21.2
Ontario	33.2	44.5	19.3	32.0
Manitoba	29.3	38.3	13.7	24.7
Saskatchewan	27.2	39.9	12.3	23.6
Alberta	34.5	50.8	18.7	34.1
British Columbia	33.6	48.1	19.9	35.8

Source: Statistics Canada, *The Daily*, Friday, May 19, 2000.

charge through the local telephone system. Though failing to generate enthusiasm in the telephone-company community, "cells" of this sort are reported in many if not most large cities in the world. Similar efforts to divert voice telephone traffic onto the Internet to avoid toll calls are in progress. Some programs offer users the opportunity to use advanced encryption scrambling to avoid being overheard. The present problem of being overheard is currently particularly acute for conventional analog cellphones users. Scanners that cover the cellphone band of the spectrum can be purchased in Canada for about $300. Digital PCS mobile phones operate in a much higher frequency band and are less vulnerable to casual eavesdroppers. Scanners covering these high-frequency bands are much more expensive and are not generally to be found in the homes of amateurs.

The effect of joining the capabilities of two or more machines electronically is not one of simple addition. Rather, the combined capabilities of two connected machines extend the range of what each can do independently. Conceptually, as Roger Penrose has pointed out, when two or more devices communicate as a network "then in effect, they are just a single device."[19] In other words, the network itself is a computer made up of dispersed processors. The combined capabilities of network-linked machines, such as modem-equipped personal computers in the home, can be harnessed through the network linkage to a single purpose, be that transmission of messages or the application of brute computing power half a world away.

The central feature of the emerging Internet is the availability of extremely fast high-volume data transmission on dedicated-trunk optic-fibre lines. The Canadian high-speed computer spine is called CANARIE with T3 data-transfer speeds of 45 megabits per second achieved and with an eventual speed of 1 billion bits per second and more in the foreseeable future.

The Internet, best understood as the combination of such national networks, grew from the university-based consortia (such as BITNET,[20] the network begun in 1981 by Ira Fuchs and Greydon Freeman to connect the computer centres of the dispersed campuses of New York City College, and JANET, which connects universities and colleges in the United Kingdom),[21] and ARPANET, the original U.S. defence-industry network. Subsequently added were commercial services such as AOL (now with millions of users in North America), the library-searching services such as Dialog, the SABRE airline-reservation system available to the public, securities-trading services, millions of Web pages of all sorts and purposes, plus tens of thousands of specialized-topic list servers.

The Internet may be one of those pivotal technological developments that drives observers many years later to remark that "everything has changed as a result." It is probable that decades hence it will be seen as a truly important innovation of the telecommunications expansion period of the late 1980s and early 1990s, since it connects the intelligentsia of the world in a single chattering tribe.

With the spread of personal computers throughout the workplace and into Canadian households, we have also installed this interactive information-exchange capacity. Though seen as incidental when the machines first appeared, the serial-interface port has become a window on the world through which much of the world's supply of wisdom and information can pass if one knows the electronic gateways.

Personal computers now send and receive large chunks of data, pictures, sound, text–anything that can be reduced to digitized code–including the pages of newspapers, which can now be printed in dispersed locations at the same time. For example, the *International Herald Tribune* is available all over Europe and the Middle East on the same day from headquarters in Frankfurt. *The Globe and Mail* (Toronto) is now printed in many locations across Canada, employing satellite transmission of finished pages to remote printing plants as is the *National Post* in facilities shared with other Southam newspapers. According to the Pew Research Center for the People and the Press, Web surfing for news is in the process of undermining the influence of both the network TV newscast and local television newscasts, especially in younger age groups.[22]

Modem connections have sparked renewed interest in the "electronic cottage"-dispersed workforce concept. As previously mentioned in connection with employer-sponsored, work-at-home projects, there is no inherent reason why many workers cannot do their work at home as independent contractors, communicating back and forth with an employer's computer by means of a modem or high-speed cable link. There are many attractions to this sort of arrangement, particularly where the daily commute to work and back may consume three hours or more. Around the major population centres of the world, such as London, the prospect of reducing this dead time is alluring–and there is some evidence that it is being taken up.[23] It may also offer the prospect of farming out repetitive data-entry work to low-wage areas and part-time workers with computers in their own homes. Of advantage to cost-conscious employers, the reappearance of this "putting out" system of work after almost 200 years of disuse is both ironic and ominous in terms of the contractual relationship between such data-entry workers and their remote and faceless employers.

Also worth mentioning in this context are a whole range of devices designed to assist persons with disabilities. The Kurzweil scanner takes printed text and "reads" it aloud or stores it in a text file, which can in turn be "read" by any personal computer equipped with a sound card as most now are. These devices are all now small enough and light enough to be considered movable, if not yet easily portable. Devices such as Vista, a computer image-enlarging system for persons with low vision, and the Versapoint Braille Embosser for producing Braille computer output are also available for those with vision problems. DragonDictate is a voice-recognition system that assists persons with mobility impairments by accepting orally dictated words and then entering them as portions of text files. It can also read aloud any file produced by a common word-processing program or in plain text format. Spell checkers and grammar cleansers are also aids for the less conspicuously disabled.

Anonymous Peer-to-Peer Communication

In the well-established model of mass communications, a single piece of information is conveyed to many consumers by the distribution of identical interchangeable copies. The most obvious examples of this time-honoured process are the television network newscast and the daily newspaper. Lately, however, a new type of distribution model has appeared that offers an alternative. This is peer-to-peer distribution.

In the peer-to-peer model, a single copy of a piece of digital information already in the hands of a consumer (acquired how it matters not) is shared with whomever wants a copy without the disclosure of identities on the part of either the donor or the donee. The obvious current example is *Napster*, a clearinghouse of musical selections. The principle could also be applied to any form of digital information resource such as a motion picture, a book, or a file of voice conversations.

There is no central distribution point in the *Napster* model, only a real-time index of what is available and on which on-line computer. A further development of this model, *Gnutella*, has no central index at all. The user makes his or her own index of availability by means of a ramifying *"what's online?"* information request to the network when logging on. The actual information, for example, a file of music in MP3 (digitally sampled and compressed) format, can be located and subsequently downloaded without the user knowing where the source file is physically located in the world or who is hosting the file. In this anonymous exchange, copyright becomes moot. By extension, all digital exchanges of a peer-to-peer nature undermine intellectual property rights, which in the extreme become a dead letter of law. If there is no clearinghouse, no tollbooth, and no record keeping involved in such anonymous transfers, there is no one to sue for redress for copyright violations and indeed no clue as to where to bring such a lawsuit since the physical location in legal jurisdiction is unclear both with respect to the copier and the copiee.

Newer peer-to-peer sites have appeared on the World Wide Web for the distribution of video clips and whole motion pictures and even secret documents that have somehow fallen into the possession of a single individual somewhere.[24] Sites such as iMesh have been established to promote such exchanges. If there is no central real-time index to legally enjoin, there would seem to be no impediment to the sharing of any resource that can take digital form in complete disregard for the world's intellectual property protection and licensing regime. Anyone can make an MP3 music file from a vinyl record, a cassette tape, a music CD, or a video tape for that matter. Likewise, anyone with the appropriate software and access to the source files for a book can make an Acrobat digital file of the contents for sharing, or scan a document, or make a compressed copy of a motion picture. It only takes one copy somewhere in the world on an on-line computer to get the process of perfect geometric reproduction going.

This new distribution model is an unmistakable threat to the entertainment industry, which derives the bulk of its revenues from licensing products to individual consumers (as in collecting admission fees at movie theatres), thereby recovering the costs of their production and accumulating funds to make more products. It is also a potential threat to the book publishing industry, and to the holders of copyright of television shows, or indeed any person, corporation, or government whose business model relies on the collection of revenues from consumers of digitized (or potentially digitized) products, or whose grasp of the levers of social control is predicated on controlling the flow of information, goods, or benefits. The model is thus also a threat to the machinery of the modern state in that secrets are now much harder to keep.

Cyberspace: The Village Common of the Twenty-First Century

As the worlds of telephone and computer, and work and leisure converged, the concept of cyberspace was coined to describe the "place" in which personal communications, images, sounds, and news streams meet. It is not a physical place but rather a space one enters with a computer. One can read the continuing 24-hour-a-day stream of information from any of the millions of Internet participants and one can respond with comments, questions, or merely "lurk" in the background as a passive receiver. Much of the world's information, rumour, and idle conjecture now moves in this manner.

One of the important aspects of this trade in information is that a user can broadcast his thoughts to untold millions of other participants with one message (by posting to all the USENET newsgroups for example). This dynamic defeats the simple mathematics of the usual oral flow of rumours, from person to person, and accelerates the process as well as reducing the noise produced in multiple imperfect replications. Slanders and libels, unfounded judgments, and dangerous truths pass through the system with equal ease as the message escapes jurisdictional bounds, the competence of courts, and the technical ability to censor.

The New World of Television

We need not dwell here on the prominence of TV in modern life in Western countries. It is simply ubiquitous, and its content is rapidly being integrated across the Western world, in no small part thanks to Ted Turner of CNN and the various European direct-to-home broadcast services such as BskyB in the U.K. Though various national technical standards exist, they do not seriously interfere with the transmission of pictures and commentary from the remotest corners of the world. There is plenty of spare capacity for future expansion, particularly where advanced digital cable-TV systems are involved, and plenty of interest in still further choice on the part of Canadians. Table 4 gives a breakdown of the number of Canadian households with colour TV sets, cable TV, VCRs, and home computers among other devices and amenities in 1998 and 1999. Telephones have become so common they no longer appear in the standard tables (a fate soon to be suffered by colour televisions as a category), and cellular telephones (or more properly mobile phones since there are several technical standards in simultaneous use) were

TABLE 4: Household Facilities in Canada

	Percentage of Households	
	1997	1998
Washing machine	81	81
Clothes dryer	77	79
Dishwasher	49	51
Freezer	59	59
Microwave oven	88	89
Cellular telephone	22	26
Compact disc player	65	67
Cablevision	75	73
Video cassette recorder	87	88
Home computer	40	45
Modem	25	32
Internet use from home	17	25
Colour television	99	99
Owned vehicle	79	79
Automobile	67	65
Van and truck	31	32

Source: Statistics Canada, Survey of Household Spending 1998, *The Daily*, December 13, 1999.

taken up rapidly as the price for the service declined in the late 1990s.

The technical means for delivering "500 channel service" to households exists and has already been installed in some Canadian households. It is designed to facilitate viewer selection and custom-signal delivery to the household including limited text messaging from the cable operator to the viewer directly. In some Canadian locales, the introduction of digital cable alongside the older analog service has progressed to the point where a digital control box is required to view any premium television service. The digital set top box itself is expensive (a retail price of $350 plus taxes has been established in the author's coverage area by Shaw Cable) but can be rented from the operator. The analog cable system continues to work in parallel with the newer digital service though the channel assignment is slightly different, leading to confusion since there is only one program listing published in the newspaper. Of course, one of the charms of digital cable is that it is self-documenting. Program listings and summaries are constantly being downloaded over the cable into the digital control box. The viewer need only press the appropriate button to retrieve the schedule and also schedule reminders of future broadcasts and obtain more background information on a future or present broadcast.

Competing directly with digital cable are direct-to-home satellite services and so-called "wireless cable," which uses the PCS mobile-telephone network to deliver television services as well as high-speed Internet connections. Home satellite receivers were first, beginning with the relatively gigantic eight- and ten-foot dishes of the 1980s, followed in the mid-1990s by pizza-plate-sized dishes first used in North America by DirectTV (known popularly at that time as the Death Star). DirectTV is a venture of GM Hughes Electronics, together with the National Rural Telecommunications Cooperative in the U.S., which sold services to Canadian households even though it was not strictly speaking allowed. Seizures of equipment, though they did take place, were few and far between. Comparable Canadian services are now available and countenanced by the CRTC. These services do not deliver popular U.S. programming such as HBO, and it could be speculated that in an open North American television market, many Canadians would still opt for DirectTV were they able to do so legally and easily. As it stands, Canadian viewers are prevented from watching many high-quality news and entertainment television services by the regulator, a situation that strikes more and more Canadians as an anachronism.

These services taken together reduce broadcasting to narrowcasting directed to discrete bands of the potential viewing audience. Some, such as wireless Internet and digital cable, will also start the flow of domestic data *back into the system* from the household. Detailed viewer profiles will be captured as they are now by major Internet portal sites.

Although they have provided a great diversification of services, cable-TV systems have proven costly to install and even more costly to upgrade to broad-band fibre-optics service. This conversion has proceeded in fits and starts and few Canadian households have a fibre-optic terminus at the present time. Industry consolidation has meant the emergence of a few very large firms, most notably Rogers Communications Inc., which continues to report operating losses.[25] The Home Shopping Network, also controlled by Rogers, continues to lose money; Rogers-ATT (formerly Cantel), the cellular-phone network whose controlling shareholder is Ted Rogers, is also showing an operating loss through a period of heavy investment and expansion.[26]

TABLE 5: Cable Television in Canada

	1994	1998
	Thousands $	
Operating Revenues	1,759,126	2,008,990 .
Operating Expenses	1,535,035	2,218,676
Program Origination	80,197	83,496
Technical Services	415,714	665,891
Sales and Promotions	49,650	106,880
Administration and General	355,609	470,918
Depreciation	275,369	409,572
Interest Expense	207,859	481,919
Net Profit (Loss) after Income Tax	184,349	199,235
Subscribers	7,833,000	8,254,000
Households Wired for Cable Service	9,935,000	10,595,000
Cable Length in Kilometres	180,000	202,000

Source: Statistics Canada, CANSIM, Matrix 1828.

The yet-to-be-completed expansion in programming that cabling has brought has been described elsewhere,[27] and the rapid adoption of VCRs, cable TV, and multiple colour-TV-set ownership are by now well known. Acquisition of these items rises directly with household income. Likewise, the amount and type of TV programming watched is well documented by companies for whom this measurement is the principle product.

What may be new is the ability to blur entertainment, work, and information acquisition using devices designed to blend media presentations on a single screen. For example, TV programming can now occupy a corner "window" of any Windows computer screen, the major portion of which is devoted to work (using a video card such as the ATI All-in-Wonder made in Markham, Ontario). Similarly, video capture boards allow the saving of segments of video and audio as digital resources that can be edited, sampled, and retransmitted. Playing a DVD of a motion picture on a corner of the screen is not all that difficult or expensive either. One can imagine a very large flat display hanging on the wall of the future with several different kinds of audio and video going on simultaneously, with work-related writing and a live video conference, for example. This is technically possible to arrange today but remains beyond the financial means of most Canadians. The number of open windows on such a display is limited only by the comfort level of the human observer in sorting out the various streams of information to make sense of the barrage of sound and image.

In terms of numbers of viewers, suffice it to say that the World Cup final in Italy in July 1990 was estimated by some to have had 1.5 billion viewers literally worldwide. By the time of the Cup final in France in 1998, it had become impossible to estimate the number of viewers worldwide, though the broadcast signal would have been available to the entire population of many participating states and to a large proportion of the adult population in the remainder. One in two Italian adults was said to be watching when the national team lost to France in the Euro2000 finale on July 2, 2000, for instance. Staggering in proportion, such world events are of a new order of public entertainment, holding the potential for monstrous stage fright for the players if they paused to think about it. A single miscue on this stage could lead to a lifetime of recriminations. True worldwide sharing of a point of view, even if only on a trivial matter such as professional sport, has become possible.

When wedded to the other information services, the information banquet-table of cable, satellite, and wireless TV is set with weather reports, aircraft movements from the local airport, stock-market measures, and in-home shopping services, in addition to the now standard fare of obscure sports and improbable talk shows.

Electronic Trade

Part of the new media picture involves the emergence of online retail and wholesale trade. The new media delivers customers to vendors without regard to the physical location of either, nor to the time of day or night. From the consumer's point of view, online sellers represent an unparalleled addition to the number of potential sources of supply. No longer restricted by what is available at local retailers, the online customer can range far and wide using on-line utilities to perform price and quality comparisons. Fulfillment of orders and actual delivery rise in importance, however, largely replicating the mail-order catalogue situation of the early part of the twentieth century when companies such as Eaton's and Simpsons had catalogue operations that delivered goods to isolated customers by railway freight and the post office parcel delivery services.

According to the Angus Reid survey organization, the number of Canadians buying goods on line has increased rapidly in the last couple of years. A clear majority of these purchases are now from Canadian suppliers (in contrast to the earlier experiences when American on-line retailers were quicker off the mark). Nevertheless, and notwithstanding the additional difficulties with customs duties and slower delivery, a very significant proportion of the on-line trade of Canadians is still with American suppliers in the year 2000.[28]

The Canadian Online Retailing Report, prepared by the Boston Consulting Group, suggests that Canadian retailers continue to draw an overwhelming proportion of their business from domestic consumers (96 percent) while American competitors with a history of catalogue selling have been very successful in attracting Canadian customers. This figure underlines the fact that traditional patterns of retail trade, international barriers to consumer purchases, and difficulties in international deliveries are all rapidly breaking down.[29] While the rhetoric of globalism is often used in the context of producer behaviour, it clearly has a consumer aspect as well, one which tends to dissolve the traditional ties of habit and loyalty between consumers and local retailers. The book retailing industry in Canada and the United States is a clear example of the transition being carried out with minimal regard to the future well-being of locally owned, low-volume book stores of the traditional sort. Kaplan's "resident alien," the hypothetical cybercitizen mentioned at the outset, buys books from whichever on-line retailer posts the best price and/or delivery performance and in most instances now, that means an on-line book seller, often outside the country.

The 24-Hour World

The range of computing and telecommunications devices available to those of moderate means are of such great import that it could be argued that they have created the infrastructure for a distinct culture, no longer based on the nation-state but rather on the unfettered exchange of information on a worldwide basis. Small wonder that Canadian concerns with national sovereignty should have become so convoluted in the area of communications policy. As one commentator has written, "no other Western nation has been so perplexed and preoccupied with the attempt to control its communications and broadcasting."[30]

One has only to examine the development of 24-hour securities and currency trading to see individual traders freed from national boundaries and even the solar cycle for the first time in the history of humankind. With access via modem and phone line, it is feasible to monitor trading and to actually trade in securities or currency on a succession of markets as they open and close across the time zones. This has lead to episodic mass movements of capital in very short periods of time with very unsettling effects on national currency stability.

For example, beginning in London, one can trade successively through New York, Chicago, San Francisco, Tokyo, Hong Kong, and Johannesburg, finally returning to London. One need never be idle. Betting on sporting events can similarly be freed from ordinary business hours. For those whose interests lie less in business and more in public affairs, it is possible to follow world news and developing stories through the international wire services available in the home via computer/modem, through the international radio services of major nations, and through the various communications satellites where live and unedited feeds of major news events are to be found. News services such as the Cable News Network (CNN), Headline News, the BBC World Service, and CBC Newsworld continue to function around the clock, ensuring the viewer the opportunity of access to major events immediately, without resort to the interpretive services of a newspaper.

As more and more such services appear and are made widely available through redistribution services such as home fibre-optics service, conventional cable, or direct-to-home satellite re-broadcast systems, such as StarChoice in Canada, one begins to see the outlines of a wired world in which one is never very far from an eyewitness view of the world events that shape both the news and the public debate that attends it. Indeed, major political events are now tailored to this viewing audience. The chant "The whole world is watching," first heard at the Democratic Convention in 1968 in Chicago, raised by demonstrators against police accustomed to working in anonymity, found an echo in Tienanmen Square in 1989, in the Trafalgar Square poll-tax protests of 1990, in Waco, Texas, in the spring of 1993, and on the lawn of Queen's Park in Toronto in June 2000 when the homeless gathered to focus their anger at government indifference to their plight, and in countless other locales.

Those insufficiently powerful to alter public policy or change governments seek to objectify their weakness by becoming the willing victims in public displays of physical repression. International public opinion is the audience, and a successful event consists of creating the impression of the ill-considered application of overwhelming force against a weak and vulnerable minority that nevertheless represents virtue. As such events happen again and again –Sharpeville, Bucharest, East Berlin, Prague, Jerusalem, and so on–a certain formula emerges: grasp the sleepless world television audience and demonstrate your unjust subservience graphically.

The Limits of the Technology: How Big Can a Dossier Be?

Looking to the future of the new media, it is not possible to foresee the full extent of their development. Prices keep dropping and performance increases dramatically year after year. Since telecommunications devices are now irretrievably linked to computer technology, it seems safe to assume that the future of communications will witness the further progressive integration of advances in computer hardware and software and associated telecommunications apparatus. One good guess is that the cost of storing digital information will be very modest in future, the price of storage having already declined phenomenally from introduction levels. This means that individuals will be able to acquire and store on their own equipment vast amounts of digital information, which might well include many books, motion pictures, and entire collections of musical performances. Further advances in the density of storage are announced routinely. In practice, this means one can store huge amounts of digital data–pictures,

words, sounds, and so on–without much concern for cost. The speed of the process of acquiring large digital files has also improved dramatically with the advent of cheap make-your-own compact disks and the arrival of high-speed network connections via television cable, the wireless phone network, and DSL services offered by the local telephone companies.

This potential to cheaply consolidate and share digital files has led to the very real concern that virtually all information on individuals and organizations will be integrated and stored indefinitely, perhaps to be used aggressively in some other context at a much later date.

Necessarily, then, the speed of human acceptance is a critical controlling variable. Expectations might be that acceptance will continue to be patchy and age-specific, and we might expect that those individuals and interests financially capable of meeting the initial costs of acquiring new devices will be the first to benefit, as has been the case in the past. But as acquisition costs keep coming down, and as more and more institutions offer incentives to individuals to transact with them on-line (such as major financial institutions and local municipalities), what was once an expensive self-indulgence is quite likely to become a routine feature of life in this country.

One "benefit" of this process has been the elimination by capital replacement of whole categories of occupations whose previous incumbents have understandably been inconvenienced by the process. The keypunch operators of the 1960s and the telephone receptionists of the 1970s and 1980s have now joined Ned Ludd's Yorkshire weavers of the early 1800s (who broke their new tools in disgust) on the long list of those whose lives have been summarily disrupted by major new technology introductions. Clearly this disruption is currently most felt by the lower ranks of the clerical occupations, now predominantly populated by women, often working part time. Also affected are older workers, accustomed to working in traditional ways, suddenly presented with new electronic tools but given little training in how to use them. But the changes are likely to proceed in many other directions as productivity increases are realized by the elimination of whole levels of managers whose jobs once consisted of passing information from one place to another. With dynamic on-line databases for transactions, open 24 hours a day year round, many previously secure managerial jobs seem destined to follow the key-punch operators duties into the oblivion of obsolescence. Indeed, many university administrators seem to harbour similar plans concerning classroom instructors. Replacement of these individuals with a database however would change the nature of the "product" beyond recognition. New types of products emerge from the fog of cyberspatial innovation all the time, however, and it would be folly to suggest that higher education will remain untouched by the new tools. Their power will be felt in many ways we cannot possibly foretell.

Without question there will be further rounds of such cost cutting by means of the substitution of smart technology for skilled and semi-killed labour in the future. Particularly with respect to the employment of artificial-intelligence elements, it is hard to predict who will use which device for what purpose. The question of feasible artificial intelligence is thus very relevant indeed. For example, if a program were able to mimic a person's interests in news, it could scan information holdings daily or hourly, searching for information that might be of interest. In some respects, the My Yahoo page already fulfills this function for its customizing users. Significantly, it can also systematically delete from consideration any piece of information emanating from a particular source or individual.

Artificial intelligence might go one step further and select items that, although falling outside the bounds of one's current interests, might on the basis of the individual's past information-consuming profile (which the program has "learned") nevertheless be of interest. Such felicitous accidents are a key to human intelligence and, if they could be made an integral part of an artificial intelligence, might be of inestimable value in keeping up with developments.

However, one of the central questions—whether it is possible to devise a program to replicate human thought processes, which can then practically be used as if it were human—cannot presently be resolved. Opinion is divided into two camps: there are those who maintain that it is intrinsically impossible to devise an algorithm for this purpose,[31] while others are more optimistic in their view, particularly the proponents of so-called "fuzzy logic." Suffice it to say that computing hardware will grow faster and more capable with the passage of time, and that the central question is one of devising the software. The traditional standard, the "Turing test," which is met if a human observer is incapable of distinguishing between human and machine responses in a blind test, can probably already be passed by machines in limited contexts, particularly with respect to the playing of chess, which has served as a development laboratory for software engineers.

Once proven practical, artificial intelligence could be quickly built into machines of all sorts in order to facilitate the taking of humanlike judgments unattended. The author has already been instructed, for instance, late one dark night in the Apenine mountains in northern Italy to "take the next right turn in 200 metres" by a sythesized female voice with a British accent, informed by a GPS receiver and a Compact Disk containing the entire geographic and road map database for the whole of Italy. A house could run itself in this fashion, creating desirable environmental conditions according to the known wishes of its human inhabitants, opening and shutting windows, turning lights on and off, acquiring information and sorting out the useful from the useless. It might even be able to defeat the junk-mail advertisers—something humans find difficult. A program that could prepare a customized daily news summary on the basis of known human preferences, discarding the obtuse and keeping an eye out for the unusual and felicitous innovation, would be a very useful utility—but it might well change the dynamics of creativity that seem somehow reliant on accidental discoveries and happy accidents.

In order to entrust the surveillance of information flow to a machine, a high degree of confidence in the machine's ability would be demanded, and a lot of learning about human interests and preferences would be required. Since human interests are always changing in response to conditions, the learning relationship would have to be continuous, like that between the archetypal British butler and his feckless master. One is never clear who is giving direction and who is taking it. Such would be the case with an intelligent household-manager computer and its human masters. Clearly, at the present state of development, most Canadians would be loath to entrust the management of their financial affairs to an artificial intelligence of any form. This does not mean, however, that it could never happen in the future; indeed, automated programs of precisely this sort now carry out trading in the reader's pension-plan funds and mutual funds.

If such programs can be devised for use by individuals on a routine basis, it is almost certain that they will be linked with a telecommunications capability. It has been argued in effect that the future of communications lies in a tightening bond between advancing computer technology and the network linkage of computers and computer-aided voice and data transmission. While it is clearly impossible to predict the form of such technological innovations to come, their further integration seems inevitable. Perhaps more sobering is the thought that the new devices will first appear as tools in the service of the wealthy and powerful—a development that may both further widen inequalities of all sorts and heighten, not reduce, social tensions of all sorts.

Notes

1. Robert D. Kaplan, *The Coming Anarchy* (N.Y.: Random House, 2000), p.87.

2. William Broad, "How the Net caught science," New York Times News Service, reprinted in *The Globe and Mail* (Toronto) (16 June 1993), p.A6.

3. Statistics Canada, CANSIM series D456755.

4. Connie Mabin, "Dell Exec says PC has Bright Future," Associated Press (15 June 2000).

5. Lynn White, Jr., *Medieval Technology and Social Change* (New York: Oxford University Press, 1962).

6. A myth has grown up around the initial unsuccessful product, the Xerox Telecopier, referred to at the time by its few users as the "Mojo Wire," and its supposed theft from the inventor. Anyone interested in pursuing this "urban myth" can start with the account published by Hunter Thompson in June 1972: "The McGovern Juggernaut Rolls On," reprinted in Hunter Thompson, *The Great Shark Hunt* (New York: Warner Books, 1979), n., p.227.

7. The Treasury Board produced a two-page flyer in 1992 outlining the rationale and goals of the pilot project. Other professional literature on the topic may be found in Robert E. Kraut, "Telecommuting: The Trade-Offs of Home Work," *Journal of Communication* 39, no. 3 (Summer 1989): 19–47; and Joanne H. Pratt, "Methodological Problems in Surveying the Home-Based Workforce," *Technological Forecasting and Social Change* 31, no. 1: 49–60.

8. Statistics Canada, CANSIM series D462100.

9. On April 28, 2000, London England acquired four-digit area codes (0207 and 0208) for the first time. Looked at another way, the new area code is 020 and each telephone number has eight digits instead of the habitual seven. Should the demand for telephone numbers and Internet IP addresses continue to grow rapidly, we can confidently expect such identify number inflation in other parts of the world too.

10. Lawrence Surtees, "Cellular Phone Companies Ringing in Customers," *Report on Business* (2 July 1990), pp.B1–B2.

11. James Bamford, *The Puzzle Palace* (Boston: Houghton Mifflin, 1982).

12. "Union Urges Curbs on Rise in Phone Taps," *The Manchester Guardian* (14 May 1990), p.4.

13. Declan McCullagh, "U.S. to Track Crypto Trails," *Wired News,* May 4, 2000.

14. Richard Walling, "Technology Boosts government wiretaps," *USA Today*, May 5, 2000.

15. Paul Recer, "Poll: Most of US has Computer Access," Associated Press, June 19, 2000; source for survey <http://www.nsf.gov/sbe/srs/stats.htm>.

16. Associated Press, "Japan PC Shipments Exceed TVs," June 9, 2000.

17. Ian Fried, "Salt Lake City tops PC Ownership Study," *CNET News.com*, June 16, 2000.

18. Jack Aubry, "Canadians hooked on cable Internet," *The Ottawa Citizen* (3 May 2000).

19. Roger Penrose, *The Emperor's New Mind* (New York: Oxford University Press, 1989), p.48.

20. For further information on BITNET, see *Bitnet: The 'Because It's Time' Network* (Princeton: BITNET Network Information Center, n.d.); Ira Fuchs, "Bitnet: Because It's Time," *Perspectives in Computing* 3, no. 1 (1983); Daniel J. Oberst and Sheldon B. Smith, "Bitnet: Past, Present and Future," *EDUCOM Bulletin* 21, no. 2 (Summer 1986): 10–17.

21. JANET has been the site of a number of firsts in the network world. For instance, an advertisement appeared in *The Guardian Weekly* of 11 July 1993 that read, in part, "Do you have access to Internet and Janet? From the 1st of July, you will have e-mail access to all the job opportunities at Liverpool John Moores University. Simply send your requests to JOBS@UK.AC.LIVJM. For the record, readers in North America anxious to give the system a try should change the address slightly to JOBS@LIVJM.AC.UK.

22. Mark Jurkowitz, "Broadcast TV news losing viewers to Internet," *Boston Globe Online,* June 2, 2000.

23. Andrew Bibby, "Joys of a City Job with Lochside View," *The Independent* (9 June 1990), p.41.

24. For example, see a site that published copies of original secret British documents on a failed attempt to assassinate President Ghadafi of Libya, an attempt which had been previously declared not to have taken place by Foreign Secretary Robin Cooke in the House of Commons.

25. John Partridge, "Red Ink Continues for Rogers," *Report on Business* (14 July 1990), p.B5. In 1994, Rogers took control of Maclean Hunter.

26. Lawrence Surtees, "Cellular Phone Companies," *Report on Business* (2 July 1990), pp.B1–B2. See John Hannigan's chapter in this volume for information on Rogers' continued expansion in the cable industry.

27. Ted Wannell and Craig McKie, "Expanding the Choices," *Canadian Social Trends* 1 (Summer 1986): 13–18.

28. "More Canadians Shopping Online," *BCTV News,* June 16, 2000.

29. Reuters, "Wary Canadian Online Retailers Eye U.S. Competition," June 19, 2000.

30. Thomas L. McPhail, "The Future of Canadian Communications," Benjamin D. Singer, ed., *Communications in Canadian Society,* 2nd ed. (Don Mills, Ont.: Addison-Wesley, 1983), pp.73–82.

31. "Yet beneath all this technicality is the feeling that it is indeed 'obvious' that the conscious mind cannot work like a computer, even though much of what is actually involved in mental activity might do so." Penrose, *The Emperor's New Mind,* p.448.

8

The Emergence of Orgamedia

Benjamin D. Singer

The computer ... has within it the potential for completely remolding the organization. –Martin Greenberg[1]

All social phenomena are ultimately a function of communication. –Lee Thayer[2]

National boundaries grow increasingly meaningless. –Ben Bagdikian[3]

For some years idealistic writers have been suggesting that new organizational communication technology–and particularly the computer–will usher in an innovative era of democratic participation and decentralization. Rather than the centralization that some pessimists had predicted, the new communication–the World Wide Web, e-mail, the fax machine, mobile phones and pagers, satellite TV, cable, satellite, and the whole range of office electronics, including photocopiers, answering machines, word processors, and varied electronic networks–will lead to decentralized communication. Instead of such communication technology "by its nature reinforcing the powerful," as Alan Westin[4] once observed, everybody's voice will be equal; everybody will have access.

Such social and organizational barriers as status, power, personal appearance, charisma, past achievements, and communication ability will now count for considerably less than they once did.

According to this argument, the positive benefits to flow from the decentralization made possible by the new means of communication include an increase in social interaction leading to greater social integration. Typical has been the analysis of one writer that new organizational media, by facilitating the flow of information, will "increase organizational cohesion and member identification with the organization's aims,"[5] or Manfred Kochen's argument that computer conferencing could lead to an increase in thoughtful interaction.[6] However, many communication theorists and researchers were beginning, as early as the 1960s and 1970s, to see the effects of the new media–computers, fax, electronic networks–as ways of disrupting the normal patterns of social organization and as engendering new forms of social disorientation–what the French sociologist Emile Durkheim called *anomie*.

The Dissolution of Traditional Structures

The key to this process is the ability of the new media to dissolve the traditional boundaries and barriers of social structures. The breakdown of social organization resembles the entropic breakdown of systems in general. They lose their distinctiveness; the borders separating organization from organization, organization from non-organization, dissolve. As Karl Deutsch said, the boundaries or "limits of an autonomous organization" are determined by the differential between internal and external communication.[7]

Moreover, things that used to be done in *organizations* were now being done within the new media, and the borders that once delimited organizations were eroding into shapelessness. As one early researcher put it, company boundaries were no longer "the most meaningful system boundaries."[8] *Place* began to disappear, as the new media replaced traditional institutions and their geographical locales. Rather than simply facilitating decentralized power sharing, the new organizational media may presage a disassembly of organizations, the breakdown of social organization as we have known it, carrying with it a dissolution of traditional social authority.

As we moved into the twenty-first century, Greenberg, Thayer, and Bagdikian have proven themselves to be remarkably prescient. Organizations have been remolded and are continuing to change to conform to the imperatives of the new media; institutional communication now plays a much more powerful role in social affairs than ever in the past, and national boundaries are giving way to Web sites as the locus of authority. The borders separating organization from organization and organization from non-organization, *have* been dissolving with the advent of the personal computer revolution. We have been witnessing a breakdown of boundaries within and between organizations, bred by increasing interconnectivity and by the speed of the new media. We have entered the age of *Orgamedia*–a state in which organization and media become inextricably intertwined, ultimately fusing to emerge as a new entity. To the naïve observer, the contemporary organization, its electronic persona, and its capacity to shape it's environment have become an amorphous whole often signified by a memorable logo.

Organic Media and the State

The hyper-interconnectivity achieved by the new means of electronic communication has been described by such metaphors as "highways" and "central nervous systems." An early report by the electronics industry in Canada correctly predicted that what were separate services—telephone, broadcasting, data processing, telegraph, and telex—would be linked together by technology, with an "eventual single national electronic highway transmitting all forms of communications.[9] This remarkable prediction had come true by the early 1990s when U.S. President Clinton made an "information highway" one of the cornerstones of policy for the U.S. government. Its investment in electronic infrastructure has been crucial to the process.

During the adolescence of the computer age, computer experts foresaw a parallel "technology merger" within organizations "in which the flow of information would be viewed as a single function within a corporation."[10] In observing the ongoing integration of hardware and software within organizations, a government specialist in communications argued that "the boundaries between what is communication and what is processing blur and become for all practical purposes indistinguishable." He predicted the merger of information handling, telecommunications, and data handling systems into one ultimate system.[11] The transmission networks in place in Canada as early as 1980 led Canadian Communications Minister Francis Fox to call them "already the central nervous system of the country."[12]

Despite the metaphor, technological integration does not necessarily lead to social integration. By the late 1970s, research was pointing to the sociological consequences of the new electronic networks. Research conducted on what were called "electronic groups" indicated that they caused borders between organizations to erode and group processes to break down. Research by Nicole Leduc, among others, confirmed that there was a bypassing of traditional organizational barriers in organizations experimenting with computer conferencing. In her study, she found a decrease in the proportion of intraorganizational messages compared with interorganizational ones.[13] These findings, combined with others indicating hierarchical communication

within the organization had diminished, led James Taylor to conclude that "the boundaries of the traditional organization are crumbling."[14] Viewed from another perspective, this suggests that bits and pieces of old organizations are combining with each other electronically, all the while losing contact with their erstwhile leaders. Organizationally, this often takes the form of "spinning off" parts of the company, governmental privatization, and merger mania.

As well, a study of professionals, including engineers, statisticians, and psychologists using electronic mail networks indicated they felt socially isolated and lacked group influence, and showed they were unable as an electronic group to "develop or maintain contact" with each other, resulting in a "breakdown in group processes," a cornerstone of social organization,[15] thus leading to a kind of electronic anomie. The decline in social organization—group processes—as a result of organizational telecommunication was also noted by Albertson, and led him to conclude that while dyads might function satisfactorily, the group, per se, would become "less salient."[16] Allegiances between individuals in the future might then be expected to be based less on status and occupational role considerations and more on opportunistic communications patterns which may well conflict with the employer's goals and objectives.

Dissolving Organizations

A cornerstone of social organization, at least in the stable social organizations we have come to know and understand, is physical territory or "place." But increasing numbers of organizations can and do now exist only in "communication space." Massive transnational corporations and conglomerates that move component bureaucracies and production services from one place to another with ease have been emerging and rapidly becoming the norm, made possible by the high interconnectivity and speed of the new media.[17] Floors of stock exchanges and other "places" that are responsible for vast sums of money are disappearing, replaced by electronic signals only. Banks—which once required face, place, and presence to impress—now are rapidly closing branches, increasingly relocating functions to electronic communication systems, and the majority of younger customers today rarely have to have contact with a human teller, using bank machines and modems instead. Never again could a Stephen Leacock write of the way in which the physical grandiosity of the bank—the authority of place—inspired so much awe in him that he fled rather than deposit his money.

Orgamedia have made physical location unnecessary.

Just as the distinctions between communications, information processing, and organizations blur and dissolve, the boundaries and operational distinctions between the media of mass communication and other organizations and systems are rapidly breaking down. The development of communications and information hardware has increasingly changed the relationship between the organization and client into that of mass communicator and audience. While barriers within and between organizations have been dissolving, organizations–in their relations to their clients–have been transformed into mass communication machines. The bank that so awed Leacock has now, like all other financial institutions, become a mass medium. It has become primarily an information source since very little physical money now moves between public and bank.

The critical media that link organizations to people, as well as to other organizations, have now become the computer and its networks, the ubiquitous fax machine (which is giving way to e-mail though still employed where signatures are required by law), the automatic dialer ("Put it on your desk in the morning, and let it make 1000 calls"), the word processor, and the cellular phone. To this array have been added automatic devices that delay messages and then phone back with the messages, and the surging "call broadcasting centres" for cellular phones and pagers.

The same processes that have lowered organizational barriers within and between organizations paradoxically have caused organizations to turn to the outside client a one-way face.[18] Typically, large and small organizations alike have automated telephone answering with the recorded voice that tells callers that "your call is important to us," something that the long automated wait proves is a meaningless message. With the advent first of xerography and then of the computer, followed by its hybrid of photocopy and computer–the word processor–every large organization has now become a mass communication machine, capable of reaching mass audiences very cheaply with the same message under the guise of an individual communiqué. We are thus reminded of the traditional definition of *mass* communication: that communications hardware transmits identical or near-identical messages to mass audiences in a one-way fashion, with a marked distinction between the roles of sender and receiver, and in which the possibility for feedback–real feedback–is low.

Diagnostics of the New Media

While traditional disciplinary distinctions have separated the study of mass communications from complex organization (except for hints and suggestions in the works of some mass theorists such as Arendt, Mannheim, and Mills whose work suggests the permeability of the disciplinary boundaries), during the decades of the 1980s and 1990s, organizational hardware and software have become one and the same with the traditional hardware and software of the mass media. The tools of mass communication analysis may now be brought to bear in the field of organization analysis as *organizations* increasingly become recognized as communication devices, and the new communications media function as organizations have in the past.

While organizations have been becoming mass communication institutions, the mass media themselves have been sensitive and responsive to change in the technology of the new organizational communication. Douglas Parkhill has said, "As technology advances and general information utilities evolve, it is likely that they will gradually replace the more orthodox media–newspapers, radio, and television–as methods of mass communication."[19] His prediction has become true as individuals and organizations use electronic databases and networks to keep up with the news on a demand basis, although there has been more amalgamation of the new media by the traditional media than replacement. For example, most newspapers (such as *The Globe and Mail*) now make available compressed editions through the Internet.

If the boundaries that once separated organizations in general from mass communication media have faded, it is also true that boundaries *between media* that formerly distinguished and separated *them* have been rapidly dissolving. Rather than the "clash" between media that Innis[20] so often described, particularly with the advent of a new medium, there has instead been coalescence. Because of the loss of media boundaries, media identities, as we have known them for the past century, now more than overlap: cable, television, newspapers, and the new media have become fused. As Alvin and Heidi Toffler point out in *Power Shift,* "Unlike the Second Wave media, each of which operated more or less independently of the other, the new media are closely interlinked and fused together, feeding data, images, and symbols back and forth to one another." They then give an example of the breakdown of boundaries between media: "TV talk-show producers get ideas for subjects and guests from the newspapers. All of them depend on fax, computers, word processors, electronic typesetters, digitized imagery, electronic networks, satellites, or other interlinked technologies."[21]

The fusion of media is equalled by the merging of roles within media. Who can remember the days when newspaper writers–before computers–were not typesetters as well? And today, to become a journalist, one must be trained in Web page technology.

Paralleling the overlapping of identities, and probably in great part because of this, media ownership patterns increasingly reflect the permeability of distinctions and identities. As a syndicated financial writer once said,

> So you thought CBS was in the broadcasting business. And you thought *Time* was in the publishing business. Well, you're right. Both companies are in those businesses. But the lines between them have become fuzzier as each has invaded the other's territory. CBS is now a major force in the publishing world. And *Time* is moving into a major role in the broadcasting industry.[22]

By the end of the 1980s, international media mega-empires had blurred the differences between forms of media and made national boundaries "increasingly meaningless," as Bagdikian has shown. To demonstrate that such integration applies not just to media forms but also to the mass media conglomeration of ownership, Bagdikian provides the following scenario: Giant Corporation buys an article for one of its magazines, converts it into a book, the author is interviewed on its television stations, the book is converted into a company-produced movie, the sound track comes out as a cassette or compact disc through the firm's record company and is then played by its radio stations, following which the film becomes a videocassette to be shown on company television stations.[23]

The Centre Cannot Hold

Where there is no organization, there is no authority.
– Robert Bierstedt[24]

A number of writers have drawn our attention to the connection between social authority, social cohesion, and organizational communication. Some begin with the fact of communication and assert that social organization per se is an outcome. Boulding says that the very meaning of social organization is based upon the "hierarchical structure of communication and authority."[25] Hugh Dalziel Duncan says simply, "Communicative forms *determine* social order."[26] The well-established experimental studies by Bavelas[27] and Leavitt[28] among others, amply attest to this–when the pattern of communication channels

is changed, there is a corresponding transformation in social authority, hence a change in social organization.

Research by Taylor and Schutze on the effect of communication technology in eroding barriers against communication points to its diluting effect upon authority. Tayor and Schutz say that while traditional organizational communication supported organizational authority, the technologies of communication introduced around 1975 dilute authority within and without organizations–"with radical implications for how our society works, how it comes to take decisions, how interests are represented in public debate, how politics are conducted and how order is maintained." They further suggest this leads to the vanishing of organizational identities "into the depths of an undifferentiated sea of communications."[29] The unprecedented organizational restructuring, mergers, buyouts, and corporate deaths in the 1980s and 1990s may be seen to be evidence of this.

Many writers have recognized that open communication channels can be dysfunctional to social organization, either directly eroding it, or affecting it indirectly through the dissolution of organizational identity. Anything that threatens the hierarchical nature of information (i.e., that it is passed through open channels rather than through successive filters) is threatening to this aspect of order. In point of fact, this rupture of traditional communication patterns is the very essence of the new organizational media. And there is a second process engendered by the new media for, while opening up organization and attacking the hierarchical dimensions of institutions, the message content undergoes changes–subtle but with definite social consequences.

The ability to modify messages by social cues and social contexts is, as Pettigrew points out in his research, a determinant of social authority.[30] The new communication changes the nature of information and of the symbols through which social order is expressed and reinforced. The meta-information that in former systems consistently modified the message content is eroded by the new communication because of its stripped-down nature. As Grande points out, in databases prepared for the information retrieval upon which modern organizational systems now depend, too many of the contextual cues to meaning are missing, and "one cannot possibly predict all possible contexts."[31] I give this example of organizational ambiguity because systems of this kind, without the social cues of traditional interpersonal communication, are replacing people as authorities within organizations. Alvin Toffler describes Third Wave communication systems as delivering "short modular blips of information that refuse to fit neatly into our existing mental files," adding that they do not "easily organize into larger wholes."[32] He is in fact describing the socially decontextualized information shaped by the new organizational media, and of course, the hypertext engines of the Internet.

Another important dimension of social organization—social stratification—is expressed and maintained both by the substantive content of communication and by form: in voice by paralinguistic phenomena, such as intonation and vocal quality, and by vocabulary selection.[33] As a participant in computer-mediated communication (CMC) once pointed out on the Internet, "CMC is much different (from "real world communication") due to the anonymity, the lack of facial features, hand signs, body language." As well, such traditional paralinguistic communication, along with forms of address, contribute to the maintenance of social order: the use of plurality, formal versus informal address, and use of titles all symbolize and reinforce a set of relationships—authority, prestige, power, distance.

When we meet people, we are influenced by prejudices about their appearance, the sound of their voice, their age. "With computers we have no prejudices," an airline pilot who participated in a computer-based electronic "bulletin board" has pointed out. As in the classic New Yorker cartoon, "nobody knows you're a dog on the Internet." When people transact their affairs within or between organizations using traditional communication, such social-emotional interaction content has played a critical role in their conduct and in maintaining a pattern of relationships that is an important dimension of social organization as we have known it. However, the new media in place by 2000 have precluded many of these meta-information cues, and particularly the forms of address that relate, differentiate, and reinforce social authority patterns.[34] When personal meetings and personal letters are replaced by electronic mail, for example, what develops is "very informal and to the point." When it replaces the telephone, the organization member "doesn't have to deal with phone etiquette."[35] Messages are short, informal, and status references are "downplayed."[36] There is consistent evidence that individuals in organizations surveyed after using one of the new media forms, teleconferencing, expressed their distress about the difficulty of "getting to know someone."[37] There was a kind of social disorientation brought about by the absence of social cues engendered by the new communication.

For similar reasons, most participants in the pioneering computer conferencing research reported by Guillaume preferred face-to-face discussions,[38] as was true of individuals asked to compare personal communication with the use of the telephone for most matters.[39] A Danish educator, after using computer-mediated communication for six months, contrasted it with in-person communication in the following way: "Most of us would find it an incivility not reacting in some way when spoken to, for example, looking at the person addressing us, and we draw conclusions on how to interpret interpersonal communication from rich sources besides the verbal action such as body language, expressions, intonations, etc.... CMC is an open landscape with very little signposting to guide you."[40]

The new organizational media are suited to the transmission of hard, clean information, abstracted and telegraphic, without social modifiers or appurtenances—Toffler's "information blips." Further suggestions concerning the role of these social modifiers come from several writers. Hartle, in his economic studies of bureaucracy, has found that high officials eschew stripped-down hard information, moving instead to the soft, fuzzy kind redolent of social input and implications (the kind that is difficult for the new media to handle well), fearful their social antennae may be dulled by the former kind.[41] As well, Kursh has informed us of the social benefits of "poor communication" in promoting social cohesion, "to assert social solidarity."[42] But the sharply defined, hard information not subject to social influence or social qualifiers weakens this aspect of social organization; fuzziness serves as a buffer in social communication and thus aids in consensus:

> A better understanding of the situation might serve only to underline the differences rather than to resolve them. Indeed many of the techniques thought of as poor communication were apparently developed with the aim of bypassing or avoiding confrontation, and some of them continue to be reasonably successful in this aim.[43]

In similar vein, social psychiatrist Elliott Jacques has pointed to the necessity of creating "constructive barriers against free communication" within organizations. He stresses the importance of "the process of keeping communications between groups at an optimum level by the creative use of selective barriers."[44] Or as Jeffrey Rosen put it, "Perhaps someday we will look back with nostalgia on a society that still believed opacity was possible and was shocked to discover what happened when it was not."[45]

It can be seen that there is a social role played by the resistance, constraints, and social modifiers described above. They function as barriers against open communication. Openness–the lack of barriers bred by the Internet–may lead to a breakdown of conventional etiquette and civility. Anybody who has participated in computer network hotlines in the 1990s has experienced the common phenomenon of "flaming"–hot, insulting, often *ad hominem* messages posted between participants, the communications equivalent of road rage. Survey any of the interactive newsgroups, and what will often be found is sharp and incessant conflict, much of it insulting if not actually destructive. As Nicol N. Schraudolph of the University of California (San Diego) says in describing a typical electronic social network, "its non-physical nature tends to lower inhibitions. To get a feeling for how closely beneath our civilized surface the caveman is lurking, and what kind of social situations can bring him out, just observe a flame war–you will find the same kind of dynamics."[46] Electronic communication, when it isn't simply cold and factual, is pugnacious, adversarial, and bereft of the kind of social responsibility upon which social organization must be built, and yet it is the wave of the future.

Others have sensed the role of communications for organizational image and identity, important contributors to social cohesion. Boulding has argued that removal of communication barriers results in changes in organizational images or identities,[47] and that organizational structure, not to mention the organization's overall ability to survive, depends upon such images. Similarly, Klapp attacks the "free-market of information"–the process that the new communication engenders–because open communication degrades system identities. He adds that collective identity requires gatekeepers, and that exogenous signals are the more substantial threat to organizational identities.[48] Alvin and Heidi Toffler have gone further, pointing out what is happening at the most general system level: "The old hard edges of the nation-state are eroding."[49]

A United Nations report in the 1980s warned against the threat of new communication technology destroying traditional forms of communication.[50] By the 1990s, others were sounding similar warnings concerning the anomie the new media would generate. As Zoglin has said, people interacting with the new media "may have trouble interacting with one another in the real world. One hypothesis: people will become more self-centred, less attuned to their neighbours and society. Bridging the gap between cultures and races could become more difficult. Civility will suffer too."[51]

This process begins with the breakdown of intercultural differences. As Clausen points out in his analysis of "post-culturalism," diversity is a victim of electronic networks that leads to anomie:

> On the Internet or in a world of permeable borders, different cultures should flourish side by side in relationships unmarked by either dominance or submission. In practice, however, such an environment rapidly breaks down not merely boundaries but cultures themselves.[52]

Evidence supporting the ideas of such analysts on the negative effect of the new communication on identity and its potential effect on social durability comes from empirical investigation by Albertson on teleconferencing, which he predicted "would have far reaching effects on the nature of organizations." One consequence would be "the erosion of corporate identity and the expectation that organizations have continuity over time."[53]

Linked to the anxiety over whether organizations will persist as they have in the past is a similar concern with the fate of professions in such domains as medicine, law, and finance and the apprehension that they are becoming attenuated or transformed into something less than they have been–that they are en route to becoming adjuncts of the new media. The professional relationships people have had with physicians, lawyers, tax accountants, financial advisers, journalists et al. have been eroding, as people turn to the Internet for expert advice Thus, to take the case of medicine, there is a breakdown in the authority and credibility of family doctors and even specialists, as patients gain immediate access to information and advice never before so freely available to them, and often in advance of its receipt by doctors. One doctors' website pointed out, following an informal poll, that 77 percent of doctors report that patients inform them of medical news through the Web and that 78 percent of doctors refer patients to websites for advice.[54] The taxpayer who once depended upon a tax consultant now has access to virtually the same software the consultant uses. Law compendia can be easily searched by keyword, as can expert reports on stocks and mutual funds. The financial adviser has been replaced by many easy-to-use forms that deliver a full report and recommendations. The hierarchical social relationships once built on the trust and credibility of professionals have diminished in importance and relevance and this process will accelerate, leading inevitably to greater scrutiny of the high incomes traditionally accorded to professionals. As a lawyer told her friend, "Why pay to see a lawyer about your will? The same boilerplate he uses is available on the Web."

In this chapter, I have attempted to draw together many of the diverse threads of the matrix connecting social organization to the new media. I have argued that the new media facilitate what I have called social disassembly, that they attenuate traditional stanchions of social organization, thus, that the rules of social organization are dramatically changing. What is pointed to as a consequence of the new communication are many of the problems traditionally linked to the mass society—a new, unexpected kind of social isolation, a severing of many traditional social relationships, and group breakdown—which is potentially and paradoxically a product of the high connectivity and openness of "decentralized" two-way communication.

One cannot, as in the past, separate the structure of media from that of social organization as they jointly metamorphose, becoming one and the same phenomenon. What we will need to do is to face the task of learning to adapt to an increasingly ambiguous existence in which media develop the attributes of organizations and organizations are transformed into media, as we continue our passage into the new civilization which rests on, and is enveloped by, a seamless tissue of media and institutions.

Notes

1. Martin Greenberg, "The Uses of Computers in Organizations," in *Scientific American Information* (San Francisco: Freeman Publishing Co.), 1966.

2. Lee Thayer, "Communications and Organization theory," in F.X. Dance (ed.), *Human Communication Theory* (New York: Holt, Rinehart and Winston, 1967).

3. Ben H. Bagdikian, "The Lords of the Global Village," *The Nation*, June 12, 1989, pp 805-820.

4. Allan Westin, *Instant World* (Department of Communications, 1971), p.29.

5. L.A. Albertson, "Telecommunications as a Travel Substitute: Some Psychological, Organizational, and Social Aspects," *Journal of Communication* 27, no. 2 (Spring): 32-43.

6. Manfred Kochen, "Technology and Communication in the Future," *Journal of the American society for Information Science* 32, no.1 (March 1981):148-57.

7. Karl Deutsch, *The Nerves of Government* (New York: The Free Press, 1969), p.197.

8. F. Kaufman, "Data Systems That Cross Company Boundaries," *Harvard Business Review* 44, no.1 (January/February 1966): 141-55.

9. "Report Urges New Look at Technology Policies," *London Free Press*, Nov. 19, 1973.

10. R. Stephens, "Effective Management Control Urged for Data Communications," *The Globe and Mail* (12 September 1978).

11. D. Parkhill, "Who's Afraid of Computer Communications?" *In Search: The Canadian Communications Quarterly* 4, 1976, p.10.

12. F. Fox, "The Eighties—New Opportunities in Communications," Speech to the Annual Convention of the Canadian Telecommunications Carriers Association, Vancouver, Canada, 1980.

13. N.F. Leduc, "Communication Through Computers," *Telecommunication Policy* (September 1979), pp.235-44; 241.

14. J.R. Taylor, "The Office of the Future: Weber and Innis Revisited," *In Search: The Canadian Communications Quarterly* 3, pp.4-13; p.10.

15. J. Guillaume, "Computer Conferencing and the Development of an Electronic Journal," *The Canadian Journal of Information Science* (5 May 1980): 21-29.

16. Albertson, "Telecommunication," p.37.

17. G. Adam, "Multinational Corporations and Worldwide Sourcing," H. Radice, ed., *International Firms and Modern Imperialism* (New York: Penguin Books,1979), p.98; A. Toffler, *The Eco-Spasm Report* (New York: Bantam Books, 1975).

18. B. Singer, "Incommunicado Social Machines," *Social Policy* 8, no. 3 (November/December): 88-93.

19. Parkhill, *op. cit.*, p.12.

20. H.A. Innis, *Empire and Communications* (Toronto: University of Toronto Press, 1972).

21. Alvin Toffler, *Power Shift* (New York: Bantam Books, 1990), p.32.

22. M. Moskovitz, "Money Tree," *San Francisco Chronicle*, November 23, 1980.

23. Ben H. Bagdikian, "The Lords of the Global Village," *The Nation*, June 12, 1989, pp.805-20.

24. Robert Bierstedt, "The Problem of Authority," in M. Berger et al. (eds.), *Freedom and Control in Modern Society* (New York: Van Nostrand, 1954).

25. K.E. Boulding, *The Image* (Ann Arbour: University of Michigan Press, 1973), p.27.

26. H.D. Duncan, "The Search for a Social Theory of Communication," in Dance, *Human Communication Theory*, p.251.

27. A. Bavelas, "Communication Patterns in Task-Oriented Groups," *Journal of the Acoustical Society of America* 22: 725-30.

28. H.J. Leavitt, "Some Effects of Certain Communication Patterns on Group Performance," *Journal of Abnormal and Social Psychology* 46: 38-50.

29. J.R. Taylor and B. Schultze, "The erosion of authority in the information society," Unpublished Paper, University of Montreal, September 1990.

30. A.M. Pettigrew, "Information Control as a Power Resource," *Sociology* 6, no. 2: 186-204; 189.

31. S. Grande, "Aspects of Pre-Literate Culture Shared by On-line Searching and Videotex," 5, pp.125-31; p.28.

32. A. Toffler, *The Third Wave* (New York: William Morrow, 1980), p.182.

33. R. Brown, *Social Psychology* (New York: The Free Press, 1965), p.66.

34. Ibid., p.62

35. Steklasa, *op. cit.*, pp.4-5.

36. Taylor, *op. cit.*, p.10.

37. Albertson, *op. cit.*, pp.33-34.

38. Guillaume, *op. cit.*, p.24.

39. B.D. Singer, *Social Functions of the Telephone* (Palo Alto, Calif.: R & E Research Associates, 1981), p.72.

40. Sisse Siggarard Jensen, Internet Posting, Computer Mediated Communication Group, "Workplace Resistance," 6 October 1990.

41. D.G. Hartle, *A Theory of the Expenditure Budgetary Process* (Toronto: University of Toronto Press, 1976), pp.82-83.

42. C.O. Kursh, "The Benefits of Poor Communication," *The Psychoanalytic Review* 58, no.2 (1971):189-208; 200.

43. Ibid., p.189.

44. E. Jacques, *The Changing Culture of a Factory* (London: Tavistock, 1957), pp.302-3.

45. J. Rosen, "The Eroded Sef," *The New York Times Magazine*, April 2000, p.66.

46. Posting by Nicol N. Schraudolph in Bitnet Group, "Soc.cultur.Jewish," Subject: Re: Post Holocaust Racism," Item 10984, 1 October 1990.

47. Boulding, *op. cit.*, p.146.

48. O.E. Klapp, *Opening and Closing* (Cambridge: Cambridge University Press, 1978), pp. 17, 21-22.

49. Alvin Toffler and Heidi Toffler, *War and Anti-War* (Boston: Little, Brown and Company, 1993), p.243.

50. D. Fisher, *The Right to Communicate: A Status Report* (Paris: UNESCO, 1982), p.47.

51. Richard Zoglin, "Beyond Your Wildest Dreams," *Time*, Special Edition (Fall 1992), p.23.

52. Christopher Clausen, "Welcome to Post-Culturalism," *The American Scholar* 65, no. 3 (Summer 1996): 380.

53. Albertson, *op. cit.*, p.37.

54. Website "Doctor's Guide to Medical and Other News," 7 January 2000.

9

Deconstruction

Philip Evans and Thomas S. Wurster

[The following are excerpts from Chapter 4 of Blown to Bits: How the New Economics of Information Transforms Strategy *(Boston, MA: Harvard Business School Press, 1999).]*

"Deconstruction" is the dismantling and reformulation of traditional business structures. It results from two forces: the separation of the economics of information from the economics of things, and the blowup (*within* the economics of information) of the trade-off between richness and reach. Traditional business structures include value chains, supply chains, organizations, and consumer franchises. When the trade-off between richness and reach is blown up, there is no longer a need for the components of these business structures to be integrated. The new economics of information blows all these structures to bits. The pieces will then recombine into new business structures, based on the separate economics of information and things.

Newspapers

Consider the newspaper business. It has a vertically and horizontally integrated value chain. Journalists and advertisers supply copy, editors and subeditors lay it out, the press prints the physical product, and an elaborate distribution system delivers it to readers each morning. Newspapers exist, and can survive and profit as intermediaries between journalists and readers, because of the economies of scale in the printing press. Writers cannot reach readers directly because they cannot cheaply print and distribute their work alone. Given its economies of scale, it makes sense for the newspaper to bundle multiple news services together, and it makes further sense to add all the other material that benefits from the same method of reproduction and distribution: classifieds, display advertisements, inserts, stock quotes, features, cartoons, TV listings, and so forth. These products cross-subsidize each other: some pull in particular segments of readers, others pull in particular segments of advertisers. All contribute to the overall fixed costs of production and distribution.

Gurus have been forecasting for years the possibility of a high-resolution electronic "tablet" newspaper, which would be loaded with daily content over the phone line, support full-motion video, offer all the advantages of electronic intelligence, and cost less per day than the price of a paper newspaper.[1] Like the equally famous "paperless office," it has not happened yet, and is not likely to become popular in the foreseeable future. As newspaper executives point out, the broadsheet is an extraordinarily cheap, convenient, and user-friendly way to distribute information. Electronic tablets are not going to replace it very soon.

However, that response is to misunderstand the nature of the challenge facing newspapers: it assumes that the transformation of the business is an all-or-nothing proposition. The question is not whether and when newspapers will go electronic. The question is more basic: will newspapers still remain a vertically and horizontally integrated business?

Deconstruction posits a melting of the glue that binds the newspaper value chain together. The glue in this case is the economics of things—printing presses and distribution—tying together the informational content. Once other means of distribution become possible, *the bundle can no longer be taken for granted.*

Liberated from the economics of things, journalists will be able to e-mail content directly to readers. Readers will be able to mix and match content from an unlimited number of sources. They will be able to download news daily (or several times a day) from multiple news services. They will be able to obtain movie reviews, travel features, and recipes directly from magazines, book publishers, and master chefs. Star columnists, cartoonists, or the Weather Service can send their content directly to subscribers. Intermediaries—Internet portals, intelligent agents, formatting software, or, for that matter, editorial teams—can format and package content to meet readers' individual interests. The "daily us" of the traditional newspaper could be replaced by a customized "daily me."[2]

Almost all these things are already happening. On-line journalism is burgeoning. Most traditional newspaper content is available somewhere on the Web. Portals offer quite sophisticated customization of home pages, including on-line tracking of an investment portfolio, continuous weather updates, local entertainment listings, and alerts on topics of special interest. But still, convenient and nifty as these services are, there is little evidence that they are drawing readers away from the daily newspaper.

However, deconstruction does not have to occur—indeed rarely will occur—across the board. Deconstruction does not mean that the newspaper business as a whole is vulnerable, but rather that the critical pieces of the business are vulnerable.

Classified advertising is a natural on-line product. When posted and accessed electronically, classified advertisers can offer continuously updated listings, extensive text and pictures, prospectively even video clips. Buyers can search systematically by whatever criteria they choose, set alerts, access related information, and respond via e-mail. The inconvenience of booting a computer is a minor consideration when selling a car or buying a house.

The migration of classified advertising has a compelling logic and is already well under way.[3] However, classifieds account for about 40 percent of the revenues of the typical newspaper but only 10 percent of its costs. The 30 percent contribution from classifieds is well in excess of the margin of just about every newspaper. If classifieds were lost, most newspapers would become financially unsustainable. *That* is the threat of deconstruction. Not electronic tablets, not Yahoo providing a customized "daily me," but the loss of classifieds. Deconstruction is most likely to strike precisely that sliver of the value chain where the incumbent can least afford to let it happen.

Newspapers are fighting back. They have moved aggressively into the electronic classified business. They have exploited their advantage as incumbents in print to provide an integrated print and electronic classified offering that reaches the widest population of buyers and sellers. And because they currently own the biggest classified "marketplace," bringing together the largest number of buyers and sellers, they are well positioned to translate their dominance of the old business into dominance of the new.

But how much is that marketplace advantage worth? Can newspapers price electronic classifieds at the same rates they charge for print? Viewed as a stand-alone business, they are charging $40 in revenues for every $10 in costs, a 75 percent operating margin. (The only reason they are able to get away with that kind of pricing is that it *isn't* a stand-alone business.) Can they get away with that kind of pricing when there are no barriers to entry, and when costs, incidentally, have dropped by a factor of over half? If newspapers preserve their price level, they risk ceding the marketplace to an electronic-only competitor who is less greedy. If they give up enough of the margin to keep the business, they lose the cash flow that supports the economics of the print product.

Either way, the subsidy that supports the print product plummets. The print business is then caught between reduced revenues and its high level of fixed costs. Newspapers cut content or raise subscription and newsstand prices, which drives down readership. Readership losses drive down the price that display advertisers are willing to pay. The loss of reader and advertiser revenues in turn necessitates further cost cutting. This downward spiral then creates opportunities for focussed competitors to pick off other parts of the value chain: second-order deconstructions that would not have been economic otherwise. So the greatest threat to newspapers is not the total substitution of a new business model, but steady erosion of the business through a sequence of partial substitutions.

This does not mean the demise of newspapers. There is a powerful rationale for a bundle of news and commentary, something to do with editorial voice, shared daily experience, brand, authority, and the reader's simple desire to be surprised by the unexpected. And people are clearly willing to pay for it: the actual cost of editorial content today is about equal to the average price of a subscription. After the deconstruction of the old bundle, which was shaped by the shared economics of presses and distribution, we shall see the rise of a new bundle (or new bundles; there is no reason to presume only one solution) that will reflect the liberated economics of information....

Implications of Deconstruction for Competitive Advantage

By transforming business and industry structure, deconstruction alters the sources of competitive advantage. The shifts will occur at different speeds and with varying intensities from industry to industry, but the consequences are the same for all businesses or industries vulnerable to deconstruction.

Competitive Advantage is "De-Averaged"

As value chains deconstruct, they will fragment into multiple businesses that have separate sources of competitive advantage. This results in the de-averaging of competitive advantage. When all the functions in a value chain are bundled together, what matters is competitive advantage over *the entire chain*. As long as the sum is advantaged, it does not matter where specifically that advantage comes from, still less whether the business is advantaged in each constituent activity. Car dealers have managed to survive despite being disadvantaged in almost every aspect of their chain, when each is viewed in isolation. Superiority in some functions offsets mediocrity in others.

But when a value chain is deconstructed, this logic unravels. Advantage on average no longer matters. Companies can no longer subsidize poor performance in one activity by combining it with others in which they are advantaged. In each separable activity, new competitors emerge who focus on maximizing performance in just that specific step. Banks are attacked by financial specialists, car dealers by local repair shops. So to survive, a competitor has to be advantaged in each and every activity in which he chooses to continue to participate....

New Opportunities Arise for Physical Businesses

In many businesses today, the physical value chain is compromised for the purposes of delivering information. The new economics of information therefore creates opportunities to rationalize the logistical value chain and build businesses whose physically based sources of competitive advantage are more sustainable.

Federal Express and UPS are among the biggest potential winners from the growth of electronic commerce. Supermarkets can take over the cash dispensing and collection function from banks. Hertz can provide the test drive. In dozens of businesses, the focussed provider of physical services, uncompromised by informational distractions (except insofar as they related to logistics), is a big future winner.

In some cases, the physical business proves a surprising source of competitive advantage. Consider the celebrated example of the electronic book seller. Amazon.com, an electronic retailer on the Web, has no physical stores and started with little inventory. It offers an electronic list of 3 million books, 20 times

larger than that of the largest chain store.[4] Customers can search through that catalog via the Web. Amazon, in its early days, ordered almost all of its books from two industry wholesalers in response to customers' requests. It then unpacked, repacked, and mailed them from its distribution facility in Seattle.

Amazon established a variety of informational advantages: the 3-million-item catalog, a user-friendly interface, reviews, customized recommendations, and so forth. But there is nothing obviously defensible about all of this. The database is owned and operated by wholesalers (originally for the benefit of small book shops) and is open to anybody. The interface, reviews, and recommendations are easy to replicate. And by double-handling the books, Amazon incurred unnecessary physical costs.

Had Amazon sat still, the wholesalers could have put dozens of Amazons into business. Indeed, they could have created a lower-cost distribution system by encouraging portals like Yahoo to serve as pure navigators, paying them a finder's fee, and then selling and shipping the book directly to the consumer. That would have eliminated the double handling. Electronic retailers would then have become mere search engines connected to somebody else's database, adding little value, and achieving little competitive advantage. The wholesalers would be the big winners.

However, the electronic book sellers did not sit still. Amazon is growing its inventory, building regional distribution centers, and backward integrating into wholesaling. And Barnes and Noble tried to acquire the largest wholesaler, Ingram, whose platform originally put Amazon into business. In the battle of the books, it is physical logistics as much as informational franchise that will determine the winner....

The Challenge to the Incumbent

Incumbents can behave like the owners of *Encyclopedia Britannica*. They can become paralyzed by their reluctance to cannibalize their established business model. Newspapers pricing themselves out of the business in an attempt to maintain revenues; banks ganging up to create a standard that limits the customer's ability to make choices; car manufacturers trying to mollify their dealers by refusing to deal with new distribution channels: all are pursuing strategies eerily similar to those that led *Britannica* to its downfall.

The paralysis of the leading incumbent is the greatest competitive advantage enjoyed by new competitors. It is an advantage that they often do not deserve, since if the incumbent would only fight all-out by the new rules, the incumbent would often win. The paralysis of the leading incumbent is also the greatest competitive advantage for the *marginal* incumbent, who has lost the old game and has every motive to change the rules. Deconstructed distribution, for example, is a huge opportunity for *offshore* car manufacturers, since they have inferior conventional distributor networks and more to gain than lose from blowing them up.

It is difficult to downsize assets that have high fixed costs when so many customers still prefer the current business model. It is difficult to cannibalize current profits. It is difficult to walk away from core competencies that were built over decades, the object of personal and collective pride and identity. And it can be even harder to squeeze the profits of partners and distributors to whom one is tied by long-standing relationships or contractual obligation.

But a greater vulnerability than legacy assets is a legacy mindset. It may be easy to grasp this point intellectually, but it is profoundly difficult in practice. Managers must put aside the presuppositions of the old competitive world and compete according to totally new rules of engagement. They must make decisions at a different speed, long before the numbers

are in place and the plans formalized. They must acquire new technical and entrepreneurial skills, quite different from what made their organization (and them personally) so successful. They must manage for maximal opportunity, not minimum risk. They must devolve decision making, install different reward structures, and perhaps even devise different ownership structures. They have little choice. If they don't deconstruct their own businesses, somebody else will do it to them.

Notes

[1] See for example Roger Fidler, *Mediamorphosis: Understanding New Media* (Thousand Oaks, Calif.: Pine Forge Press, 1997).

[2] The prototype customized electronic newspaper was developed at the MIT Media Lab and called "Fishwrap" after the journalist's proverb "Yesterday's news wraps today's fish." For a detailed description see <http://fishwrap-docs.www.media.mit.edu/docs/diev/CNGlue/conglue.html>.

[3] The most immediately vulnerable segment is job classifieds (especially for higher-skill jobs), which accounts for about one-third of classified revenues. The vulnerability of newspapers in the real estate and automotive categories is compounded by the vulnerabilities of realtors to disintermediation and of automotive dealers to a deconstruction of their own.

[4] Amazon.com Web site: <http://www.amazon.com>.

PART 3

PROCESS AND IMPACT OF THE MEDIA

Media impact can be explored from diverse points of view, ranging from the individual effects of a specific powerful medium to the broad impact of media on such issues as political process or national identity.

However, as is repeatedly acknowledged in the literature, media effects are difficult to measure. One starting point is the assessment of who is watching and listening to which electronic media programming. Today's ratings determine tomorrow's content. Hence it is important for an industry that accounts for so much of our time to understand the mechanisms by which such decisions are made.

Given that, we may ask not only what such measurement reveals about broadcast audiences, but about the very accuracy of their portraits of audiences. Edward Withers and Robert S. Brown attempt to answer such questions by providing a revealing picture of both Canadian audience behaviour and of the methods and problems of assessing audiences.

Their chapter suggests that tomorrow's TV content may be a function not only of audience choice but also of the idiosyncracies of the tools of measurement. The traditional measurements of audiences, which have been primary determinants of future content and advertising expenditures, are being replaced by new technologies of assessment, "people meters," which sharply reduce turn-around time for the data and, more importantly, may be a more accurate tool of the ratings society.

Jonathan Rose's chapter deals with a specific form of impact: political advertising. It shows that government advertising campaigns are not a recent innovation. They have been used for decades to shape public opinion about public policy and programs. And far from declining in importance and impact, they have become larger, more sophisticated, and better co-ordinated attempts to secure public support as time has gone by. He suggests there is a fine line between informing the public and actually creating support in the Canadian public. Sometimes, this support seems destined to promote the views and objectives of the party in power at the time rather than those of the government as a whole. Such a use of advertising might well be considered an abuse of public office and funds by some.

Another way to approach the role of mass media with respect to politics might be to question the impact of differential coverage of the parties on their individual fortunes, and to consider such traditional issues as media bias. We might also concern ourselves with the quality of coverage, the backgrounding of issues, and the efficacy of attempts to measure the impact of media on elections. Some of this, the most visible aspects of the media's contact with politics—the flash and show-business aspects of mass media coverage of elections—is described by Robert Everett and Frederick J. Fletcher as "horserace journalism."

In fact, Everett and Fletcher go well beyond such issues, examining the way in which the media "frame the context for political communication," a step beyond traditional research concerns (such as the coverage of politics during campaigns). The authors describe the parties' "permanent campaign footing" (between elections), when indirect forms of political visibility are bought by those in power through various kinds of paid ads or through the use of public buildings for display of symbols and messages that function as subtle testimonials to their good works. Everett and Fletcher also draw our attention to the agenda-setting function of the mass media for other communication channels, such as interpersonal networks, and remind us of the didactic function of the media, which educate the electorate by demonstrating how the system works—something that the abstraction of formal education often fails to do.

The media, they conclude, do not merely reflect the political process but are inextricably part of the process.

Another starting point for many researchers is the analysis of specific types of media content. Probably the question most addressed by content analysis, other than violence, is the representation of women. A recent Canadian study informs us that the pattern of media treatment of women has not changed much during the past decade, that women are considerably underrepresented in all areas of Canadian broadcasting, as well as restricted in the diversity of roles they portray.[1]

Shari Graydon further tests the content issue with her comprehensive overview of the portrayal of women in the mass media. She examines a broad range of studies dealing with women's portrayal in varied Canadian and U.S. media, and of attempts by organized groups to combat the pervasive underrepresentation and distortions of the images of woman, and suggests in her conclusion a powerful weapon, economic clout, that can transform women's relationship to the mass media. It should be pointed out that although Graydon's inquiry is based on North American work, the patterns she found seem to be universal: research, even in such progressive societies as Scandinavian ones, reveals the differential treatment of women–their low numbers and selective roles in the media.[2]

Tannis MacBeth, in highly acclaimed Canadian research, takes a step beyond content, examining the influence of television (our most "massified" medium) on both children and adults. The central question (one of the most persistently asked in recent decades) is: What *is* the nature of TV's impact? Three of her most important findings deal with the impact of TV in displacing other activities, its power to socialize, and its role in promoting aggression in everyday life.

First, one of the most powerful potential effects of TV is displacement of other activities, such as participation in community activities and the use of other media, the latter possibly affecting the development of reading skills.

Second, TV has a discernible impact upon the acquisition of gender-role norms. One of the potential effects of TV upon socialization (individual identity building) is its power to reinforce traditional images or norms. Peer-scale analysis reveals that TV does affect young people's perceptions of gender roles in the direction of traditional stereotypes. Early development of normative images–beliefs, expectations, and stereotypes–whether resulting from direct experience or from TV helps to direct future perceptions and expectations. As a Swedish research report posed the question of the potential impact of media's power to socialize, "televised fiction (on the whole) fosters self-confident, resolute males, while it cautions young women to remain passive, to avoid risks, to seek shelter."[3] While not discounting the power of other influences in the social system, MacBeth was surprised to find how measurably strong was TV's impact, over and above that of other forces.

Third, the most often investigated specific question in the history of mass communication research is whether media content stimulates aggressive behaviour. MacBeth does find an increase in indicators of aggression in boys and girls after TV is introduced. However, she qualifies this finding by pointing out that TV effects do not occur in a social vacuum: where social controls against the commission of aggression are sufficient, violent behaviour is not inevitable.

MacBeth's research indicates that TV not only plays an important role in psychosocial processes, but that the nature of its effects are decidedly measurable.

According to Duncan Cameron, "Canada continues to be a dumping ground" for foreign TV and film productions. Furthermore, correction of this problem is hampered by the tendency of Canadian media to "understate their own influence" in spite of evidence, such as that of MacBeth and others, that indicates the discernible influence of media, particularly TV, on the development of attitudes and behaviour.

But how do you measure something as intangible as national or cultural identity? Some suggest that we begin with the building blocks of national identity–knowledge of important facts about one's own country. Many Canadians are confused about their history, their geography, the great figures who have contributed to the building of their society. Researchers have found that Canadians confuse U.S. facts with Canadian facts, and are more able to identify U.S. politicians, journalists, and historical figures than Canadian ones. They seem to know more U.S. authors and musicians, and they substitute U.S. language customs for Canadian ones.

Canadian policy, both past and projected, in weakening the financial power of Canadian media while further reducing trade barriers to the U.S., may well accelerate this process of acculturation of Canadians by American media. One must ask whether the mass media are different from other national institutions that remain "in the way of two winds of change that pay no heed to borders: free trade and technology."[4]

Notes

[1] *Gender and Violence in the Mass Media* (Ottawa: Health Canada, 1993), pp.10-12.

[2] Vibeke Pedersen, "Soap, Pin-up and Burlesque: Commercialization and Femininity in Danish Television," *The Nordicom Review of Nordic Mass Communication Research*, no. 2 (1993): 26.

[3] Charly Hulten, "Does television promote equality?" *Sveriges Radio Audience and Programme Research* (December 1993): 44.

[4] "The day of the national car industry is over," *The Globe and Mail* (7 February 1994), p.A11.

10

The Broadcast Audience: A Sociological Perspective

Edward J. Withers and Robert S. Brown

For most of the twentieth century, radio and TV have been considered the most important of the mass media. The reach of the two broadcast media far outstrips the circulation of newspapers or magazines. Broadcast outlets serve as sources of both news and entertainment. In addition, TV is an important medium in the socialization and education of children. Even infants too young to be included in standard estimates of audience size will watch TV intently, and will develop programming preferences.[1]

As a result, there has been ongoing discussion and debate about the impact of the broadcast media, the messages and content that they carry, and the social problems thought to be associated with media consumption. Many participants in the debate have offered theories on the basis of assumed patterns of media use, or critics' impressions about how the public might be influenced. Fewer have taken as their starting point the actual media behaviour of the population.

This chapter will present a non-technical review of the media habits of Canadian TV viewers and radio listeners. It will also discuss research methods and provide a portrait of the social and economic context within which audience research is undertaken and used.

Why Measure Broadcast Audiences?

The measurement of broadcast audiences is critical because it provides feedback as to the size and internal composition of program, station, and network audiences to programmers and broadcast managers. Perhaps more importantly, audience data provide the basis for the buying and selling of commercial air time. For most broadcasters, these transactions determine station and network revenues (and in the private sector, profits or losses as well). Early in broadcast history, though, the situation was different. When radio broadcasting first began in the 1920s, transmission stations were operated by radio manufacturers in order to stimulate the sale of receiving sets. Quite rapidly, however, radio's economic basis shifted from the promotion of receivers to the sale of broadcast time to commercial sponsors. Television (with only a few non-commercial exceptions) has also adopted this pattern.[2]

In 1998, revenue from the sale of advertising time in the Canadian TV and radio industry totalled $3 billion.[3] Television accounted for $2.07 billion—just over two-thirds of this total—while radio advertising supplied slightly less than one-third of all industry advertising revenue at $0.93 billion. Aside from a limited number of publicly funded non-commercial broadcast outlets (such as the CBC's AM and FM radio systems and provincial educational TV networks), broadcasting's economic basis is this sale of advertising time. It is not simply the "time" that is being sold, however. The actual "commodity" is the listening or viewing audience exposed to the commercial message. As one might expect, larger audiences will generally produce greater revenues than smaller ones, although the internal composition of an audience also has a bearing upon its commercial value. Audiences with large proportions of viewers and/or listeners with certain characteristics (such as individuals with high disposable income, households' principal shoppers, persons who are generally light users of TV or radio, or who are difficult to reach through other advertising vehicles) will command a premium.

Even in non-commercial broadcast settings, audience data are important (though not all-important). Broadcasters with public or educational—rather than commercial—mandates are still anxious to know about the size and nature of their audiences. The study of audience size and composition can help non-commercial broadcasters better understand their audiences and how to communicate with them. Such information is helpful in station or network planning, management, and scheduling. Extreme cases can also be instructive, suggesting broadly which approaches "work" and which do not. Unexpectedly low audience estimates can provide a "flag" to program management, and can be of assistance in deciding which series should be shifted to a less prominent position in the broadcast schedule, or perhaps undergo program evaluation. By contrast, upbeat audience estimates can be used in negotiations with funding agencies and in promotional activities. If the aim of a broadcast organization is to serve the public in some specified manner, this goal cannot be fulfilled if few are watching or listening, or if certain sociodemographic groups are not being served. Non-commercial broadcasters cannot afford to turn their backs on measures of audience performance.

In terms of traditional means of tracking business activity or rates of service provision (such as records of purchase transactions), broadcasting audiences are intangible.[4] From a radio- or TV-control room, it is impossible to tell how many listeners or viewers are tuned to the outgoing programming. Broadcasters do receive audience response in the form of unsolicited letters or phone calls—but this type of feedback, while valuable, is not systematic, and attempts to generalize from it are perilous. There is no way to determine whether those who phone or write are indeed typical of the general audience. Nor is it safe to assume that a program that draws a great deal of unsolicited response has a larger audience than one that does not. If anything, unsolicited audience reaction can be thought of as providing an indication of the intensity of audience reaction.

Commercial broadcasters and their clients make use of data from third-party audience measurement services. Underlying every "media buy," there must be at least a minimal level of agreement about the expectations of the buyer and the obligations of the seller in terms of audience "delivery." Audience data provides a lingua franca for the parties to commercial transactions to work from a common set of measurements and operational definitions.

Unfortunately, standard measures of the size and nature of the audience present only part of the picture. Quantitative estimates do not reveal what viewers thought about a program, how much they enjoyed it, whether it touched their emotions, whether they learned anything from it, were changed by it, or embarked on some course of action as a result of the experience. Customized program evaluation research is undertaken by broadcasters and producers of TV materials in order to answer some of these open questions.

Who Measures Audiences? And By What Means?

The broadcast industry in Canada is served by two major syndicated audience-measurement organizations. One is the BBM Bureau of Measurement (initially, but no longer, known as the Bureau of Broadcast Measurement—hence the "BBM"). The organization is a Canadian, not-for-profit, "tripartite" co-operative of broadcasters, advertisers, and advertising agencies, all having an interest in the objective measurement of broadcast audiences.[5] By contrast, Nielsen Media Research (Canada) is a private, profit-making enterprise owned by its American parent Nielsen Media Research and—since 1999, all of Nielsen Media Research has been owned in turn by VNU, Inc. of the Netherlands. Nielsen Media Research has no continuing relationship to the market research firm A.C. Nielsen, though they were both founded by Arthur Nielsen Sr. and for years were part of the same company. The combined A.C. Nielsen companies were, for a period, owned by U.S. business information broker Dun and Bradstreet.

BBM and Nielsen Media Research both offer TV-audience data, while radio is measured only by BBM. The services have been described as "syndicated" because they spread their operating costs across a large number of subscribers who then all have access to the common pool of data. Over the course of time, BBM and Nielsen—usually competing but sometimes co-operating—have altered their services according to the levels of television measurement they have offered, and the measurement technologies they have used. Levels of TV measurement have been historically described as "market" and "network" (see comments immediately below). The technologies employed have been viewing diaries and electronic people meters (see details in later sections).

For much of its history, television measurement in Canada had been segmented into "market" and "network" services. This long-standing distinction has been to some degree overtaken by recent developments in the industry, but the notions remain useful in explaining how measurements are made and reported, how audience measurement in Canada has evolved, and how the relationship between the BBM and Nielsen organizations has changed over time.

"Market" measurement and reporting is geographically localized and is designed to serve broadcast stations that originate from a particular city or adjacent set of cities (e.g., Vancouver/Victoria, or

Ottawa/Hull). Each TV market is served by at least one and usually several originating stations that can be individually reported and identified by call letters (e.g., CFCN, Calgary). Signals can "spill" into neighbouring markets when two or more market areas are close to one another, or when cable companies import "distant" signals not ordinarily receivable by antenna alone. As a result, stations typically attract some fraction of their total audience from areas outside their own home markets. To some stations, "spill" is extremely important. Station CKVR serves Barrie, Ontario, but its signal is widely available via cable in Toronto and its suburbs–allowing CKVR to attract far larger audiences than could otherwise be expected from its home market alone.

"Network" measurements are based on regional and national units of geography–much larger areas than local markets. Network measurements combine the audiences of several affiliated broadcast stations (e.g., CTV or CBC), or particular local stations that have acquired a regional presence by virtue of repeater transmitters and extensive cable or satellite carriage. Widely available cable specialty services are also interested in "network" level measurement and reporting, because it is suited to their patterns of signal distribution. When programs are broadcast simultaneously, or in comparable time periods, or across time zones, "network" audiences can be combined and reported in a unified manner. Even though affiliated stations contribute audiences to network totals, the local sample sizes will be too small to report reliable estimates for individual affiliates.

Prior to 1989, both BBM and Nielsen operated market and network services using viewing diaries. In addition to their differing geographic bases, network surveys were in the field more often than market surveys, but with much smaller sample sizes. Nielsen shifted its network service from diaries to people meters in 1989, but continued to operate a diary-based service for Canadian markets. The Nielsen Canada people-meter service used technology similar to that of its parent U.S. company. The Nielsen national service is called, in both countries, the NTI or "Nielsen Television Index." (Nielsen local market-level measurements are known as the "NBI," for "Nielsen Broadcast Index.")

In 1995, Nielsen Canada and BBM reached an "accord" that segmented the nation's television audience measurement system and established a division of labour between the two organizations. Under the terms of the accord, Nielsen meters would provide the only national-level measurement service. Nielsen would also provide metered measurement of the Ontario region and the Toronto/Hamilton market. To do this, the number of people-meter households in the market area was to be increased in order for the market to be independently reportable via people meter. Nielsen agreed to withdraw from market measurement elsewhere in Canada, although the accord did set a timetable for the potential future expansion of Nielsen people meters into the Vancouver/Victoria market and into Quebec for regional network reporting.

BBM became the exclusive measurement service for all non-Toronto markets as a result of the accord–though with the prospect of losing additional major markets as the Nielsen meter panel expanded. In exchange, BBM agreed to withdraw both its diary-based network service and its reporting of the Toronto/Hamilton market (although a limited number of diaries were placed in Toronto/Hamilton in order to estimate the "spill" into the area from stations in Barrie, Kitchener/Waterloo, and Peterborough). BBM was permitted, under the accord, to continue to develop new forms of meter technology. Since 1992, BBM had been co-operating with Arbitron of the United States in an effort to develop a personal, portable, passive people meter. BBM also worked with Taylor Nelson Sofres of the U.K., testing "picture matching"–a novel and unconventional method of making channel identification available to people meter systems.

The accord was presented to the industry as an opportunity to end the expensive "duplication" of competing measurements. This had been a sore point with subscribers, many of whom previously felt compelled to sign on with both services. Subscribers were also hoping to–but did not necessarily–obtain lower fees and a "common currency" of audience estimates. The accord also allowed each service's ongoing production stream to specialize in the methods and technologies that it knew best. Finally, the agreement was hailed as a chance for the industry to catch its collective breath and plan rationally for the future in a less turbulent environment.

The 1995 accord was to have been in effect for a four-year term, but each of the measurement services had the option to pull out with a six-month notification period. Some eighteen months into the accord, BBM announced its intent to withdraw in order to test and implement new people-meter technology that it felt was, in several respects, superior to the system used by Nielsen. BBM's system determined the channel being viewed by virtue of the "picture matching" process (described later). BBM maintained that "picture matching" is compatible with the impending shift to digital (as opposed to current-day analog) broadcast signals. Most importantly, BBM argued that, in a digital environment with multiplexed channels, Nielsen's analog tuner-probe technology will no longer be capable of correctly identifying the channel being viewed. BBM's test and initial roll-out were both conducted in the Vancouver/Victoria market, where Nielsen had enlarged its own meter sample for local market reporting roughly one year earlier.

The two organizations are currently involved in a "shoot-out" with potentially dramatic consequences. Many observers feel that the "winner" in Vancouver will gain an insurmountable advantage, and that the "loser" will be in danger of being driven from the Canadian TV audience-measurement landscape. This battle, however, may be a long one. Both are capable and determined organizations, and Nielsen, in particular, has the capacity to persevere through many lean years, provided that its multinational and American parent corporations feel that such a strategy is worthwhile. At this writing, it is still far too early to predict a winner.

Two Types of Television Measurement Systems: A Closer Look at Diaries and People Meters

Audience measurement in Canada is conducted using two different technologies: viewing diaries and electronic people meters. Details of the systems' operations appear below. The two systems produce related but not directly comparable results.

Viewing and Listening Diary Measurement Procedures

Until 1989 when Nielsen Media Research launched a national system for electronic measurement of television audiences, all syndicated audience measurement in Canada relied upon the use of viewing and listening diaries distributed to a sample of households. Diaries continue to provide measurement for all Canadian radio markets, and all but the very largest Canadian television markets. In vastly simplified form, diary-based audience surveys are organized as follows: the measurement service contacts selected sample households by telephone and asks them to accept, complete, and return specially prepared diaries in which household members record their TV or radio use for a period of one week. Thus, reports will be based upon estimates of the number

of viewers or listeners attracted to a given station, channel, network, or program in a particular week.

The TV diary is printed in the form of a booklet and is structured so that for each measured day, a viewing entry can be made for any 15-minute period from 6:00 a.m. until 2:00 a.m. the following morning. A typical TV record entry consists of the station tuned (by channel number), the call letters or network identification, and the title of the program seen. The viewing of any person two years of age and over (2+) will be recorded in this manner. To anticipate later discussion, the age threshold for radio measurement is slightly higher, with reports collected on the behaviour of any person 12 years and older (12+), while the measured radio day begins at 5:00 a.m. and ends at 1:00 am.[6]

"Market" or "sweep" surveys using diaries are conducted on a seasonal basis, with the largest taking place during the fall and spring, when data are collected during November and March respectively. Sweeps represent intensive periods of TV measurement and are designed to produce data for local broadcasters, although sweep data can be aggregated across local markets and reported on the basis of larger geographic units. With a few exceptions, stations in all but the largest of markets receive data only during sweep periods.

Seasonal "sweep" surveys are multi-week enterprises, but with each week measured independently (i.e., even when adjacent weeks are surveyed, the second week is measured using a new and different set of respondents). Because program scheduling tends to be based on a weekly program grid, reported estimates often represent averages computed across the number of weeks contained in the survey, although single-week estimates are also available. However, no household participating in the "sweep" survey does so for more than one of the measured weeks.

Due to the commitment to reporting at the level of local-station audiences, sweep surveys are obliged to have a sufficient number of respondents in each TV market to generate reliable local estimates and information on the composition of program audiences. Therefore, sweep samples are very large when compared to the samples of other institutions that engage in survey research. For example, a national public-opinion poll found in a newspaper might contain between 1,500 and 2,500 respondents nationwide. The fall and spring sweep surveys conducted by

BBM contain roughly 85,000 persons (averaging slightly more than 20,000 per week over four weeks).

Despite the effort invested in their execution, diary-based surveys have a number of shortcomings. The Canadian media environment is very sophisticated. Roughly 75 percent of Canadians live in households with cable-TV service, and many cabled households can receive 50 or more channels. It is often difficult for respondents to correctly identify and report the stations and programs that they have watched, even when they try their best to provide an accurate record of their TV-viewing behaviour. Due to respondent confusion, a certain number of diary entries will erroneously attribute viewing to a station other than the one being watched. Cable simulcast-substitution policies add to the difficulty in correctly identifying the station tuned. When Canadian and American stations are both showing the same program, cable companies will often substitute or duplicate the Canadian station's signal on the American station's assigned cable channel. The proliferation of remote-control devices further confounds diary measurement. Viewers will often switch back and forth between several channels during each 15-minute reporting period, only to find that the design of the diary permits only one station or program to be entered for each quarter-hour.[7] Finally, viewing is not always recorded as it takes place, but is often reconstructed from memory after the fact. This practice will also contribute to reporting error, as high-profile "hit" programs or programming on frequently watched or heavily promoted channels will stand the best chance of being recalled. Lightly viewed channels or less-prominent programs may be missed in the recall process and underreported as a result.

The growth of cable-specialty channels poses an additional problem for diary measurement. Remembering that diary-based audience estimates are produced in weekly "snapshots" (where the only viewing credited to a channel is that recorded during the week when survey participants hold viewing diaries), it is difficult to measure the behaviour of viewers who tune to specialty channels on an occasional basis (not once every week, but once every *few* weeks). Such a viewing pattern does not lend itself to measurement using one-week diary-based survey procedures. The problem here, of course, is that "occasional" viewers who hold diaries can "look like non-viewers" if their tuning happens to occur in weeks before or after—but not during—the measured survey week. A longer base measurement period would restate and enlarge the estimated cumulative number of viewers over that longer-time interval, in a manner consistent with the way viewers actually use certain specialty services.

People-Meter Methods in Television Research

The response of TV-audience measurement services to the problems outlined has been the people meter—an electronic device designed to collect and record a log of viewing behaviour as it occurs. The Nielsen meter is connected to the TV set by a probe attached to the tuner. The probe automatically monitors the status of the set by tracking the day, time, set on or off, and station tuned.[8] Associated devices containing tuners of their own (e.g., VCR's or set-top cable boxes) have a potential impact on channel selection, and so these must also be wired by Nielsen in order to determine which channel the household is watching.

The new meters deployed by BBM carry out these same functions, but do not use a tuner-probe method to determine the station tuned. By contrast, the "picture matching" system used by BBM's meter determines the channel in a multi-step process. First, whenever a metered set is in use, the meter evaluates and records the characteristics of a stream of sampled elements from the pictures being displayed by the set. This summarized information is time-stamped and stored. Second, the summarized picture data is later forwarded to BBM by the meter. Finally, the channel tuned is identified by matching the meter's time-stamped and summarized picture elements against a master reference database. The reference database is constructed at a central site where all channels or stations receivable in the area are continuously monitored. "Monitoring" consists of applying the same process used by the meters in the field: picture sampling, the evaluation of sampled elements, and the storage of time-stamped summarized data on picture characteristics.

The "people" element of the people meter is achieved by further co-operation of household members. The system seeks not only the "behaviour" of the TV set, but also specific information on who is watching. All members are asked to indicate their presence in the audience by pressing a numbered or lettered button on a remote-control device. Every household member has a button, and the system's design allows the individual's demographic characteristics (age, gender, language, and others) to be attached to all viewing records generated by any individual known to the system. Participants are expected to log themselves in when the television is first turned on, and to log in and out as they enter and leave the room where viewing is taking place.

Meter measurement uses a panel-sample design; households remain members of the people-meter sample for an extended period (two years or more). This characteristic enables researchers to track individual and household viewing patterns over longer periods and moderates the "snapshot" quality of diary-based measurement. A panel design has its own limitations, however. Large samples are important in measuring the composition of specialty audiences but the number of respondents in the people-meter panel is basically constant from week to week, unlike diary designs where multi-week averages can dramatically increase the number of cases available for analysis.[9]

In a people-meter system, meters automatically report a day's set of records to the host computer at the offices of the measurement service. This transaction is conducted via modem and telephone late at night. Transmission and recovery of data takes only a few seconds and does not disturb the participating household or interfere with its use of the telephone. The speed of electronic measurement is in sharp contrast to the diary system, where paper booklets must be distributed and returned through the mail (and their contents edited and then keypunched into computer records before processing can begin in earnest). Compared with the diary system, turn-around time is dramatically reduced for the calculation and publication of audience estimates. Where broadcast managers once had to wait weeks for estimates for a given program, people meters have the capacity to provide audience estimates only days after the show went to air.

Nielsen Media Research launched its Canadian national people-meter service in September 1989 as a counterpart to the one its parent company was already operating in the United States. At first, sample sizes were only large enough to produce national, and not local, estimates, but since then, Nielsen has expanded its sample of households and established North America's first people-meter market in Toronto/Hamilton in 1995. Nielsen added the Vancouver/Victoria market in 1997.

BBM has also been active in developing and testing people-meter systems, but did not deploy a system on a permanent basis until 1998, in the Vancouver/Victoria market. BBM plans to have meters in the Toronto market and Ontario region and in Quebec by fall 2000, with a full national service available

in 2001. Prior to the 1998 launch, BBM intensively tested an earlier people-meter design in the summer of 1990, but ultimately abandoned that initiative citing high costs and reservations about the quality of panel members' button-pushing behaviour—an abiding concern in any system dependent on the unfailing co-operation of household members. Meanwhile, BBM continues to work with Arbitron on the development of its portable passive people meter.

Reporting Terminology: What Is a Rating?

Audience estimates are produced in a number of different ways, reflecting different methods of "scorekeeping" applied to the basic data generated by diary- and meter-based measurement technologies. Since those technologies are in flux, this discussion will steer away from yet another underlying set of operational definitions—specifying exactly what qualifies as listening or viewing.[10] One of the most stunning differences produced by the changing technology is in the interval of measurement. Diaries use 15-minute measurement and recording intervals. By contrast, people meters can measure and record intervals as short as several seconds. Again, however, the intent here is to provide an intuitive rather than an intensely technical understanding of commonly used audience-research measures.

Audience measurement "ratings" should *not* be confused with other kinds of "ratings" proclaiming that movies or TV programs are suitable, in terms of content, for particular kinds of audiences. Nor should they be confused with measures of the degree to which programming is "liked" or "enjoyed" by its audience. In the realm of television audience measurement, "ratings" (when used in a collective sense) will refer to estimates of the size and composition of program audiences. However, estimates expressed in "rating points" are but one of several ways of summarizing the size and nature of broadcast audiences.

The common element underling all summary measures is an estimate of the number of viewers or listeners for a given program, time block, day, or measured week. This estimate is based upon a projection to the larger population of the viewing and listening patterns observed in the research sample recruited by the measurement service. "Projection to the population" implies the ability to do four related things. First, one must have a research sample of a size and quality suitable for generating projectable results. Second, one must have a reliable method for recording what was watched, and when, and by whom in the sample. Third, one must be able to define the relevant units of geography where the measurements are taken. Fourth, one must make use of a detailed knowledge of the population residing in those same areas–its overall size, with breakdowns by age, gender, and other characteristics.

For audience estimates dealing with programs and coherent time blocks, the basic measurements are the "average minute audience" (for people meters) and the "average quarter-hour audience" (in diary systems). In order to summarize people meter data in "average minute audience" form, a program or time block will be broken down into a series of minute-by-minute estimates that are then averaged across the number of minutes in the analysis. The reported "average minute audience" is the result of that final averaging process. The detailed individual-minute estimates required to perform the calculations are typically used only as behind-the-scenes "ingredients" by computerized systems–although individual-minute data can be extracted, if necessary. With diary data, a program or time block is broken into its component 15-minute measurement periods, and the individual estimates for each period are averaged, yielding the "average quarter-hour audience."

A rating point is a population-based measure where the estimated audience (from within a defined geographic area) is equal to one percent of the population of that same area. So if a program has a rating of 12, the average audience was equal to 12 percent of the area's population. In a slightly looser interpretation, 12 percent of the area's population was watching the program. Given the population basis for the calculation, an area must always be defined in order for the rating proportion to be computed and reported. Rating points can also be computed in group-specific terms (e.g., among children, teens, or women 18-49 years of age, again always in some defined area). In each case, the underlying calculation reflects the estimated number of group members viewing, divided by the group population. Ratings are usually associated with local TV markets, where all or most of the population has access to the signals of broadcasters with stations originating in the central city (or cities) of the area. Boundaries for these market areas are defined by negotiated consensus within the broadcast industry.

Also prominent as a summary measure is station or network reach. Those encountering references to "reach" for the first time may expect it to have to do with signal access–but this is not the case. Instead, reach is another measure of viewing behaviour. Reach estimates are unduplicated counts of the number of viewers or listeners attracted by a station or network in a defined time period (such as a time block, a broadcast day, or a measured week). The term "unduplicated" implies that audience members are counted once and only once, no matter how often they appear and reappear in the audience, and no matter how long they spend with the broadcast service in question. The reach estimate therefore produces a two-fold classification, distinguishing between those who viewed and those who failed to do so during the time period stated. Over a measured week, almost all Canadians will be counted as having been "reached" by at least one broadcast or cable service, and the vast majority will have been reached by several. A measured viewer who samples many channels over the course of a week can, in theory, contribute to the reach of as many TV services as can be received in the measured household. Reach estimates are typically based on the smallest unit of viewing available from the system of measurement at hand. With diaries, the smallest unit collected is the quarter-hour, so viewers have to log at least one quarter-hour of tuning to a given channel in order to contribute to its reach. By contrast, the smallest unit in meter systems is the measured minute, and this brief duration is all that is required for a viewer to be classified as having been "reached." Reach estimates are not directly comparable between the two technologies. Meter systems, with their comparatively "low" one-minute behavioural hurdle, will produce very liberal, high-magnitude reach estimates. Diary systems, with a "higher" 15-minute qualifying hurdle, will produce far more conservative estimates.

A final commonly used measure is audience share, which expresses the amount of time viewers spent with a given program or network as a percentage of the total number of minutes (or quarter-hours, in a diary system) spent by the population with all TV services during a specified time period. Weekly station or network shares, then, really represent the proportion of all viewing time (as opposed to an estimated number of persons) devoted to a given broadcaster. This rule linking share to viewing time is often bent, however, for 30- or 60-minute periods that correspond to the duration of an individual program. In such a case, share values are often loosely described *as if* the calculation were based on "viewers" instead of "viewing time." The "viewers" interpretation is technically incorrect, but over short measurement intervals, it does not do a severe injustice to the data. Share calculations are distinct from the computation of rating points, where the entire population is used as the basis for the calculation. In off-peak hours (when the number of available viewers or listeners is small), program audiences may not be reportable in rating points, but often will be reportable in terms of share values—indicating that the program may have attracted a relatively large "slice" of a small available viewing "pie."

Television Audience Measurement in Transition

The Launch of the People Meter and Its Impact on the Broadcast Industry

Any period of change in the "industry standard" for doing business is always an anxious one. To a large degree, the acceptability of diary-based data was a negotiated agreement among its various users. A change in the practice of measurement, however, implies that there can also be changes to these negotiated understandings. If prompted to focus upon the diary system, most users of audience research could produce a long list of deficiencies in data-collection procedures. At the same time, system users were, on most occasions, willing to overlook these shortcomings in favour of getting on with business.[11]

Commercial-broadcast management practices are, in many respects, accommodations to the prevailing form of measurement. When research methods change, often the data change as well. The commercial implications of the advent of the people meter have sent shock waves through the industry. Commercial broadcasters are concerned that their advertising revenues will decline if the people meter should report smaller audiences than had customarily been reported under diary measurement. Many advertisers, by contrast, would welcome this outcome, feeling that they could reduce their costs at the broadcasters' expense. Ironically, disruptions due to changes in the measurement system are not directly linked to the actual viewing behaviour of the Canadian population. On the day that diary measurement ceased and metered measurement began, there was no massive change in the viewing habits of Canadians. What did change, however, was the *industry's method of knowing* about those habits. To the extent that different methods produce different results, the industry's *understanding* of the audience changes, as does its practices of responding to that understanding.

Consider the challenge of measuring the viewing of young children between the ages of two and six. Without parental assistance in completing children's

diary entries, the viewing of young children will most likely be underreported. The same is true of metered measurement. Unless parents are willing to intervene, very young children may not be able to log themselves into and out of the people-meter audience with the accuracy generally expected of panel participants.

Unlogged children's viewing is a topic of serious concern in meter-based systems, but was never a major focus of attention under the diary system. In diary-based measurement, underreporting of unsupervised children's viewing is "invisible." It is gone without a trace—and without any reminder that it has been missed or underreported. There may be error, but no unacceptable contradiction in the returned data. By contrast, when confronted with improperly reported children's viewing, the ever-vigilant people meter will detect that the TV set was on and a particular channel tuned, or even that channel changes were taking place—but the meter record will also show that no household member was properly logged into the audience. This is a thoroughly undesirable state of affairs under the rules established for people-meter data, since a record of the set's behaviour alone (without at least one viewer's presence declared to the meter) is insufficient to attribute an audience to the program tuned. Children are a major source of unlogged viewing, but as culprits, they are by no means the only ones. Anyone living in a metered household can generate records of "null viewing," where the set is on but no audience member is logged into the system.

There is no perfect system of measurement, and as a consequence people-meter data also has its shortcomings. Problems with metered data and even the basic ground rules for editing and processing the data must be handled through a process of negotiation. In spite of its microchips, modems, host computers, and other advanced hardware, a people-meter system is in part a technical enterprise and in part social construction. Broadcasters and advertisers are lobbying for the establishment of subtly different sets of measurement and reporting practices that they feel will be to their own long-term advantage. Each group is pushing for a distinct and competing standard in an effort to ensure economically favourable results for its sector of the industry.

Advertisers have long feared that viewers' efforts at "commercial avoidance" reduce the size of the audience viewing the messages, compared to the programming minutes on either side of a commercial pod. Viewer behaviours such as channel-flipping via the TV remote control and taking trips out of the room (and away from the TV) during commercial breaks are held to be responsible. Given this premise, program-length average-minute audiences are claimed to overstate the number of viewers that were actually exposed to the commercials. Since the people meter has the capacity to report audiences on a minute-by-minute basis, many advertisers are pressing for the reporting of audiences for individual commercials (or the specific minutes that contain them) as well as for programs. If the reporting of commercial minutes were to become accepted as common practice, the commercial's own audience—rather than that of the programing that contains or surrounds it—would determine the value of the advertising time.

The process is by no means strictly technical. It is also driven by industry politics and economics, the level of co-operation that research participants are willing to provide, and the level of intrusion that respondents are willing to tolerate. The ideal system is a tall order. It must be acceptable to broadcasters, advertisers, and agencies as providing detailed credible data from large research samples, all at reasonable cost. Such a system would obtain voluminous quantities of detailed information, and yet be relatively unobtrusive to those supplying the data to the measurement service.

New Developments in the Viewing Environment and Audience-Measurement Technology

The technical aspects of audience measurement, however, present interesting challenges. Part of the challenge lies in the expectation that the television environment of the future will likely be very different from the one seen in the year 2000. Further, the shape and speed of these changes cannot yet be specified, except for a few initial generalizations. Digital broadcasting will prompt a convergence between TV sets and personal computers; between programming and on-line information services. Computers will be capable of showing high definition television transmissions. Viewers will be able to link on the fly to related websites for additional detail or background information. In this portrait, video will become an increasingly customized and interactive experience. Fragmentation will likely increase as a result of the availability of additional signals, since several multiplexed digital signals can be carried where a single conventional signal currently resides. Several of the cable specialty channels licensed by the CRTC in 1996 currently realize only a portion of

their eventual signal access. In specific areas and cable systems, these services are in a holding pattern due to the scarcity of traditional analog channels. Once the broadcast system converts to digital distribution, these barriers will disappear. Television signals will appear on wider, flatter screens and with greater clarity than is currently available.

BBM and Nielsen, rivals in Canadian television audience measurement, are deploying new technologies and developing new and competing lines of business that both reflect and foreshadow changes in the technical, viewing, and commercial environments. In response to the emergence of the Internet as an advertising medium, both organizations are now actively measuring Internet use, in addition to their traditional broadcast measurement activities. The New Media Division of BBM (created in 1996) participated in the fall 1998 launch of Media Metrix Canada, a joint venture with Media Metrix, Inc. of New York, a leading provider of Internet measurement. By May 2000, BBM was installing measurement software on the personal computers of its people-meter panel households in order to track TV viewing done on computer. For its part, Nielsen U.S. announced a strategic alliance with NetRatings Inc. and launched a Nielsen/NetRatings service in 1999. Nielsen Canada announced the creation of a parallel service in January 2000, with ongoing measurement scheduled to begin by mid-year.

The emerging digital television environment poses a challenge in positively identifying the channel to which the TV sets of meter panel members are tuned. Nielson's traditional people-meter technology employed one or more analog probes to determine the status of the tuner on the set, and the tuner of any other device (e.g., VCR, set-top converter/decoder) capable of resolving a signal itself and passing it on to the set. Nielsen's rival, BBM, claims that this system will not be able to measure digital broadcasts because carried within the bandwidth allocated to each current "channel" will ultimately be two or more different digital signals, which will need to be distinguished from one another and measured independently. Nielsen, while admitting the long-term vulnerability of the tuner-probe approach, issued a counterclaim that BBM's "picture matching" is just an interim solution because signals in a fully digital environment will eventually be customized by viewers to such an extent that the image presented to the viewer is no longer likely to match against a standard, non-customized benchmark reference. Nielsen claims that, if this should happen, rates of "unattributed viewing" in picture-matching measurement systems (e.g., tuning to signals that the picture-matching system cannot identify) will climb to unacceptable levels. Nielsen's answer is found in a devices like the A/P (Active/Passive) Meter, which reads codes that identify program content and commercials, and the Software Meter, which is being developed in co-operation with the Microsoft Corporation and is designed to enable measurement of television signals viewed on a personal computer.

A Canadian Internet-TV news service, "WorkdayTV" (www.workdaytv.com), is in the forefront of the delivery of live audio and video to desktop computers. Launched in April 2000, WorkdayTV transmits direct to the Internet from a mobile truck based in Toronto's business district. The service broadcasts live reports and interviews whenever financial markets are open. It is designed to bring breaking news to the computers of workers in the financial sector and those who follow financial markets at home. The service launched using a commercial model, selling both Internet-style "banner" advertising and television-style 30-second commercial time units (one of the first examples of the sale of "commercial time" on the Internet). As Internet broadcast services of this type mature and multiply, they will require a reliable system of audience measurement in order to justify continued investment by sponsors, and to allow broadcasters and advertisers to agree on the value of the commercial time sold.

In addition to adapting to a changing technical environment, research into new methods of television audience measurement has also been directed towards making measurement observations more automated and less dependent on the compliance of respondents as perennial button-pushers. New measurement systems on the horizon are designed to be as "passive" as possible, and often use high-tech electronics and elements of "artificial intelligence" to replace the information currently supplied by panel members. In response to the burden of logging oneself into and out of the people-meter audience, Nielsen Media Research in the U.S. was at one time developing a "passive people meter" system that it believed would be the successor to the push-button people meter. This system was to have used visual imaging and image-recognition systems to scan the room containing the TV, identify household members by comparing them to stored data from reference photographs, and automatically log them into and out of the audience whenever the TV set is on and they are in the room. In this way,

participants would no longer have to press buttons to indicate their presence in or absence from the audience. Sceptics felt that this system traded one form of intrusiveness for another more ominous pattern of surveillance, although Nielsen representatives maintained that they anticipated no difficulties with household acceptance if the system were to replace existing meters. For whatever reason, discussion of this proposed system has cooled in recent years.

Nielsen has several other less radical developments under way. One is the Active/Passive (A/P) meter, which will be able to identify digital signals by codes that they carry and generate interim codes for programs that lack them. The A/P meter is a clear alternative to the current analog probe method of determining the station tuned. Nielsen Canada does not expect to conduct a rapid wholesale conversion of existing meters to the A/P system, but does plan to install A/P devices on a gradual basis, where changes in household circumstances warrant it.

BBM, in co-operation with Arbitron in the U.S., is developing a competing device–the personal, portable, passive people meter. The unit was initially known as the "4-P" meter, but is now simply referred to as the Arbitron PPM (the portable people meter). This device, about the size of a current-day pager, would be carried or worn by survey participants but would require no further button pushing or other intervention, other than docking in a "hub" at home each night. The "hub" would both re-charge the portable unit and download the information collected and retained from the previous day. The meter is designed to listen for and detect highly subtle codes that can be embedded in television sound tracks and radio broadcast signals, supplying programming streams with acoustic "fingerprints" that are inaudible to viewers and listeners. The meter will recognize and record the code, which can later be identified as belonging to a particular TV or radio station. The detection technology was developed by Arbitron with the assistance of Lockheed Martin, which had been a major U.S. defense contractor. The division that is working on the coding and decoding of inaudible signals was famous, during the Cold War, for making sonar arrays for nuclear submarines.

Originally, BBM and Arbitron had hoped to deploy the "4-P" meter in large-scale tests in 1995. But shortly after BBM announced its intended timetable for testing and roll-out, Arbitron stunned the industry in November 1993 by announcing that it would terminate its U.S. television measurement service–effectively ceding the marketplace to Nielsen as a monopoly supplier. Arbitron continued to operate its U.S. radio measurement service, and proclaimed a commitment to further development of the "4-P" meter (which could also measure radio audiences) in spite of the television measurement shutdown. Development has indeed continued, though at a slower pace than had previously been forecast.

The Arbitron PPM, as the "4-P" meter came to be known, offers the intriguing capacity to combine TV- and radio-measurement activity with a unified research sample. If realized, this could moderate the effective cost of operating the service, enable researchers to conduct cross-medium analyses, and could also provide estimates of out-of-home TV viewing (not presently available from existing measurement systems that are connected in one way or another to the television sets that "host" them). In June 2000, Arbitron announced that a radio measurement field trial for the PPM would be conducted in Wilmington, Delaware, beginning in fall 2000. Increases in sample size and test-area geography to the full Philadelphia market (within which Wilmington is nested) are planned for late 2001.

Also in June 2000, the U.S. branch of Nielsen Media Research agreed to participate in the Arbitron Wilmington and Philadelphia PPM field trials and simultaneously acquired the option to participate in the deployment of the Arbitron PPM in the United States. In Canada, however, circumstances are different. BBM—due to its participation in the early development of the Arbitron meter—holds the exclusive Canadian rights to the signal-encoding technology central to the operation of the system. This condition potentially confines Nielsen's North American use of the Arbitron PPM to the United States, unless an accommodation can be worked out with BBM.

Audience Research Findings: A Viewer-Centred Portrait of Canadian Broadcast Audiences

The Television Environment, Viewing Habits, and Behaviour

Television is present in almost every Canadian home. In 1997, an estimated 99.2 percent of Canadian households had at least one TV set, and 98.7 percent had at least one colour TV.[12] During 1998, programming was provided by 155 originating Canadian TV stations, 129 of which were commercial ventures. In addition, the nation was served by 47 cable specialty and pay-specialty networks.[13] In addition, the BBM Bureau of Measurement in its fall 1999 survey, estimated that 86 percent of Canadians (2+) live in households containing videocassette recorders (VCRs), which are used to play back time-shifted broadcast and cable programming, purchased or rented tapes, or home movies produced by Camcorders. An estimated 75 percent of Canadians (2+) live in homes with cable-TV service, and 8 percent of Canadians (2+) live in homes with satellite dishes—further expanding the range of available viewing choices by providing both "distant signals" (difficult or impossible to receive by antenna alone) and a number of specialty channels. With the recent introduction of "small" satellite dishes intended for direct-to-home transmission, satellite is becoming an increasingly popular choice for Canadians. The proportion of persons in satellite-equipped homes has almost tripled in two years (from an estimated 3 percent in fall 1997). The "small" dishes are still about the size of large pizza pans, but they are much smaller than the traditional satellite dishes that used to dominate the occasional Canadian back yard.

Not only are TVs and TV services themselves ubiquitous, but almost all Canadians come into contact with TV at some time each week. Reach estimates for "all stations" illustrate this fact. During the fall 1999 BBM seasonal-survey period, an estimated 96 percent of the Canadian population watched at least some TV each week. Most people use TV on a daily basis. On a typical day, 76 percent of Canadians (2+) will use TV. Figure 1 shows how Canadians use TV across the broadcast day. The line chart shows the proportions of adults (18+), teens (12-17), and children (2-11) using TV at different times.[14]

Audiences are at their highest during prime time (7:00 p.m. to 11:00 p.m.), with a peak between 8:00 p.m. and 10:00 p.m., when 39 percent of the population, and 43 percent of adult Canadians, will be watching TV. Morning, daytime, and late-night use of TV is considerably lower than the prime-time peak. During the morning, roughly 15 percent of children will be using TV and much of this viewing is supplied by pre-schoolers at the lower end of the children's 2-11 age continuum. Teens and older children are typically in school during weekday-morning and early-afternoon hours, while on weekdays adults are often at work, either in or out of the home. Prior to noon, less than 10 percent of the population is using TV, followed by a slight local peak at lunchtime. In the early afternoon, the proportion of Canadian adults using TV hovers at about 10 percent before beginning (at about 3:00 p.m.) a gradual climb towards the evening peak viewing

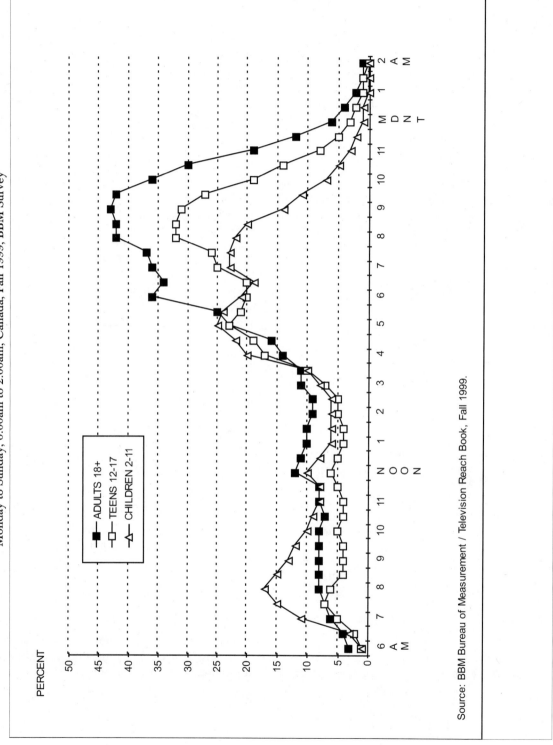

FIGURE 1: Percentage of Adults (18+), Teens (12-17), and Children (1-11) in the Television Audience, Monday to Sunday, 6:00am to 2:00am, Canada, Fall 1999, BBM Survey

Source: BBM Bureau of Measurement / Television Reach Book, Fall 1999.

FIGURE 2: Percentage Distribution by Daypart, Weekly Broadcast Hours, and Television Viewing Hours, Canada, All Persons 2+, Fall 1999

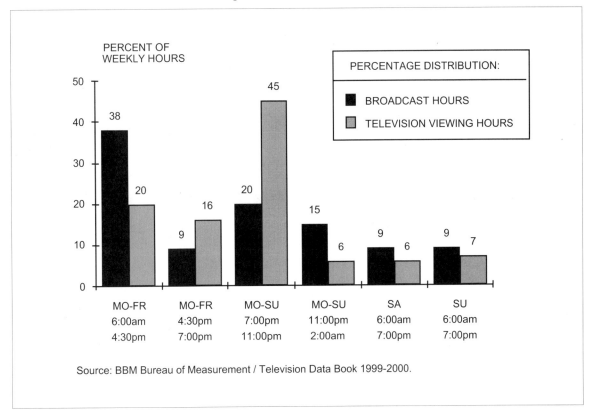

Source: BBM Bureau of Measurement / Television Data Book 1999-2000.

hours. In the late evening, the proportion of the population using TV declines rapidly. Clearly, what is "late" varies by age group. Children begin leaving the TV audience first, followed by teens. Adults persist later into the evening than do the two younger groups, but even here the proportion using TV is in rapid decline by 10:30 p.m.

A different perspective on TV viewing is obtained by examining the number of hours of TV viewing at different times of the day or week. Segmenting the week into a series of "dayparts," Figure 2 contains a percentage distribution of weekly measured broadcast hours on the one hand, and TV viewing hours devoted by the national audience on the other. Once again, the importance of the prime-time (7:00 p.m.-11:00 p.m.) block from Monday to Sunday is unmistakable. This period contains 20 percent of the measured week, but receives 45 percent of all hours spent with TV by the Canadian population.

How much time does the typical Canadian spend with TV each week? Expressed on a per-capita basis, Canadians (2+) watched an average of 21.6 hours per week during the fall 1999 BBM survey period. To anticipate later discussion, women (18+) reported the heaviest levels of TV use (at 25.5 hours per week), and children (2-11) and teens (12-17) reported the lightest levels (each at 15.5 hours per week). The heaviest viewers in the Canadian population tend to be older adults (60+).

Viewing time has been trending gradually downward in recent years, as illustrated in Figure 3, which shows per capita viewing hours for Canadians (2+) over the period 1989-99. There is considerable debate over the extent to which time spent with the Internet is responsible for declining hours of TV viewing in recent years, although the trend was already in progress prior to the explosion of Internet access. In spite of this gradual decline, television continues to represent a major component of Canadians' leisure time.

Figure 4 presents findings from an analysis of data provided by the fall 1999 BBM seasonal survey. The figure profiles the per-capita average viewing hours by major age and/or sex groupings. Children and

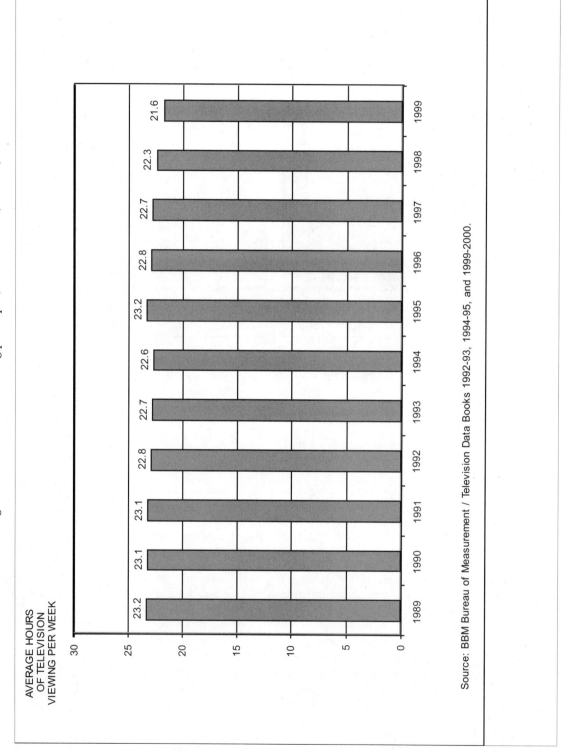

FIGURE 3: Average Hours of Television Viewing per Capita, All Persons 2+, Canada, 1989-99

Source: BBM Bureau of Measurement / Television Data Books 1992-93, 1994-95, and 1999-2000.

FIGURE 4: Average Hours per Week Spent with Television
by BBM Age and Sex Groupings, Canada, Fall 1999

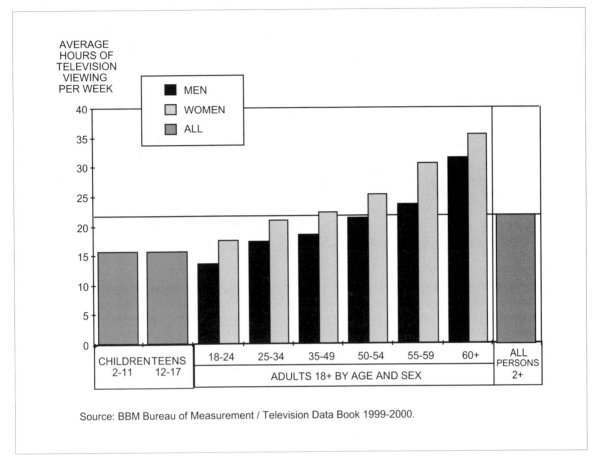

Source: BBM Bureau of Measurement / Television Data Book 1999-2000.

teens are presented together without differentiation by sex, while adults are classified by both age and sex in the analysis. Older adults tend to spend a larger number of hours watching TV than younger adults, with a close relationship observed between increasing age and increasing time spent with TV. Within each adult age group, women tended to be heavier viewers than men. Among all the groupings, children, teens and the youngest adults (18-24) were the lightest viewers.

Per-capita measures and grouped data, however, hide a great deal of individual variation. Differences in time spent with TV are shown in dramatic fashion by BBM's TV viewing quintiles (Figure 5). The quintile groupings are constructed in a two-step process: first, the national BBM sample is rank ordered according to the time each respondent spent with TV; second, this rank-ordered array is segmented into five equal parts called "quintiles," each containing 20 percent of the sample. In this way, the

quintiles themselves represent groupings that can be used as categories in other analyses.

The lightest-viewing quintile (or the 20 percent of the Canadian population that watched the fewest number of hours) accounted for less than 3 percent of all hours spent with TV. Members of this group spent less than 8.25 hours with TV during the measured week, and collectively averaged only 4.0 hours per week. By contrast, the heaviest-viewing 20 percent of the population supplied just over 44 percent of all TV viewing hours. Members of the heaviest-viewing quintile devoted a minimum of 34.25 hours per week to the medium, and averaged 47.7 hours–more than 10 times the average viewing time observed in the lightest-viewing quintile.

Television viewing, like many other behaviours, is subject to seasonal variation, and for TV a prominent characteristic of this variation is a decline during the summer months (see Figure 6). Late fall and winter/spring represent peak periods of viewing, as

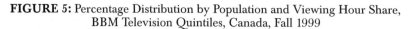

FIGURE 5: Percentage Distribution by Population and Viewing Hour Share,
BBM Television Quintiles, Canada, Fall 1999

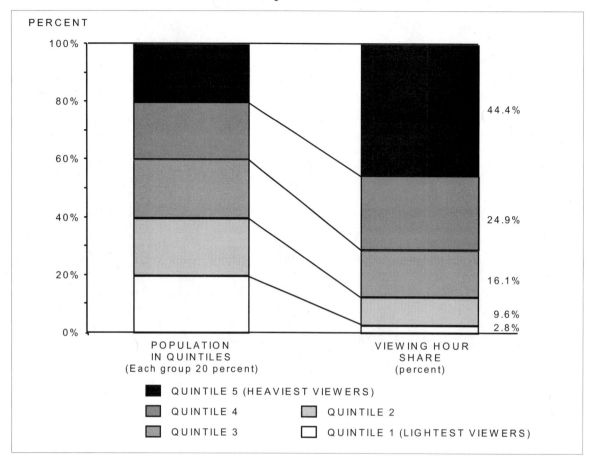

people spend less time outdoors.[15] Over the course of a measured summer week, almost the same number of persons will use TV as come into contact with the medium at other times of the year. However, the average number of hours spent with TV declines markedly during the summer period. Per-capita viewing (2+) during the summer tends to be about 20 percent below the levels observed during the fall and spring measurement periods. In addition to this overall decline in viewing time, viewers also re-apportion their viewing—distributing their viewing time in a different pattern across dayparts. Late night hours receive a slightly higher proportion of time during the summer than in spring and fall. Some groups have dramatically different summer viewing habits relative to the patterns seen in the rest of the year. Teens (12-17), for example, "freed" from school obligations during the summer months, show marked increases in their proportion of time spent with television in the daytime and late-night dayparts.

Viewing by Type of Television Service

Canadians spend more than three-quarters of their viewing time with conventional TV stations and networks, with the bulk clearly devoted to the viewing of Canadian stations. Figure 7 provides a portrait of TV viewing-hour shares by station group, and shows Canadian English and French networks, independent stations, and cable-specialty channels strongly represented.

The distribution of viewing hours by station group also indicates the changing and increasingly competitive and fragmented nature of the Canadian TV industry. In the fall of 1999, almost 30 percent of Canadian viewing time was devoted either to programming played back on a VCR, or to Canadian or American cable-specialty services. This is double the proportion observed in 1992. These are categories that barely existed in the mid 1980s. Their emergence was dramatic, and collectively, these new

FIGURE 6: Summer Season Declines in Viewing Time: Percentage Changes by Age and Sex, Relative to the Average of Spring and Fall Levels, Selected BBM Television Markets,* BBM Television Surveys, 1999

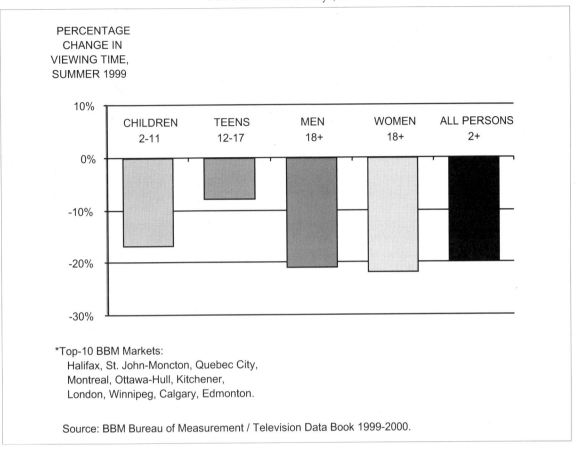

PERCENTAGE CHANGE IN VIEWING TIME, SUMMER 1999

*Top-10 BBM Markets:
Halifax, St. John-Moncton, Quebec City, Montreal, Ottawa-Hull, Kitchener, London, Winnipeg, Calgary, Edmonton.

Source: BBM Bureau of Measurement / Television Data Book 1999-2000.

signal sources have irrevocably changed the Canadian TV environment.

The Sports Network (TSN), which attracts more viewing hours than any other cable-specialty service, first appeared on Canadian cable systems in the fall of 1984, as did MuchMusic. These services were originally pay-discretionary, but later migrated to "extended basic" cable and became available to (and viewed in) many more households than had initially subscribed under pay-TV marketing arrangements. Other cable-specialty services quickly followed. Many more were launched in 1988: YTV Canada (with programming for youth and children), The Family Channel (with a core inventory of Walt Disney programming for children), Vision-TV (featuring multifaith religious programming, documentaries, and arts performances). After clearing some regulatory hurdles, CBC Newsworld (specializing in news and current affairs) was launched in 1989. French-language cable-specialty channels also

commenced operations, with services such as Le Canal Famille (with programming for younger viewers and families), MusiquePlus (a counterpart to MuchMusic), Le Réseau des Sports (companion to TSN), TV-5 (featuring Canadian and international programming in the French language), and Super Écran (movies).

In the 1990s, the number of specialty services grew at a phenomenal rate. In 1996, the CRTC licenced 23 new specialty services–so many that most cable systems could not accommodate all the fledgling channels at once. Several had to go into a holding pattern, awaiting the channel-capacity expansion that will be provided by conversion to digital signal handling. Many of the owners for this fleet of services were already involved in traditional broadcasting–a pattern that had not been seen in the early days of cable-specialty channel development. Among the later group of specialty channels,

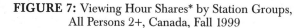

FIGURE 7: Viewing Hour Shares* by Station Groups,
All Persons 2+, Canada, Fall 1999

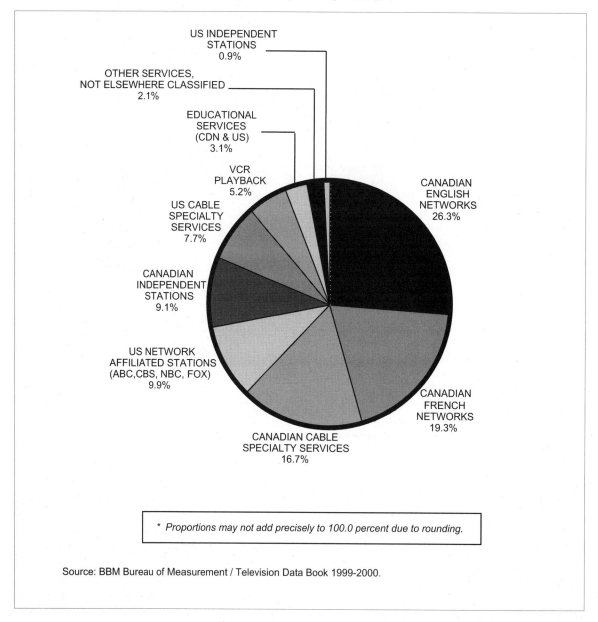

* Proportions may not add precisely to 100.0 percent due to rounding.

Source: BBM Bureau of Measurement / Television Data Book 1999-2000.

Teletoon and CTV Sportsnet have been the quickest to catch on with Canadian viewers.

Pay-per-view television, a different way of organizing and marketing a cable specialty service, first became available on cable in fall 1991. Viewer's Choice offers several channels of programming (with a mixture of movies, concerts, and selected sporting events) available on a pay-per-view basis. The service employs a special addressable-cable decoder that will de-scramble the network's signals when

suitable arrangements have been made in advance between the subscribing household and the cable company. Fees for programs ordered in this manner are added to the household's standard cable charges.

Cable-specialty services are noteworthy both for the share of tuning hours that they attract and for the kinds of material that they deliver. In contrast to the program-driven orientation of conventional TV stations and networks (where widely different kinds of programming will be aired for different target

FIGURE 8: Percentage Distribution of Television Viewing Time by Program Origin: Anglophones, Francophones, and Total Canada, All Persons 2+, Fall 1995

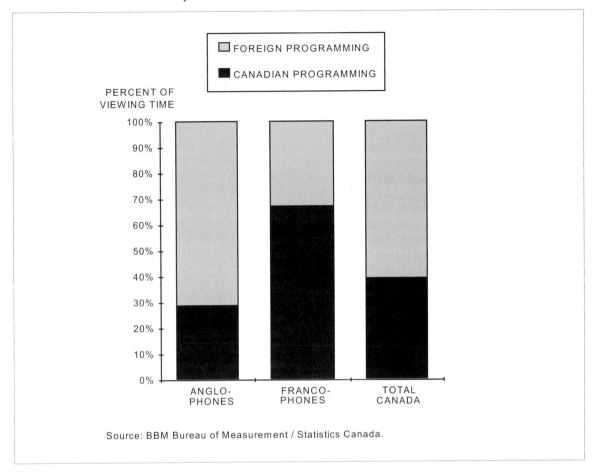

audiences over the course of the broadcast week), cable-specialty services tend to be format-driven, operating within relatively narrow parameters of style and content. Format-driven services also tend to attract audiences that exhibit specific demographic skews. For example, YTV seeks a younger audience of children and teens; TSN attracts an audience primarily (though by no means exclusively), composed of men 18+. There are clear parallels between the format specialization of cable-specialty channels and the historical development of radio (see later discussion on the origin of radio formats).

Videocassette recorders have also changed the competitive TV environment. During the early 1980s, VCRs began appearing in greater numbers. The videocassette recorder was featured on the cover of *Time* magazine in late December 1984, with the accompanying story billing it as "Santa's hottest gift ... a magic box that revolutionizes home viewing."[16] VCR sales were fuelled by a combination of declining

prices and an expanding inventory of prerecorded cassettes for sale or rent. As a result the VCR quickly made its way into Canadian homes. Access to VCRs almost doubled in a single year, from fall 1983, when an estimated 13 percent of Canadians (2+) lived in households containing a VCR, to fall 1984, when 24 percent of Canadians had a VCR at home. Steady growth continued, and by fall 1999 an estimated 86 percent of Canadians had VCRs in their homes.[17]

Not all those with access to a VCR will actually use it in a given week. VCR playback was reported by 28 percent of the Canadian population (2+) in fall 1999, and, as shown in the viewing-hour-share pie chart (Figure 7), VCR playback accounted for 5.2 percent of all hours spent with TV by Canadians. The grand lesson, however, is that VCRs and cable-specialty services have collectively cut into the viewing-hour shares of traditional broadcast stations and networks.

FIGURE 9: Percent of Viewing Time by Program Genre and Origin,
All Persons 2+, Canada, Fall 1995, BBM Survey

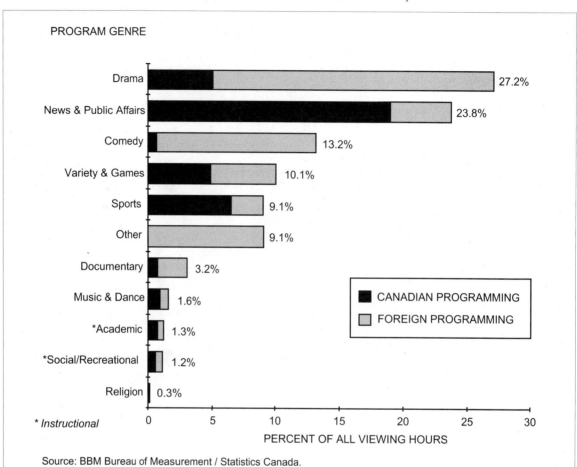

Viewing by Program Origin and Genre

The prominence of Canadian stations and networks seen in Figure 7 does not necessarily mean that viewers are watching Canadian programming. Even on Canadian TV services, the most heavily viewed programs are often those that originate elsewhere—typically in the United States. Figure 8 illustrates a Statistics Canada analysis of fall 1995 BBM data that partitions the viewing hours of Canadians (in three categories: Anglophones, Francophones, and total population) according to the origin of the programming viewed. Among English-speaking Canadians in particular, the proportion of viewing time spent with foreign (again, primarily American) programming is stunning. As a group, Anglophones spend less than 30 percent of their TV viewing time with domestic programming. Francophones are much more heavily reliant on Canadian

programming (spending 67 percent of their viewing time with domestically produced programs), but still devote roughly one-third of their TV viewing time to foreign content. Overall, 61 percent of all TV viewing time of Canadians was spent with imported programming.

What kinds of programming do Canadians watch the most? What are the most popular program genres, and does domestic programming account for more viewing hours within some categories than others? When the time that Canadians spend viewing TV is divided by program genre, the largest quantities of viewing hours are devoted to drama, news and public affairs, comedy, and variety and game shows (see Figure 9, based upon a Statistics Canada analysis of BBM data from the fall 1995 seasonal survey).[18] Roughly three in ten Canadian viewing hours are devoted to drama, while news and public affairs account for 24 percent of viewing time. Comedy and variety and games comprise 13 and 10 percent of viewing time respectively.

Much has been written about Canadians' taste for foreign (generally American) TV programming. An inspection of Figure 9, however, clearly shows that the balance between viewing time devoted to domestic and foreign programming in fact varies widely with program genre. Canadians spend a considerable amount of time following foreign-produced dramatic and comedy productions, but the proportions are markedly reversed for news and public affairs, as well as sports. Within the variety-and-games classification, the balance between domestic and foreign programming is roughly equal.

Readers should also be aware that there are further distinctions to be made in Canadian viewing behaviour by language. Those who follow French-language broadcasts are more likely to watch Canadian-produced programs than are those who spend most of their time with English-language TV. Therefore, if the analysis presented in Figure 9 were reproduced for Anglophones and Francophones, very different results on the dimension of program origin would be observed for each group, as might be expected based on the findings contained in Figure 8.[19]

An analysis geared only to viewing time does not take into account the relative availability of Canadian programming by genre. The proportions reported here reflect a real-life combination of the "menu" (what is offered) and the "diet" (what is consumed).[20] The number of viewing hours devoted to Canadian dramatic productions is limited by a general reluctance, particularly on the part of private broadcasters, to underwrite the production of dramatic series, for a number of reasons. First, it is far less costly to acquire programming than it is to produce it from scratch. Second, regulations allowing simultaneous cable substitution permit Canadian broadcasters to obtain credit for cabled audiences tuned to programming that originates with American networks, since these viewers will see the commercial messages carried by the Canadian station. Third, the "traditional wisdom" within the industry has held that domestic productions have severe difficulties in attracting Canadian audiences in the face of stiff competition from American programming. Finally, Canadian productions have had limited marketing opportunities in the international TV marketplace, with a massively lopsided flow to the exchange of programming between the U.S. and Canada.

Canadian dramatic programming has made the occasional successful foray into the schedules of U.S. broadcast and cable networks, but the histories of these programs remain counterexamples to the U.S. networks' tendency *not* to acquire Canadian adult programming (although Canada has been very successful in exporting children's programming, even to the United States). The notable exceptions include CBC's *Anne of Green Gables* series, and the CBC drama specials *Love and Hate* and *Conspiracy of Silence* that appeared during the summers of 1990 (on NBC) and 1992 (on CBS), respectively. In 1994, the comedy adventure *Due South* became the first Canadian series (as opposed to single-program "specials") to run in prime time on one of the major American networks (CBS). CBS renewed *Due South* for 1995 after initially announcing its intention to cancel the program, but did not renew the series again. Two additional seasons of *Due South* were produced for the Canadian domestic market (on CTV) and for syndication and sale to U.S. cable channels and to broadcasters in Europe and Australia; production ended in March 1998.

Radio—The Other Broadcast Mass Medium in Canada

As of 1999 there were 910 radio stations in Canada: 793 private stations and 117 CBC stations. This was an increase of 200 stations over the 710 existing in 1991. AM frequency radio has declined in importance over the years. In 1991 AM radio had the greatest number of stations (377 stations versus FM's 333), but AM and FM had exact parity in the proportion of Canadians reached (66 percent each of all Canadians 12 years of age or older), and each had an equal share of total hours tuned. By 1999 the situation had entirely changed. FM radio had the greatest number of stations (564 compared to AM's 346), it had the greatest proportion of Canadians reached (78 percent of all Canadians 12 years of age or older, compared to 44 percent for AM), and it had more than two-thirds of total listenership. The popularity of FM stations is now highest with young listeners, while men and women over 65 prefer AM stations.[21]

Like TV, radio is present in almost all Canadian homes (99 percent by 1992). Over three-quarters had two or more radios, which is not surprising. Canadians on average listen to between 21 and 22 hours per week, about the same time as spent with TV and about the same time spent with radio in 1990.[22]

Radio listening is fairly consistent throughout the year. Canadians spend the least amount of time with radio in the fall (21.8 hours per week in 1999). While

FIGURE 10: Average Hours of Radio Tuning by Gender,
Adults 18+, Fall 1999

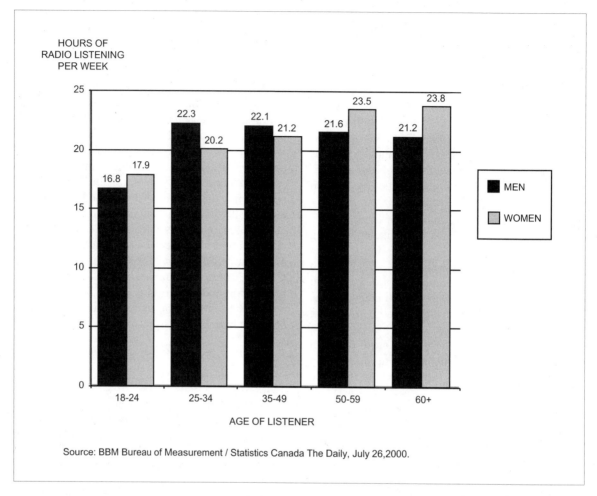

Source: BBM Bureau of Measurement / Statistics Canada The Daily, July 26,2000.

TV viewing decreases in the summer, radio listening increases somewhat (from 22.0 hours per week in spring 1999 to 22.4 hours in summer). Radio has the advantage of portability: when Canadians go to the cottage or beach, they can take their radio with them, or they can listen in the car (95 percent of car commuters listen to radio while travelling to and from work). Seventy-nine percent of adults listen to radio at home, 72 percent listen in vehicles, and nearly one-quarter (24 percent) listen at work.

Adult women listen to radio the most (around 21.4 hours per week), with adult men a close second (21.3 hours). Figure 10 illustrates that, as adult Canadians age, their listening to radio increases somewhat, especially among women over 50 (after age 50, male listening declines slightly). Teens spend much less time with radio: 11 hours per week. Radio reach increases with income, like newspapers and

magazines, but unlike TV.[23] As seen in Figure 11, radio listening peaks in the early morning, between 7:00 and 9:00 a.m., when people get up. Among adults, listening declines in the evening, after people get home from work and school, and when many watch TV. Among teens, listening levels increase in the afternoon and are above adult levels in the evening, a pattern that has remained consistent in recent years.[24]

As the oldest electronic mass medium, radio demonstrates some of the difficulties of measurement: the nature of the technology and its content has changed beyond recognition from the first Canadian radio broadcast in 1920. The penetration of radio was unprecedented in its heyday. The daily "soap opera" format of TV was perfected on radio, and the format of the first dramatic and comic TV programs were directly taken from radio (including many of the

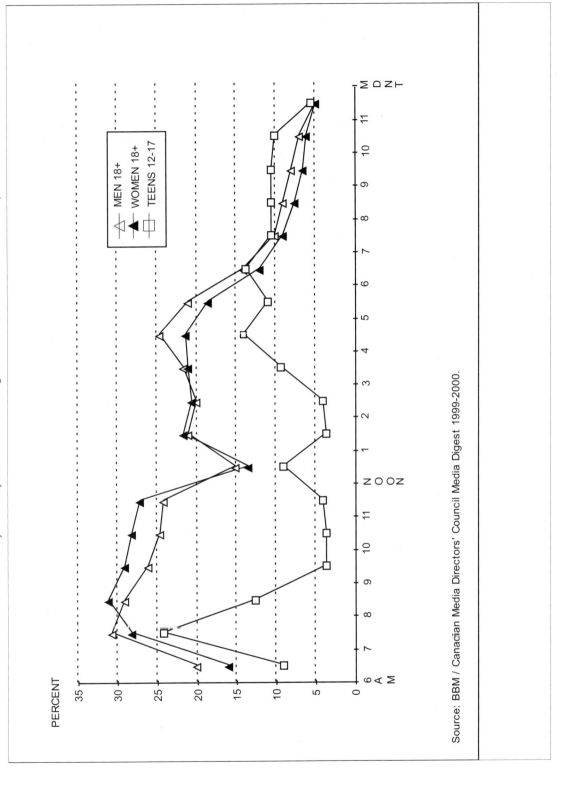

FIGURE 11: Percentage of Men (18+), Women (18+), and Teens (12-17) in the Radio Audience, Monday to Friday, 6:00am to Midnight, Canada, Fall 1999, BBM Survey

Source: BBM / Canadian Media Directors' Council Media Digest 1999-2000.

original radio stars and characters). Radio news was responsible for the decline of evening newspapers and the virtual disappearance of the "extra" from city streets.[25] With the rise of television following the Second World War, there was fear that radio might disappear. The same concerns surrounded the movie industry, which did indeed go through a major post-war slump. Radio survived as the result of an extraordinary adaptation: the medium entirely changed its format, to supplement rather than directly compete with TV.[26]

At present, radio seems to have found a workable formula: it caters to its audience during times when TV is inappropriate. People listen when they wake up in the morning, while they are working, driving, playing, and the like. But when evening comes and they settle down in their living rooms, the radio dial is turned off in favour of the TV. Nevertheless, radio remains one of the most massive of our mass media in terms of the ownership of sets. And there is evidence that radio is adapting itself to the most recent technological innovation, the Internet: studies of heavy Internet users show that of all major media, radio had the lowest decline of time spent.[27]

Radio today is an illustration of successful "narrowcasting"—the targeting of broadcast content to a particular subgroup within the larger population, with the subgroup defined in terms of its programming tastes, its demographics, or both. In its heyday, radio's success was built upon the production and transmission of general programming that attracted large and relatively undifferentiated mass audiences. Now, radio programmers target very specific demographic subgroups in their marketing (at times not entirely to the liking of Canadian Radio-television and Telecommunications Commission [CRTC] regulators). In fact "programs" in the traditional sense are secondary in the presentation of music for most of these subgroups. The exceptions are public broadcasters such as CJRT in Toronto, and the CBC, perhaps the last of the traditional radio networks. For most radio services, the broadcast day is organized around a consistent format rather than around a sequence of distinct and identifiable programs. The focus on narrowcasting explains how the total number of radio stations in Canada grew by 200 over 10 years, while the total listening remained constant over the same time.

As a result, format changes, when they occur, tend to be dramatic. Toronto station CISS-FM, which had been operating profitably as a country music station, was sold and changed format (to contemporary hit

radio, billing itself as "Power 92") all on the same day in February 1999. In the past few years many AM stations have switched to talk radio format. An example was the instant switch (at 6:00 a.m. on June 7, 1993) of Toronto's CFTR-AM radio from Top 40 or Contemporary hit radio (targeting younger listeners 12-24) to an all-news format attracting older listeners more preferred by advertisers. Also in Toronto in 1999, the CBC's AM programming stream migrated to FM in an effort to supply a clearer signal to local listeners whose AM reception was impaired. The service also became known as "CBC Radio One," with the loss of the distinction between AM and FM modes of delivery.[28]

The listing below provides a portrait of the most prominent formats adopted by commercial Canadian radio stations. These format descriptions show the extreme importance placed on audience targeting: the demographic subgroups reached are as important as the programming content itself.

- *Adult contemporary:* largely music from current and mainstream pop hits targeting adults 25-49.
- *Album-oriented rock:* largely harder rock music using mostly cuts from CD's in rock genre, including hits and non-hits, targeting adults 18-34.
- *Contemporary hit radio, or "Top 40":* music based on current hits, targeting 12-24-year-olds.
- *Country or "country and western":* contemporary or traditional music in the "Nashville" and/or "bluegrass" genre.
- *Easy listening, also known as "beautiful music":* largely featuring cover versions of hits and instrumentals. The target audience consists of adults aged 35+.
- *Gold/Oldies, pop music hits from 1950s-1990s:* sometimes called "classic hits."
- *Middle-of-the-road:* predominantly softer vocal hits from all eras, targeting adults aged 35+.[29]

Figure 12 shows radio tuning by station format for Canadians (12+) in fall 1999. Two-thirds of Canadian listening time was taken by adult contemporary, country, contemporary, talk, and gold formats. Adult contemporary music tends to be strong in the 25-54 age group, while those 12-24 are more likely to tune to contemporary. Listening time to the CBC and talk radio increases with age. CBC listeners tend to be more frequent among highly educated Canadians, while country has a lower listenership in that group.[30]

FIGURE 12: Percent of Radio Tunings by Station Format, All Persons (12+),
Canada, Fall 1999

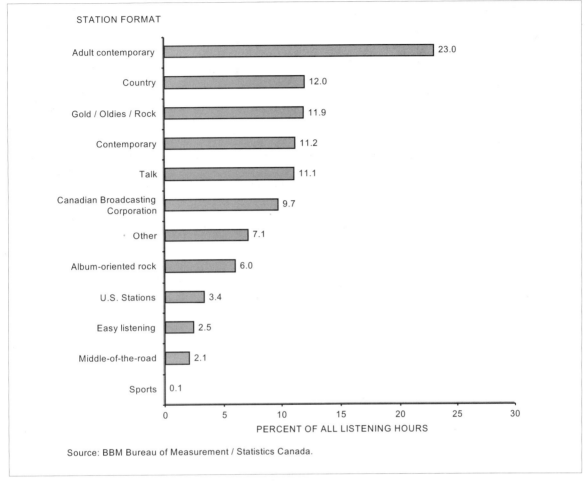

STATION FORMAT

Adult contemporary — 23.0
Country — 12.0
Gold / Oldies / Rock — 11.9
Contemporary — 11.2
Talk — 11.1
Canadian Broadcasting Corporation — 9.7
Other — 7.1
Album-oriented rock — 6.0
U.S. Stations — 3.4
Easy listening — 2.5
Middle-of-the-road — 2.1
Sports — 0.1

PERCENT OF ALL LISTENING HOURS

Source: BBM Bureau of Measurement / Statistics Canada.

Similarities to and Differences from Television Measurement

Radio data are collected through diaries in much the same way as TV data: both measure audiences in terms of reach or share, rather than the quality of response. There are, however, some serious structural differences in the measurements. First, radio measures all those 12 years of age and older (BBM used to measure children 7-11 but has excluded all children under 12 since fall 1990), while TV measures all those 2 years of age and older. Second, BBM radio measurement starts at 5:00 a.m. and ends at 1:00 a.m., whereas TV measurement starts at 6:00 a.m. and terminates at 2:00 a.m. (Because radio is more background oriented, people will "get up" with radio, hence its earlier measurement time.) Third, radio broadcasting is not organized on a program basis as is TV, but rather on the basis of station format, which remains relatively consistent throughout a given broadcast day; and radio estimates are reported accordingly, by station and daypart.

Methods for measuring radio will no doubt change as the medium itself changes. The Internet is already having an impact on how people listen to radio, and it is also becoming another means through which radio is transmitted. Currently, any Internet user with entry-level computer equipment can listen to thousands of radio stations, from classical music on KDFC in San Francisco (www.kdfc.com) to zydeco on the "Bayou Beat" in Alexandria, Louisiana (www.thetowntalk.com). The Montreal Expos baseball team decided to broadcast its English-language play-by-play coverage of the 2000 season exclusively over the Internet. (This move did not stem purely from a desire to be avant garde; it was linked to the team's failure to negotiate a satisfactory broadcast rights agreement with any local English-language radio station.) As full band Net access becomes more widespread, Internet radio may well become the biggest change in radio use since the rise of FM. Researchers will no doubt develop new methods to capture listenership of this latest radio development.

Program Evaluation: Formative and Summative Research

Ratings provide detail on viewing habits and audience composition, but they do not indicate how and why viewers react to programming. A TV program is a very complex entity, with a multitude of variables that can be measured. Kuplowska (1985)[31] notes just some of these elements in TV:

- characters, hosts
- plot, storyline
- dialogue, script
- content, message
- music (lyrics, melody)
- visuals (stills, graphics)
- pacing, effects
- story-telling, rhymes, quizzes, problem solving.

What happens when individual audience members watch or listen to a program? Will they like a host or particular character? Does the music enhance or detract from the program? Does the magazine format of a science series "work" with its intended teenage audience? These are the types of questions program evaluators deal with.

Although there are several types of program-evaluation techniques, two are especially important: formative and summative research.[32] Formative research takes place during a media product's developmental stages; summative research measures effectiveness of a product after its completion. The terms originated in 1967, although formative research is usually considered to have started in 1921 with evaluation of First World War training films on civilian audiences. Formative research on radio programming in the U.S. dates from the 1930s.[33]

What Is Tested?

Program research is, if anything, a reductive process. It is impossible to research all aspects of a program. To do so would exceed the resources of even the most munificent department, would take too long, and would provide too much information (i.e., producers and directors would be overwhelmed with factual information). Over a number of years, TVOntario has sponsored a large number of formative and summative research and evaluations. Such research is usually undertaken at the request of producers or directors. The production staff will have a variety of program elements they want tested, and evaluation instruments are written with these in mind.

Parsons and Lemire note that formative evaluations should measure the level of appreciation for a program, and its intellectual (i.e., cognitive) impact. Level of appreciation goes beyond general interest in a program; it should be interesting enough that viewers will watch the entire program as well as future programs in the series. Factors evaluated should include interest in the program subject (e.g., interest in science if a science magazine show is tested), how the subject is treated, and reaction to style and presentation elements such as pace, continuity, and background music. Intellectual impact is not measured directly, because it is difficult to determine how much someone learned from a program. Instead, evaluators look for reaction to the level and amount of information, the comprehension of concepts, and possible problem areas.[34]

Although formative and summative research was originally aimed at radio and television programs, the process has expanded to investigate learning systems or multimedia packages. An early example was a formative evaluation of "Automating the Office," developed in the early 1980s to explain the new role of computers in the workplace. The learning system included television programs, print support materials, an optional telephone tutor, and computerized assignments. More recently, multimedia curriculum packages known as VClips have been produced for Ontario classrooms; these consist of short videos, related Internet/CD ROM games, and a teacher lesson plan. Formative and summative research is especially important for examining multimedia packages because it may be one of the few ways to determine how effectively the various components interact with each other.[35]

While research is undertaken with a limited number of objectives, other useful information will often come to the surface. One research project tested two hosts for a film series. The movie buffs researchers talked to had as much to say about the look of the set as they did about the hosts, and some of their suggestions about the set were adopted by the series producers.[36] Parsons and Lemire point out that "pilot testing can often alert production people to inconsistencies, errors, or faulty assumptions that develop during the rush of putting a program or package together." They give an example of a TV pilot for pre-schoolers where print appeared on the screen without the characters saying the words aloud; the scriptwriters had forgotten that most pre-school children cannot read.

Who Is Tested?

BBM and Nielsen measure ratings and reach in Canada, using respondents that are selected to be representative of the general population. It may not be viable for program evaluators to test such large and generalized samples. Educational programs are usually designed with specific population subgroups (or target audiences) in mind. So for evaluation purposes, programs are tested with members of those intended audiences. TVOntario's *The Science Edition* was primarily targeted at adults interested in science, while *The Successful Landlord* was aimed at small landlords in Ontario who wanted to learn more about property management. Mainstream TV is not as closely targeted, but distinctions are a matter of degree. Commercial network revenues are derived from advertising, and therefore shows may be designed to attract target audiences of interest to advertisers, such as 25 to 39-year-old females or 18 to 49-year-old middle-class males. Researchers will be most interested in knowing how people from target subgroups react to the programs and will therefore look within these subgroups to select evaluation participants.

When Does Testing Take Place?

Testing can be done at any stage of production, from initial conceptualization to completion of a series. At TVOntario, for example:

- Adults interested in politics were presented with general ideas about a series on Canadian government and politics and asked to comment about these ideas.

- Four-year-olds were shown graphics of an animated character in a program for pre-schoolers and were asked probing questions about that character.

- Facilitators of a four-session virtual course for early childhood educators discussed their experiences, with the intent of increasing the effectiveness of virtual learning courses being developed by TVOntario.

- General-public adults, teachers, and students of English-as-a-Second-Language tested the first two programs of a series on Canadian history.

- Elementary-school children and their teachers were involved in a four-month test of a completed series on French intended for children in Grades 4-6.

- Grade 4-6 students with reading difficulties and teachers from a reading clinic were shown the pilot program of a series aimed at these students.[37]

The methodologies used will vary from project to project. As a rule of thumb, formative evaluation is usually qualitative in nature. Focus groups are a key method of gathering research. In a typical focus group, a small number of participants (6 to 10) will view a program or set of programs, write their reactions on a questionnaire, and talk about the programming in a discussion moderated by the researcher. Depending on the nature of what is being tested, such evaluations may involve anywhere from 10 to several hundred respondents over a series of test sessions.

Summative research also involves a range of methods. Focus groups, most often identified with formative research, are also an essential tool in summative evaluations. In one evaluation, Grade 6 teachers and students used a leaning module on science and technology, consisting of videos, teacher-training workshops, teacher guides, hands-on materials for classroom use, and CD ROM materials. The primary evaluation instrument was focus groups where participants discussed their experiences. Summative research can be more quantitative, involving statistical analysis. Information is collected through such methods as telephone interviews and examination of pre- and post-test knowledge. Often, several qualitative and quantitative methodologies will be used simultaneously. The evaluation of TVOntario's *Habitat* science series included focus groups of elementary-school students and teachers, and knowledge tests administered before and after program viewing.[38]

How Effective Is This Research?

One answer to this question is that it is difficult to say. When properly utilized, formative and summative evaluation is such an intrinsic part of television production that it is difficult to isolate its contribution from other elements in the process. However, there is some evidence to suggest its importance in the success or failure of TV programs. For example, Mayo et al. looked at the transfer of *Sesame Street* to Mexico and Brazil. The first Latin American programs enjoyed great initial success, but ultimately failed after only a few seasons. Mayo et al.

concluded that a major reason for the failure was that the type of formative evaluation successfully used in American development of *Sesame Street* was not used in the production of the Latin American programs.[39]

Research Communications, an American research firm, reviewed 100 research studies on programming for public, cable, and commercial TV to examine the validity of formative evaluation. Formative findings were compared with appropriate survey and ratings data. In two focus-group studies, appeal ratings of TV programs were compared with ratings for those programs, and found to be almost identical. In other cases, responses to group testing in focus-group studies were the same as those of telephone-survey respondents interviewed at home after watching the same programs (e.g., grading a new children's series with target-age viewers in focus groups and then in a separate telephone survey).[40] Still, the research is only effective if it is properly used. The extensive formative and summative component of *Today's Special* may have been pivotal in the development of that very successful children's show, but only because the producer and production staff were familiar with research and responsive to it.[41]

How Widespread Is This Research?

Summative research is best suited to short-run educational programs: most TVOntario summative evaluations test series that are used in the school system or by registrants in non-credit educational programs. It is therefore restricted to the major educational broadcasters. Formative testing is also undertaken by provincial educational broadcasters (such as TVOntario, Tele-Quebec), the CBC, and, to a limited extent, CTV. However, such research is not widespread for several reasons.

Educational broadcasters have a mandate to instruct the public and to provide material to be used in learning. They therefore have a desire and need to find out more about viewing reaction than is provided through ratings figures. Detailed analysis of this type is best provided by formative and summative evaluation. The programming of other broadcasters, however, typically does not carry explicitly stated educational objectives, so the need for this type of research is not as acute. The cost of formative research is another major barrier. Many TV series in Canada originate from independent production companies who sell the series to a network. They do not have access to staff researchers and may not want to add the cost of research to already strained budgets. Research rarely provides any "magic answers" to production executives, who may not be comfortable with (or may be distrustful of) the conditional findings provided by social science research. However, the process can supply direction and assistance, and can provide practical solutions to production problems. Finally, program research (especially formative research) is, by its very nature, subject to time constraints. A director may wish to test program elements, but may not have the time to wait until results are tabled before proceeding with full production.

Many media workers, therefore, may consider this type of audience research interesting but marginal (although this attitude is changing as the increasingly competitive media environment motivates producers to take advantage of formative and summative research). Producers of commercial advertising messages, by contrast, tend to test them diligently. It is probable that the combined budgets for all formative research done in Toronto on TV commercials (paid for by advertising agencies and their clients) exceeds the total budget for all programming research in Canada. The result is a situation where commercial messages are often more thoroughly tested than the programs that surround them. However, the value of program research cannot be questioned, as Aimee Dorr observes in her discussion of formative research on children's programming:

> Formative research is neither theoretical in its questions nor ideal in its methods ... but it invariably improves the television content created for children. When formative research is combined with a highly skilled staff and appropriate expert advice, the television content that is created will be attractive and understandable to children. It may not be a million dollar winner, but it will always be better than it would have been.[42]

Summary and Discussion

Syndicated audience research has many similarities to public-opinion measurement. Both enterprises attempt to quantify the opinions and behaviours of the Canadian public regarding important areas of their lives. Polling and audience measurement also rely upon the projection of findings and observations from a research sample to the population at large. For practical reasons, these are useful activities, but neither will produce perfect results. A number of different kinds of error are present in all research efforts, and although researchers work to minimize them, they cannot be eliminated. There is always some question as to whether the results produced actually conform to the behaviours or opinions that researchers are attempting to measure.

Another shortcoming of syndicated audience measurement is that it does not report the interest of viewers or listeners in the programming, their depth of feeling, or their level of involvement. Ratings measure what people listen to or watch, but not the quality or intensity of the listening or viewing experience. In radio, the intensity of the experience is not a major issue, as the medium is often used as "background" while listeners are engaged in other activities. Television, however, is watched in a variety of settings—at times as background—but it may also be watched quite intensely (as an activity in itself and with a minimum of distraction).

Formative and summative program research can provide supplementary information: attitudes towards program formats, components, and characters, as well as reaction to pace and type of information. Studies of this type, however, are conducted erratically, on only a limited number of productions. Further, it is difficult to extrapolate findings from formative and summative research to the population at large because of the nature of sample selection and the small sample sizes typically employed. In addition, program research focus groups are often conducted in office or hotel meeting rooms, where participants devote their entire attention to a program and discuss it afterward. These test settings and the procedures associated with them are very different from the casual listening and viewing habits of most Canadians.

Syndicated audience measurement has evolved primarily as a means of determining commercial costs and revenues. Formative and summative research has contributed by helping production staff make programs more effective in accomplishing their intended objectives, whether these are educational or commercial. These activities are neither as perfect as the day-to-day behaviour of the broadcast industry might suggest, nor as defective as their more vocal critics would claim. There are indeed limitations, but audience research is still capable of providing useful feedback to program producers, managers, and policy-makers.

Notes

1. For a study of infants' TV behaviour in a Japanese setting, see Takashiro Akiyama and Sachiko Imaizumi Kodaira, "TV Viewing by Infants, Age 4-35 Months," a paper presented at the EBU Tel Aviv Research Seminar 1990: ETV Broadcasting Research in the Nineties.

2. Melvin DeFleur and Sandra Ball-Rokeach, *Theories of Mass Communication,* 4th ed. (New York: Longman, 1982), pp.81–88.

3. Data from Statistics Canada's *Radio and Television Broadcasting 1998* (document number 56-204-XIB).

4. Hugh Beville Jr., *Audience Ratings: Radio, Television, and Cable* (Hillsdale, N.J.: Lawrence Erlbaum Associates, 1985), pp.xii–xiii.

5. Though remaining a not-for-profit enterprise, BBM has adopted more of a business orientation in the last few years, and in 1989 created a new custom-research division known as ComQuest, which undertakes a wide range of market research and public-opinion polling projects for corporate clients of all kinds. In December 1992, BBM announced that it was entering into a project partnership with Arbitron, a private-sector audience-measurement service from the U.S., in an effort to develop and launch advanced measurement technologies. (See later discussion of the "4-P" meter.)

6. Prior to the fall of 1990, BBM measured radio audiences using a lower audience-age threshold, reporting listeners aged seven and older.

7. Many industry personnel, particularly those representing advertisers and advertising agencies, believe that remote-control devices—and the "zapping" and "grazing" tuning behaviours that are alleged to follow from them—have destroyed the ability of the diary's 15-minute recording interval to capture and reflect modern tuning patterns accurately. BBM used data from its people-meter field trial to test claims about channel-switching behaviour and presented findings suggesting that compulsive channel-changing is not nearly as widespread as is generally assumed. BBM argued that for most quarter-hours, there really was a clear "winning" station. Further, BBM found that viewing patterns characterized by frequent channel changes tended to be concentrated in a minority of metered households. See Ken Purdye and Gérard Malo, "Don't Count the Paper Diary Out Yet!" a paper presented at the Worldwide Broadcast Audience Research Symposium, Toronto, 1992.

8. Prior to the development of the people meter, A.C. Nielsen (as well as Arbitron) operated set meters in the U.S. for many years. Set meters, which record household tuning but not the viewing behaviour of individual household members, were never used in Canada, so the Canadian measurement system has "leapfrogged" directly from diaries to people meters. For more information on the Nielsen set meters, see Beville, *Audience Ratings,* pp.70–75.

9. There are indeed advantages to be gained in constructing multi-week averages from meter-panel data—but the effective sample size does not increase as quickly as it does when aggregating across the independent weekly samples that are characteristic of diary measurement. This limitation of meter sample size has been moderated by the installation of additional meters designed to measure selected local markets, although the sample size expansion is restricted to particular geographic areas.

10. Such a task appears obvious: after all, viewing is viewing, isn't it? Around the world, however, some operators of national audience-measurement systems have tended to develop their own distinct sets of operational definitions. Others have provided no explicit instructions on what should be coded as viewing, effectively leaving the operational definition of viewing up to respondents (so that viewing is whatever respondents feel or think it is). The following questions illustrate the difficulties. Who is measurable as an audience member? European systems of audience measurement, for example, tend to exclude young children, who are typically reportable under North American ground rules. In some nations, people count as "viewers" merely by being in the same room with an operating TV. In other systems of measurement, proximity to the set is not sufficient, and persons must be paying attention in order to qualify as "viewers." Also, how long must a viewer be tuned to a channel in order to be credited to its audience? With the advent of remote-control devices, "zipping and zapping" viewing behaviours can wreak havoc with the attempts of measurement services to devise acceptable operational definitions. Technical advances introduce further complications. Many TV sets are now capable of showing more than one picture at a time. When this happens, to which broadcaster should the audience be attributed? So an apparently "simple" question can have multiple (and complicated) answers.

11. See David L. Altheide and John M. Johnson, *Bureaucratic Propaganda* (Boston: Allyn & Bacon, 1980), pp.77–107. Altheide and Johnson conclude tersely that "media agents act as if the facts are in."

12. Statistics Canada, *Household Facilities and Equipment 1997* (document 64-202-XPB).

13. The Television Bureau of Canada, *Public TV Basics, 1999-2000.*

14. It is important to note that percentages provide comparable data across groups on a proportional basis—but in doing so, the within-group percentage values obscure the tremendous differences in overall group sizes. Adults (18+) comprise the largest of the three groups by far, making up an estimated 79 percent of the Canadian (2+) population, according to fall 1999 BBM population estimates.

Teens and children represent 8 and 13 percent of the (2+) total respectively. If numerical estimates were plotted in Figure 1, instead of percentages, any chart scaled to accommodate adults would show the trend lines for children and teens compressed against the axis at the bottom of the chart. This is because a small proportion of adults could outnumber even a large proportion of children or teens. At 8:00 a.m.–when children clearly lead the rest of the population in TV use on a within-group percentage basis, as shown in Figure 1–adults would still dominate numerically, supplying 70 percent of all persons using TV at that hour, followed by children (25 percent) and teens (5 percent).

15. Commercial broadcasters lament the fact that the peak viewing months of January and February follow, rather than precede, the pre-Christmas period that is so important to retail merchants. When TV audiences are at their highest, retail sales are sluggish, and merchants are more reluctant to continue existing advertising campaigns or launch new ones.

16. *Time* magazine (24 December 1984), pp.44–50.

17. BBM surveys, fall 1983 through fall 1999 (presenting data on persons living in households containing VCRs). The recurring and somewhat peculiar phrase "persons living in households" is intentional, and reflects data-handling practices at BBM. In executing its sweep surveys, BBM recruits the co-operation of households, and gathers data on all available members. But when it tabulates results, BBM "explodes" all of its participating households and reports its findings in terms of the component persons. So percentages are calculated against a base of persons–who collectively represent 100 percent–and *not* a base of all households. Aside from tracking response rates to its sweep surveys, no BBM results are percentaged against a base of households or reported in absolute numbers of households. The persons versus households distinction is subtle but can produce differences between measures calculated in different ways. If, for example, certain devices or services are found predominantly in larger households, the "percent of persons living in households with those characteristics" would be slightly higher than the alternative "percent of households" having those same traits.

18. Data are drawn from *Television Viewing in Canada 1995* (document number 87–F0006XPE), one of a series of reports–unfortunately now discontinued–on culture produced by Statistics Canada.

19. Analysis by genre and language group is presented in the Statistics Canada document *Television Viewing in Canada*, for those who are seeking additional detail.

20. The distinction between the "menu" and the "diet" first appeared in Gary Steiner, *The People Look at Television: A Study of Audience Attitudes* (New York: Alfred A. Knopf, 1963).

21. The Canadian Media Directors' Council *Media Digest 1992-3* (Toronto: Canadian Media Directors' Council, 1993), p.15; The Canadian Media Directors' Council *Media Digest 1999-2000* (Toronto: Canadian Media Directors' Council, 1999), p.27; Statistics Canada, "Radio Listening," *The Daily*, July 22, 1999.

22. Statistics Canada, *Household Facilities and Equipment 1992*, p.17; *1993 Radio Facts Book* (Toronto: Radio Marketing Bureau of Canada, 1993); *1992-1993 Radio Data Book* (Toronto: BBM Bureau of Measurement, 1993), p.2; *2000 Radio Marketing Guide* (Toronto: Radio Marketing Bureau of Canada, 2000), p.5.

23. *2000 Radio Marketing Guide*, pp.5, 6, 9, 24, 33. The Canadian Media Directors' Council *Media Digest 1999-2000*, p.28; Statistics Canada, *The Daily*, July 22, 1999.

24. The Canadian Media Directors' Council *Media Digest 1999-2000*, p.29.

25. Ben H. Bagdikian, *The Information Machines: Their Impact on Men and the Media* (New York: Harper & Row, 1971), p.56.

26. Bagdikian, *The Information Machines*, p.163.

27. DeFleur and Ball-Rokeach, *Theories of Mass Communication*, p.92; *Radio Marketing Guide, 2000*, p.13.

28. *The Globe and Mail*, 21 June 1993. See also the CISS sale press release (available at <http://www.newswire.ca/releases/February1999/05/c3302.html>) and a brief synopsis in *Strategy Magazine*, "Consolidation to put big boys in control," November 8, 1999, p.B16.

29. *1990 Radio Facts Book* (Toronto: Radio Marketing Bureau of Canada, 1990), Section 2.2.

30. Statistics Canada, "Radio Listening," *The Daily*, July 26, 2000.

31. Olga Kuplowska, "Formative Evaluation in Children's Programming: Methods, Results, Applications," a paper presented at the Annual Convention of the American Theater Association, Toronto, 4 August 1985.

32. These are not the only types of programming research. There are also market research and ascertainment studies, to assess needs and interests of target audiences. These studies are used in early stages of series planning to determine the nature and general direction of programming. Radio broadcasts do not have these testing procedures because most radio stations are more format-oriented than program-oriented.

33. Marjorie A. Cambre, "Historical Overview of Formative Evaluation of Instructional Media Products," *Educational Communications and Technology* 29, no. 1 (Spring 1981): 3-6.

34. Patricia Parsons and Anne-Marie Lemire, "Formative Evaluation: The TVOntario Perspective," *Canadian Journal of Educational Communications* 15, no. 1 (Winter 1986).

35. Robert Stewart Brown and Pat Parsons, *Summative Evaluation of Automating the Office*, Office of Project Research Report No.3, 1985-86 (Toronto, TVOntario); Giuliana Colalillo, *Evaluation of the Grade 7 VClips Curriculum Package*, Report 6 1998-99 (Toronto, TVOntario).

36. Avi Soudak, *Formative Evaluation of Film International*, EPR Report no. 22, 1985-86.

37. Patricia Parsons, *Evaluation of "The Member From,"* EPR Report no. 3, 1987-88 (Toronto: TVOntario); K. Duggan, P. Parsons, and B. Karam, *Today's Special: Formative Evaluation of Two Pilot Programs*, EPR Report no. 5, 1981 (Toronto: TVOntario); Giuliana Colalillo, *Evaluation of the ECE Virtual Classroom Project: Facilitator's Focus Group*, Report no. 4 1998-1999 (Toronto, TVOntario); P. Parsons and R.S. Brown, *Origins: Formative Evaluation*, EPR Report no. 17, 1986-87 (Toronto: TVOntario); R.S. Brown and K. Duggan, *Summative Evaluation of the Telefrancais Learning System*, EPR Report no. 14, 1986-87 (Toronto: TVOntario); Dianne Davis, *Reading Rap: Formative Evaluation*, EPR Report no. 15, 1990-91 (Toronto: TVOntario).

38. Robert Stewart Brown, *Summative Evaluation of the Habitat Learning System*, EPR Report no. 3, 1989-90 (Toronto: TVOntario).

39. J.K. Mayo et al., "The transfer of *Sesame Street* to Latin America," *Communication Research* 11, no. 2 (April 1984): 259-80.

40. Research Communications Ltd., "Formative Research for Television: Believe It or Not?" Paper presented at the Association for Educational Communications and Technology 1985; AECT Annual Conference, Anaheim, California, 1985. In the evaluation of TV Ontario's *Habitat*, focus groups of teachers pointed out the same strengths and weaknesses of the learning system as a utilization study of in-school use. See Brown, *Summative Evaluation of the Habitat Learning System*.

41. Kay Duggan and Pat Parsons, *Today's Special: A Summary of the Research*, EPR Report, 1983 (Toronto: TVOntario).

42. Aimee Dorr, *Television and Children: A Special Medium for a Special Audience* (Beverly Hills, Calif.: Sage Publications, 1986), p.58.

The Advertising of Politics and the Politics of Advertising

Jonathan Rose

Governments talk. They listen and they speak. Government communication occurs in a number of different ways. Historically, political parties, mass media, interest groups have all contributed to our public conversation directly and routinely. In the past these methods were *supplemented* by advertising. Now, seemingly, the previously normal means have been overshadowed by the power and presence of government advertising. It is not confined to any one political party or any region. We see it everywhere: the government of Ontario, for instance, spent $4 million on a series of health-care ads, one of which showed a young boy with a Band-Aid and a tag line that said "sometimes change hurts";[1] the government of Québec used it to complain that Ottawa was short-changing Quebecers in transfer payments[2] (see Figure 5); the government of British Columbia spent $5 million to persuade its citizens that the Nisga'a treaty was a sound one;[3] the federal government bombards our homes around Canada Day reminding us that, according to the United Nations, Canada is the best place to live in the world.[4] Recently, the federal government spent $6 million on a television advertising campaign designed to give it major credit for a federal-provincial health agreement.[5] All of these ads are similar in one way: they are designed to persuade mass publics of the virtues of a government initiative. This chapter will explore the advertisement as an increasingly used tool of the state in an effort to show how governments communicate and what they are saying through this mode of communication.

Rhetoric and Advertising

All advertising is a form of rhetoric. In common parlance, we often use the word rhetoric to mean something vacuous or meaningless or something that does not require a response, such as a rhetorical question. Its original meaning is far from that. In ancient Greece, Plato believed that rhetoric was the art of flattery and had no use in seeking the truth. His disdain for rhetoric was a philosophical one in that rhetoricians were not interested in transcendental truths but rather in persuading the audience of an argument. Plato's student, Aristotle, in his book *Rhetoric*, disagreed with his teacher, arguing instead that rhetoric could be used for both good or evil. Unlike Plato's *dialectic*, which dealt with broad philosophical principles and certainty, Aristotle's *rhetoric* dealt with specific issues and probability based on how plausible the audience found the argument. In its most general sense, rhetoric is about finding the best mode of persuasion. Aristotle wrote:

> Rhetoric may be defined as the faculty of observing in any given case the available means of persuasion. This is not a function of any other art. Every other art can instruct or persuade about its own particular subject-matter; for instance medicine about what is healthy and unhealthy; geometry about the properties of magnitude, arithmetic about numbers and the same is true of the other arts and sciences. But rhetoric we look upon as the power of observing the means of persuasion on almost any subject presented to us; and that is why we say that, in its technical character, it is not concerned with any special or definite class of subjects.[6]

The great Canadian literary critic Northrop Frye said that "rhetoric has from the beginning meant two things: ornamental speech and persuasive speech. These two things seem psychologically opposed to each other, as the desire to ornament is essentially disinterested, and the desire to persuade the reverse."[7] In this chapter we will use the word rhetoric in the Aristotelian sense, namely any form of persuasion. One of its most familiar forms is judicial speech, such as the closing arguments of a lawyer; it can also be deliberative such as Martin Luther King's "I Have A Dream" speech. Rhetoric can also be ceremonial, designed to praise, such as the Speech from the Throne that occurs at the beginning of every Parliament in Canada. The eulogy given by Justin Trudeau praising his father is a notable recent example of epideictic or ceremonial rhetoric. Rhetoric need not be verbal. It can also be visual. When Alliance Party leader Stockwell Day entered the House of

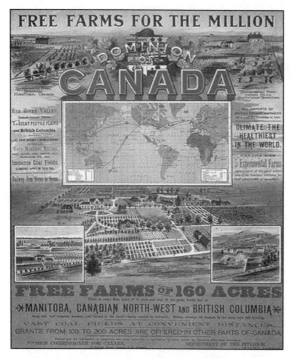

FIGURE 1: Nineteenth-century Canadian goverment immigration advertisement

Commons in September 2000, he told the national press gallery that he would no longer participate in "scrums" (the ad hoc media interviews that take place outside of the legislature) preferring instead to speak at scheduled press conferences in front of a podium with a background of Canadian flags. The rhetoric here was clear. In choosing this venue he was attempting to portray himself as a prime minister rather than an opposition leader. Linking disparate images (prime ministerial podium/opposition leader) he makes an implicit argument about how he wants to be portrayed. This is called "associative logic" and is a staple in advertising where implicit connections are made between a product and a certain kind of lifestyle or values. We see rhetoric everywhere, from ads on television to the fashion sense of university students[8] to architecture such as the gleaming-gold bank towers in Toronto or the classical Greek architecture that adorns many court houses. This chapter will examine rhetoric or the art of persuasion through advertisements of the federal government in Canada.

Increasingly, advertising is an important component of any government's communication arsenal. An examination of it will tell us what rhetorical messages are being communicated, how arguments are made semantically, and how advertising by government is stretching to new boundaries and creating a new and potentially harmful way of communicating with mass publics. This chapter will also review some common arguments made against government advertising and why advertising may have a corrosive effect on public deliberation.

Is Government Advertising New?

Government advertising in Canada has been around since before Confederation. In Canada it originated in a myriad of official gazettes and unofficial government newspapers. After Confederation, the federal government's first large-scale campaign was advertising for immigration. It appears that advertising was a vitally important component of the government's communication campaign in support of immigration well into the twentieth century. This early campaign had much to do with Clifford Sifton, the Minister of the Interior in Wilfrid Laurier's government, who was one of the early enthusiastic proponents of advertising. Not only did he use it to attract "desirable" immigrants, but he also used advertising as a form of subsidy to newspaper publishing. Sifton had this to say about selling Canada to immigrants: "In my judgement, and in the judgement of my officers, the immigration work has to be carried on in the same manner as the sale of any commodity; just as soon as you stop advertising and missionary work the movement is going to stop."[9]

In American newspapers, the Canadian federal government ran ads under the slogan of "Free Land Clubs." One ad proclaimed "Free Farms for the Million" (Figure 1). Language was carefully parsed to ensure that the correct tone was used in the ad. Certain words, such as "pioneer," were never used, perhaps because of the negative association conveyed by them. "Snow" was never mentioned and "cold" was replaced with "invigorating" and "bracing" in advertisements. In "Free Farms" the weather is described as "the healthiest in the world." Pierre Berton writes that one immigrant said that

> the kindest thing to say about [the advertisements] is that [they were] a little on the optimistic side. Canada was said to have a healthy climate guaranteed to be free of malaria. One has to admit that this was true. It was said that while the prairie summers were hot, the heat was delightfully invigorating and while it got cold in winter the cold was dry and not unpleasant. I used to recall those glowing words as I pitches sheaves with temperatures at 95 in the shade, and as I ran behind the sleigh at 30 below to keep from freezing.[10]

In "Western Canada, the New Eldorado" (Figure 2) the concerns of potential immigrants were anticipated: Western Canada is "easy to reach," there's

FIGURE 2: "Western Canada: The New Eldorado"

"nothing to fear," and perhaps responding to fears of the west being too "wild," families would be "protected by government." The juxtaposition of the horse-drawn carriage on the left with the expansive farm house on the right makes a visual argument about claims of material prosperity that await new immigrants. Underneath the pictures is a warrant, or reason, for immigrating to Canada: "This is your opportunity. Why not embrace it?" beckons the ad.

While the rhetoric of these early immigration ads may have been as overheated as the prairie summers they advertised, it established the federal government as an important player in the advertising business. The two world wars also saw the federal government as an active participant in propaganda, which took the euphemism of "Victory Bond campaigns." Using some of the most visually evocative images that have ever appeared in print advertising, the federal government was able to portray the enemy as blood-thirsty while at the same time portraying "our boys" as shining knights, keeping the world safe for democracy.[11] After the Second World War, the welfare state was significantly expanded. The advent of medicare and social welfare policies blurred the lines between federal and provincial responsibilities. Those complex arrangements made

between Ottawa and the provinces muddied the jurisdictional waters with each side claiming credit for having the burden of funding the growing social welfare state. Advertising became an important method for the federal government to claim its share of credit for policies and programs that it funded. With Canada's centennial and Expo in 1967, the federal government's appetite for advertising grew even more. While the dominant kinds of ads during this period were "feel good" ads, the style portended the present-day Canada Day and Olympic ads, which make a virtue out of citizenship. This period also marked the introduction of the Canada "word mark" or logo on all of its ads. The federal government completed its transformation from political entity to brand name. Throughout the 1970s and 1980s it had entrenched itself as the largest advertiser in the country. Virtually every year, it had spent more money on advertising than large corporations such as General Motors or Proctor and Gamble. While it is no longer the largest advertiser, it is consistently among the top five.

The Politics of Advertising

Advertising may be the most common form of mass persuasion that we come across in our lives. Arguably, it rivals almost all other institutions in terms of influence and pervasiveness. It infuses our habits, customs, and language. It shapes our mores and reinforces class, gender, and racial distinctions. Advertising has a profound effect on children's socialization. This should not be a surprise since a typical child may view 45,000 television ads in a year.[12] In fact, one of the most familiar and easily recognized icons for children is Joe Camel, a cartoon character from an advertising campaign designed to sell cigarettes.[13] Benjamin Singer argues that children's advertising is a science that employs sophisticated psychological techniques to reach its audience.[14] The United States spends more money on advertising than 66 other nations combined, including all of the other members of the G-7 economies.[15] Gillian Dyer suggests that "it could be argued that advertising nowadays fulfils a function traditionally met by art or religion."[16] Though we may not recognize it, advertising is deeply political. It is one of the most powerful social forces in advanced industrialized economies. Because of its political nature, advertising is deeply ideological. This section will explore the ideological implications of all forms of advertising. In doing so, an argument will be made that government advertising, which employs the same vocabulary as commercial advertising, forces citizens to think like consumers and treats public institutions like brand names. The effect of this can only be corrosive on democratic deliberation and further inhibits a robust form of citizen participation.

It is precisely because of its ubiquity that we may not see the ideological implications of advertisements. We may see them as vehicles merely to sell products and their ostensible purpose is certainly just that. But they can be read at a deeper level as well. Like any visual representation, such as a painting, film, or photograph, advertisements have certain rules and codes which, when put together, constitute a grammar. This grammar is so widely shared that we fail to see how these rules socially construct and help make sense of the world around us. C.B. Macpherson used the cliché "conspicuous consumption" (originally coined by Thorstein Veblen in *The Theory of the Leisure Class* in 1899), to analyze advanced capitalist economies such as Canada in which individual worth is measured by our ability to possess or consume. Our involvement in the wider world is dictated by the possessions that we own. As a result, we retreat from the public sphere into our own private world where possessions instead of community are what link us to others. Building on the work of Macpherson, William Leiss in his book *Limits to Satisfaction* argues that marketing in late capitalism is noteworthy for its fusion of the symbolic and material benefits of goods sold through advertising. Goods, such as SUVs or Nike clothing, have less intrinsic value than they do symbolic value.

The ideological component of ads is transparent to us because it reinforces our value system. One ad from the American Association of Advertising Agencies makes the claim that "advertising is a mirror of society's tastes." The tag line bluntly reads, "Advertising. Another word for Freedom of Choice."[17] From this we can construct a simple syllogism that may help us understand the rhetoric of this ad:

> Major premise: Advertising is freedom of choice.
> Minor premise: We believe in freedom of choice.
> Conclusion: Therefore we believe in advertising.

The major premise is clearly stated in the tag line. What is missing is the minor premise. In order to make sense of the message, the reader must provide a missing premise. It is supplied easily because it is an important tenet of our belief system, and as such has an ideological component. This kind of rhetoric is called an "enthymeme."

One of the most famous modern political speeches relied on an enthymeme to persuade the audience. Martin Luther King Jr.'s "I Have a Dream" speech can be expressed in the following syllogism:

> Major premise: God will reward non-violence.
> Minor premise: We are pursuing our dream non-violently.
> Conclusion: God will grant us our dream.

According to Em Griffen, "King used the first two-thirds of the speech to establish the validity of the minor premise.... King used the last third of his speech to establish his conclusion.... But he never articulated the major premise."[18] The argument made sense only if the listener provided it. One of the reasons "I Have a Dream" was such a powerful speech was that the missing premise was so clearly understood by the audience. Aristotle called the rhetorical technique of the enthymeme the "most effective of all forms of persuasion."[19] As we will see, it is used often in government advertising.

Andrew Wernick provides an excellent example of a recent advertising campaign that may be perceived to be non-ideological because it presents as "natural" a worldview that does not challenge our own. He writes that "Bennetton's 'Colours of the World' Campaign makes a liberal virtue out of its cosmopolitan ambition to capture a global market for its kiddie fashion clothes. For the affluent, new, middle-class stratum at which it is aimed, its vapid, feel-good colour-blindness will not, perhaps seem ideological at all."[20] Louis Althusser reminds us that we need not be conscious of ideology for it to be present: "Ideology represents the imaginary relationship of individuals to their real conditions of existence." In other words, individuals internalize ideology but our behaviour is guided by the demands of the ideological apparatus that is liberal democratic capitalism. Developing the arguments made by Althusser and applying them to advertising, Raymond Williams has written that advertising employs its own ideology or "magic system." He writes, "If the consumption of individual goods leaves that whole area of human need unsatisfied, the attempt is made, by magic, to associate this consumption with human desires to which it has no real reference."

In commercial advertising, the relationship between the product and a human desire is known to all of us. Lexus cars are sold as displays or indicators of success, beer of all varieties is sold as a promoter of popularity, DeBeers markets diamonds as testaments of love—the bigger the diamond the greater the love. Lest you buy too small a diamond, their ads even provide the helpful advice of how much money

FIGURE 3: Bennetton's "Burning Car"

FIGURE 4: Bennetton's "Refugees"

should be spent on an engagement ring. (Three months salary, in case you wanted to know.) All of these examples demonstrate the associative properties of advertising. If the ad is to "work," the connection between the product and the value must be rhetorically clear. Often there are divergent ways of viewing an ad. This is called "polysemy" and occasionally it is the point that the advertiser wishes to communicate. In an infamous series of ads, Bennetton, the clothing manufacturer, chose to market its clothing by portraying a burning car or a truck full of refugees (see Figures 3 and 4). In these ads, the image portrayed seems to have little or no bearing on the product. According to John Fiske, this kind of communication is called entropy, which is "less comfortable, more stimulating, more shocking perhaps but harder to communicate effectively."[21] When communication is entropic, it has high informational value because it challenges our expectations.

While Bennetton's advertising agency likely wants to shock the reader as a rhetorical technique, in other cases this is entirely inadvertent. This was the case in a recent dispute between an American shoe manufacturer called Just For Feet and its advertising agency, Saatchi and Saatchi. The agency, which was paid $7 million to produce an advertisement during the 1998 Superbowl, is being sued by the client who claims that the ad has tarnished its reputation by contributing to the "entirely unfounded and unintended public perception that it is a racist or racially insensitive company." According to *Salon* magazine, "The ad opens with a shot of white men in a military Humvee tracking the footprints of a barefoot black Kenyan runner. The men drive ahead to offer the runner a cup of water laced with a knockout drug. The runner drinks the water, and immediately collapses to the ground, unconscious. While he is passed

out, the white men force a pair of Nikes on his feet. When the runner awakens, he sees the sneakers and begins shouting and flailing. 'No! No!' he cries. He then scrambles to his feet and runs away, still trying to shake the shoes from his feet."[22] The ad, whose argument was supposed to be that Just for Feet will do just about anything to put shoes on its customers, was read as "This is a shoe firm that is racially and culturally insensitive." In this and other controversial campaigns, the advertising agency may have a different understanding than its client of the public mood or tolerance of irony, exaggeration, litotes, or other rhetorical tropes. When advertisers misjudge a product it may have an effect on the sales of the company. When government advertisements fail it may be because the viewer draws the wrong inference but it may also be a consequence of the "product" itself. As we shall see, government advertising of certain policies is viewed with equanimity; others are seen as blatantly propagandistic.

Do Ads Work?

Advertising agencies and all forms of mass media make their money from the belief that advertising works. There is an industry of experts whose livelihood depends on society's belief that advertising successfully persuades people to buy. Foremost among these is Nielsen Media Research, which measures audience share of television programs, which in turn is the basis of how much media organizations charge for a commercial. Below that are advertising agencies that produce the ads, and polling companies and firms that engage in focus-group testing to assess the consumer's response to the messages. Data vendors sell statistics to confirm the target audience and help show how well an ad will do in a particular context. Often these data serve as a legitimating device for the client who is more likely to understand the origin of decisions based on "numbers" than the often more chaotic and idiosyncratic creative process. However sophisticated these techniques may be, attempting to infer behaviour after an ad, as a result of the ad, may be somewhat tenuous.

There are several problems with the effects literature. The first is its assumption that the basic unit of society is a rational, self-reflexive individual. In reality, the compulsion to buy is a result of a complex bundle of diverse and sometimes conflicting motivations, of which advertising is only one. A second problem concerns whether advertising is an effective channel of communication for persuasion. As the title of Michael Schudson's famous book *Advertising, the Uneasy Persuasion: Its Dubious Impact on American Society* suggests, the impact of advertising may be overblown. According to Schudson, the influence of advertising is greatly exaggerated because "advertising is propaganda and everyone knows it."[23] For him, the effect of advertising is evident in creating and sustaining a consumer culture. We may remember a slogan or be able to recreate the argument of an ad, but this does not mean we will purchase a product. The effect of advertising is in shaping "our sense of values even under conditions where it does not greatly corrupt our buying habits."[24] In a similar vein, Stephen Kline sees "advertising not as manipulation but as a vehicle for situating ... brands within established cultural patterns and ideas."[25] A third issue, and one that has salience for government advertising, is how advertising effects are measured when there is no product to purchase. Government advertising, which is assessed and produced in the same ways as commercial advertising, rarely motivates one to purchase and in some cases does not require behavioural change of any sort. Finally, a further problem in the effects literature is that most versions of effects see the audience as somewhat passive—it is the object of communication. Older versions, such as the "magic bullet" approach, saw advertising as a one-way flow. While that has largely been repudiated, the dominant assumption is that receivers of an ad understand the messages in virtually the same way.

Other theories, such as the uses and gratifications approach,[26] when applied to advertising argue that people are selective in how they understand, process, and mediate advertising. Culture, the environment in which the ad is viewed, the viewer's education, and the degree to which ads are used as a basis for social interaction are some of the intervening variables that may mitigate the effect of an ad. A new model of communication theory called "constructionism" advances the uses and gratifications approach by suggesting that the public has considerable agency in interpreting messages, including ads. Ann Crigler defines it as an approach that "admits all people to roles of interpretation and issue definition limited only by their interest and attention to the topic."[27] What constructionism suggests is that less attention should be placed on impact and behavioural change and more on the dynamic way in which meaning is generated and the motivations of the sender.

The true effects of advertising, therefore, may not exist in the micro world of purchase, but in the larger ideological world. For consumer goods, the ethic of capitalism and consumer sovereignty is reinforced in all advertising. In the case of advertising by government, the values or cultural patterns and ideas that may be affected are things such as our faith in government, our trust in politicians, or our sense of efficacy in the political system. It may be here where the real power of social marketing lies.

This section has attempted to demonstrate several things about the politics of advertising. Advertising employs a code or grammar called rhetoric. Rhetoric allows the reader of an ad to understand its message and it is what makes an advertisement persuasive. It provides us with the tools to examine and take apart the apparent intention of the sender. While one may infer the intentions from the kind of arguments that are made, understanding the effects of an advertisement is more difficult. Aristotle himself argued that the audience would find speeches persuasive based on a number of external factors, such as the mood of the audience or the character of the speaker who should have "good sense, good moral character and goodwill."[28] Appropriate style, delivery, and rhythm are also factors that affect rhetoric. These may be peculiar to each individual, so we must be circumspect when drawing conclusions about the success of a speaker. This section also has argued that, because advertising is an ideological instrument, we cannot view it "objectively" but must understand it through the lens of our culture.

The Advertising of Politics

The adoption by politics of the language and rhetoric of a communication tool whose purpose is to sell products raises a number of issues that will be explored in this section. Government's use of advertising as a means of communicating to mass publics has important implications for democracy. Such advertising may radically change the relationship between the citizen and the state. While much has been written on political parties and their advertising efforts, very little attention has been devoted to governments. This may be because during election campaigns all parties engage in an orgy of advertising that has become, for some, the primary source of information about the differences between parties. The fact that researchers have found that viewers were more likely to remember negative ads than positive ones[29] further contributes to the apparent power of party advertising. While election periods offer us a condensed and intense period of political advertising, it is the periods *between* elections that offer us real insight into the nature of political persuasion.

Government advertising has several broad functions. The first thing that all government advertising does is to attempt to change attitudes. This may be done explicitly, as in the case of anti-racism or Canada Day ads, or implicitly by cultivating a favourable attitude towards an issue or policy. Second, government ads inform citizens about programs, policies, benefits. Ads in this way could provide an important and efficient way for the state to communicate on administrative matters to citizens. The third thing that they do is frame issues in certain ways. The introduction of a contentious policy, such as gun registration or the implementation of the GST, may be advertised as simply an administrative change in an effort to blunt criticism. The fourth function of government ads is to modify behaviour. Anti-drinking and driving or anti-smoking ads are the clearest example of this sort of ad. Each of these will be examined in greater detail below.

Attitude Change

Elsewhere I have argued that an appropriate metaphor for government advertising is, to borrow a phrase from Walter Lippmann, "making pictures in our heads."[30] In his masterful book *Public Opinion*, Lippmann argues that "the health of society depends on the quality of information it receives." In a mass-media-saturated world, we are inundated with a variety of information sources that vary significantly in their quality. Lippmann suggests that our environment is "too big, too complex and too fleeting for direct acquaintance,"[31] so the public relies on business and political elites to make sense of the world outside. Demonstrating remarkable prescience, Lippmann suggests that "the world outside" is created by "making pictures in our heads." "What each man does is based not on direct and certain knowledge, but on pictures made by himself or given

to him."[32] In other words, we are no longer able to apprehend the vast array of conflicts, personalities, and issues but, according to Lippmann, require others to analyze and make sense of the world. While this is clear enough in terms of the role of the mass media, how does it relate to government advertising? The pictures created by government advertising make up the face that government presents to the public and, in some respects, the face that the public understands as government. State advertising is the primary means of cultivating these images and reinforcing the values of liberal democracy.

Rhetoric teaches us that there are explicit and implicit purposes to arguments. The explicit purpose relates to the ostensible, immediate goal of the communicator. For example, when a lawyer argues on behalf of a person accused of murder, she is primarily concerned with persuading the jury of her client's innocence. As anyone who has seen any number of Hollywood films can attest, there is also often an implicit purpose to the defence. Perhaps the lawyer wants to expose racism in the justice system or perhaps she is making a claim about police powers. The rhetoric of government advertising is no different. Canada Day ads not only remind Canadians of the importance of a national holiday but provide an opportunity to reinforce a long-standing message of the federal government: the importance of a strong and united Canada.

Sometimes the attempt at attitude change is transparent. In 1980, during the Québec referendum, the federal government ran anti-smoking ads that said in big letters, "SAY NO!". In smaller letters below was "to smoking." In this case the ad was an obvious attempt to influence Quebecers on the appropriate way to vote. Before the 1975 Ontario election, the Progressive Conservative government of Bill Davis was criticized for its tourism ads that read, "Life is good Ontario. Preserve It. Conserve It." The slogan was so close to Progressive Conservative that it almost appeared as a sound-alike or malaprop for the party name. One of the most famous ads prior to the patriation of the Constitution in 1982 was one called "Flight." The federal government defended it as a feel-good ad about our democratic ideals, but given the context, it was an attempt to persuade citizens about the importance of a patriated Constitution. The spot opened with a slow-motion shot of geese flying a few feet above the water. A woman hums the first four notes of "Oh, Canada." As we see the geese flying, the narrator intones:

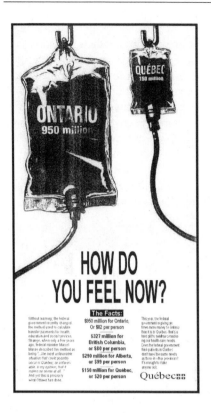

FIGURE 5: Quebec's "Blood-bag" ad, 1999

Freedom is an important part of our heritage. As Canadians. [The woman continues to hum "Oh, Canada."] The right of each and every one of us to strive. To rise. [The geese take off.] To be free. Riding the wings of freedom, working together to make our hope and dreams come true. For all Canadians. [The woman finishes a verse of the national anthem and the screen fades to black.] Brought to you by the government of Canada. [The Canada wordmark is displayed.][33]

"Flight" is an enthymeme whose missing premise may not be evident to those who view it 20 years later but whose argument was clear when it was first broadcast. The syllogism would look like the following:

Major premise: Freedom is an important value.
Minor premise: A constitution preserves freedom.
Conclusion: Supporting a patriated constitution will preserve freedom.

The major premise was the content of the ad. The minor premise is not stated but the conclusion is alluded to in the phrases "working together to make our hope and dreams come true" and "for all Canadians." "Flight" is a good example of how advertising must be viewed in historical context to understand its full meaning.

Though it may be somewhat crude, other federal government ads make a more nuanced, implicit argument for federalism. Just as there is an ideological backdrop for commercial ads, so too is there a mythic context for understanding federal government advertising. According to Murray Edelman, myths simplify a complicated world and act as important signs to guide our beliefs and actions.[34] This is especially true in Québec where, to use the language of Roland Barthes, myths take simple first-order signs and imbue them with a greater secondary meaning. The myths become a second language that speaks about the assumptions of the first.

An excellent case study of the role of myths in attitude change can be seen through an examination of two ads of a campaign that ran in Québec newspapers following the 1999 federal budget (see Figures 5 and 6). The government of Québec spent $320,000 on a campaign designed to tell Quebecers that, according to Premier Bouchard, "there will be less money for health than we had hoped."[35] The way that it chose to portray this was to use blood bags to illustrate the difference in federal funding for health care for Ontario versus Québec. The rhetorical techniques that were used here were an ethical appeal, *ethos*, and an emotional appeal, *pathos*. The disparity in size of blood bags is an obvious appeal to our sense of fair play. The ethical argument of this ad is that all Canadians are not treated alike. The emotional appeal is made in large letters: "How do you feel now?" The text elaborates the claim that the province of Québec is getting short-changed in health-care transfers by quoting a former federal government minister who echoes the same sentiments. Above the government of Québec wordmark in the bottom right corner, the last sentence of the text reads, "It's enough to make anyone sick." In this ad, the text is secondary to the visual, providing evidence to support the claims made in pictures. In the ad, the blood bags function as a kind of "metonymy," a common rhetorical technique that means a part standing for the whole. The blood bag stands for the disparate health of the two provinces. In other words, the ad tells us that metaphorically and literally, the lifeblood of the province is being taken away.

The federal government countered the Québec claims with the fleur-de-lis ad (Figure 6). Fleur de lis with dollar signs running through them spreading out over the country is a strong visual response to the Québec government ad. The large text which reads, "24% of the population [but] 34% of new transfer payments" invites the reader to look again at claims

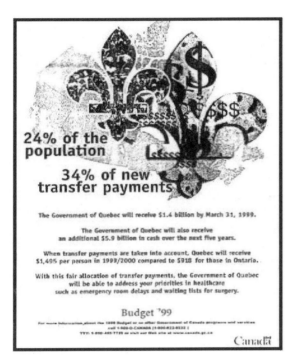

FIGURE 6: **The Federal Government's Response**

of unfairness. In response to Québec's argument that all Canadians are not treated alike, the federal government agrees, turning the argument on its head. The ad suggests: "It's true. Canadians are not treated alike. Québec is treated more favourably than other provinces." The fleur-de-lis, which extends far beyond the province, is a visual reinforcement of the written claims.

Though the explicit discussion that is occurring between the two governments in these ads is about different interpretations for health-care funding, the implicit point is equally important. This ad must be viewed in the context of the relations between the federal and Québec governments. Seen as such, it is part of the ongoing and historic claims of grievances by Québec against Ottawa. It attempts to change attitudes towards federalism as much as it does towards health care. Much of federal government advertising, both in and outside of Québec, has this function. While the ostensible purpose may be benign, the second-order meaning is deeply political. In this sense, government advertising develops and propagates large-scale myths (or stories) to ensure the social cohesion of society. Jacques Ellul called this "integration propaganda."[36] These grand stories, or "noble lies" to use Plato's phrase, are vital to creating a quiescent mass public. They tell us who we are, remind us of our shared identity, and offer "moments of truth," as Hannah Arendt called them. The death of Pierre Trudeau in October 2000 offered this important moment of truth where the death of a former prime minister served as an opportunity to remind Canadians of who we are. Defining moments such as this become formative events in the life of a nation and are integral to myth making.

Information

In addition to changing attitudes, advertising by governments also provides information. In fact, this is often governments' defence of it. Premier Bouchard's justification of the blood bag ad was that it was important to inform Quebecers about the impact of the recent budget. In October 2000, Health Minister Alan Rock justified his department's $6 million advertising expenditure by saying it was "public information about a public asset." The importance of education and ensuring that the public is knowledgeable about policies is a long-standing principle in democracies. Progressive thinkers in the early twentieth century, such as John Dewey, argued that having access to information was the means to enlightenment and rational political action. An informed citizenry is more effectively able to participate in public affairs, the argument goes. Dewey observed that "one great trouble at present is that the data for good judgment are lacking; and that no innate faculty of mind can make up the absence of facts."[37] Many citizens are uninformed about basic political information, and without it they are unable to make judgements that liberal democracy demands of them.

Whether government advertising provides adequate "information" to fulfil a democratic obligation is an important issue. It is not clear that it does. While some ads do provide a wealth of information, others such as "Flight" are not informative at all. The GST ad illustrated in Figure 7 seems to be a classic example of an ad that aids in democratic deliberation by providing feedback (a 1-800 number) and access to pamphlets. In this 1990 ad, the word "information" or "info" appears five times. The lack of any graphic image, compared to Figures 5 and 6, aids in conveying a high degree of impartiality. Compared to the *ethos* and *pathos* of these other ads, the GST ad uses *logos* or a rational appeal to make its case. The tag line, "Information you should know," reinforces the government's argument that it is educating consumers about a proposed tax. While this might be true, the provision of information is itself a rhetorical

FIGURE 7: GST ad, 1990

technique designed to persuade. The GST was sold to Canadians as an administrative change in the tax system rather than a fundamental one.[38] On controversial issues, such as the GST or transfer payments, governments are more likely to use *logos* as a technique as it gives the appearance of objectivity. But ads, of course, can never be objective. Ads are inherently persuasive instruments. On controversial issues, governments run the risk of propagandizing as they are seen to intervene in a public debate that has not yet been resolved. In an effort to minimize this, controversial issues are sold as information. This may be evident in an ad by the appearance of statistics (see Figure 6), a text-heavy presentation, and the spartan use of graphics (see Figure 7), which often make a visually persuasive claim.

Framing

According to Matthew Mendelsohn, "frames are persistent patterns of interpretation, presentation, emphasis and exclusion by which symbol-handlers routinely organize discourse."[39] We all know that during an election campaign ads are used by political parties to frame issues in specific ways.[40] One of the arguments this chapter makes is that while election campaigns offer an intense period of advertising by political parties, the advertising between elections by governments is as significant. The period between elections offers political elites the opportunity to frame issues that will be important during an election. By doing so, they are better able to control the agenda and discuss the election on their own terms. What frames do is present a version of reality that may become the dominant image in the minds of viewers. For example, George Gerbner has suggested that the proliferation of violence on television

has cultivated a more violent society than one that exists. In this case, the fictional world of television frames our version of reality. When governments discuss the debt as one of the most important issues facing Canadians, they are engaged in framing. By not talking about social welfare programs, unemployment, education, or other issues, they are attempting to make pictures in our heads. A common frame during an election campaign is that of a "horse race," with reporters covering who is ahead and who needs to make up ground.

Like myths, frames are essential tools for understanding and simplifying a complex reality. One of the features that makes an advertisement work is its associative logic. Is a 30-second spot able to distil an issue into a concise message? Inasmuch as ads shape the attitudes and beliefs towards something, they can be said to be about framing. The GST was framed not as the controversial tax measure it was but as an administrative issue. Ads for gun registration are framed as an issue of responsibility. Early immigration ads framed Canada as a land of great expanse and freedom. It is important to recall that frames constructing the political spectacle are created by political elites and as such reinforce established power structures and values. Murray Edelman puts it succinctly when he writes that

> language about politics is a clue to the speaker's view of reality at the time, just as an audience's interpretation of the same language is a clue to what may be a different reality for them. If there are no conflicts over meaning, the issue is not political, by definition.[41]

Because all advertising uses frames and because frames are created from strategic decisions, government advertising can never be value-free or objective. Common frames used in state ads revolve around economics, human impact, or control. As I suggested in the previous section, even the most prosaic of ads–those that provide seemingly benign information, such as notice of government tenders–are political because they use frames to communicate a second-order message.

Behavioural Change

A final function of government advertising is to modify behaviour. In this category we can put non-contentious kinds of behavioural change, such as ads that discourage drinking and driving or smoking or those that encourage one to vote. In the 1980s, the federal government produced a series of ads extolling the virtues of fitness and bemoaning the relatively unfit nature of the average Canadian. These

"Participaction" ads used rich symbolism in their messages and even claimed that the average 30-year old Canadian was only, and possibly not, as fit as the average 60-year-old Swede, a claim that would later prove to be completely unfounded.[42]

Advertising by government may not be an effective means of changing the short-term behaviour of citizens. (Behaviour, however, may change over time as attitudes evolve.) States are in a unique position in society in that they are able to constrain behaviour and provide sanctions for those who violate these constraints. Advertising as a tool of behavioural change is a rather blunt instrument because there are no means of compliance. In other words, there is nothing that compels the audience to follow the strictures of the ad. In this way, they may more properly be seen as exhortations.

Government ads that encourage behavioural change are often non-controversial and therefore may take liberties in terms of their use of symbolism, images, and even truth as the "Participaction" ads demonstrate. Health and Welfare Canada hired McKim Advertising in 1993 to create an ad called "Morphing" that used Hollywood-style digital technology to show an adolescent being transformed into a cigarette, while other kids looked on in horror. After being transformed back into her normal state, all three children throw away their cigarettes and continue playing. The tag line says, "All you need is you." This kind of hard-hitting symbolism would not be used on controversial issues. Evocative symbols that may suggest an overt persuasive function are more likely to be used in campaigns where there is agreement surrounding the claims made in the ad.

Demonstrating the difficulty advertising has in changing behaviour, focus-group testing of this campaign by Tandemar Research for Health and Welfare Canada said that "the ads were perceived as unique and memorable.... Messages were considered thought provoking and effective."[43] And yet, according to campaign tracking done by The Creative Research Group, 92 percent of those people who had seen the ad "probably will not or definitely will not" change their behaviour. This is 1 percent more than those who had not seen the campaign.[44] The inherent paradox of this, and much advertising, is that to like or remember an advertisement does not mean that one will be motivated to change one's behaviour because of it. While behavioural change is a function of government advertising, demonstrating it conclusively is fraught with ambiguity.

Some Common Complaints

Government ads are nearly universally disparaged and disdained. Writing about political rhetoric, but in words that seem equally appropriate to state propaganda, Kenneth Burke wrote that it serves to "sharpen up the pointless and blunt the too sharply pointed."[45] This section will examine some of the more common complaints and explore the democratic implications of these. These concerns can be summarized as: government advertising is a waste of taxpayers' money; is a proxy for political party ads; is a denigration of Parliament; and represents a further commodification of culture.

Waste of Money

The way that government advertising is framed by the mass media is through the lens of a waste of taxpayers' money. Recent newspaper headlines tell the story: "Federal Media Spending Called Orwellian Overkill"; "Ottawa Accused of Wasting Money on Propaganda"; "Ads Waste Money"; and "Public Funds are not for Politicking."[46] The foremost criticism of government expenditure on advertising has been that it is a task that should not be done, or if it is, political parties should pay for it. When concerns are raised that advertising is a waste of money, there are really several related claims being made. First, government advertising is a waste because it does not work. In our media-savvy society, people know what the government is up to, and they won't let themselves be fooled by government ads, the critics say. Second, the messages being communicated are not the sorts of things on which governments should spend our tax dollars. Telling us to feel good about being Canadian is not something on which the government should advertise. Third, advertising is a waste of money because governments are not in the business of "selling" and ads are all about selling.

A Proxy for Political Ads

Another common refrain against government advertising is that it uses public funds too often to do partisan work. Policies that are appropriately those of the governing party should be advertised by the party and not the state. Brian Mulroney's Conservative government was censured by the Speaker for advertising the GST using taxpayers' funds before it had been approved by Parliament. Until it had been declared law, it was merely the policy of the sponsoring party. Any advertising at this stage should be paid by the party and not government. In other cases, it is less clear. Is the federal government acting unethically by advertising policies that it enacted and that will form the basis of the governing parties' platform in the next election? In October 2000, the federal Department of Justice ran an ad campaign called "Children Come First." The prime minister had said, just before the election, that children would be a priority for his government if they were re-elected. This kind of election priming raises questions about when an issue ceases to be partisan. One criterion we can make is that no government should advertise legislation that has not yet received the royal assent. The conflation of party and government ads that happens close to an election might be made clearer by imposing limits on advertising in the last year of a government's mandate. Unfortunately, since the lifespan of any Parliament is not fixed, such limits could be evaded by simply calling an "early" election.

Denigration of Parliament

The criticism that government advertising denigrates Parliament is made regularly by opposition M.P.s. The full argument is that by using advertising to persuade citizens, governments are ignoring Parliament as the "talking place," which, etymologically, is what the word *parliament* means. The representative democratic imperative says that collective decisions taken by the people must be made by Parliament where citizens have given M.P.s the right to speak on their behalf. Government advertising by-passes this role and relegates the legislature as a passive participant. Liberal leader John Turner was furious when Brian Mulroney's Progressive Conservative government advertised the GST as a fait accompli when the legislation was still before Parliament. Turner said, "The words [in the ad] constitute a contempt of Parliament, constitute an intimidation of Parliament, because ... the only inference to be drawn [from it] is that it does not matter what members of Parliament do in dealing with these taxes."[47]

There are, however, equally compelling democratic reasons for state advertising. Governments have always argued that it is one of the few ways in which they can communicate with mass publics in an unfiltered and unmediated way. Government advertising may symbolize the decline of Parliament but also the increasing government-by-plebiscite tendencies in Canadian politics in which the state feels the need to communicate directly with citizens. While its practice does not preclude creating stronger ties with citizens, the reality is that government advertising further marginalizes Canadians by speaking at them and not involving them in genuine conversation. It is

as much a denigration of Parliament as it is of the precepts that underlie a more direct kind of democracy.

Commodification of Citizenship

Perhaps one of the most troubling aspects of government advertising is that, by employing the techniques, grammar, and codes of a mode of communication designed to sell products, it debases the entire political process. A 30-second spot is not an appropriate method to engage citizens on the complexities and subtleties faced by a multicultural citizenship. Ads reduce Canadian identity to mere slogans and create a hollow nationalism. At its worst, it is patronizing to speak to citizens on important matters of the state through a channel of communication that is designed to sell soap. Political and commercial advertising is becoming increasingly blurred. Both are adopting the language of the other. For example, during the 1995 Quebec referendum, the *Oui* side adopted the daffodil, peace sign, and daisy as integral icons in its campaign. By cashing in on the revival of 1960s retro-fashion that was popular at the time, the *Oui* side was metaphorically saying that choosing to embrace sovereignty was no different than choosing fashion. In the 1998 Winter Olympics in Nagano, Japan, the federal government spent over $5 million on advertising "Our athletes, the pride of a nation." By branding our athletes with this slogan, the federal government was making us feel proud of our citizenship. Rhetorically, the ads were not much different from Roots, the clothing manufacturer that outfitted the Canadian Olympic team. Roots used our pride to sell clothing. The government used our pride to sell its version of nationalism. Though the products were different, emotional appeals (*pathos*) were the same. Bell Canada's "Dieppe" ad shows a young man who, in his trek through Europe, stops at Dieppe to call his grandfather to thank him for his wartime efforts. Molson's "I am Canadian" ad, which extols the cultural differences between Canada and the United States, has elevated a struggling actor into a nationalist hero and used patriotism to sell beer.[48] If not for the product, the federal government could not have written a better script. In some cases, such as the Air Canada ad that ran in newspapers following the 1998 Supreme Court of Canada reference, companies make bolder claims about federalism than any government could. It showed row upon row of stop signs that filled two-thirds of the ad. In the closest row, the word "non" was spray-painted on a sign in the same way that stop signs were defaced in Québec during the referendum. Except, as the text below the stop signs indicate, the "non" was not an explicit endorsement of the federal position in a referendum, but rather was ostensibly meant to be read as "non-stop" as in Air Canada has more non-stops to the United States.[49]

Conclusion

This chapter has tried to show how politics informs advertising and how advertising is directing more and more of politics. Just as commercial advertising is driven by ideological messages, so too is political advertising. Examining the rhetoric of government advertising, one finds that within all ads are carefully crafted arguments designed to persuade the reader. Rather than engaging citizens in the *res publica*, advertising marginalizes them and treats them as spectators. Government advertising may be a response to the general malaise that afflicts a growing number of citizens. It may further the perception that politics is about posturing and hype and governments are not willing to have serious discussions with citizens about issues that demand our attention. By exposing the limitations of state advertising and arguing its importance in the government's communications arsenal, this chapter has tried to suggest that we should not take government advertising for granted as first and foremost a source of information for citizens. On the contrary, its persistence and growth may suggest a new and possibly undesirable relationship between citizen and state.

Notes

[1] Jane Coutts, "Ontario health-care TV ads Provoke Opposition Criticism," *Globe and Mail,* October 29, 1998, A6.

[2] Danny Kucharsky, "Waving the Flag," *Marketing,* June 12, 2000, 19.

[3] Eve Lazarus, "B.C.'s Nisga'a Treaty sold on Emotion," *Marketing,* November 2, 1998, 4.

[4] Anne Marie Owens, "Author says UN Report not Meant to be Political," *National Post,* July 1, 2000, 4.

[5] Hugh Winsor, "Exactly how much clout can $21.2-billion buy?", *Globe and Mail,* September 27, 2000.

[6] Aristotle, *The Rhetoric and the New Poetics* (New York: Modern Library, 1954), Book 1, Chapter 2.

[7] Northrop Frye, *Anatomy of Criticism: Four Essays* (New York: Atheneum, 1967), 245.

[8] An excellent book on this subject is Dick Hebdige, *Subculture: The Meaning of Style* (London: Routledge, 1987).

[9] House of Commons, *Debates,* July 27, 1899. Cols. 8654-8655.

[10] Pierre Berton, *The Promised Land: Settling the Canadian West 1896-1914* (Toronto: McClelland and Stewart, 1984), 16-17.

[11] See Jonathan Rose, *"Making Pictures in Our Heads": Government Advertising In Canada* (Westport, CT: Praeger, 2000), 56-67.

[12] Quoted in Jeffrey L. Derevensky and Carolyn Klein, "Children and Television: A Contemporary Look" in Helen Holmes and David Taras, *Seeing Ourselves: Media Power and Policy in Canada,* 2nd ed. (Toronto: Harcourt Brace, 1996), 51.

[13] Mangini v. R.J. Reynolds Tobacco Company, San Francisco Superior Ct. No. 959516. Accessible at <http://www.library.ucsf.edu/tobacco/mangini/report/>.

[14] See Benjamin Singer, "Advertising: A Socio-cultural Force" in the 4th edition of this book and especially the section called Advertising directed to Children.

[15] Kim B. Rotzoll and James E. Haefner with Steven Hall, *Advertising in Contemporary Society: Perspectives Toward Understanding,* 3rd ed. (Chicago: University of Chicago Press, 1996), 2.

[16] Gillian Dyer, *Advertising as Communication* (London: Methuen, 1986), 2.

[17] The ad is reproduced in Robert Goldman, *Reading Ads Socially* (London: Routledge, 1992), 4.

[18] Em Griffen, *A First Look at Communication Theory* (New York: McGraw Hill, 1991), 269.

[19] See *Rhetoric and New Poetics,* Book 2, Chapter 21.

[20] Andrew Wernick, *Promotional Culture: Advertising, Ideology and Symbolic Expression* (London: Sage, 1991), 23.

[21] John Fiske, *Introduction to Communication Studies,* 2nd ed. (London: Methuen, 1990), 16.

[22] Ruth Shalit, "The Ad From Hell," *Salon* on-line magazine, May 29, 1999.

[23] Michael Schudson's famous book, *Advertising, the Uneasy Persuasion: Its Dubious Impact on American Society* (New York: Basic Books, 1984), 4.

[24] Ibid., 210.

[25] Stephen Kline, *Out of the Garden: Toys, TV and Children's Culture in the Age of Marketing* (Toronto: Garamond, 1993), 27.

[26] See J. G. Blumer and Elihu Katz, *The Uses of Mass Communication: Current Perspectives on Gratifications Research* (Beverly Hills: Sage, 1974).

[27] Ann Crigler, "Introduction, Making Sense of Politics: Constructing Political Messages and Meanings" in Ann Crigler (ed.), *The Psychology of Political Communication* (Ann Arbor, MI: University of Michigan Press, 1996), 1.

[28] Aristotle, *Rhetoric,* Book II, 1378a, line 6.

[29] Kathy Kellerman, "The Negativity Effect and Its Implications for Initial Interaction" in *Communication Monographs* 51 (1984), 37.

[30] See Jonathan Rose, *"Making Pictures in Our Heads."*

[31] Walter Lippmann, *Public Opinion,* (New York: Macmillan, 1922), 16.

[32] Ibid., 25.

[33] This ad can be viewed at <http://politicalads.ca>.

[34] See his *Constructing the Political Spectacle* (Chicago: University of Chicago Press, 1988)

[35] David Gamble and Paul Cherry, "Bouchard defends blood-bag campaign," *Montreal Gazette,* February 23, 1999, A1.

[36] Jacques Ellul, *Propaganda: The Formation of Men's Attitudes* (New York: Knopf, 1972).

[37] John Dewey, *The Public and Its Problems* (London: George Allen & Unwin, 1927), 209.

[38] See Jonathan Rose and Alasdair Roberts, "Selling the Goods and Services Tax: Government Advertising and Public Discourse In Canada," *Canadian Journal of Political Science* 28:2 (June 1995).

[39] Matthew Mendelsohn, "Television News Frames in the 1993 Canadian Election" in Helen Holmes and David Taras (eds.), *Seeing Ourselves, Media Power and Policy in Canada,* 2nd ed. (Toronto: Harcourt Brace Canada, 1996).

[40] See <http://politicalads.ca> for examples of some recent election ads.

[41] Murray Edelman, *Constructing the Political Spectacle* (Chicago: University of Chicago Press, 1988), 104.

[42] James Christie, "Participaction's Propaganda," *The Globe and Mail,* May 7, 1990, A1.

[43] Tandemar Research Inc. "A Disaster Ad Check for Health and Welfare's Anti-Substance Campaign, 'Morphing,'" TR#32137, February 1993. Data received from author's Access to Information Request.

[44] The Creative Research Group Limited, "Health and Welfare Campaign Tracking Presentation," May 1991. Data received from author's Access to Information Request.

[45] Kenneth Burke, *A Grammar of Motives* (New York: Prentice Hall, 1945), 393.

46. *Montreal Gazette*, November 8, 1980, 8; *London Free Press*, May 4, 1982, A3; *Times Colonist*, February 1, 1999, A1; *National Post*, June 12, 1999, B8.

47. House of Commons, *Debates*, September 25, 1989, 3819.

48. The ad can be viewed at <http://politicalads.ca>.

49. This verbal pun in rhetoric is called "syllepsis." It refers to a word (usually a verb) that lacks congruence with one subject it governs. The "non" refers to the non-stop flights of an airline but also the French "non," the way in which federalists would vote in a referendum on secession. The ad can be seen in *The Wall Street Journal*, May 27, 1998, A17.

12

The Mass Media and Political Communication in Canada

Robert Everett and Frederick J. Fletcher

The mass media form the stage upon which the most visible aspects of Canadian politics are played out. The print and broadcast media, especially television, have an important influence on the agenda for public debate and on how Canadians perceive politics. Issues that gain the attention of major news media become those that are defined as political by the general public and political elites. Moreover, the media have considerable influence on the nature of political discourse, the context in which political matters are understood, and the standards by which they are judged.

It is a mistake, however, to define political communication–communication about public institutions and policies–in terms of the media alone. In fact, political communication is conducted through a variety of channels, including the interpersonal networks formed by political parties, interest groups, and also within families, groups of friends, or in the places where we work, learn, and pursue recreational activities The development of the Internet has led to the emergence of a wide range of forms of public communication that are playing an increasingly important role in political discourse. The mass media continue to provide the context for other channels of communication, but these have a life of their own. Communication scholars agree that messages have their greatest influence when they move from the mass media into interpersonal communication. In an era of increasing distrust of large organizations, it is important to remember that the media filter and amplify political ideas that they select from a vast array of sources but rarely originate.

The limits of short-term media influence can be demonstrated quite easily. Individuals can and do respond quite differently to the news of the day depending on their own political points of view or the perceived impact of issues on their lives. One notable Canadian example of media limitations was revealed during the national referendum on the Charlottetown constitutional accord of 1992. A majority of Canadian voters rejected the accord despite a massive advertising blitz, the exhortations of the country's political elites, and the endorsements of pundits, editorialists, and columnists. A more recent case involves the evolution of Reform into the Canadian Alliance. Coverage of the party and its leadership contest was almost unprecedented in scope and intensity. Yet popular support was virtually unchanged when the transformation was complete and a new leader was in place. (The 2000 election did not produce much change, despite a vigorous–and negative–campaign.) From a political communication perspective, these and other cases serve to remind us that, while the mass media occupy a central place in the political process, their day-to-day influence is neither uniform nor wholly predicable. Media power is constrained by a variety of influences, particularly the capacity of audiences to ignore or resist persuasive messages.

With these qualifications in mind, it is important to recognize that the mass media are so pervasive in Canadian society that they help to form our ideological environment and personal worldviews. This is particularly true of those elements of media content that we usually do not think of as political, such as advertising and entertainment programming. Over the long term, these forms reflect and reinforce the beliefs, ideas, and values that form the context of Canadian politics. The media content made available to us is influenced in turn by a wide range of social, economic, and political factors, including commercial considerations, government regulations, audience interests and tastes, advertiser preferences, cultural styles, media fashions (often imported from the U.S.), and the values and professional practices of media owners, managers, and producers, including news workers. In their turn, audiences select, interpret, and react to media messages in different ways, depending on their education, age, social class, ideological perspectives, place of residence, interests, and other social and personal traits. In their role as political communicators, the media operate in a complex milieu, with conflicting expectations and audiences with minds of their own.

Although still not available to many Canadians, the rapidly growing array of new forms of public communication on the Internet–from specialized news services and advocacy group websites to chat rooms, news groups and partisan propaganda–are opening up new possibilities for democratic discourse. However, while the new information technology permits various innovations to empower ordinary citizens, this potential can "easily be overwhelmed by other factors," particularly commercial considerations and the actual scope for effective participation in decision making.[1] Citizens will have little incentive to avail themselves of these new sources of information and communication if their views are perceived to have no effect on policy. In addition, the new technologies are creating new opportunities for control and manipulation of information by those who control the services and the portals into them, including effective new ways of gathering information on individuals. The growth of expensive, specialized news services is widening the gap between the information rich and the information poor.

Expectations and Explanations: Normative Roles and Analytic Approaches

As mass media have grown in their diversity, reach, and prominence in everyday life, theories of democracy have assigned them a concomitantly greater importance in the political process. With what appear to be worldwide populist pressures for more citizen involvement in politics, the quality of information available to citizens becomes increasingly important. The existence of "public space," in which debate over issues of public importance can take place, has never been more important. Yet we entrust the main public-information function to a mass media system that has many concerns other than public education.

Despite the media's intense engagement in the process, their role differs from that played by other political institutions. In Canada, the majority of media concerns are profit-making enterprises that seek to maximize audiences and attract the advertising revenue on which they depend. The idea that news work is a calling with a higher moral purpose frequently clashes with the reality that mainstream mass media are businesses.[2] Some legislative initiatives and regulatory practices charge mass media,

even those controlled by private interests, with certain social, economic, and political responsibilities: values of nation building, diversity, and equity are embedded in successive broadcasting acts. However, many of these principles are diluted by economic considerations, the influence of private-sector interests on regulatory decisions, and a lack of will to implement declared principles. The Charter of Rights and Freedoms proclaims the freedom of the press and other media, recognizing the central place occupied by the media in the political realm.[3] Yet this very right, said to be a requirement of democracy and pluralism, grants media organizations freedom to pursue interests that may not coincide with broader social objectives and needs. Finally, mass media fulfil a variety of roles and are used for numerous reasons. Entertaining fare is the chief staple of radio and TV, and their pervasiveness has made them important parts of everyday human experiences. Mass media do not exist primarily for the purpose of enhancing political communication.

Both the theory and practice of the Canadian media reflect a tension between conflicting theories. The "libertarian" (or free market) theory, with its origins in nascent liberalism and confrontations with authoritarian rule, posits the rationality of humankind, the necessity of an unfettered and diversified ownership, and the utility of a vigilant press in maintaining a check on government abuse.[4] In the main, the theory is identified with print media and grew alongside the establishment of the mass, urban newspaper of the nineteenth century.[5] The second theory is that of "social responsibility," the tenets of which evolved out of experience with the diffusion of radio. It was spurred by practical limitations on the number of available frequencies and the disappointing lack of public spirit among early radio proprietors. Given these problems, the state has a legitimate (if generally limited) role in helping to ensure that the media are open to a variety of opinions, are manifestly balanced and self-conscious in discharging a public trust, and respect society's legal and political framework.[6] Although the articulation of obligations and fulfilment of social purpose is usually attributed to the American Commission on Freedom of the Press (1944-47),[7] it is evident in the thrust behind the creation of the Canadian Radio Broadcast Commission (CRBC) in 1932, a state agency responsible for both regulating and broadcasting. The agency evolved over time into the current division between the Canadian Broadcasting Corporation (CBC), a broadcaster, and the Canadian Radio-television and

Telecommunications Commission (CRTC), which regulates broadcasting and is charged with enforcing the public-service responsibilities of all broadcasters.

Although the libertarian theory underlies the Charter of Rights provisions, and is favoured by proprietors, there are substantial elements of the social-responsibility doctrine in the Canadian political culture. Most media organizations acknowledge their responsibilities, and these are manifested in membership of press councils, the Canadian Advertising Foundation, and the Canadian Broadcast Standards Council. These voluntary agencies promote adherence to certain public-interest standards, but exist primarily to stave off the imposition of government regulations and polish the image of their respective industries. The influence of the social-responsibility approach shows up more clearly in the public spirit that has animated CRTC regulations and policies that attempt to ensure diversity, balance, and a modicum of Canadian content in the broadcast media. While media managers and owners acknowledge certain social responsibilities in return for legal protection, they frequently cite libertarian ideals to support their independence to pursue commercial and sometimes ideological imperatives.

Regardless of the operative theory, Canadian mass media are expected to perform multiple political roles, some of which take on special significance in the domestic context. For the majority of citizens in mass societies such as Canada, the principal continuing connection to leaders and institutions is provided by the words, sounds, and images circulating in the mass media.

The media convey basic information about political systems by identifying elementary and more complex symbols, imparting knowledge of how the system functions, providing models of citizen behaviour, and orienting citizens to both institutions and issues. In this sense the media are expected to impart both values and the kind and quality of information that can support an interested, active population.[8] The media should not only help alert citizens to major issues but also monitor the activities of government, raise alarms when powers are abused, and scan the horizon for looming social trends. Media content ought to help clarify political priorities, assist in the creation of public opinion, and maintain links between government and the governed. None of these roles should be confined to the domestic environment. Media should also contribute to international understanding on a global scale. This inventory is not exhaustive, but it represents some of the

key functions that fall to the media and, as Denis McQuail argues, criteria by which to "assess how the media actually do their work in practice."[9]

Not surprisingly, the media frequently fall short of these ideals. Scholars tend to employ one of two broad analytical frameworks for understanding the role of mass media in political settings and for explaining shortcomings. One builds on liberal-democratic theory, which posits a society composed of both individuals and groups, endowed with different skills and resources, competing for political goods. The media are expected to provide a full and fair account of this complex interaction. When they fail to meet these expectations, critics point to the nature of news work as the central cause. They blame journalists' values and practices, including lack of expertise and resources, as well as the influence of official sources and of owners, media managers, and advertisers. The other perspective, more critical of fundamental political structures, descends from Marxist theorizing about the media. In this perspective, the mass media serve to buttress the power of the ruling classes by reproducing dominant ideologies.[10] In what Marchak calls "relatively moral societies," where brute force is normally illegitimate,[11] the mass media appear to be a key means by which social control is maintained. A variant of this perspective is offered by Noam Chomsky, who employs what he calls a "propaganda model," whereby the media sharply delimit "the bounds of the expressible" and, in excluding dissent from entrenched, official positions, serve the interlocking interests of state and corporate power.[12]

Although there are differences in premises and conclusions in these two broad perspectives, certain common elements can be observed in various critical analyses. There is wide agreement that the mass media are conservative, protective of the status quo. This conservatism stems from the mass media's relationship to other institutions and groups within society. Media absorb and reflect values and ideas, reinforce and legitimize existing arrangements, and settle into conventional relationships with other politically salient institutions. For these reasons, it is appropriate to question the independence of mass media from the prevailing political order, despite the claims and aspirations of many news workers. Groups advocating social change often find themselves frustrated in their quest to promote ideas that challenge conventional wisdom through the mainstream media.

In the Canadian case, the media have traditionally been seen not only as an essential component of representative democracy but also a crucial instrument for the promotion of national unity and identity. When the media fail to bridge regional and linguistic divisions or to provide Canadians with salient information about public policy, it is difficult for Canadians to participate in a meaningful and productive debate about their country and its future. In the new century, the Canadian media system, long confronted by regional divisions and the powerful appeal of American popular culture, faces new challenges from direct broadcast satellites and other technological innovations that threaten the already limited space in the media system for Canadian ideas, values, and issues. New communication technologies promise increased choice and the illusion of consumer sovereignty, but this may come at the expense of Canadian culture and the shared public space necessary for the development of the political consensus for effective representative democracy.

The Manufacture of News

Stuart Adam has argued that news work is concerned with producing a form of knowledge that differs from that of disciplined scholarship or artistry, and should be judged from that perspective.[13] In a similar vein, Ross Eaman refers to a notion of journalism as "front-line humanism," which aspires to provide a "preliminary picture of the world."[14] This is a useful corrective to the sometimes exaggerated expectations that impose a falsely idealistic standard on the practitioners of news work. Yet this conception obscures the relationship between news values and practices and the political realm. Journalists' "instincts" are not inborn but are grounded in professional practices, and their judgments are guided by what Ericson, Baranek, and Chan describe as a "vocabulary of precedents."[15] This language conveys an occupational ideology comprised of assumptions about the world, and is transmitted through accumulated practices and values. If the picture of the world that emerges is preliminary, it is also highly predictable. If it is impressionistic, it is also structured.

One of the chief tenets of journalism is "objectivity." The concept suggests a number of attributes, including independence, impartiality, factuality, and truthfulness. Many practitioners understand objectivity as a balanced perspective. In this sense, hard news stories should acknowledge that there are "two sides" to every story. In reality, genuine objectivity is fundamentally an ideal rather than a wholly plausible standard by which to judge media. Even so, as Hackett and Zhao have argued, the persisting reign of objectivity tends to reinforce the perception of a supposed social consensus around basic political assumptions while screening out ideologies that fall outside the mainstream.[16]

Another dominant (and limiting) trait in news is the focus on elites occupying positions of authority within government and elsewhere. This attention confers legitimacy on conventional political institutions and high-status incumbents of offices at the apex of power. Consequently, issues passing onto the political agenda reflect the priorities and prescriptive approaches of officials, one aspect of a phenomenon called "framing." It is difficult for those outside the political mainstream to receive coverage except under unusual circumstances or through a willingness to enter into routine relationships with news workers. This has a number of implications. On the one hand, political discourse is narrowed and conditioned by elites. On the other, media attention magnifies the power of certain offices and distorts the nature of the political process. For example, Canadian prime ministers have much opportunity to communicate directly with the public and to take advantage of ceaseless attention.[17] There are risks for leaders as well, and TV in particular has established additional criteria for the evaluation of leaders. However, the accent on "leadership," and the emphasis on individual personalities as an expression of leadership, help mask the origins and exertion of political power. Matthew Mendelsohn argues that election coverage, with its focus on leadership and short-term issues, obscures the fundamental interests of classes and other social groups and promotes a non-ideological politics that leaves voters with little choice but to vote on the basis of leadership, since alternative frameworks for interpreting election campaigns are not provided. This is particularly true of TV coverage, which is the major source of information for most voters.[18]

News is sometimes likened to "history on the run,"[19] a fast-paced assembling of facts and pertinent data. News is presented in short, discrete segments that lack connections to previous experience and explanation. The world is presented as an array of events and a parade of personalities engaged in activities that are at once novel and familiar. This can leave audiences anxious and uncertain, and increases the need for what Nelson describes as "reassurance" from both the presenters of news and political authorities.[20] News values also place a premium on factual information that is deemed to be accurate and thorough. This gives another advantage to official sources who are in positions of some authority.

Over time their interpretation of events and understanding of the political process become "naturalized," unquestioned as the basis for political discussion and policy development.

Attention to official sources narrows political discourse and thereby lends credence to the notion of "consensus" formation–decisions apparently arrived at by negotiated compromise and based on middle-of-the-road approaches. Conversely, and not surprisingly, other voices often go unheard. The experiences, causes, and perspectives of many people are, if not entirely absent, consigned to the margins of media content. Fletcher, Marino, and Everett have described media content dealing with persons with disabilities as "sporadic, limited and distorted."[21] This conclusion could apply, with equal justice, to others. The portrayal of women, Native peoples, people of colour, the young, and the old also suffers.[22] In Canada, media attention is disproportionately focussed on central Canada and, to a lesser extent, major cities elsewhere in the country. This is not an insignificant feature of media-content marginalization. By obscuring or devaluing, the media also alienate on the one hand, and impede entry to the political process on the other.

Other values can be inferred from the study of news and other forms of media content. A premium is placed on stories that are recent, unambiguous, predictable in their outcome, immediate to the lives of audiences, focussed on government and business, contain elements of conflict (including violence), or are negative.[23] Events take precedence over concepts or stories that unfold over a long term. News resembles drama in personification of issues, the narrative structure, and its colourful, and indeed trivial, diversions. The world is portrayed as chaotic and random.

These are some of the durable characteristics of political news and commentary. There are also several new phenomena in Canada. Some observers have decried the growing conservatism of the media at the expense of a wider spectrum of perspectives in reporting and opinion. David Taras has written of the "winds of right-wing change" that have swept over the media. He traces this to the creation of a "right wing information infrastucture" over the last two decades, one which has witnessed the flourishing of conservative pundits, the growing influence of right-wing think tanks, the deliberate and direct control of media content by partisan owners, and the corporate "boosterism" of Canadian newspapers.[24] This may also reflect trends in the United States.

Trudy Lieberman has documented the investment of considerable money and the utilization of sophisticated public relations techniques by corporations in alliances with conservative public policy institutes.[25] It has not been uncommon in the past for powerful groups to complain about negative coverage though what Edward Herman calls "flak": petitions, lawsuits, speeches, calls, and letters.[26] These interests are increasingly proactive in trying to shape the news and public opinion. At the same time, media are redefining themselves, first and foremost, as profit-seeking enterprises that are governed to an ever-greater extent by business imperatives and sensitivities to advertisers.[27] This has often resulted in a thinning of the ranks of news workers.

These attributes are a function of various aspects of news work. In part they stem from perceptions that the audience expects or demands an accustomed style of reporting. More than this, news work is tied to routines imposed by deadlines and the orchestration of activities by the institutions news workers cover. Press galleries have not been representative of the population at large, lack sufficient resources and incentives to widen their field of vision, and develop routine relationships with the sources they encounter. By travelling in packs and converging on beats, news workers learn that it is better not to be scooped than to scoop, and acquire a shared view of the world. Indeed, much of the political content of the media fails to connect public issues with the everyday lives of citizens, leaving many with the feeling that politics is somehow separate from their lives and their primary function is to watch, and occasionally vote.[28]

The Canadian Media System and Communications Network

Virtually all mass media in Canada share certain characteristics, such as adherence to professional norms, reliance on advertising revenue, a tendency towards a shared worldview, and private ownership. Even public radio and TV networks adopt similar practices, styles, and outlooks in order to compete for audiences and remain in good standing with political masters. Yet the Canadian system is not monolithic. There are differences in the reach, impact, and kind of content conveyed. Moreover, the mass media system operates alongside, and in conjunction with, other communication networks and alternative media.

One way to classify elements of the media system is suggested by Elkin, who distinguishes between mass media that contribute to the goal of creating distinctive Canadian identities and cultures, and those that frustrate attainment of this objective.[29] On the one hand, national identity is promoted by mass media that span the country, encourage recognition of common symbols and themes, draw upon the talents of indigenous producers, or are attuned to Canadian political issues and debates. On the other hand, certain characteristics of the mass media system, such as the penetration of American content, regionalism, and linguistic divisions, are contrary to the formation of national identity.

Identity is not forged simply on the basis of nationality. While some media cater to elite or mass audiences, others are aimed at small groups outside the mainstream. A few media enterprises help shape the media agenda, and others are consciously dedicated to challenging their agendas. For some the accent is on education; for others, entertainment. The mass media "system" is not composed exclusively of enterprises in the business of delivering programming; audiences themselves are relevant actors, and mass media-policy contests involve the state and all those who seek to influence policy outcomes. By the same token, political communication is not monopolized by mass media per se. Face-to-face encounters and exchanges within other social institutions are also relevant, even if they are not fully independent of mass media. The political communication network is, in this light, both multifaceted and complex. It draws together a number of components, including those that predate mass media. Yet all of these elements are now defined in terms of their relationship to the mass media system, even those that resist its messages. This is perhaps the most considerable power of the mass media: to enlarge the public domain and to create a Canadian communication system. Technological change and the pressures of globalization and U.S. interests continue to make the system an embattled one.

Despite—or perhaps because of—these external pressures, Canada has one of the world's most highly developed communication networks. The media system—including national, regional and local media—is heavily dependent upon a vast infrastructure of copper wire, microwave relays, satellites, and cellular systems to receive and deliver information. This network brings telephone and television services as well as the Internet into our homes and businesses. Without it, the world would be a very different place. The network continues to evolve, providing new services almost daily, and moving towards broadband distribution systems that will bring a vast array of new information and entertainment forms to Canadian audiences. The network brings to Canadians not only domestic programming but also a wide range of foreign content, not only American popular culture but increasingly materials targeted at—or sought out by—the many linguistic and cultural communities in Canada. The "third media"—both domestic and foreign—are an important new development. Canadians with Internet capacity are increasingly proactive in seeking out programming, including content outside the mainstream, that pleases them. The consequences for Canada's sense of identity are not yet clear.

Ownership and Control

Issues surrounding the ownership of mass media enterprises remain at the heart of much recent scholarship on media and politics. Broadly speaking, interest in the problem is attracted by the historical link drawn between diversity of opinion in a democracy and the need to maintain plural ownership of the sources of that opinion. Given a tendency towards uniformity in content and outlook, however, the debate is not confined to concerns about the number of owners. Other factors include the nature of companies holding mass media portfolios, managerial styles, relationships between owners and their employees, and the resources directed towards news-gathering operations. In essence, the question is whether ownership patterns are in conflict with what the Royal Commission on Newspapers described as the "public trust" residing in newspapers and other mass media.[30]

It is possible to control any company without holding all or even a majority of shares. By the same token, influence over the affairs of a company can be subtle rather than direct. Consequently, the search for evidence that owners dictate the editorial policy of their mass media enterprises, if it is predicated on uncovering examples of overt manipulation by proprietors, can prove frustrating. Indeed, the differences between comparable media organizations are frequently narrow.[31] A more revealing angle is to examine the consequences of general tendencies in ownership.

In Canada, mass media ownership has been increasingly concentrated under the ownership of fewer, larger corporations. There are several types of concentration: the linked company (or classic chain) in which one corporation owns more than one enterprise in the same business; the vertically integrated company, which both produces and consumes products; cross-ownership, consisting of corporations owning enterprises in different media fields; and the conglomerate, which controls mass media assets and other sorts of business.[32] All of these types are represented in Canada, with growth driven by a number of economic impulses.[33] Not the least of these is the profitability of mass media enterprises in Canada (despite some areas of risk, such as AM radio and competition from new services). Concentration is visible in every sector of mass media and telecommunications. The trend of the 2000s is the convergence of content production and channels of distribution, with the purchase of the CTV television network by BCE, which offers satellite and Internet delivery services. The risk is that a few large companies may soon control the entire network of media production and distribution, creating the potential for abuses of power. For the most part, domestic radio, TV, newspaper, and magazine outlets are Canadian-owned (a result of ownership regulations that require that Canadians own a controlling interest in media organizations). The main issue remains one of how corporate ownership may affect media performance.

The state's licensing of TV and radio stations, and the CRTC's insistence on their economic stability, has helped to create natural concentrations of networks. It is in the print media that the impact of concentration is at once most stark and most troubling. Ottawa has twice sanctioned comprehensive studies of the phenomenon, at some risk, given the sanctity of the "free" press: the Special Senate Committee on the Mass Media (chaired by Senator Keith Davey) and the Royal Commission on Newspapers (chaired by Tom Kent). In the decade between these studies (the Davey Committee reported in 1970), concentration in the newspaper sector had continued apace, further reducing the number of independent owners and lessening newspaper competition. Equally worrisome was the introduction of new management structures and the intrusion of boardroom priorities on editorial expenditures.[34] Mass media are expected to produce regular, healthy returns on investment, often at the expense of staff coverage, investigative reporting, and other attributes of quality journalism.

Both Davey and Kent came under fire for proposing measures sponsored by the state intended to promote news workers' resources and autonomy, which were portrayed as attacks on press freedom, and severe criticism was triggered by their proposals for some regulation of ownership. The Senate Committee recommended establishment of a Press Ownership Review Board to monitor and prevent acquisitions not in the public interest.[35] Ottawa failed to act on most of the suggestions contained in the two reports. It is unlikely that newspapers and magazines will ever be regulated in the same fashion as the broadcasting industry, and control of all mass media will almost certainly continue to reside with large corporations. Recent mergers, such as the purchase of a large newspaper chain and a share of the *National Post* by CanWest Global, which also owns a major television network and is moving into Internet services, have put the issue on the public agenda once again.

Regulation

It has often been remarked that the establishment of infrastructure, control over content, and political guidance have been more crucial in Canada than in many other countries. This view, expressed by politicians and scholars alike, derives from a belief that Canada is presented with a unique and sometimes daunting set of problems. Proximity to the American border, a vast and sparsely inhabited land mass, linguistic duality, and cultural diversity are conditions that pose special challenges and demand concerted, organized efforts to overcome them. Consequently, the state is said to have played a legitimate and significant role in presiding over the development of the Canadian media system in the twentieth century.

While Canada continues to face these problems, the concept of an active regulatory regime, which was always exaggerated and romanticized, has yielded to a quite different vision. Over time, the regulatory powers of the federal government have eroded due to atrophy and the steadily growing influence of private-sector broadcasters, an erosion that has occurred despite scores of investigations. Many commentators share the conclusion of Frank Peers that "there have been increasing contradictions between the objectives declared by Parliament and the broadcasting pattern that has emerged in practice."[36]

Regulation can be understood in two senses. On the one hand, media can be subject to stipulated performance criteria and face penalties for noncompliance. On the other, media can be supported by direct subsidies and other material assistance, technical exchanges and advice, and policies that indirectly promote media goals. In Canada, the tendency has been to associate regulation with punitive measures or with an interventionist or statist public policy. This reflects philosophical objections to media regulation registered by private-broadcasting interests and the enduring image of Canada's initial responses to the introduction of radio and television, which focussed on a national public service. Yet in June of 1990, the head of the CRTC declared that "we're not looking for ways to punish broadcasters; we'd rather use positive reinforcement."[37] This quotation fairly illustrates an approach that has gained favour since the beginning of regulation. The federal government and, to a more modest degree, its provincial counterparts have infrequently resorted to sanctions, instead of proffering incentives and forgiving failures.

After a short period of unregulated development,[38] in 1928 the federal government struck the Royal Commission on Broadcasting to inquire into the appropriate regulatory model and delivery system. The commission's recommendations paved the way for the creation of the Canadian Radio Broadcasting Commission, which in 1932 became Ottawa's regulatory agency and the country's primary broadcasting system. Although capital investment was curtailed and private stations had already been established, the fusion of functions under the auspices of the state appeared to rest on a number of implicit principles. Among them is a strong presence for the state and its regulatory agencies, the notion of a "single system" wherein private as well as public broadcasters will participate in the attainment of policy objectives, and an emphasis on nation building.

These principles were not self-evident, enduring, and incontestable. Over the years, dozens of inquiries have been conducted by the federal government. The changes in the intervening span have taken Canada some distance from these apparent founding doctrines. In a sense, the regulatory burden has shifted from the state onto corporations operating in high-technology, capital-intensive sectors such as broadcasting. The pivotal lesson to be learned from this history is that regulation is very much tied to political forces. The ideological orientation and partisan composition of governments, along with the pressures brought to bear by various groups, have affected the evolution of policy. Many policies initiated by the Progressive Conservatives after they assumed power in 1984 indicate that they were dedicated to free-market operations, deregulation, and withdrawal of support for publicly owned and alternative media. This led to doubts about the continuing viability of the domestic magazine industry,[39] fears that the CBC will be unable to fulfil its legislated mandate, and concerns that commercial considerations will prevail over cultural aspirations. The Liberal

government, elected in 1993, has continued to seek ways to protect the magazine industry, but has done little to stop the erosion of the CBC.

New technologies have made it possible to greatly expand the choices available to media audiences. Cable, satellite, and Internet transmissions hold out the potential of creating almost limitless options for Canadians. This prospect—and the natural concern that American signals will overwhelm Canadian outlets—as led to the licensing of dozens of new, domestic cable channels. The strategy adopted by the CRTC is to establish Canadian channels as soon as it is feasible to do so. But the rapid multiplication of options runs the risk of further fragmenting the audience. Moreover these new speciality services are all narrowly focussed in terms of content, and not obliged to offer a full range of programming. National networks continue to provide local and national newscasts, but the networks' share of the audience is ebbing and their investment in public affairs programs is dropping. New technologies have also helped to whet the appetite for media convergences. The trend is for Canadians to be offered new forms of delivery, with the merging of television and the Internet, with a strong effort to develop a distinctive "brand" of Canadian popular culture to compete with imported materials.

The history of Canadian regulation is tempered by some successes. In terms of ownership, key media operations, notably radio and TV stations and newspapers, remain in Canadian hands for the most part. This situation can be contrasted with that in other sectors of the economy controlled by foreign enterprises, where local control is not the norm. Employment opportunities have been created or preserved for many working in various branches of the media through Canadian-content regulations and other incentives. Applicants for licences are compelled to address the principles articulated within the regulatory framework. Canadian audiences continue to register preferences for domestic news and current events programming, support that has been heeded by the CRTC. Nevertheless, the willingness and capacity of regulators to resist global trends towards concentration, privatization, and a U.S.-led popular culture are limited. Indeed, the CRTC has accepted the argument that effective regulation of Internet services is not feasible.

Elections

Although the relationship between media and politics is an ongoing one, it is in sharpest relief during election campaigns. These offer a paradigm case for media researchers because they have stated objectives (conversion or reinforcement of voting behaviour), are short term, enjoy exceptionally intense coverage, and generate numerous polls that offer plausible evidence of the relationship between content and opinion. Scholars are attracted to the possibility of testing agenda-setting theory because this conjunction satisfies the minimum requirements to substantiate claims about the ability of mass media to affect voting outcomes.

Coverage of elections has been criticized for a number of reasons. One trait that has been noted is the accent on what has been called "horserace journalism"[40]–coverage that revolves around winners and losers. This can be observed in the frequent citation of polling data, speculation about the relative fortunes of parties, and fascination with campaign strategists and their tactics. An impression is left that Canadian elections are fought in earnest only by those parties that held seats in Parliament prior to dissolution. Other parties receive cursory mentions and appear to be registering mere protests rather than presenting plausible alternative prescriptions. Campaign coverage is usually oriented to major party leaders, who are accompanied by an entourage of Ottawa-based correspondents and joined at intervals by local journalists.

The highlight of recent campaigns has been the televised leaders' debates. Although they often appear to be tests of personal stamina, sincerity, linguistic skill, and quick thinking rather than an opportunity to illuminate party differences, they nevertheless provide voters with a unique opportunity to compare the leaders and the priorities they are able to articulate.[41] The 1984 and 1988 debates were clearly turning points in those campaigns, though they did not determine the outcome in either case. The 1993 debate lacked the "defining moment"–the one news clip that grabbed media attention–of the two previous encounters but it did probably enhance the standing of the Reform and BQ leaders, who were presented on an equal footing with the leaders of three traditional parties. The performance of former Conservative leader Kim Campbell simply confirmed for many voters the impression that she did not represent a departure from the Mulroney years, already conveyed by the media. The 1997 debate–with five party leaders in a news conference format–provided the leaders with an opportunity to express their priorities but did not have much influence on voters, despite evidence that Jean Charest,

then leader of the Progressive Conservative Party of Canada, won the debate.[42] A similar pattern was observed in 2000, when P.C. leader Joe Clark was seen to have won the debates, but delivered only 12 Conservative seats in the House of Commons.

Leader-focussed coverage fosters the perception that the campaign is national, a depiction that has little regard for the diversity of issues that affect the regions and peoples of Canada. Coverage of the leaders is also compressed into "sound bites," with each day bringing a new, carefully crafted but succinct utterance that will ring in the ears of the trailing pack of journalists. It is notable that sound bites have been much briefer in recent campaigns, declining from some 60 seconds in the 1960s to an average of under 10 seconds in the most recent elections. It is difficult, if not impossible, to convey a complex thought in such a short span of time. News items themselves are somewhat shorter but the major trend has been to substitute the voices of journalists, paraphrasing and interpreting the statements of party leaders, for the voices of the leaders themselves. In the midst of campaign jousting, performance substitutes for principled debate and journalists play the role of critics.

Increasingly, forecasting the outcomes of elections is done by means of polling. Party standings become the obvious background for much of the analysis in campaign coverage and colour the narrative lines used to depict leaders and their relative fortunes. As Peter Desbarats has remarked of polls in general, they serve to "heighten the impression of a simplistic contest of opposing forces."[43] There has in recent elections been increasing competition among polls, often with somewhat divergent results. Nevertheless, poll results continued to shape the overall coverage, providing interim scores in the election "horse race."

A number of consequences flow from these patterns. While concrete issues are not entirely ignored by the media, the style of coverage offers a disincentive for parties to produce substantively different platforms.[44] Ironically, in an era in which partisan loyalties are declining, parties themselves continue to exert enormous influence over the content of campaign coverage. Campaign managers, sensitive to the media's preferences and predilections, attempt to seize on the close attention paid to leaders and viable parties to pitch alleged strengths in terms of superior leadership, ability to unite all Canadians, or fidelity with the true values underlying the Canadian system. While issues still matter to the electorate, the demand is met with bland or vague promises. This has contributed to an increase in voting volatility and, in all likelihood, voter disaffection. The federal election campaign of 1988, which ultimately pivoted on the crucial issue of the proposed free-trade pact with the U.S., produced a glut of negative, personality-centred advertising and platitudes. Perhaps more than any other recent election, a substantive issue emerged with crystal clarity; at the same time, media coverage of free trade as an economic matter of some consequence was deeper than usual. Yet the leaders were ill prepared to engage in a substantive debate, and the mass media waited on the parties to define the campaign agenda.

The Canadian system of electoral democracy is one of "regulated competition." In order to promote the values of equity, transparency, and accessibility, and an informed vote, the *Canada Elections Act* sets out regulations that limit the expenditures of registered parties, candidates, and others (including advocacy groups) during the actual election campaign, as well as providing an allocation of paid and free broadcast advertising time to registered parties. Parties qualify for broadcast time and the use of tax credits for contributors if they nominate at least 50 candidates in the election. The regulations also require parties and candidates to identify all contributors who give over a certain amount and to report their expenditures. Some public funding is available to parties and candidates. These provisions–along with a requirement that all partisan advertising carry sponsor identification–help to make an informed vote possible and have worked to keep the costs of campaigning under control so that ordinary citizens can afford to seek office if they wish. The maximum expenditure permitted for a candidate is about $62,000 (depending on the number of voters in the constituency) and about $11.5 million for a party that nominates candidates in all 301 ridings. Individuals and advocacy groups are limited to spending no more than $3,000 in a constituency or $150,000 overall on partisan advertising during the campaign. These restrictions limit the freedom of expression of all of the participants but are intended to help maintain a relatively level playing field for those seeking office and to limit the influence of money in Canadian elections, avoiding the excesses of American elections.[45] Smaller parties receive limited media coverage and are usually not represented in televised leaders debates, but the free time provided on the major broadcast networks ensures that their proposals receive at least some exposure.

Election communication is often the subject of controversy, with attention often focussed on negative advertising and alleged bias in news coverage. In the 1993 election, for example, the Conservatives broadcast a television ad that appeared to be mocking Jean Chrétien's facial deformity. The ad provoked a substantial backlash and was withdrawn, but not before it damaged an already faltering Conservative campaign. In 1997, the Reform Party (now the Canadian Alliance) ran a television ad that was seen as an attack on French-speaking political leaders. The ad might have strengthened Reform support in some areas, but it appears to have reduced support in crucial Ontario ridings.[46] Attack ads may be effective at times, but there is always the risk of backlash. In addition, they can be seen as debasing electoral discourse.

News coverage is seen as an important source of balanced information for voters. However, allegations of bias are common and sometimes they can be substantiated. Three examples can be noted. That all but two major dailies supported the Progressive Conservatives in 1988 raised concerns about partisan bias in the news coverage.[47] In 1993, controversy arose over the perception that news media gave overwhelmingly favourable coverage to Kim Campbell during the Conservative leadership race and during the post-convention euphoria over a new leader, but then seemed to subject her to unrelenting scrutiny and negative coverage after the election was called. In 1997, it was suggested that the NDP was simply ignored, not giving it much opportunity to make its case in the mainstream news media.[48] A similar pattern was observed in 2000. Whether there is any truth in these claims, debate over the fairness of coverage and the quality of information provided to voters is likely to remain a feature of Canadian campaigns, a recognition of the potential influence of the news media on voters.

Government Information and Advertising

One relatively neglected field in political communication has been the role of government information services. The study of information circulation, socialization, ideology, and agenda construction has focussed mainly on news media. Attention is often drawn to controversial, highly visible publicity campaigns,[49] the operations of partisan appointees in press offices, and relations between sources and news workers.[50] The state's own permanent resources are less well understood in this context. Yet total expenditures on the range of government information services and policies (including advertising) are enormous. Ottawa is thought to spend in excess of $1 billion annually, although precise figures are difficult to determine; costs are spread throughout the government, and even top-level officials are unable to provide accurate details.[51] Information and advertising contribute to various aims: to encourage awareness of a branch of government or, of more concern, to polish its reputation; to announce and detail particular programs and policies; to alter public attitudes or behaviour in line with policy objectives; and to condition acceptance of long-term government directions. As should be clear, the legitimacy of each depends on the extent to which campaigns are restrained by sensitivity to partisan and ideological considerations. The federal government spent a great deal of public money to support the Yes campaign during the 1992 referendum, for example.[52]

Governments have an assortment of techniques that enable some form of communication to take place; paid advertising is probably the most visible and controversial of these methods. The range is striking, and includes signs on government buildings, messages enclosed in mailings of government cheques, flyers and posters, subsidized copy carried by private media (with the community press a favoured channel), agencies such as Statistics Canada, departmental press offices, listings in the Blue Pages of telephone directories, and enquiry services such as the Reference Canada hotlines. Most government information and advertising is conducted through permanent agencies staffed by government employees, or under the auspices of private companies working under contract. Information policy encompasses related legislation affecting access to information provisions, privacy laws, polling, archival services, document classification, the circulation or censorship of media content, and immigration regulations.[53] All of these can be employed to affect the flow of information between citizens and the state.

The impressive growth in information services is sometimes justified on the grounds that the state has an obligation to persuade rather than coerce, and engage in practices that will project symbols of sovereignty and political aspirations, educate citizens in the political process, disclose long-term government intentions, and promote conditions that will enhance opportunities for participation. It has also been stimulated by a desire to by-pass news workers who may not replicate an official pronouncement without some interpretation or balance. Parties are now on something akin to a permanent campaign footing, and the availability of a host of techniques to reach voters is sometimes an irresistible temptation to the

governing party. Some scholars have concluded that government information services can be judged in a positive light, finding that they generally succeed in meeting professional standards and maintaining their independence against the temptations for partisan abuse.[54] But these sanguine evaluations tend to discount the extent to which government services dispense information that conforms to both short-term partisan impulses and more enduring ideas, values, and beliefs. Government information services are also used to frame issues on the political agenda. A recent case study concluded that the information campaign supporting Ottawa's Goods and Services Tax (GST) presented the legislation as a long-delayed technical adjustment rather than a contentious policy issue.[55] This campaign was conducted by means of paid advertising, telephone "hotlines," brochures, and speakers. Other putatively neutral agencies, such as Information Canada and the Canadian Unity Information Office, both created in the 1970s, advanced views on "federalism" in response to the growing power of the Quebec independence movement and the electoral victories of the Parti Québécois.[56]

While direct communication is both necessary and legitimate, neither the philosophy behind government information services nor the practices that have developed contain sufficient safeguards against abuse. Even modest protection afforded by automatic parliamentary scrutiny or independent auditing are missing. The Mulroney government was chastised by the Speaker of the House of Commons and the Canadian Advertising Foundation for misleading advertisements regarding the GST.[57] However, both judgements were rendered in response to complaints made by members of opposition parties. For the most part, controls are a matter of partisan political debate rather than fixed, elaborated, acknowledged principles. The increased use of partisan-style advertising by governments as well as by advocacy groups, especially in the period just prior to elections, raises questions not only of fairness but also of the quality of public debate. In 1999 and 2000, for example, the Ontario and federal governments attacked one another over health-care spending in 30-second television and radio spots that were often misleading and, in any event, too brief to convey the complexity of the issues involved. While this form of public discourse may reach more citizens than any other more reasoned approaches, it has been criticized for degrading the level of public discourse.[58]

Mass Media and Political Communication: Illusions and Realities

Mass media are indeed pervasive and influential. They are not, however, all-powerful. Nor are they distinct from other communication processes and other political forces. Political communication occurs in a variety of social situations and is conducted through a number of channels. Although it is difficult to summarize simply the role played by mass media, it seems clear that they tend to reinforce and legitimize rather than challenge political institutions, dominant political ideas, and prevailing political norms. However, the mere presence of the mass media changes the political world in some significant ways, not least by altering the rituals and rhythms of political life for everyone. Television has had a particularly profound impact in this regard. While there is little doubt that TV has permitted a greater proportion of the population to know about politics, and perhaps to feel a pseudo-involvement in the process, it has not ushered in a new era of participatory politics. For some, television has debased political discourse[59] or reduced political affairs to a parade of spectacles staged by a new breed of image-makers.[60] By implication, these distractions impair the utility of TV to build upon its reach and attractiveness to viewers of all kinds.

In certain instances and under the appropriate conditions, the media can have a demonstrable positive effect. Exposure to media content can raise awareness of pressing political issues or help close gaps in knowledge. This has led to calls for greater media literacy—understanding of media style, content, and construction. This assumes that the mass media will continue to dominate political communication channels, and suggests that audiences should take greater responsibility for the wise use of content, albeit still relying on mass media sources. Another, more comprehensive approach lies with what Denis McQuail describes as a "democratic-participant theory."[61] As he outlines it, the theory posits a system where citizens have access rights, organize small-scale, interactive media, communicate free of government and professional control, and, in effect, become both senders and receivers. It is difficult to imagine this approach entirely supplanting current mass media systems: a mixed system is a more realistic vision. However, many groups are seeking to create their own co-operative ventures for communication within, and outside, their communities. For example, community-based services have been established by or are open to groups in urban settings, among aboriginal peoples, or on campuses. Not all of these endeavours are made possible by state assistance, but many rely on grants from government agencies. Although the CRTC has been somewhat resistant, and government funding cannot be assumed, this model is gaining some favour among those who feel neglected or alienated by mainstream mass media. The Internet offers intriguing new possibilities for marginalized groups to reach their own communities and perhaps the larger society. To date, however, few Internet services have made any substantial inroads into the public space inhabited by the mainstream media.

If the theorists we have cited are correct in their view that the mass media frame the context for political communication, the patterns we have noted are of considerable importance for the political process. The observation that the mass media present the illusion of participation and the reality, under most conditions, of elite domination is important information for citizens. The extent to which the opportunities presented by new communication technologies for more interactive and participatory forms of political communication are realized depends largely on the distribution of social power. Even in a relatively open and pluralistic society such as Canada, dissident groups are frequently denied access to the mainstream media or presented as marginal. Other channels, such as community radio and the alternative press, may be open to them, but their public influence is limited. Presently, new ideas can get wider currency only through the larger media. It can be argued that the media respond more quickly than other political institutions to new issues. However, they generally present them in a conventional context, focussing on dramatic events and leaders rather than the issues themselves.

As we pointed out in the beginning of this essay, mass media are only one of several communications systems that influence the political process. Citizens hoping to make informed choices must be aware that the mass media, as is the case with the other less obvious channels of communication, are themselves part of that process—and therefore of the problem of politics—rather than a mere reflection of it.

Notes

[1] Leslie A. Pal, "Wired Governance: The Political Implications of the Information Revolution," Robert Boyce, ed., *The Communication Revolution at Work: The Social, Economic and Political Impacts of Technological Change* (Montreal: McGill-Queen's University Press, 1999), pp.11-37. See also Bill Cross, "Teledemocracy: Canadian Political Parties Listening To Their Constituents," Cynthia J. Alexander and Leslie A. Pal,

eds., *Digital Democracy: Policy and Politics in the Wired World* (Toronto: Oxford University Press, 1998), pp.132-48.

2. George Pollard, "Profile of Canadian Radio Newsworkers," *Journalism Quarterly* 66, no. 4 (Autumn 1989): 85-86. Pollard is primarily concerned with "ethics," but he contrasts professional experiences with the expectations of novice news workers.

3. *Constitution Act,* 1981, Part I, Schedule B (*Charter of Rights and Freedoms*), 2 (b).

4. Ross A. Eaman, *The Media Society: Basic Issues and Controversies* (Toronto: Butterworths, 1987), pp.73-81. Eaman, like many other scholars, uses a typology first constructed by Fred S. Siebert, Theodore Peterson, and Wilbur Schramm. See their *Four Theories of the Press: The Authoritarian, Libertarian, Social Responsibility and Soviet Communist Concepts of What the Press Should Be and Do* (Urbana, Ill.: University of Illinois Press, 1956). Contemporary theorists in this vein sometimes note the Cold War prejudices behind the original work (Eaman refers to the "socialist" rather than "Soviet Communist" theory), and have refined it to include "developmental" and "participatory" theories. See Denis McQuail, *Mass Communication Theory: An Introduction* (Beverly Hills, Calif.: Sage, 1987), pp.107-34.

5. For a history of this development in Canada, see Paul Rutherford, *The Making of the Canadian Media* (Toronto: McGraw-Hill Ryerson, 1978).

6. Eaman, *The Media Society,* pp.81-84.

7. Eaman follows Siebert, Peterson, and Schramm in this contention. See Eaman, *The Media Society,* p.83.

8. See Frederick J. Fletcher, "The Mass Media and Political Education," Jon H. Pammett and Jean-Luc Pepin, eds., *Political Education in Canada* (Halifax: Institute for Research on Public Policy, 1988), pp.89-95.

9. McQuail, *Mass Communication Theory,* p.124.

10. Wallace Clement, *The Canadian Corporate Elite: An Analysis of Economic Power* (Toronto: McClelland & Stewart, 1975), pp.270-86. See also Dallas Smythe, *Dependency Road: Communications, Capitalism, Consciousness and Canada* (Norwood, N.J.: Ablex, 1981).

11. Patricia Marchak, *Ideological Perspectives on Canada,* 3rd ed. (Toronto: McGraw-Hill Ryerson, 1988).

12. Noam Chomsky, *Necessary Illusions: Thought Control in Democratic Societies* (Toronto: CBC Enterprises, 1989), p.10.

13. G. Stuart Adam, "The Journalistic Imagination," G. Stuart Adam, ed., *Journalism, Communication and the Law* (Scarborough, Ont.: Prentice-Hall, 1976), pp.7-9.

14. Eaman, *The Media Society,* pp.46-50.

15. Richard V. Ericson, Patricia M. Baranek, and Janet B.L. Chan, *Visualizing Deviance: A Study of News Organization* (Toronto: University of Toronto Press, 1987), p.348.

16. Robert A. Hackett and Yuezhi Zhao, *Sustaining Democracy: Journalism and the Politics of Objectivity* (Toronto: Garamond Press, 1998).

17. See Frederick J. Fletcher, "The Prime Minister as Public Persuader," Thomas Hockin, ed., *The Apex of Power: The Prime Minister and Political Leadership in Canada,* 2nd ed. (Scarborough, Ont.: Prentice-Hall, 1977), pp.86-111. See also David Taras, *The Newsmakers: The Media's Influence on Canadian Politics* (Scarborough, Ont.: Nelson Canada, 1990), pp.119-51.

18. Matthew Mendelsohn, "Television Frames in the 1988 Canadian Election," *Canadian Journal of Communication* 18 (1993): 149-71. See also M. Mendelsohn, "Television News Frames in the 1993 Election," David Taras and Helen Holmes, eds., *Seeing Ourselves: Media Power and Policy in Canada* (Toronto: Harcourt Brace, 1996), pp.8-22, and M. Mendelsohn and Richard Nadeau, "Good People and Bad Politicians: TV News, Public Opinion and Elections Outcomes," *Harvard International Journal of Press and Politics* 4 (1999): 63-76.

19. This is the title of a documentary film about media coverage of the 1979 federal election campaign in Canada, produced by Peter Raymont.

20. Joyce Nelson, *The Perfect Machine: TV in the Nuclear Age* (Toronto: Between the Lines, 1987), pp.98-104.

21. See Frederick J. Fletcher, Dian Marino, and Robert Everett, "News Coverage of Disabilities and Disabled Persons in the Canadian Media," a study presented to the House of Commons Standing Committee on the Status of Disabled Persons, Ottawa, April 1988.

22. Eileen Saunders, "Mass Media and the Reproduction of Marginalization," Frederick Fletcher, ed., *Reporting the Campaign: Election Coverage in Canada,* volume 22 of the Research Studies of the Royal Commission on Electoral Reform and Party Financing (Toronto: Dundurn Press, 1991), pp.273-321.

23. Tim O'Sullivan et al., *Key Concepts in Communication* (New York: Methuen, 1983), pp.153-54.

24. David Taras, *Power and Betrayal in the Canadian Media* (Peterborough, Ontario: Broadview Press, 1999), p.200.

25. Trudy Lieberman, *Slanting the Story: the Forces that Shape the News* (New York: The New Press, 2000).

26. Edward Herman, "Media in the US Political Economy," John Downing et al, eds., *Questioning the Media: A Critical Introduction* (Newbury Park, California: Sage, 1990), pp.82-83.

27. Robert Hackett and Richard Gruneau, *The Missing News: Filters and Blind Spots in Canada's Press* (Aurora, Ontario: Garamond, 2000), pp.58-64.

28. David V.J. Bell, Frederick Fletcher, and Cathy Bolan, "Conclusion," Frederick Fletcher, ed., *Reaching the Voter: Constituency Campaigning in Canada,* vol. 20 of the Research Studies of the Royal Commission on Electoral Reform and Party Financing (Toronto: Dundurn Press, 1991), pp.179-200.

29. Frederick Elkin, "Communications Media and Identity Formation in Canada," Benjamin Singer, ed., *Communications in Canadian Society,* 2nd ed. (Don Mills, Ont.: Addison-Wesley, 1983), pp.147-57.

30. Royal Commission on Newspapers, *Report* (Ottawa: Supply and Services, 1981), p.21. The royal commission was struck by the federal government in the wake of the simultaneous closing of newspapers in Ottawa and Winnipeg on August 27, 1980. The day's events gave the Thomson and Southam chains an effective daily-newspaper monopoly in the respective cities.

31. Frederick J. Fletcher, *The Newspaper and Public Affairs* (Ottawa: Supply and Services, 1981).

32. Royal Commission on Newspapers, *Report,* pp.1-4. See also the data compiled by the Special Senate Committee on the Mass Media, *Report,* Vol. 1, *The Uncertain Mirror* (Ottawa: Information Canada, 1970), pp.1-37.

33. The economic factors involved include the enhanced borrowing power of large entities, the high cost of operating "big media," restrictions against foreign ownership, and generous taxation and regulatory policies that encourage rather than discourage mergers.

34. Special Senate Committee, *Report,* pp.71-73.

35. Royal Commission on Newspapers, *Report,* pp.241-44.

36. Frank Peers, *The Public Eye: Television and the Politics of Canadian Broadcasting, 1952-1968* (Toronto: University of Toronto Press, 1979), p.248.

37. John Haslett Cuff, "CRTC's Watchdog Role to be Maintained, Broadcasters Told," *The Globe and Mail* (5 June 1990), p.A19.

38. This is Arthur Siegel's description of the situation in the 1920s. See his *Politics and the Media in Canada* (Toronto: McGraw-Hill Ryerson, 1983), pp.162-65. Although licences were issued by the Ministry of Marine and Fisheries, regulatory powers were not exerted in the sense of establishing principles and concrete objectives.

39. The globalization of mass media ownership in step with other businesses has fostered calls for an end to the practice of prohibiting extensive foreign ownership of mass media, a regulation adopted by many, if not most, countries. Pressures to abandon such stipulations have emanated from multinational corporations and are also being exerted by governments such as the U.S. For a detailed discussion of the impact of these factors in Canada, see Frederick J. Fletcher and Robert Everett, "The Media and Canadian Politics in an Era of Globalization," Michael Whittington and Glen Williams, eds., *Canadian Politics in the 21st Century* (Toronto: Nelson, 2000), pp 381-402.

40. R. Jeremy Wilson, "Media Coverage of Canadian Election Campaigns: Horserace Journalism and the Meta-Campaign," *Journal of Canadian Studies* 4, no. 4 (Winter 1980-81).

41. See Cathy Barr, "The Importance of Televised Leaders Debates," pp.107-56; and Robert Bernier and Denis Monière, "The Organization of Televised Leaders Debates in the United States, Europe, Australia and Canada," in Frederick Fletcher, ed., *Media and Voters in Canadian Election Campaigns,* volume 18 of the Research Studies of the Royal Commission on Electoral Reform and Party Financing (Toronto: Dundurn Press, 1991), pp.157-211.

42. N. Nevitte, A. Blais, E. Gidengil, and R. Nadeau, *Unsteady State: The 1997 Canadian Federal Election* (Toronto: Oxford University Press, 2000), p.17, 85.

43. Peter Desbarats, "Meech Lake: Polls, Power and Too Much Privacy," *The Globe and Mail* (8 June 1990), p.A7.

44. Harold Clarke et al., *Absent Mandate: The Politics of Discontent in Canada* (Toronto: Gage, 1984), pp.87-97.

45. These provisions are under appeal at this writing. For a detailed discussion of electoral regulation in Canada and the contrast with the United States, see Jennifer Smith and Herman Bakvis, *Changing Dynamics of Election Campaign Finance: Critical Issues in Canada and the United States* (Montreal: Institute for Research on Public Policy, July 2000) <www.irpp.org/pm/index.htm>.

46. Frederick J. Fletcher and and Robert MacDermid, "Reading the Spots: the 1997 Federal Campaign," Paper presented at the annual meeting of the Canadian Political Science Association, Ottawa, June, 1998. See also Nevitte et al., pp.90-102.

47. James Winter, *Common Cents* (Montreal: Black Rose Books, 1992), p.74.

48. Nevitte et al., *Unsteady State*, p.40.

49. See, for example, T. Joseph Scanlon, "How Government Uses the Media," G. Stuart Adam, ed., *Journalism, Communication and the Law* (Scarborough, Ont.: Prentice-Hall, 1976).

50. Robert Everett, "Information Canada and the Politics of Participation," Ph.D. dissertation, Graduate Program in Political Science, York University, Toronto, 1990.

51. Brian Mulroney's former communications adviser, Bill Fox, conceded that the dollar amount is impossible to calculate. See Martin Cohn, "Free Trade: A Product in the Making," *The Toronto Star* (11 March 1987), p.A20.

52. "Two Agencies Spent Nearly $6 Million on Yes Vote," *The Toronto Star* (26 December 1993), p. A31.

53. See Donna Demac, *Keeping America Uninformed: Government Secrecy in the 1980s* (New York: Pilgrim, 1984), pp.4-5.

54. See O.J. Firestone, *The Public Persuader: Government Advertising* (Toronto: Methuen, 1970), and Malcolm Erb, "Public Relations in Government," Walter B. Herbert and John Jenkins, eds., *Public Relations in Canada: Some Perspectives* (Markham, Ont.: Fitzhenry & Whiteside, 1984), p.167.

55. Jonathan Rose, *Making "Pictures in Our Heads": Government Advertising in Canada* (Westport, Conn.: Praeger, 2000), pp.155-183.

56. Everett, "Information Canada," pp.110-13.

57. The Speaker ruled that early advertisements wrongly indicated that the tax would come into effect when the law had not been passed in Parliament. The Canadian Advertising Foundation objected that the GST was portrayed as a simple replacement rather than a new tax measure. See Alan Freeman, "GST Radio Ads Called 'Deceptive,'" *The Globe and Mail* (22 August 1990), pp.A1, A2.

58. See Neil Postman, *Amusing Ourselves to Death: Public Discourse in the Age of Show Business* (New York: Penguin, 1984), pp.16-29.

59. Taras, *The Newsmakers*, pp.233-39.

60. Postman, *Amusing Ourselves to Death: Public Discourse in the Age of Show Business*, pp.16-29.

61. McQuail, *Mass Communication Theory*, pp.121-23.

13

The Portrayal of Women in Media: The Good, the Bad, and the Beautiful

Shari Graydon

An oft-repeated media joke suggests that if extraterrestrials were to land on the planet Earth and draw conclusions about female human beings based on how women are depicted in contemporary mass media, the outer space creatures might conclude that women—who constitute about 30 percent of the population—are uniformly beautiful, obsessively thin, surgically reconstructed, and scantily dressed objects of male sexual desire, who derive pleasure primarily from clean dishes and being dominated by men. Furthermore, they conveniently die off before reaching middle age, no doubt in order to avoid the mortification of gray hair, wrinkles, and cellulite.

Although clearly an exaggeration, the joke often evokes the laughter of recognition. In fact, since the 1960s, feminists, social commentators, and media researchers alike have been expressing concern about the pervasive underrepresentation and stereotypical portrayal of women in mass media. From television news programming and situation comedies to print advertisements, music videos, and mainstream movies, the inequitable image of women and its concomitant social implications have been the subject of extensive investigation.

Mass media and popular culture have become constitutive elements of our social environment. Television alone, as MacBeth notes elsewhere in this volume, has dominated our leisure time since the 1960s. The average North American child spends more hours in front of the television set than attending school. This, in conjunction with additional time spent interacting with video games, comic books, and teen magazines, arguably comprises an alternative—not to mention more engaging—curriculum; and one that is hardly informed by the same values as our formal education system. Many argue that the crafted images and constructed messages of mass media are among the most effective means of reinforcing notions considered by the dominant forces in society to be normal, acceptable, and ideal.

Inevitably, this hegemonic process is believed to naturalize and legitimize systemic forms of oppression affecting those who are already less powerful, including women, ethnic minorities, the elderly, gays and lesbians, and people with disabilities.[1]

As early as 1954, Dallas Smythe drew attention to the fundamental inequities of the media's "alternative curriculum" with respect to women and its negative socializing potential.[2] Betty Friedan's pioneering feminist work *The Feminine Mystique*, published in 1963, was based in part on a content analysis of women's magazines and precipitated a widespread critical review of the image of women in mass media.[3] Entire bibliographies of in-depth research into the problematic portrayal of women have been compiled, dating from the 1970s to the present.[4] Hundreds of studies document in repetitive detail the limiting roles and characteristics accorded to women in media forms, ranging from television dramas and children's cartoons to the photographs and comic strips in daily newspapers. In Canada, the Royal Commission on the Status of Women convened in 1967 received more than 30 separate briefs from women's groups addressing the issue.[5] Almost three decades later, government panels on a variety of tangentially related issues continued to publish reports recommending the need to improve gender portrayal in the mass media.[6]

MediaWatch, a national, volunteer-based feminist organization established in 1981 to work for change in the media's treatment of women, identifies some of the most pervasive and troubling trends, particularly in advertising, as follows:

- *Objectification:* Equating women with objects is dehumanizing and encourages the notion that women can be bought, owned, and disposed of.

- *Irrelevant sexualization:* Using women's bodies in a sexual way in order to attract attention perpetuates the attitude that women's primary function is to serve men sexually.

Strong enough for a man... [handwritten note]

advtzrs know they need 5 appt em [handwritten note]

- *Infanticization:* Presenting women as silly, childish, and coy, or passive and vulnerable, waiting to be rescued (especially in contrast to men, who are generally portrayed as strong, serious, and assertive) undermines women's need for independence and reinforces the perception of women as victims.

- *Domestication:* Defining women always in relationship to their husbands, children, or parents, and showing them predominantly in a home environment, denies the complexity of women's lives and their contributions to society.

- *Victimization:* Portraying women as the natural victims of male brutality, either overtly or by implication, is particularly troubling given the incidence of violent acts experienced by women both within and outside of their homes.[7]

Nancy Signorielli, author of numerous studies into the portrayal of women in media during two decades, noted in a 1989 article that over a period of more than 15 years, the image of women was consistent in its traditionality and generally upheld the status quo: women were, on average, younger, more attractive, and more nurturing than men; more likely to be victimized, married, or involved in romantic activity; and, when married, less likely to work outside the home, or more likely to be employed in traditionally female occupations such as nursing or secretarial work. Citing U.S. demographic statistics, Signorielli pointed out the inaccuracies of the television picture in relation to reality, concluding that "the image conveyed by prime time television is that women, especially if married, should stay home and leave the world of work to men."[8]

Subsequent content analysis research undertaken by Signorielli and Bacue comparing three decades of prime time portrayal trends, and including sample programming from as recently as 1998, found that although women continue to receive less *recognition* than men on television, they do experience more *respect* than they previously enjoyed.[9] Female characters remain younger overall than their male counterparts, but more of them are depicted as working outside the home in more prestigious occupations. TV in the late 1990s reflected fewer nurses and teachers and significantly more women employed in traditional male, or gender-neutral, jobs.

Other recent research into the portrayal of women in a variety forms of media suggest that despite persistent areas of concern, some aspects of the picture are changing, albeit slowly. Regulatory initiatives and continued lobbying efforts by women's organizations, which have historically had little impact on "adjusting the image,"[10] are gradually being supplemented by evolving commercial interests. In an increasingly fragmented and competitive communications environment, advertisers and programmers alike are beginning to pay greater attention to the manner in which they depict a significant portion of the consuming public.

The Advertiser's Woman (or "Who's Come a Long Way, Baby?")[11]

Although research studies cataloguing inequitable representation and portrayal trends cross all media forms, much of the most prominent discussion of the negative stereotyping of women in media has focussed on advertising. This is understandable: advertising has sustained a long tradition of criticism, from consumer concerns about false claims to Marcuse's notion of "false needs."[12] In addition, the vast majority of media images are at least indirectly underwritten by—and therefore potentially subject to interference from—commercial advertisers.[13]

Furthermore, the money invested in the creation of advertising campaigns often exceeds that spent on the accompanying programming or editorial copy.[14] Indeed, many of the most memorable messages constituting the shared cultural vocabulary of late twentieth century North America have been brought to us by commercial sponsors. Campaign slogans such as Clairol's "Does she, or doesn't she?", or Virginia Slims' "You've come a long way, baby" are ingrained upon our collective psyche with the permanence of nursery rhymes and parental admonishments. Moreover, the consumption ethos of advertising is directly implicated in the general media tendency to commodify women. As one research team put it, "For the male consumer, the implicit promise is that, if you buy product x, you will also get the sweet young thing associated with it. For the female, the dynamics are those of incorporation: buy product x and *be* the sweet young thing."[15]

John Berger's seminal book and TV series *Ways of Seeing* effectively linked the historical subjugation of women evident in Renaissance art to contemporary advertising imagery in the early 1970s.[16] Erving Goffman's 1979 study *Gender Advertisements*, which analyzed the physically subordinate positioning of women in a select sample of print images, has continued to inspire subsequent research seeking to extend his approach to more current and randomized samples.[17] Later, the widely viewed video *Still Killing Us Softly*, by Jean Kilbourne, introduced a great many teachers and students throughout Canada and the U.S. to Kilbourne's feminist critique of advertising.[18]

Previous reviews of the extensive body of research into this area have cited evidence that demonstrates that, throughout the 1960s and 1970s, both in broadcasting and print media, the advertiser's woman was one who was more likely than her male counterpart to be seen in the home using household cleaning products, or, if employed, working in a stereotypically female (and by implication, subservient) position. Many studies found that a significant portion of prime-time television advertisements locating women outside of the home appeared to present women as sex objects whose primary focus was to attract and hold the attention of men. Women were largely excluded from playing the "voice-of-authority," which, in narrating TV commercials, reinforces the frequent on-camera positioning of men as experts. In contrast, men have traditionally been depicted as independent, intelligent, and ambitious. They have been much more typically featured selling *and* using important and/or "big ticket" items such as pharmaceutical products, cars, and gas (whereas women have been more frequently depicted as authorities about personal care items).[19]

In a replication of one of the earliest comprehensive analyses of network TV commercials, Ferrante, Haynes, and Kingsley determined, from an analysis of almost 1,400 ads appearing in 1986, that there was no significant change with regard to the kinds of products typically associated with women in advertising, the percentage of female voice-overs, or the frequency with which women were used as on-camera authorities.[20] Although women were shown less often at home and in a greater number of roles than in the earlier study, the researchers concluded that "these results reinforce the fact women and men are [still] not treated equally in television advertising."

Similarly, in a 1989 analysis of 353 prime-time television commercials, analyzing voice-overs, products, product representatives, and settings, Lovdal found that all categories were unchanged from a similar 1978 study, except female product representatives.[21] Overall, men were portrayed in three times as many occupations as women, who were instead presented in "a plethora of stereotyped roles, including wife, mother, bride, waitress, actress, dancer, and in a dearth of professional roles such as photographer,

athlete, dentist, and businesswoman." Men continued to dominate 90 percent of voice-overs, and women were seen speaking only to those considered to be of inferior status (pets, children, and other women) about a narrow range of issues such as feminine hygiene, headaches, and diets.

Bretl and Cantor's content analysis of a 1985 sample of television commercials, while confirming the findings cited above regarding both voice-over statistics and the continuing association of female characters with domestic-based products, nevertheless also identified several areas of small, but statistically significant improvement. Compared to a study done on a 1971 sample of advertisements, Bretl and Cantor found that almost as many women as men appeared as the main characters in ads; and that the difference between the numbers of men and women depicted inside the home had decreased. Although women were still less likely to be employed, the gap between men and women in high-status jobs was much lower than previously noted, and the proportion of men depicted as spouses or parents, with no other occupation, had increased.[22] Similar changes were reflected in a 1992 study of print advertisements in the business-oriented publications *Time, Newsweek,* and *The Economist.* Stephenson, Stover, and Villamor found that, although women remained underrepresented overall, they were less often depicted in clerical roles, and more likely to be seen as realtors, interior designers, and small business owners.[23]

Clearly, portrayal trends are influenced by the audience being targeted. Coding a sample of more than 2,000 commercials aired in 1990, Craig determined that advertisements aimed at women homemakers viewing daytime television tended to feature more traditional roles and emphasize domestic duties and maintaining one's appearance.[24] In the evening, however, women were more likely to be seen in authoritative positions away from the home; and on the weekend, advertisements tended to emphasize traditional stereotypes of masculinity (aggressiveness, independence, competitiveness) and to cater to "male fantasy," featuring women in subservient or sex-object roles.

Several studies extending Goffman's seminal work reinforce the persistent disparities.[25] Research in the late 1980s and early 1990s found that women were considerably more likely than men to be portrayed alone, as narcissistic, subordinate, and/or dismembered, while men were more likely than women to be shown engaged in a purposeful activity. (It is worth noting here that "purposeful activity" was tellingly defined by the authors as "sailing a boat, versus kicking up your heels alone in the kitchen.") Interestingly enough, stereotypical gender displays appeared more frequently in advertisements found in the more "modern"–i.e. *MS., GQ,* and *Rolling Stone*–of the six magazines sampled, causing one group of researchers to question whether or not "traditional" publications (in this case, *Good Housekeeping, Sports Illustrated,* and *Time*) were ultimately more progressive than those considered modern.[26]

The most comprehensive Canadian research comes from the content analysis conducted by Erin Research on behalf of the Canadian Radio-television and Telecommunications Commission (CRTC) in 1984 and again in 1988.[27] The 1988 data determined that advertising on Canadian television included fewer female characters than male (41 percent versus 59 percent), and in particular, fewer women over age 35; significantly fewer female voice-overs (14 percent versus 86 percent); and a strong tendency to associate women with home and family roles. In addition, women were more likely to appear in ads for household consumer goods such as detergent or plastic wrap (67 percent), but considerably less visible in paid political announcements (18 percent) or automobile commercials (20 percent). In a sample of 2,000 alcohol ads (at one time seen to be among the most sexist) appearing on Canadian TV, only 7 percent of female characters in beer commercials were found to have speaking roles (versus 29 percent of males); in cooler advertisements, none of the women spoke (versus 49 percent of the men).

In French-language television advertisements in Canada, male and female characters are more evenly split (53 percent and 47 percent respectively), female voice-overs account for 23 percent of the total, and there were less significant gender differences in assigned roles than in English-language ads. The most recent analysis of Canadian print advertising consisted of MediaWatch's recommendations to the Canadian Advertising Foundation in 1993 in response to the latter organization's request for submissions pertaining to its Sex-Role Stereotyping Guidelines, designed to help advertisers voluntarily eliminate sexism. Although not an empirical study, the MediaWatch report provided an anecdotal assessment of the ways in which the guidelines had failed to have any measurable effect on the image of women, and included print advertisements selected from 1992-93 Canadian consumer magazines on the basis of their sexist content. In addition to comments addressing the underrepresentation of women in authoritative roles, the report focussed primarily on the objectification and irrelevant sexualization of women and girls, and the implied linking of sexual "fun" with "danger" or violence.[28]

Indeed, despite the improvements noted above in the range of roles accorded women in advertising, sexualization remains an issue. Plous and Neptune's review of 1,800 advertisements from U.S. fashion publications *Cosmopolitan, Glamour, GQ, Esquire, Ebony,* and *Essence* found that the body exposure of women increased between 1985 and 1994, and that female flesh was approximately four times as common as male skin.[29] Interestingly enough, over the last five years, anecdotal evidence of greater male exposure–most notably in underwear and cologne ads[30]–has suggested that the male-female inequity is changing in this regard. However, the increase in male nudity does not appear to have diminished the incidence of female body exposure. As Plous and Neptune noted, "increases in work-role equity seem to have been offset by a concomitant trend towards displaying women as decorative and sexualized."[31]

In a review of the TV commercials aired during the 1999 Superbowl game, *Advertising Age* observed: "After three decades of gradually weaning itself from naked objectification, advertising has apparently decided that the benefit of crudely impressing men trumps the disadvantages of honouring women. It's as if Madison Avenue sneaked into the nation's psyche and absconded with 30 years of feminist awareness."[32]

It is difficult to determine whether or not such dramatic examples are evident of a more pervasive trend, however. After a spate of content analysis studies in the 1970s and 1980s, the last decade has yielded comparatively little documentation. It is possible that the relative consistency of limiting and sexist depictions over time may have served to discourage more contemporary advertising research in both Canada and the US.

Women in Entertainment Media: What's Wrong with This Picture?

The image of women in contemporary entertainment media has also been the subject of much investigation. The tradition of studies into the roles accorded to women in television series has expanded into analyses of how women fare in feature films, cartoons, and comics, and more recently, music videos and electronic games. As in advertising, dominant messages in the portrayal of women in entertainment programming have included the tendency to portray women as less intelligent and capable, overly emotional and dependent, and in roles that emphasized their domesticity or sexuality.[33] Most notable and consistent of the results of such research is the evidence demonstrating how vastly underrepresented women are in virtually all forms of mainstream entertainment.

Television's Woman (or "Why Do They Call It the 'Boob Tube,' Mommy?")

The most comprehensive research into the status of women in television has been a long-term study by George Gerbner, drawing on the Cultural Indicators research project data archives, which began documenting television trends in 1969. The most recent report, released in 1998, was commissioned by the Screen Actors Guild and provided an update on the findings of a 1993 analysis of prime-time and daytime fictional television programming, including series, films, and animated cartoons. The sample programming studied included 6,882 characters appearing in 440 prime time episodes, and 2,137 characters appearing in 205 episodes of daytime network serial dramas.

The 1993 analysis found that, in terms of sheer numbers, women did best in daytime serials and game shows, where they comprised 45.5 percent of the characters and 55.3 percent of the contestants, respectively. In all other programming formats, women made up one-third or fewer of the on-screen participants, hitting lows of 23.4 percent in children's programming and 27.8 percent in the news. These figures remained remarkably stable from 1982 to 1992, with 1992 statistics accurately reflecting those of a decade earlier.

Some trends were particularly troubling. For instance, although in general "good" characters outnumber "bad" ones in both sexes (2 to 1 for men, and 5 to 1 for women), among older characters, the proportion of female villains was more than eight times that of male villains. In addition, the picture in children's television was found to be the "harshest and most exploitive. The inequities of prime time are magnified Saturday morning. A girl will see about 123 characters ... but rarely, if ever, a role model of her gender as leader."[34]

The 1998 update found that women's representation had increased by 3.5 percent since 1993, from 33.2 percent of the roles to 36.7 percent.[35] However, female characters on television continued to age faster than men, with almost 9 out of 10 being under the age of 46. The roles assigned to them remained primarily romantic, with female characters under age 18 engaging in sexual interaction in more than a quarter of their appearances, while their male counterparts did so in less than a fifth of theirs. Sexual interaction decreased significantly for older female (but not male) characters, and women continued to grow more evil as they aged. Women of colour were even less well represented than their white counterparts.

A more focussed analysis of prime-time portrayal using the Cultural Indicators methodology was conducted using 1992-93 data by Alasmar, Hasegawa, and Brain.[36] In examining the proportion of major versus minor roles in 42 hours of programming culled from 60 different shows, they found that although females represented approximately 39 percent of all speaking roles overall, they accounted for less than 18 percent of major roles. More encouragingly, they also found many more single women in professional, white-collar positions and fewer women who were defined by their romantic links or marital status. Female characters were also less likely to be seen caring for children than in earlier studies.

Canadian data is less readily available: however, what information there is appears to correspond to the results of U.S. research. The CRTC/Erin research, which assessed daytime as well as prime-time dramatic programming, found 43 percent female characters in the former and only 34 percent in the latter. Action dramas were typically found to have the smallest proportion—30 percent or fewer female characters—and situation comedies and soap operas had the highest, at approximately 45 percent. In terms of the roles accorded to women, the authors concluded that, "like female characters in U.S. drama, those seen on Canadian stations tend toward marriage, children, and romance, while men tend toward paid work, vehicles and violence." Furthermore, unlike the findings in advertising, small differences were seen between French and English programming, primarily because 80 percent of characters on Canadian television, in both languages, appear in U.S. productions, a fact which also accounts for the pervasive similarities in media gender imbalance between the two countries.[37]

A television monitoring study conducted by MediaWatch in 1992, which coded 1,295 characters in 75 episodes of nine Canadian-made dramatic series, found that only 33.6 percent of all characters were female. As in the US data, women of colour fared even worse, making up only 4.2 percent of all characters, compared to 12.4 percent of characters

men should change to be like women,
agree.

who were men of colour.[38] In an informal and much less comprehensive review of CTV programming, MediaWatch also noted that in the eight shows planned for the Canadian network's fall 1993 schedule, only 3 female lead characters were featured, compared to 12 male leads.[39]

This is not to say that the television arena has not seen some changes in the portrayal of women over the years. In a comparison of 1987 programming to data from the 1950s, Davis noted a seemingly progressive phenomenon that occurred in the 1970s, when a number of programs featuring female leads seemed to dominate the small screen. Closer analysis, however, revealed that–from the provocatively-dressed "Charlie's Angels" ordered about by the invisible male authority figure, to Mary Tyler Moore, who although independent and single was rarely assertive (always calling her boss "Mr. Grant" when everyone else addressed him as "Lou")–the picture was not particularly indicative of an increase in autonomous and intelligent women.[40]

A number of studies have focussed specifically on the image of women and work. Vande Berg and Streckfuss reviewed three decades of studies on the portrayal of gender and occupation on prime-time television, and extended previous work by examining in their study the organizational actions performed by men and women in a sampling of network television news, sports, and entertainment programming during 1986 and 1987.[41] Their findings, in addition to confirming the unrealistically low percentage of women seen as being employed outside the home, also demonstrated that although women on television were almost as likely as men to be professionals, they still tended to hold lower-status positions (i.e., nurse versus doctor). Women were often seen as inheriting their status from their spouses or relatives and tended to be shown performing proportionately more relationship-oriented actions, such as motivating, socializing, and counselling, and fewer of the political and decision-making actions seemingly reserved for male characters.

In their analysis of these results, the study's authors argued that, from a humanist/feminist perspective (versus through the dominant lens of corporate capitalism), the activities being performed by women may well be seen as measures of success, not failure. Further, they proposed that less attention should be paid to eradicating images of women who are "enacting a humane, interpersonally-focussed, cooperative concerned information-sharing style of working and managing," and more emphasis instead should be given to changing the depiction of television's working men, who are characterized by toughness, self-centeredness, and aggressive competitiveness.

A second study by Atkin, Moorman, and Lin investigating working female leads in prime-time network series during the 1980s did so in the context of structural factors. Their hypothesis about the degree to which market conditions may have played an influential role in the development of and support for strong female-driven series such as *Murphy Brown, Designing Women, Murder She Wrote* and *Roseanne* appears to have potentially significant implications for positive portrayal trends in the future. These implications will be discussed at greater length further on.[42]

Finally, a review of portrayals of women in prime-time promotional announcements during the 1995 television season across both established and emerging US networks determined that female characters were generally portrayed in more provocative attire, as more attractive, and more physically fit than their male counterparts.[43]

It is unfortunate that at this writing, more recent analyses of contemporary programming are not available. In the late 1990s, a number of new television shows featuring female characters in prominent roles certainly contributed to the impression that women's share of the small screen might be on the increase. Although on an anecdotal basis, it may be clear how programs such as *Friends, Ally McBeal, Xena: Warrior Princess, Buffy the Vampire Slayer, Sex in the City,* and *West Wing* reinforce and/or challenge established trends, it would be more telling to have the benefit of research that positions these shows in the context of the rest of the television environment.

Movies: More of the Same (and Good Girls Don't Die)

The analysis of women's representation in film has tended to focus on genre studies or in-depth discussions of individual portrayals, yielding little empirical evidence. In 1989, the U.S. Screen Actors Guild reported that only 14 percent of that year's total number of lead characters were female, and that an increasing number of women's roles were for rape victims or prostitutes.[44] Susan Faludi's analysis of Hollywood portrayal trends in the 1980s, although anecdotal, nevertheless documented some equally disturbing trends. In 1987, for instance, she noted that the "good" women–"subservient and bland housewives, babies, or voiceless babes"–were rewarded (as in *Fatal Attraction, Three Men and a Baby,* and *Beverly Hills Cop*), while the "bad" women–who failed to give up their independence (appearing in the same movies as a "homicidal career woman," a "mannish and child-hating shrew," and a "hip-booted gunwoman")–were punished.[45]

More recently, *Premiere* magazine published a statistical overview of women's status in Hollywood showing some progress. Thirty-four percent of all movies made in 1995, for instance, boasted female protagonists. At the same time, however, the article reported that the average age of best actress Oscar winners had dropped from 45 in the 1980s to 39 in the 1990s, suggesting that television trends continue to be reflective of movie practices.[46]

Film critic Molly Haskell once lamented Hollywood's treatment of women in the 1960s as being characterized by "amoral pinup girls, molls taking guff from their gangsters ... and thirty-year-olds reduced to playing undergraduates.... With the substitution of violence and sexuality for romance, there was less need for exciting and interesting women; any bouncing nymphet whose curves looked good in ketchup would do."[47]

Two analyses dealing with popular "slasher" films targeted mostly to teen viewers and commonly perceived as focussing on the brutal killing of primarily young women suggest that Haskell's complaints remain timely, in at least one genre. The results of Weaver's 1991 investigation into the extent to which male and female characters were victimized by violence in 10 slasher titles contradicted earlier work by Donnerstein, Linz, and Penrod, which concluded that women were far more likely to be brutalized than men.[48] However, although the Weaver study found no significant difference between the number of male and female victims, and no rapes in the films sampled, sexist messages were conveyed by a tendency to reward "virginal" female characters with escape while punishing their more promiscuous friends. In addition, when women were killed, their death scenes were significantly longer than those of their male counterparts.

Cowan and O'Brien's analysis of a considerably larger sample of 56 movies confirmed Weaver's results regarding the equitable victimization of male and female characters, but suggested the common perception that more women die in slasher films may be attributable to the fact that women's "protected" status makes their deaths more memorable and the best-known titles have a preponderance of female victims. Cowan and O'Brien also found evidence to support Donnerstein et al.'s contention about a significant link between sex and violence. Not only did they, like Weaver, note a higher incidence of survival rate among "good" girls, but in addition, their sample revealed 15 instances of rape.[49]

Women in Music Videos: Sex Sells

Sex and violence have formed a potent mixture in another medium aimed primarily at young audiences: music videos. Since the introduction of MTV (Music Television) in 1981, and its Canadian counterpart, MuchMusic, several years later, the derogatory, sexualized image of women in this advertising-cum-art form has also spawned numerous studies. Much of the early research, in addition to reflecting stereotypical occupational roles and a two-to-one ratio of male characters over female (consistent with television data generally), also determined that women were much more likely than men to be dressed provocatively (50 percent versus 10 percent). A majority of videos were found both to depict scenarios in which women were denigrated by men and to include violent, sexual, and criminal activities.[50]

Two analyses of videos broadcast in 1987 tended to support such findings, confirming women's low status, revealing attire, and stereotypical behaviour[51] while demonstrating that male characters were also frequently objectified and shown as engaging in sexually explicit actions.[52] Subsequent U.S. research in the early 1990s continued to document an overemphasis on women's physical features and sexuality,[53] but a decrease in the number of females depicted as dependent and fearful.[54] The latter study also found an increase in the number of female prostitutes appearing in 1993 videos.

Several Canadian studies identified an increase in videos containing sexist portrayals from 46 percent in 1988 to 55 percent in 1992.[55] Sexist videos were also found to get more airtime than non-sexist videos. More than three-quarters of the women depicted were approximately 25 years or younger and portrayed as being "dependent on men, dancing and posing seductively. Women over 25 years of age were typically ugly, badly dressed, and neglected." Although between the two samples, explicit portrayals of violence decreased from 27 percent of videos in 1988 to 16 percent in 1992, implicit violence remained through symbolic representations that used special effects and image juxtaposition. According to the aggregated data from the CRTC's 1984 and 1988 studies, women constitute 3 percent of instrumental players, 19 percent of singers, and 40 percent of dancers.

In 1996, MediaWatch undertook a more recent analysis of MuchMusic programming. However, the group's failure to predict that "prostitute" would constitute a significant occupation category so skewed the data (and demoralized the coders) that the volunteer-driven project was abandoned.[56] Interestingly enough, the most recent analysis–a review of country music videos airing in 1997–confirmed earlier trends in rock and rap genres (regarding underrepresentation, stereotypes, and appearance emphasis), with one exception: country music videos do not feature sexual violence against women; nor do they portray women as strippers and prostitutes.[57]

Women and the News: "And that's the kind of day it's been..."[58]

George Gerbner describes the thematic structure of news as dealing with "the exercise of power: who has it, who uses it, who seeks it, and most of all, who threatens it."[59] This analysis provides a disturbing, if partial, explanation for the invisibility and imposed irrelevancy of women in both print and broadcast news programming. Often referred to as a "window" on the world in general, and on one's own society specifically, news, because it is a selective process of construction, is also widely accepted as serving "a narrative function ... circulating meanings that in general confirm and conserve existing social and economic relationships."[60] As Stuart Hall notes,

> The choice of *this* moment of an event as against that, of *this* person rather than that, of *this* angle rather than any other, indeed, the selection of this photographed incident to represent a whole complex chain of events and meanings, is a highly ideological procedure.[61]

Although one might expect women to appear less often as newsmakers, given the fact that they occupy fewer positions of power and authority in society, this is inevitably compounded by a situation in which the definition of news, and the criteria governing the selection process Hall describes, remain predominantly determined by men.

Women in Newsprint: Dying to Make Headlines[62]

Davis' 1982 analysis of 5,500 stories in eight newspapers revealed the following trends in the portrayal of women in newspapers: women were rarely the main characters in news stories and when they were, the headlines were smaller and the stories shorter; women were rarely present in sports or business stories, but appeared more often in "soft" features; and they were rarely quoted. More often than men,

women were referred to by their first names, described in personal ways (rather than by occupation or experience), and defined by their spousal relationships.[63]

These trends–although gradually changing–are reflected in more current studies, as well. MediaWatch's national newspaper survey of 15 or more English language Canadian dailies gathered annual statistics between 1990 and 1993, and again in 1998, confirming that, on average, female reporters and columnists comprised just under 30 percent of those shaping the print news and less than 20 percent of those whose activities are considered newsworthy or whose opinions are considered worth soliciting. Three French-language papers, analyzed in 1993 only, and the *National Post*, introduced in 1998, reflected on average 20 percent female bylines and 15 percent or fewer references made to women. The MediaWatch surveys cited evidence of all of the trends observed by Davis, as well as the presence–albeit declining–of sexist language. Common examples included the frequent use of false generics (such as "chairman" or "spokesman," even when referring to a woman); or descriptions of female musicians and athletes that focus on their physical appearance and sexuality (in a manner rarely used to describe male performers) and de-emphasize their professional skill and achievements.[64]

In fact, separate studies exploring the coverage of women's sports document a particularly inequitable picture. An analysis of national U.S. television sports programs in 1995 found that both ESPN and CNN devoted only about 5 percent of their stories to women's sports, and the stories tended to be significantly shorter than those on male athletes and/or activities.[65] Olympic coverage is kinder to women in terms of volume of coverage, although undue attention continues to be focussed on their marital status, emotionality, and appearance.[66]

In 1995, MediaWatch and Erin Research co-ordinated researchers in 71 countries to create a database on the participation and portrayal of women in the world's radio, television, and print news media. The resulting report drew on 49,000 data records representing information on more than 40,000 journalists and interviewees appearing in over 15,000 news stories. Although regional differences were evident–most notably in India, where 71 percent of journalists were female, concentrated mostly in broadcasting–the findings of this *Global Media Monitoring Project* reflect trends similar to those of earlier, less comprehensive studies: excluding

India, women represented 36 percent of all journalists and 19 percent of interviewees.[67]

On a qualitative level, Columbia journalism professor Helen Benedict conducted a comprehensive analysis of the way in which the press treats female rape victims. Her study documented the extent to which entrenched but false assumptions about rape, underlying and reflected in U.S. media coverage of sex crimes, result in the perpetuation of a virgin or vamp dichotomy and pervasive "blame-the-victim" mentality.[68] Examining in exhaustive detail the newspaper reporting of four high-profile cases (some covered extensively by Canadian media, as well, such as that of the "Central Park Jogger"), Benedict described problematic journalistic practices that include the use of sexist and sexually charged language to describe victims; the tendency to focus on the woman's lifestyle and past, despite its frequently questionable relevance; and the failure to provide context for a particular crime, which would locate it within a larger social phenomenon. Benedict's microanalysis provides a useful and compelling counterpoint to the more readily available empirical studies, which often fail to address relevant social and institutional contexts.

Women in Television News: Reading the Teleprompter

In its assessment of gender representation in Canadian broadcasting, the CRTC-commissioned Erin study determined from the 1988 sampling of English-language television news that women were most likely to appear as anchors (39 percent) than reporters (28 percent), and least often as those interviewed (22 percent). French-language news representation was marginally better. In addition, female reporters were found to cover proportionately more "soft" and local stories than their male counterparts. These results echoed those of Soderlund, Surlin, and Romanow in their examination of on-air staff in local newscasts from a selection of 21 stations across Canada in 1985.[69] Later, MediaWatch, in its submission to the CRTC licence renewal hearings for CTV in 1993, cited evidence regarding Canada's largest private broadcaster's predominance of male hosts and experts.[70]

The "host" category is subject to employment equity initiatives and appears to be improving at a faster rate than the latter, in which the low numbers are explained in part by reporters' tendency to rely on traditional sources (typically male-dominated government and industry networks) and by the perceived relative scarcity of female experts.[71]

Data pertaining to U.S. television news reports, many of which are also seen by Canadian viewers, reveal similar trends. In Gerbner's survey of 31 U.S. newscasts during the spring of 1992, women comprised only 35.4 percent of news deliverers, 20 percent of authorities cited, and 17.4 percent of newsmakers. The U.S. study also noted that the only significant attention paid by the news to women's rights related to the contentious abortion issue (6 percent of news items in 31 newscasts over a period of eight days in 1992).[72]

Many of these reports have suggested that better representation of women in the profession of journalism–both print and broadcasting–will necessarily ensure that news content itself begins better to reflect women's experiences and voices. However, an analysis of 159 stories broadcast on major U.S. networks during the first 100 days of the Clinton administration in the early 1990s found little difference between the way male and female journalists reported the news.[73] Authors Liebler and Smith concurred with earlier researchers Rakow and Kranich[74] in suggesting that changing the way in which current news practices marginalize women requires not simply more female journalists and more extensive coverage of issues directly involving women, but profound structural change. The latter argue, for instance, that news is an essentially masculine narrative, in which women's relative absence as sources and subjects is made even more problematic by the fact that, when they do appear, they serve more as a ritualized notion of "women," acting as "no less the bearers of meaning, the objects of male fantasy than other representations of women."[75]

The Impact of Gender Portrayal

The implicit hypothesis inspiring virtually all of the studies into gender portrayal in mass media is that stereotyping and underrepresentation have a negative socializing influence. Considering the weight of evidence already cited regarding the biased nature of gender portrayal in the context of a society still struggling with persistent and systemic sexism, such attention would not seem unwarranted. Nevertheless, measuring the socializing effects of media in this area (as in others) has proven to be a significant challenge.

The bulk of the research into the media effects of gender portrayal has focussed on the extent to which children learn sex-role attitudes and behaviours from television. Early experimental studies summarized by Signorielli[76] suggest that boys and girls identify with same-sex TV characters (including those in cartoons) whom they perceive to be exhibiting sex-typed attributes (i.e., boys respond to physical strength and activity level, and girls to physical attractiveness). Furthermore, heavy television viewing in children and teens has been found to correlate to stereotyping of occupational roles; increased agreement with statements such as "women are happiest at home raising children" and "men are born with more ambition than women"; the exhibition of greater sex-typing behaviour for gender-related qualities and activities (i.e., independence and sports for boys; warmth and cooking for girls); and the increased likelihood that children will identify domestic chores as being associated with either men or women along traditional lines.[77]

One of the most compelling pieces of research into media effects is the widely cited natural experiment conducted by MacBeth (and discussed at greater length elsewhere in this volume).[78] Capitalizing on the much-delayed introduction of television into a small British Columbia community ("Notel"), MacBeth and her colleagues assembled before-and-after data that, among other things, demonstrated that children's perceptions with regards to sex roles were less strongly sex typed prior to the presence of TV, and only became comparable to the perceptions of children in other communities ("Unitel" and "Multitel"), which were already receiving one or two stations after the medium's introduction. The unique opportunity to measure the impact of television as an isolated variable makes the findings of this study particularly persuasive.

 The literature investigating effects of gender portrayal on adult subjects is much more limited, but several small-sample studies suggest that positive relationships exist between the viewing of entertainment programming and the acceptance of traditional sex roles; the viewing of daytime serials and the support of traditional family structures and values; and the viewing of stereotyped material and the amount of sex-role stereotyping in self-descriptions.[79] Research conducted by Geis, Brown, Walstedt, and Porter on the effects of traditional and non-traditional gender roles in TV commercials found that the viewing of sex stereotypes in ads prompted women to downplay achievement in favour of homemaking as compared to men, and as compared to women who had viewed reversed sex role commercials.[80]

A number of studies have responded to the growing rates of anorexia and bulimia among young women, as viewed in the context of a media image of women that is defined by the bodies of fashion models who weigh 23 percent less than the average North American woman, and—along with female actors and dancers—are estimated to be thinner than 95 percent of the population.[81] Earlier research has determined that media generally emphasize women's appearance to a greater extent than men's and present a steadily thinning female ideal; women are more likely than men to overestimate their body size; and extra weight has become associated with poor health and lack of control.[82]

Building on this material, Myers and Biocca conducted an experimental study exposing affluent young women to some combination of body image-oriented and/or non-body image-oriented TV commercials and/or programming. Although the women overestimated their body sizes as expected after viewing commercials that focussed attention on body image and products or services designed to achieve a thin shape, the subjects tended to feel slightly euphoric and thinner than they normally would. The response to the programming was much weaker, and the authors hypothesized that the advertisements' first-person address effectively invited viewers to fantasize that they could attain their ideal bodies (albeit with help). The authors suspected that the slightly improved mood registered by the women immediately after viewing the commercials would diminish (and perhaps translate into the more commonly documented "self-loathing") when confronted by "the cold reality of the mirror." Nevertheless, they concluded that the most significant aspect of the experiment was the implication that "watching even 30 minutes of television programming and advertising can alter a woman's perception of the shape of her body." Subsequent research found women's body image satisfaction was affected by even 13 minutes of exposure to fashion magazines; the subjects' preoccupation with thinness was heightened after viewing the thin models featured in the publications.[83]

Although a discussion of mainstream pornography and the related effects research is outside the scope of this chapter, it is useful to refer to this body of literature, given the increasing concern about violence against women in the media already mentioned, the infiltration of pornographic imagery into mainstream media forms,[84] and the growth of the pornography industry itself, which now generates more money worldwide than the "legitimate" film and music industries combined.[85] Augustine Brannigan points out elsewhere in this volume that research has not established a definitive link between use of pornography and criminal behaviour. Nevertheless, the experimental evidence suggesting that exposure to sexually violent films desensitizes both male and female viewers to victims of violence, and increases acceptance of rape myths,[86] is problematic enough in a society struggling with the consequences of high incidences of real sexual violence against women.[87]

Research Challenges

Much of the content analysis research has assessed portrayal trends in empirical terms, and then simply hypothesized possible effects, drawing on theory or literature from psychology and other related fields. Because of the impossibility of isolating the impact of one or more media forms from the myriad of other influences on sex-role socialization (such as family, school, or friends), even those studies that have attempted to draw conclusions based on experimental evidence have been met with some scepticism. The cultivation model used by Gerbner and Signorielli, because it seeks global impacts, is able to identify only small effects, due to the extent to which individual viewers respond differently. At the same time, lab experiments, which take personal and situational variables into consideration, are able to predict results only within the narrow field of the individual experiments themselves, making it difficult to generalize their findings. Tuchman, in her 1979 summary of the available research on media effects, argued that any conclusions made at that point in time about the impact of gender portrayal would have to mirror those made by the then-recent Surgeon-General's report on violence, and go only so far as to suggest that "for some children, under some circumstances, televised sex-role stereotypes may be harmful to optimal personal development."[88]

Despite the multitude of research on gender roles undertaken in the intervening years, this perspective appears to remain. As Spears and Seydegart point out, despite common sense conclusions that might be drawn from the existing body of evidence regarding the likelihood of a preponderance effect, the systemic discrimination quantified by the research and the evidence supporting at least the potential for harm have failed to translate into truly effective policy.[89]

The Regulatory Environment: Ineffective and Increasingly Irrelevant

In 1932, then Prime Minister R.B. Bennett declared the airwaves a "national resource" that should be protected from "private exploitation" and reserved for the use of the people. Implicit in this statement, and in the radio broadcasting act that followed it, was the notion that such a powerful means of communication should be used for the benefit of *all* Canadians. Almost 70 years later, the evidence demonstrates that the system continues to fail to reflect Canadian women in a fair and equitable manner.

From the Canadian Radio League in the 1930s, through the Massey Commission on broadcast policy in 1949, the Fowler Commission on television policy in 1955, and the Royal Commission on the Status of Women in 1967, women and women's groups have been actively lobbying the government, urging that they be portrayed "as free human beings with the same capacities as men."[90] Finally, in 1979, continued pressure led to the establishment of the Task Force on Sex-Role Stereotyping in the Broadcast Media by the CRTC. For the next three years, public representatives worked with members of the broadcasting and advertising industries to develop guidelines that would eliminate gender stereotyping. In its 1982 report, *Images of Women*, the commission recommended that the guidelines be voluntary for a two-year period of self-regulation, after which industry initiatives towards addressing the problems would be assessed.[91]

As previously mentioned, in 1984, the CRTC commissioned an independent firm, Erin Research, to conduct a comprehensive content analysis documenting the portrayal of gender roles in Canadian broadcasting. Published in 1985, the first Erin report revealed that there were fewer women than men in virtually all aspects of Canadian broadcasting, both programming and advertising, and that the roles of women and men differed qualitatively in every area. In light of this, and after additional presentations at public hearings during April of 1986, the CRTC acknowledged that, although industry had shown greater sensitivity to the problem, this had not translated into sufficient improvement. As a result, compliance with the sex-role stereotyping guidelines—which the CRTC asked the Canadian Association of Broadcasters (CAB) to strengthen—was made mandatory and a condition of licence for radio and television licencees. The commission further indicated that broadcasters would be required to describe at licence renewal hearings the efforts they were making and policies they had developed to address the issue of sex-role stereotyping. (Unfortunately, despite the fact that presenters at the CRTC hearings and the commissioners themselves all acknowledged that getting women into key decision-making positions would be the most effective solution to media sexism,[92] no measures were taken on employment equity. The CRTC indicated that under the then-current *Broadcasting Act*, it had no authority over broadcasters' hiring practices.)

In 1988, the CRTC had Erin Research conduct a second, follow-up study of gender portrayal in Canadian broadcasting, mirroring the methodology of the original 1984 research. Published in 1990, this report found that, based on its review of the gender-portrayal data, the 1984 to 1988 period was "characterized much more by stability than by change." Although some improvement was noted, women still lagged behind men in both quantitative and qualitative measures.

In 1990, after several delays and amendments, the CRTC finally approved the CAB's new guidelines, which include specifics relating to women's changing roles; the presentation of a diversity of lifestyles, ages, races, and appearances; the avoidance of exploitation; the use of non-sexist language; and balance in expert representation, among other things.[93] While an important step, these guidelines nevertheless still lacked easily measurable goals and dates for achieving targets. Furthermore, since the CRTC would not be measuring the broadcasters' compliance with the guidelines, determination of their failure to adhere was dependent on a public complaint process. This required not only that groups and individuals know the guidelines and regulations, but also that they monitor radio and television stations and submit formal complaints or intervene in licence-renewal hearings. In addition, the CRTC's assessment of any such complaints would be in some part reliant on a subjective evaluation of the licensee's goodwill and intention to comply.

In fact, a comprehensive analysis of the 1988 licence-renewal hearings conducted by Linda Trimble determined that the commission failed to assess industry actions regarding gender stereotyping to any significant degree. Few questions were asked of licensees about the issue (usually only one, of a general nature) and the condition of licence requirement was rarely mentioned. Further, Trimble noted that the commission was satisfied by mere assurances by licensees that they were attempting to educate

staff or monitor programming and advertising.[94] A subsequent survey by MediaWatch of transcript hearings from 18 stations across Canada confirmed these findings.[95]

The new broadcast act, passed by Parliament in September of 1991 and which the CRTC is under obligation to enforce, now states:

> Canadian broadcasting should through its programming and the employment opportunities arising out of its operations, serve the needs and interests and reflect the circumstances and aspirations of Canadian men, women and children, including equal rights.[96]

This wording gave the CRTC new authority, paving the way for the commission's 1992 announcement that the employment equity practices of its licensees would subsequently be subject to review during licencing hearings. Chairman Keith Spicer noted that

> despite the efforts by broadcasters in recent years, there is still much to be done to eliminate barriers to employment for ... traditionally under-represented groups....

and further stated that

> the Commission recognizes that the Canadian broadcasting system has a unique and ... influential role to play by providing realistic, equitable portrayal of men and women in the programming and advertising it brings into Canadian homes. This is why we intend to maintain a strong presence in the area of gender portrayal.[97]

Despite these words, however, the CRTC also indicated in its 1992 Policy on Gender Portrayal (CRTC 1192-58) that it would drop the condition of licence regarding adherence to the sex-role portrayal code—its only measure of enforcement—for broadcasters who had been members of the Canadian Broadcast Standards Council (CBSC), an industry body, for six months. Far from reflecting Spicer's contention about "maintaining a strong presence in the area of gender portrayal," this effectively constitutes an abandonment of the issue to an industry that had already demonstrated its unwillingness to follow voluntarily imposed guidelines under self-regulation. Although the CBSC positions itself as an organization designed to administer the code and inform and educate broadcasters about emerging social trends, its role, too, is a passive one; action is taken only if members of the public knowledgeable about the system register formal complaints.[98] The discrepancy between the situation requiring improvement and the measures in place to effect the necessary change is considerable. Although the evidence demonstrates that media discrimination against women is systemic, the complaint-driven, and therefore piecemeal, process by which change is theoretically being supported is not conducive to tangible, let alone pervasive, improvement.

Much like the CAB, the Canadian Advertising Foundation (CAF) has long argued for and managed to maintain a position of self-regulation regarding gender portrayal. The CAF guidelines are purely voluntary; even when–as the result of consumer complaints–an advertiser is found by the CAF to be in contravention of the guidelines (which deal with issues such as equality in roles of authority, the avoidance of sexual exploitation, and the use of inclusive language), the industry body merely informs the advertiser of the infraction by letter, and may suggest ways of altering the depiction. In rare cases, CAF has suggested that an ad be discontinued, but the voluntary nature of the guidelines and the fact that not all advertisers and media outlets support the organization prevent CAF from enforcing any of its recommendations. A case in point is the experience with other media. Films, magazines and books–although classified by provincial film review boards according to the difficult-to-define "community standards" criteria, or regulated by Criminal Code obscenity provisions, are not subject to any equality regulations. Films receiving a restricted rating may not be shown or rented to persons under the age of 18, although an informal survey of video store employees suggests that such rules are by no means universally enforced.

Exerting an impact on video games and computer pornography has also proved enormously difficult. The failure of existing regulations to deliver greater equity in traditional media disinclines both advocates and government to invest additional energy in developing rules for newer media forms. This does not mean that occasional efforts to encourage more responsible practices are not being made; however, such efforts tend to focus primarily on restricting the accessibility of violent material by children and youth,[99] rather than on the more ambiguous and contentious issues relating to the portrayal of gender. Bureaucratic processes designed to deal with sexually degrading material available in print have been notoriously ineffective; the rate of technological change renders the application of anti-pornography and equity regulations even less likely in electronic media.

Indeed, in this age of rapid technological change, some expect regulatory measures to become increasingly irrelevant, as a continually shifting communications environment renders policies developed to suit today's circumstances inapplicable tomorrow.

A History of Activism

From the introduction of broadcasting in Canada in the 1930s through to the present day, women's groups have been integrally involved in the debate and research into gender portrayal and representation in the media. MediaWatch, founded in 1981 as a result of the findings of the 1979 CRTC Task Force, was the first group established specifically to address the issue and has been among the most active and influential in its lobbying, educational, and advocacy efforts. Located in Toronto, and dependent on a national network of volunteers, MediaWatch has published numerous research studies on the portrayal and representation of women in Canadian media; is a regular intervener in CRTC hearings; supports consumers in their efforts to be heard by broadcasters, publishers, and advertisers; and has developed and distributed a wide variety of print and video educational materials for both industry and the public. The organization has a history of successful advocacy initiatives at municipal, provincial, and federal levels. Influential in the development of many of the regulatory measures described above, MediaWatch is recognized internationally by organizations seeking to improve the media portrayal of women elsewhere.[100]

Most of the other Canadian organizations formed specifically to address women's inequity in media are professional groups seeking primarily to improve the opportunities for and presence of women in the communications industries. These include Toronto Women in Film and Television (TWIFT; formed in 1984), and its regional counterparts in Vancouver and Montreal. In 1991 TWIFT published *A Statistical Profile of Women in Canadian Film and Television Industry,* documenting the extent to which women are underrepresented both generally (composing 35 percent of industry employees overall) and in management (14 percent). The three organizations develop training courses for women, present briefs to the government on equity issues, and support women's networking in the industry.

Canadian Women in Radio and Television (CWRT), and the Canadian Association of Journalists women's caucus, both established in 1991, also work to promote women in their respective industries, as does the National ACTRA (Alliance of Canadian Cinema, Television and Radio Artists) Women's Committee. In 1991, a number of high-profile Canadian women's organizations and concerned individuals co-operated in the formation of CASandRA (Coalition Against Sexism and Racism in Advertising). CASandRA's first initiative was to lobby for regulation in Ontario to eliminate sexism and racism in beer and liquor advertisements deemed at the time to be the worst offenders in their portrayal of women.

Conclusion

Ironically, the advertising industry may, in the final analysis, become responsible for initiating the much-needed shift in the way in which women are portrayed in, and by, contemporary mass media. Where empirical documentation of systemic underrepresentation and the lobbying efforts of women's groups have failed, bottom-line considerations may ultimately prevail. Although the industry has been slow to respond to trends such as the fact that women purchase the majority of men's clothing and half of all automobiles sold in the United States (worth many billions annually),[101] there is evidence to suggest that this reluctance is becoming an unaffordable luxury.

As the lifeblood of commercial media, advertising not only has some influence over programming content, scheduling, and lifespan, it also must demonstrate some level of sensitivity to consumers, who are becoming increasingly cynical and sophisticated in their engagement with a media environment in which technology appears to be poised to expand their choices exponentially. In the past, advertisers (and, to a lesser extent, programmers) have defended their portrayal practices by arguing that as individual creative teams they cannot be held responsible for the aggregate image that emerges; stereotypes are (in an age of 15-second TV commercials) necessary cultural shorthand;[102] the products of their efforts are essentially mythical narratives designed not to reflect realities, but to evoke desires;[103] and finally, people seek identification with their ideal selves and don't want to be shown reality-based portrayals.[104]

The first two defences might carry some weight if media sexism were not systemic, and if men were as victimized as women by portrayal practices; the latter two contentions are increasingly questionable. Although it is clear that women derive pleasure from even some of the media products that carry the most limiting imagery (women's magazines, for instance, represent a "multi-million dollar business which presents pleasurable, value-laden semiotic systems to immense numbers of women"),[105] nevertheless, there is increasing evidence that female audiences are also becoming much more discriminating about portrayal issues. Advertising executive Rena Bartos' research into how homemakers and working women responded to traditional and progressive portrayals determined that both groups "responded most

positively to contemporary commercials and imagery, and most negatively to traditional ones." She found that women were particularly offended by exploitative ads portraying women as sex objects, and cited a National Advertising Review Board (NARB) study that found that "the most vocal critics of advertising as 'sexist' are younger, better educated, more articulate women who often are opinion leaders."[106]

Why then, do women continue to purchase products—or watch programs—that they feel insult their intelligence? The empirical evidence cited here supports Bartos' explanation that it is because they have no choice; virtually all advertising (television programming, and so forth) discriminates against women, so boycotting media or advertisers on the basis of inequity would mean severely limiting their cultural participation. Indeed, a second NARB study into complaints against advertising concluded that people buy products *despite* being offended by ad messages, not because of them.

More recently, Canadian data gathered by CompuSearch/InfoGroup for a specialty-television service applicant determined that a significant percentage of Canadian women—with higher education and income levels—agreed that women are, by and large, negatively portrayed in the media.[107] At the same time, even though viewers with lower income and less education appeared less aware of negative portrayals, women in these categories expressed a particularly strong preference for TV programs depicting women in "smart, confident yet feminine roles." These survey findings were further confirmed by independently conducted focus-group research, which determined that women with young families were critical of broadcasters for airing programs rife with poor role models. Perceiving television to be an influential medium helping to shape children's values, they felt that broadcasters "should take more responsibility to help expose young children of both sexes to realistic and positive portrayals of women living and successfully coping with a variety of different situations and lifestyles."[108]

Although there has been no comprehensive analysis of the extent to which women respond to alternative imagery when they *are* given a choice, anecdotal evidence from various media is relevant. A 1993 review of trade and academic literature relating to female audiences and supplemented by audience-rating statistics found that programs produced by women and featuring strong female leads (such as *Murphy Brown, Roseanne,* and Canadian productions *ENG* and *North of 60*) were more popular among female audiences than, for instance, police dramas featuring very few women.[109] Moreover, a competitive environment was found to be conducive to the production of more women-oriented programming. Two studies noted that the number of single-female leads and their range of occupations expanded during the 1970s, a time characterized by network rivalry, and again during the late 1980s, when cable expansion increased competition. This suggests that given the opportunity, women will choose progressive imagery over that which is traditional or stereotypic.

No similar evidence is available in the advertising arena, although the phenomenal success of The Body Shop, a rapidly growing retail empire competing in the highly saturated and advertising-obsessed personal care industry, is an instructive case. The Body Shop does no traditional advertising, relying instead on word-of-mouth, a Web presence, and publicity generated largely by news and feature interviews with the corporation's female president, who is openly critical of the cosmetic industry's traditional advertising appeals to women's insecurities.[110] As one marketing columnist noted: "The reality watch already is evident as cosmetic and hair companies increasingly try to lure the older woman by recycling the models of the seventies—laugh lines, crow's feet and all."[111]

As the marketplace is increasingly forced to recognize women's economic clout, the portrayal picture may well improve. Women's continued striving for more equitable treatment in media, in the context of the struggle for equity in society at large, may ultimately be achieved primarily because media and advertising industries decide that "sex sells" has become secondary to "money talks." Indeed, if this trend is realized, it will underline the extent to which, in the world of commercial media at least, equity comes with a price tag: for an underrepresented group to be treated fairly by mass culture, its members must first acquire sufficient spending power to be perceived as a viable audience and/or commodity.

Notes

1. Gramsci's concept of hegemony informs and is central to a large body of work; see for instance Todd Gitlin, "Television's Screens: hegemony in transition" in *Cultural and Economic Reproduction in Education*, ed. M. Apple (London: Rutledge and Kegan Paul, 1982), p.203; and, especially relevant to this paper, Ellen McCracken, *Decoding Women's Magazines From Mademoiselle to Ms.* (London: The MacMillan Press Ltd., 1993), p.3; and Karen M. Stoddard, *Saints and Shrews: Women and Aging in American Popular Film* (Westport, Connecticut: Greenwood Press, 1983), p.5.

2. Dallas W. Smythe, "Reality as Presented by Television" in *Public Opinion Quarterly*, 18, 1954, pp.143-156. In an analysis of one week of dramatic programming on several New York stations, Smythe noted that only a third of the characters were women; that they were on average five years younger than the men; and that women who remained in the home were more likely to be considered "good."

3. Gaye Tuchman, "Women's Depiction by the Mass Media" in *Signs*, 4.3, 1979, p.530.

4. *Role Portrayal and Stereotyping on TV: An Annotated Bibliography of Studies Relating to Women, Minorities, Aging, Sexual Behaviour, Health and Handicaps*, compiled and edited by Nancy Signorielli (Westport, Connecticut: Greenwood Press, 1985), pp.3-89; and *Women and the Media: Resources for Analysis and Action*, compiled by Michelle Valiquette (Toronto: MediaWatch, 1993).

5. MediaWatch, *Tracing the Roots of MediaWatch*, 1993, p.5.

6. See, for instance, three reports released in 1993 by various federal government departments or organizations, including: *Gender Equality in the Justice System* (Department of Justice); *Living Without Fear: Everyone's Goal, Every Women's Right* (Status of Women Canada); and *Changing the Landscape: Ending Violence–Achieving Equality* (Canadian Panel on Violence Against Women).

7. These categories represent a condensed version of trends described in MediaWatch's *Objection Letter Guide*, 1992, p.4.

8. Nancy Signorielli, "Television and Conceptions About Sex Roles: Maintaining Conventiality and the Status Quo" in *Sex Roles*, Vol. 21, Nos. 5/6, 1989, pp.341-360. See also studies cited in Signorielli, *Role Portrayal and Stereotyping on TV: An Annotated Bibliography of Studies Relating to Women, Minorities, Aging, Sexual Behaviour, Health and Handicap*.

9. Nancy Signorielli and Aaron Bacue, "Recognition and Respect: A Content Analysis of Prime-Time Television Characters Across Three Decades" in *Sex Roles*, Vol.40, No. 7/8, 1999, pp.527-545.

10. This reference is taken from a 1987 MediaWatch-sponsored conference entitled *Adjusting the Image*.

11. The Virginia Slims campaign slogan, arguably one of the longest running lines in advertising history, is also one of the most inflammatory. Jean Kilbourne criticizes the concept on two counts: for trivializing a woman's real need for independence by equating the escape from restrictive traditions with the freedom to ruin one's health by smoking; and for targeting young women already concerned about achieving an unrealistically slim body image with a campaign that constructs a deliberate association between weight loss and a habit that kills. *Still Killing Us Softly* (Cambridge, Massachusetts: Cambridge Documentary Films, 1987).

12. For a discussion of the dominant critiques of advertising, see William Leiss, Stephen Kline, and Sut Jhally, *Social Communication in Advertising* (Toronto: Nelson Canada, 1990), pp.15-33.

13. Although editors and programmers typically deny that advertisers are permitted to influence content, Gloria Steinem provides an especially relevant description of advertiser influence on the non-advertising content of women's magazines in "Sex, Lies and Advertising" in *Ms.* July/August 1990, pp.18-28. Ben Bagdikian also documents a number of cases in *The Media Monopoly* (Boston: Beacon Press, 4th edition, 1992), especially pp.152-173.

14. Sut Jhally, *The Codes of Advertising: Fetishism and the Political Economy of Meaning in the Consumer Society*, (London: Pinter, 1987), p.103.

15. Michelle A. Masse and Karen Rosenblum, "Male and Female Created They Them: The Depiction of Gender in the Advertising of Traditional Women's and Men's Magazines" in *Women Studies International Forum*, 1988, Vol. 11, No. 2, p.143.

16. John Berger, *Ways of Seeing* (London: British Broadcasting Corporation/Penguin Books, 1973), especially pp.36-64.

17. Penny Belknap and Wilbert M. Leonard II, "A Conceptual Replication and Extension of Erving Goffman's Study of Gender Advertisements," in *Sex Roles*, Vol. 25, Nos. 3/4, 1991, pp.103-118, and Masse and Rosenblum, "Male and Female Created They Them: The Depiction of Gender in the Advertising of Traditional Women's and Men's Magazines," pp.127-144.

18. The video has been broadcast frequently on public television and disseminated through educational video distribution networks throughout North America.

19. For reviews of the earlier literature in this area, see Benjamin D. Singer, *Advertising and Society* (Toronto: Addison-Wesley, 1986), pp.104-108; Alice E. Courtney and Thomas W. Whipple, *Sex Stereotyping in Advertising* (Massachusetts: Lexington Books, 1983); and Lynn T. Lovdal, "Sex Role Messages in Television Commercials: An Update" in *Sex Roles*, Vol. 21, Nos. 11/12, 1989, pp.715-724.

20. Carol L. Ferrante, Andrew M. Haynes, and Sarah M. Kingsley, "Image of Women in Television Advertising," in *Journal of Broadcasting & Electronic Media*, Volume 32, Number 2, Spring 1988, pp.231-237.

21. Lovdal, "Sex Role Messages in Television Commercials: An Update," pp.715-724.

22. Daniel J. Bretl and Joanne Cantor, "The Portrayal of Men and Women in U.S. Television Commercials: A Recent Content Analysis and Trends Over 15 Years" in *Sex Roles*, Vol. 18, Nos. 9/10, 1988, pp.595-609.

23. Theresa Stephenson, William J. Stover, and Mike Villamor, "Sell Me Some Prestige! The Portrayal of Women in Business-Related Ads" in *Journal of Popular Culture*, Vol. 3, No. 4, Spring 1997, pp.255-271.

24. R. Stephen Craig, "The Effect of Day Part on Gender Portrayals in Television Commercials: A Content Analysis" in *Sex Roles*, Vol. 26, Nos. 5/6, 1992, pp.197-211.

25. See Belknap and Leonard, "A Conceptual Replication and Extension of Erving Goffman's Study of Gender Advertisements," pp.103-118; Masse and Rosenblum, "Male and Female Created They Them: The Depiction of Gender in the Advertising of Traditional Women's and Men's Magazines," pp.127-144; and Mee-Eun Kang, "The Portrayal of Women's Images in Magazine Advertisements: Goffman's Gender Analysis Revisited," in *Sex Roles*, Vol. 37, Nos. 11/12, 1997.

26. Belknap and Leonard, "A Conceptual Replication and Extension of Erving Goffman's Study of Gender Advertisements," pp.103-118.

27. CRTC *Portrayal of Gender in Canadian Broadcasting: 1984-1988*. Prepared by George Spears and Kasia Seydegart, Erin Research Inc. (Ottawa: CRTC, 1990), as cited in George Spears and Kasia Seydegart, *Gender and Violence in the Mass Media*, Report Prepared for the Family Violence Prevention Division, Health and Welfare, Canada, Erin Research, 1993, pp.32-33.

28. "Submission to the Canadian Advertising Foundation Re: Revision of Sex-Role Stereotyping Guidelines" (Toronto: MediaWatch, 1993).

29. Plous and Neptune, "Racial and Gender Bias in Magazine Advertising," pp.627-644.

30. Shari Graydon, "Reverse Sexism in Advertising," CBC Radio Commentary, broadcast in various Canadian markets, 30 June 1999.

31. S. Plous and Dominique Neptune, "Racial and Gender Bias in Magazine Advertising" in *Psychology of Women Quarterly*, 21, 1997, pp.627-644.

32. B. Garfield, "Chauvinist Pigskin: Ad review: Super Bowl advertisers set the world back 30 years with naked appeals to guys," *Advertising Age*, 1 February 1999, p.1.

33. A brief review of the literature pertaining to women in television can be found in Donald M. Davis, "Portrayals of Women in Prime-Time Network Television: Some Demographic Characteristics" in *Sex Roles*, Vol. 23, Nos. 5/6, 1990, pp.325-332.

34. George Gerbner, "Women and Minorities on Television: A study in casting and fate," A report to the Screen Actors Guild and The American Federation of Radio and Television Artists, June 15, 1993, pp.1-14.

35. George Gerbner, "The 1998 Screen Actors Guild Report: Casting the American Scene–Fairness and Diversity in Television: Update and Trends since the 1993 Screen Actors Guild Report," A Cultural Indicators Project Report, December 1998.

36. Michael Elasmar, Kazumi Hasegawa, and Mary Brain, "The Portrayal of Women in Prime Time Television" in *Journal of Broadcasting & Electronic Media*, Winter 1999, pp.20-34.

37. George Spears and Kasia Seydegart, *Gender and Violence in the Mass Media*, pp.24-25.

38. *Front and Centre* (Toronto: MediaWatch, forthcoming in 1994).

39. Unpublished *Submission for CTV Application for Renewal of License*, provided to the CRTC Hearing Committee, September 1993, p.3.

40. Donald M. Davis, "Portrayals of Women in Prime-Time Network Television: Some Demographic Characteristics," pp.326-327.

41. Leah R. Vande Berg and Diane Streckfuss, "Prime-Time Television's Portrayal of Women and the World of Work: A Demographic Profile" in *Journal of Broadcasting and Electronic Media*, Spring 1992, pp.195-207.

42. David J. Atkin, Jay Moorman and Carolyn Lin, "Ready for Prime Time: Network Series Devoted to Working Women in the 1980s" in *Sex Roles*, Vol. 25, Nos. 11/12, 1991.

43. Carol Eaton, "Prime Time Stereotyping on the New Television Networks," in *Journalism & Mass Communication Quarterly*, Vol. 74, No. 4, Winter 1997.

44. As cited in Naomi Wolf, *The Beauty Myth*, p.137.

45. Susan Faludi, *Backlash: The Undeclared War Against American Women* (New York: Doubleday, 1991), pp.112-139.

46. Milena Damjanov (compiled by) "Women's Studies: Tracking the Progress of Women in the Industry," in *Premier Magazine*, Special Issue 1997, pp.47-51.

47. Molly Haskell, *From Reverence to Rape: The Treatment of Women in the Movies* (Chicago: University of Chicago Press, 1973).

48. James B. Weaver, III, "Are 'Slasher' Horror Films Sexually Violent? A Content Analysis" in *Journal of Broadcasting & Electronic Media*, Vol. 35, No. 3, Summer 1991, pp.385-392.

49. Gloria Cowan and Margaret O'Brien, "Gender and Survival vs. Death in Slasher Films: A Content Analysis" in *Sex Roles*, Vol. 23, Nos. 3/4, 1990, pp.187-196.

50. Literature reviews of the earliest studies of music television are provided by Rita Sommers-Flanagan, John Sommers-Flanagan, and Britta Davis, "What's Happening on Music Television? A Gender Role Content Analysis" in *Sex Roles*, Vol. 28, Nos. 11/12, 1993; and Steven A. Seidman, "An Investigation of Sex-Role Stereotyping in Music Videos" in the *Journal of Broadcasting and Electronic Media*, Spring 1992, pp.209-216.

51. Steven A. Seidman, "An Investigation of Sex-Role Stereotyping in Music Videos," pp.211-215.

52. Rita Sommers-Flanagan, John Sommers-Flanagan, and Britta Davis, "What's Happening on Music Television? A Gender Role Content Analysis," p.746.

53. Joe Gow, "Reconsidering Gender Roles on MTV: Depictions in the Most Popular Music Videos of the Early 1990s" in *Communication Reports*, Summer 1996, Vol. 9, Issue 2, pp.152-163.

54. Steven Seidman, "Revisiting Sex-Role Stereotyping in MTV Videos" in *International Journal of Instructional Media*, 1999, Vol.26, Issue 1, pp.11-23.

55. Baby, Chene, and Viens, 1988, and Baby, Chene, and Dugas, 1992, as cited by George Spears and Kasia Seydegart, *Gender and Violence in the Mass Media*, p.28.

56. The author was president of MediaWatch at the time.

57. Julie L. Andsager and Kimberly Roe, "Country Music Video in Country's Year of the Woman" in *Journal of Communication*, Winter 1999, Vol. 49, No. 1, pp.69-82.

58. At the end of the nightly CTV national newscast, anchor Lloyd Robertson intones, "And that's the kind of day it's been, here at CTV News." The subtle reinforcement of the notion that the highly selected and constructed series of news stories is simply a mirror of reality, when in fact it invariably fails to adequately reflect the perspective or give voice to the experience of at least half of the population, strikes the author as presumptuous, at best.

59. George Gerbner, *Women and Minorities on Television: A Study in Casting and Fate*, pp.12-13.

60. Lana F. Rakow and Kimberlie Kranich, "Woman as Sign in Television News" in *Journal of Communications*, 41 (1), Winter 1991, p.9, citing various sources and in the conclusions of Dhyanan Ziegler and Alisa White in "Women and Minorities on Network Television News: An Examination of Correspondents and Newsmakers" in *Journal of Broadcasting and Electronic Media*, Vol. 34, No. 2, Spring 1990, p.215.

61. As cited by Barbara F. Luebke in "Out of Focus: Images of Women and Men in Newspaper Photographs" in *Sex Roles*, Vol. 20, Nos. 3/4, 1989 p.124.

62. As Helen Benedict notes in *Virgin or Vamp: How the Press Covers Sex Crimes* (New York: Oxford University Press, 1992), violent crimes have been "the meat and potatoes of daily American newspapers since the mid-1980s" (p.25) and because women are so underrepresented, the extent to which they do appear as victims seems proportionately larger. Furthermore, news by definition focuses on the unusual and since women are less frequently the victims of crime, their victimization may be more likely to position them in headlines than any other (self-determined) activity. In fact, in MediaWatch's most recent newspaper study, *Focus on Violence: A Survey of Women in Canadian Newspapers*, June 1993, the slight increase in women as newsmakers over previous years (22 percent versus 17-19 percent) appeared in part to result from the arrest of Paul Teale for the rapes and murders of several young women in Southern Ontario on the day of the survey.

63. Luebke, "Out of Focus: Images of Women and Men in Newspaper Photographs," p.122.

64. MediaWatch, *Women Strike Out*, Nov. 1998, *Focus on Violence: A Survey of Women in Canadian Newspapers*, June 1993, and *A Good Day To Be Female? A Three Year Overview of Sexism in Canadian Newspapers*, June 1992. Similar statistics are found in U.S. dailies. See Debra Gersh, "Women Still Underrepresented," *Editor and Publisher*, May 15, 1993, and Rebecca Ross Alders, "Women: Minor Figures in News," *Presstime*, May 1993.

65. C.A. Tuggle, "Differences in Television Sports Reporting of Men's and Women's Athletics: ESPN SportsCentre and CNN Sports Tonight" in *Journal of Broadcasting & Electronic Media*, Vol. 41, Winter 1997, pp.14-24.

66. Katherine N. Kinnick, "Gender Bias in Newspaper Profiles of 1996 Olympic Athletes: A Content Analysis of Five Major Dailies," in

Women's Studies in Communications, Vol. 21, No. 2, Fall 1998, pp.212-237.

67. MediaWatch, *Global Media Monitoring Project,* Toronto, Canada 1995.

68. Helen Benedict, *Virgin or Vamp: How the Press Covers Sex Crimes,* (New York: Oxford University Press, 1992).

69. CRTC *Portrayal of Gender in Canadian Broadcasting: 1984-1988* and Soderlund, Surlin, and Romanow, 1985, as cited by George Spears and Kasia Seydegart, *Gender and Violence in the Mass Media,* pp.17-21.

70. MediaWatch, *Submission for CTV Application for Renewal of License,* 1993, pp.1-2.

71. George Spears and Kasia Seydegart, *Gender and Violence in the Mass Media,* p.21.

72. George Gerbner, "Women and Minorities on Television: A study in casting and fate," A report to the Screen Actors Guild and The American Federation of Radio and Television Artists, June 15, 1993, pp.1-14.

73. Carol M. Liebler and Susan J. Smith, "Tracking Gender Differences: A Comparative Analysis of Network Correspondents and Their Sources" in *Journal of Broadcasting & Electronic Media,* Winter 1997.

74. Lana F. Rakow and Kimberlie Kranich, "Woman as Sign in Television News" in *Journal of Communication,* 41(1) Winter 1991, p.12.

75. Ibid.

76. See Nancy Signorielli, "Television and Conceptions About Sex Roles: Maintaining Conventiality and the Status Quo," pp.341-343.

77. Nancy Signorielli, "Children, Television, and Conceptions about Chores: Attitudes and Behaviours" in *Sex Roles,* Vol. 27, Nos. 3/4, 1992, pp.57-170.

78. See Tannis MacBeth Williams, "The Impact of Television: A Longitudinal Canadian Study" in this volume, and Meredith M. Kimball, "Television and Sex Role Attitudes" in Williams, ed., "The Impact of Television: A Natural Experiment in Three Communities" (New York: Academic Press, 1986) pp.265-301.

79. As reviewed by Nancy Signorielli, "Television and Conceptions About Sex Roles: Maintaining Conventiality and the Status Quo," p.343.

80. As cited by Lynn T. Lovdal, "Sex Role Messages in Television Commercials: An Update" in *Sex Roles,* Vol. 21, Nos. 11/12, 1989, p.717.

81. See Naomi Wolf, *The Beauty Myth* (Toronto: Vintage Books, 1990) pp.184-185.

82. Philip N. Myers, Jr., and Frank A. Biocca, "The Elastic Body Image: The Effect of Television Advertising and Programming on Body Image Distortions in Young Women" in *Journal of Communications,* 42(3), Summer 1992, pp.108-133.

83. Sherry L. Turner, Heather Hamilton, Meija Jacobs, Laurie M. Angood, and Deanne Jovde Dwyer, "The Influence of Fashion Magazines on the Body Image Satisfaction of College Women: An Exploratory Analysis" in *Adolescence,* Vol. 32, No. 127, Fall 1997, pp.603-614.

84. See Patricia Sawatsky, "After the Butler Decision: Sex, Violence and Entertainment in Canada" in MediaWatch *Bulletin,* Vol. 5, No. 3, Fall 1992, p.3; and Rosemarie Tong, *Women, Sex and the Law,* 1984 as cited in Naomi Wolf, *The Beauty Myth,* p.51. The latter refers to a U.S. court decision which "upheld the right of male workers to display pornography in the workplace, no matter how offensive to women workers, on the grounds that the landscape is steeped in that sort of imagery anyway."

85. Naomi Wolf, *The Beauty Myth,* p.79.

86. Neil Malamuth and Edward Donnerstein, eds. *Pornography and Aggression,* 1984; Wendy Stock, "The effects of pornography on women," testimony for the Attorney General's Commission on Pornography, 1985, as cited by Susan Cole, *Pornography and the Sex Crisis* (Toronto: Amanita Enterprises, 1989) pp.49-52.

87. Moreover, a recent study of 26 prime-time television dramas dealing with rape found the perpetuation of rape myths is also prevalent in mainstream television programming, as well, a fact that will inevitably make it more difficult to isolate the factors potentially contributing to the real-life phenomenon; see Susan Brinson, "The Use and Opposition of Rape Myths in Prime Time Television Dramas" in *Sex Roles,* Vol. 27. Nos. 7/8, 1992.

88. Gaye Tuchman, "Women's Depiction by the Mass Media," p.539.

89. George Spears and Kasia Seydegart, *Gender and Violence in the Mass Media,* pp.6-7.

90. MediaWatch, *Tracing the Roots of MediaWatch,* 1993, p.5.

91. The history of this process is described in both George Spears and Kasia Seydegart, *Gender and Violence in the Mass Media,* pp.65-71, and MediaWatch, *Review of Policy on Sex-Role Stereotyping* in response to Public Notice CRTC 1990-114, June 1991, pp.4-6.

92. While this contention has been debated (see Gaye Tuchman, "Women's Depiction by the Mass Media," p.534), there is also significant support for the notion that more women directors, writers, and producers in media industries would affect a shift in portrayal trends. See for instance Catherine Murray, Shari Graydon, Theresa Kiefer, and Jacqie Botterill, *It Matters Who Makes It: A Review of Research on Women, Audiences and The Media* (Lifestyles Television Inc. 1993) especially pp.28-32; and Eva Pomice, "A Few Good Women ... and how they're changing the way advertising addresses us," in *Lears,* March 1993, pp.103-107, 130.

93. CAB, *Sex-Role Portrayal Code for Television and Radio Programming,* 1990.

94. Linda J. Trimble, "Coming To A Station Near You: The Process and Impact of The Canadian Radio-television and Telecommunication Commission's Involvement in Sex-Role Stereotyping," unpublished doctoral dissertation, Queen's University, 1990.

95. MediaWatch, *Review of Policy on Sex-Role Stereotyping,* p.14. The report quantifies the number of licencees asked about the issue, and the kinds of initiatives they referenced in response.

96. The Broadcasting Act, 1991, as cited in George Spears and Kasia Seydegart, *Gender and Violence in the Mass Media,* p.65.

97. CRTC news release, September 1, 1992.

98. CRTC, 1992 Policy on Gender Portrayal, Public Notice 1992-58, pp.8-11.

99. In the summer of 2000, for instance, British Columbia's Attorney General announced that the province would be developing a new classification system to protect children from violent video and computer games. (See Andrew Petter, "Guarding parents' right to chose," in *The Victoria Times Colonist,* 27 July 2000, p.A15).

100. MediaWatch, *Women as Equal Partners in the New Broadcast Environment,* Submission to the CRTC Structural Hearings, 1993.

101. Eva Pomice, "A Few Good Women ... and how they're changing the way advertising addresses us," p.103.

102. Benjamin D. Singer, *Advertising and Society,* p.114.

103. Karen M. Stoddard, *Saints and Shrews: Women and Aging in American Popular Film,* p.8.

104. Roland Marchand, *Advertising the American Dream* (Berkeley: University of California Press, 1985).

105. See Ellen McCracken, *Decoding Women's Magazines From Mademoiselle to Ms.,* p.1.

106. Rena Bartos, "Women and Advertising" in *International Journal of Advertising,* 1983, 2, pp.37-38.

107. CompuSearch/InfoGroup Inc., *Quantitative Research Study Produced for Lifestyles TV Inc.,* 1993, pp.24-27.

108. ComQuest Research Group, *Lifestyles Television Focus Group Report,* 1993, pp.7-9.

109. Murray, Graydon, Kiefer, and Botterill, *It Matters Who Makes It: A Review of Research on Women, Audiences and The Media,* p.19.

110. "Body Shop succeeds without advertising" in *The Globe and Mail,* March 2, 1988, p.E1.

111. Marina Strauss, "Marketing tries new wrinkles," in *The Globe and Mail,* December 29, 1993, p.B1.

14

The Impact of Television: A Canadian Natural Experiment

Tannis M. MacBeth[1]

By the 1960s, almost all North American homes had at least one television set, and watching TV had become the preferred leisure activity of children and adults. Despite increasing use since then of new technologies such as the Internet, at the turn of this century only sleeping and school and/or work occupy more time than television. What effects, if any, does TV have on viewers' attitudes and behaviour? Does it affect reading skills, creativity, vocabulary, aggressive behaviour, gender-role attitudes, participation in community activities, or use of other media? These questions prompted our research. An unusual opportunity in the form of a natural experiment enabled us to avoid a major problem faced by researchers interested in the effects of TV: how to determine whether viewers are affected by TV in each of these areas, whether viewers who differ on these dimensions use TV differently, or whether both influences occur in a transactional relationship, as some researchers[2] contend. This "chicken and egg" problem prompted the U.S. Surgeon General's Commission[3] to lament in 1972 that there was no longer a North American community without TV reception. Such a town would provide a natural experiment in which to study residents before and after they became regular viewers. It would enable researchers to make causal inferences, provided careful consideration was given to other possible influences, including change due to maturation (normal age-related change), history (other important events occurring in the community during the same period), regression towards the mean (high scores are more likely than low scores to decrease, and vice versa), and so on.[4]

To my astonishment, shortly after the publication of the Surgeon General's report, I heard about a Canadian town still without TV reception but due to receive it within a year.[5] It was July 1973. Our elation at finding a town without TV quickly turned to horror, however, when I learned in September that we did not have 10-12 months to organize the details of our project before the transmitter would be installed. Instead, every effort was being made to have it operational for the Grey Cup, only two months hence in November. With great effort, we managed to obtain local permission, funding, assemble all the necessary materials and personnel, and collect baseline data before the town's residents celebrated the arrival of both TV reception and the Grey Cup. We in turn celebrated the beginning of an exciting, extensive, and demanding research project.[6] The details of the methodology and results of this research have been published as a book; this chapter provides a summary and overview of what we did, why we did it, and what we found.[7] The overall design of the project is described first, followed by the substudies presented in the following order: creativity, vocabulary and spatial ability, IQ scores, reading skills, participation in other leisure activities, gender-role attitudes and perceptions, aggressive behaviour, and use of TV and other media. This is followed by discussion of the processes underlying the effects of TV and then by some general conclusions regarding our study. The essay ends with a postscript section providing a brief update on related research and conclusions.

Design of the Study[8]

The name Notel was chosen for the town without TV.[9] If only Notel had been studied, however, it would have been impossible to know whether any changes that occurred were due to the effects of TV or to the effects of some other event that occurred simultaneously with the introduction of TV to Notel. At least one comparison or control town was needed. The first comparison community, about an hour's drive away, was suggested by Notel residents. We gave it the name Unitel because it had had one TV channel, CBC English, for seven years. Notel was going to obtain that same (and only) channel. Residents of both Notel and Unitel agreed that the two towns were similar. We wondered whether the effects of TV might vary depending on whether viewers could watch one channel or several, so a second comparison town was selected. Multitel had had four channels for 15 years: one Canadian channel (CBC English) and three major private networks from the U.S., ABC, CBS, and NBC. As far as could be ascertained, using data from Statistics Canada and other sources, the three towns were similar in size, in demographic variables such as socioeconomic status (SES) and cultural backgrounds of the residents, and in the types of industry in the area. Each village, with a population of about 700, served an area about four times as large, in terms of schools, services, and so on.

One important feature of this experiment is that the people without TV in Notel were not self-selected. Comparisons between those who choose to have or not to have TV are a problem because the two groups also vary considerably on several other dimensions. It is difficult to rule out the likelihood that effects apparently due to TV really are due to other differences between the groups.

Notel, like Unitel and Multitel, was not isolated. This is important because the effects of TV in a community accessible only by sea or by air, as is true of many small Canadian communities, may be different from the effects in a non-isolated community. Notel should have had TV, but the transmitter meant to bring TV to both Notel and Unitel wasn't very successful. Notel was located in a valley in such a way that most residents could not pick up the transmitter's signal most of the time. Some residents could pick up a poor signal occasionally and did so. We heard amusing stories of people never seeing the puck while watching hockey games apparently played in snowstorms, and of families driving camper trucks just far enough to pick up a clear TV signal. Notel residents knew what TV was and watched it when they were elsewhere, but most could not watch on a regular basis. The median number of hours viewed per week by Notel school children, i.e., the number above and below which 50 percent watched, was zero. By comparison, the median for Unitel was 23.5 hours, and for Multitel, 29.3. That some Notel residents sometimes watched TV made it less likely that there would be differences amongst the towns, so our research provides a conservative test of TV's effects.

All three towns were studied just before Notel obtained TV (Phase 1) and again two years later (Phase 2). This interval was chosen because it seemed long enough for any TV effects to be clearly evident, but not so long that other major changes of a historical nature were likely to occur or that many residents would have moved. Attrition from Phase 1 to 2 was relatively low and did not differ significantly for the three towns (mean = 28.5 percent).

The topics we chose to study had been identified in previous literature as potentially influenced by TV, either positively or negatively. Some of the studies within this project focussed on children, elementary and/or high-school students, and others focussed on adults. Unfortunately, our resources did not enable us to study pre-school children. Some of the comparisons were cross-sectional, i.e., comparisons among the three towns within each phase of the study, and comparisons from Phase 1 to Phase 2 that involved different people. A comparison between Grades 3 and 5 students in Phase 1, or between Grade 3 students in Phase 1 and Grade 3 students in Phase 2, is cross-sectional because the two groups are comprised of different students. Some other comparisons were longitudinal, i.e., the same students were studied in Phase 1, for example, when they were in Grade 3, and then again in Phase 2, when they were two years older and in Grade 5. Statistical analyses were used to evaluate whether statistically significant differences occurred among the groups within each phase, or for each town from Phase 1 to Phase 2, and whether patterns of similarities and differences varied according to other factors, e.g., Grade or gender. The details of these analyses are provided more comprehensively in our book;[10] in this chapter only significant results are discussed.

Creativity

The question of whether TV facilitates or inhibits various aspects of viewers' thinking is much debated. When we designed this project, claims that TV has a negative impact on children's imagination or creative thinking were heard frequently, but the empirical evidence was sparse. A few researchers had found a negative relationship between creativity scores and amount of TV viewing and offered the interpretation that the more creative students tend to limit their use of TV. But the correlational nature of their data could not rule out the alternative and widely heard hypothesis that creativity is itself affected by TV. This hypothesis is consistent with theorizing about creativity, which tends to emphasize the role of experience in developing fluidity of ideas. For example, Suler[11] contends that creativity is a cognitive activity shaped by both the immediate environment and the larger cultural and historical context. When this study was designed there had been relatively little research on the relationship between creativity and TV exposure, but the evidence that did exist indicated a negative relationship. For these theoretical and empirical reasons, we hypothesized that TV would have a negative effect on creativity.

Creativity is difficult to define and even more difficult to measure, but there is some agreement that it includes ideational fluency (ability to generate ideas that fulfil particular requirements) and originality (ability to generate unique or unusual ideas). We examined these abilities in both children and adults.

Children

L. Harrison[12] and I assessed children's creativity with the Alternate Uses Task. This is considered a good measure of both ideational fluency and originality. A sample item is, "Tell me all the different ways to use a newspaper." The children were assessed individually, in a relaxed atmosphere, with no time limits. Both the total number of responses and the uniqueness or originality of each response were scored. In Phase 1, a total of 160 students in Grades 4 and 7 were assessed. Two years later, in Phase 2, 137 of the same students, now in Grades 6 and 9 (the longitudinal sample), were reassessed, along with 147 students who were in Grades 4 and 7 (the cross-sectional sample).

The results were clear. The pattern was similar for number and uniqueness of ideas and for cross-sectional and longitudinal comparisons. Before their town had TV reception, Notel students scored higher on average than the students in Unitel and Multitel. When Notel had had TV for two years, however, the scores of Notel, Unitel, and Multitel students did not differ. From Phase 1 to Phase 2, only the scores of Notel students changed significantly, and they decreased.

The same students also were given a figural measure of creativity. They were shown a series of simple designs and for each one asked to "tell me all the different things it might be." The pattern of results for this task, a less widely used measure of creativity than the Alternate Uses Task, did not indicate any relationship between performance and exposure to TV. Our hypotheses to explain the creativity findings for children are discussed under the heading "Interpretation," along with the results for adults.

Adults

Creative problem solving by adults was assessed by P. Suedfeld, B. Little, A. Rank, D. Rank, and E.

Ballard[13] using tasks that require the individual to "break set," i.e., to think of the materials presented to them in a different, unusual way. The adults (60 per town per phase) were tested individually in their homes, and they were a random, representative sample of their respective communities.

In Phase 1, before Notel had TV, the Duncker Candle Problem was used. Each person was given a box of tacks, a vertical cardboard surface, a candle, and a book of matches. They were told to "affix the candle to the cardboard wall, using any of the objects on the table, so that it stays there and burns freely without being held." The trick is to think of the tack box as separate from the tacks, and as a potential support for the candle. One merely has to tack the box to the cardboard surface and then stand the candle in the box. The differences among the proportions solving the problem were in the hypothesized direction but not statistically significant: 40 percent in Notel, 25 percent in Unitel, and 30 percent in Multitel. There was a significant difference, however, in the speed with which the problem was solved. Of those who succeeded, Notel adults did so significantly faster (150.6 seconds) than Unitel adults (251.0) and marginally faster than Multitel (263.1) adults.[14] Most people, however, never did solve the problem. Among those who didn't, Notel adults kept trying significantly longer (401.0 seconds) than did the unsuccessful adults in Unitel (279.9) and marginally longer than those in Multitel (332.4). This is an interesting finding because it is the only one we know that indicates a potential long-term effect of TV on persistence at problem solving. Teachers often complain that children aren't able to concentrate or persist as long as they used to, and attribute this to TV, but there is very little evidence for children concerning long-term effects of TV on persistence.[15]

In Phase 2, the creative problem-solving task was the 9-Dot Problem, in which people are shown nine dots, three in each of three rows, forming a square. The goal is to join all the dots, "using no more than four lines without lifting your pen off the paper or retracing any line." The solution requires going outside the square twice in order to connect the nine dots. This problem turned out to be very difficult; only 7 of 180 adults in the three towns actually solved it. It was not possible, therefore, to compare the three towns in terms of success, but it was possible to consider persistence. Among those who did not solve the problem, Notel adults persisted significantly longer (292.8 seconds) than Unitel adults (263.8) and marginally longer than Multitel adults (277.3). Change in persistence from Phase 1 to Phase 2 cannot be evaluated statistically because the problem and its difficulty level changed, but in absolute terms the drop in persistence in Notel (108.2 seconds) was noticeably larger than the drop in the other towns (16.1 seconds in Unitel; 55.1 seconds in Multitel).

Interpretation

This set of results indicates that the performance of both children and adults on creativity tasks was better in the absence of TV than when TV was available. Several explanations seem plausible, and they are not mutually exclusive. The first set of hypotheses revolves around the notion that, for at least some children, watching TV displaced other activities that might have facilitated creativity or creative problem solving. In particular, some other activities could provide experiences that would be helpful on these tasks. For example, in the absence of TV, children might play games that facilitate creativity. These might involve thinking about how various things could be used in a way similar to the questions asked on the Alternate Uses Task given in this study. Television also may displace "doing nothing," and the latter may encourage reflection and thinking about ideas more than does TV.

Another possibility is that TV displaces some activities that require deeper information processing than does watching TV. Gavriel Salomon[16] has reported some evidence that the *amount of invested mental effort* (AIME) required to watch North American TV is small. Children and adults are aware of this and, according to Salomon, tend to watch TV most of the time in a relatively mindless as opposed to a relatively mindful way.[17] Salomon contends that children learn when very young that TV requires only lower levels of information processing, i.e., encoding (taking in information directly) and chunking (parsing or grouping information), but not mental elaboration. In other words, TV does not require working over or transforming information. Children accustomed to using these relatively mindless processing skills with TV also may use them to process information in other situations, even when they are not adequate. For example, the Alternate Uses Task clearly requires mental elaboration, as do the Duncker Candle and 9-Dot Problems. The content of TV also may provide relatively few models of divergent thinking (coming up with many plausible answers or solutions) as opposed to convergent thinking (one correct answer). In short, this set of hypotheses revolves around the notion that North American TV and

perhaps North American culture tend to be oriented more towards entertainment than towards reflective thinking and persistence, so TV viewing does not facilitate performance on tasks that require these skills. Whatever the processes involved, the creativity findings for children indicate that the better performance of Notel students on creativity tasks in the absence of TV was not maintained once it became available. This finding contrasts with that for fluent reading skill, discussed later in this chapter.

Vocabulary and Spatial Ability

Not all of our hypotheses about the effects of TV were negative. We predicted that TV would have a positive effect on vocabulary,[18] particularly in the early grades for children not yet able to read for pleasure themselves. In Phase 1, M. Morrison gave the Peabody Picture Vocabulary Test (PPVT) to 61 children in Kindergarten and Grade 1 in Notel and Unitel, and L. Harrison and I gave the Wechsler Intelligence Scale for Children (WISC) vocabulary test to 160 children in all three towns in Grades 4 and 7. In Phase 2, L. Harrison and I gave the WISC vocabulary test to 284 students in Grades 4, 6, 7, and 9. The results provided no evidence to support the hypothesis that TV has a positive effect on children's vocabulary.

In interpreting the vocabulary findings it should be noted that our measures also are considered to be good measures of general verbal intelligence. For example, the child was required to give definitions for a series of words. Whereas one would hypothesize a positive effect of TV on vocabulary, as we did, IQ scores tend to be relatively stable across these age ranges, so little change might be expected for a vocabulary measure of IQ. Even for the PPVT measure of receptive vocabulary given in Kindergarten and Grade 1, requiring only word comprehension, however, there was no evidence of any effect of TV. With hindsight, we think that people do learn some vocabulary from TV but that other sources may be at least as important. For example, in the absence of TV, parents and older siblings may read to young children more than they do when TV is available. Children also may experience more social interaction with adults. They probably learn the kinds of vocabulary that vocabulary tests assess from conversation, from being read to, and later on from reading themselves, as much as or more than they learn such vocabulary from TV.[19] They may also learn some specific vocabulary from TV, but perhaps not the kind assessed by vocabulary tests.

We studied spatial ability,[20] assessed by the WISC Block Design task requiring the child to arrange a set of blocks so the surface duplicates a series of two-dimensional spatial designs. In becoming TV "literate," viewers learn to decode two-dimensional spatial representations of three-dimensional space. It seemed reasonable, therefore, to hypothesize that TV experience would be positively related to spatial ability, either because children high in this ability are more attracted to TV or because TV facilitates performance on spatial-ability tasks. In Phase 1, spatial ability was assessed for students in Grades 4 and 7, and in Phase 2, for students in Grades 4, 6, 7, and 9. We found no evidence for either a positive or negative effect of TV.

IQ Scores

As mentioned in the previous section, the vocabulary and spatial ability tests L. Harrison and I gave in Grades 4 and 7 in Phase 1, and in Grades 4, 6, 7 and 9 in Phase 2, were the WISC Vocabulary and Block Design IQ tests. In addition, in Phase 1 we obtained group test IQ scores from the permanent school records of 631 students across the three towns. IQ scores from individual tests administered by professionals are considered to be more valid and reliable assessments than are scores from group tests, in part because the latter depend on reading ability and because other factors such as fatigue and attention are not part of the assessment. We used the group test IQ scores primarily as a control when assessing the role of TV in relation to other variables potentially related to IQ, but we also conducted some other analyses of the IQ data.[21]

We found reasonably strong evidence that children's use of television and other media varies with IQ, as measured both individually and by group tests. Lower IQ students watched more television and used less print than did higher IQ students. To me, one of our most intriguing sets of findings in the entire project concerned the relations among IQ scores, reading ability, print use, and the availability of TV. Typically in research, as was the case in our towns when TV was available, substantial interrelations are found amongst IQ scores, reading skill, amount of reading, and type of material read. In our study, however, in the absence of television, IQ was more independent of reading skill and print use. In Phase 1, Notel students' IQ scores were not related to their print use, and were not related to their performance on an individual measure of fluent reading skill (described below in the next section). In addition, although Notel students' IQ scores were significantly related to their Phase 1 group reading test scores, they were statistically significantly less strongly related to those scores than was the case for Unitel and Multitel students. As I discuss in the next section, these findings have prompted me to wonder whether one of the effects of television is to produce more reading dropouts than when it is not available.

Reading Skills

A number of other researchers have found that in the late elementary grades and in high school, students who report watching more TV tend to be poorer readers and to do worse in school than students who watch less TV. Why would reading achievement be negatively related to amount of TV viewing? One possibility is that it interferes with acquisition and/or maintenance of good reading skills. Another possibility is self-selection; poor readers may choose to watch more TV than do good readers. On average, students who do worse on IQ tests also tend to be poorer readers, to read less, to read different material, to do worse in school, and to watch more TV. Most researchers have found that significant relationships or correlations between reading achievement and TV become insignificant or even drop to zero after the relationship of IQ to both of these variables is removed. The many difficulties in interpreting correlational data regarding TV and school achievement underscore the importance of the opportunity to study students in Notel before and after reception became available.

In the early stages of learning to read,[22] children focus on decoding individual letters and words. Later, reading becomes more fluent and automatic; a brief glance is sufficient to process an entire phrase. R. Corteen and I[23] studied the fluent reading or automated reading skills of students in Grades 2, 3, and 8 in Phase 1, and, in Phase 2, students in Grades 2, 3, 4, 5, 8, and 10. We also assessed Grade 2 students in all three towns two years after Phase 2.[24] Each student was tested individually. The items of a standardized reading test were given in a tachistoscope, a device that controls the amount of time the item is available to be seen, or in this case, to be read. The student had to read a series of items each presented very briefly. Some were words, some phrases, and some nonsense words, i.e., words that follow the spelling rules of English but are not true words (e.g., sked). About 500 students were tested. In addition to this individual measure of fluent reading skill, Phase 1 students also were tested on a group reading test that assessed both vocabulary and comprehension. Group reading tests were given in all three towns to 813 students in Grades 1 through 7, six months after the arrival of TV in Notel.

The reading results were complicated and varied according to both grade and gender, but the pattern was clearer when the relationship of IQ scores to other variables was controlled. When all of the findings from the individual reading test were considered, the weight of the evidence suggested that TV slows down the acquisition of fluent reading skills in the early elementary grades, but once good reading skills are acquired, they are not lost. The group test results corroborated these individual results. In particular, Notel students in Grades 2 and 3 obtained higher comprehension and vocabulary scores than did Unitel and Multitel students, who did not differ.

We did not observe directly the relationship between use of TV and acquisition of reading skills, so we can only speculate about the process, but the pattern of results obtained in this and other studies is consistent with the following set of hypotheses. When no TV is available, most children may practise reading enough to become fluent in the early elementary grades. For most children, however, learning to read is difficult. They have to "crack the code," and when they are first reading, they do so only with great difficulty and slowly. At the initial decoding stage, they are unable to read for entertainment or pleasure and still enjoy having adults or older siblings read to them for these purposes. Reading is hard work, and watching TV probably is more fun. Children who have the most difficulty learning to read may find TV most attractive. The brighter children without learning disabilities may obtain sufficient reading practice in school or may read more at home than others, either on their own or with the aid of parents or siblings.

The rewards associated with the process of learning to read probably are greater for those who acquire the skills more quickly. To the extent that parents consider reading to be an important activity or skill, they may provide more encouragement. Or, parents with a greater orientation to print than to other media may more often encourage and provide help with reading. By the later elementary grades, children who are poor readers will obtain little practice in school. The school curriculum focusses on acquisition of reading skills only in the early grades, and these children are likely to read less outside school and to watch more TV. As other researchers have found and as we noted earlier, by this stage use

of TV, IQ scores, reading skills, and amount and type of reading are interrelated. In effect, we are suggesting that TV may lead to an increase in the proportion of reading dropouts, especially among the less intelligent students in the early grades. Note, however, that this hypothesized influence of TV is indirect; the real cause is insufficient reading practice, so cutting down on time with TV might be necessary but would not be sufficient to produce good readers. In our view, the correlations between reading achievement and use of TV typically found in the later elementary grades and in high school are the outgrowth of a process that began in the early elementary grades, and not primarily due to the current influence of TV on reading skill. Older students who watch a lot of TV and read relatively little probably do so because they are poor readers, rather than the other way round.

Participation in Other Leisure Activities

In addition to habitually being chosen over other in-home activities, TV viewing may also displace a number of activities typically conducted outside the home, either indoors, in other dwellings, or out of doors. G. Handford and I[25] studied participation in other leisure activities by the residents of Notel, Unitel, and Multitel. The main focus was on adolescents (students in Grades 7 to 12) and on adults (young, middle-aged, and older).

A method called ecological psychology,[26] or behaviour-settings analysis, was particularly well suited for this study. In the 1950s Barker and Wright did a behaviour-settings analysis of a town in the U.S. they called "Midwest."[27] They theorized that each unit of the environment, or behaviour setting, places limits on the range and types of behaviour likely to occur there, sometimes for physical reasons but also because of social and other conventions. Their system provides a method for specifying units of the environment in a way that could be applied to entire communities such as Notel, Unitel, and Multitel, towns of about the same size as Midwest.

The public behaviour settings for each community for the previous year were determined in each phase by visiting the town and interviewing several people in each of the following categories: clergy, retailers, town clerks and elected officials, officers of community clubs/organizations, recreation-commission personnel, school teachers, editors of the newspaper, police, and children. In addition, copies of the community newspaper were obtained for the preceding year and items referring to community activities, organizations, meetings, special events, and so on were gleaned.

The list of activities and events unique to each town was organized into the 12 categories that Barker and Wright had used to describe Midwest. These were *Sports; Open Areas,* such as parks, playgrounds, swimming holes; *Businesses,* such as stores and offices; *Civic Activities,* such as the post office and town hall; out-of-school *Educational Activities,* such as open houses, music lessons, and adult classes; *Meetings* of clubs and other non-sports organizations for both children and adults; *Medical Activities,* such as visits to the hospital, doctors' offices, and so on; *Dances, Parties, and Suppers; Special Days,* such as weddings, funerals, and elections; *Religious Activities* of the churches and Bible camps; *Entertainment,* such as special movies, parades, bingo; and *Other Activities,* which included fundraising events, clean-up campaigns, and so on. A questionnaire was developed to cover these 12 categories of community activities, with about 275 individual items in total. Another questionnaire assessed participation in 58 private leisure activities (e.g., reading books, bicycling). Whereas separate community-activity/behaviour-setting questionnaires were developed for each phase of the study in each town, the same private leisure activity questionnaire was given in all towns in both phases.

Each person indicated whether and how he or she was involved in each activity during the preceding year. All students in Grades 7 through 12 completed questionnaires at school. The adults were surveyed by mail using a random sample from the electoral lists. Phase 1 questionnaires were completed by 1,023 people and Phase 2 questionnaires by 1,369.

Participation in private leisure activities varied considerably by age and gender, but only minimally by town or phase of the study, so there was little evidence of any impact of TV.

The number of community activities did not vary according to whether TV was available, but participation in those activities did vary. When total participation was considered, i.e., summing across the 12 activity categories, residents of Notel in Phase 1 reported participating in more of their community's activities than did residents of both Unitel and Multitel, and the difference between Unitel and Multitel also was statistically significant. During the second year after the introduction of TV to Notel, total participation by the Notel residents remained greater than that for Unitel, and Unitel participation remained

greater than that for Multitel, but the differences were much smaller than in Phase 1. From Phase 1 to Phase 2 total participation by the longitudinal sample (i.e., the same) youths (18 and younger) decreased significantly in Notel, but did not change in Unitel or Multitel. For longitudinal-sample adults (19 and over) there was a decrease in total participation in all three towns, but the decrease in Notel was 33 percent greater than in Unitel and 40 percent greater than in Multitel.

The negative effect of TV was especially strong for *Sports* (both active and spectator), but there also was evidence that TV affected attendance at *Dances, Parties, and Suppers,* particularly by youths, as well as attendance at *Meetings* of clubs and other non-sports organizations, particularly by adults. The results for participation in the categories *Special Days* and *Entertainment* were not as clear, but there was some evidence that TV also had a negative effect for these activities. There were no systematic differences among the towns in attendance at *Medical* and *Religious* activities. There were some differences among the towns for *Open Areas, Businesses, Civic, Educational* (non-school), and *Other* activities, but the pattern of results suggested that TV did not play a role in these differences.

Television's apparent effect on participation in community activities was found for both adolescents and adults, but the effect was particularly strong for the oldest age group (56 and over). Before reception was available in Notel, adults in this group participated in the activities of their community at about the same rate as middle-aged adults (36–55 years), but two years after the arrival of TV there had been a dramatic decrease in their relative participation. This occurred for sports as well as for total activities. This decreased participation by the oldest age group (by comparison with adults in the middle years) found in Notel in Phase 2 also was evident in Unitel and Multitel in both phases, which would explain the decrease in total participation for the longitudinal sample of adults but not for youths in Unitel and Multitel from Phase 1 to 2. This pattern of findings suggests that one of the effects of TV may be greater age segregation. These age-related results also are provocative because other research indicates that people age more successfully in later life if they are involved in active rather than just passive leisure pursuits.

The finding that participation in total community activities was greater in both phases in Unitel than in Multitel is striking. It was particularly strong for *Sports,* and is one of only a few results in the entire project indicating that, beyond the presence versus absence of TV, the number and/or type of channels available and/or their use makes a difference. One possible explanation is that the mean difference in hours of TV viewing between Unitel and Multitel (about 7 hours per week for youths and 6 hours for adults) accounts for some of the difference in participation in community activities. Another possibility is that decreases in participation in community activities occur gradually following the introduction of TV reception. Such habits may change slowly. In Phase 1 Multitel had had TV twice as long (15 years) as Unitel (7 years). This hypothesis is consistent with the finding that, whereas participation by Notel residents dropped significantly from the year preceding the arrival of TV (Phase 1) to the second year after its arrival (Phase 2), in Phase 2 it remained higher than participation in both Unitel and Multitel. The theory of ecological psychology would predict these findings on the basis that behaviour settings constrain and influence people's behaviour. If the continued existence of a community activity became threatened by a drop-off in participation, formal and informal pressure would be exerted on participants.

Gender-Role Attitudes and Perceptions

Attitudes and perceptions regarding gender roles may be acquired through observation of real life, the media, or some combination of the two. From the 1950s onward, content analyses have consistently demonstrated that there are two or three times as many male as female characters on TV, and that both females and males typically are portrayed in traditional gender roles, i.e., in sex-typed ways. Evidence regarding the effects of such portrayals is more limited than the evidence regarding how the genders are portrayed, and has more often focussed on effects of counter-stereotypical than typical content, since the effects of typical content are more difficult to isolate from the influences of other media and real life. The gender-role perceptions of students in Notel, Unitel, and Multitel therefore promised to yield important insights regarding media effects and were studied in this project by M. Kimball.[28]

Perceptions about appropriate and typical behaviours of girls and boys "your own age" (Peer Scale) were assessed using the Sex-Role Differentiation scale (SRD) developed by Lambert.[29] Students also were asked to rate how frequently their own mother and father performed certain tasks (Parent Scale). For each item on the Peer Scale, the child rated on a seven-point scale how typical a certain behaviour, a

certain characteristic, or the future suitability of a certain job was for boys their own age. The child then rated how typical the same item was for girls their own age. Their score for each item was the difference between their ratings for boys and girls. This scale measures degree of sex-typing—in other words, the extent to which the students differentiated or sex-typed their peers. For the Parent scales, the children rated how often their mothers and their fathers each performed certain tasks, so the difference scores reflected the students' perceptions of their parents' division of activities, discipline, support, and power.

In both phases, all students in Grades 6 and 9 in each of the three towns completed the scales, a total of approximately 150 students. Longitudinal data were not obtained. Data were also analyzed for a group of Grade 5 and Grade 8 children from Vancouver who had completed the scales eight months prior to the Phase 1 testing in Notel, Unitel, and Multitel. This was done to determine whether the scores of students in these small communities were similar to or varied significantly from the scores of children growing up in an urban environment.

The bulk of the evidence for the Peer scales indicated that TV did affect students' perceptions of gender roles, and that effect was to make perceptions more sex-typed or traditionally stereotyped. Before their town had TV, Notel students held more egalitarian gender-role perceptions of their peers than did students in Unitel and Multitel. Two years after the introduction of TV, Notel students' gender-role perceptions had become more sex-typed. In Phase 2 there were no significant differences among the towns. With regard to the students' perceptions of their own parents' behaviour, there was no evidence that exposure to TV had any effect; the Parent scores did not vary according to the town or phase of the study. The results for both the Peer and Parent scales for students who had grown up with TV in Vancouver were similar to those for students who had grown up with TV in Unitel and Multitel. This and other evidence that the data from residents of Notel, Unitel, and Multitel were similar to other North American data supports the generalizability of the project's results regarding the effects of TV.

These findings concerning gender-role attitudes are in some ways surprising. They indicate that TV's impact was sufficiently strong to be measurable over and above the impact of many other influences. When the data for this study were collected, most of the gender-related influences from real-life, from TV, and from other media were relatively traditional. Television may be an especially effective teacher of gender roles, since it provides more models than most children encounter in real life, and during the 1970s, when this study was conducted, they were presented similarly and stereotypically in most TV programs and commercials. All theories of gender-role acquisition emphasize the importance of models. Other processes whereby TV may influence gender-role perceptions are discussed later.

The results of this research corroborate findings obtained in other studies indicating that the media play an important role in the development of gender-role attitudes. What has yet to be demonstrated, however, is the extent to which the media influence gender-role behaviour (e.g., assertiveness in female-male interactions). This project did not directly address that question, but did produce some provocative hints concerning gender-related behaviour. In several substudies, there was a stereotypical gender difference in the towns with TV (Unitel and Multitel in both phases, Notel in Phase 2), but no gender difference in the absence of TV (Notel in Phase 1). This pattern was evident in performance on the spatial-ability task (Block Design), for fluent or automated reading skill, for participation in community activities, and for gender-role perceptions.

Aggressive Behaviour

Perhaps the most widely studied effect of TV is its influence on viewers' aggressive behaviour. The U.S. Surgeon General's investigation in the early 1970s focussed mainly on this issue. The topic continues to be widely discussed and controversial.[30] Most academic researchers, after reviewing the literature, have concluded that the weight of the evidence from laboratory experiments, field observational studies, field experiments, and natural experiments, indicates that exposure to violence in the media can, and for some viewers does, cause an increase in aggressive behaviour. Moreover, there is evidence that aggressive behaviour is stable from childhood to adulthood, so to the extent that TV has an influence during childhood, this effect is likely to be maintained into adulthood. The American Psychological Association's (APA) Board on Social and Ethical Responsibility for Psychology reviewed the available research and concluded that repeated observation of real and dramatized violence during childhood is one factor contributing to the development of stable patterns of aggressive and anti-social behaviour.[31]

Laboratory studies have the advantage that researchers can control both the filmed or televised aggressive content and some other variables that might interact with or be confounded with that content in influencing aggressive behaviour. They have the disadvantage that they are not naturalistic. For example, children may have fewer inhibitions about behaving aggressively when they believe they are not being observed by adults or when the target of their aggression is an inflated plastic Bobo Doll rather than another human being. In other words, laboratory studies indicate whether the media in general or TV in particular *can* in a controlled setting cause an increase in aggressive behaviour. They do not indicate whether, given the vicissitudes of daily life, social controls regarding aggression, and so on, TV *does* cause an increase in real life. Most of the field observational studies have the advantage of being more naturalistic than the laboratory studies but the disadvantage that the data are correlational in nature. This raises the question mentioned earlier of whether children who are more aggressive choose to watch more TV aggression and violence, whether TV causes an increase in aggressive behaviour, or whether, as some researchers[32] contend, the relationship is transactional, i.e., there is influence in both directions. The natural experiment in Notel, Unitel, and Multitel therefore promised to provide an important new kind of information on this controversial topic. L. Joy, M. Kimball, and M. Zabrack conducted this study.[33]

Children's aggressive behaviour was observed during free play on school playgrounds, before school, at recess, at lunchtime, and after school. In Phase 1, children in Grades 1, 2, 4, and 5 were observed in all three towns. In Phase 2, children in Grades 1, 2, 3, and 4 were observed. This provided before-and-after cross-sectional comparisons between the phases for children in Grades 1 and 2, and provided longitudinal comparisons for the children who were in Grades 1 and 2 in Phase 1, and two years later in Grades 3 and 4 in Phase 2. In addition, cross-sectional comparisons were made among the four grades within each phase. A total of 120 children from the three towns were observed in each phase, each for 21 minutes. Five girls and five boys were observed in each grade in each town in each phase. The observations were time-sampled across different days of the week and periods during the day, so each child was observed on a number of different occasions, with the order randomly predetermined and not dictated by the action of the moment. Neither the children nor the teachers were told that these observers were interested in aggressive behaviour.

The two observers used checklists of 14 physically aggressive behaviours, such as hits, slaps, punches, kicks, bites, pushes, holds, and grabs, and 9 verbally aggressive behaviours, such as disparages, mocks, curses, and commands in a loud, angry tone of voice. For each interval, the observer noted the number of times that each physically and each verbally aggressive behaviour occurred. Accidental aggression and rough-and-tumble play were not included. Observer reliability was established initially during training in each phase, checked periodically during the observations, and was found to be high in both phases. The Phase 2 observers were different from those who observed the children in Phase 1.

In addition to the behavioural observations on the school grounds, peer ratings and teacher ratings of aggression were obtained for each child. In individual interviews each child indicated the three students in his or her class who were the bossiest, fought the most, talked back to the teacher the most, argued and disagreed the most, and pushed, shoved, and poked the most. Each teacher rated each child in her or his class on several seven-point scales ranging from not at all characteristic to very characteristic (of the child being rated). Both positive and negative behaviours were rated and grouped into four composite teaching ratings: (1) aggressive, argumentative, bossy, and hostile; (2) active and loud; (3) competitive and dominant; and (4) friendly and honest.

There were no differences in aggressive behaviour related to grade level. The most important question was whether there would be an increase in the aggressive behaviour of Notel children following the inception of TV in their community, and there was. Notel children in the longitudinal sample increased from Phase 1 to 2 in both physical and verbal aggression. This could not be attributed to maturation (being two years older), since there was no evidence of differences in aggressive behaviour among the grades in either phase, and since there was no change for longitudinal-sample Unitel or Multitel children, who also were two years older. Twelve cross-sectional comparisons from Phase 1 to Phase 2 were made in each town (physical aggression: Grades 1 and 2 girls in Phase 1 versus Grades 1and 2 girls in Phase 2, the same comparison for boys, the same comparison for the girls and boys combined, a similar set of three comparisons for Grades 3 and 4 versus 4 and 5, and a similar set of six comparisons for verbal aggression). In Notel, 10 of the 12 comparisons revealed a statistically significant increase in aggression; the other two increases were not significant.

None of the 12 Unitel comparisons and only 2 of the Multitel comparisons (for girls, Grades 1 and 2, verbal aggression decreased; for boys and girls combined, Grades 3 and 4, physical aggression increased) was statistically significant. The increases in Notel occurred not only for both physically and verbally aggressive behaviour, for both girls and boys, but also for children who were initially low in aggressive behaviour as well as those who were initially high. This latter finding is noteworthy because some people have contended that only children initially high in aggression are affected by violence on TV. It makes sense that children with the least inhibitions against behaving aggressively would be most likely initially to imitate aggression, and that may have happened in Notel. These findings indicate, however, that it is not just these children who are influenced in the longer run, in this case over a period of two years.

The catharsis hypothesis would predict a decrease in aggression in Notel following the introduction of TV, due to vicarious release of aggressive impulses while viewing. All other theories (modelling/imitation, disinhibition, desensitization, arousal, and so on) about the effects of media violence on aggression would predict an increase in Notel, but predictions about comparisons among the towns within each phase are less clear. Most groups have dominance hierarchies and methods of controlling aggression among members, but tolerance of aggression varies considerably (motorcycle gangs and nuns might be extreme examples). It would not necessarily be expected, therefore, that the mean levels of aggression for the three towns would form a sensible pattern in relation to the availability of TV. In Phase 1, the mean level of verbal aggression in Notel and Unitel was lower than that in Multitel, and there were no Phase 1 differences in physical aggression. Two years after the arrival of TV in Notel, the level of verbal aggression was significantly higher than that for both Unitel and Multitel, which did not differ. In Phase 2, Notel children were highest in physical aggression, exhibiting more than Unitel children, who were lowest; Multitel children were in between and not significantly different from Notel or Unitel.

The pattern of findings obtained in this study suggests that the social milieu is important. When social controls are adequate, either for individuals or groups, aggressive behaviours acquired from various models, including TV, may not be performed because of the individual's inhibitions against behaving aggressively. When the social controls are disrupted, however (which may have been what happened with the advent of TV in Notel), behaviours learned from all sources may be more likely to be performed. When considering these and other results regarding the influence of TV on aggression, it is important to remember that aggression is a socially disapproved behaviour, albeit sometimes associated with mixed messages. Parents, teachers, and others generally try to teach children not to be physically and verbally aggressive. This is sufficiently successful that researchers who wish to study aggression beyond the middle school years have considerable difficulty doing so. Thus, in studies such as this, for an effect to be measurable it has to be sufficiently strong to overcome or go beyond the individual's inhibitions against behaving aggressively.

In general, the peer and teacher ratings of aggression were consistent with the researchers' observations of aggressive behaviour on the school playground. This indicates that the observed behaviours had external validity, i.e., that the children observed during this study to be relatively aggressive also were considered by the other children and their teachers to be aggressive relative to their peers.

The processes through which TV is theorized to influence aggressive behaviour are discussed later, and an "update" is provided at the end.

Use of Television and Other Media

Was Notel really a town without TV in Phase 1? Were Unitel and Multitel residents similar to or different from each other in amount of TV viewing? Information about TV use that would answer these and other questions was obtained from 1,168 children and 239 adults in Phase 1 and from 1,206 children and 741 adults in Phase 2. In Phase 1, students from all grades in Notel and Unitel were interviewed individually at school about their TV viewing. In Phase 1 in Multitel, students in Grades 1 to 8 were interviewed individually, and those in Grades 9 to 12 described their TV viewing habits on the questionnaire regarding participation in community activities. In Phase 2, information was obtained not only about TV use but also about the use of other media, including radio, magazines, book reading, use of the library, and parental control of children's TV viewing. In Phase 1, information about adults' use of TV was obtained via mailed questionnaires, primarily in Unitel and Multitel, and in Phase 2, some adults were interviewed in their homes about their use of TV and other media, whereas others provided information via mailed questionnaires. For both children and

adults, the interview and questionnaire samples yielded comparable and reliable results.

M. Boyes and I[34] analyzed the media-use data. The evidence obtained via interviews and questionnaires confirmed that, for most residents, Notel was indeed a town without TV in Phase 1. Fully 76 percent of the Notel students in Grades 1 through 12 reported watching zero hours of TV per week, by comparison with 8 percent of Unitel and 3 percent of Multitel students. These Unitel and Multitel percentages are very close to the figure of 5 percent reported by Hirsch[35] for large representative samples of U.S. residents in 1975, 1976, and 1977. Two years later, in Phase 2, only 11 percent of Notel students reported watching zero hours per week; the Phase 2 figures for Unitel and Multitel were 13.8 percent and 2.8 percent, respectively.

Students in Multitel, where four channels were available, did report watching more hours per week on average than Phase 1 students in Unitel and more than both Notel and Unitel students in Phase 2, but the differences were not great. In Phase 1, Unitel students in Grades 4 through 10 reported watching a mean of 25.4 hours per week by comparison with 33.6 hours for Multitel students in Grades 4 through 10.[36] In Phase 2, data were obtained from students in Grades 1 through 12; the mean for Multitel (26.9 hours per week) was significantly greater than the means for both Unitel (21.0) and Notel (20.9), which did not differ. Since the U.S. networks had longer broadcast days than did CBC, TV was available to Multitel children more hours per week. For example, Notel and Unitel children did not have access to TV prior to 9:00 a.m. on weekdays, whereas Multitel children could watch before school. Given that, it is even more surprising that children with one channel of CBC TV watched only 25 percent fewer hours than did children with access to the three privately owned U.S. networks in addition to CBC. The pattern of results for adult TV use was similar. In Phase 2, Multitel adults reported watching a mean of 27.6 hours per week by comparison with 23.8 for Unitel adults and 22.0 for Notel adults.

In Phase 2, when data for other media were obtained, radio use was more similar than different across the towns. Multitel adults reported reading fewer books (2.36) per month than did adults in both Notel (4.68) and Unitel (4.39), and the same was true for checking books out of the library for their own use. More Notel (76.3 percent) than Multitel (68.0 percent) children reported ever going to their local library; Unitel children (70.4 percent) did not differ from either Notel or Multitel children. Averaging across the towns, children who watched more TV reported reading more comics, fewer books, and listening to the radio less than did those who watched less television. The findings concerning availability of TV, IQ as a measure of intelligence, book reading, use of other media, and amount of TV viewing two years after the arrival of TV in Notel were consistent with the findings described earlier in this essay for the relations among ability to read, IQ, and TV use. Children varied less, according to IQ, in their use of print (and to some extent radio), when TV was not available than when it was. And when it was available there was some evidence that the students with lower IQ scores tended to drop some activities in favour of TV viewing, especially those requiring the most mental effort, i.e., book reading.

In general, these findings regarding media use corroborate the evidence regarding the effects of TV in this project. Presence versus absence of television was more important than the number of channels or the nature of the channels available.

Processes Underlying the Effects of Television[37]

Many discussions of the effects of television have been based on overly simplistic models. In my view, the processes through which TV influences its viewers are complex. At a minimum the following points need to be considered.

When watching TV, people usually do not behave in a stereotypically passive or mesmerized fashion. There is a good deal of evidence that children as well as adults are actively engaged.[38] The effects of TV result from an interaction of the characteristics of the viewer and the characteristics of the medium. With regard to viewers, the outcome depends in part on whether they approach TV in a relatively mindful or relatively mindless way, and whether their goal is to seek information, entertainment, or some combination of the two. Viewers frequently time-share television with other activities, and sometimes this is appropriate. Ironing or shoe polishing are less onerous if time-shared with TV, but some activities such as playing or practising a musical instrument are difficult if not impossible to time-share with TV. Doing homework or studying are important examples of activities probably not best time-shared with TV. In surveys conducted in the United States (Grades 7 to 9)[39] and in the Netherlands (Grades 8 to 10),[40] students agreed on the negative impact of TV on homework, whereas in research conducted in the United

Kingdom, students who studied while watching TV believed that they could do so effectively.[41] All three studies focussed on use of media while doing homework rather than on the effects of that practice. In other experimental studies conducted with U.S. university students, background TV interfered with performance on difficult cognitive tasks.[42] Children and adults vary in their knowledge of their own thinking processes (metacognition), including, perhaps, their knowledge of their ability to time-share one or another kind of activity with TV. Good high-school and university students may be aware that it is better not to study while watching TV, whereas students who do less well may not realize that this practice may affect their school achievement.[43]

The individual's habits regarding TV–i.e., amount of TV and kinds of programming viewed–are relevant when considering effects. It has been found, for example, in longitudinal studies in both Sweden[44] and the United States[45] that pre-schoolers who watch more children's educational TV programming and less fictional programming intended for children (including cartoons) and for adults do better at school entry and beyond than do children with the opposite viewing patterns in the pre-school years, even after socioeconomic status (SES) variables are controlled. What the individual would have done in lieu of watching TV is also important. Would the alternative activities have some other potential benefit (e.g., mental stimulation or physical activity) or might they have been detrimental? In addition, the viewer's stable and transient characteristics play a role in the communication outcome. The person's state of arousal, in terms of relative wakefulness or sleepiness, past experience, cultural background, political views, and so on, will influence comprehension and the impact of the content. McLuhan contended that the medium is the message, i.e., that the characteristics of TV itself are important in its influence. These include *formal* characteristics, i.e., those of its form, including music, action, camera angle, and type of shot.[46] The content of TV varies both within a culture and between cultures. Moreover, TV content is by no means stable, but is continuously evolving, which makes it difficult to study both its content and its effects.[47] There are also differences among individuals within a culture in the biases and expectations they bring to the TV-viewing situation. In sum, many factors play a role in the influence of television, and simplistic analyses such as an assumption of all-or-nothing effects should be viewed with scepticism.

In hypothesizing about the processes through which the content of TV influences viewers (for example, with regard to gender-role perceptions and aggression), a psychological theory called *schema theory* or *schematic information processing* theory[48] is helpful. A schema is a self-relevant belief or expectation, and a script is a schema for a sequence of events. The closest everyday concept is a stereotype. Schemata, scripts, and stereotypes tend to direct attention, perceptions, and memory. Once established, they are resistant to change. For example, in one study children were shown either a film of a female physician and a male nurse or a film of a male physician and a female nurse.[47] The children who saw the male physician and the female nurse all recalled the situation correctly, but only half of those who saw the female physician and the male nurse did so; the other half reversed their roles. The most likely explanation is that the children processed the information via their gender-role schemata, and they either didn't notice the discrepancy when initially watching the film or subsequently altered their memory to be consistent with their gender schemata. This phenomenon is well known with regard to prejudice. People who hold the view that a particular group is lazy, and then encounter a hardworking member of that group, typically do not change their stereotypes on the basis of the contradictory information. They either do not notice that the individual is both hardworking and a member of that group, or they make that individual an exception. Schemata and stereotypes are formed through both direct experience, e.g., nurses and physicians encountered in real life, and from indirect experience, e.g., hearing physicians (of unknown as well as known gender) referred to with male pronouns and nurses referred to with female pronouns, and via the media. Since children in North America typically begin watching TV regularly at two to three years of age, its content must play an important role in both the initial formation and the subsequent maintenance of their schemata and stereotypes in a number of areas, including minorities, aggression, and gender roles.

Among the other ways in which TV content has been shown to influence viewers, *observational learning* via the *imitation of models and their behaviours* is one of the most important.[50] Television provides many models, including models of gender-role behaviour, aggressive behaviour, and pro-social behaviours such as sharing. It is important to recognize that learning consists of two steps, acquisition and performance.[51] Acquisition would include the initial

formation of a schema or stereotype. Behaviours acquired through observation may not be performed because of inhibition, or there may be a gap between acquisition and performance of the modelled behaviour. Another possibility is that performance does not occur unless there is some cue in the environment that cognitively triggers the acquired behaviour and provides a link for the individual from the previously observed model to the current situation.[52] Moreover, the environmental cue may be linked up through a network of associative pathways with related thoughts and feelings. Activation of any one component spreads along the pathway to activate the others (e.g., feeling activated ideas, thought activated feelings). Researchers have shown, for example, connections among violent cues in media, violent thoughts, and hostile feelings.[53]

The viewer's state of *arousal* also plays a role in the effects of TV content. This is true not only in terms of physiological arousal such as sleepiness or wakefulness, as mentioned earlier, but also with regard to attentiveness or cognitive arousal. Salomon's concept of amount of invested mental effort, or AIME, is relevant in this regard.[54] As he has found, North American children tend to believe that TV is a relatively easy medium from which to learn, and that they are good at learning from TV, so they watch with relatively little AIME. This will make it difficult for programming intended to be educational or informative to be effective. It also may make it more likely that children will notice, remember, and acquire negative behaviours (e.g., aggression) but not notice the sanctions portrayed for that behaviour (e.g., punishment), particularly if they are imposed much later in the film or TV program. By comparison with the amount of mental effort they invest in watching TV, North American children tend to believe that print is a more difficult medium and to report investing more mental effort when processing information from print. Not surprisingly, these same children have been found to remember more from print than from television.

As mentioned in the earlier discussion of the effects of TV on creativity, it may influence the manner in which people *process information*. As Salomon contends,[55] television requires primarily encoding and chunking of information but does not require or encourage mental elaboration. Indeed, TV and visual media in general may interfere with or prohibit mental elaboration. One cannot stop the flow of incoming information to pose critical questions, whereas while reading one can look up from the page and try to think of counter-examples, ponder the evidence, and then continue without losing one's place. Doing the same thing while watching an audio-visual presentation will result in new information being lost.

Another process underlying some effects of television is *desensitization* or habituation.[56] Viewers may become accustomed to certain behaviours or models, even ones they initially found offensive. Habituation or desensitization to media content may in turn result in *disinhibition* or reduction in inhibitions regarding certain attitudes and/or behaviours. Desensitization and disinhibition apply potentially not only to such behaviours as violence but also to sexist and/or racist comments, the portrayal of women or men as sex objects, and so on. There is empirical evidence that viewers become desensitized to media violence through exposure to it, but there is as yet no evidence on the question of whether media violence desensitizes them to violence in real life.

Finally, as outlined earlier for some of the phenomena we studied, certain effects seem to occur because watching TV is done in lieu of other activities that could have had a different consequence, at least for some people. These effects include direct *displacement* of other activities, such as sports or attending a community meeting. They also include *indirect* displacement, e.g., through problem-solving games that might contribute to creativity or problem-solving performance. Another indirect example would be reading or discussing with others either feminist or very traditional views regarding gender roles as opposed to exposure to the sorts of portrayals shown on television. The issue of *time-sharing* television with appropriate versus inappropriate activities also comes under the rubric of indirect consequences. Finally, as was noted earlier, displacement by TV of doing nothing, i.e., boredom, also may be important if during those bored periods the individual is reflecting upon ideas or engaging in some form of mental elaboration.

Summary and Conclusions

When we designed this research we hypothesized that television influences its viewers in a number of ways, both positively and negatively, based on previous research and theories. The natural experiment provided by the imminent arrival of TV reception in Notel was a wonderful opportunity. But, to be frank, we were sceptical that any effects of TV would be measurable over and above the many other influences that operate in a naturalistic setting. They were. To summarize:

- TV had a negative effect on creativity, as indicated by the number and unusualness of children's ideas and the speed and persistence of adults in a problem-solving task.

- A negative effect on the acquisition of reading skills in the early elementary grades was found for both an individual fluent-reading task and for a group comprehension and vocabulary test.

- TV negatively affected participation in community activities, particularly *Sports, Meetings* of clubs and organizations, and *Dances, Parties, and Suppers*, and to a lesser extent, *Special Days* and *Entertainment*. Participation decreased for both adolescents and adults, including older adults.

- Students' attitudes and perceptions regarding gender roles became more sex-typed as a result of TV, a finding we also interpret as negative.

- The introduction of TV to Notel led to an increase in children's aggressive behaviour; this was true of both verbal and physical aggression for both boys and girls, and for children initially low as well as those initially high in aggression.

- For the areas in which we hypothesized that TV would or might have a positive impact, including vocabulary, spatial ability, field independence, and fineness of information processing, there was little, if any, evidence to support those hypotheses, but also no contradictory evidence.[57]

- Some additional areas in which there was no evidence, positive or negative, of effects of TV were participation in private leisure activities and in certain kinds of community activities (e.g., *Religious, Medical*).

- Finally, because of various constraints we were not able to study the impact of TV in all potentially important areas. Among the areas in which it is likely that TV does have an impact are consumer behaviour (as a result of the content of both programs and commercials); information and/or general knowledge (especially type of knowledge, e.g., regarding entertainers versus history); physical fitness and obesity; and attitudes regarding racial and/or ethnic groups.

Update

In almost all cases, the academic community's response to the publication of our findings has been positive. For example, the American Psychological Association's (APA) Task Force on Television and Society[58] reviewed research on the positive and negative effects of TV advertising and programming, emphasizing research conducted since the early 1980s. They cited our findings for gender-role attitudes[59] in stating that "demonstrating causal influences of television on sex stereotypes is difficult because such stereotypes abound throughout the society, not just on television" (p.29). Our findings regarding participation in community and other leisure activities[60] were cited as evidence for a modified version of the displacement hypothesis, i.e., that "television viewing does displace other activities, but not at random" (p.86). It displaces "activities that serve functions similar to TV (e.g., entertainment) and those that are incompatible with viewing (e.g., attending a local sports event)" (p.86). Along with evidence from other studies, our findings[61] were cited as evidence that reading is the one academic "subject that may be negatively influenced by TV viewing, but the effects are small" (p.87).

With regard to our analysis of the processes whereby television may influence acquisition of fluent reading skills, Comstock[62] quoted our hypothesis, and went on to say that the model we proposed also could readily apply to mathematical and writing skills.

With regard to our other major findings, the APA Task Force's report[63] did not mention those concerning vocabulary,[64] persistence at problem-solving tasks,[65] or media use.[66] The only instance in which their conclusions differed from ours was with regard to creativity. In citing our study they noted that "children showed reduced performance on one of two measures of creativity after television was introduced" (p.90), and, on balance, they agreed with the conclusions reached by Anderson and Collins[67] that "there is little evidence that television as a medium has any effects on such cognitive processes as attention, creativity, impulsivity, or attention span" (p.91)[68] In my opinion, our finding that prior to the arrival of TV, Notel children scored higher than both Unitel and Multitel children on the ideational fluency Alternate Uses Task (which is acknowledged to be the better measure)[69] and our findings regarding persistence on problem solving by adults,[70] are more important than the preceding quote acknowledges.

Indeed, some of those same authors have more recently pursued the issue empirically by analyzing data from two samples they studied longitudinally.[71] They found that viewing by pre-schoolers of informative TV programing intended for children (especially *Mister Rogers*) predicted higher creativity scores on the Alternate Uses ideational fluency task in adolescence, whereas entertainment viewing in the pre-school years predicted lower creativity scores in adolescence. Their findings do not permit causal inferences, but are consistent with our conclusions regarding our own results, and call into question Anderson and Collins' conclusions cited earlier. In the third edition of their textbook, Liebert and Sprafkin[72] displayed our before-and-after creativity results in a figure and concluded that, when taken together with the findings of other researchers, our data "suggest that heavy exposure to standard commercial television may inhibit children's imaginative and creativity abilities" (p.15). Citing our results and those of others, Greenfield and her co-authors[73] concluded that "the majority of the research on television and imagination indicates a detrimental effect of the medium" (p.55), and Singer[74] concluded that the evidence for negative effects on creativity appears to be stronger than for positive effects. These differing interpretations of similar evidence provide a good illustration of the importance to readers of evaluating published evidence in its original form for themselves, rather than relying on summaries provided by others.[75]

The topic of violence in the media and its effects on aggressive attitudes and behaviour has continued to receive a great deal of attention from both researchers and the public. The consensus in both groups is that viewing violence does lead to aggressive attitudes and behaviour, and that this is a problem in North American society. Freedman,[76] a social psychologist at the University of Toronto, reviewed some of the literature and stated that it did not support that conclusion, but Friedrich-Cofer and Huston[77] took issue with his analysis of the evidence, including his interpretations of their own field experiment results. In addition to the points they raised, I would highlight a "Catch-22" in Freedman's argumentation. He did not consider the evidence from any laboratory studies, on the basis that they cannot reveal whether media violence causes aggressive behaviour in daily life. But he then ruled out the evidence from correlational real-life studies, on the basis that they do not permit causal inferences, which, as I noted earlier, is precisely the strength of laboratory studies. Laboratory studies indicate whether viewing violence *can* cause aggressive behaviour, and field studies indicate whether this violence-aggression link *does* occur in real life. Our natural experiment was, when published, one of the relatively small number of studies that provided evidence on both the "can" and "does" questions, but Freedman did not include it in his review, as it was then in press and not yet published. More recently, the APA Task Force's report[78] cited our study as "one unique source of information" (p.56) that, along with other kinds of research evidence they reviewed, supports "the conclusion that viewing television violence leads to aggression that becomes a lasting part of individual behavior patterns" (p.56).

Since the publication of our study, a number of researchers have demonstrated in both laboratory and field experiments[79] that violence viewing causes children as well as adults to have emotional responses and violent thoughts as well as to behave more aggressively towards other humans, not just inanimate objects. Several of these studies included random assignment of individuals to experimental conditions, so causal inferences can be made. In other longitudinal field observational studies it has been demonstrated that TV-violence viewing in childhood predicts later aggressive and anti-social behaviour, even after early aggressive behaviour is statistically controlled.[80] Researchers who have recently reviewed the research on media (TV and film) and aggression using the technique called meta-analysis to statistically evaluate the entire body of evidence have concluded that exposure significantly enhances aggressive behaviour.[81] Information-processing theories have been used to develop models for understanding *how* TV exposure influences aggressive behaviour, including the roles of individual characteristics and situational influences.[82] As Dubow and Miller pointed out, most researchers[83] who have considered the body of evidence "acknowledge that television violence viewing is only one of many causes of aggression (other causes include family environment characteristics) but conclude that it is nevertheless of social significance."[84]

In both Canada and the U.S., public concern about violence on television has become increasingly evident. The 1992 Larivière petition, begun by a teenager in Quebec who blamed TV violence for her sister's rape and murder, was signed by over one million people. In response to government warnings, the Canadian Association of Broadcasters (CAB) developed a self-regulatory code for private broadcasters that was approved by the CRTC in October 1993. The CRTC has requested that the public networks (including CBC), cable, pay TV, and specialty services also develop self-regulatory standards. Also in October 1993, the U.S. Attorney General Janet Reno warned media executives during a Senate Commerce Committee hearing that if immediate steps were not taken to reduce violent content and deadlines were not established, the government should respond. Such events led some prominent researchers to conclude that the 1992-93 television season was a turning point from research on television violence to widespread agreement about the need for action to create a cultural environment that is free, diverse, fair, and not threatening to human potentials.[85] Ratings for violent content in network and cable programs have since been developed for both Canadian and U.S. television programs.

In sum, the empirical evidence and theorizing in recent years in the area of media violence and aggressive behaviour has been consistent with and has extended our findings and conclusions, and the public has expressed increasing rather than decreasing concern about violence in the media.

Our research findings have been carefully reviewed[86] and widely cited.[87] Almost all of these responses have been positive and have concurred with our interpretations. More recent research has tended to support rather than contradict our findings and conclusions.

No single study can be definitive. Laboratory studies, field experiments, field observational studies, and natural experiments such as our Notel, Unitel, and Multitel study provide different and complementary kinds of evidence concerning the effects of television and other media on human behaviour. The results of our research, when added to the converging evidence that has accumulated from other research over the years, indicate that TV does affect its viewers. The hypothesis of no effects, once popular, is no longer tenable. This is certainly not to argue that television is the only or most important influence, but to state that over and above the myriad other influences on human behaviour, television plays a role that is measurable on average, despite the many individual differences among viewers.[88]

Notes

[1.] In previous editions of *Communications in Canadian Society*, and in some other descriptions of this research, I wrote under my former name, Tannis MacBeth Williams. I have since reverted to Tannis M. MacBeth.

2. See for example Karl Erik Rosengren, K. Roe, and I. Sonesson, *Finality and Causality in Adolescents: Mass Media Use.* Paper presented at the meeting of the International Communication Association, Dallas, May 1983; Lynette Friedrich-Cofer and Aletha C. Huston, "Television Violence and Aggression: The Debate Continues," *Psychological Bulletin* 100 (1986): 364-71.

3. National Institute of Mental Health, *Report of the Surgeon General's Scientific Advisory Committee on Television and Social Behavior* (Rockville, MD.: 1972).

4. For a detailed general discussion of these and other threats to internal validity see Thomas D. Cook, Donald T. Campbell, and Laura Peracchio, "Quasiexperimentation," M.D. Dunnette and L.M. Hough, eds., *Handbook of Industrial and Organizational Psychology,* 2nd ed., Vol. 1 (Chicago: Rand McNally, 1990), pp.491-576. For a detailed discussion of threats to internal validity in quasiexperimental studies of television, see Tannis M. MacBeth, "Quasiexperimental Research on Television and Behavior," Joy Keiko Asamen and Gordon L. Berry, *Research Paradigms, Television, and Social Behavior* (Thousand Oaks: Sage, 1998), pp.109-151. For a detailed discussion of threats to internal validity in the context of this research, see Tannis MacBeth Williams, "Background and Overview," in Tannis MacBeth Williams, ed., *The Impact of Television: A Natural Experiment in Three Communities* (New York: Academic Press, 1986), p.138.

5. I would like to express my gratitude to Mary Morrison, a Vancouver psychologist who brought this town without TV to my attention.

6. We are grateful to the Canada Council (later the Social Sciences and Humanities Research Council of Canada) for funding both this research and sabbatical leave fellowships that enabled me to complete the data analyses and writing.

7. It is impossible in a chapter of this length to provide the many details regarding literature, citations, results, appropriate qualifying statements, and complex statistical analyses that are provided in a book of more than 400 pages. Readers of this chapter are cautioned that it provides only a summary and overview, and are encouraged to obtain details from Tannis MacBeth Williams, ed., *The Impact of Television: A Natural Experiment in Three Communities* (New York: Academic Press, 1986).

8. Details are provided in Tannis MacBeth Williams, "Background and Overview," Williams, *The Impact of Television,* pp.1-38.

9. Pseudonyms are used for all three towns to protect the anonymity ethically required and promised to the individuals and communities studied.

10. Williams, *The Impact of Television.*

11. John R. Suler, "Primary Process Thinking and Creativity," *Psychological Bulletin* 88 (1980): 144-65.

12. Linda F. Harrison and Tannis MacBeth Williams, "Television and Cognitive Development," Williams, *The Impact of Television,* pp.87-142.

13. Peter Suedfeld, Brian R. Little, A. Dennis Rank, Darilynn Rank, and Elizabeth J. Ballard, "Television and Adults: Thinking, Personality, and Attitudes," Williams, *The Impact of Television,* pp.361-93).

14. The reason that the difference between 150.6 and 251.0 is statistically significant ($p < .05$) but that the difference between 150.6 and 263.1 is only marginally significant ($p < .10$) has to do with controlling the alpha (Type I) error level according to the number of comparisons made (3 in this case), and in particular, the distance between comparisons.

15. Tannis M. MacBeth, "Indirect Effects of Television," Tannis M. MacBeth, ed., *Tuning in to Young Viewers: Social Science Perspectives on Television* (Thousand Oaks, CA: Sage, 1996), pp.149-219.

16. Gavriel Salomon, "Television Watching and Mental Effort: A Social Psychological View," Jennings Bryant and Daniel R. Anderson, eds., *Children's Understanding of Television: Research on Attention and Comprehension* (New York: Academic Press, 1983), pp.181-198.

17. Ellen J. Langer and A. Piper, "Television from a Mindful/Mindless Perspective," Stuart Oskamp, ed., *Applied Social Psychology Annual: Television as a Social Issue, Vol. 8* (Newbury Park, CA: Sage, 1998), pp.247-260.

18. Harrison and Williams, "Television and Cognitive Development."

19. George A. Miller and Patricia M. Gildea, "How Children Learn Words," *Scientific American* 259, no. 2 (1988): 94-99.

20. Harrison and Williams, "Television and Cognitive Development."

21. The results are described in detail in MacBeth, "Indirect Effects of Television," as well as in Harrison and Williams, "Television and Cognitive Development," and in Tannis MacBeth Williams and Michael C. Boyes, "Television viewing patterns and use of other media," Williams, *The Impact of Television,* pp.215-63.

22. Jeanne Sternlicht Chall, *Stages of Reading Development* (New York: McGraw-Hill, 1983).

23. Raymond Corteen and Tannis MacBeth Williams, "Television and Reading Skills," Williams, *The Impact of Television,* pp.39-86.

24. We decided to collect Phase 3 data from Grade 2 students because Unitel students in Grade 2 obtained very low Phase 2 scores. This is the only instance in the project in which Phase 3 data were obtained.

25. Tannis MacBeth Williams and Gordon C. Handford, "Television and Other Leisure Activities," Williams, *The Impact of Television,* pp.143-213.

26. Roger G. Barker, *Ecological Psychology: Concepts and Methods for Studying the Environment of Human Behavior* (Stanford, Calif.: Stanford University Press, 1968).

27. Roger G. Barker and Herbert R. Wright, *Midwest and Its Children* (Hamden, Conn.: Archon Books, 1971, originally published 1955).

28. Meredith M. Kimball, "Television and Sex-Role Attitudes," Williams, *The Impact of Television,* pp.265-301.

29. R.D. Lambert, *Sex Role Imagery in Children: Social Origins of the Mind,* Studies of the Royal Commission on the Status of Women in Canada, no. 6 (Ottawa: Information Canada, 1971).

30. See, for example, the following exchange: Jonathan L. Freedman, "Effect of Television Violence on Aggressiveness," *Psychological Bulletin* 96 (1984): 227-46; Lynette Friedrich-Cofer and Aletha C. Huston, "Television Violence and Aggression: The Debate Continues," *Psychological Bulletin* 100 (1986): 364-71; Jonathan L. Freedman, "Television Violence and Aggression: A Rejoinder," *Psychological Bulletin* 100 (1986): 372-78.

31. American Psychological Association, *Violence on Television* (Washington, D.C.: APA Board of Social and Ethical Responsibility for Psychology, 1985).

32. See note 2, above.

33. Lesley A. Joy, Meredith M. Kimball, and Merle L. Zabrack, "Television and Children's Aggressive Behavior," Williams, *The Impact of Television,* pp.303-60.

34. Williams and Boyes, "Television-Viewing Patterns and Use of Other Media."

35. Paul Hirsch, "The 'Scary World' of the Non-Viewer and Other Anomalies: A Re-analysis of Gerbner et al.'s Findings of Cultivation Analysis," *Communication Research* 7 (1980): 403-56.

36. In Phase 1, data were obtained from students in all grades in each town, but comparisons in hours of TV viewing were made only for Grades 4 through 10. This was because we were not confident in the reports of children in the early grades and because the Unitel high school ended with Grade 10 (Grade 11 and 12 students went elsewhere, including some to Notel). In Phase 2, improved interview methods gave us more confidence in the younger children's reports, and the schools in all three towns went to Grade 12.

37. For more details see Tannis MacBeth Williams, "Summary, Conclusions, and Implications" (pp.395-443) as well as other chapters in Williams, *The Impact of Television.*

38. Aimee Dorr, *Television and Children: A Special Medium for a Special Audience* (Beverly Hills, Calif.: Sage, 1986); Elihu Katz, "On Conceptualizing Media Effects: Another Look," Stuart Oskamp, ed., *Television as a Social Issue,* pp.361-74; Aletha C. Huston and John Wright, "Television and Socialization of Young Children," MacBeth, *Tuning in to Young Viewers,* pp.37-60.

39. James E. Patton, Thomas A. Stinard, and Donald K. Routh, "Where do Children Study?", *Journal of Educational Research* 76 (1983): 280-286.

40. Johannes W.J. Beentjes, Cees M. Koolstra, and Tom H.A. van der Voort, "Combining Background Media with Doing Homework: Incidence of Background Media Use and Perceived Effects," *Communication Education* 45 (1996): 59-72.

41. J. Mallory Wober, "Text in a Texture of Television: Children's Homework Experience," *Journal of Educational Television* 18, no. 1 (1992): 23-24.

42. G. Blake Armstrong, "Cognitive Interference from Background TV: Structural Effects on Verbal and Spatial Processing," *Communication Studies* 44 (1993): 56-70; G. Blake Armstrong, Greg A. Bioarsky, and MarieLouise L. Mares, "Background TV and Reading Performance," *Communication Monographs* 58 (1991): 235-253; G. Blake Armstrong and Bradley S. Greenberg, "Background TV as an Inhibitor of Cognitive Processing," *Human Communication Research* 16 (1990): 355-386.

43. Tannis M. MacBeth, "Indirect Effects of Television," and it was subsequently supported by the results of the Netherlands study.[40]

44. Karl Erik Rosengren and Sven Windahl, *Media Matter: TV Use in Childhood and Adolescence*, (Norwood, NJ: Ablex, 1989).

45. Huston and Wright, "Television and Socialization of Young Children."

46. Aletha C. Huston and John C. Wright, "Children's Processing of Television: The Informative Functions of Formal Features," Jennings Bryant and Daniel R. Anderson, eds., *Children's Understanding of Television: Research on Attention and Comprehension* (New York: Academic Press, 1983).

47. George Comstock, "Television Research: Past Problems and Present Issues," Asamen and Berry, eds., *Research Paradigms, Television, and Social Behavior,* pp.11-36.

48. Shelley E. Taylor and Jennifer Crocker, "Schematic Bases of Social Information Processing," E. Tory Higgins, C. Peter Herman, and Mark P. Zanna, eds., *Social Cognition: The Ontario Symposium in Personality and Social Psychology* (Hillsdale, N.J.: Erlbaum, 1978), pp.89-135.

49. Glenn D. Cordua, Kenneth O. McGraw, and Ronald S. Drabman, "Doctor or Nurse: Children's Perceptions of Sex-Typed Occupations," *Child Development* 50 (1979): pp.590-93.

50. Albert Bandura, *Social Learning Theory* (Englewood Cliffs, N.J.: Prentice-Hall, 1977); for a review of the ways in which imitation interacts with other processes with regard to aggressive behaviour, see Eric F. Dubow and Laurie S. Miller, "Television Violence Viewing and Aggressive Behavior," MacBeth, *Tuning in to Young Viewers*, pp.117-147; for another, detailed review of the processes whereby mass media influence aggression, see Russell G. Geen, "The Influence of the Mass Media," Russell G. Geen, *Human Aggression* (Pacific Grove, CA: Brooks Cole, 1990), pp.83-112.

51. Bandura, *Social Learning Theory.*

52. L. Rowell Huesmann, "Television Violence and Aggressive Behavior," David Pearl, Lorraine Bouthilet, and Joyce Lazar, eds., *Television and Behavior: Ten Years of Scientific Progress and Implications for the 80s*, Vol. 2 (Rockville, Md.: National Institute of Mental Health, 1982), pp.126-137.

53. Brad J. Bushman and Russell G. Geen, "Role of Cognitive-emotional Mediators and Individual Differences in the Effects of Media Violence on Aggression," *Journal of Personality and Social Psychology* 58 (1990): 156-163; also see Dubow and Miller, "Television violence viewing and aggressive behavior," for a discussion of these processes.

54. Salomon, "Television Watching and Mental Effort."

55. Ibid.

56. Albert Bandura, "Social Learning of Aggression," *Journal of Communication* 28, no. 3 (1978): 12-29; George Comstock, "New Emphases in Research on the Effects of Television and Film Violence," Edward L. Palmer and Aimee Dorr, eds., *Children and the Faces of Television* (New York: Academic Press, 1980); Monroe M. Lefkowitz and L. Rowell Huesmann, "Concomitants of Television Violence Viewing in Children," Palmer and Dorr, *Children and the Faces of Television.*

57. Findings on field independence and fineness of information processing have not been discussed in this chapter; details can be found in Suedfeld et al., "Television and Adults."

58. Aletha C. Huston, Edward Donnerstein, Halford Fairchild, Norma D. Feshbach, Phyllis A. Katz, John P. Murray, Eli A. Rubinstein, Brian L. Wilcox, and Diana Zuckerman, *Big World, Small Screen: The Role of Television in American Society* (Lincoln: University of Nebraska Press, 1992).

59. Kimball, "Television and Sex-Role Attitudes."

60. Williams and Handford, "Television and Other Leisure Activities."

61. Corteen and Williams, "Television and Reading Skills."

62. George Comstock, *The Evolution of American Television* (Newbury Park, Calif.: Sage, 1989).

63. Huston et al., *Big World, Small Screen.*

64. Harrison and Williams, "Television and Cognitive Development."

65. Suedfeld et al., "Television and Adults."

66. Williams and Boyes, "Television-Viewing Patterns."

67. Anderson and Collins, *The Impact on Children's Education.*

68. Huston et al., *Big World, Small Screen.*

69. Harrison and Williams, "Television and Cognitive Development."

70. Suedfeld et al., "Television and Adults."

71. Aletha C. Huston, personal communication, June 2000, based on an unpublished manuscript by Daniel R. Anderson, Aletha C. Huston, Kelly L. Schmitt, Deborah L. Linebarger, and John C. Wright, "Adolescent Outcomes Associated with Early Childhood Television Viewing: The Recontact Study."

72. Robert M. Liebert and Joyce Sprafkin, *The Early Window,* 3rd ed. (Toronto: Pergamon, 1988).

73. Patricia Marks Greenfield, Emily Yut, Mabel Chung, Deborah Land, Holly Kreider, Maurice Pantoja, and Kris Horsley, "The Program-Length Commercial: A Study of the Effects of Television/Toy Tie-Ins on Imaginative Play," Gordon L. Berry and Joy Keiko Asamen, eds., *Children and Television: Images in a Changing Sociocultural World* (Newbury Park, Calif.: Sage, 1993), pp.53-73.

74. Dorothy S. Singer, "Creativity of Children in a Television World," Berry and Asamen, *Children and Television: Images in a Changing Sociocultural World*, pp.73-88.

75. For my own relatively recent review of the literature on creativity, imagination, persistence, IQ, school achievement, participation in other activities, and television, see Tannis M. MacBeth, "Indirect Effects of Television."

76. Freedman, "Effect of Television Violence on Aggressiveness"; Friedrich-Cofer and Huston, "Television Violence and Aggression"; Freedman, "Television Violence and Aggression."

77. Ibid.

78. Huston et al., *Big World, Small Screen.*

79. See for example Kaj Bjorkvist, *Violent Films, Anxiety, and Aggression* (Helsinki: Finnish Society of Sciences and Letters, 1985); Brad J. Bushman, "Moderating Role of Trait Aggressiveness in the Effects of Violent Media on Aggression," *Journal of Personality and Social Psychology* 69 (1995): 950-960; Russell G. Geen, "Role of Cognitive-Emotional Mediators and Individual Differences in the Effects of Media Violence on Aggression"; Wendy L. Josephson, "Television Violence and Children's Aggression: Testing the Priming, Social Script, and Disinhibition Predictions," *Journal of Personality and Social Psychology* 53 (1987): 882-890.

80. For example, Martin Botha and Gerhard Mels, "Stability of aggression among adolescents over time: A South African study," *Aggressive Behavior* 16, (1990) 361-380.; L. Rowell Huesmann and Leonard D. Eron, *Television and the Aggressive Child: A Cross-National Comparison* (Hillsdale, N.J.: Erlbaum, 1986); Monroe M. Lefkowitz, Leonard D. Eron, Leopold O. Walder, and L. Rowell Huesmann, *Growing Up to Be Violent* (New York: Pergamon, 1977); O. Weigman, M. Kuttschreuter, and B. Baarda, *Television Viewing Related to Aggressive and Prosocial Behavior* (The Hague: Stitching voor Onderzoek van het Onderwijs, 1986).

81. Haejung Paik and George Comstock, "The Effects of Television Violence on Antisocial Behavior: A Meta-Analysis," *Communication Research* 21(1994): 516-546; Wendy Wood, Frank Y. Wong, and J. Gregory Chachere, "Effects of Media Violence on Viewers' Aggression in Unconstrained Social Interaction," *Psychological Bulletin* 109 (1991): 371-83.

82. Leonard Berkowitz and Karen Heimer, "On the Construction of the Anger Experience: Aversive Events and Negative Priming in the Formation of Feelings," *Advances in Experimental Social Psychology* 22 (1989): 1-37; L. Rowell Huesmann, "An Information Processing Model for the Development of Aggression," *Aggressive Behavior* 14 (1988): 13-24.

83. For example, see Huston et al., *Big World, Small Screen,* and Liebert and Sprafkin, *The Early Window.*

84. Eric F. Dubow and Laurie Miler, "Television Violence Viewing and Aggressive Behavior," Tannis M. MacBeth, ed., *Tuning in to Young Viewers*, pp.117-147.

85. George Gerbner, Michael Morgan, and Nancy Signorielli, *Television Violence Profile No. 16: The Turning Point from Research to Action,* (Philadelphia; The University of Pennslyvania, Annenberg School of Communication, 1994).

86. In, for example, *Journal of Communication* 36, no. 4 (1986): 140-44; *Contemporary Psychology* 32, no. 4 (1987): 309-10; *etcetera* 44, no. 2 (1987): 201-4; *Canadian Psychology* 28, no. 3 (1987): 298-99; *Die Zeit* (13 November 1987); *Journalism Quarterly* (Winter 1987); *New Zealand Journal of Educational Studies* 22 (1987): 131-34; *Contemporary Sociology* (1987): 553-54; *Communication Research Trend* 10, no. 3 (1990).

87. For example: Berry and Asamen, *Children and Television: Images in a Changing Sociocultural World*; John P. Murray, "Studying Television Violence: A Research Agenda for the 21st Century," Asamen and Berry, *Research Paradigms, Television, and Social Behavior*; Karl Erik Rosengren and Sven Windahl, *Media Matter: TV Use in Childhood and Adolescence*; Victor C. Strasburger, "Adolescents and the Media: Medical and Psychological Impact," *Developmental Clinical Psychology and Psychiatry* 33 (Thousand Oaks, CA: 1995). See also Huston et al., *Big World, Small Screen*; Comstock, *The Evolution of American Television*; Liebert and Sprafkin, *The Early Window.*

88. I would like to express my gratitude to Janet Werker for her very helpful comments on an earlier draft of this chapter.

PART 4

CONTROL AND POLICY

ass media and cultural industries occupy an ambiguous status in Canada. Many Canadians feel that such institutions, because of their power and influence, must be subject to some kind of control. Yet we are ambivalent about this. The resulting tension is reflected in the many forms and the extent of such control.

Control can be exerted in many different ways, of which the most visible are formal institutions charged with this responsibility: regulatory bureaucracies such as the Canadian Radio-television and Telecommunications Commission (CRTC), which answer to Parliament and whose constituency is both the public and the mass media organizations. Another means of control is the official inquiry—a royal commission, or an investigation by Parliament or by a ministry—any of which may suggest new laws and regulations or, at least, policy initiatives to be carried out by ministries or other organs of government. Yet another type of control is exerted by the rules of international trade administered by the World Trade Organization (WTO). These rules now prevent the legislation of certain types of subsidies and restrictions on media ownership and behaviour that were once used to protect domestic markets.

Although these methods are the obvious means of asserting official authority, there is a competing form of control that the power of ownership of media conveys—one increasingly difficult to contain in modern society. This difficulty is the product of increasing complexity, rapidly changing identities and functions of media and cultural industries, as well as the incessant shifts in national auspices of the conglomerates that own the newspapers and magazines, broadcast stations, music companies, film producers, and publishers. It is to such issues of control and policy that our authors turn their attention.

The CRTC is a large, sometimes confusing organization, which many Canadians do not understand. It is also Canada's most prominent and most important control institution. It develops broadcast policies, makes regulations that carry out those policies, issues licences, and exercises powers of suasion, meeting

with politicians, trade groups, and representatives of consumer groups, as John Meisel, a former chair of the CRTC, explains. In fact, its overt regulation of broadcasting is only the most visible aspect of its armamentarium, for it also seeks to "help the broadcasting industry to internalize the values which animate the *Broadcasting Act*," as Meisel points out. The values to which he refers are in part a reflection of unique challenges that Canada faces, which include the strengthening of unity and national identity as well as facilitating the expression of multiculturalism.

By its nature, the CRTC is an institution that is engaged in an ongoing dialogue, often controversial, with critics representing the audience, the industry owners, and other groups. Meisel informs us that the process of regulating Canadian broadcasting must be seen in the light of the difficulty of achieving the lofty goals of broadcasting acts, the complexity of Canadian society, the disparities of the Canadian value systems, and complications in regulating engendered by rapid change in communications technology, particularly that of expanded cable and satellite operations. Complicating the picture further, the Commission's use of the term "consumer-driven TV" seems to be pointing to a future characterized by greater choice and less regulation.

Professor Meisel's essay is a highly salient contribution to our knowledge of Canada's most important communications control institution. Because of his intimate and comprehensive knowledge of the agency he once headed, we are reprinting his original paper with a few amendments and the addendum of a policy statement by the CRTC in 1999 dealing with Internet regulation, an issue that had not been taken up earlier in the decade.

Throughout their history, Canadians have learned to depend upon the press for their most important information needs. From this, it follows that the role of governmental commissions that undertake to study the press is a delicate one. They are forms of social control, even if they do not "censor" the news manifestly. They can make recommendations, which, in theory, can become the basis of legislation (as happened following the report of a Senate committee on hate literature in the 1960s) that inevitably resonates throughout news content. Inquiries, such as that carried out by the Kent Commission, as described by Andrew Osler, may have impact on newspapers, even though they do not become the basis for press laws per se, for scrutiny of this nature indirectly influences the policy of newspapers.

Professor Osler asks why newspapers should be "singled out as objects for both public and political concern" in a world of increasing "giantism" and conglomeration of industries. His answer is, as the Davey report put it, that media control is passing "into fewer and fewer hands," and that with an increase in size and ownership by non-professionals, as is often the case in media conglomerates, journalistic process, objectives, and norms are likely to be determined by cost accountants–at the expense of quality. Too much centralization of power in a critical industry such as newspaper publishing is socially unhealthy by any standard.

While Osler examines mechanisms of control of the press by a governmental control mechanism within Canada, John Hannigan's perspective is that of "control of information, ideas, entertainment, and popular culture by a handful of mammoth private organizations" at the international level. Information now flows freely across borders, aided by vast advances in communications technology, with nationality being "largely irrelevant."

Hannigan focusses on three issues bearing on the control of content: the "synergism" between media empires and other business interests that may be affected by media content (news, opinion, popular culture); the loss of emphasis on traditional media values, particularly those of the journalism profession; the demonstrated habit by multimedia empires of recycling tried-and-true material from one medium to another, thus constituting a Gresham's law in which the bad and the redundant drive out the good and the innovative.

Canada has been spared penetration by the global giants of media so far, but a relatively few Canadian mini-empires do control the majority of Canadian media. However, the "commodification," or free market and recycling of media content at the global level does present a challenge as Canadian media become integrated into the international network, because of the increasing links generated by communication technology–a necessity in order to compete effectively. Control may be subtly lost as highly capitalized new technology threatens Canadian facilities with obsolescence, leading to more dependence on the giants outside who gain control as the builders and operators of the new systems. This threat is exacerbated by the accelerating obsolescence of older communications technology and the high capital cost to replace existing equipment as we are further transformed into an information-exchange-based society.

Jody Berland and Will Straw draw our attention to the relationship between governments' cultural policies and the promotion of cultural production, raising the question of the increasing loss of distinction between culture and commodity. Berland and Straw document the reality that governments increasingly play a key role in the management of culture through policy initiatives, which often have paradoxical effects, as in the initiatives to preserve identity and cultural sovereignty. Berland and Straw focus their attention on the recording, film, and book industries, but their analysis would generally apply to other parts of the culture industry such as broadcasting, magazines, theatre, and museums.

The principal problems of the Canadian culture industry are economic: most of its products are more costly to produce in Canada than to import, resources for national distribution and promotion are inadequate, and there is a need for government financial support for many kinds of cultural products. But the economic infrastructure of the Canadian culture industry does not seem to naturally support important aspects of cultural production–a problem that is in part due to Canada's relatively small population base. As Alvin Toffler once noted, describing what he called the "law of the inefficiency of art," there is a sharper rise in cost to produce culture than other goods and services. Government policy encourages the production of that which will be economically successful, rather than experimentation and risk taking.

Canada's culture industry faces dilemmas that government policy has not ameliorated. By distributing the products–whether films, records, or books–of transnational firms, Canadian organizations can earn money to promote their own cultural productions, and also meet a key objective of government policy–to become "more market- based," or "propelled by consumer demand." The irony is that when Canadian firms meet that criterion, the products (from abroad) that are given emphasis detract from attempts to build the inventory of grassroots Canadian cultural products.

15

Stroking the Airwaves: The Regulation of Broadcasting by the CRTC

John Meisel

nyone enjoying even a nodding acquaintance with the subject of this book need not be told that communications is of the greatest possible importance to society and individuals alike. This being so, it will not surprise the reader that so critical an area is subject to pervasive efforts aimed at ensuring that communications processes and content enhance social goals and do not undermine the well-being of the whole community. This is more easily said than done. Take body language, for instance, the most pervasive form of communication. How is a society to guide and police such things as shrugs of the shoulder, undulating hips, raised eyebrows, or rude gestures of the finger? Although efforts to control such minutiae of human behaviour have been and are being made, they are rarely successful for long.

It is when people send signals to one another through a public medium that the community finds it easier to become involved and to exercise control. Books, plays, films, newspapers and journals, posters–these are the preferred targets of public concern (often resulting in thought control and censorship.) These constraints are usually applied by the state to reinforce prevailing moral codes or to weaken political opposition. Even liberal democracies, imbued with civil-libertarian values and respect for freedom, attempt to prevent certain types of messages from being exchanged freely. But such efforts invariably cause concern and bring forth cries of outrage from those committed to the idea that the unfettered exchange of ideas is a *sine qua non* of free democratic societies.

But in one domain, even highly permissive and open societies have accepted the need for governments to become involved in, and to direct and regulate, the most influential means of communication. That area is broadcasting. The reason for pervasive state involvement in the first instance was technological. The scarcity of frequencies made it essential that they be allocated to specific broadcasters so as to prevent more than one from sending signals on the same wavelength in any listening area. Technological innovation has taken the pressure off this aspect somewhat since, in the era of fibre optics, digital compression, and satellites, we are capable of receiving hundreds of radio and television services. But the number of available frequencies is still not unlimited and, as we shall see, there are other reasons for regulating broadcasting, particularly in countries like Canada.

Before zeroing in on the Canadian Radio-television and Telecommunications Commission (CRTC)–the centrepiece of the Canadian broadcasting regulatory regime[1]–we must note that there are other instruments for the imposition of societal values on communication. They include informal social pressure; censorship boards such as those that classify films; laws governing obscenity or hate literature; the structure of communications industries and the practices of their unions; and public ownership of broadcasting facilities. In some countries, as the McCarthy experience in the U.S. showed, legislative committees can terrorize the public and communications industries into quite appalling forms of self-censorship. In recent times, efforts are increasingly being made to prevent exhibitions from being mounted or theatrical performances presented that are deemed by some minorities to be racist or otherwise offensive. All these means are widely used in different jurisdictions for the purpose of influencing the manner in which individuals and groups interact with one another by spoken or written word and in other ways as well. One particularly important device for guiding a country's communications is the so-called independent regulatory agency, such as the Federal Communications Commission (FCC) in the U.S. and our own CRTC. These are responsible for ensuring that broadcasting and other telecommunications, such as telephone service, are used in the public interest, as defined by governments.

The CRTC is the successor to a number of earlier broadcast regulators, some of which did double duty as the board of directors of the public broadcasting company and the overseer of the private sector.[2] This occurred because initially the Canadian broadcasting system was intended to be overwhelmingly public with only modest participation by private firms. For a number of reasons this perspective changed, and a mixed regime in which the public sector was paramount became one dominated by the private sector. Now the board of the Canadian Broadcasting Corporation (CBC) is responsible solely for the corporation, and the CRTC regulates and supervises the whole system.

In what follows, we shall discuss the role, structure, and modus operandi of the federal regulator as background for a consideration of some of the major issues and controversies its existence has generated in recent years. But before tackling these tasks, it is necessary to sketch the context in which the CRTC operates.

First, it is important to note that regulation is not the same thing as censorship, despite the previous discussion. Indeed, the *Broadcasting Act* specifically places responsibility for programming on the shoulders of the broadcasters themselves, who are ultimately held accountable for all material they air–advertisements as well as programming. The CRTC has no authority to tell a broadcaster what it must or must not broadcast. The 1991 *Broadcasting Act* (often referred to as Bill C-40) requires that the programming available on the whole system "provide a reasonable opportunity for the public to be exposed to the expression of differing views on matters of public concern."[3] Similarly, the commission has regulations in place that prohibit the broadcast of "any abusive comment ... that, when taken in context, tends or is likely to expose an individual or a group or class of individuals to hatred or contempt on the basis of race, national or ethnic origin, colour, religion, sex, sexual orientation, age or mental and physical disability."[4]

However, even if the CRTC knew in advance that a station planned to air a program that would incontrovertibly snub these (or other) regulations, it has no power to act until *after* the program in question has been broadcast. Thus, freedom of speech is enshrined in the *Broadcasting Act*, but likewise, so is accountability. To repeat, regulation, at least in Canada, is not to be confused with censorship.

The Regulatory Environment

That Canada is a sparsely populated country, living in the shadow of the American colossus, is nowhere more evident and more significant than in the field of broadcasting. The scattered population, stretched out in a thin line of settlement along the U.S. border, has required assistance in maintaining communications from the very beginning in order for the country to constitute a viable political community. That is why the entry of British Columbia into Confederation was dependent on the completion of the transcontinental rail link and why early Canadian governments became so deeply embroiled in the affairs of the companies constructing it. Broadcasting and telecommunications are the contemporary equivalents of the railway and play equally critical nation-building (or nation-defending) roles. The way in which they perform them and the way in which the government can assist them are affected by a number of factors.

Canada not only has a much smaller population than its neighbour, but it is also economically dependent on it in myriad ways. Its population is divided into two linguistic families and two quite distinct societies. A significant proportion of Canadians are descended from neither of the two charter groups, including, of course, the first settlers–the aboriginal population. While the early immigrants were largely European, the recent newcomers are more likely to be Asian, West Indian, or Latin American. Because of the country's history and its demographic makeup, and also because of the massive exposure to American political culture, Canadians have, comparatively, a very low sense of national cohesion and a low sense of national identity.

While distinct from Americans, Canadians nevertheless share many of their neighbours' characteristics and values. One of the differences concerns their respective perception of the roles of the state. We have been more disposed to rely on the state to provide certain kinds of services than Americans, although the privatizing zeal of a recent government (1984–93) seems to have diminished this difference. Nevertheless, Canadians have traditionally opted for a much more mixed economy in which both the public and private sectors played major parts. We are more deferential, more conciliatory, less violent and litigious, and lacking in the messianism so characteristic of our neighbours. But, there are a great many similarities between the two cultures, similarities that are evident among both Francophones and Anglophones.[5]

These similarities in part explain why Canadians are so fond of American TV programs, but there are other reasons. American programs were available before indigenous ones, and so our tastes were developed by imported shows. Many of the performers on

TABLE 1: Percentage Distribution of TV Viewing Time on Canadian Stations by Origin and Type of Program (Fall 1991, All Persons Two Years and Older)

Type of Program	Canadian Programs	Foreign Programs	Total
News, public affairs, and documentaries	18.0	6.4	24.3
Instruction	2.4	0.8	3.1
Religion	0.2	0.1	0.3
Sports	5.0	2.4	7.3
Variety and games	5.5	5.0	9.5
Music and dance	0.6	0.5	1.1
Comedy	1.4	15.6	17.0
Drama	4.5	24.7	29.2
Other		8.2	8.2
Total	36.5	63.5	100.0

Source: Adapted from Statistics Canada, *Television Viewing, 1991* (Culture Statistics) (Ottawa: Minister of Industry, Science and Technology, 1993), Table 2, p. 20. Note: Figures may not add to totals owing to rounding.

American TV have become household names all over the world and are powerful magnets attracting large audiences. Furthermore, the productions of the U.S. networks are carried not only on American channels available to most Canadians with ordinary rooftop antennas or rabbit ears, and on cable and satellite dishes, but are also presented by the Canadian networks and independent stations. They are ubiquitous and have become part of the daily lives of large numbers of Canadians. In addition, the production values of the major U.S. dramas are extraordinarily high; the programs are therefore technically very strong.

The appeal of TV programs varies considerably among Canadians, depending on the type involved. Table 1 presents the percentage distribution of TV viewing time by origin and type of program. It tells us that the four most viewed kinds of programs are drama (29.2 percent), news, public affairs, and documentaries (24.3 percent), comedy (17.0 percent), and variety and games (9.5 percent). In the news and public affairs category, Canadian presentations outdraw American ones by almost three to one (18.0:6.4)–a margin that is, however, narrowing. As recently as three years ago, as the previous editions of this book showed, the difference was more than four to one. The recent American predominance in the variety and games category has been reversed (5.5:5.0). But when it comes to comedy and drama, the situation is decidedly lopsided. In the former, the pull of U.S. programs is 11 times greater than that of those originating in Canada (15.6:1.4). In the latter

category, Canadians watch programs from across the border five and a half times as often as they do those originating at home (24.7:4.5).[6]

It has been argued that the main reason for the attraction for Canadians of American comedy and drama programs is that such homegrown programs simply are not available. Viewers have little choice in the matter because Canadian broadcasters, particularly the private ones, present virtually no Canadian programs in these categories.[7] The argument that the proportion of viewing of Canadian programs is related to their availability is supported by the differences between recent statistics and those used in the previous edition of this text. In the three years from 1988 to 1991, during which the availability of Canadian programs increased, the gap between the consumption of American and Canadian variety and drama programs narrowed slightly. The ratio for the former, which was 13.1:0.8, changed, as we saw, to 15.6:1.4; for the latter it dropped to 24.7:4.5 from 25.7:4.0. Still, the viewing of American programs, compared with Canadian ones, is very substantial.

A great deal of soul searching has gone into the matter of why so few Canadian programs are available in the all-important entertainment category. Although the policies of broadcasters and governments, as well as the nature of the Canadian community, have something to do with it,[8] a major reason is economic. It costs well over $1 million to produce an hour-long, top-quality drama. In the American market this expense can be amortized by selling the program to a large number of stations.

Canadian plays of equal quality carry a similar price tag but, because of the disparity in the size of the American and Canadian markets, the number of potential buyers (and advertisers) is substantially lower. The per-unit cost is therefore incomparably higher and unattractive to commercial Canadian broadcasters who can acquire rights to sure-fire American hits for a fraction of the price of creating Canadian shows.

This partial sketch of the relevant background indicates what challenges have confronted, and still confront, broadcast regulation in Canada. The consequences arising from Canada's small, fragmented, and scattered population who live in a huge space next to a vital, gigantic, and attractive neighbour make up most of the fundamental preoccupations of the CRTC.

To carry out a mandate based on such preoccupations, one may ask how the CRTC is organized and how it goes about carrying out its business.

Role of the CRTC[9]

The *Broadcasting Act* stipulates that the CRTC "shall regulate and supervise all aspects of the Canadian broadcasting system with a view to implementing the broadcasting policy," Section 5(1), which is set out quite elaborately in Section 3 of the Act, and in conformity with a regulatory policy that is also specified in Section 5(2). These mandatory guidelines were articulated by Parliament as the result of an unusually long and complex process of study, consultation, deliberation, and legislative debate.[10] There was no doubt in the legislators' minds that the broadcasting system was to serve an extremely wide range of social purposes. These include the encouragement of "the development of Canadian expression by providing a wide range of programming that reflects Canadian attitudes, opinions, ideas, values and artistic creativity," Section 3(1)(d)(ii); the safeguarding, enriching, and strengthening of the cultural, political, social, and economic fabric of Canada, Section 3(1)(d)(i); serving "the needs and interests, and reflecting the circumstances and aspirations of Canadian men, women and children, including equal rights, the linguistic duality and multicultural nature of Canadian society and the special place of aboriginal peoples within that society," Section 3(1)(d)(iii). Each broadcasting undertaking "shall make maximum use, and in no case less than predominant use, of Canadian creative and other resources in the creation and presentation of programming," Section 3(1)(f). Furthermore, the latter should

"be varied and comprehensive, providing a balance of information, enlightenment, and entertainment for men and women of all ages, interests and tastes," Section 3(1)(i)(i).

These and many other provisions of the act give the CRTC sweeping powers to regulate virtually every aspect of radio and television in the country. Since its inception, the CRTC has not been shy about interpreting its parliamentary mandate aggressively. It has been encouraged to do so by the general absence of government policy, which left a vacuum someone had to fill, and by the courts who have supported the commission's generous interpretation of the *Broadcasting Act.* The most recent legislation, which on the one hand suggests some curbs on the regulator's long reach,[11] substantially expands the scope of the CRTC by charging the broadcasting system with many responsibilities that were not identified in previous Acts. References to employment opportunities for men and women, to multiculturalism, the special place of aboriginal peoples, or to programming that includes a significant contribution from the Canadian independent production sector invite the commission to become much more exacting in scrutinizing the performance of its licensees.

Another expansion of the CRTC's already generous ambit can be detected in recent changes in cable policy. The commission, having in 1986 largely vacated the field of cable-rate regulation, returned to it four years later because it found that subscribers had to be protected against the somewhat predatory practices of some companies.[12]

So, although, as we shall see, the commission has attempted to accommodate itself to the deregulatory rhetoric and program of recent governments by stressing its more permissive supervisory mandate at the expense of the more intrusive regulatory one, technological change, and societal and economic developments continue to steer it towards a commanding role in Canadian broadcasting. However, new broadcasting technology, as we shall see, also makes regulation more difficult.

Structure of the CRTC

Although the CRTC maintains several regional offices, its headquarters are located in a vast Kafkaesque complex of government buildings in Hull.[13] The staff numbers 400, one-quarter of whom specialize in telecommunications. The chairman performs a double function: that of CEO and that of "political" head who, by virtue of leading the team of commissioners, has considerable influence on the policy decisions they reach. The chairman is also the principal spokesperson who, consequently, exercises a good deal of influence on the broadcasting industry through speeches and informal contacts with the public and the regulated industries.

Bill C-40 provides for up to 13 full-time and 6 part-time commissioners. All are appointed for five-year renewable terms by the governor in council (the cabinet) and hold their positions during "good behaviour" (i.e., they can only be fired for very good cause). In the past, most, although by no means all, have been patronage appointments of Liberal or Conservative governments. It appears that when Keith Spicer, the head at the time of writing, was made chairman, he was assured by the prime minister that during his term of office he would have a say in the filling of vacancies on the commission.[14]

Part-time commissioners live in different parts of the country and hence bring to their job a more regional perspective than that likely to be espoused by an Ottawa resident. The new Act also provides for some geographic decentralization among the 13 full-time commissioners. Six part-time members are also inclined to view the world from the vantage point of a citizen rather than a bureaucrat or at least a government person. Although all of the latter used to live in the Ottawa area, Bill C-40 now stipulates that a full-time commissioner must reside wherever in the country the CRTC has an office—and the number of regional offices is expected to grow from four to seven or eight. By autumn 1993, commissioners had been appointed to posts in Halifax, Winnipeg, Montreal, Toronto, Edmonton, and Vancouver. Before the passage of the new legislation, it was fiercely opposed by CRTC chairmen who doubted whether this arrangement could work since the full-time members, constituting the commission's executive committee, used to meet once a week, if not more often, and frequently held ad hoc sessions on short notice to deal with the ever-present emergencies confronting the CRTC. The government and Parliament were not deterred from their wish to implant a decentralized element into the regulator's structure, however.

The commission's modus operandi has changed substantially since the new Act came into effect. The weekly meetings of the executive committee are no longer held: the committee itself, in fact, has vanished. Much of its work has fallen on the shoulders of a smaller committee, called the Public Hearings and Cable Rate Committee, chaired by the commission's vice-chair responsible for broadcasting. The use of

teleconferencing and other electronic aids has enabled the commission to function effectively even under the new geographically decentralized regime.

In a significant clause, both novel in the annals of Canadian law making and indicative of how information technology is transforming modern decision making, Canada's law-makers invented a metaphysical conceit enabling a person to be in two places at the same time. According to the amended CRTC Act,

> A member may participate in a meeting of the Commission ... by means of such telephone or other communication facilities as permit all persons participating in the meeting to hear each other, and a member who participates in such a meeting by those means is deemed for the purposes of this Act to be present at the meeting. (Section 10 (4) of the CRTC Act, as amended by Bill 40).

While the CRTC's internal structure tends to undergo changes from time to time, certain features are constant. Thus, there is always quite a pronounced separation between the staff working on broadcasting and those working on telecommunications. A legal directorate serves both these groups, as does the commission's secretariat, which is responsible not only for all housekeeping, but also for work connected with licensing and public hearings. In addition, distinct directorates are responsible for the three major areas of broadcasting—radio, television, and cable. A significant change, noted with displeasure by the Report of the Caplan-Sauvageau Task Force (p.182), relates to a special research unit. It was abandoned in 1984, although research activities continue to be undertaken at diverse sites within the commission.

Modus Operandi

The work of the commission falls mainly into four major categories, although there are many other, less central tasks to be performed. These are: the development of policies, the making of regulations, the issuing of licences, and the exercising of powers of suasion, in the hope that this will result in a climate conducive to the realization of the goals of the *Broadcasting Act*. In the past, some of the policy making took place by default, as noted earlier, because governments of the day failed to provide policy guidance. Such strategic decisions as the role to be played by cable or the timing of the introduction of pay-TV services fall into this category. Bill C-40 gives the cabinet substantially greater powers of direction and, since the responsible ministry has become very active in broadcasting, it can be expected that more broad policy decisions will henceforth emanate from the politicians. But there are still innumerable fields to be tackled, such as general policies affecting the relations between cable and conventional broadcasters; the role of telephone companies in broadcasting, if any; AM, FM, and TV policies; violence on television; how to handle sex stereotyping; matters related to advertising and so on.

Many of the policies developed by the CRTC find expression in regulations adopted through a rigorously formal procedure. These regulations are in fact delegated legislation, filling out in detail the intentions sketched in the Act by Parliament. Their violation is a breach of the law and may be followed by court action.

The procedure followed by the CRTC in devising policies and regulations usually involves a good deal of public consultation. A policy paper is usually published and made widely available to interested parties for comment. The latter may be in the form of written submissions but in almost all important cases also involves the appearance of witnesses at one or more public hearings. These are an essential feature of the commission's modus operandi.

They play a central role not only in the development of policies and regulations but also in the licensing process. The law states that the airwaves are public property and are to be used in the public interest. The chief mechanism for ensuring that this is done is the CRTC and its licensing regime. At the heart of the latter is the fact that one can only broadcast legally in Canada if one has received a licence from the federal regulator. Each licence specifies precisely what the CRTC expects from the licensee, whether the proportion of a particular type of music to be played on a radio station or the hours of original Canadian drama on TV. The most important features of the TV licence are usually enshrined in specific conditions of licence that spell out the licensee's commitments. The penalty for breaching a condition of licence can be non-renewal of a licence or renewal for only a short time.

The normal procedure before a licence is awarded is for several companies or individuals to submit carefully prepared applications and all sorts of supporting documents. Every such application is made available to competing applicants and the general public. In due course, a public hearing takes place at which a panel of commissioners hears evidence in support of the various applications and such criticisms as potential competitors and other interested parties may wish to present. Members of

the panel will have studied detailed analyses and comparisons of the competing applications prepared by the commission staff, and are therefore well briefed about the areas to be explored in detail with the applicants. Although the CRTC's counsel is always present at the hearings, witnesses at broadcasting hearings are not under oath, and most of the questioning is done by commissioners rather than the commission's legal officers.

After the hearing, the panel and staff review the evidence heard and eventually, after having consulted the other commissioners, the panel makes the final decision about who is to receive a licence, and under what conditions. The commission's decision can be appealed either to the courts, on questions of law, or to the federal cabinet. The latter cannot vary the CRTC's determination of the case, but it can set a decision aside or send it back for re-hearing. Both legal and cabinet appeals are rare.

Insofar as the final principal function of the commission is concerned–that of influencing the milieu in which it operates–the task is less clearly defined and largely informal. It falls primarily on the shoulders of the chair, who regularly meets with all the major players in the broadcasting world, whether they are in the public or private sector, with government officials, parliamentarians, and from time to time also with representatives of provincial governments. The commission head also makes a large number of speeches to trade and other associations and interest groups, attempting to inform the world of the CRTC's plans and reactions. At the heart of this activity is the need to persuade the industry that it should do all it can to realize the goals of the *Broadcasting Act*, not only because of the formal rules and decisions of the CRTC but particularly because such action is intrinsically desirable. In a sense, the commission must attempt to help the broadcasting industry internalize the values that animate the *Broadcasting Act*.

A Case in Point: Revising the System

The foregoing discussion was, perforce, rather general. Many of the points made will become more concrete if we consider a recent major initiative of the commission, in which it attempted to create a new television scenario so as to implement the goals of the *Broadcasting Act* in the face of new technical and economic realities. The impetus for this initiative was, as usual, complex: the development of a new satellite-distribution technology in the U.S., dubbed "Death Stars," capable of delivering over 200 channels to subscribers equipped with a receiving dish the size of a dinner plate; the emergence of "digital-video compression" (DVC)–the ability to "squeeze," with the aid of a "black box," a dramatically increased number of services into currently available TV receivers; the increasing convergence of broadcasting and telephonic technologies; the wish of many Canadian entrepreneurs to offer heretofore unavailable TV programming and other services; the continuing and growing clamour of conventional broadcasters demanding that they be compensated by the cable companies for their programs presented on cable; dissatisfaction with the billing and other policies of cable companies. Over and above these concerns was the fundamental strategic question of whether the future course of broadcasting in Canada would be based on a satellite-to-home delivery system or on one relying on cable.

To address these and other issues, the CRTC announced that in September 1992 it would hold a major "structural hearing" in which it would "review … the evolving communications environment, and its impact on the existing and future structure of the Canadian Broadcasting system."[15] Its concerns were identified and discussed in a lengthy Public Notice, which elicited over 700 written submissions from interested parties even before the month-long hearing took place in March of 1993, at which 126 witnesses presented their views. On June 3, 1993, the commission released four Public Notices, taking up 76 pages, to announce its findings.[16] Even then, these documents were essentially declarations of intent to be followed by implementation through additional proceedings and decisions.

The commission's strategy is encapsulated in the title it gave to the news release accompanying the bundle of its notices: "Consumer-Driven TV: A Canadian Bridge to the Future." In keeping with the prevailing public-policy ethos, and in the light of new available technologies, regulation is to be kept to a minimum and the viewers are to have a greater choice; but it is also recognized that it will take a long time for the new technologies to be fully established. The decisions growing out of the "structural hearing" are therefore a bridge towards the future. The latter will offer not only digital-video compression (and hence an explosion of new services) but also "universal addressability offering 'pick-and-pay' choice from eventually hundreds of channels."[17]

Cable is favoured over direct-to-home service (DHS), although the latter is recognized as a valid component of the broadcasting scene. The commission failed to heed the broadcasters' call for a ruling compelling cable companies to pay royalties for carrying the latters' programs. This issue was judged to fall primarily under copyright law. In view of the increasingly converging character of the relevant technologies, telephone and cable companies are encouraged to explore opportunities for co-operative ventures for the shared use of network infrastructures. Important changes are announced affecting billing formulas and practices of cable companies, as well as the manner in which they are to be regulated.

Three decisions, in particular, will fundamentally affect the structure of our future broadcasting system. The first relates to the upgrading of hardware, so as to permit the interactive (addressable) use of cable. The majority of the commission, with some abstentions, allowed the cable companies to raise part of the capital needed from a monthly addition to subscriber fees.

However, in the second of the ground-breaking new developments, cable companies are required to contribute to a production fund, estimated to reach about $300 million, over five years.

Third, the commission's Notice called for applications for a new range of Canadian specialty, pay-TV, and pay-per-view services.

The overall changes foreshadowed in these decisions are designed to make the Canadian system more flexible and in some respects less regulated, while at the same time strengthening as much as possible its Canadian flavour. It remains to be seen how the intentions will be realized and whether they will have the desired effect.

June 3, 1993, the day on which the path-setting "structural" blueprint was unveiled, saw the release of another, related, historic decision. It concerned religious broadcasting. The commission, mindful of the *Broadcasting Act*'s insistence that programming must be balanced when matters of public concern are involved, had heretofore refused to license any religious-broadcast undertaking representing a single faith or group of faiths on the ground that it or they would not be able to offer balanced programming. The steadily increasing number of available channels, vigorous agitation by some religious groups, and the presence of single-faith broadcasters in Western Canada importing unauthorized American religious programs were among the reasons for which the commission called a hearing in October 1992 to review its policies on religious broadcasting. In this instance, over 2,600 written and 56 oral presentations were received.

With no fewer than six commissioners dissenting, the majority decided to authorize the licensing of single or limited point-of-view religious services, but stipulated that they could only be seen on cable on a discretionary basis and that they may only be packaged with other Canadian religious services. Only individuals willing to subscribe to a religious tier will be able to see the programs of the single-faith broadcasters that do not adhere to the balance rule; subscribers to only the basic service will not receive these programs. The commission also announced that the new services will be subject "to a rigorous code of ethics assuring honest fund-raising and accounting, as well as respect for other religious groups."[18] At the time of writing, almost 50 licenses have been issued under the new policy. It is too soon to tell whether the forebodings of the dissenting commissioners were justified. In their minority opinion they expressed the fear that "removing the requirement for balance in discretionary religious broadcasting will promote religious, cultural and racial intolerance in Canada and will lead to a weakening of the cultural, political, social and economic fabric of Canada."[19]

The processes through which the commission reached its decisions on the new structure of the broadcasting system, and on the role of religious broadcasting within it, illustrate all four of the aspects of the CRTC's work noted in the previous section. Firstly, major innovations in policy were involved. Secondly, although no final regulations or licenses have yet emerged, considerable thought and guidance on these follow-up matters are to be found in the Public Notices discussed here. The die is cast. Finally, the documents to which we have referred fairly bristle with suggestions, recommendations, and advice, which, while not formally binding, clearly fall under the category of exercising powers of suasion.

In addition, the cases we have summarized illustrate eloquently the considerable degree to which the commission consults interested parties, the sensitivity it displays towards new technologies and their consequences, the stubborn nature of the problems it must resolve, and the fact that some of the issues it confronts lead to deep divisions within it. The cases also suggest that the realism and insight displayed by the CRTC at this stage of major transformation have yet to be tested.

Controversies about Regulation

Few government agencies receive as much public attention as the CRTC. Among the reasons for this attention are the wide-ranging scope of its activities in the broadcasting and telecommunications sectors, the narcissism of the media that leads them to lavish disproportionate attention on themselves and all things affecting them, the far-reaching consequences of the commission's decisions and their impact on the lives of most Canadians, and the number, wealth, and media access of the parties directly affected by the regulatory decisions. At any rate, the commission often finds itself at the centre of lively controversy. Most of these disputes fall into two categories: those relating to regulation as such and those emanating from specific practices of the regulator.

Some critics question whether it is appropriate for a liberal democracy to have the state interfere at all in the free exchange of ideas. These arguments are strengthened by the libertarian, privatizing tendencies associated with the 1980s and 1990s. The parallel is often drawn between print and electronic media. Political freedom, it is argued, depends on the unhindered exchange of ideas made possible by a virtually unlimited freedom of the press in most respectable democratic polities. The unfettered conditions of the print media should, in this view, also prevail in the electronic sector. Government control of broadcasting is, therefore, seen as an unwarranted intrusion into matters the state should leave alone. While it may be necessary for a government department to allocate radio frequencies, and for the courts to watch over such matters as libel, any interference beyond that is unacceptable.

This argument may have some abstract appeal, but it is not convincing at a practical level. At least two major factors weaken it fatally. One arises from the fact that the economic structure of publishing is such that certain individuals or interests are clearly favoured in being able to present their views. The preferences and interests of owners and advertisers often influence content with the result that views challenging the socioeconomic status quo are silenced or minimized. The other is that it is relatively easy and inexpensive to produce and disseminate printed material, particularly with the advent of desktop publishing, whereas access to broadcasting, notably TV, is extraordinarily expensive. These two compelling, universally applicable arguments are strengthened immeasurably in Canada by a third: without the active intervention of the state, there would be hardly any Canadian programs on the air, particularly on TV, and particularly entertainment programming. The widespread anti-regulatory rhetoric espoused by the business community and marketeering economists is therefore misdirected when applied to broadcasting.

Broadcasters themselves seem to be rather ambivalent about the controversies affecting the desirability of regulation. Individually, and through their trade organizations, the Canadian Association of Broadcasters (CAB) and the Canadian Cable Television Association (CCTA), they complain bitterly about regulatory intrusion into their business, but on the other hand they seem to like the stability and predictability resulting from regulation. During the discussions about whether the new legislation should give the government greater powers of direction, the CAB was among the commission's staunchest supporters. Both conventional broadcasters and cable operators have done amazingly well economically while regulated by the CRTC[20] and it is therefore likely that in general they would just as soon be guided by it than not.

There is, nevertheless, considerable objection to the commission's unceasing efforts to make broadcasters present a reasonable proportion of Canadian programs. Although even the private companies are now beginning to spend a little on providing indigenous drama, historically they have fought the commission tooth and nail on this point, even in periods, unlike the present, when they were reaping immense profits. The so-called bottom line has always won over whatever sense of patriotic duty may have stirred in the broadcasters' breasts. The logic of the pocket book is invariably supplemented by the rhetoric of freedom: "give the public what it wants, and it clearly wants U.S. shows," the argument runs—and it is widely echoed by numerous journalists and members of the public.

We have already noted that tastes in viewing and listening are not innate qualities of the human species but are acquired by exposure and are shaped by what is available. One reason, as we saw, for Canadians liking American TV is that they are used to it. If more Canadian material were available and had been there during the formative stages of TV, audience tastes would differ It is nevertheless the case that the quality of many domestic programs used to be decidedly inferior to the imported product, and that this has given our own productions a bad name. One reason for this difference was the small amounts of money allocated to Canadian drama by the broadcasters. Recent experience shows that when sufficient funds are made available, Canadian programs compete effectively with foreign ones. The resources available are still inadequate, however, to support

competition in this domain on an even playing field. We cannot invest as much as our neighbours in the production of regular TV programs, and we cannot afford the system of "pilots," which, in the U.S., ensures that only the most popular programs are retained in each year's schedule. Under these conditions, it is necessary for the television industry and the government to undertake a variety of measures designed to improve the quality and augment the quantity of Canadian shows in neglected programming areas.

Two aspects of Canada's regulatory regime were at one time the subject of great controversy, but the heat formerly generated by them has now abated. One concerned which level of government should have responsibility for broadcasting, and the other, the respective place of the private and public sectors. With respect to the former, provincial challenges to federal jurisdiction were resolved by the courts in favour of Ottawa.[21] After the Meech Lake debacle, the government of Quebec has again raised this issue, however. The original idea recommended by the Aird Commission,[22] of fostering an exclusively public system, gradually gave way to a mixed regime in which the CBC was dominant. Eventually, as we noted, the private sector gained the upper hand, and there is no question that at present the CBC is no more than one of many players, albeit an enormously important one, in the line-up of Canadian broadcasters.[23] Currently, the Canadian system is therefore a mixed one with the private sector dominating. While a small but vociferous group of Canadians strongly deplore this change, the present political and economic realities make its cause all but futile. The controversies over the respective place to be occupied by the public and private sectors have been resolved. The best the Friends of Canadian Broadcasting (the major pro-CBC lobby) can hope for is the survival and reasonable funding of the CBC as one of the key members of the Canadian broadcasting family.

Controversies about the CRTC

A perennial issue concerning the CRTC arises from its status as an *independent* regulatory agency. These types of government instruments are not fully autonomous but are at what is termed an "arm's length" distance from the government of the day. The controversies range over the extent to which the politicians or officials in regular government departments affect the day-to-day operations and decisions of the regulator and, obversely, the degree to which the agency marches to its own drummer, irrespective of the priorities and direction of the government. In the past, the CRTC enjoyed a very high level of independence, and governments, other than through their appointments, could do little about it. While the government had some powers of issuing directions to the agency, they were severely limited. The *Broadcasting Act* now empowers the governor in council to issue to the commission directions "of general application on broad policy matters" under Section 7(1)–i.e., with respect to just about everything except its licensing decisions, Section 7(2). The government must consult the commission before making an order, which has to be laid before the House of Commons and referred to an appropriate house committee. In combination with the government's continued powers to send back or annul any licensing decision on appeal, the new powers enable the political authorities to circumscribe the commission's freedom of action substantially more than was the case in the past.

It remains to be seen whether the new powers will be used extensively. If so, maintaining a separate regulator may become a wasteful extravagance. The chances of this happening, however, are slim. Even with curbed powers, the case for an independent agency is quite overwhelming, and for several reasons:

- At one level, it is imperative in a liberal democracy that an essential information- and news-purveying service be insulated from the immediate control of the government party or parties.

- Many owners of media are, not surprisingly, highly politicized and maintain fairly close ties with one or another of the political parties. Under such conditions it is desirable that the process of awarding licences and other matters affecting the broadcasting environment be insulated from the government of the day, which might otherwise be strongly tempted to reward its friends and punish its enemies, possibly quite unwittingly.

- The task of regulating as complex a field as broadcasting requires immensely detailed technical and social knowledge and experience. A stable, highly visible, quasi-independent agency is more likely to build up *and maintain* the necessary infrastructure than a routine government department, whose personnel are likely to be highly mobile within the overall governmental apparatus.

- We noted earlier that an important procedure used by the regulator is to exercise its power of suasion. A former CRTC chairman argued that his agency was the conscience, or moral compass, guiding the industry towards the goals set by Parliament. This kind of role can best be played by an independent, well-defined, and highly visible agency whose spokespersons are free from the restraints normally binding officials and politicians.

- Most of the decisions of the CRTC tend to antagonize more individuals than they please. Since politicians usually try to maximize support and minimize giving offense, the field of broadcast regulation is generally quite unattractive to them. It is convenient to be able to duck difficult choices and awkward decisions by having recourse to an arm's-length agency, for whose actions the government does not take immediate responsibility and which can serve as a scapegoat when unpopular policies are needed.

In view of these factors, it is probable that the new powers of direction proposed for the cabinet will be used sparingly, and that the CRTC will continue as a reasonably autonomous agency. It will, however, be easier than before to ensure that the general direction of CRTC policy and other decisions will be congruent with the predispositions of the government elected to power in Ottawa. On several occasions in the past–with respect to the timing of the introduction of pay TV, for instance, or when the government was contemplating the introduction of specialty programming services, as recommended by the Caplan-Sauvageau Report–the commission went its own way and by so doing frustrated some policy intentions of the minister responsible for communications.[24] This kind of conflict is unlikely to recur under the new legislation.

Another means through which reigning governments influence the work of the commission is their power to decide appeals brought to the cabinet by disappointed "victims" of the regulator. During the five years ending in 1993, the CRTC released over 4,500 broadcasting decisions. Of these, only six were appealed to cabinet and it referred only two back to the commission. The most recent of the two cases, which occurred in the autumn of 1993, nicely illustrates the manner in which seemingly simple licensing decisions can have far-reaching, systemic consequences, and also how the cabinet can ensure that hotly contested, important decisions can be subjected to reconsideration in the light of government concerns.

The CRTC had licensed two companies to provide digital pay-audio services. The sound quality of this technology is far superior to that of currently available transmissions. The Canadian music industry appealed the decision to cabinet, terming it "cultural assassination": the proposed services—to cost cable subscribers about $10 per month—were to consist of more than 70 channels of 24-hour programming. Fewer than one-fifth of these channels were to be Canadian. This, it was asserted, would cripple the Canadian music industry. The CRTC critics estimated that home taping of radio programs already accounted for a loss of $250 million per year in retail sales of recordings. The high quality of the new signals would lead to an additional massive flight of revenue.

In its decision on the appeal, the cabinet asked the CRTC to consider, in a new hearing, whether the service could use more Canadian programming and why the new services did not plan on using Canadian telecommunications resources to distribute Canadian material. The commission was also asked to explain why, in its decision, it approved different levels of Canadian content for the two services, and why it did not require pay-audio services to be available in all parts of Canada. Thus the appeal led to the CRTC having to reconsider the whole issue of digital-audio technology at another hearing and to take into account some of the concerns of the government.[25]

To those individuals who watch the broadcasting scene from close quarters, an interesting tension between the CRTC's regulatory and supervisory roles has become apparent. Towards the middle of the 1980s the general policy direction of the commission underwent something of a change. Greater sensitivity than heretofore was displayed towards the economic condition of applicants and licensees. As a result, and also no doubt in response to the general deregulatory climate evident in many parts of the world, the CRTC proclaimed and applied a new emphasis on the supervisory, rather than the regulatory, aspects of its mandate. In some areas the broadcasters were left to make their own decisions rather than be governed by regulations. Both the CAB and the CCTA, for instance, set up standards councils for their respective industries. But the CRTC did not abdicate its responsibility in the areas governed by

some self-regulation. Instead, it relied on the less intrusive means of supervising what was done through the requirement that reports be produced on specified occasions and through evaluations of the performance of its licensees at licence-renewal time.

Disagreements have arisen about the effectiveness of this change. The commission has generally assumed that this loosening of regulatory control has met with beneficial results, but others have argued that the approach is flawed because most broadcasters are so driven by the profit motive that they find it almost impossible to put the public interest (and their obligations to the commission) ahead of earning extra income. The commission itself acknowledged, as we saw, that its vacating of the regulation of cable rates led to the imposition of excessive charges by the companies and that it had to re-impose controls. Another area in which the lenient policy failed to produce adequate results is that of the avoidance of sex-role stereotyping.[26] The judgement most observers make on the consequences of the policy change depends to a great extent on their general attitude towards the effectiveness of market mechanisms and the integrity of the private sector. If the availability of Canadian drama is used as an indicator, then the evidence suggests that the changing emphasis in the CRTC's regulatory style has not met with unequivocal success.

Among the many charges laid against the CRTC by one of its most severe critics, Herschel Hardin, none is as stinging and troubling as the accusation that the commission sanctions the sale of radio and TV licences.[27] All broadcasting acts, from the very beginning, have asserted that the airwaves are public property. It follows from this that a broadcasting licence bestows the right on the licensee to use a frequency for a specified period of time and under certain given conditions. Hardin argues that this should make it mandatory that, when the licence period comes to an end, or when a broadcast undertaking is up for sale, competitive bids be considered by the commission for the next licence period. Canadian practice has been quite different. Once a broadcaster "acquires" the licence it is his (or hers or theirs) for as long as it is not given up or, theoretically, for as long as it is not revoked; "theoretically" because the CRTC has rarely revoked a licence, even when repeated violations of its terms occurred. Competitive bids are not allowed at licence-renewal hearings. One consequence is that, when a broadcasting undertaking is sold, the items exchanging hands are all the assets, including the remaining term of the licence and the virtual certainty that this term will be renewed. It is true that when the purchase of a broadcasting company is agreed upon, the deal is always made on the understanding that the CRTC must approve it. In practice, the commission has only rarely refused to sanction the sale of radio and TV stations and tends to approve changes in the ownership of cable companies, although there have been a few exceptions.

The commission justifies the position it has taken on competitive licence renewals by pointing to the high capital costs of most broadcast undertakings and the long term needed to develop suitable programming. The maximum licence term allowed by the 1968 Act was only five years, and the CRTC has maintained that, unless the holder of a licence was assured of having a much longer period of time available, the necessary equipment could not be acquired and the commitments exacted by the commission could not be met. Hardin and other critics have found this defence unconvincing, particularly with respect to the transfer of cable ownerships. There is no doubt that, in fact, licences seem to be bought and sold in Canada when stations change hands and that the commission's argument is less valid now that the licence period has been extended to seven years. In the U.K. and elsewhere, television licences are auctioned, admittedly for longer stretches of time than those available under current Canadian law.

The extreme leniency of the CRTC with respect to the non-revocation of the licences of delinquent licensees has also occasioned a good deal of debate. There are those who argue that the commission is much too friendly to the broadcasters and that it has consistently refused to use the powers it has available to enforce its own decisions. The CRTC's response to the charge is that to revoke a licence may not always be the best way of furthering the goals of the *Broadcasting Act.* In some communities, particularly small ones, the consequence, according to the commission, would be to deprive listeners of important sources of information and entertainment, possibly for a very long time. Furthermore, too draconian an approach by the regulator might prevent some *potentially* excellent broadcasters from developing and improving their services until they attain the desired standards. A more lenient style of regulation, the CRTC has maintained, produces better results in the long run.

Whatever the merits of these arguments, it cannot be denied that both private broadcasters and the CBC have defied the wishes of the commission from time to time, and that the latter's insistence on certain levels of Canadian programming on TV, or on the pursuit by radio stations of specified musical formats, has frequently been ignored. This, while by no means rendering the CRTC impotent, has reduced its effectiveness and has sapped its authority. The history of broadcast regulation in Canada has been a long haul in which the goal of making our airwaves in large part Canadian has been repeatedly attenuated or abandoned under pressure from the private broadcasters. A recent important illustration is the CRTC's substantial reduction in 1986 of its Canadian-content requirements for pay-television licensees.[28] It must, however, be noted in all fairness that the situation has improved somewhat recently as the result of the presence of TVO, Vision, and also the efforts of some private broadcasters.

This notwithstanding, private broadcasters have, as noted earlier, consistently fought the commission's efforts to maximize Canadian programming, particularly in the entertainment field. They assert that the commission's insistence that certain amounts of programming time be dedicated to domestic material (50 percent overall, 60 percent in evening hours, at the time of writing) is misguided. This strategy, they claim, leads to a great deal of cheap, unattractive fare on TV, which adds to the station's Canadian quota but fails to attract audiences. A better approach, they maintain, is to reduce the percentage of broadcast time allotted to Canadian programs and to compensate for this with a smaller number of high-class, very attractive, and widely watched domestic dramas and variety programs. While this strategy appears desirable in principle, it is not likely to work in practice. It would permit the broadcasters to load up their schedules with popular (and, as we have seen, relatively inexpensive) American programs, and it would unquestionably reduce the already slender Canadian component in the private stations' schedules. The *Broadcasting Act*'s strictures that each broadcasting undertaking make predominant use of Canadian creative and other resources as in Section 3(1)(e), and that the system provide programming that reflects Canadian attitudes, opinions, ideas, and values as per Section 3(1)(c)(ii), would certainly not be met under a "qualitative" rather than a "quantitative" approach. In addition, it is exceedingly difficult to define high-quality and attractive programming, and it would be virtually impossible to administer such a system. The latter is nevertheless compelling and, as we saw earlier, the CRTC is once again implementing a strategy that it hopes will lead to higher quality domestic production while at least maintaining the current levels of Canadian content.

Finally, among the controversies affecting the way in which the commission carries out its business, there is one which relates to public hearings. A striking contrast is evident between the telecommunications hearings and its broadcasting ones. This, of course, is in part because the two areas of regulation are governed by different Acts. Broadcasting hearings, as mentioned, are much less formal; lawyers play only a minor role and witnesses are not under oath or subject to cross-examination. This informal, relaxed atmosphere is alleged by some to contribute to the tendency of the CRTC to be too lenient and compliant insofar as its broadcast licensees are concerned. The commission, however, does not see the matter in this light. Informal hearings, it believes, reveal as much, if not more, information than highly formal ones; they are less onerous for all parties concerned; they avoid the opaque obfuscation of legal discourse; they permit ordinary citizens to take part; and they enhance the generally constructive symbiosis between the broadcasters and the commission—a relationship that overall, in the CRTC's view, has salutary consequences for Canada's broadcasting system and for the realization of the design implicit in the *Broadcasting Act*.

Conclusion

What can we conclude from the above discussion, particularly with respect to probable future developments? The regulatory environment is clearly changing and the regulatory process is adapting to the new circumstances. The chief variables in these ongoing developments are the continuing rapid technological innovations on the one hand, and the deregulatory climate in the world on the other. These two factors may, to some extent, neutralize each other. New equipment and emerging new services de-stabilize the broadcasting scene and generally lead to demands for some sort of supervision and regulation that would enable interested parties to plan rationally for the future and that would protect the investment of established players. The sociopolitical climate inimical to government encroachments into the economy, however, inhibits officials and regulatory agencies from providing the needed stabilizing measures. In this tug of war, the intrusive reach of government is almost certain to win out. It is generally the case in Canada that, while deregulation is taking place in some sectors of life (air transport, for

instance), new and increased control is being imposed elsewhere (environmental control). Considerable doubt exists, in fact, about the depth and extent of the public's hostility to regulation. Many people are highly selective in their views on these matters; the libertarian philosophy applied to some fields is less evident in broadcasting. Discussions about the new broadcasting legislation, despite the deregulatory rhetoric of some participants, furnished many inducements for an extensive involvement by government in the work of broadcasting undertakings.

But modifications are occurring with respect to the division of labour among various units of the government involved in guiding what is available on the airwaves. These modifications are almost certain to continue and will have an impact on the future role of the CRTC. Two aspects of these changes are striking.

Firstly, it is becoming increasingly obvious that the desire, enshrined in all broadcasting acts since the 1930s, to strengthen the Canadian character of programming requires more than mere regulation. Tax measures, treaties, and agreements affecting transborder co-productions, and the provision of loans or outright grants for Canadian productions are needed to enable indigenous writers, artists, and production companies to compete effectively with American networks and independents. In recent years, the most visible and effective extra-regulatory program has been that of Telefilm Canada, a government agency that makes substantial sums of money available, under conditions designed to further Canadian content, to Canadians engaged in the creation of television drama. Another instrument for strengthening Canadian content is the public broadcaster—the CBC. Although it is financially squeezed at present, future governments may, particularly if the economy picks up, charge the CBC with an even greater role in providing indigenous shows. Other than regulatory measures therefore affect the broadcasting scene, and the CRTC's role is complemented by programs and agencies over which it has no control. Its influence is, therefore, correspondingly reduced.

Secondly, even within the regulatory ambit, some power is being transferred from the CRTC to the political players—cabinet, the minister, and government (as distinct from agency) officials. Extending the cabinet's powers of issuing directions to the CRTC, provided for in the new Act, indicates that the regulator's freedom of action will be circumscribed. The cabinet requires supporting paperwork before it can become involved in these matters—work that falls on the shoulders of the minister responsible for communications and his officials. As the result, and also as the consequence of the factors noted in the previous paragraph, the position of the CRTC as the grand panjandrum of broadcasting will become less monopolistic.

The commission's continuance was not always a foregone conclusion. Both the Caplan-Sauvageau Commission and the federal government considered, in the course of devising their new policies, whether a different regulatory regime, and a different regulator, might not serve the country better. That the CRTC was, in the end, given a vote of confidence and enhanced powers is perhaps less an unqualified expression of approval than a recognition that the task of administering the *Broadcasting Act* and of regulating the airwaves in Canada is an extraordinarily difficult one, defying a perfect solution.

Some observers would have preferred a more radical course. Thus Liora Salter, a highly qualified expert who wrote a number of studies for the Caplan-Sauvageau Commission, recommended in one that a completely new approach (building on the past, to be sure) was in order.[29] After identifying three phases in the commission's history (the pro-active phase, 1968-73/5, the managerial one, 1975-81/2, and supervisory regulation, 1982–present), she proposed a regime that would be preemptive in orientation (pp.3-10, 25-8). Much greater emphasis would be given detailed legislation, some fields would be deregulated, and the CRTC (which was to continue) would have many of its powers curtailed, as well as, however, receiving substantially more effective instruments of enforcement.

In the end, less sweeping changes found their way into the *Broadcasting Act*, regrettably perhaps ignoring some useful suggestions made by Caplan-Sauvageau and others. Among these, two are particularly attractive. Caplan-Sauvageau recommended the appointment of a public advocate in each of the CRTC's regional offices, who would ensure public participation and who would act as a broadcasting ombudsperson.[30] Others, including Salter, suggested that ways be found of enabling public interveners in commission hearings to be funded out of public funds or, as is done in telecommunications proceedings, by the regulated industries. A less cut-and-dried reform, but one likely to pay high dividends, would be to devise an open, systematic, and quality-conscious process of appointing commissioners.

While the past performance of the CRTC suggests that, on the whole, persons of considerable skill and integrity have served on the commission, the patronage aspect has led to the appointment of commissioners who were weak or misguided. But even when first-rate individuals are named, the government rarely pays much attention to the philosophy a nominee brings to issues affecting broadcasting and telecommunications in Canada. This ought to change.

In the light of all the above, what lessons can we learn from Canada's experience with regulating broadcasting? First is the aforementioned immense difficulty of realizing the goals specified in our recent and current broadcasting acts. The reasons must be sought in the complexity of Canada's society, in the incongruities marking Canadian value systems, and in the challenges provided by a dramatically accelerating change in communications technology, including the growing convergence between telephony and cable, entertainment and data management. Second is that the process of guiding radio, TV, and cable is inevitably linked in the most sensitive way to political and administrative structures and forces. Third is the importance the electronic media possess in this country as demonstrated by the deep and sustained interest they elicit among an extremely wide and numerous group of Canadians. Finally, although the broadcasting scene in Canada is far from perfect, it nevertheless provides an opportunity to Canadians for the consumption and enjoyment of an unrivalled varied and rich source of radio and TV programs, catering to every conceivable taste and providing quite remarkable opportunities for choice. The cardinal weakness—the relatively small number of available Canadian dramas on TV—is still evident, but the immense attention it attracts from all sides suggests that in due course even this conundrum will, particularly under some of the provisions of the new *Broadcasting Act* and some recent CRTC decisions, elicit promising solutions.

In any event, the CRTC offers an important and fascinating case study of broadcasting and telecommunications. It is a major force with respect to the electronic media, to be sure, but it also provides an ideal subject for the study of other forms of communication. Its own decision-making process involves an immensely complex communications network. What the agency does is vitally affected by the communications webs characteristic of all large-scale organizations. In addition, there is the delicate interaction among the regulator and the public, the regulated industries, the minister responsible for communications and the officials in that department, the central agencies in Ottawa, some professional and industry groups, and interested parties at the provincial level. Furthermore, no national broadcasting system can avoid becoming involved in the global scene. Internally, the work of the commission results from a continuous process of communications between its principal components: the chair, the commissioners, officials in different branches of the organization, and consultants.

A circular communications process is, therefore, manifest in the CRTC and its outside relations. It is among the most powerful determinants of what happens in Canada's communications infrastructure. At the same time, it also is subject to extensive communications processes that affect its behaviour. This in turn influences, through the national communications system, some of the messages that determine its own actions, and so on, and on and on.

The regulatory process in broadcasting therefore consists of two continually interacting communications cycles that are, because of their importance to the country and because of their intrinsic interest, a most suitable subject of study for the student of communications.

Editorial Afterword – CM/BS

Since Professor Meisel's paper appeared in 1995, the CRTC has taken further policy action concerning the issue of regulation of the Internet. In 1999, following an extensive review, the CRTC "concluded that the new media on the Internet are achieving the goals of the Broadcasting Act *and are vibrant, highly competitive and successful without regulation." Francoise Bertrand, CRTC Chairperson explained that "by not regulating, we hope to support the growth of new media services in Canada." She added, "Our message is clear. We are not regulating any portion of the Internet."*

The rationales for this decision were:

1. That Internet content "that is predominantly alphanumeric text is by definition not broadcasting under the Broadcasting Act."

2. What is transmitted can be "customized" or "uniquely tailored by the individual user, does not involve the transmission of programs for reception by the public and is, therefore, not broadcasting."

3. Any material that might be defined as "broadcasting" will be exempt because "the new media complement, rather than substitute for traditional broadcasting. Before the new media could substitute for traditional media, key technological and other developments would have to take place."

This sweeping hands-off policy decision of the CRTC concerning the Internet in an era of "media convergence" has attracted remarkably little criticism even though there is much content on the Internet that has offended Canadians. Some of it is indeed broadcast material from the U.S. There is a fear that the current CRTC stance foreshadows a diminution of the entire Canadian broadcasting system as a result of the withdrawal of the regulator from its fastest growing component.

"What Ms. Bertrand didn't say, but what is clearly possible," according to an editorial in The Globe and Mail, *"is that the infinitely elastic Internet may well herald the demise of the federal regulator as far as broadcasting is concerned.... Some radio stations are already transmitting over the Web. By declining to regulate them, the CRTC is sending a go-ahead signal to other broadcasters and neophytes who feel constrained by the content shackles that the federal communications watchdog has imposed on traditional radio and television networks."* [31]

Notes

[1.] Although the CRTC regulates both broadcasting and telecommunications, this chapter focusses almost exclusively on the former.

[2.] For details about the earlier regulatory bodies, see relevant sections of Roger Bird, ed., *Documents of Canadian Broadcasting* (Ottawa: Carleton University Press, 1988); Frank W. Peers, *The Politics of Canadian Broadcasting 1920–1951* (Toronto: University of Toronto Press, 1969); and Frank W. Peers, *The Public Eye: Television and the Politics of Canadian Broadcasting 1952–1968* (Toronto: University of Toronto Press, 1979).

[3.] Bill C–40. An Act respecting broadcasting and to amend certain Acts in relation thereto and in relation to radiocommunication. Second Session, Thirty-fourth Parliament, 38–39 Elizabeth II, 1989–90–91. Statutes of Canada 1991, Ch. 11, Section 3(i), IV.

[4.] CRTC, *Television Broadcasting Regulations 1987,* as amended in 1991, 5(b); and CRTC, *Radio Regulations 1986* 3(b), as amended in 1991.

[5.] For an exhaustive treatment of this comparison see S.M. Lipset, *Continental Divide: The Values and Institutions of the United States and Canada* (New York: Routledge, 1990).

[6.] Statistics Canada, *Television Viewing 1991, Culture Statistics* (Ottawa: Minister of Industry, Science and Technology, 1993).

[7.] See W.A. Johnson, "Canadian Programming in Television. Do Canadians Want It?" Address to the Broadcast Executive Society, Toronto, February 19, 1981.

[8.] John Meisel, "Fanning the Air: The Canadian State and Broadcasting," *Transactions of the Royal Society of Canada,* Series V, Vol. IV (1989, 1990).

[9.] The two basic Acts defining the CRTC mandate and its structure are the *Broadcasting Act,* cited in endnote 3, and *The Canadian Radio-television and Telecommunications Commission Act* (RSC 1985, c22 and p.6 amendments).

[10.] Task Force on Broadcasting Policy, *Report* (Ottawa: Minister of Supply and Services, 1986), cited henceforth as Task Force *Report;* Paul Audley, "The Agenda for Broadcasting Policy: Reflections on the Caplan-Sauvageau Task Force," R. Lorimer and D. Wilson, eds., *Communication Canada* (Toronto: Kagan and Woo, 1988), pp.199–213; John Meisel, "Near Hit: The Parturition of a Broadcasting Policy," K. Graham, ed., *How Ottawa Spends 1989/90* (Ottawa: Carleton University Press), pp.132–63.

[11.] Section 5(2) states that "the broadcasting system should be regulated and supervised in a flexible manner that ... is sensitive to the administrative burden that, as a consequence of such regulation and supervision, may be imposed on persons carrying on broadcasting undertakings." Compared to previous Acts, Bill C–40 also substantially enlarges the power of the cabinet to issue directives to the CRTC.

12. CRTC PN 1990–53, "Cable Television Regulation, 1986–Changes in the Regulation of Subscriber Fees and Related Matters."

13. The seven-storey CRTC building is adjacent to a large hotel, a happy siting that enabled one former chairman of the CRTC occasionally to take a break in his daily 12-hour (or more) schedule for a quick swim.

14. Sarah Jennings, "I'm a chameleon—I like to re-invent myself," *The Globe and Mail,* 12 May 1990, p.C1.

15. CRTC, *Public Notice,* June 3; CRTC 1993–74, *Structural Public Hearing,* p.1.

16. Ibid; and CRTC, *Public Notices,* CRTC 1993–75, CRTC 1993–76 and CRTC 1993–77, 3 June 1993, with appendices.

17. CRTC news release, 3 June 1993, "Consumer Driven TV: A Canadian Bridge to the Future," p.1.

18. CRTC news release, 3 June 1993, "Freedom of Expression Balanced by Tolerance: Cornerstones of a New CRTC Religious Broadcasting Policy," p.3. See also CRTC Notice, CRTC 1993–78.

19. CRTC news release, "Freedom of Expression," p.3.

20. See Task Force *Report,* pp.391–400, 422–29.

21. Supreme Court of Canada, "In the matter of reference as to jurisdiction of Parliament to regulate and control radio communication," 30 June 1931, *Supreme Court Reports* 541 (1931); Judicial Committee of the Privy Council, "*Re* regulation and control of radio communication," 9 February 1932, *Dominion Law Reports* (1932) 2D.L.R., 81–88; *Capital Cities Communications v. Canadian Radio-television and Telecommunications Commission. 1978. 2RCS 141; Public Service Board v. Dionne. 1978. 2RCS 191.* See Roger Bird, ed., *Documents of Canadian Broadcasting* (Ottawa: Carleton University Press, 1988), pp.70–110; and R. Brian Woodrow et al., *Conflict over Communications Public Policy,* unpublished (C.D. Howe Institute, 1980), passim.

22. *Report* of the Royal Commission on Radio Broadcasting (1929).

23. For a succinct review of the evolution, see David Ellis, *Evaluation of the Canadian Broadcasting System* (Ottawa: Minister of Supply and Services), 1979.

24. Meisel, "Near Hit."

25. CRTC, Decision CRTC 93–236, Cogeco Radio-Télévision Inc., *New Pay Audio Programming Undertaking Canadian Digital Radio* (Ottawa, 25 June 1993); "CRTC assailed for cable audio plan," *The Globe and Mail,* 1 July 1993, p.C1; Canadian Press, "CRTC pay-audio decision protested," *Calgary Herald,* 2 July 1993, p.C10; Harvey Enchin, "Ottawa stalls pay-audio licenses," *The Globe and Mail,* 24 September 1993, p.B3.

26. For a detailed analysis, see Linda Trimble, "Coming Soon to a Station Near You: The Process and Impact of the Canadian Radio-television and Telecommunication Commission's Involvement in Sex-Role Stereotyping," Ph.D. thesis, Queen's University, 1990.

27. Herschel Hardin, *Closed Circuits. The Sellout of Canadian Television* (Vancouver: Douglas & McIntyre, 1985), passim.

28. CRTC, *Annual Report 1986–87* (Ottawa: Minister of Supply and Services, 1987), pp.51–52.

29. Liora Salter, "Issues in Broadcasting," unpublished Research Report to the Caplan–Sauvageau Task Force.

30. Task Force *Report,* p.196.

31. "Net gains for the CRTC Deciding not to regulate the Internet makes a virtual win out of Necessity," *The Globe and Mail,* 19 May 1999.

The Evolution of a National Press Policy: Ownership and Social Control in the 1990s

Andrew M. Osler

[Because of the untimely death of Professor Osler, this article has been lightly revised by the editors from the version which appeared in the 4th edition. There have been no changes at all to the central themes presented. They remain as germane today as when they were written– eds.]

Canada has a long history in developing legislative instruments that generally seek to contain the nation's media and to co-opt them to purposes of national policy. While the process always has been more obvious in the case of the broadcast media, the printed media, too, have been subject to periodic efforts to mount regulatory initiatives of one sort of another. Thus, the failure of the federal Parliament to pass a much-anticipated national press act in the early 1980s seems more surprising in hindsight than that the passing of such would have made Canada unique at that time among the established democracies of the English-speaking world.

In fact, with other democratic jurisdictions experimenting with approaches to press regulation, the Canadian experience in the 1990s can no longer be described as exceptional.

As might be expected, given the continuing strength of the Constitution's first amendment provisions there is little such activity in the U.S. of the 1990s. But in Britain the government put the press on notice in 1990 that it had 18 months to set up an effective voluntary regulation system or else face legislated constraints. Had it been enacted, the contemplated statute would have reached considerably beyond the regulatory framework envisaged in Canada's aborted press legislation of almost two decades ago. Like its predecessor, the British Press Council, which was disbanded on December 31, 1990, Britain's Press Complaints Commission is a voluntary body, and financed by an industry levy. It was established on the forceful recommendation of the government's 1990 Home Office Privacy Committee after the committee had completed its investigation of a long list of alleged press excesses and other offences, including alleged unethical and inappropriate approaches to coverage of the comings and goings of members of the royal family. The present government, elected in 1997, has made clear its support for effective self-regulation and for the work of the Press Complaints Commission.

Compliance with the rules of proper publishing behaviour is a matter of continuing government interest. The Conservative government of John Major (with unusual official support from the then official opposition Labour Party) gave notice that it would impose provisions of a statutory code of press practice should the complaints commission fail in future to function satisfactorily on a voluntary basis. In the words of Home Secretary of that day, Tim Renton, the British press is "on probation."[1]

While evidently more draconian in intent, the British moves of the early 1990s lack the breadth and sophistication of the earlier Canadian initiative. Canada's position in the early 1980s actually was the logical manifestation at the time of forces long at work in our national political life. It was immediately inspired, however, by the recommendations of the Report of the Royal Commission on Newspapers (Kent Commission), published in August 1981.[2] Draft legislation based upon the report's recommendations was announced by Jim Fleming, a junior minister of state in the Liberal government of then Prime Minister Pierre Trudeau. With established responsibility in the federal cabinet for matters relating to multiculturalism, Fleming was given the added duty of dealing with the recommendations of the Kent Commission, perhaps to attempt to incorporate them in the law of the land. He chose (presumably with full cabinet and prime ministerial approval) to develop them as legislation, and he announced his general intentions to do so in a speech to members of the University of Western Ontario's Graduate School of Journalism in May 1982.[3] Fleming further formalized his ideas, introducing them in the House of Commons in the form of a draft *Daily Newspapers Act* on July 6, 1983.[4]

In themselves, the legislative measures were not strong, and they would probably have had little immediate impact on the conduct of the nation's press. But they were remarkable nonetheless, because they made the concept of a general press law politically viable in the Canadian democracy, where no such acceptance previously had existed, and because they constituted a dramatic leap forward in a long-standing evolutionary process leading towards a national press policy. This was first evident in Canadian political culture at least a generation earlier.

The Canadian Roots

The roots of the Canadian position are complex, but readily traced. Federal interest in the printed media as potential objects of policy concern, especially as the journalism of these media relates to questions of national unity and national cultural development, dates back at least to the publication in 1951 of the report of Vincent Massey's Royal Commission on National Development in the Arts, Letters and Sciences in Canada. But it was a dramatic sequence of events in 1980, involving newspaper closures and corporate mergers, that had the immediate effect, politically, of moving the federal government to create the catalytic Royal Commission on Newspapers under the chairmanship of Thomas Kent, a professor of Management Studies at Dalhousie University in Halifax. This commission's recommendations, and the general sense of public urgency that surrounded its year-long processes of research and public hearings, provided the impetus that brought long-developing federal policy interest in the nation's press to a new maturity.

While the broadcast industry, since its inception early in this century, has been not only heavily regulated but also an important object of direct federal capital investment (the latter most significantly in the Crown-owned Canadian Broadcasting Corporation), the country's print media have remained comparatively untouched by government. Certain areas of the law, notably Criminal Code provisions relating to contempt of court and criminal libel, and provincial statutes pertaining to civil defamation, have traditionally provided public protection against journalistic excesses.[5] But there has been no statute specifically designed to regulate the press as an industry. Neither (with several specifically framed exceptions of recent decades, such as the obscenity and hate-literature amendments to the Criminal Code) has there been any law touching upon the general quality or content of print journalism, or seeking to give it any form of overall direction.

The greatest long-term consequence of the events of the early 1980s, especially of the draft press legislation of the summer of 1983, is that new political ground was clearly spaded. Should political circumstances justifying renewed federal interest in our daily newspapers arise again (and it seems entirely probable), federal politicians doubtless will find useful precedent in the events of the early 1980s to justify direct government intervention. The more immediate government concern when the Kent Commission was established, however, was clearly with economic patterns in the press industries, especially those that gradually led, in the latter half of the twentieth century, to a most extraordinary concentration of newspaper ownership in a very few hands. This process accelerated dramatically in the decade of the 1970s—a circumstance that prompted the royal commissioners of 1981 to open their report with the words: "This commission was born out of shock and trauma."[6] Indeed it was.

Black Wednesday

Two major dailies, the *Ottawa Journal* and the *Winnipeg Tribune*, had been permanently closed by their respective owners, Thomson Newspapers and Southam Inc., within hours of each other on August 27, 1980. On the same day, Thomson sold its 50 percent interest in Pacific Press Ltd., which publishes Vancouver's two dailies, the *Sun* and the *Province*, to the firm's only other investor, Southam Inc. Meanwhile, in Montreal, Thomson sold to Southam its one-third minority interest in the *Montreal Gazette*.

Southam thus was left as the sole owner of the only English-language daily newspaper in each of Montreal and Ottawa, and of the two dailies in Vancouver. Thomson's *Free Press* became the only daily newspaper in the lucrative Winnipeg advertising market until the unexpected emergence in November 1981 of the *Winnipeg Sun*, an independent morning tabloid, not associated with the Toronto-based Sun group.

These arrangements (excluding those involving the *Winnipeg Sun*, of course) were subsequently investigated by the federal Department of Corporate and Consumer Affairs. Though they failed in the final analysis to produce convictions, seven charges based on questions involving the merger, conspiracy, and monopoly provisions of the *Combines Investigation Act* were laid by federal authorities against each of the Southam and Thomson organizations. Four similar charges were laid against the corporate ghost of FP Publications, and some individual executive officers of these companies were also charged.[7]

In addition to the dramatic events of August 27, 1980 (since dubbed Black Wednesday in journalistic circles), other dailies also disappeared during the difficult decade of the 1970s. The *Toronto Telegram* and the *Montreal Star* were perhaps the best known of these, but important papers such as *Montréal-Matin* and Quebec City's *l'Action* also ceased publication. *The Calgary Albertan* died, but was resurrected by the Sun Group, which bought its corpse from Thomson Newspapers, and re-established it as *The Calgary Sun*. On the west coast, the *Times* and the *Colonist*, published in Victoria, were merged to form the single Thomson-owned *Times-Colonist*.[8]

By far the most significant development of the decade, however, was the purchase of FP Publications by Thomson in January 1980. In this single move, the Thomson group acquired eight daily newspapers, among them the Toronto *Globe and Mail*, the *Winnipeg Free Press*, and the *Times* and *Colonist* in Victoria. This takeover left the Thomson organization with 40 of Canada's 117 newspaper "titles."[9] Southam Inc., however, with just 14 titles, emerged from the activities of 1980 as the largest newspaper group in terms of circulation statistics. In 1980 it controlled 32.8 percent of English-language Canadian daily-newspaper circulation, while the Thomson organization controlled 25.9 percent. The actual figures have not changed greatly since 1980, but according to Senator Keith Davey (whose 1970 Special Senate Committee on the Mass Media provided Canada's first major study of its daily newspaper industry), the situation has deteriorated considerably since the failure of the parliamentary initiative of the early 1980s. In his words:

> The situation was bad enough in 1970. Twenty years later it is that much worse. In 1970 there were 116 dailies, of which 60 percent were group-owned. In 1980 there were 117 dailies, 75 percent of which were group-owned. In 1989 there were 116 dailies, 80 percent of which were group-owned.[10]

Senator Davey correctly notes in the same article that the most dramatic change in the decade of the 1980s occurred in French Canada, where fully 90 percent of daily newspapers had become group-owned by 1989, compared with just 50 percent a decade earlier. In English-language journalism, Thomson holdings remained more or less static, but those of the Southam organization were expanded by the acquisition of the *Kitchener-Waterloo Record* in 1989.[11] Southam's growth (despite a generally poor

showing at the corporate bottom line in recent years) continued in the 1990s with the acquisition of the venerable and well-respected Kingston, Ontario, *Whig-Standard* in 1990 from the independent hands of the Davies family.[12]

In fairness, one must note that new newspapers emerged during the decade of the 1970s and continued to do so. But the more significant of these in terms of circulation figures were all sensational morning tabloids. Their presence on the publishing scene is clearly a mixed blessing from the point of view of anyone concerned about the quality of daily journalism. Pierre Peladeau's *Le Journal de Montréal* and *Le Journal de Québec* began publication in the early 1970s, as did the *The Toronto Sun*, spiritual successor to the defunct *Telegram*. The *Sun* subsequently expanded to mini-chain status with its purchase of the old *Calgary Albertan* (promptly renamed *The Calgary Sun*), and its somewhat earlier launching of a new tabloid in Edmonton, predictably christened *The Edmonton Sun*. In very recent years, a *Sun* also has risen in Ottawa where it competes with Southam's well-established *Citizen*.

The Sun group (from its inception a doubtful financial venture when one considers its Toronto competition, Torstar Corp. and the Thomson-owned *Globe and Mail*) achieved instant financial security in February 1982, when Maclean Hunter Ltd., the Toronto-based magazine publisher with extensive television, radio, and nationwide cable-TV interests, became the Sun group's major shareholder. It has since been acquired by the Quebecor group.

Since then, Hollinger-Southam's *National Post* has been added to the mix, as well as three "commuter newspapers" distributed free of charge during the morning rushhour in the Toronto public transportation system. Two of these are products of existing newspapers (the *Sun* and the *Star*) but one is published by Swedish newspaper interests.

Of course, processes of corporate concentration and rationalization of assets are not unique to the newspaper industry. Indeed, they are descriptive of a generalized private-sector trend in recent decades, accelerating in very recent years towards the concentration of smaller firms (whatever their service or product of manufacture) under the corporate umbrellas of a shrinking number of large conglomerate entities. Nowhere, however, have the negative effects of industrial concentration been so singled out as objects for both public and political concern as in the newspaper business. The decision of the Thomson

Corporation in the year 2000 to divest all of its newspaper holdings save only the Toronto *Globe and Mail* [eventually folded into a new joint venture with BCE Enterprises] potentially lends itself to a further reduction in the diversity of voices and opinions since it is quickly coming to dominate the business information collection and dissemination niche of the new media of the entire Western world. And by concentrating its formidable financial resources in Web publishing ventures (while selling nearly all of its newspapers and weeklies to CanWest Global Communications), the Hollinger-Southam group is also creating a dominant position in electronic publishing and broadcasting that is potentially just as controversial as its previous commanding position in the Canadian newspaper business.

Senator Davey's Point of View

Corporate concentration in the news business became clearly focussed as problematic in the minds of citizens and politicians with the publication in 1970 of the exhaustive report of the Davey Committee. In the language of the report:

> What matters is the fact that control of the media is passing into fewer and fewer hands, and that the experts agree that this trend is likely to continue and perhaps accelerate. The logical … outcome of this process is that one man or corporation could own every media outlet in the country except the CBC. The committee believes that at some point before this hypothetical extreme is reached, a line must be drawn.[13]

By 1981, in response to criticisms levelled at the Kent Report, Senator Davey was using more urgent language:

> The situation that confronted the Kent commission was alarmingly simple. Press concentration in Canada has become almost total. Fewer and fewer voices are speaking to more and more Canadians. Ten years ago the Senate committee reported that 77 percent of Canadian daily newspaper circulation was involved in some form of common ownership. Three big chains controlled 44.7 percent of readership. Comparable figures today are 88 percent with just two big chains controlling 47.2 percent of all English-language readers.[14]

As we have seen, Senator Davey's concerns continue to be pertinent to the present day.

Further concentration would have been prevented under the provisions of the draft legislation of the early 1980s, the objective being to limit newspaper holdings of any owner or ownership group to 20 percent of the country's total average daily circulation.[15] In his policy announcement of May 1982, then Minister of State Fleming spoke of a need to encourage the Canadian Radio-television and Telecommunications Commission (CRTC) to use its regulatory powers under the *Broadcasting Act* to break up local mixed-media monopolies and near monopolies.[16]

It appears that these and other containment measures continue to be as strongly advocated as ever by Senator Davey, by his spiritual successor Professor Tom Kent, and by most others who fear the consequences of daily journalism's continuing corporate concentration.

Southam, Torstar, and Conrad Black

Southam and Torstar figured prominently in what many observers initially assumed might prove to be the great further rationalization of the 1990s. Fearing possible unfriendly takeover bids from a number of sources, Southam in 1985 entered a defensive agreement with the mighty Torstar Corporation in which Torstar (owners of *The Toronto Star* among its other assets) *acquired 25 percent of So*utham's voting shares, while Southam acquired 30 percent of Torstar's non-voting shares. Describing Southam Inc. as a "flabby, rambling, underproductive old soldier of a corporation," *The Globe and Mail's* William Thorsell at the time saw Torstar's role in this odd-couple relationship as that of "boyfriend and bodyguard." The deal was based on a Torstar pledge that it would not turn corporate predator, but would act as Southam's protector for a 10-year period.

Interestingly, the deal between the two media giants, which clearly had the effect of moving Canada's newspapers in the direction of whole new possibilities for ownership concentration, was not at all unwelcome among working journalists. Nor was it by any means rejected out of hand by the country's media watchers and critics.

As Thorsell noted (with obvious full appreciation of the inherent irony), media bellwethers and critics of the early 1980s almost unanimously tended to identify the large, established media corporations—Thomson in particular, but also Southam, and such regional interests as those of the Irving family in New Brunswick, or the Blackburns in London, Ontario—as the villains in the piece. By 1989, however, such organizations were being seen more as old friends than ancient enemies and certainly to be preferred to unknown outsiders.

Rightly noting that the Torstar-Southam deal of 1985 "should have appalled Canada's intelligentsia in principle," and wondering that it was in fact greeted with "indifference, silence or approval," Thorsell suggested that latter-day thinking among the reluctant critics of corporate "giantism" in the media industries might have been running something like this: Better to see Anglophone Canada dominated by even fewer big newspaper companies than to see Southam gobbled up by some parvenu who might have the "wrong" values or do the "wrong" kinds of things. In 1985, the most interested observers feared that the civilized press would fall into the hands of manipulators or boors.[17]

It was precisely the dreaded parvenus who did emerge, however, when federal regulators obliged Southam and Torstar to terminate their standstill agreement five years ahead of schedule in September 1990, and everything was thrown back into the fire. With recession-bound Torstar generating less-than-satisfactory corporate balance sheets, there was little inclination in that quarter to turn corporate predator.

Instead, new investment funds came from Paul Desmarais and his Quebec-based Power Corporation, which by March 1993 had acquired just under 19 percent of Southam's common stock.[18] Even more interesting, however, was the arrival on the Southam scene of Conrad Black and Hollinger Corporation. By November 1992, the Black interests had acquired some 23 percent of Southam's common stock, most of which had been held by Torstar during the years of the Southam-Torstar agreement.[19] Between them, the Black and Desmarais groups also acquired an influential six-seat block on the Southam board. The Desmarais interests have had significant newspaper investments in Quebec for many years (notably La Presse of Montreal), but their venture via Southam into English-Canadian newspaper ownership is a new departure.

Conrad Black's Hollinger group had owned a number of small newspapers, mostly in Western Canada, for many years, but had never been perceived as a central player. In the following years, Black acquired a number of major British publications (among them the Daily Telegraph and the conservative opinion-and-commentary magazine The Spectator, and The Jerusalem Post), along with newspaper properties in Australia and elsewhere. His investment in Southam now clearly casts him not only as a major international newspaper investor, but one with dominant Canadian holdings. In a word, Conrad Black emerged as the dreaded parvenu, and the Canadian newspaper business suddenly became much more interesting.

The problem of ownership concentration remains, and if anything it has become more intense in recent years. There are fewer and fewer truly independent newspapers in the country (as Southam's acquisition of the Kitchener-Waterloo Record and The Whig-Standard of Kingston, among others, demonstrates).

Thus it's not that the problem of ownership concentration has left us, or even become muted in any way. It has simply become a lot more complicated. The shift of investment away from print newspapers in the direction of electronic publishing by the major corporate interests (Thomson, Southam-Hollinger, and Quebecor) merely further complicates the corporate entanglements.

The Rest of the Story

While fascinating in themselves, economic patterns and ownership machinations tell only part of the Canadian newspaper story of the late decades of the twentieth century and the beginnings of the new millennium. The intent that there should be federal involvement in matters related to the quality and social purposes of print journalism, as well as in the economics of the press industries, has long been a part of the equation and was evident, for instance, in the provisions of the 1983 draft legislation relating to the establishment of a Canadian Advisory Council on Newspapers. This agency was intended to

> have the objectives of receiving complaints about press reporting in daily newspapers that are not members of effective press councils, promoting public debate, complementing the press councils and ombudsmen that already exist locally, and reporting biennially (to Parliament) on the state of the industry on the basis of its own research and analysis.[20]

Whether Minister of State Fleming and his cabinet colleagues ever intended that a council should emerge in this form is debatable. As events unfolded, a great many newspaper publishers (who clearly saw the scheme as the serious intent of the government of the day) took advantage of a "loophole" offered by Fleming, and moved during the fall of 1982 and the early months of 1983 not only to join the country's existing voluntary councils, but to create new ones in regions of the country where such councils had not previously existed.[21] In a statement in January 1983, Fleming said the national council concept would be reviewed if momentum was maintained in the growth and development of voluntary councils. Though some form of federal involvement was assured by the minister,[22] its precise nature was never revealed. The Newspaper Bill died on the Order Paper when Parliament was prorogued in December 1983; the minister himself was dropped from the cabinet in a year-end cabinet shuffle.

Tom Kent, who chaired the original royal commission, clearly was bitter at this turn of events. "The retreat from the commission's recommendations to Fleming's (considerably weaker) proposals was understandable," Mr. Kent said in a newspaper interview at the time. "But the retreat to doing nothing at all I consider very weak indeed."[23]

The Kent proposals in fact were significantly different from the provisions of the draft legislation, primarily in their greater severity. There was little difference in matters of principle. Instead of the 20 percent ownership limitation contained in the legislation, for instance, Kent and his colleagues of the royal commission (retired *Toronto Star* ombudsman Borden Spears and Laurent Picard, a former president of the CBC) sought to place the general ownership limitation at 5 percent of total national daily circulation.[24] "Grandparent" loopholes were to have been granted to the large existing ownership groups, but none of these would have been left entirely untouched. The Thomson organization, for instance, would have been required to divest itself either of the Toronto *Globe and Mail*, or of all the other newspapers in its possession. It is ironic indeed that Thomson chose to do the latter voluntarily in the year 2000, selling its considerable travel agency assets as well, in order to pursue its attempt to dominate electronic information publishing worldwide.

The rationale behind the Kent proposal for Thomson divestiture was that the *Globe and Mail*, which prints simultaneously via satellite in six Canadian cities[25] and has significant same-day circulation in most major population centres in the country, would be in a form of regional or local competition with many other Thomson newspapers.[26] Such same-owner competition was deemed to be undesirable.

The royal commission also recommended the establishment, under federal statute, of a so-called press rights panel. This proposed body (much more powerful than the Canadian Advisory Council on Newspapers described in the legislation) was envisaged as having authority to review all proposals for newspaper-ownership changes, including proposals for newspaper closures, and generally to monitor journalistic performance.[27]

Why the Newspapers?

While such details relating to the ownership-concentration phenomenon and what should be done about it are important and interesting in their own right, one should not lose sight of the fact that

there is an important prior consideration: Why should newspapers be singled out for special legislative consideration? After all, they constitute collectively but one industry in a general climate in the Western world where the overwhelming trend is towards Brobdingnagian economic entities. The authors of the Kent Report seemed, at first glance, to dismiss the issue: "Whether the country should change its general policy towards economic concentration is not a subject of this report."[28] Like their counterparts in the Davey group of 1970, however, the royal commissioners of the 1980s identified three phenomena that at least separate newspapers from other forms of economic endeavour, and that are of continuing interest in the 1990s.

First, newspapers deal in public information, not in shoes or butter. It is peculiar to the nature of information that it requires many independent approaches to processing and production if the many and varied requirements of the democratic marketplace are to be met. The authors of the Kent Report note in several places that the efficiencies of corporate systems and economic rationalizations, both within and among the chains, tend to reduce the critically important element of journalistic diversity. When journalistic diversity disappears, the flow of ideas to the marketplace becomes less rich and varied. "In writing style, presentation and display, newspapers become more alike, less individual, less distinctive."[29]

Second, as newspapers become larger in themselves (and parts of still larger chains and conglomerate enterprises), the people who run them are less and less likely to be professional journalists. The needs of the journalistic process therefore lose their significance in the corporate hierarchy of values. In the words of the Kent Report: "From a narrow business viewpoint, what is spent on editorial content becomes simply a cost."[30]

It is in the context of these first two concerns that one best sees the rationale behind William Thorsell's frustration with those muted latter-day critics of the system, who seem more exercised about the possibility of newspapers falling into the corporate hands of organizations other than the traditional major chains, or even from outside the news business altogether, than with further expansions of the existing media giants. Perhaps anticipating the arrival on the scene of new major investors, such as Conrad Black, Thorsell offered this rather prophetic observation in 1989, when the possibility of new entrepreneurial players entering the game still seemed rather remote:

"Common ownership, not conglomerate ownership, bedevils Canadian journalism.... We should welcome outside bidders, accepting that a new owner likely will have other major economic interests."[31]

Third, too much potential power is put in too few hands, and it is power without accountability. "Whether the power is in practice well used or ill used or not used at all is beside the point. The point is that how it is used is subject to the indifference or to the whim of a few individuals, whether hidden or not in faceless corporations."[32]

In the final analysis, this question of power and its applications may be the most important element. Lists of items of special concern can be generated to support a case for the containment of most any industry in a structure of special legislation, but the journalists of the newspaper industry, and the already well-regulated broadcast industry, are closer to politicians and bureaucrats, and touch their lives more directly than workers in any other field of endeavour, with the possible exception of the civil service itself.

Power and Its "Consequences"

At the very least, politicians cannot help but be sensitive to the workplace concerns of the journalists with whom they share daily existence in a nearly symbiotic relationship. There is, however, an important and healthy tension in the relationship that the American columnist George Will described as succinctly as any observer when he wrote about the exercise of democratic power as being absolutely the prerogative of the politicians of the moment, with "consequences" being the prerogative of their attending journalists.[33] In 1852, however, when the British Foreign Minister Lord Derby sought to inform the press of its "sacred duty to maintain that tone of moderation and respect even in frankly expressing their opinions" on issues of the day, the *London Times* offered what remains the classic description of the tension phenomenon:

> The press lives by disclosures, whatever passes into its hands becomes part of the knowledge of our times, it is daily and forever appealing to the enlightened force of public opinion.... [T]he statesman's duty is precisely the reverse. He cautiously guards from the public eye the information by which his actions and opinions are regulated.[34]

The Canadian economist and communication theorist Harold Innis postulated the existence of a much more profound dynamic in the relationship between all social institutions (including those of government) and the mass media, of which the symbiotic tension between journalist and politician would be only a symptom. It was Innis's thesis, briefly stated, that a cultural "bias" that both accommodates and reflects the technical possibilities and limitations of its communication system will develop in any given society. Change in the communication system, therefore, will have nothing less than a revolutionary effect on social institutions, including governmental ones. In Innis's own cautious language:

> We can perhaps assume that the use of a medium of communication over a long period will to some extent determine the character of knowledge to be communicated and suggest that its pervasive influence will eventually create a civilization in which life and flexibility will become exceedingly difficult to maintain and that the advantages of a new medium will become such as to lead to the emergence of a new civilization.[35]

Enormous technical changes took place in the newspaper business in the twentieth century. Early mechanical developments (revolutionary in their own time) gave way gradually to automated production and information-handling systems between about 1950 and 1970, and the effectiveness of these systems has since been enhanced enormously by computerization. When one surrounds the changing newspaper business with the reality of the rapid evolution of the electronic media in this century, from the crude beginnings of radio broadcasting in the early decades to the contemporary developments in, for instance, computer-governed fibre-optic transmission systems, it is not difficult to see an Innis-style revolution in the making. Certainly, it is not unreasonable to assume that democratic politicians, with their natural inclination to favour the established order of things, will seek in such circumstances to apply social-control mechanisms to all the mass media, including the press. In Canada, special conditions of extraordinary foreign cultural influence provide the federal government with added incentive.

In terms of practical expression of all this, we have in Canada the clear example of the *Broadcasting Act*, and the policies and regulatory mechanisms that exist therein. The act spawned the Crown-owned CBC, with generous federal funding, as a dominant national system for both radio and television broadcasting; private-sector broadcasting is restricted to a secondary role under an elaborate licencing and regulatory structure. The combined public and private system, under the provisions of the act, is monitored and periodically adjusted by the federal regulatory body, the CRTC.

It is intended that the domestic broadcasting system should compete effectively with the enormous outpouring of American electronic culture across the international border and into the homes and minds of Canadians. Among other provisions related to content, the *Broadcasting Act* contains a general "mandate," which requires that all broadcasting outlets be effectively owned and controlled by Canadians, and that the broadcasting system should "serve to safeguard, enrich and strengthen the cultural, political, social and economic fabric of Canada." Broadcasters also are required to use Canadian talent and resources wherever possible in their programming.

In addition to these general provisos, the CBC (described in the Act as the national public broadcaster) has further mandate obligations to provide all Canadians with a wide range of programming that informs, enlightens, and entertains, and to do so in both official languages. Most importantly the CBC must "contribute to shared national consciousness and identity," and reflect the "multiracial and multicultural nature of Canada."[36]

Discussion of the *Broadcasting Act* and its provisions is not a purpose here, of course. It is sufficient to say that the concept of co-opting the broadcasting media, at least in part, to purposes of national policy has been a central aspect of public philosophy related to broadcasting since it was first enunciated by the Royal Commission on Broadcasting in 1929. What is important for present purposes is that similar policy postures, the reaction to similar concerns of national identity and cultural integrity, also have been evolving with regard to print media in Canada for many years.

For reasons primarily pertaining to limitations on political opportunity imposed by the ancient laissez-faire tradition that surrounds printed journalism in the public imagination, federal policy towards newspapers necessarily has evolved much more slowly. Indeed, the evolutionary process will have to expand well beyond the legislative departure of the early 1980s before anything comparable to the mature structure of the broadcasting policy will exist for the print media.

A Single Alien Source

The tradition of federal concern is a long one, however. Indeed, the beginnings of a clear pattern of events leading to the Kent Report, and to the press legislation which it inspired, are evident at least as early as 1951, with the publication that year of the report of the Royal Commission on National Development in the Arts Letters and Sciences in Canada. The commission actually made only passing reference to the print media as "the chief source of knowledge to Canadians of their country,"[37] noting in a context of general concern that "a vast and disproportionate amount of (media) material coming from a single alien (American) source may stifle rather than stimulate our own creative effort."[38]

This was a statement of the obvious, but given the immense prestige and influence of this royal commission, it was enough to lend important credence to later public arguments in support of the principle of a government obligation to concern itself with the quality and social purposes of newspapers and magazines. A number of royal commissions, task forces, and other public inquiries have followed, and each has added its brush strokes to the canvas put in place by Vincent Massey.

It may be useful to note here in passing that royal commissions and other forms of federal-investigatory devices, with their personnel appointed from outside the civil service, have played an extremely important role in the long-term formulation of social policy in Canada. As J.E. Hodgetts has written,

> royal commissions appear to remain the chief source of "outside" inspiration for longer term program development.... [T]hey become temporary research institutes, assembling the best available outside (non-governmental) talent to carry on sophisticated analyses of complex social and economic problems.[39]

The Royal Commission on Publications, which reported in 1961, was responsible for the first significant post-Massey developments in press policy evolution. Chaired by the well-regarded Ottawa newspaper editor Senator Grattan O'Leary, it also provided a classic demonstration of both the long-term policy influence that a good royal commission report can have, and of government use of the royal commission device to test the waters of public opinion.

Actually more concerned with periodicals than with daily newspapers, the O'Leary Commission proposed tax-law changes to make it impossible for Canadian advertisers to write off, for income tax purposes, the cost of advertising in periodicals owned by foreigners and published in Canada.[40] These proposals received mixed reactions from Canadians, but were roundly condemned in official Washington, and by the powerful publishers of such American publications as *Time* and *Reader's Digest*, both of which at the time produced branch-plant Canadian editions with large circulations. Parliament passed a form of window-dressing legislation that left *Time*, *Reader's Digest*, and a long list of other U.S.-based publications untouched for the time being in their lucrative Canadian operations.

The measures eventually were given solid effect, however, by legislation in 1976, which forced, among other changes to tax law affecting Canadian publishing, the dramatic closing of Time Inc.'s Canadian edition. (*Reader's Digest* was able to alter both its corporate structure and its editorial policies sufficiently to meet the new Canadian requirements.)

The O'Leary Commission clearly established the political principle of a federal right to involvement in regulating the fiscal affairs of the print media. It is important to note, however, that this commission also gave important, if general, encouragement to the principle of government involvement in questions of journalistic quality and cultural influence. Stating that "there must be few left to deny the right–indeed the duty of government to act ... if faced with demonstrable community necessity," the report offers this statement of principle: "Only a truly Canadian printing press, one with the 'feel' of Canada and directly responsible to Canada, can give us the critical analysis, informed discourse and dialogue which are indispensable in a sovereign society."[41]

While the several royal commissions from Massey to Kent, along with the Senate study of 1970, provide the most important landmarks in the evolution of Canada's federal press policy, a number of lesser task forces and inquiries also have made their contributions and deserve comment here. In 1977, the CRTC was required by the cabinet to investigate allegations of pro-separatist bias in the news and public-affairs programming of the CBC's Francophone arm, Radio-Canada. It is noteworthy, as a comment on evolving government attitudes, that the resultant Committee of Inquiry into the National Broadcasting Service was given a very broad mandate under which it examined many aspects of media performance on a national scale, including aspects of print-media performance. Among other things, the committee suggested (this with reference to an analysis it commissioned of the content of the Canadian Press wire service)[42] that Canadians receive an unbalanced view of their country in the print as well as the broadcast media, with too much concentration on news emerging from the major eastern power centres of Toronto, Montreal, and Ottawa.[43]

Reference also should be made to the 1977 Ontario Royal Commission on Violence in the Communications Industry. This provincial study (which cannot be seen as having direct relationship to the various federal studies primarily under examination here) is interesting in the present context because it was chaired by the late Judy LaMarsh, Secretary of State in the federal Liberal governments of Lester Pearson during the 1960s. The present *Broadcasting Act* was developed under her ministry. The tentative observation might be made that the powerful press legislation proposed by Miss LaMarsh in her 1977 Ontario report, complete with an elaborate structure of press councils and various devices for the regulation of print journalism and the improvement of its quality, are similar to much that is contained in the Kent recommendations.[44]

Information Canada

Of more direct interest in the present discussion is the Task Force on Government Information, which was created by federal order-in-council to examine and report upon conditions in the federal government's various public information services. Reporting in 1969, this group powerfully and directly criticized the nation's media, especially the press, for failing to report the nation's business adequately to the people of Canada. Using critical language stronger than that employed by any previous federal study group, the authors of this report stated:

> A Greshem's Law of mass media starts to operate with bad communication driving out good.... Complex issues and events lose out to simplification. Harmony is eroded by emphasis on discord. Faith is undermined by day-to-day emphasis on the attention-getting substance of crisis, lust, incompetence and sloth.[45]

The major recommendation of the task force was that a federal information agency be established, and the cabinet acted almost immediately with the creation in 1970 of Information Canada. Its life was short: Information Canada was dismantled in 1975 as part of a government austerity drive that year. In terms of its contribution to an evolving national press policy, Information Canada might best be regarded as an interesting, but abortive, experiment. It was, in effect, an attempt to find avenues around the news media, rather than to seek to co-opt them more directly to national policy purposes. As Joe Clark, then the backbench member for Rocky Mountain, put it in a House of Commons debate in 1973, "it is, in short, an attempt to get around the normal filters of democracy; an attempt not to present information, but to manage it."[46]

Vastly more important than either the Information Canada experiment, or the task force that gave it birth, was the exhaustive Senate examination of the mass media chaired by Senator Keith Davey (which as noted earlier) reported in 1970, at about the time the Information Canada experiment was being launched. There is no need to add significantly here to our earlier discussion of the Davey Report, other perhaps than to emphasize that this investigation must be regarded as the single most important step taken in the evolution of a comprehensive federal press policy prior to the work of the Royal Commission on Newspapers. The Davey study not only provided the first detailed public examination of media economics and ownership relationships, but explored deeply such hitherto untrodden territory (at least in terms of government-sponsored research) as the values and traditions of journalism, news-flow and news-definition patterns, journalism education and standards of professionalism, and working conditions in the industry. Public attitudes towards newspapers were explored, as were the dynamics of intermedia relationships, and a number of questions pertaining to the cultural impact of the mass press.

While the actual recommendations of the Senate committee were mild and often generalized, proposals were made for the establishment of a federal Press Ownership Review Board and a federal Publications Development Loan Fund. The committee also urged the industry itself to establish a voluntary national press council.[47] None of these suggestions were ever adopted in the legislative sense, but the Canadian voluntary press council movement, already discussed, clearly had its beginning with Senator Davey's recommendations. Most of the issues raised by the Davey Committee were revived by the Royal Commission on Newspapers and continue to feed public discussion on the subject of the country's daily newspapers.

A Right of the People

It is important to emphasize by way of summation a point that has been made several times in this discussion: the press legislation of the 1980s was the end product (in its time and place) of an evolutionary process that began much earlier in Canadian national development. The legislative proposals of the early 1980s would have been politically unthinkable prior to the time of the Massey Commission, and the question remains as to whether they were in reality

any more appropriate at the time of the Kent Commission, or for that matter during the 1990s, than they would have been perceived as being at mid-century. The fundamental Kent argument, so strongly reflected in the abortive legislation, was that economic trends in the newspaper industry had created a threat to press freedom (and by implication to national development) at least as great as any potential threat from an overly ambitious government. As the authors of the Kent Report have expressed the problem,

> freedom of the press is not a property right of owners. It is a right of the people. It is part of their right to free expression, inseparable from their right to inform themselves. The commission believes that the key problem ... is the limitation of these rights by undue concentration of ownership and control of the Canadian daily newspaper industry.[48]

The point is well taken. But it does not consider the inextricably related point on the obverse side of the coin: that an invitation to government to rectify these presumed economic ills is also an invitation to government to concern itself with the quality and social purposes of journalism. That government has quite willingly accepted this second "invitation" is amply demonstrated in many of the provisions of the draft legislation. Both the Kent Report and the draft legislation received public criticism from a number of quarters on this score, but the case was perhaps best put by Lord McGregor of Durris, who chaired a British royal commission on the press between 1974 and 1977. On the Kent Commission's press rights panel concept (and by implication on the advisory council of the legislation), Lord McGregor said:

> It is here that we meet the fundamental difference between the Canadian and the British reports. The British commission was urged by several groups to recommend the creation, by or through governmental intervention, of new agencies to control the press. It rejected all such proposals on the ground that government intervention would undermine the independence of the press and soon involve persons who owed their position to government acting in practice as censors.[49]

It is more than a little ironic that just a decade later, Lord McGregor, a man with a long record as one of the most knowledgeable and sympathetic of press critics in all of Britain, found himself serving as chair of his country's new Press Complaints Commission, and evidently much less worried about the consequences of government intervention. In 1991 he offered this observation about the looming possibility of the commission shifting from voluntary to government-imposed status: "It would require only one word from us (the members of the commission) that the press was not giving its full commitment to enforcing its (voluntary) code ... and statutory intervention would be on the cards."[50]

One must presume that political interest in the printed media in Canada (admittedly more or less dormant since the Fleming legislation died on the Order Paper in December 1983) could be revived at any time. What is perhaps most important to keep in mind is that nothing really has changed. Processes leading to further economic concentration, though somewhat more complicated, have not changed in their fundamentals; the dynamics of the media-political relationship increasingly overwhelm traditional ways of doing things within our political organizations; and the political temptation to seek to co-opt the media (including the printed media as the British experience clearly suggests) remain very much with us.

Notes

1. "World Press Freedom Review," *IPI Report: Monthly Bulletin of the International Press Institute*, December 1991.

2. *Royal Commission on Newspapers, Report* (Ottawa: Supply and Services, 1981).

3. Jim Fleming, "Government Proposals on Freedom of the Press in Relation to the Canadian Daily Newspaper Industry," an address to the Graduate School of Journalism, University of Western Ontario, London, Ont., 25 May 1982.

4. James Rusk, "Press bill proposes new limits on chains," *The Globe and Mail* (7 July 1983).

5. Robert Martin and Stuart Adam, *A Sourcebook of Canadian Media Law* (Ottawa: Carleton University Press, 1991). The interested reader will find a comprehensive discussion of the law as it applies to Canadian media in this thorough summary and introduction to the subject.

6. *Royal Commission on Newspapers, Report*, p.Xi.

7. "Two newspaper chains ordered to stand trial on combined charges," *The Globe and Mail* (6 May 1982).

8. *Royal Commission on Newspapers*, Report, pp.4–9.

9. *Royal Commission on Newspapers, Report*, p.90. The royal commissioners noted a number of local situations in Canada where two seemingly separate newspapers are published under common ownership, printed on the same presses, and even produced by common news, advertising, and business staffs. Examples include the Irving-owned *Times* and *Transcript* in Moncton, and the independently owned *Chronicle-Herald* and *Mail-Star* in Halifax. In order to produce realistic statistics, the Royal Commission selected the rather peculiar word "title," to describe each newspaper-production situation. Thus *The London Free Press* is designated a single "title," but so are the fictionally multiplied papers in Moncton, Halifax, and elsewhere.

10. Senator Keith Davey, "Getting the media we deserve?" *Content* (July/August 1990).

11. "Southam buys the KW Record," *The Globe and Mail* (25 November 1989). This was not entirely unexpected, as Southam had been a significant minority shareholder in the Record property for many years.

12. Charlene Yarrow, "Hail and Farewell to the Whig," *Ryerson Journalism Review* (Summer 1993).

13. *Special Senate Committee on the Mass Media, Report*, Vol. 1, The Uncertain Mirror (Ottawa: Queen's Printer, 1970), p.6.

14. Keith Davey, "Newspapers jolted into hysteria," *The Globe and Mail* (16 September 1981).

15. The two largest chains, Southam Inc. and Thomson Newspapers, then as now exceeded the 20 percent limitation. However, a "grandparent" clause in the legislation would have left these chains intact, at least for the time being.

16. In London, Ontario, for instance, London Free Press Holdings Ltd. could have been a candidate for enforced divestiture. At that time, the company owned the city's only daily newspaper, its television station (since sold to Baton Broadcasting interests in Toronto), and two of its radio stations. In New Brunswick, the late K.C. Irving, whose holdings included all the English-language daily newspapers and extensive broadcast interests in that province, also could have been affected. (Members of his family continue to hold the media properties once owned by Mr. Irving.)

17. William Thorsell, "The Paper Chase," *Report on Business Magazine* (March 1989).

18. Harvey Enchin, "Power adds to stake in Southam," *The Globe and Mail* (20 March 1993).

19. "Hollinger gets three seats on Southam board," *The Globe and Mail* (22 January 1993).

20. Fleming, "Government Proposals," p.15.

21. The Ontario Press Council and the Alberta Press Council were both established in 1972. The Quebec Press Council, the only council that operates as a tribunal rather than relying on the membership principle, was established a year later in 1973. The QPC hears complaints relating to all media, not just newspapers. Growth in the council movement in the wake of Minister of State Fleming's announcement of his legislative proposals in May 1982, was phenomenal. The Ontario council, which could claim just 10 of the province's dailies as members in September 1982, saw its membership climb to 31 of the province's 42 dailies by January 1983. All 43 of the province's dailies (including such newly established ones as the *Ottawa Sun* and the *Burlington Spectator*, which joined in 1989 and 1987, respectively) were listed as members in the Council's Annual Report for 1989. During the decade of the 1980s, all eight of Alberta's dailies became members of that province's press council. New councils were organized in the Atlantic provinces, in British Columbia, and in Manitoba and Saskatchewan.

22. Jim Fleming, interview on "The Nation's Business," *CBC Television*, 16 January 1983. Further information was obtained in conversations with officials in the minister's office.

23. "Kent feels Ottawa bowed to publishers' pressure," *London Free Press* (7 April 1984).

24. *Royal Commission on Newspapers, Report*, p.239.

25. "New plant allows earlier delivery," *The Globe and Mail* (3 September 1990). In addition to its main plant in Toronto, the Globe now has five remote plants served by satellite transmission. This most recent satellite printing plant is located at Boucherville, near Montreal.

26. *Royal Commission on Newspapers, Report*, p.243.

27. It was proposed that the council should, in effect, monitor the quality of Canadian daily journalism, and especially that it should oversee the relationship between all chain or conglomerate owners and the editors employed by them. Under these proposals, editors were to function under contracts "detailed by statute" with their publisher-employers. These contracts would have required the creation of local advisory committees to hear public complaints and to which editors would have been required to make annual reports. It was proposed that these reports also should go to the national Press Rights Panel, which in turn would have had the statutory obligation to make periodic recommendations to Parliament touching individual newspapers, specific ownership groups, or the industry in its entirety.

28. *Royal Commission on Newspapers, Report*, p.219.

29. Ibid., p.166

30. Ibid., p.89.

31. Thorsell, "The Paper Chase."

32. *Royal Commission on Newspapers, Report*, p.220.

33. George F. Will, "The Problem Isn't Bias," *Nieman Reports* (Autumn 1978).

34. Harold Herd, *The March of Journalism* (Westport, Conn.: Greenwood Press, 1976), p.142.

35. Harold A. Innis, *The Bias of Communication* (Toronto: University of Toronto Press, 1973), p.34.

36. These mandate provisions are described in the *Broadcasting Act*, 1991, Section 3. The place of the legislated mandate is further described in an internal CBC policy document *Journalistic Policy* (Ottawa: Canadian Broadcasting Corporation, 1988). This document recognizes the mandate provisions as the "legislated objectives by which the corporation is governed."

37. *Royal Commission on National Development in the Arts, Letters and Sciences, Report* (Ottawa: King's Printer, 1951), p.61.

38. *Royal Commission on National Development, Report*, p.18.

39. J.E. Hodgetts, *The Canadian Public Service: A Physiology of Government* (Toronto: University of Toronto Press, 1976), p.217.

40. *Royal Commission on Publications, Report* (Ottawa: Queen's Printer, 1961).

41. Ibid., p.2.

42. Andrew M. Osler, *An Analysis of Some Aspects of French and English Content in the Canadian Press Wire Service, May 2–6, 1977*, a report of commissioned research to the Committee of Inquiry into the National Broadcasting Service (Canadian Radio-television and Telecommunications Commission, 1977), CRTC Library, Ottawa.

43. *CRTC Committee of Inquiry into the National Broadcasting Service, Report* (Ottawa: CRTC, 1977), pp.20–21.

44. *Royal Commission on Violence in the Communications Industry, Report*, Vol. 1 (Toronto: Queen's Printer for Ontario, 1977).

45. *Task Force on Government Information, Report*, Vol. 1 (Ottawa: Queen's Printer, 1969), p.10.

46. Hansard, July 23, 1973.

47. *Special Senate Committee on the Mass Media, Report*, Vol. 1 (Ottawa: Queen's Printer, 1970), pp.255–60.

48. *Royal Commission on Newspapers, Report*, p.1.

49. Lord McGregor of Durris, "Commissions differ on state of newspaper industry," *London Free Press* (23 October 1981).

50. Brian MacArthur, "Deadline looms as editors press on with reform," *The Sunday Times* (6 January 1991).

17

Canadian Media Ownership and Control in an Age of the Internet and Global Megamedia Empires

John A. Hannigan

At the stroke of midnight on April 30, 2000, Time Warner Cable TV subscribers in New York, Los Angeles, and Houston who were watching the ABC channel witnessed something very strange. After becoming fuzzy, and then snowing over, their television screens turned a flat blue, followed by the appearance of a written message that began, "Disney has taken ABC away from you." In fact, Time Warner itself had pulled the plug on ABC as a tactical move in a commercial dispute with the Disney-owned network over the terms of renewal of a "retransmission consent agreement." The agreement defined the terms under which the ABC programs would be carried in the future on Time Warner Cable.[1] While Time Warner and Disney have since forged a truce and Disney is back on the cable system, "Black Monday," as it is now being called in the broadcasting industry, can be interpreted as a cautionary tale on several accounts.

Looking to the immediate future, it raises some disturbing questions about the willingness of telecommunications carriers to ensure the free flow of content through the channels that they own. This is especially salient in light of the escalating trend towards the convergence of television and computers. If, as is now widely predicted, the Internet is transformed into a mass medium, then those companies who control access through telephone lines, or, more likely, through broadband ("big pipe") cable linkups, will instantly become powerful gatekeepers possessing the capability and incentive to shape their customers' experience of the cable and the Web. Indeed, the Black Monday crisis was ultimately all about Disney's growing fear that once the proposed merger of Time Warner and America On Line (AOL) is consummated, ABC programming would not be treated equally, especially once AOL got broadband distribution over Time Warner's cable wires.[2]

More broadly, the experience of Black Monday spotlights a trend that has alarmed many contemporary media analysts–the mushrooming global control of information, ideas, entertainment, and popular culture by a handful of mammoth private organizations such as Time Warner/AOL and Disney. Whereas in the past, media ownership and control have been concentrated in the hands of local, regional, and national elites, today it is feared that the world's mass media are increasingly dominated by a dozen corporate giants, nicknamed by American investigative journalist Ben Bagdikian as "the Lords of the Global Village."[3]

The globalization of the world media has raised a number of concerns about the homogenization, access to, and suppression of information and ideas. Some observers have seen the rise of global megamedia empires as the final step in the historical shift towards a mass society presided over by a cynical, manipulative, and conservative power elite–an oligopoly, members of which have their own agenda and who resist economic changes that do not support their own financial interest. In this view, new media technologies, which hold the potential to advance widespread public participation and equality in social life through their interactive capacity, are instead being employed to create a system of global consumer markets.[4] As such, mass communication has become a mediator between mass production and mass consumption. Not only can this mediating function be understood in terms of new forms of labour and social control (offshore information processing, computerized job performance monitoring), but it is also said to represent a means of facilitating the circulation of "cultural capital" through both economic and cultural circuits.[5] Each of these roles (redistribution of work, new forms of social control, new organization of consumption), appear to restrict rather than open up equality in social relations.

This chapter focusses on the issues of Canadian media ownership and control in an age of the Internet and global megamedia empires. In presenting this material, I first describe the changes in markets, competition, ownership, and media technologies that have occurred worldwide over the last 30 years and then analyze the extent to which Canada has been affected by these changes. I start with an overview of the changing international media marketplace, highlighting in particular the upsurge in transnational information flows, which has been precipitated by the deregulation of the communications industry in the U.S. and Western Europe.

Globalization of the World Media

The Changing International Media Marketplace: Deregulation and Competition

For most of the last three decades, media sociologists have expressed alarm at the global penetration of Anglo-American media content. In its strongest form, this concern took the shape of the "media imperialism thesis," which stated that the expansion of American TV worldwide was part of an orchestrated attempt by the U.S. military-industrial complex to prevent popular unrest in Third World countries by employing homogenized, American, commercial culture as a prophylactic.[6] Others were less inclined to suspect a concerted conspiracy, but, nonetheless, decried the rising internationalization of the consumption, leisure patterns, youth culture, education, language, and consciousness of overseas nations.[7]

Since the mid-1970s, the flow of information across national borders has dramatically intensified. One of the major reasons for this has been the growth of new multimedia giants as a result of the deregulation of telecommunications, notably in the United States and Europe.

From 1975 onward, a "free marketplace" approach to new communications technologies began to assume dominance in U.S. regulatory circles, replacing an earlier commitment to the principle of defending the "public interest."[8] While this partly echoed the influence of "Reaganomics," it was also a reflection of the so-called "electronics revolution" which originated in the 1970s and 1980s and has continued up through the present era. The development of microwave, coaxial cable, (communications) satellites, fibre optics, and, above all, the merging of computer and telecommunications

technologies made competition "both possible and inevitable."[9] While there have been a number of important milestones here, two developments have been of particular note.

In 1982, the Bell Telephone system in the U.S. was broken up when its parent company, AT&T, settled a long-running anti-trust suit by agreeing to divest itself of its regional companies, which represented about two-thirds of its employees and three-quarters of its assets. The decision did not apply directly to Canada, although Bell Canada did reorganize in the early 1980s by creating Bell Canada Enterprises (BCE), a move which enabled the company to enter a new range of markets. While the federal court in the U.S. did restrict AT&T in some ways, notably by imposing a seven-year moratorium on its entry into the electronic Yellow Pages business, it essentially left AT&T free for the first time to compete in the generation of telecommunications services as well as their provision. AT&T thus became a major player in the growing computer-related and information markets populated by other corporate giants such as IBM (through its investment in MCI) and General Motors.[10]

Fourteen years later, another major milestone was marked by the passing of the U.S. *Telecommunications Act* of 1996. Designed to replace a regulated marketplace with a more highly competitive one, which would be characterized by a multitude of competing communications carriers and programs, the Act eliminated the ceiling on total radio ownership nationwide, eased restrictions on ownership concentration in the broadcast media, and repealed rules against telephone companies entering the cable TV business. Even more significant in the future may be the decision to give existing television networks and station owners the right to broadcast digitally in their assigned frequencies. Since each new digital channel could be split six ways, it will allow the use of the public airwaves for cellular phones, pagers, computer modems, and other electronic businesses.[11]

The escalating competition and deregulation seen in the United States has also occurred in Europe, most notably in Germany, Ireland, and France, where government-broadcasting monopolies have been dismantled and domestic communications opened up to multinational capital. One of the most visible indicators of this has been the launching of communications satellites, which are used to beam services such as Rupert Murdoch's "B Sky B" to European audiences. Increasingly, the footprints of these direct-broadcast satellites has spread beyond political boundaries, fragmenting national audiences and abolishing traditional monopolies.[12] Unlike TV networks tied to a single country, these satellite stations have no public-service responsibilities; consequently, they are a sink for endless hours of syndicated reruns and second-run movies, many purchased from American producers—"commercial operations with advertising increasingly aimed at megamarkets that stretch across continents."[13] In similar fashion, the global media firms have discovered Asian markets, where two-thirds of the world's potential viewers reside. This is particularly evident in Hong Kong, the region's most intensive media centre. Murdoch is a presence here too, operating STAR (Satellite Television Asian Region) TV which carries the BBC News,[14] Prime Sports, and MTV Asia.

The Global Media Oligopoly

Media concentration is by no means a new phenomenon. Desbarats[15] has noted that as early as 1884 a syndicate headed by the Scottish-American steel magnate Andrew Carnegie controlled 8 daily newspapers and 10 weeklies in Britain; by 1937, four men—Lords Beaverbrook, Rothmere, Camrose, and Kemsley—owned nearly one of every two national and local daily newspapers sold in Britain. During the same era, three American press magnates—Joseph Pulitzer, William Randolph Hearst, and Edward Wyllis Scripps—established burgeoning newspaper chains through a combination of mergers, shutdowns, and circulation-boosting sensationalist reporting.

What distinguishes the current "Lords of the Global Village" is the size, scope, and degree of multimedia ownership of their holdings. In 1988, the world's top 10 media giants collectively generated revenues of $51 billion, twice the Canadian national debt for the same year.[16] Nearly a decade later (1997), the top four (Disney, Time Warner, News Corp. and Bertelsmann) together had revenues of $US60 billion.[17] Of the "dominant dozen" global media corporations in 1997, 10 were headquartered in the United States, one in France, and one in Germany. Nationality, however, is largely irrelevant as each has extensive holdings abroad. While the majority of the contemporary media barons started out in the print media, today their empires include newspapers, magazines, book publishers, scholarly journals, TV stations, pay TV, satellite channels, cable networks, record companies, movie studios, and computer databanks. While some are divisions of multinational

manufacturing-and-services conglomerates such as General Electric, most are first and foremost creatures of the communications world. A few (e.g., Rupert Murdoch's News Corp) are controlled by flamboyant media "buccaneers" whose takeover actions, lawsuits, and lifestyles are considered to be newsworthy in themselves. Most are operated by low-key millionaires and/or professional managers who avoid the limelight as much as possible. Nevertheless, as Bagdikian has noted, many of these media magnates indulge in various forms of "synergism" with other multinational corporations.[18] It is not unusual to find interlocks between the large media firms and financial and commercial operations that are affected by news, opinion, and popular culture. The chairman of Hachette, a French media Goliath, is Jean-Luc Lagardère, who also heads one of that country's largest military defence contractors. Silvio Berlusconi, nicknamed the "green octopus," served as premier of Italy from 1994 to 1996. At one time the sole owner of all national commercial TV in Italy, Berlusconi openly acknowledged his strategy of using his three channels to promote sales in his retail chain, Standa, the largest in Italy.[19] Bagdikian identifies the "Lords of the Global Village" as constituting part of a powerful troika in conjunction with worldwide advertising agencies and the multinational manufacturers of consumer goods.[20] This alliance has the potential to powerfully affect the cultural, social, and political values in much of the world.

In the past, the scholarly examination of the relationship between chain ownership and the quality of the media product has been undertaken primarily for the case of newspapers. The underlying assumption here has been that concentrated ownership results in a standardized, homogenized form of news. Drawing on a comprehensive review by Edwin Baker,[21] Dean Alger concludes that, while the results are "somewhat mixed," generally, "the weight of the evidence leans decidedly in the direction of suggesting that newspaper ownership by media chains tends to have deleterious impacts on newspaper quality, diversity and editorial independence."[22] Accordingly, one major study of front-page articles in British newspapers in 1987, 1989, and 1991 found that independently owned dailies, as compared to those owned by conglomerates, printed more articles by their own staff rather than generic news-service stories; did more journalistic digging rather than just relying on standard news releases; and covered more stories requiring reportorial effort.[23] After reviewing a number of Canadian and American empirical studies of chain versus independent ownership, Glasser et al. concluded that chains may extend to their member newspapers a considerable degree of autonomy in the day-to-day production of news, but will, at the same time, retain control over the kinds of allocative decisions that determine basic policies, long-term goals, and the general disposition of resources.[24]

Critics of the new multimedia behemoths have similarly raised the spectre of homogenization. They portray the new media barons first and foremost as deal-makers to whom journalistic values are secondary, if not unknown, Followers rather than leaders of public opinion, they are said to approximate the profit maximizers of traditional economic theory.[25] As such, they are depicted as imitators, promoters, and packagers rather than creators and crusaders. Significantly, upon assuming ownership of *TV Guide*, Rupert Murdoch dispensed with the magazine's "critical" stance towards the entertainment industry, substituting Murdoch's standard diet of health, fashion, celebrity lives and loves, human interest, and horoscopes.[26]

While the notion that increasing corporate size will lead to profitable synergies "may rest more on hype than reality,"[27] nevertheless it is a quest that threatens to reduce culture production to a relative handful of packaged products where "spinoff" is the key, operative phrase. Multimedia companies such as Time Warner are able to morph a cultural property through a range of genre formats while spreading their production costs broadly. For example, the Robert James Waller novel *Bridges of Madison County* variously appeared as a best-selling book, music video and recording, which was promoted and sold through Time Warner's magazine and mail-order outlets before re-appearing three years later as a motion picture that was cross-promoted through its magazines and CNN, then redistributed through its television stations and cable franchises.[28]

Further, the media watchdogs fear that the increasing power of the global companies will give their owners a stranglehold over information that would almost certainly be employed in order to "promote their political and economic views."[29] Simon Regan, a biographer of Rupert Murdoch, identifies two strategies that are used in order to make this happen. The first is to work out a general editorial policy, especially with regards to current affairs; the second is when owners insidiously promote or suppress news and views about their

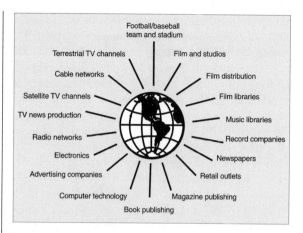

Figure 1: Elements of a Modern Media Empire

influential friends.[30] The line between these two widely differing sorts of influence has occasionally been drawn very thinly by Murdoch, Regan claims, and the same charge is often implied in the criticism of other media barons. Almost invariably, both they and their friends are deeply conservative.[31] This conservatism, it is suggested, is translated into media content.

Media analysts are concerned also that the new global conglomerates are increasingly gaining control over both the hardware and software of communications. Perhaps the leading illustration of this is Time Warner.

From its roots as an American publishing magnate (*Time, Fortune, Sports Illustrated, People*), Time Inc. expanded aggressively into the electronic media, assembling the second-largest cable-television system in the United States, as well as acquiring Home Box Office (HBO) whose premium cable television fare today includes the Emmy-award-winning comedy show *Sex and the City*. In a $US14.1 billion deal in 1989, Time Inc. bought the film, television, and recording-music giant Warner Communications, contributing to its holdings a broadcast network, a film studio, and a chain of stores selling themed merchandise featuring Bugs Bunny, Road Runner, and other cartoon characters from the Warner Brothers stable. Once again, in 1995, Time Warner engineered a megadeal, buying out Turner Communications for $7.2 billion. With the addition of prime cable-TV channels CNN, TBS, and TNT, a library of classic American films, and the Atlanta Braves (baseball) and Hawks (basketball) teams, Time Warner transformed itself into "the largest multimedia corporation in the world."[32]

Now Time Warner is poised to conclude a merger with AOL, which would make it a leading player in the convergence of television, cable, and computers. In very much the same spirit, billionaire Paul Allen, co-founder with Bill Gates of Microsoft, has been steadily reworking his investments to enable something he calls the "wired world." Allen describes this as a collection of intertwined businesses that would combine content with cable systems for broadband distribution to on-line consumers. Among his significant holdings are Charter Communications, a $US4.6 billion cable-TV operator created from 12 systems across the United States; DreamWorks SKG, the entertainment company whose *American Beauty* won the Academy Award for best film of 1999; Oxygen Media, a magazine and start-up cable channel that produces television shows and Internet content for women; and Digeo Broadband, which aims to create content for high-bandwidth cable TV.[33] With what seems now like remarkable foresight, Rupert Murdoch foresaw such a development nearly a decade ago when he predicted the breakdown of traditional barriers separating five of the world's biggest industries–computing, communications, consumer electronics, publishing, and entertainment–and their transformation into a dynamic whole.[34]

The Impact of New Media Technologies

As David Hutchison has observed, technological breakthroughs by themselves are not sufficient explanations for the changes that ensue as a result of these innovations. Rather, technological change interacts with political, economic, and social forces to determine how and where new inventions are utilized.[35] This has particular relevance to the issue of media ownership and control in a global context.

In the original image of a "global village" as promoted by Marshall McLuhan, the electronic media were seen as a means by which the control over print-based information by bureaucratic-national structures would be shattered. Instead, the world would move towards a "new age," which would be characterized by both decentralization and global integration. By annihilating the constraints imposed by space and time, the way would be opened for the regaining of a sense of social identity and harmony.[36]

While the technological revolution predicted by McLuhan is not yet complete, in retrospect it appears that he was both right and wrong.

On the one hand, the past decade has seen the emergence of global politics, communities of concern, and social movement networks. This can be identified in the success of media events such as the Live-Aid concerts, the establishment of international networks for peace, ecology, and human rights, and the effective use of the Internet in the 1998 global campaign against the Multilateral Agreement on Investment (MAI). Without leaving their living rooms, TV viewers have experienced the horrors of war in Bosnia and Kosovo, the joy that greeted the dismantling of the Berlin Wall, and the shock and tragedy of the Concorde jet crashing into a Paris hotel. Changes in media-delivery systems, particularly the widening availability and spread of the videocassette recorder (VCR) in Eastern Europe and Third World countries, have prompted some media scholars to rethink the media-imperialism thesis.[37]

On the other hand, it is increasingly evident that most new media technologies so far have not been instruments for human liberation and identity building. The most popular destinations on the World Wide Web are those connected to sex and pornography. According to America Online, "the largest ongoing webcast in history" is the 24-hour-a-day feed of the CBS reality show *Big Brother*, evidently, over half a million "web zombies" tune in hoping to catch something spicy.[38] Similarly, while the hybrid of video games and interactive telemedia may produce new, more sophisticated levels of graphic reality, these games frequently engage their users, especially children, in aggressive and sometimes brutal acts. These new products and services are generally characterized by "a wealth of possibility and a dearth of direction."[39] At present, all indications are that the next generation of media technologies will be absorbed into what Morris-Suzuki has termed "information capitalism."[40] One of the characteristics of this information capitalism is that corporations are able to tap a new source of profit by their use of freely obtained social knowledge to create private knowledge.[41] This is especially evident in the growth of "user pay" databanks that are increasingly controlled by a few giant media firms such as Thomson Corporation and the Knight-Ridder newspaper chain. Even government data are fast disappearing into private companies, which then lobby to forbid the government to make that data available free or inexpensively.[42] Similarly, the lucrative business in computer networks is not in global networking but in private corporate networks.[43] The same holds true for "teleconferencing"–the video-telephone innovation that was trumpeted in the 1970s as having so much value for grassroots communication.

Internationally, then, the flow of information across national borders has intensified. This reflects both a trend towards the deregulation of telecommunications in the U.S. and Western Europe and the rise of giant multimedia firms, to whom increasing corporate size represents a profit-maximizing "synergy." New media technologies combine computing and communications in ways which create a wealth of possibilities; however, this new generation of interactive systems is likely to become absorbed into an "information capitalism," wherein corporations profit by using freely obtained social knowledge to create private knowledge. Contrary to McLuhan's prediction, then, the "global village" of the future may be privatized, exclusive, and inhospitable to the emergence of new collective identities.

Globalization and the Canadian Media

Patterns of Concentration and Monopoly

Throughout the last century, there has been a steady trend towards increasing concentration of media control in the hands of a decreasing pool of owners. In 1930 in Canada, for example, 116 daily newspapers were under the control of 99 publishers; by 1953, the start of the TV era, 89 were under the control of 57 publishers, with 11 publishers accounting for 42 dailies, about one-half the total.[44] As newspapers became more and more dependent upon revenues from readers and advertisers, survival became more and more difficult for smaller newspapers, who lacked the access to capital funds and administrative expertise possessed by larger newspapers or newspaper chains.

Concern over increasing newspaper concentration peaked at two points during the 1970s and 1980s. In 1970, the Special Senate Committee on Mass Media brought down its report (usually referred to as the Davey Report[45] after its chairman, Senator Keith Davey), in which it was claimed that Canada's mass media were "becoming increasingly concentrated in the hands of a smaller, privileged group of businessmen."[46] Of Canada's 11 largest cities, chains were found to enjoy a monopoly in seven. The three biggest newspaper chains–Thomson, Southam, and F.P. Publications–controlled 44.7 percent of the circulation of all Canadian daily newspapers, up from 25 percent a dozen years earlier. The newsrooms of Canadian newspapers, the Davey Committee concluded, were nothing less than "the bone yards of broken dreams."[47] Furthermore, the Davey Report noted a pattern of multimedia ownership by corporate groups. Just under two-thirds (66.4 percent) of Canada's daily newspapers were owned or partially controlled by "media groups" along with 48.5 percent of Canadian TV stations and 47.4 percent of radio stations. To help control this increasing concentration of the country's mass media, the Davey Report recommended the establishment of a press ownership review board, patterned after the British Monopolies Commission, which would have the power to approve or disapprove mergers between, or acquisitions of, newspapers and periodicals. Its guiding principle would be that all transactions that increase concentration of ownership in the mass media are undesirable and contrary to the public interest–unless shown to be otherwise. This recommendation was never implemented.

A decade later, the closings on the same day of the *Winnipeg Tribune* and the *Ottawa Journal*–thus eliminating direct competition between the Thomson and Southam chains in those cities–prompted the federal government to appoint a Royal Commission on Newspapers under the chairmanship of a former journalist and civil servant, Tom Kent. The Kent Report, released in 1981, documented a further deterioration in the independent ownership of Canadian newspapers since the Davey Committee had done its work. Two chains, Thomson and Southam, were found to be dominant with a combined aggregate circulation of close to 15 million readers, 58.7 percent of the circulation of all English-language newspapers. Also noteworthy were financier Conrad Black's Sterling Newspapers, owner of 11 small dailies; Torstar Corporation, publisher of *The Toronto Star*, Canada's largest newspaper by circulation, and 31 weeklies; Pierre Peladeau's Quebecor Inc., operator of two French-language tabloids–*Le Journal de Montreal* and *Le Journal de Quebec*–and 28 weeklies; Power Corporation (four dailies); Toronto Sun Publishing Corp. (three tabloids in Toronto, Calgary, and Edmonton) and a handful of regional monopolies in south-western Ontario (Blackburn Group) and New Brunswick (Irving Group).

Like the Davey Committee, the Kent Commission came up with several controversial recommendations that were designed to limit the future growth of the chains: a general ownership limitation of 5 percent of total daily circulation in cases of new acquisitions, immediate divestiture of selected holdings by the Thomson organization and several regional owners, the establishment under federal statute of a "press rights panel" that would have the authority to review all proposals for newspaper ownership changes, including proposals for newspaper clo-sures.[48] As was the case with the Davey Report, the key recommendations of the Kent Report were never legislatively enacted. Unwilling to risk attack in the press and on television and radio, the government preferred to accept newspaper proprietors' claims that they could and should regulate themselves.[49]

In the years since the Kent Report, the situation has not improved. Addressing the Canadian Advertising Foundation (CAF) in the spring of 1990, Senator Davey observed that "the country's major media operations control more today than they did twenty years ago—and the situation is worse still in Quebec."[50] Today, about 72 percent of Canada's newspapers belong to chains, with a little over half belonging to just one—CanWest Global Communications (which purchased them from Conrad Black's Hollinger Inc.).[51] Increasingly, as the CanWest/Hollinger deal illustrates, ownership changes no longer involve the transfer of ownership of a newspaper (or a radio/TV station or cable company) from independent ownership to chain ownership but, rather, from one multimedia chain owner to another.[52]

Penetration by Global Megamedia Empires

In contrast to the U.S., Canada generally has not been a fertile ground for the expansionary ambitions of the global media barons. There are several reasons for this. First, a combination of tax restrictions, regulatory constraints, Canadian-content quotas, and foreign-ownership rules has not made the purchase of Canadian media properties very easy or attractive. This was especially the case during the Trudeau years when the CRTC and the Foreign Investment Review Agency (FIRA) represented obstacles to non-Canadian investors. Even today, non-Canadians are not permitted to own a controlling interest in Canadian newspapers and 80 percent of the voting stock and paid-up capital of a cable-TV or broadcasting company must be owned by Canadians. Second, compared with the U.S., the number of media units for sale in Canada is usually minimal, and those that are available are usually snapped up by domestic communications giants such as CanWest Global, Quebecor, and Rogers.

Nevertheless, foreign media conglomerates have penetrated the Canadian media market in a variety of ways.

According to *Globalization of the Mass Media*,[53] a 1973 report issued by the U.S. Department of Commerce, there are three main methods by which firms have globalized the electronic mass media and other markets: complementary expansion, horizontal expansion, and vertical expansion. Complementary expansion occurs when a firm is engaged in the production of mass media products that are functionally related, e.g., videocassette recorders (VCRs) and videocassettes. Typically, a company that manufactures "hardware" (TV sets, satellite dishes) will purchase companies that produce "software" (films, TV programs, video games) in order to control both price and supply. Horizontal expansion occurs when a firm sells the same product in at least two different foreign markets, either through foreign direct investment or through exports. The former is illustrated through the control of the recorded-music industry by a handful of giant corporations, while the latter is typified by the global export dominance of American motion pictures and TV programming. Globalization through "vertical expansion" occurs when a firm controls more than one stage in the production chain, and this combined ownership transcends national borders. For example, a record label may be distributed domestically by a multinational distributor or a film studio with headquarters in a foreign country may enhance its profits by building theatres abroad.

Aside from record (CD, laser disc, tape), film, and periodical distribution, which has mostly escaped the reach of government regulation, globalization has impacted the Canadian media primarily through joint ventures between Canadian and foreign firms that involve "complementary" aspects. Rogers Communications Inc., a major player in the Canadian telecommunications industry, has linked up with the American computer behemoth Microsoft. As part of its July 1999 $US400 million investment in the Canadian company, Microsoft has requested that Rogers field-test the Microsoft TV Platform, first in Toronto, and later, nationwide. This will allow TV viewers to utilize their existing television set and cable connection to seamlessly switch from video channels to the Internet using a wireless keyboard. Eventually, Rogers will deliver additional enhanced TV services via digital cable and the Platform.[54] A more direct entry into the Canadian market may come from Time Warner/AOL. Through its Canadian subsidiary, AOL Canada, AOL is capable of importing, via the Internet, American cable superchannels such as HBO, which cannot at present be legally broadcast north of the border. What opens

**TABLE 1: The Leading Multimedia Companies in Canada and
1999 Year-End Operating Revenues, by Rank**

Company	Operating Revenues
Quebecor Inc	$10.83 billion
The Thomson Corp.	$8.54 billion
Hollinger Inc	$3.24 billion
Rogers Communications Inc.	$3.11 billion
Le Groupe Vidéotron Ltée	$936 million
Shaw Communications Inc.	$728 million
Alliance Atlantis Communications Inc	$633 million
Canwest Global Communications Corp.	$602 million
CTV Inc.*	$528 million
Canadian Broadcasting Corp.	$484 million

* CTV is now part of BCE Inc. In 1999, BCE's revenues were $14.21 billion, making it the second-highest ranked (by operating revenues) telecommunications company in Canada.

Source: National Post Business, "Canada's 500 Largest Corporations," June, 2000.

the door to this is the CRTC's 1999 decision not to regulate the Internet.[55]

Finally, American companies who are legally prohibited from controlling Canadian media outlets have entered the country as minority owners. For example, BCE is partially owned by Ameritech, the Chicago-based Regional Bell Operating Company (RBOC); NetStar Communications (taken over in 1999 by CTV) by the Disney company ESPN; and Corus (controlled by the Shaw family) by Liberty Media, a subsidiary of TCI (which is in turn owned by AT&T). If Canadian ownership rules were to be relaxed in the future, we could probably expect at least some of these minority stakes to grow significantly.

Canadian "Lords of the Global Village"

Throughout the 1990s, there were only two Canadian media companies that could justifiably lay claim to global status—Thomson Corporation and Hollinger Inc. At its zenith, Thomson Corp. was a leading second-tier megamedia corporation with annual revenues of about $US8 billion (1997). With a portfolio of 237 daily newspapers in Canada and the U.S. and another 151 in the United Kingdom, it was the largest newspaper company in North America (in terms of number of properties).[56] Hollinger, presided over by business legend Conrad Black, operated the third-largest newspaper chain worldwide, behind News Corp. and Gannett. By 1998, Hollinger had acquired 58 of Canada's 106 dailies with 37 percent of the total circulation.[57]

Recently, both Thomson and Hollinger have suddenly withdrawn from the newspaper business in North America to pursue other interests. In the former case, the Thomson board has opted to put all of its newspaper properties except *The Globe and Mail* up for sale so as to be able to focus entirely on opportunities in e-commerce, specifically the provision of legal data. In the latter instance, Black negotiated a $3.5 billion deal with CanWest Global Communications in July 2000 that includes 13 major daily newspapers in Canada, 136 small newspapers, 85 trade publications, and a 50 percent interest in the *National Post*, which Black started in 1998. Soon after, in a separate deal, Black spun off Hollinger's newspapers in the U.S. Remaining in the Hollinger newspaper portfolio are the *Daily Telegraph*, a high-circulation conservative daily in Britain; the *Chicago Sun-Times*, the second-ranked newspaper (by circulation) in that city; and the *Jerusalem Post*. There has been much speculation as to why Black bowed out of North America; the most convincing theory seems to be that the company's debt was too high while it's stock was undervalued in the market, making it impossible to expand into new frontiers such as multimedia ownership.

With Thomson and Hollinger largely out of the picture, there are now four[58] main corporations that are poised to dominate the Canadian media landscape: Rogers Communications, CanWest Global, Quebecor, and BCE.

After a series of bold initiatives and strategic retreats over the last quarter century, Edward (Ted) Rogers Jr. appears to be finally hitting his stride. For a time, Rogers Communications Inc. was the largest Canadian cable operator in the U.S., with over half a million subscribers in systems in Texas, Minnesota, and Oregon, as well as having set up a cable system in the Republic of Ireland. However, in 1989, Rogers suddenly sold its U.S. cable holdings for $US1.27 billion and announced that it would spend the proceeds in order to complete a national cellular network for Cantel, its cellular-telephone company, and to upgrade the entire Rogers cable system in Canada. For most of the 1990s, the company lost money and shouldered a $5 billion debt load. Then, in 1994, Rogers surprised its annual shareholders meeting by announcing the takeover of Maclean Hunter, a venerable Canadian media conglomerate with a stable of trade and mass media periodicals, radio and television holdings, and one of the 20 largest cable-TV systems in North America. With its coffers swelled by investments from Microsoft, British Telecommunications, and AT&T, and with a $4 billion swap of cable-TV assets with Shaw Communications Inc. in place, Rogers stock rose 35 percent in 1999-2000, elevating Ted Rogers to the number nine position on *Canadian Business'* "Rich 100" list of wealthy Canadians. And, the company's purchase of the Toronto Blue Jays baseball club gives it a significant new source of content for this cable empire.

The most recent superstar on the Canadian communications firmament is Israel (Izzy) Asper, a Winnipeg businessman and former provincial Liberal leader, who controls CanWest Global Communications. The crown jewel of CanWest is the Global TV network, which has long claimed the title of Canada's "third national television network," but, with only seven stations, has been closer to a regional network with strengths in Ontario and the Prairies. By acquiring eight more television stations from WIC Western International Communications Ltd. for $800 million, as well as independent outlets in Hamilton and Victoria, CanWest, the largest buyer of U.S. television programs in the country, has dramatically raised its profile. And, by virtue of CanWest's acquisition of Hollinger's newspaper properties, Asper has become an instant media baron. An experienced player in foreign markets, CanWest has significant holdings in Australia,[50] New Zealand, and Ireland.

The Péladeau family of Montreal operate a multibillion-dollar printing, publishing, and media empire, which includes *Le Journal de Montreal*, the market leader in Quebec, and Television Quatre Saisons, Quebec's second-biggest private TV network. Established by their late father, Pierre, once described as "the most powerful Francophone press lord outside France,"[60] the company is now run by his two sons Pierre Karl (chairman and CEO) and

Erik (vice-chairman). Pierre Péladeau, a self-made millionaire who rose to become Canada's largest commercial printer, was always viewed as an outsider by the media establishment in English Canada, where his racy tabloid papers and separatist political views were frowned upon. Pierre Karl has been more successful in penetrating the Anglo media scene, engineering a takeover of Sun Media Corp., which publishes a chain of dailies, as well as operating CANOE, an Internet portal that rates as the 20th-largest website in Canada (by number of visitors). Most recently, Quebecor has joined forces with its major shareholder, the provincial pension fund, Caisse de dépôt et placement du Québec, to mount a successful $4.9 billion cash counter-offer for Groupe Vidéotron.[61]

Finally, there is BCE Inc., which was created when the Bell Canada system was broken up in the 1980s. Since its creation, BCE has had a chequered career. After enduring some extensive losses as a result of an ill-considered detour into commercial real estate investment, BCE successfully nurtured the growth of Nortel Networks Corp., the high-technology firm whose spectacular growth has made it the toast of the Toronto Stock Exchange. BCE has steadily built a nest of Internet, satellite, and wireless businesses, notably Sympatico/Lycos, the fifth and seventh most popular Canadian websites respectively, and Bell ExpressVu, a direct-to-home satellite broadcaster. In May 2000, BCE struck a deal to purchase the CTV television network, Canada's largest private broadcaster, giving it significant content to stream onto its Internet sites.

Conclusion

Has the globalization of the world's media affected Canada? For the most part there seems to be little direct penetration by foreign conglomerates into the ownership structure of Canadian newspaper, radio/television, and cable services. Instead, a handful of Canadian media giants have grown even larger by cannibalizing smaller chains. Indirectly, however, the growth of global megamedia empires has potentially serious implications for Canadian media and society. Above all, the danger is that worldwide media and culture are being inexorably reduced to the level of a mass-produced commodity whose origin is irrelevant.

Further, the growth of global megamedia empires has begun to shift the balance between national cultures and the interests of transnational business in favour of the latter. In broadcasting, the contradictions between the internationalizing tendencies of markets and the imperatives of national institutions is particularly sharp.[62] In the future, Mosco foresees the right of businesses to pursue commerce and set social and public policy taking precedence over the political rights of national citizens and their governments, thus contributing to the creation of a new "transnational information order."[63]

Moreover, the rising fortunes of media conglomerates, national and global, means that the scope for innovation in programming and creative output may be curtailed. Keith Davey has spoken to this point when he observed that "the fact is, the owners and controllers of the newspapers and other media in this country are all the same kind of people doing the same kind of thing with the same kind of private-enterprise rationale."[64] While some media barons have kept money-losing "prestige" publications going beyond their natural life (e.g., Rupert Murdoch's newspaper, *The Australian*), generally they are committed to projects that follow a tested formula and produce a high circulation or ratings. As the Consumers' Association of Canada has suggested, the concentration of media ownership and cross-media ownership can lead to a situation where "the diverse range of opinion, ideas and attitudes that exist within Canada on issues of public concern" may not be adequately reflected.[65]

Canada thus stands at a crossroads. As has been the case with some countries in the European Community, the rise of pay TV, satellite-TV programming, and so on has been allowed to take place in a commercial context, in part because national governments have sought to stifle the influence of public networks and channels whose ideology they suspect of being contrary to the interest of business.[66] While non-Canadian owners have been mostly shut out of many aspects of Canadian media ownership, domestic chains and media groups have, with few exceptions, been allowed to grow with impunity; and, with the recent spate of multimedia mergers, this is even more the case today. To date, most have been reasonably responsible; almost all documented instances of the flagrant abuse of power have occurred when regional monopolies develop control of all the media in a given region.[67]

In the future, however, the rapid development of new interactive media technologies and broadband synergies will raise the ante. It may be rather extreme to claim, as have the U.S.-based consultants, Forrester Research Inc.,[68] that only live-event programming (sports, political coverage, award shows) will survive the onset of interactive TV and retain a mass audience of real-time viewers. Nevertheless, the convergence of the computer and television worlds is clearly of major significance. Existing communications-delivery systems could become obsolete very quickly, leaving independent operators and cash-starved public institutions on the outside. While their comments are no doubt prompted by a degree of commercial envy, it is still worth heeding the cautions issued by Time Warner/AOL rivals in their written filings with the FCC concerning the proposed merger. In its deposition, Disney worries that the new Time Warner/AOL giant could discriminate against competitors and "impede the free flow of news, information, entertainment, services, and commerce to consumers."[69] NBC, which is owned by General Electric, warns that the $124 billion union could create an all-powerful gatekeeper able to control the free flow of content through state-of-the-art technology.[70] In scenarios such as this, only global media conglomerates whose resources are in the billions of dollars, and who have forged convergences around multiple-media content and marketing, will be in a position to build and operate these new systems. If this should be the case, then, the spectres raised by Bagdikian, Alger, and others may become more immediate and pervasive.

Notes

1. James B. Stewart, "Mousetrap: What Time Warner Didn't Consider When It Unplugged Disney," *The New Yorker* (31 July 2000), pp.28-34.

2. Stewart, "Mousetrap," pp.30-31.

3. Ben H. Bagdikian, "The Lords of the Global Village," *The Nation* (12 June 1989), pp.805-20.

4. Vincent Mosco, *The Pay-Per Society: Computers and Communication in the Information Age* (Toronto: Garamond Press, 1989), p.54.

5. The recent revival of Karl Marx's concept of "circuits of capital" can be traced to the British urban geographer David Harvey. It refers to the principle that investment capital must always be kept in continuous circulation in order to keep its value increasing. See David Harvey, *The Urbanization of Capital* (Baltimore: The John Hopkins University Press, 1985). For more about the circulation of cultural capital in an urban setting, see Sharon Zukin, "Socio-spatial Prototypes of a New Organization of Consumption: The Role of Cultural Capital," *Sociology* 24 (1990): 37-56.

6. Herbert I. Schiller, *Mass Communication and American Empire* (New York: Augustus M. Kelley, 1969); Alan Wells, *Picture Tube Imperialism? The Impact of U.S. Television on Latin America* (Maryknoll, N.Y.: Orbis Books, 1972).

7. Jeremy Tunstall, *The Media Are American* (New York: Columbia University Press, 1977), p.273.

8. Jeremy Tunstall, *Communications Deregulation: The Unleashing of America's Communications Industry* (Oxford: Basil Blackwell, 1986), p.3.

9. Henry Geller, "Foreward" in Stuart N. Brotman, ed., *The Telecommunications Deregulation Sourcebook* (Boston and London: Artech House, 1987), p.vii.

10. In 1984, GM bought EDS (Electronic Data Systems), the leading software company in the U.S. at the time. A year later, it purchased Hughes Aircraft, the "leader in space vehicles." See Tunstall, *Communications Deregulation*, p.288.

11. Dean Alger, *Megamedia: How Giant Corporations Dominate Mass Media, Distort Competition and Endanger Democracy* (Lanham, Maryland: Rowman & Littlefield, 1998), pp.101-3.

12. Desmond Bell and Neil Meehan, "Telecommunications Deregulation and Ireland's Domestic Communications Policy," *Journal of Communication* 38 (1988), pp.70-71.

13. Bagdikian, "The Lords," p.805.

14. In late 1994, just three years after its launch, STAR TV summarily removed the BBC from its northern beam that reached mainland China after authorities complained about the BBC coverage of the country. See Daya Kishan Thussa, "Infotainment International: A View from the South," D. K. Thusson, ed., *Electronic Empires: Global Media and Local Resistance* (London: Arnold, 1998). Cited in Alger, *Megamedia*, pp.73-74.

15. Peter Desbarats, *Guide to Canadian News Media* (Toronto: Harcourt Brace Jovanovich, 1990), pp.54-55.

16. D'Arcy Jenish, "Media Wars," *Maclean's* (17 July 1989), p.29.

17. Alger, *Megamedia*, p.33.

18. Bagdikian, "The Lords," p.815.

19. Neville Clarke and Edwin Riddell, *The Sky Barons* (London: Methuen, 1992), p.10.

20. Bagdikian, "The Lords," p.816.

21. C. Edwin Baker, "Ownership of Newspapers: The View from Positivist Social Science," Research Paper R-12, Shorenstein Center, Kennedy School of Government, Harvard University, September, 1994.

22. Alger, *Megamedia*, p.180.

23. Kimberley E. Fradgely and Walter N. Niebauer Jr., "London's Quality Newspapers: Newspaper Ownership and Reporting Patterns," *Journalism & Mass Communication Quarterly* 72 (1995): 902-12.

24. T.L. Glasser, D.S. Allen, and S.E. Blanks, "The Influence of Chain Ownership on Newsplay: A Case Study," *Journalism Quarterly* 66 (1989): 607-14.

25. Peter J.S. Dunnett, *The World Newspaper Industry* (London: Croom Helm, 1988), p.36.

26. Richard Belfield, Christopher Hird, and Sharon Kelly, *Murdoch: The Decline of an Empire* (London: Macdonald, 1991), p.214.

27. Joshua Hammer, "The Myth of Global Synergy," *Newsweek* (26 June 1989), p.54.

28. Heather Menzies, "Media Mergers, Logos and the Damned Old CPR," *Canadian Forum* (June 2000), p.26.

29. Jenish, "Media Wars," p.28.

30. Simon Regan, *Rupert Murdoch: A Business Biography* (London: Argus and Robertson, 1976), pp.198-99.

31. Some exceptions are the late Robert Maxwell, who was long associated with the moderate left in Britain, and Silvio Berlusconi, whose connections with the Socialist Party in Italy ultimately led to a term as premier.

32. Alger, *Megamedia*, p.7.

33. David Kirkpatrick, "Why We're Betting Billions on TV," *Fortune* (15 May 2000): 249-61.

34. "B Sky B Turns First Profit: Satellite Broadcaster Key Part of 'Superhighway of the Air,'" *The Globe and Mail* (9 September 1993), p.B20.

35. David Hutchison, "Broadcasting Policy in Canada and the United Kingdom: Politics, Technology and Ideology," *Canadian Journal of Communication* 15 (1990): 91-92

36. Ian Parker, "Option in Telecommunications Regulation," *Canadian Journal of Communication* 15 (1990): 40.

37. See, for example, Christine Ogan, "Media Imperialism and the Videocassette Recorder: The Case of Turkey," *Journal of Communication* 38 (1988): 93-106.

38. Anita Hamilton, "I'm a Web Zombie," *Time* (31 July 2000), p.53.

39. Karen Wright, "The Road to the Global Village," *Scientific American* 262, no. 30 (1990): 83-94.

40. Tessa Morris-Suzuki, *Beyond Computopia: Information Automation and Democracy in Japan* (London: Kegan Paul, 1988).

41. Joji Watanuke, "Development of Information Technology and Its Impacts on Society: The Case of Japan," a paper presented to the XIIth World Congress of Sociology, Madrid, Spain, July 1990.

42. Bagdikian, "The Lords," p.815.

43. Wright, "The Road," p.93.

44. Wilfred Kesterton, "The Growth of the Newspaper in Canada," B.D. Singer, ed., *Communications in Canadian Society*, 2nd ed. (Don Mills, Ont.: Addison-Wesley, 1983), p.9.

45. Senator Keith Davey, Chairman, *Report of the Special Senate Committee on Mass Media* (Ottawa, Queen's Printer, 1970).

46. T.C. Seacrest, "The Davey Report: Main Findings and Recommendations," B.D. Singer, ed., *Communications in Canadian Society*, 2nd ed. (Don Mills, Ont.: Addison-Wesley, 1983), p.117.

47. David F. Rooney, "The Bone Yards of Broken Dreams," *Media* (Spring 2000): 6.

48. Thomas Kent, Chairman, *Report of the Royal Commission on Newspapers* (Ottawa: Ministry of Supply and Services, 1981).

49. Rooney, "Broken Dreams," p.7.

50. Randy Scotland, "Rainmaker Raises a Cloudy Spectre; Media Concentration Increasing," *Marketing* 95, no. 19 (1990): 9.

51. Rooney, "Broken Dreams," p.7.

52. Walter I.. Romanow and Walter C. Soderlund, "Thomson Newspapers' Acquisition of the Globe and Mail: a Case Study of Content Change," *Gazette* (International Journal for Mass Communications) 41 (1988): 7.

53. U.S. Department of Commerce (National Telecommunications and Information Administration), *Globalization and the Mass Media* (Washington, D.C.: U.S. Government Printing Office, January 1993), pp.53-68.

54. "Rogers to Bring WebTV Services to Cable," *Broadcaster* (June 2000), p.15.

55. John Bugailiskis, "Working Up an Appetite for iCraveTV," *Broadcaster* (January 2000), p.4.

56. Lucia Moses, "Let's Make a Deal," *Editor & Publisher* (20 March 2000): 22.

57. Alger, *Megamedia*, p.130.

58. A possible fifth is Shaw Communications, the second-largest cable television operator in Canada. From its roots as a mid-size regional operator in western Canada, Shaw has assembled a varied portfolio which includes cable television channels YTV, Treehouse, Teletoon, and the Comedy Network; 14 radio stations in Ontario, British Columbia, and Alberta; and Shaw Home Service, which provides high-speed Internet access. See Renee Huang and Douglas Coull, "Modern Moguls," *The Globe and Mail* (1 August 2000), p.B8.

59. For a time in the late 1990s, CanWest owned as much as 76 percent of Network Ten, Australia's third-largest television network but was ordered by the Australian government to pare this back to 57.5 percent. Recent reports in the Australian business media have suggested that Asper may be planning to sell his New Zealand radio and television assets, which include two national television networks, to Network Ten.

60. Kevin Daugherty, "Péladeau Eyes France as Quebecor Net Triples," *The Financial Post* (30 April 1993) p.23.

61. Groupe Vidéotron is considered a major prize by Quebecor, not only because of its dominance on the Quebec media scene and its reputation as an innovator in interactive television, but because its subsidiary, TVA, was recently granted national cable carriage status. This means that it is able to compete with Radio Canada for advertisers on a national basis. See Noel Myer, "The Monster Network : How TVA Continues to Dominate the Quebec Market," *Broadcaster* (October 1999), pp.10-12.

62. Richard Collins, "Broadcasting and National Culture in Canada," *British Journal of Canadian Studies* 4 (1989): 35-57.

63. Vincent Mosco, "Towards a World Information Order: The Canada-U.S. Free Trade Agreement," *Canadian Journal of Communication* 15 (1990): 46-63.

64. Scotland, "Rainmaker Raises a Cloudy Sceptre," p.9.

65. Nickolas Murray, "Bigger Isn't Better: The Need to Curb Media Takeovers," *Canadian Consumer* 17, no. 9 (1989): 30.

66. Hutchison, "Broadcasting Policy."

67. Dunnett, *The World Newspaper Industry*, p.196.

68. Forrester's claim is contained in a report authored by television industry analyst Josh Bernoff, "Interactive TV Cash Flows." It is cited in John Bugailiskis, "TV Fully Gets Interactive and This Time It's Personal," *Broadcaster* (April 2000), p.13. Bernoff also cites the new "black box" technology pioneered by two high-technology companies, TIVO and Replay, which would unravel the mass market and destroy prime time by permitting the viewer to "watch anything you want to watch when you want to watch it." See Michael Lewis, "Boom Box," *The New York Times Magazine* (13 August 2000): 36-41; 51; 65-7.

69. "NBC Worried About Time-AOL Merger," *Metro* (Toronto edition) (26 July 2000), p.16.

70. Marc Gunther, "Dumb & Dumber," *Fortune* (29 May 2000), p.146.

Getting Down to Business: Cultural Politics and Policies in Canada

Jody Berland and Will Straw

For over half a century, the cultural industries in Canada have been the focus of public opinion and ongoing debate. Royal commissions, books and articles, studies and surveys, newspaper editorials, trade journals, and government position papers have repeatedly put forward positions and arguments concerning the ownership and control of Canada's cultural industries. Each decade has produced new regulations, policies, and controversies addressing the organization and administration of culture. The underlying issues, nevertheless, have remained relatively constant: the high costs of producing in Canada compared to those of importing programs and cultural commodities; the lack of adequate national distribution and promotion for books, films, and recordings; the dependence on government support of some type for the production of works by Canadian companies–all of these arise from a well-documented economic and structural imbalance in the political economy of Canada's culture, which has kept culture (and government policy) very much in the public eye.

Over the last two decades, however, public discussion of the arts and culture in Canada has evolved in distinctive, revealing ways. While each day's newspaper brings announcements of new convergences within and between the telecommunications and entertainment industries, the sense that these developments are the legitimate focus of collective attention and debate has receded in the face of an implicit claim that they are inevitable. Discussion of the specific character (or very existence) of new TV-specialty channels, digital-radio services, or cross-media conglomerates has been confined to the circumscribed circles of those with an economic stake in the decisions that will bring them into being.

At the same time, recent controversies in Canadian cultural life have had little to do with the contours of life in the age of New Media. Unexpectedly, perhaps, on those occasions when relationships between money and art or culture and political

control have become the focus of public debate, it has been in connection with cultural institutions that some may consider marginal or anachronistic: the art gallery, the theatre, and–catalyzing a debate that is clearly transitional in relation to earlier times–the commercial market for books.

In the early 1990s, a series of controversies over the acquisition policies of the National Gallery of Canada brought the thorny issue of political control over cultural decision making into barbershops and radio phone-in programs all over the country. The revival of the musical play *Show Boat* at the North York Performing Arts Centre in 1993 provoked widespread debate, not simply about the place of such a work within a cultural canon, but over the extent of the responsibility borne by public or quasi-public institutions towards the communities in which they are based. The imposition of the Goods and Services Tax (GST) on books, implemented in 1991, was met by fierce opposition, not only from publishers and book sellers wishing to protect the fragile Canadian publishing industry, but also from a vocal community of readers and educators defending the rights of a non-professional reading public. Was their reading to be defined as a product of commerce or culture? In hindsight, we can see the 1980s and 1990s as one long contentious process of shifting books–and, indeed, cultural production and consumption in general–from the cultural into the commercial domain. In each of these debates, meanwhile, culture was being evoked as everybody's business; but these issues arose in contexts different from those that Canadian editorialists, researchers, and consultants had grown to know so well.

As the audiences for electronically based entertainment forms become more fragmented and globally dispersed, there is a certain aptness in the fact that galleries and performing-arts centres became the focus of public controversies over cultural identity and policy. At one level, this is symptomatic of the growing, often deliberate, obscurity that surrounds the more large-scale transformation of our communications and media structures. Unable to follow or distinguish between the corporate mergers, imminent new services, and legislative or regulatory hearings announced or promised with monotonous regularity in the business sections of our newspapers, we may lose the sense that it is within such changes that the character of a national culture is being re-made.

At the same time, the movement of the art gallery or musical play to centre stage in the debate over cultural value is itself revealing of new economic and social logics at work. Musical theatre, we are told, is now the second-largest employer of musicians in Canada (after the Canadian Broadcasting Corporation), and a major force in establishing Toronto as a tourist destination for those seeking a safe alternative to the United States.[1] Galleries, like museums and cultural festivals, have become the perennial bright hopes of municipal and regional economies, seized upon as antidotes to de-industrialization and spurs to gentrification. While both galleries and municipal theatres are increasingly dependent on touring blockbuster shows for financial stability, both are housed in buildings that seem to represent the very heart of their city and even their country, and so to safeguard the liveliness and continuity of urban and national cultural activity. As the focus of so many hopes, they have become, as well, the ground on which controversies over cultural identity are played out. In many respects, they fulfil the *monumental* function that was once that of such institutions as the Canadian Broadcasting Corporation (CBC) or the National Film Board (NFB); they are looked to for the ways in which they condense and express a collective sense of cultural purpose.

The present-day character of Canada's cultural industries has its roots in the 1980s, a time of significant growth and change within these industries. By 1980, the transnational entertainment industries were among the largest integrated corporate conglomerates in the world, and their products and innovations increasingly set standards (and obstacles) for cultural enterprises in other countries. Culture and communications were among the fastest-growing sectors of the economy, and by the early 1980s, they contributed more to Canada's gross domestic product (GDP) than the textile, aircraft, and chemical industries combined.[2] While employment and income were declining in both manufacturing and resource extraction, they were exploding in the cultural and information industries. This continued throughout the decade: by 1988, cultural industries in Canada

accounted for approximately 450,000 jobs and $10 billion (Cdn.) in revenues.[3] However, these revenues were draining south, rather than staying in the country for reinvestment in Canadian production. In 1980, Paul Audley noted in his ground-breaking study that Canada had a deficit in commodity trade, royalties, and licence payments in the cultural-industries sector in excess of three-quarters of a billion dollars.[4] On the basis of both economic loss and cultural disenfranchisement, it seemed logical (if not long overdue) to suggest that more direct support for the cultural industries would be economically and culturally advantageous to Canadian society. These pressures precipitated a period of fundamental change in the management of cultural production in Canada.

The shifting direction of government policy was made evident in a number of published statements in the early 1980s, which expressed a new realization of the growing economic importance of culture for the Canadian economy. Rather than posing Canadian culture and the marketplace as opposed or antithetical, as, for instance, the influential Massey Commission had done in 1951, such statements emphasized their compatibility and promoted new government measures in that light, with a view to making Canadian production more profitable. The first major study by the newly mandated Department of Communications (DOC)–the 1982 report of the federal Task Force on Cultural Policy (or Appelbaum-Hebert Report)–promoted the notion that a more market-based cultural-industrial policy could also advance the long-cherished goals of Canadian cultural autonomy. While few of its proposals were followed (for instance, that the CBC and the NFB turn over production to the private sector), its orientation helped set the tone for coming changes.

This new mandate for the DOC (which was subsequently split, in 1993, into Industry Canada and the Department of Heritage), in conjunction with subsequent policy statements and initiatives, led to a number of tangible and related effects in the management of culture. The most immediately visible was an increase in direct support for types of cultural production that could most easily be made self-sufficient within the marketplace. Thus, new programs were introduced to subsidize book publishing (the Book Publishing Development Program, initiated in 1979), sound recording (the Sound Recording Development Program, begun in 1986), and film (the Feature Film Fund, set up by Telefilm in 1986), all of which were explicitly oriented towards the production of

Canadian commodities for circulation within the existing distribution, retail, and broadcast structure of the respective markets.

This shift was also evident in the changing proportions of government expenditures on culture throughout the decade. While such expenditures remained almost constant as a share of total government expenditures, there was a substantial increase in support for film and video production, a somewhat smaller increase for the performing and visual arts, but a decreased amount, proportionately, given to broadcasting, heritage, and the literary arts.[5] Major cuts to the CBC followed the Conservative victory in 1984, and, in the years that followed, an increasing proportion of government expenditure was administered through the DOC relative to that granted to such traditional arm's-length agencies as the Canada Council and the NFB.

In direct relation to this, a second important effect was the increased emphasis on what was seen as inevitable technological change. This emphasis was one factor underlying the government's decision to shift responsibility for culture to the DOC, and was evident in subsequent attempts to encourage investment in the private sector through changing patterns of public support. This orientation was given public expression by the first Minister of Communications of the new DOC, who represented communications and culture as part of the larger, inexorable transformation of industry, work, and economy propelled by the new information technologies. As Francis Fox stated in his brief to the Royal Commission on the Economic Union and Development Prospects for Canada, in 1983,

> this brief ... argues that we must approach culture and technology together, since both are critical components of future industrial sense.... Increasingly we are coming to understand that any policy which fails to take adequate account of the cultural dimension will result in a weakening of our capacity to respond to the changing circumstances of international industrial competition.... Although not generally recognized, arts and cultural activities may have as much to contribute to economic performance as information technology.[6]

This orientation had the advantage of legitimating new government expenditures on culture, but it had the disadvantage, as Audley has observed, of promoting expanded production and sales in culture as an end in itself–i.e., with the same economic goals as other industries–rather than as a means to a further end that could be defined only in cultural terms.[7] Thus, a third ramification of the new approach that has influenced both policy and the culture industries

has been the idea that cultural products worthy of support in Canada should be able to compete in an international market. This idea was introduced and disseminated to the public through the frequent use of the phrase "world class," which by the mid-1980s had come to pepper ministerial speeches and reports. This emphasis came to play an important role in the Conservative government's defence of the unpopular Canada-U.S. Free Trade Agreement, which many Canadian artists, publishers, and producers saw as a dangerous threat to Canadian production and cultural sovereignty. Its one positive feature, from the vantage point of cultural producers, was the greater accessibility of American markets to circuits of multinational distribution. A further (and certainly related) effect of government's new interest in and attitude towards the cultural industries was a greater tolerance for the rising concentration in domestic-ownership structures, an expression of the new determination to compete in an international market increasingly shaped by gigantic mergers and corporate conglomerates. Nowhere was this more evident than in book publishing, wherein the Foreign Investment Review Agency (FIRA), which had previously overruled foreign purchases of Canadian publishers, reversed its policy and allowed Random House to be taken over by an American publisher in 1982.[8] This was followed by other similar decisions, foreshadowing the later abolition of FIRA by the Conservative government. Later legislation allowed foreign companies to purchase Canadian companies if they sold back a majority share to Canadian interests within two years. The DOC's criticism of the "chainstore environment"[9] notwithstanding, this program did little to alter the high levels of concentration threatening publishers and controlling important sectors of the cultural industries, such as book, film, and recorded-music distribution and retailing. The arrival of the Chapters and Indigo book retailing superstores on the scene in the late 1990s, and with them their electronic Web marketing arms, simply built on this established policy platform.

Finally, the new era was marked by a subtle but significant shift in the balance of administrative powers through which the Canadian government managed the regulation and financing of culture. This shift was evident in two types of development. The first was the increasing participation of provincial governments in arts funding and a greater interjurisdictional collaboration between the federal government and the provinces. This, too, was initiated in 1980, with the first federal conference of provincial ministers of culture. Especially since the federal election of the Conservatives in 1984, federal agencies have tended to emphasize the cultural industries and related trade relations with the U.S. and to mandate an arts-funding strategy more decentralized towards the provinces and private sector.[10] The second type was the greater degree of decision making appropriated by the DOC and other government bodies in proportion to traditional "arm's-length" agencies such as the Canada Council and NFB. One instance was the DOC's Cultural Initiatives Program, initiated in 1980, which distributed millions in lottery and government funds to cultural and arts projects, with the mandate of promoting the innovative use of new communication technologies in cultural organizations, increasing public participation and access, and fostering community identity and exchange.[11]

The shift to more direct governmental action was also encouraged by a number of overt pressures during the 1980s. Most visible of these was the pressure on cabinet from private broadcasters to overturn a controversial CRTC decision licensing the CBC to run the all-news cable-TV service, and a demand from black cultural-community organizations that cabinet overturn the unpopular CRTC licensing of a country-music radio station in Toronto in favour of a dance-music station supported by groups representing ethnic and immigrant groups in the city. Since then, Parliament's Standing Committee on Communications and Culture came to play a much more prominent role in the development of cultural policy in a number of areas. In the 1991 *Broadcasting Act*, the CRTC was given a stronger mandate to adopt regulatory measures to various market environments; at the same time, the federal government's power to direct and veto CRTC decisions was strengthened, thus reducing the traditional "arms-length" relationship between cabinet and Canada's cultural agencies. In the 1991 *Broadcasting Act,* the CRTC was given a stronger mandate to adapt regulatory measures to various market environments; at the same time, the federal government's power to direct and veto CRTC decisions was strengthened, thus reducing the traditional "arms-length" relationship between cabinet and Canada's cultural agencies.[12]

This same historical conjuncture saw two developments with far-reaching effects on the cultural industries–the federal government's first round of revisions in the *Copyright Act,* passed in 1988, and the signing of the Free Trade Agreement (FTA) in 1989. Both were achieved in the midst of large-scale debate

and political controversy, demonstrating the degree to which the changing political and economic climate had contributed to the growth of major political lobbies of artists and producers throughout the country. While artists were able to win a greater protection of their rights in revisions to the *Copyright Act* (though the same, regrettably, cannot be said for academics), few saw the FTA as a positive development for Canadian culture. Artists and producers, and their trade and professional associations, were among the most vocal opponents of the agreement, which, in their view, would threaten cultural sovereignty because of the decreased economic viability of production within Canada, in conjunction with the diminished political scope for public subsidies and interventions.[13]

There are no conclusive assessments of the impact of the FTA and its successor, NAFTA, on culture. It is evident that the greater emphasis on competition in an "open" continental market helped to shape many of the strategies for government support that have emerged in recent years. It is also clear that the government's heightened interest in the financial efficacy of cultural production did not result in a decline in levels of intervention but rather in a change in the types of intervention being employed. In the following discussion, we will review some developments in the areas of sound recording, filmmaking, and book publishing, and compare the range of effects that such changes have brought about.

The Recorded-Music Industries

One of the distinctive features of the cultural industries, Bernard Miège has suggested, is the extent to which so much of the work upon which they depend takes place prior to intervention and investment by large-scale commercial concerns. The economic rationale of many cultural industries is such that firms operating within them need not normally invest in the training or equipping of the creative personnel whose work they bring to the market.[14] These activities–underwritten, for the most part, by cultural practitioners themselves–will, nevertheless, be perceived as valuable only once they have been subjected to processes that performers themselves are unable to set in motion: those involving the creation of celebrity and conformity to forms and techniques deemed to have value within a particular market.

Major firms within a cultural industry possess a double advantage–for it is essential to their functioning that creative personnel undertake and subsidize their own training, but the results of this training are deemed to be without value in the absence of activities (such as promotion and widespread distribution) that large-scale cultural industries alone appear able to undertake.

Prior to the 1980s, Canadian initiatives in the field of popular music reflected the belief that a significant level of musical activity was, in many ways, a given. While policies directed at the film industry throughout the 1970s privileged the moment of production—out of an often ill-defined conviction that continued activity at this level would eventually leave in its wake an audience for Canadian films—efforts to strengthen the recorded-music industries worked, above all, to build audiences for a Canadian music that was assumed to be already flourishing in a creative (if not commercial) sense.

If the 1970s represent a turning point in the history of Canada's sound-recording industry, this is only partially the result of Canadian-content regulations for radio broadcasters, introduced in 1970. These regulations, which require that a certain percentage of music played on radio stations meet specified criteria so as to be considered "Canadian," are still in effect, despite significant modifications. Their effectiveness in building and maintaining an audience for certain Canadian performers and composers has been widely acknowledged; nevertheless, the decade following their implementation saw a significant restructuring of Canada's recording industry, one in which Canadian-content regulations played a relatively minor role.

The modern history of the domestic recording industry has been shaped by two developments. The first was the growth of a domestic "independent" sector within this industry, consisting of firms that were Canadian-owned and did not possess their own distribution systems. The second was the consolidation, by major multinational firms, of a "branch"-distribution system in Canada, whereby the Canadian subsidiaries of these firms control coast-to-coast distribution of musical recordings in Canada. This development followed trends within the U.S. market during the late 1960s, through which major recording firms moved from using independent distributors to get records into stores and established their own elaborate structures. They were then compelled to purchase or affiliate themselves with smaller record labels to maintain the steady flow of product on which an efficient use of these structures depended.

One striking characteristic of the Canadian recording industry is the extent to which these two developments became intertwined. The growth of an independent, domestically owned recording sector, throughout the 1970s and 1980s, served to strengthen the position of a nationwide distribution network owned by multinational firms. Just as these new independent companies turned to multinational distributors as a means of achieving a national presence within record retail stores, multinational firms themselves regarded Canadian-owned companies as vehicles for extending their product lines. Since 1987, the percentage of new releases in Canada that qualify as Canadian content has remained relatively steady, at roughly 15 percent of the total new titles issued. The percentage of total revenues attributable to Canadian recordings, however, has hovered around 10 percent.

Prior to the 1970s, Canadian-owned recording firms typically evolved out of record pressing or distribution concerns. Throughout the course of that decade, however, they increasingly tended to be based in artist management or other "talent"-oriented activities. Management firms representing one or more artists would form small recording firms for the purpose of producing recordings by these artists. An affiliation agreement with a multinational record company would be sought for the purposes of attaining distribution across the country. If these recordings were successful, the smaller label would expand. It might license recordings or masters from other foreign firms—those passed over by multinational firms operating in Canada—or sign other domestic performers. In either case, the Canadian-based company would make use of its multinational parent for distribution purposes.

Many of the most successful Canadian recording labels to have emerged, such as Attic or Aquarius, grew out of arrangements of this sort. Such firms functioned both as independent labels—in the sense that they seek to market their own acts domestically and abroad, and to license foreign acts for release within Canada—and as custom labels for multinationals, who employ them as a means of being involved in local musical cultures. This latter function has converged with the growing tendency for multinational firms to function primarily as distributors of custom labels, employing them as means of monitoring and profiting from musical activity in distinct geographical or generic sectors.

With their lower costs, small firms could operate profitably within musical genres whose potential

space much larger than that of the traditional record store. Nevertheless, the significant growth in the size of music retail outlets in the 1990s had, by the end of the century, run up against two countervailing tendencies. One of these was the growth in digital means for circulating music. Web-based systems, such as Napster, further complicated and threatened to undermine the traditional music retailing business. At the same time, the growth in the teen and pre-teen market for pop music (best exemplified in the extraordinary success of Britney Spears), suggested that the industry was once again dependent on the success of a limited number of superstar performers. In this context, the investment by retailers in enormous, exhaustive inventories seemed to make less economic sense.

All of these developments, incremental on their own, have altered the music industries in Canada in profound ways. A recording industry dependent on the recycling of back catalogues is one in which countries with long-standing traditions of successful musical recordings are likely to prosper. On the other hand, an industry dependent on a handful of teen idols is unlikely to leave such idols in the hands of domestically owned record companies; rather, they will be signed directly to their U.S. headquarters. Similarly, a retail industry organized around the multi-levelled superstore is one closed to all but the most highly capitalized firms. A&A Records, one of the major Canadian-owned retail chains, declared bankruptcy in March 1993 after it was unable to raise the funds needed to compete with other, superstore-oriented chains such as the British-owned HMV.

These shifts represent the beginning of broader transformations in the ways in which music is made available to listeners and buyers. Digital broadcasting (some Web-born and totally unregulated) and cable-based home-music services, each of which cater to more specialized musical tastes than those currently served by radio broadcasters, have begun to arrive. As people come to choose the narrowly defined musical genres that will enter their homes, the feasibility or acceptability of Canadian-content regulation will almost certainly be called into question. (How, after all, can one enforce a 30 percent Canadian-content quota for formats specializing in opera or swing music of the 1940s?) At the same time, the imminence of these developments pushed the Canadian government to introduce a public performance royalty for musicians and record companies, through which the inclusion of songs on radio play-lists will result in payments to artists and record labels and not

simply to composers. This development, while introduced amidst claims of its benefits to artists, positions multinational rights holders to benefit from the new, technologically mediated ways in which music will be consumed and acquired.

Government policies to nourish a domestic recording industry in the 1970s were directed at radio broadcasting, then considered the principal means for ensuring an audience and market for musical recordings. In the 1980s, the barriers to success that policy sought to remedy were those relating to the expense and skill required for international promotion. In the new century, government policy-makers face the same uncertainties as the music industries overall. What business model will govern the marketing of music? What will be the impact on national markets of distribution systems that are increasingly global in reach and concentrated in ownership?

Film in Canada

In December 1993, after France and other members of the European Economic Community (EEC) refused to capitulate to U.S. pressures, policies designed to protect the European film industry were left intact when a round of negotiations over the General Agreement on Tariffs and Trade (GATT) came to an end. One prominent Canadian film producer expressed disappointment that the Canadian government had "hidden behind the French and let the French fight the battle. We're going to benefit without having fought."[20] Canada's passivity on the subject of film imports came as no surprise; the cinema has long been the Canadian cultural industry in which foreign control has been strongest and the political will to resist, the weakest.

Less obvious, perhaps, were the benefits to Canada of European intransigence. France's 40 percent ceiling on TV programming made outside the European community included a provision treating co-productions of the Canadian and French industries as European content. These co-productions have involved investments worth approximately $100 million (Cdn.) per year–a major source of revenue for Canadian production companies. That Canada should have a stake in a trade dispute between France and the U.S. is revealing of two realities in today's markets for audio-visual products. The first is that the crucial battles to come will have less and less to do with the desire to protect one national culture from another, as the question of access by all producers to international markets moves to centre stage. The second is that the extent of Canada's involvement in co-productions for European TV reveals how little the health of the Canadian film and TV industries may be deduced from the numbers of Canadian feature films winning prizes or garnering significant box-office revenues. In an industry increasingly split between a stratum of international blockbusters produced largely in the U.S., and another level producing thousands of hours of programs destined for home-video and TV services, money by Canadian producers is increasingly accumulated in the thin margins of profitability associated with the latter.

The weakness of the Canadian feature-film industry, and the reasons for that weakness, are among the most well-documented features of Canadian cultural life. Pendakur has traced the long historical process whereby the distribution sector of the film industry in Canada—that which determines where revenues will go—came to be dominated by the distribution arms of Hollywood producers, who achieved levels of industrial integration in Canada outlawed by the Supreme Court in their own country.[21] More recently, investigative reporting made public a secret agreement between the Mulroney government and a trade group representing U.S.-based distributors operating in Canada; in order not to jeopardize ongoing free-trade negotiations, Canada agreed to weaken a Bill that would have limited the activities of U.S. distributors in Canada.[22] As with the sound-recording industry, public policy designed to support the production of films in Canada has moved towards increasingly direct forms of subsidy in the last two decades. In the 1970s, the federal government sought to stimulate film production by extending the Capital Cost Allowance (CCA), a form of tax relief available to investors in a range of industries, to the production of feature films. Between 1978 and 1980, as a result of the CCA, $125 million in indirect federal subsidies went to support the production of privately produced films within Canada.[23] These films, for the most part inexpensive imitations of U.S. productions, were generally box-office failures. In 1981, for a variety of reasons (such as a rise in interest rates and a general overheating of the production industry the previous year), investors withdrew or withheld films from Canadian film production, and banks refused to provide bridge financing to producers.

Arguments over the success of this program—and its larger effects on the structure of a Canadian film industry—continued throughout the 1980s. The application of the CCA to film remains one of the best-known cultural-policy initiatives in recent history. In many respects, the CCA and the films resulting from it nourished the ritual re-enactment of age-old arguments over the purpose of Canadian cultural policy. Should this policy serve primarily to stimulate a distinctly Canadian cinema, or would the latter be the eventual side effect of a profitable, popular Canadian cinema that, even if it began by imitating Hollywood, would lay the foundation for a domestic industrial infrastructure? Was the most appropriate vehicle for exposing Canadian films to a domestic audience the system of film theatres, by now firmly in U.S. hands, or a protected and regulated broadcasting system? Was the "Canadianness" of domestically produced films to be a function of easily observable points of reference (settings, historical events, and so on) or of a more elusive complex of national-cultural characteristics? Is the historical failure of English Canada to develop an economically stable film industry the result of existing political and economic forces (the distribution problem, once again) that might be altered, or is it the inevitable effect of a small population in which profitability is almost impossible?

In no small way the terms in which these questions were posed reflected dilemmas specific to English-Canadian content. French-language audio-visual culture within Canada has long been characterized by a relatively greater two-way flow of production personnel and audiences between popular TV and a cinéma d'auteur. The French-language films of the National Film Board, from the 1950s through the early 1970s, were obviously examples of a fully subsidized and somewhat "official" cinema, but this did not stop them from registering and inspiring shifts of popular consciousness. While the Quebec feature-film industry has, over the last 20 years, partaken of the idioms of an international art cinema, its films draw, at the same time, upon a culture of celebrity and promotion that is noticeably lacking in English Canada.

In the aftermath of the CCA's acknowledged failure, federal policy towards the cinema shifted in important ways during the 1980s. The Canadian Film Development Corporation, created in 1967, was renamed Telefilm Canada in 1983, and this change in name reflected a new emphasis on the production of programming for television. Telefilm Canada's major programs—the Canadian Broadcasting Program Development Fund, introduced in 1983, and the Feature Film Fund, initiated in 1986—were partially a response to economic recession, but they paralleled changes in the structure of film financing throughout the world. The much-ridiculed dentists, whose tax-sheltered investments spurred production during the years of the Capital Cost Allowance, were replaced as sources of funding by a constellation of federal and provincial agencies and the buyers of broadcasting and ancillary rights. To a certain extent, the highly speculative aspect of film production has declined with this shift, as pre-sales to a series of "windows" (theatrical release, pay TV, videocassette markets, and broadcast TV) increase the percentage of budgets guaranteed from the outset.

While intermittent calls for a unified film policy that would co-ordinate the activities of the CBC, NFB, and other government agencies have gone unheeded, all these actors are now free to participate as partners in individual ventures. In the early 1990s, two developments long urged by the independent film-production sector in Canada became realities. In the first, the CBC began to broadcast independent Canadian feature films on a regular basis, finding an audience for works that, while winning prizes around the world, had been notably absent from Canadian television screens. In a more gradual and imperceptible development, the NFB has emerged as a significant supplier of services and programs for independent, often very marginal, sorts of filmmaking, overcoming an isolationism that many saw as symptomatic of a crisis of institutional purpose.

In the 1990s, the successful producers of audiovisual programming in Canada are those companies, such as Alliance-Atlantis, that have deliberately withdrawn from the lottery of producing large-budget films for theatrical release.[24] The emergence of an international market for television co-productions and the co-existence of several public-funding agencies has increased the stability of funding, but they have required that greater energies be spent in pre-production phases of filmmaking. In 1988, Micheline Lanctôt and others involved in the Québécois industry regretted the uniformity of vision now enforced by a seemingly endless series of reader reports and co-production committees, as a particular treatment or proposal went from one funding source to another.[25]

In a broader sense, the film and TV-program industries in Canada at present stand as evidence of a new international division of labour and of the emergence of distinctive new global markets. If Canada is now a world leader in the production of animated TV programs, this may be taken as proof of our ability to build upon past and glorious traditions, such as that of Norman MacLaren and the NFB. Nevertheless, as animation studios based in Ottawa or Vancouver send preliminary drawings to Korea or elsewhere for the labour-intensive copying and detail work on which the animation industry depends, we are dealing with an industry as rationalized and placeless as that which produces computer or automobile parts. Similarly, the markets for children's TV programming, in which Canadian producers have a significant presence, are ones in which budgets and wages have been driven downward by competition and audience fragmentation. As more and more Hollywood films are shot in Canada, the last few years have witnessed a decline in the number of independent, "artistic" features made here.

Film and television policy in Canada has long been based on an implicit double agenda. There has been a persistent conviction that policies intended to stimulate a domestic industry must be temporary and contingent, preparatory to that day when Canadian films and TV programs will have won over their domestic audience and subsidies will no longer be required. The Capital Cost Allowance of the 1970s was the most obvious of initiatives intended to be short-lived, but its eventual failure strengthened an opposing argument: that the production industry in Canada required permanent, stable, and public-sponsored forms of funding.

The tension between a narrative of eventual triumph—in which Canadians, now accustomed to seeing their collective experience represented in their films and TV programs, will happily support a domestic industry—and the realistic recognition that domestic production will perennially require some combination of private and public monies remains at the heart of debates over a Canadian film policy. In some cases, Canadian film policy is defended in the name of a "trickle up" scenario, in which investments in Canadian TV or popular-film genres will provide the infrastructure for a more serious and distinctly Canadian cinema. From other quarters, a process of "trickle down" is envisioned: a cinéma d'auteur will create the international audience for Canadian films upon which an appeal to the elusive, domestic general public and stable market support will be based.

Publishing

Perhaps because Canadian writers have achieved so much success nationally and abroad, the book-

publishing sector has been relatively successful at
bringing its problems into the public eye. The artistic
achievements of writers may not have ensured
greater economic success for Canadian publishers,
but the financial problems, foreign acquisitions, and
government bail-outs of Canadian book publishers
have received exceptional levels of public attention.
The "Don't Tax Reading" coalition, formed in 1987,
succeeded in publicizing the new GST as the most invidious attack on culture under the Conservative regime, taking their cause to the Senate as well as to the
national press. Perhaps ironically, two years earlier
the 1985 "Baie Comeau" policy on foreign acquisitions of book publishers, in response to pressures
from Canadian publishers and the reading public,
helped position the government as being committed
to the country's cultural identity while it pursued free
trade. "Arguably," suggests one commentator, "without it [or some equivalent] the forces arraigned
against free trade might have been victorious."[26]
Whether because of the link between education and
reading, because the print media is especially attuned to problems of writers and publishers, because
of the nationalism of prominent Canadian writers, or
because "culture" seems to cling more visibly to a
capital "C" in the older world of publishing, this ability to mobilize widespread public concern about
government management of a cultural industry has
been unique to Canadian publishers. In book publishing, patterns of foreign and Canadian ownership
are much the same as in sound recording: a 1983
DOC study of book publishing found that 84 percent
of the responding companies were owned by Canadians, but that these accounted for less than 25 percent of the domestic market.[27] Today, Canadian-owned firms produce nearly 90 percent of
Canadian books; studies suggest that through the
1990s Canadian authors increased their share of both
leisure reading and trade book publishing.[28] Most
books sold in Canada are manufactured from imported titles or imported directly from abroad. (The
percentage of books imported is predictably higher
in the English than in the French market. Canada
seems to have a strong book-export record, but if you
exclude Harlequin Books, a Toronto publisher of romance in 12 languages (which many studies do, since
the company is so uncharacteristically large: it accounts for 90 percent of book exports), the picture is
quite different.

Does this extensive sale of imported books within
the country support or supplant the publication of
Canadian books? This depends largely on the
structure of financing and distribution within the
domestic industry. To strengthen this structure,
contemporary policies include the Book Publishing
Development Program (BPDP), established in 1979,
and the Baie Comeau policy, an anti-foreign-
investment book-publishing policy announced by
then Minister of Communications Marcel Masse in
1985.

The BPDP's mandate was "to ensure the development of Canadian-authored titles through the medium of a strong, profitable Canadian-controlled
publishing industry."[29] The program, administered
by the DOC after 1980, emphasized subsidies based
on past sales. Publishers responded positively to the
prospect that government subsidy would strengthen
the business end of Canadian publishing, although
some argued that the program's emphasis on commercial viability and success could endanger the het-
erogeneity of the book-publishing industry by reinforcing the economic status and size of large
companies. Not surprisingly, larger companies, according to the DOC, supported the program's emphasis on rewarding "success."[30] But smaller companies found that the program's emphasis on financial
stability counteracted the program's own stated
goals, since it is precisely the smaller, more risk-
oriented companies that publish the largest number
of original titles.

Later, seeking to counteract growing industry concentration, the DOC was careful to emphasize the diversity of size, type, and region in book publishers eligible for BPDP support. The BPDP was renewed
and expanded in 1986, and, as the renamed Book
Publishing Industry Development Program
(BPIDP), was able to draw on funds from both the
DOC and the Canada Council to support Canadian-controlled book publishers. Offering both grant
funds (for culturally worthy books) and project grants
(to entice companies into profitable market sectors
like educational publishing), the BPIDP was rede-
signed to help publishers expand operations rather
than use funds to cover existing deficits.[31] Its purpose
was to improve the financial viability of publishers as
they attempted to "adjust," as Masse stated in 1986,
"to the program's orientation towards industrial development, as distinct from cultural support."[32] A
1983 report on book publishing had emphasized the
"blockages" in distribution and promotion that prevent books from reaching consumers in both domestic and export markets.[33] The BPIDP therefore
placed a greater emphasis on sales and marketing. It
succeeded in strengthening the economic position of

some publishers, but again raised concern among others that success was being measured and rewarded in purely industrial or marketing terms. This strategy was, however, defended by the Canadian Book Publishers Council, which argued (as some in the film industry have done) that indigenous publishing depends on a strong economic infrastructure.[34]

The BPIDP adopted a project-based granting formula to correct the failings of its predecessor, the BPDP, such as perceived grant dependency and the perceived failings of publishers to account for how the money was spent. In 1993, after another DOC review, the program was again replaced; the new program was re-titled the BPDP. This newest industrial-support program does away with the project-based granting formula and eliminates the long-term Postal Subsidy for publishers (122 years old at the time of its death), neither of which, they claimed, had managed to counter the problems of marketing Canadian books. The postal-rate subsidy had lowered the cost of book distribution for Canadian and foreign distributors equally, they argued; the government promised to replace it with special funds targeting the distribution of Canadian materials. So far, such funds have not caught up with the subsidies. Since the demise of the postal rates subsidy, a number of Canadian journals and periodicals have folded, citing loss of the postal subsidy as immediate cause. Perrin Beatty, final Minister of Communications with the Conservative government, explained that the postal subsidy and the Baie Comeau policy of reviewing foreign acquisitions, both of which he had decided to abandon, were "unfair"—almost certainly a response to pressures from U.S. publishers subsequent to the signing of the Free Trade Agreement. Beatty reportedly vetted the proposed policy changes with American publishers before proceeding.[35]

The Baie Comeau policy was an article on foreign purchase in book publishing attached to the Investment Canada Act, which the Conservatives had passed to replace the Foreign Investment Review Agency. The Baie Comeau policy required foreign companies that acquired Canadian assets in the publishing industry to sell at least 51 percent control to Canadians within two years of acquisition. Direct purchases of Canadian publishers could not be approved through normal procedures within Investment Canada. Thus, Baie Comeau permitted government to define the book trade as "culture" rather than as "commerce." Subsequently, the policy was enshrined in the Free Trade Agreement as Article

1607, in direct opposition to other articles of the FTA that define cultural industries as businesses first (we return to this point in our conclusion.)

The Baie Comeau policy produced a number of conflicts with American publishers, lobbyists, and members of congress. The most prominent conflict occurred with Gulf + Western, which threatened a "scorched earth" policy if forced to divest itself of all its Canadian acquisitions.[36] In May 1989, Masse and McDermid (Minister of Privatization) announced that the government had signed an agreement with Gulf + Western to purchase 51 percent of Ginn & Co. (Canada) and GLC publishers. As with opposition to Canadian-film distribution policy mounted by the U.S. chairman of the Motion Pictures Export Association, Jack Valenti, the Baie Comeau policy demonstrated "the capacity of U.S. stakeholders to command the involvement of elected officials in cultural policy issues; that those officials are prepared to protest to the highest level of the Canadian government; and that the Canadian government was receiving protests on more than one cultural policy issue as it was trying to negotiate a FTA with the U.S. and sustain sufficient domestic support for that project."[37]

As communications minister responsible for abandoning Baie Comeau, Beatty emphasized its limited effectiveness since "the technical definition of Canadian control can be met without real control resting with Canadians."[38] The policy had also been criticized for increasing the market price of American holdings while depressing the value of domestic companies prohibited from seeking foreign purchasers. Beatty promised stronger limitations on new foreign investments in, and indirect acquisitions of, publishing companies. Canadian companies can now be purchased by foreign companies providing owners can prove "clear financial distress," but foreign owners face stronger requirements to support the development of Canadian authors, book distribution, and publishing education.[39] Between 1987 and 1992, the market share of foreign-owned firms declined. But, as publishing researcher Roland Lorimer observes, the change was as much to do with who was importing (increasingly, agency-controlled firms) as with how much was imported. Book exports also increased significantly in the same period, assisted by publishers and government through the Association for the Export of Canadian Books. But 90 percent of books written by Canadian authors are sold within Canada, and their publication continues to require subsidies; today "the industry is overall, marginally profitable but only after grants."[40] Critics were not convinced that abandoning Baie Comeau was the right solution, however, even with the increased grants Beatty promised in its place. As columnist Rick Salutin explained, it "left basic economic structure to the mercies of the marketplace."[41] Canadian publishers rely on a retail sector that is dominated by chain stores, notably Chapters, Rénaud-Bray, and Indigo, with the former, alone, responsible for more than $500 million in sales per annum. Despite the apparently greater inventories of the new superstores, their competitive advantage is derived just as much from the discounted prices that they apply to new blockbuster titles. The strategies that have allowed the new chains to dominate their markets—an insistence on the right to return unlimited numbers of books to publishers for refunds, for example, and heavy investments in e-commerce—have rendered the Canadian publishing industry fragile even as it seems to be under the control of a small number of powerful players.

Conclusion

Books, journals, and newspapers in Canada are affected by the same legislative and economic changes that define globalization everywhere. The increased influence of the doctrine and practice of "free flow" in information, the growth of a transnational, technical infrastructure to enable low-cost local production, increased vertical and horizontal integration among global industries, the removal of trade barriers between countries, and the rise of financing through advertising, marketing, and corporate support, along with the decline of financing through state subsidy—all of these combined have helped to change the shape of cultural production around the world. The situation in Canada is no exception.

Current developments in copyright legislation are one area where such influences are apparent. In Canada, changes in copyright law appear to strengthen the rights of authors, but they also strengthen the rights of publishers over authors and users and facilitate the general transfer of funds from the public to the private sector. Technological advances, however, work against the integrity of copyright as an enforceable property right. This can be seen in increased limitations on "fair use" in educational contexts, which force educators to pay fees for classroom use of copyrighted materials, but at the same time, the increasingly widespread flouting of these principles by individuals, especially on

the Internet. As researchers observed in a recent study,

recent trends in copyright legislation have been aimed at strengthening the potential benefits to creators. In fact, such changes have been more effective in strengthening the monopoly position of the publisher as the effective exploiter of intellectual property. This strengthened monopoly position encourages producing nations to seek to bolster their already dominant position and ensure that it is not undermined by international behaviour of other nations.[42]

What is often framed as an international effort to acknowledge the rights of intellectual-property holders is recognizably rooted in the need to overcome national particularities in copyright and related fields so as to standardize the international flow of cultural products and revenues. It is grounded, as well, in the shift of many cultural industries from manufacturers of concrete objects to marketers of rights and back catalogues. This trend has led to considerable conflict between national and transnational publishers over the control of markets and territories. The conflict between Canada and the U.S. over the Baie Comeau policy on foreign acquisitions was one instance of this emergent global pattern.

The tension between national and international publishers has also produced a number of policy compromises, such as the Book Industry Support Program devised by the Canadian government. This program has helped to strengthen the market position of major companies preparing to enter the global market, but it has not significantly strengthened the publication of Canadian books for Canadian readers. The decline of small, independent publishers, who produce the vast majority of such books, has been one direct effect of the Canadian government's emphasis on industrial policy in the name of cultural sovereignty.[43]

As the Liberal government, first elected in 1993, continues to assess its policies and priorities, many controversial and important issues confront the Minister of Heritage. Specific policies aimed at the cultural industries will undoubtedly continue to be affected by two major trends influencing cultural industries in Canada and, indeed, globally.

One is the trend towards global ownership and marketing, and the related tendency for national protectionist policies to give way to a more open market economy. The accompanying claim that Canadian-based cultural producers must now compete in an international marketplace occludes the extent to which that marketplace is less and less "open" in any real sense. Attic Records of Canada, which has for many years bought the Canadian rights to market foreign record company back catalogues and music-publishing inventories in Canada, now finds these rights increasingly controlled on an international basis by multinational firms.[44]

One result of these shifts, as we have seen in discussing the publishing industry, is the erosion of the distinction between "culture" and "commodity," which has traditionally held important political, legislative, and cultural implications for Canadians. This was evident in the sections of the FTA pertaining to culture, which entitle the U.S. to counter cultural subsidies with commercial sanctions of equal value. In other words, the U.S. may choose to evaluate the commercial value of policies that directly or indirectly subsidize the production of films, records, or books, and retaliate by imposing commercial sanctions of equal value on, for example, lumber or car parts. This clause does not directly prohibit cultural subsidies, but it discourages them by making it possible and legal for such subsidies to be opposed by U.S. lobbyists and politicians. More fundamentally, it radically alters the status of culture as a special domain not entirely circumscribed by the marketplace, one in which governments had been previously entitled to intervene legislatively in the name of national sovereignty.[45]

The other trend shaping public policies is the collapse of traditional distinctions between different sectors of cultural production (broadcasting, cable, telecommunications, information, and the classic "culture industries") brought about by the expansion and integration of new technologies in the communications and information spheres. In this respect, the Conservative government's final restructuring of government departments, in 1993, stands as an interesting clue to new attitudes concerning the relations between industrial and cultural policy. While the joining together of culture and communications (or "hardware" and "software") in the newly formed Department of Communications in 1980 signalled a new emphasis on the cultural industries as a motor and site of economic development, the movement of "hardware" questions out of the DOC (now renamed the Department of Heritage) in 1993 could be taken to signal the return of cultural questions to a circumscribed administrative ghetto.

The rhetoric that currently surrounds promised or emergent new media services (such as on-line music-delivery and television systems) is founded on two premises: that these services are inevitable, the result of forces (such as industrial convergence and technical digitization) beyond national control, and that they are propelled by consumer demand. Leaving aside doubts one might have concerning either of these premises taken alone, it is clear that they are in significant ways contradictory. As the presumed engines of technological development, each is conveniently anonymous, and those who claim to speak in their name resist challenge. It is typical of Canadians to decry the perpetual re-emergence of long-standing debates over national identity and purpose. As we write this, however, dozens of digital specialty-TV services, radical changes in the nature of radio broadcasting, and new alliances between telephone companies, television networks, sports promoters, and cable concerns are all being considered in the absence of noticeable public debate or concern.

It is the silent, apparently inevitable quality of these changes, rather than the possible effects attributable to any one of them, that is most disconcerting.

Notes

1. Harvey Enchin, "Livent plays lead in stage revival," *The Globe and Mail* (16 October 1993), p.B1.

2. Francis Fox, Minister of Communications, *Culture and Communications: Key Elements of Canada's Economic Future*, a brief to the Royal Commission on the Economic Union and Economic Development Prospects for Canada, 1983, p.13; Department of Communications, *Canadian Cultural Industries* (Ottawa: Supply and Services, 1985), p.1; John Meisel, "Flora and Fauna on the Rideau: The Making of Cultural Policy," Katherine A. Graham, ed., *How Ottawa Spends: 1988–89: The Conservatives Heading into the Stretch* (Ottawa: Carleton University, 1988), p.50.

3. Canada, Department of Communications, 1987–1988 Preliminary Statistics.

4. Paul Audley, *Canada's Cultural Industries: Broadcasting, Publishing, Records and Film* (Toronto: James Lorimer, 1983), p.xxviii.

5. Meisel, "Flora and Fauna," p.55.

6. Fox, *Culture and Communications*, pp.1–2.

7. Audley, *Canada's Cultural Industries*, p.123.

8. Ibid., p.320.

9. Department of Communications, *Vital Links-Canadian Cultural Industries* (Ottawa: Department of Communications, 1987), p.17.

10. D. Paul Schafer and André Fortier, *Review of Federal Policies for the Arts in Canada (1944–1948)*, prepared for the DOC (Ottawa: Canadian Conference for the Arts, 1989), pp.46, 56.

11. Department of Communications, *An Overview of the Cultural Initiatives Program 1980–1985* (Ottawa: DOC, Government of Canada, 1985). Also see Meisel, "Flora and Fauna," p.58.

12. Liss Jeffrey, "Private Televisions and Cable" in Michael Donland, ed. *The Cultural Industries in Canada: Problems, Policies and Prospects* (Toronto: James Lorimer & Co., 1996), pp.250-51.

13. "Free Trade and Culture: Who Cares?" *Arts Bulletin* 11, no. 1 (Fall 1986), Special Edition, Canadian Conference of the Arts; John Hutcheson, "The Thief of Arts: Will Free Trade Rob Us of Our Culture?" *Canadian Forum* (February 1987): 9–18; Vincent Mosco, "Towards a Transnational World Information Order: The Canada–U.S. Free Trade Agreement," *Canadian Journal of Communications* 15, no. 2 (1990): 46–63; Lanie Patrick, "Global Economy, Global Communication: The Canada–U.S. Free Trade Agreement," Mark Raboy and Peter Bruck, eds., *Communication For and Against Democracy* (Montreal: Black Rose Books, 1989).

14. Bernard Miège, *The Capitalization of Cultural Production*, trans. Nicholas Garnham (New York: International General, 1989), p.23.

15. Karyna Laroche and Will Straw, "Radio and Sound Recording Policy in Canada," *Australian–Canadian Studies* 7, nos. 1–2 (1989): 164.

16. Larry Leblanc, "Many Canadian Acts Still Outside the Int'l Spotlight," *Billboard* (23 March 1991), p.72.

17. Larry LeBlanc, "Attic Records Tops Canada Indies: Keeps Competitive with Changing Focus," *Billboard* (31 July 1993), p.40.

18. Brendan Kelly, "Alternative rockers thrive thanks to free trade, GST," *MTL* (April 1991), pp.40–41.

19. Larry Leblanc, "MCA Taking Stock in Cargo Records: Distrib/One-Stop Gets Boost in Alternative Camp," *Billboard* (26 June 1993), p.54.

20. "Canadian film sector pleased with GATT," *The Globe and Mail* (16 December 1993), p.B8.

21. Manjunath Pendakur, *Canadian Dreams & American Control: The Political Economy of the Canadian Film Industry* (Toronto: Garamond Press, 1990); see also Mike Gasher, "Le vrai chef-d'oeuvre d'Hollywood," *Le Devoir* (11–12 December 1993), p.A11.

22. See Stephen Godfrey, "Film rights: How Ottawa bowed to pressure," *The Globe and Mail* (28 March 1992), p.A1.

23. Federal Cultural Policy Review Committee, *Summary of Briefs and Hearings* (Ottawa: Supply and Services, 1982), p.197.

24. See, for example, Murray Campbell, "To live and learn in L.A.," *The Globe and Mail* (16 January 1992), p.A8.

25. "Lendemains d'euphorie/Cinéma québécois: table ronde," *24 Images* 37 (1988): 12– 23.

26. Roy Norton, *Canada's Nationalistic Book Publishing Policy: A Review of Stakeholders' Criticisms, 1985–1990* (Cambridge, Mass.: Center for Information Policy Research, Harvard University, 1991), p.3.

27. Roland Lorimer, "Book Publishing" in Michael Donland, ed. *The Cultural Industries in Canada: Problems, Policies and Prospects* (Toronto: James Lorimer & Co., 1996), pp.10-11, 14.

28. CPER Management Consulting Inc., *Profile of the Book Publishing Industry in Canada* (Ottawa, 1983), pp.ii–iii.

29. Depoartment Of Communications, *Vital Links*, p.28.

30. Rowland Lorimer, "Book Publishing in English Canada in the Context of Free Trade," *Canadian Journal of Communication* 16 (1991): 58–72.

31. "Communications Probes Future of BPIDP," *Quill & Quire* (January 1990), p.10.

32. CPER, *Profile*, p.46.

33. "Communications Probes Future," *Quill & Quire.*

34. John Lorinc, "Nothing for Granted: 'Good old days are gone' as federal publishing policy tilts towards bottom line," *Quill & Quire*, (December 1992), 1/10; Rick Salutin, "$102 million for publishers? Well, whoopee," *The Globe and Mail* (14 February 1992), p.C1, column: Ted Mumford, "Proof's in Pudding," *Quill & Quire* (March 1992), p.6.

35. Lorimer, "Book Publishing in English Canada," p.67.

36. Norton, *Canada's Nationalistic Book Publishing Policy*, p.20.

37. Mumford, "Proof's in Pudding," p.6.

38. Ibid.

39. Salutin, "$102 million for publishers?"

40. Roland Lorimer, "Book Publishing" in Michael Donland, ed., *The Cultural Industries in Canada: Problems, Policies and Prospects* (Toronto: James Lorimer & Co., 1996), pp.10-11, 14.

41. Rowland Lorimer and Eleanor O'Donnell, "Globalization and Internationalization in Publishing," *Canadian Journal of Communication* 17, no. 4 (Autumn 1992): 501.

42. See ibid. for a longer discussion of this.

43. Leblanc, "Attic Records Tops Canada Indies."

44. Jody Berland, "Free Trade and Canadian Music: Level Playing Field or Scorched Earth?" *Cultural Studies* 5, no. 3 (October 1991): 317–25.

45. See, for example, the Green Paper *New Media, New Choices* (Ottawa: Department of Communications, 1993).

PART 5

SOCIAL PROBLEMS AND THE MEDIA

The mass media have long been blamed for social problems. The tradition of blame goes back to Plato's time, when the great Greek philosopher warned of the harm that would come from young people's exposure to the works of poets.

Each time a new medium emerges, there is fear that it will have undue influence on society (or will be inordinately influenced by powerful groups). Hence, the famous Payne studies of films in the U.S. in the late 1920s, the investigation of comic books in the 1940s, of TV in the 1960s in the U.S., and in Canada in the 1970s, and the renewed emphasis concerning the effects of TV in 1993 and 1994. The latter concern has been translated into new codes on TV violence announced by the Canadian Radio-television and Telecommunications Commission (CRTC) in 1993 to deal with the problem of "gratuitous" violence on Canadian TV screens.

The authors in this section have chosen to examine controversies in four different domains in which mass media have been the subject of scrutiny. The apprehension over violence continues to be the foremost issue, but concern over pornography has been mounting in recent years. During the past decade, Canadians have also become particularly aware of complaints from members of visible-minority groups over their treatment by the media, and there have been increasing questions about the use of public-relations activities by powerful groups to influence Canadian media.

Eugene D. Tate and Kathleen McConnell have reviewed the debate over the connection between mass media violence and real-life violence, tracing some of the theories and research back to Aristotle. They provide a critical analysis of the literature on the media and violence, reviewing, particularly, four prominent theoretical perspectives.

One of the dominant theories is the classical mass society notion that suggests a linear model of effects (sometimes called the "magic bullet theory"). It in turn has spawned three mini-theories—the "devil theory," the "cultivation theory," and the "mean world theory"—which the authors describe and assess. A

second theoretical perspective, mostly the work of social psychologists, is based on audience differences and media reinforcement, in which cue-and-reinforcement theories and learning theories predominate. A third perspective is the "limited effects" model, which includes as factors such sociological determinants of behaviour and socialization as family, peer, and friendship groups, and which views the media as reinforcing their influence. The fourth perspective is that of the "active audience"–an antidote to the classical mass theory.

The authors are dissatisfied with the explanatory power of these perspectives, mainly because they implicitly employ reductionism to explain potential media effects: they are limited to one or two strong but general independent variables, ignoring the complexity of individual developmental determinants or facilitators and of social context, a point made as well by media theorist Thelma McCormack.[1] Tate and McConnell argue for a holistic, multidimensional approach geared to the concept of the "social person" as an alternative to the numerous one-factor theories.

Controversy over the effects of pornography and violent erotic literature has led to varied research and many court cases. As well, investigators have conducted research to assess the role of pornography and aggressive sexual depictions in arousing hostile sexual behaviour in males towards females,[2] some of which has suggested that pornography is a causal factor in violence towards women.

However, sociologist Augustine Brannigan disagrees with bland assertions of causation. He examines the recent history of protest against the growth of pornography, and the rationales of key court decisions, and takes a position consistent with that of feminist scholar Thelma McCormack who wrote: "The old hardcore pornography is becoming middlebrow kitsch ... pornography has ceased to be a dangerous influence on behaviour, but has instead become a form of entertainment, a diversion that does not require any grandiose explanation."[3] He would agree with the words of Alan Borovoy, head of the Canadian Civil Liberties Association, in defending the right of artists to depict unwholesome sexual activities without fear of criminal prosecution: "Art cannot be confined to the portrayal of virtue."[4]

Of course, other voices contradict the civil-libertarian view. As one critic said, the "shock artists" who use pornography to arouse extreme reactions believe "that if something is shockingly degrading and dehumanizing, it is, perforce, art." An ironic and perhaps inevitable outcome is censorship and repression.[5]

Brannigan parallels the current concern over pornography in Canada with past actions taken against comics and even such "objectionable literature" as the Hardy Boys novels. He points out that two models have been the basis of public inquiries–the political/moralistic versus the rational/scientific, one based on public opinion and popular morality, the other on the scientific measurement of effects--and draws out the implications of their application.

The mass media have great power to define the identities of social groups, for their own members as well as for outsiders, as Augie Fleras points out. From this power, two problems emerge for minority-group members, particularly "visible minorities." The first is their visibility (or invisibility), and the second is the manner in which they have been portrayed. For many years Canadian media have substantially underrepresented and misrepresented visible-minority groups in TV programs and in advertising, as Fleras asserts, in his discussion of television.

The press and TV news with their power to select and position the news, as well as to control the way in which content is presented, have also been subjects of great concern by members of minority groups. News coverage tends to emphasize minority-group members as social problems, as violent, sometimes identifying criminals by race or ethnic origin, and as objects of ridicule.

Fleras draws our attention to the mechanisms by which some of these injustices to minorities arise. While he identifies a number of causes, a powerful underlying mechanism, "systemic discrimination," may be generated in part by media concern with audience size and advertising revenues. Fleras surveys a number of proposed solutions to such problems, and hopes that the media will work towards a "post-multicultural" position through greater consciousness of their treatment of minority-group members.[6]

Notes

[1] Thelma McCormack, "Codes, Ratings and Rights," *Institute for Social Research Newsletter* (Winter 1994): 4.

[2] See, for example, Evelyn K. Sommers and James V. Check, "An Empirical Investigation of the Role of Pornography in the Verbal and Physical Abuse of Women," *Violence and Victims* 2, no. 3 (Fall 1987): 189-209; Neil M. Malamuth and James V. Check, "The Effects of Aggressive Pornography on Beliefs in Rape Myths: Individual Differences," *Journal of Research in Personality* 19, no. 3 (September 1985): 299-320; Gordon E. Barnes, Neil M. Malamuth, and James V. Check, "Psychoticism and Sexual Arousal to Rape Depictions," *Personality and Individual Differences* 5, no. 3 (1984): 273-79.

[3] Thelma McCormack, "Censorship and 'Community Standards' in Canada," Benjamin D. Singer, ed., *Communications in Canadian Society*, 2nd ed. (Don Mills, Ont.: Addison-Wesley, 1983), p.216.

[4] Farhan Memom, "Boyd urged to drop child-porn charges," *The Globe and Mail* (10 January 1994), p.A8.

[5] Martha Bayles, "The Shock-Art Fallacy," *The Atlantic* (February 1994) p.20.

[6] However, not everybody agrees that state policy should continue to promote what is called multiculturalism. The noted journalist Robert Fulford (whose passionate criticism of racism is cited by Fleras) also believes excesses in the name of multiculturalism have generated serious new problems in recent years: "Instead of dissolving racism, multicultural policies emphasize and harden it." See Robert Fulford, "Down the garden path of multiculturalism," *The Globe and Mail* (9 June 1994), p.C1.

19

The Mass Media and Violence

Eugene D. Tate and Kathleen McConnell

Two boys, aged 11 and 13, dressed in camouflage clothes, hide in a wood three hundred feet from a school. The fire alarm of the school rings and children file in an orderly manner out onto the playground. As the classes gather at their assigned places on the playground, the boys quietly wait, guns in hand. After the building is completely evacuated, an automatic locking system seals all entrances to the school. Only then do the boys open fire, killing four girls and one teacher while wounding eleven other children.

This is the third playground attack in the United States in six months. The Governor of Arkansas, where the attack occurred, immediately focusses on the role of television in de-sensitizing "our society into a state of callousness and disregard." Others in authority blame the Hollywood violence industry and video games. The video game *Red Neck Revenge* is especially popular in Arkansas as it features a Southern man who scores points by running down people with his pick-up truck or randomly shooting people with a shotgun. Some people blame a culture that celebrates guns and violence. "After all," they say, "they gave the younger boy an air rifle before he could even read or write."[1]

If you think this only happens in the United States, consider these incidents:

- In England two boys kidnap a younger boy from a shopping mall and murder him, copying an act they are supposed to have seen on television.[2]

- In November 1997, a 14-year-old girl is beaten and drowned by teenagers in Victoria, B.C.

- In February 1998, six youths attack a 17-year-old in Sault Ste. Marie, Ontario, with a hatchet. The victim requires twenty hours of surgery to re-attach his arm, fingers, and ear.

- A 14-year-old stabs two Winnipeg girls.

- A 13-year old girl is found guilty in London, Ontario, of attempted murder after stabbing a 9-year-old boy on a school playground.

- A schoolyard scuffle in Toronto turns violent when the 17-year-old brother of one of the four 11-year-old assailants of another 11-year-old Russian boy joins in the fight. The 17-year-old grabs a hockey stick and beats the immigrant boy into a coma near death. The Russian boy is a recent immigrant who has only been in Canada for about a year.[3]

Violence among children and teenagers is a serious problem in North America. We may wish to argue that it is not as serious in Canada as in the United States but the argument fails in light of the facts. It is true that in Canada only 30 percent of homicides involve guns while in the United States 70 to 80 percent of murders involve guns. Canadians pride themselves on not having a gun culture in comparison to United States. Yet, when the federal government passes a gun registration law hundreds of Canadians refuse to obey the new law. Arguments given are the same arguments given in the United States against gun registration.

Playground violence is a very real problem in Canada as in the United States. Is the Governor of Arkansas correct that this brutality is related to media violence? How much of the aggression in Canadian society can be attributed to violent media content? Consider the following scenario.

Imagine for a moment that you are a jury member in the trial of a teenager accused of murdering his elderly next door neighbour.[4] The prosecution has shown that the teenager and a friend broke into the neighbour's home looking for money. When she returned home and surprised them, the defendant shot her with her own gun. She died before the police could get her to a hospital. The teenager was arrested and admitted shooting his neighbour because she got in his way while he was robbing her house.

The defence attorney is presenting the argument that the teenager did not know right from wrong because he had watched too much television. The attorney argues that the defendant lives in the world of *Kojak*, *Hunter*, and *Police Story*–the world of the TV crime drama. Thus, he saw nothing wrong with shooting his neighbour because this is what he saw people do on TV.

The courtroom drama unfolds as the defence attorney sets the stage by suggesting the defendant was a lonely, rejected child. First his father and later his stepfather rejected the boy. The crux of the defence attorney's argument centres on negative rejection from his mother, who would say to him, "Barry, we never wanted you. We found you in a garbage dumpster. Now don't bother us and go watch television." The family had moved to your city a little over a year ago, and students at the school had rejected Barry.

Driven into the world of TV after being rejected in the real world, the defence attorney continues, Barry came to believe that what he saw on television comprised reality. Therefore, he saw nothing wrong with shooting someone because this was a common occurrence on TV.

The defence attorney admits that Barry shot and killed his neighbour. The defence does not contest this aspect of the case, but nevertheless argues that Barry was not guilty because of his addiction to TV and his attempt to live within the world he experienced vicariously through this medium.

Barry is a TV junkie and not responsible for his own acts, argues the attorney. The violent content of TV crime shows caused the teenager to act in this manner. The defense implores you to find Barry not guilty because of his TV addiction. As a juror in this case, how would you vote? What is the relationship, if any, between media violence and aggressive, abusive behaviour in society?

Historical Perspectives on the Problem

The relationship between the media and violence has been an issue since the beginning of what can be characterized as modern society. The question of the precise nature of this relationship has been raised to major importance with the communications revolution[5] and the rapid increase in the development of technology for mass communication.[6] The introduction of each new technology evokes questions about its effect on individuals and society. With each advancement, concern has been expressed about the deterioration of lifestyles, the de-personalization of everyday relationships, the increase of violence in society, and the decline of morals among the populace.

The invention of the printing press and the subsequent rise of newspapers, books, pamphlets, broadsides, the Penny Press, and finally paperback books caused societal pressures for censorship, the introduction of codes of journalistic ethics, libel laws, and licensing laws. Self-declared guardians of public purity prepared lists of banned books based on religious or moral grounds.[7]

The introduction of radio gave rise to new licensing laws and the creation of governing boards, such as the Bureau of Broadcast Governors and later the Canadian Radio-television and Telecommunications Commission (CRTC), to control the use of the airwaves.[8] Concerns about the anti-social effects of radio were mixed with similar ones that motion pictures were creating a generation of juvenile delinquents.[9]

After the controversies of the mid-1940s and early 1950s about a causal relationship between crime comics and children turning to a life of crime, the introduction of the Comic Book Code led to the demise of several popular comic book titles. This controversy reappeared in the 1990s with the introduction of a series of urban comics.

Since 1990, there have been a number of new comic books written specifically for urban blacks with superheroes such as *Brotherman*. In 1993, the creation of the comic *Flatbush Native* introduced the inner-city realist who witnesses violence but does not react to it, but who, if forced, reacts in an extremely violent manner. The editor of Flatline Comics, producers of *Flatbush Native*, denies that they seek to glorify violence. Instead, he argues, they are trying to present a realistic portrayal of inner-city life. "We're not trying to glorify violence, but at the same time we're not trying to sugarcoat reality. If there's violence it's in relation to what's going on in the story." Critics of the comic book argue that it simply reinforces stereotypical portrayals of African-Americans as violent people.[10]

Interestingly the debate over motion pictures has resurfaced in the latter part of this decade. Since 1992 there has been an increase in the publication of books with titles like *Screen Violence; Laughing Screaming: Modern Hollywood Horror and Comedy; Down and Dirty: Hollywood's Exploitation Filmmakers and Their Movies; Shocking Entertainment: Viewer Response to Violent Media*. With the increase of violence in major Hollywood films, the issue of the relationship between delinquency and cinematic presentations of brutally realistic violence has again become the focus of researchers in mass communication and cultural studies.[11]

The rapid development of television culminated in a vast debate over its effects on children, especially the relationship between violent content and aggressive behaviour in children and youth. The Surgeon General's report in the U.S. stated the conclusions of a blue ribbon panel of broadcasters, mass media scholars, and critics concerning the relationship between violent TV content and effects on viewers. George Comstock, an adviser to the Surgeon General's Advisory Committee, summarized their conclusions:

> The Surgeon General's advisory committee, despite the sizable representation associated with broadcasting, concluded in its report *Television and Growing Up: The Impact of Television Violence* that the convergence of findings from dissimilar methods–laboratory type experiments, field experiments, and surveys–supported the hypothesis that violent programming increases the likelihood of aggressiveness among young viewers. Nothing has occurred since to make anyone think differently.[12]

The key word in Comstock's summary is "likelihood." He does not identify a direct, one-to-one relationship between violent TV content and aggressive behaviour in children; he says that it increases the possibility or probability of such behaviour. Several reports to the committee examined the complexity of the relationship between violent content and aggression in young viewers. Factors that must be considered are the viewer's age, gender, societal norms operating in the immediate environment, social class, environmental cues present in the content that are similar or dissimilar to the natural environment, reward or punishment shown for violent activity, and attitudes of family or peer group towards aggressive behaviour.

Similarly, the Ontario Royal Commission on Violence in the Communications Industry (the La Marsh Commission) reported the results of research on children and adults who viewed, listened to, or read violent media content. The commission supported 28 studies on all forms of media violence, examining magazines, books, motion pictures, newspapers, music, and television. This extensive research focussed on all major areas of concern. The commission's report stated:

> The evidence is clear that exposure to media violence can lead to aggressive or violent behaviour, although not in everyone all of the time. . . . The best evidence is that there is an interaction of personality, life experience and life circumstances, social and peer processes, distinctive or situational cue properties, and opportunity.[13]

The commission went on to discuss the complex relationships between the media, violent content, individuals, and social institutions such as the family, peer groups, and sports organizations.[14]

While the debate concerning the harmful effects of violent TV content continues, new concerns have been expressed concerning the harmful effects of video and computer games on the health and lifestyle of Canadian children. This follows on the debates about music videos, hidden messages in lyrics, and dangers from the lifestyle of the MTV generation. Recently concern has been expressed about violent and pornographic content on the Internet.

Much of this debate about Internet content centres around the definition of freedom of speech. Americans, who have largely developed the World Wide Web, argue for complete freedom of expression so that the Web will contain all types of content. Other countries in the world, contending that freedom comes only with responsibility and accountability, argue for restrictions to content on the Web. Computer programs have been developed that allow parents to block out types of net content that they find offensive.

In 1993, both the U.S. government and the CRTC in Canada moved to restrict violent content on network TV. The U.S. Senate held hearings on the effects of violent media content and aggression in children. Federal guidelines on violent content were proposed to television producers. TV producers in the U.S. voted to reject federal government restrictions on violent content. They argued that self-regulation by the industry would be preferable to governmental regulation.

In Canada, there was increasing activity between 1990 and 1993 by the CRTC concerning violence on TV. The CRTC contacted members of the industry and provincial governments concerning practices and possible new initiatives. Then, in October 1993, the CRTC announced a new violence code developed by the Canadian Association of Broadcasters (CAB), which took effect in 1994; compliance with this code was made a condition of licence.

The code's key provisions were:

- a total ban on broadcast of gratuitous violence;

- violence suitable for adults will be shown only after 9:00 p.m.;

- "sensitivity" concerning children and with respect to violence against vulnerable groups such as women and visible minorities, and against animals;

- a violence-classification system to be applied to programs.[15]

While the code is mandatory in Canada, research conducted in the United States suggests that a violence-classification system is ineffective. In a three-year study conducted by four universities for the National Cable Television Association, it was found that a rating system based on age did not consistently alert parents to violent content in a television program. Some 60 percent of programs received the TVY rating, which means the program is suitable for all children. Only 38 percent of children's programs received the TVY7 rating stating that the program is suitable for children over the age of seven. Some 9 percent of children's programming received a TVY14 rating showing that the program is unsuitable for children under the age of 14. A majority (91 percent) of children's television programs received ratings of TVG or TVPG.

In the United States, the industry began using ratings in 1997 after receiving pressure from the National Parent Teacher Association and the American Medical Association. The National Broadcasting Company (NBC) and Black Entertainment Television both refuse to use the voluntary rating system. This system flashes symbols like "v" for violence, "l" for language, "s" for sex, and "d" for suggestive dialogue for 15 seconds at the beginning of each program. If a parent misses the beginning of the program, they have no knowledge of the rating of the program.

Theoretical Approaches to the Question of Media Violence

The search for a relationship between the mass media, media content, and effects on people's lives is an ancient one. Aristotle investigated the relationship between content and social effect in his three-volume work on persuasion, *Rhetoric*. Aristotle believed that every action must have a cause—every belief, attitude, or value must arise from some specific, persuasive cause. The Aristotelian perspective has led to several different, often conflicting, answers to the causal relationship between the mass media and violence.

To understand this debate more fully, a survey of the approaches that have historically been taken to the problem will be presented. For the sake of brevity and an integrated understanding of the complexity of the issues, we have grouped these approaches under four theoretical paradigms. We focus on the theoretical assumptions about audience, media power, communication, and personhood instead of research methodology because researchers working within

each of the four paradigms have used a variety of methodological tools: experimentation, survey research, case studies, and clinical methodologies. The four broad theoretical perspectives chosen will define the issues more sharply than if we had focussed on the particular research methodology utilized in each study. To conclude, we will present a fifth paradigm, or model, which we believe is integrative and heuristic for research in the twenty-first century.

1. Mass Society and Technological Determinism

The earliest, and still popular, approach to the problem of the mass media and violence comes from the related perspectives of mass society and technological determinism. This approach has roots in the early sociological writings of Comte, Spencer, Durkheim, Tonnies, Marx, and others.

Basic to the approach is an understanding that the major revolutions experienced in the development of technological society have led to the interdependence of people, while at the same time alienating people from one another. Where once they were bound together through kinship and communal ties, in modern mass society these ties have broken down, causing people to lose a sense of self. Bloom and Selznick summarized this situation by saying that modern society is made up of masses in the sense that

> there has emerged a vast mass of segregated, isolated individuals, interdependent in all sorts of specialized ways yet lacking in any central value or purpose. The weakening of traditional bonds, the growth of rationality, and the division of labour, have created societies made up of individuals who are only loosely bound together. In this sense, the word "mass" suggests something closer to an aggregate than to a tightly knit group.[16]

Since people are isolated, they are considered susceptible to the influence of all types of propaganda. The mass society perspective fanned the foundation for propaganda studies done before and during the Second World War. The fear was that people in a mass society were open to the lies of the propagandist who was able to use the mass media to skilfully manipulate and control public opinion.[17]

In this perspective, the mass media are considered omnipotent. The model of personhood that supports this perspective is the plastic person controlled and moulded by the mass media. The audience is understood to be passive. Thus, individual audience members are shaped and controlled by those who produce and control mass media content.

The communication model proposed by researchers working in this perspective is a linear model of immediate effects, which has two names: the "hypo-dermic needle model" or the "magic bullet."[18] In this model, media content is simply injected into the minds of individuals within the mass society. The audience is passive, not too intelligent, and simply receives whatever is generated by the mass media. Communication is understood as something that someone does to someone else. Harold Lasswell's famous model for understanding the content of communication, "Who says what, through which channel, to whom, with what effect,"[19] simply reinforced this understanding of mass media effects.

Often two other related perspectives are connected with the mass society perspective: technological determinism and what James Fletcher has called the "devil hypothesis."[20] Technological determinists, such as Marshall McLuhan,[21] Harold Innis,[22] and Jacques Ellul,[23] hold that we are products of the media in our society. Most technological determinists are not concerned with media content; it is the media themselves that determine how we understand and know the world and ourselves.

The devil hypothesis holds that the media are evil because they destroy human values and culture. Thus TV is understood as the "plugged in drug"[24] that, because of its immediacy and power, controls the minds of viewers. As people use TV, they replace real-life experiences with the vicarious experiences of TV content. It is this argument that the defence attorney, in the trial discussed earlier, was using in the defence of the young killer.

While some scholars have found this perspective to be weak, it is still extremely popular among critics of the mass media and some researchers. A refinement of it, the "cultivation theory" developed by George Gerbner,[25] Herbert Schiller,[26] Hal Himmelstein,[27] and Tannis MacBeth,[28] among others, holds that the mass media, especially television, create a common symbolic environment for people. The world of TV creates reality, thus providing the symbolic framework with which people understand the world around them. Therefore, the depiction of violence on TV as a means to gain and maintain power causes people to see the world in which they live as violent. The use of violence by white males on TV to maintain power and control over women, children, the elderly, and minority groups causes viewers to accept such violence in their own lives.

The major effect of this is not so much to cause people to use violence, but to de-sensitize them to the use of violence in society, to make violence

acceptable when used by sources of power, and to bring about what is called the "mean world syndrome." The world is seen as an evil or dangerous place in which to live. People come to fear for their lives and their property as they adopt the media-generated image of a violent world; they come to accept that excessive violence is necessary to maintain law and order. This perspective of the world is directly related to the amount of television people view: specifically, the number of hours spent viewing each day. Light viewers are understood to have divergent views about the world and reality. Heavy viewers, on the other hand, are those who share in the mean world syndrome.

Research for the La Marsh Commission by Doob and MacDonald,[29] and Tate,[30] as well as British research by Wober for ITV,[31] failed to find the expected relationship between hours spent viewing TV and the mean world syndrome. Doob and MacDonald found that there was a relationship between the crime rate of the neighbourhood in which viewers lived and a belief in a mean world. People in high-crime neighbourhoods did spend more hours watching TV because of the violent environment within the neighbourhood. The effect is related to crime rate in the neighbourhood or environmental violence and not simply to the amount of time spent viewing television.

Gosselin, deGuise, and Paquette[32] conducted a multiple-step study of violence on Canadian television and its cognitive effects. The first step was to conduct a content analysis of specifically Canadian television content. In other words, while MacBeth for the La Marsh Commission drew a sample of all television channels received in Ontario, these scholars from the Université Laval analyzed only Canadian television channel content. Using Gerbner's protocol for analysis of violence, a *violence index* for Canadian television was created.

The overall violence index score for Canadian television programs was 106.1, compared to a violence index score of 169.6 for U.S. television. By this measure, Canadian television is about 34 percent less violent than that found in the U. S. Private Canadian networks had more violent programming than public networks. English- and French-language networks showed about the same amount of violence using this measure. Programs produced in Quebec had a lower violence index (49.6) than programs produced in other Canadian provinces (111.9). Children's cartoons had the highest violence index (206.8) while other children's programming had an index of only 1.9, indicating hardly any violence at all. Soap operas had a lower violence index (55.6) than films (178.4) and series (98.9).

Using this content analysis of Canadian media, these researchers developed a questionnaire related to viewing television and the mean world syndrome. The questionnaire was administered to 360 Quebec university students in a first-year media course. The results are ambiguous. There is no clear relationship between the amount of time spent viewing television and fear of the world. Women tended to view television less than men, but women under the age of 35 reported a fearful view of the world. Men and women over the age of 35 did not view the world as a fearful place even though they watched significant amounts of television.

The authors argue that the data support their hypothesis of a direct relationship between number of hours spent viewing television and fear of the world but this is not apparent to the careful reader. They report a significant linear relationship between viewing television and this cognition. They also report a direct relation between cognition and fear of the world. However, there is no significant statistical relationship between the number of hours of television viewing and fear of the world. The conclusion drawn is that the relationship is more complex than reported by Gerbner.

2. Audience Differences and Media Reinforcement

While the determinist perspective considers the audience to be plastic and controlled by media content, the audience differences and media reinforcement perspectives acknowledge a passive audience that is affected by media cues and content. In 1964, Raymond Bauer[33] identified an "obstinate audience" based on several different perspectives of individual differences among audience members. Bauer relied on psychological research on perception to explain the obstinacy of the audience. *All perception is selective:* therefore, when confronting the media, people see what they are prepared to see, understand what they have learned through past experience, and remember what they care to remember. *Selective exposure* (no one can pay attention to all media messages because they would suffer from information overload), *selective perception, selective understanding,* and *selective recall,* all work against the producer of media content and the mass media.

Perception research would lead one to conclude that the greater the violence in one's environment, the greater the probability that one will view violent TV content, accept it as true of the world in general, and act aggressively towards others. Similarly, one would expect that environmental cues portrayed in the media, such as the presence of guns, would cue aggressive behaviour in some viewers.

Two competing theories used to explain individual differences among viewers of violent TV programming are the "catharsis hypothesis" of Feshbach,[34] and Feshbach and Singer,[35] and the "stimulating effects" (aggressive cues) theory proposed by Percy Tannenbaum[36] and Leonard Berkowitz.[37] Both of these suggest that people identify with media content, which then causes them to act in a specific manner. These scholars argue that this is especially true of television with its arousing and powerful presentation of violent content.

The catharsis hypothesis argues that when an individual is feeling frustrated or disturbed over some matter, violent programming helps the individual work out this tension through involvement with the media content. Identification with the problems and activities of characters in the TV program brings about a cathartic effect within the viewer. As one views violent programming, psychological tension is discharged through empathetic identification with the violence on the screen. Thus, after viewing TV, the individual is more relaxed and less frustrated than before viewing. Feshbach and Singer have also argued that those in lower social classes show more identification and catharsis than those of higher social classes.[38]

The stimulating effects (aggressive cues) theory of Leonard Berkowitz[39] is considerably more popular among scholars than the catharsis theory. This stimulus-response theory argues that media dramatizations of violent and aggressive content increase the individual's level of emotional arousal and may cue the viewer to aggressive behaviour. Tannenbaum[40] has argued that the electronic media have a greater arousal effect than print media. This arousal may be converted into aggressive behaviour depending on the social context of the person aroused.

Berkowitz has also shown that the presence of weapons, such as guns, violent arguments, and threats in media content will act as cues to heighten arousal producing aggressive behaviour. Similarly, when the violence is presented as justified, there is a greater probability of arousing the viewer to aggressive behaviour. Again, if the individual is frustrated at the time of viewing, there will be an increase in the probability of aggressive behaviour. Finally, the similarity between the media setting and the viewer's environment may also cue the viewer to act violently against others.

Learning theories take individual differences into account when examining the relationship between the mass media and violence. The most popular has been "observational learning theory," as developed by Bandura and Walters.[41] This theory indicates that people learn aggressive behaviour from media portrayals. As one sits in front of the TV set, or reads a book, one learns about the violence in this world, how to act aggressively, and about new forms of aggressive behaviour. This is especially true for children, who have little or no experience with the real world. Just as children may acquire new patterns of conduct by observing parents or siblings, or a brother or sister, so they learn how to act when watching TV.

Bandura and Walters do not believe that children (or adults) will automatically perform these violent or aggressive behaviours. Rather, a situation must arise that has environmental cues similar to those found in the media portrayal, thus calling forth the aggressive behaviour. The probability of performing these acts is increased by other factors, such as expectation of being rewarded for being aggressive, the social situation of the child after viewing, the child's gender (boys are usually permitted to be more aggressive than girls in our society), the social norms operating in the situation, and the expectation of social support from another who viewed the same program.

3. Limited Effects/Weak Media Model

The limited effects model, or the reinforcement approach,[42] grew out of the review of mass media persuasion research done by Joseph Klapper in 1960 and Jonathan Freedman in 1984 and 1986.[43] Klapper surveyed the literature of his day and summarized his findings by formulating a reinforcement perspective. According to Klapper the media are really quite powerless in changing beliefs, attitudes, and values; rather they serve to reinforce messages provided by other parts of the social system. Rarely do the media challenge the existing business and political structure of the country. They seek, instead, to reinforce beliefs about the culture and social system in which we live.

The media do not ordinarily move people to perform aggressive behaviour but rather reinforce existing behaviour patterns. People live in environments where social norms concerning aggressive behaviour are operating. These norms regulate behaviour no matter what the content of TV or other media programming. People live within family and friendship groups that govern behaviour through pressure. Consequently, violent content on TV or in other media will not move one to aggressive behaviour. People who dwell in violent or aggressive environments will experience the violent content as reinforcing that environment and lifestyle. Those living in non-violent environments will dismiss violent media content because it is foreign to their understanding of the world in which they live.

4. The Active Audience That Uses the Media

"Uses and gratifications theory" was developed in Great Britain, Israel, and Sweden during the late 1960s and early 1970s.[44] There has been some criticism of this paradigm because it does not fit the traditional definitions of a theory. Basic to this perspective is the understanding that audience members seek out media content to meet individual needs. Contrary to the traditional linear (action and action-reaction) model of communication used by the theories already discussed, this approach uses a transactional model of communication.[45] "Uses and gratifications" scholars argue that one cannot understand the effects of the media until one understands the reason audience members use the media.

"Uses and gratifications" research has shown that audience members actively use media content in many different ways. The audience consists of rational individuals, not robots moulded or controlled by the media. The media interact with the audience members in many ways, and people use different media to meet a multiplicity of needs. Those interested in which movies are showing locally or the weekly grocery bargains will turn to print media such as the daily newspaper or weekly flyer. Those seeking current information on a disaster or weather system will most likely turn to radio or a local weather channel on cable TV. For in-depth reporting on a political incident in Latin America, one may well wait for one of the news magazines or turn to a TV documentary or news show such as *The Journal, W5,* or *The Fifth Estate.*

Tate[46] has suggested a modification of the catharsis hypothesis based on the uses and gratifications perspective. His research for the La Marsh Commission indicated that there is not one audience "out there" that watches everything on TV, as most media determinists have argued, but at least six different, clearly identifiable audiences.[47] Each audience specializes in different types of programming and media usage. For example, there is a specific audience for crime dramas and violent content, and another that watches only sports programming and rarely, if ever, views other types of programming. A third adult audience consistently views only children's, religious, and instructional programs; this audience prefers non-threatening, nonviolent programming.

Using activation theory,[48] Tate argued that people employ varied media for different psychological reduction or amplification benefits. This theory argues that each individual has a unique level of activation—either meaning, or activity, or physiological—that fluctuates in a learned pattern during waking hours. If the level of any of the three dimensions becomes too high, the individual will seek to lower it to the accustomed level for that time of day; if the level becomes too low, the individual will seek to raise it to the accustomed level.

Media use is one way to raise or lower the level of activation. Fletcher[49] reports, for example, that within two minutes of listening to any piece of music one's heartbeat synchronizes with the beat of the music. Music, then, is a socially acceptable, bidirectional "drug," which people use to raise or lower their heartbeats and hence their levels of psychological or physiological activation. Research by Houghton-Larsen[50] on media usage found that people over 30 read books for relaxation, while those under 30 use recorded music. People know which media will relax them, which will wake them up, which will energize them if they are too tired, and which will break the boredom of their activities. While growing up we learn which media will best meet our various activation needs.

Tate argued, therefore, that to understand the cathartic effect of television one must first discover the gratification that media usage provides. If a person views violent content because past experience has taught that it stimulates the intellect, then the cathartic effect will be intellectual stimulation. If, however, one views it because past experience has taught that it is relaxing, then the cathartic effect after viewing will be relaxation. Fouts reported to the La Marsh Commission that, among the children studied in his research, those who viewed the most crime shows were those who had the highest IQs and were also the least aggressive. They reported that they viewed this type of programming because the plots were the least predictable and therefore provided the most intellectual stimulation.[51]

Tate measured level of activation before and after viewing selected TV programs. Adults who reported viewing a specific genre for relaxation (i.e., crime dramas, soap operas, situation comedies, and so on) were significantly more relaxed after viewing a representative program of that genre. It seems reasonable to argue, therefore, that one must consider the use to which a medium is put before one links a specific effect to its use. Thus, it should be clear from this perspective that the study of the mass media and violence is more complex than the simple reductionist perspectives we have surveyed.

Problems with Reductionism

We need to review briefly the problem of scientific reductionism as it applies to the study of the mass media and violence. In his provocative book on the media and the public opinion process, James Lemert[52] argued that the primary reason for the conclusion that the media have little effect on people, or only minimal reinforcing effect, lies in the reductionism employed by scholars of mass communication in the past.

Reductionism is the attempt to explain behaviour on the basis of one or two simple general variables such as imitation, catharsis, attitude change, or the mass media. In other words, reductionist theories may attempt to explain aggressive behaviour in children by simply counting the number of violent acts on TV during a given week, or by pointing to the introduction of TV into a community. The mass media do not exist in a social vacuum. Yet, for 60 years or more, mass communication researchers have attempted to explain societal effects from the individual case study or the analysis of average groups of viewers.

Empirical studies of mass media effects have assumed that one can establish a uni-dimensional relationship between a few media variables and behaviours in real life. Given the complexity of the situation, the uniqueness of individuals, and the subtlety of the phenomena under examination, many scholars have had to settle for a reinforcement paradigm to explain the relationship between the mass media and violence because of the reductionist theoretical and methodological paradigms they have adopted in their research.

In his report to the La Marsh Commission, Gregory Fouts gave a comprehensive critique of the reductionist perspective in this field of research. Fouts pointed out the weaknesses in previous research conducted on a simplistic assumption that a few variables manipulated in media presentations would be directly related to, or serve as a simple cause of, observable imitative behaviours in people. Past research tended to focus on one program shown to children viewing by themselves. As he noted, "a viewer does not see just one program in which his/her attention is focussed by request of a researcher; he/she is not exposed only to the materials seen on television, nor is he/she isolated from other influences."[53] Media usage does not occur in a social vacuum.

Instead of seeking simplistic, linear, cause and effect relationships between media violence and aggressive behaviour, as empirical scholars have sought to do in the past, Fouts argues that we must use a developmental perspective to examine the complexity of relationships. Fouts outlines in some detail the differences between the reductionist-empirical perspective of the past and the developmental perspective taken in his research on children and televised violence. Instead of looking for cause and effect relationships between a few media content variables, developmentalists seek to understand the complexity of relationships, and to describe many different patterns of variable and effect relationships.

Empiricists are more likely to conceive of the audience as passive and reactive, while developmentalists understand that the audience is active and influenced by many factors, not only in the environment, but also within the viewer. The empiricist is interested in supporting a theory with aggregate data and is not usually interested in individual differences, while the developmental researcher is interested in group differences based on age, gender, and maturation.

The empiricist is not interested in what the viewer perceives or thinks about the content viewed on television; the interest is focussed on the effect of the content on the person. This emphasis on effect arises from the Aristotelian and Cartesian models of cause and effect that underlie the empirical research paradigm. The developmental researcher has rejected these cause-effect premises and examines how the media user selects, interprets, and processes media content.

Empirical researchers have often used larger groups of subjects, seeking to develop laws that govern behaviour. Developmental theorists and researchers are more likely to take a rules perspective[54] to allow for variation and uniqueness of behaviour. Finally, empiricists have been quite active in seeking to manipulate and change the environment, "while developmentalists usually try to enrich and optimize understanding with as little manipulation of the environment as possible."[55]

One of the most extensive critiques of the North American empirical effects research has been published by David Gauntlett in his book *Moving Experiences: Understanding Television's Influences and Efffects*.[56] Gauntlett summarizes his argument in his second book, *Video Critical: Children, the Environment and Media Power*.[57] David Gauntlett criticizes the effects tradition on several levels.

Gauntlett attacks North American effects research for a general lack of theory. Generally, no theoretical foundation is given for the research. This relates to the scientific reductionism we have discussed above. Many researchers simply assume a relationship between media violence and aggressive behaviour in children. No attempt is made to make a theoretical foundation to support this relationship or its existence.

Communication and cultural studies scholars in the United Kingdom are highly critical of the effects research carried on in North America. These scholars, like David Gauntlett, are critical of effects research not only for its lack of theoretical foundation but for its lack of awareness of its ideological roots. As Martin Barker wrote in *The Times Higher Education Supplement*, "the arguments about effects do not spring out of an ideological vacuum. They generally tend to spring from deeply felt beliefs about how society should and should not be organized and regulated."[58]

We must also raise the question of how the researcher defines violence. A survey of the effects research will show that violence is simply defined as physical or verbal violence—*direct violence*, as Johann Galtung[59] has defined it. In the introduction to her book *Defining Violence: Understanding the Causes and Effects of Violence*, Hannah Bradley has noted that recent thought casts doubt on "definitions of violence in a particular context of the discourses that have constructed particular forms of violence as legitimate."[60]

As Bradley notes, to define a concept is to expose it to investigation. Too often North American researchers simply define violence as a force that one person uses against another. It is easy to count the number of such acts in a television program or motion picture. On this basis, David Gauntlett has argued that most of the television programs chosen for empirical investigation in North American effects research are not particularly violent.

The second factor in this traditional definition of violence is that the aspect of intentionality is assumed to be present. Force is traditionally defined as "being employed intentionally." This means that for most people violence occurs when one person (aggressor) intentionally uses force to control another person (victim). This is the melodramatic definition of violence. Again, this definition of violence falls entirely within the scope of what Galtung defines as *direct violence*.

Such a definition of violence focusses only on interpersonal violence while ignoring other types of violence. In this perspective, wars are understood to be large-scale interpersonal conflicts. There is an aggressor who intends to harm or destroy the other group. This definition of violence masks other types and causes of violence. Empirical effects research focusses on intentional interpersonal violence of one form or another. Concern is expressed about the use of force against another person. No attention is paid to "structural violence," or forms of discrimination, stereotyping, harassment, prejudice, animosity between individuals or groups, and economic systems that produce "accidental" violence. These subtle forms of violence are passed off as a "necessary evil."

Dorothy Sayers once noted that "there is great concern for physical violence but not violence in board rooms." In other words, no consideration is given to those forms of bureaucratic violence that legitimize the use of violence against women, children, ethnic groups and racial groups. When boards of corporations make decisions or create policies that discriminate against racial or ethnic groups, they legitimate structural violence within the company and social structure. When international corporations take products developed for sale in the United States and flood markets of Third World countries with cheap products that increase the number of "lifestyle diseases" in cultures where they have been rare or unknown, the board is practicing structural violence. We must ask, "What aspects of the economic and social system produce violence against children, women, and racial or ethnic groups in Canada?" This is not a question that the effects research focusses on because it is not physical or verbal force intentionally used against another person. The definition of violence generally found in the North American effects tradition keeps researchers and critics from focussing on the more subtle forms of violence in society.

Similarly, no research is conducted on "cultural violence"[61]–those aspects of culture that legitimize structural and direct violence. We have noted above that Canadians have been generally less receptive to violent media content than people in the United States. The question then arises, "What is there in American culture that makes violence against another person or group permissible and legitimate?" Much attention is paid to violent media content but no attention is paid to those aspects of American culture that legitimate the production of such content.[62]

Media professionals will argue that they are only reflecting life in the United States. Urban life is violent, they argue, and therefore media content must reflect the authenticity of this violence. Other media professionals argue that violence makes programming interesting and exciting. Violence sells on television as violence is action and action makes the content interesting to the viewer.

Critics argue that by emphasizing violence the media increase the perception of all society as being violent. This is the mean world syndrome or "fortress mentality" identified by Gerbner and others. Some scholars have estimated that only 10 percent of societal violence is directly linked to the viewing of violent television content. However, the more important question is: What are these portrayals teaching viewers about different ethnic, racial, and national peoples in the world? What stories do they legitimate about groups and regions in the nation? What other forms of violence do they hide from the viewer by emphasizing intentional force?

Cultural studies have focussed somewhat on some aspects of the social structure that legitimize the more visible forms of violence. David Gauntlett, Sonia Livingstone, David Morley,[63] and others point out that there is often a hidden elitism in the critiques of violent media content. Too often, the message is that lower classes are more prone to be affected by violent media content than the better-educated upper classes. Too often, the concern with violent media content is an elitist prejudice against those persons of lower social classes or ethnic groups who are considered to be inferior intellectually. Since they are not well educated, they spend more time viewing television and accepting its content without thought.

In this sense, concern about violent media content and behaviour is a moral panic.[64] A moral panic is a heightened pseudo concern created by persons in power to control people and social events. It may be used to create a rush to purchase some product or media technology. A moral panic may be created to keep people from focussing on other social issues that affect their lives in economic or structural ways. A moral panic may be created by a political party to increase their chances of being elected to office or to distract voters from relevant political issues.

In many respects concerns about media content and violence in society is a moral panic. The concern about television content is used to sell newspapers, magazines, and books. It is used to increase audience ratings since a controversial film or program attracts more viewers. It is used as a part of election campaigns to garner votes. It is used to legitimize bureaucratic institutions created to control or censure the medium of film or television. As Barker wrote in the *Times Higher Education Supplement*, "media violence is the witchcraft of our society."

The assumption made by effects researchers, that what children watch now is directly linked to how they will act in the future, hides too many societal and internal causes of violence. This simplistic reductionism explaining behaviour to one aspect of media usage is meaningless. As Barker observes in his review of the literature, "it is absurd to believe that number of hours viewed is related to my doing something."

The strongest North American critic of empirical effects research is Dr. Jonathan Kellerman in his book, *Savage Spawn: Reflections on Violent Children.*[65] Kellerman declares that Mitchell Johnson and Andrew Golden, the two pre-teenagers who coldly killed the children and teacher at Jonesboro, Arkansas, are not troubled youth but psychopaths. Kellerman's case is effectively and cogently presented in his book. Those individuals whom we hear about and see on television news who have shot students and teachers at their school are young psychopaths. They kill because they are driven by a psychopathic need for stimulation and excitement. They are the modern-day manifestations of Jesse James, Billy the Kid, Butch Cassidy, and Bonnie and Clyde. Like their historical counterparts, they coolly plan, execute, and enjoy the violence they produce. From early childhood, they have manipulated, bullied, controlled, and sought power over other children and adults.

What is one to say to children of a culture that glorifies the psychopaths of society? Jesse James, William Bonney (Billy the Kid), Butch Cassidy are honoured in myth, song, story, books, and film. Yet, each one was a teenage psychopath. Each of these American folk heroes had killed in their teens. Billy the Kid killed his first victim at age 14, and by 21, was known

to have shot 21 men. Is this any different from the two teenagers at Columbine High School in Colorado?

Kellerman attacks the idea that violent media content has any relationship to aggressive behaviour in children or youth. In a chapter entitled "The Scapegoat We Love to Hate," Jonathan Kellerman discusses the diminished returns of the volume of money poured into mass communication research on violent television and violent behaviour. After examining the correlation research between media violence and aggression in children either for (1) sensitization and desensitization, (2) identification, (3) arousal, and (4) positive reinforcement, Kellerman says, "Though some statistical support has been obtained for all four suppositions, *not a single causal link between media violence and criminality has ever been produced.*" Kellerman affirms that all money now given to media research should be withdrawn and given to treatment centres to help young psychopaths learn new patterns of behaviour. After the age of 11 or 12, Kellerman says, clinical research shows that it is impossible to alter the behaviour patterns of the violent child. Therefore, an early warning system must be developed whereby potentially violent children can be identified and direct interaction taken to change the life of the child. Kellerman states that no child should have access to lethal weapons. He also says we must take very seriously the warnings troubled youth give about coming violence. Finally, there are some treatment interventions that may be successful with pre-teen psychopathic children.

A final criticism of empirical effects research lies in the methodological assumptions made by the researcher before conducting research. Cultural studies scholars argue that, instead of giving a questionnaire with pre-set categories to viewers, the researcher must use qualitative research methodologies that allow the viewer to set his or her own categories.[66] Instead of presenting children with pre-set categories for understanding television content, these researchers argue that one must listen to the child describe what he or she sees on the television. Interview techniques are used to let the child set her or his own categories of television content.

Similarly, the researcher must be thoroughly aware of his or her own motives and values underlying the research that is being undertaken. This latter concern is the problem of *reflexivity*. North American scholars are criticized for ignoring the reflexivity question. This ignorance causes them not only to ignore the ideological roots of their research but also to bias their research in such a way as to obtain a predetermined result.

The American psychiatrist Robert Coles has spoken candidly of the necessity for reflexivity—for an awareness of the researcher's own assumptions, definitions, theoretical perspectives, and even her or his own way of life—while doing research. "Those of us who want to understand children ... will often find ourselves compelled to think twice about our own assumptions, maybe even the very nature of our kind of living."[67] Too often researchers make assumptions about the children they are researching that denigrate the persons they are studying and their understanding of the television they view.

Researchers must always be aware of the hidden meanings that underlie the research they are conducting in order to let the people they are seeking understanding from to be truly human. In the following passage, Robert Coles makes clear why every social scientist must be reflexive about his or her life and work:

> Still, it is not enough for us to realize how awful life can be for so many of our fellow citizens; and I say that not only because we risk denying them their successes and victories, achieved against such high odds, but also because we ourselves pay a high price for the apparent sympathy and near-despair we demonstrate. We run the risk of becoming self-satisfied and opinionated rather than genuinely concerned and aware, and thereby we do both others and ourselves a grave injustice.... They establish islands of order and even beauty in the midst of the chaos they can't eradicate. Yes, beauty; in ghettoes I have seen the equivalent of those wild flowers.... Then, there are television programs, and not only *Sesame Street*. Out of what we call soap operas and domestic comedy shows a mother can extract a lesson, find a moment of encouragement, build a day's foundation of confidence and tenacity and inventiveness.[68]

The Ontario Royal Commission on Violence in the Communications Industry: Some Generalizations

The five volumes of research reports, along with the summary volume (Vol. 1) and the extensive bibliography (Vol. 2), make the La Marsh Commission one of the most complete mass media research projects undertaken in any country. When compared, for example, with the content analysis study conducted at UCLA from 1996 to 1999, it becomes apparent that the La Marsh Commission is much broader in approach than other major studies.[69] Throughout this article we have reported findings from many of the 28 research reports published by the commission. Several things become clear as one reads through this Canadian research.

First, one should be very careful not to transfer findings from research conducted in the U.S. to Canadian populations. We believe that the research conducted for the La Marsh Commission has shown that Canadian media users are different in their response to violence in media content from U.S. viewers. Other Canadian research supports this general rule, whether it is in audience reaction to Archie Bunker[70] or media usage in border communities.[71]

Second, Canadians have a tendency to be more innovative by accepting theory and research paradigms that are little used by scholars in the U.S. While Canadian researchers are well aware of work done in the U.S., they have also pioneered the utilization of perspectives from Europe and Asia. Our experience has been, generally, that U.S. scholars are slower in adopting new perspectives on the media. Consequently, seven to ten years after the La Marsh Commission published their final report, a report generally unknown in the U.S., scholars there began to report research methodologies and theoretical perspectives similar to those adopted by Canadian scholars under the auspices of the La Marsh Commission.

Third, the La Marsh Commission sponsored research investigations into all forms of media, thus making it more comprehensive than, for example, the Surgeon General's *Report on Television Violence*. The commission also surveyed work done in different countries around the world on violence and the media. Canadian readers are able to assess responses from many different cultural, ethnic, and national perspectives. This makes the report an important starting point for any understanding of this question. The commission also received summaries of the benefits of media usage, especially TV viewing, so that their perspective was not too one-sided.[72]

Unfortunately, like many royal commission reports, the six volumes of the La Marsh Report gather dust on the bookshelves of libraries and scholars. Some researchers have continued to pursue research begun for the La Marsh Commission while others have moved to different interests.[73] The commission's recommendations for the establishment of a multi-channel, monopolistic, national TV system, using a different broadcasting system from that used in the U.S., was broad and controversial. It further recommended that a powerful national press council be created to govern ownership and content of the print media.

The commissioners understood that Canadians cannot depend on media owners to protect the country from U.S. control and influence. We know now that the monopoly media owners of Canada are generally continentalists with nothing to lose by promoting American interests.[74]

The controversy created by these far-reaching recommendations of the La Marsh Committee reflected on all aspects of the work done for the commission, thus reducing the attention it received. Yet, some very creative research was conducted for the La Marsh Commission. This is not to say that all of the research reports are of equal value, but it is to affirm that Canadian scholars have here (as in the 1970 Davey Committee and the 1981 Kent Commission)[75] a valuable foundation for future investigations into this complex question.

Investigating the Complexity of the Relationship between the Mass Media and Violence: Some Suggestions for the Twenty-First Century

Basic to understanding the research conducted on the mass media and violence in the past is the realization that these researchers began with the assumption that the media user is a person first, who is then socialized into society by the media. We argue that this assumption, while having some merit and utility, provides for a limited path of analysis. As we have attempted to show elsewhere,[76] personhood is multidimensional. Thus, the unit of analysis is the social person who encounters the media as only one of many socializing phenomena. This allows for an eclectic approach for analysis of cognitive and affective variables. Basing our analysis on the seminal writings of the "dialogical" philosophers[77] (those who understand meaning as arising from spontaneous conversation between two or more people), we hold that personhood has four dimensions, each of which must be considered before one can begin to assess adequately the relationship between violent media content and aggression in individuals and society.

Imperative Speech: The Developing Self (Thou)

The first dimension of personhood is response to parents, siblings, relatives, institutions, media, and so on in the world to which we are born. We are socialized by our parents, grandparents, brothers and sisters, aunts and uncles, into a family and a culture. We begin life as social beings. Our families, friends, peers, religious leaders, teachers, and so on speak to us with imperative speech, calling us into being, giving us guidance, and sending us out into the world. We respond to their direction, love, support, and the stories they tell us about the world around us.

Here the media act in conjunction and/or in conflict with the primary social groups in which we are involved—some media content reinforces familial values, while other content clashes with them. That which reinforces and expands on familial beliefs, attitudes, values, stories, norms, and mores will be encouraged by parents and significant others, thus strengthening the individual's developing social value system.

At the same time, family discourse will seek to counteract conflicting media, peer, or educational influences. Fouts found that, generally, television viewing for children is a social event, with over 80 percent of the respondents reporting viewing with their parents occasionally or often. Some 43 percent of the parents in his study reported restricting programs that contained viewer discretion warnings; so parents do control the viewing patterns of their children.

Noble's[78] research supports this finding, indicating that, as parents discuss TV content with their children, they change the child's understanding of the violent content. If we are to understand the relationship between viewing violent television content and behaviour of children in this dimension of personhood, we must examine carefully the family environment. In other words, we must make the family the unit of observation and not the individual child. How tolerant is the family of aggressive behaviour, violent media content, and media content that conflicts with familial values and norms? How do parents treat violent media content when their children encounter it? What sources of violence or abuse exist within the family environment? How do these sources interact with media content and behaviour patterns within the family to legitimize the abuse of family members? What mythic structures held by significant others in the family are supported or reinforced by media content? What media content contradicts beliefs, values, and attitudes held by significant family members? In what manner do the media support and augment cultural violence within society, thus reinforcing and legitimizing the forces of discrimination, harassment, abuse, rape, death, war, and genocide in the modem world?[79]

In other words, we need a multidimensional approach that combines an analysis of media content, the cultural myths that underlie it, familial mythic structure, family environment, and aggressive behaviour. For example, James Fletcher[80] has indicated that the most popular form of media content in North America is melodrama. This is a form of drama that depicts the world and life as a constant battle between two opposing forces, most often good and evil. This theme is timeless. It is a way of working out salvation concerns that have been central to humans since people began telling stories and developing myths. The theme through which the drama is played out varies, but central to melodrama is this eternal struggle. There are no greys or neutrals in melodrama: evil is depicted as totally evil and good as totally good.

A saga is the continuing story of this eternal struggle. Melodrama is found in novels, especially the romance novel, in motion pictures, in music, and in radio or TV drama. The docudrama carries the theme into life by dramatizing fictionalized real-life events that are melodramatic in nature. The mini-series condenses the struggle between good and evil into from 6 to 15 one-hour segments. The nighttime soap operas (i.e., *Dallas, Melrose Place*) present the struggle perpetually, with dramatic pauses during the summer. These have audiences around the world waiting in suspense for the season premiere to find out who is winning the eternal struggle. Daytime soap operas portray the struggle in the lives of people living in a glamorous world quite different from the world most viewers experience daily. Melodrama is dependent on violent content because of the battle dominant to the genre.

In one of her novels, Amanda Cross refers to soap operas as "women's melodrama." This may no longer be as true as it was in the days of radio or the early days of television but, generally, the audience still consists of women. Children come to experience the soap opera as they view it with a mother or friends. Within the family context the interaction between family viewing norms, media usage, and text help to create viewer competence.

Laura Stempel Mumford[81] has argued that competence as viewers is "a creation of the text itself, for it is through watching soaps that we gain the experience necessary to decode further episodes and new series. A soap opera teaches us how to watch it, tutors us in its rules and conventions, provides us with the history and information we need, and thus makes it possible for us to understand it in the future."

Mumford does not wish to suggest that viewers are passive recipients of the all-powerful texts of the media nor does she want to imply that viewers are "simply discursive constructs created by the programs we watch." She does wish to affirm that viewers are "collaborators in the construction of the soap opera (and every other) text." She points out, "The very notion of viewer competence, at least as I am invoking it, assumes that there is active work to be done in watching soaps, especially in sorting through our knowledge of the genre's rules and our memories of a program's short- and long-term history as we attempt to make sense of each new event on the screen."

We wish to assert that media texts are only one form of narrative (story) that we learn as children. Stories are the basic factors of cognitive structure.[82] In order to understand anything in life we create a story about it. As children, our parents create stories for us as they prepare us for the activities of the day. They read stories to us from books before we go to sleep. We watch stories on television, hear them on the radio in children's programming, and listen to them in the lyrics of songs. From a very early age stories are central to our understanding of life and other people in our world.

In his recent study of leadership, Howard Gardner,[83] has shown that the first story we learn as children is what he calls the "Star Wars Scenario." This is melodrama at its best, with a battle between the hero and the forces of evil. Gardner argues that this story is so powerful that it stays with us during the rest of our life, patterning our perceptions of reality in the world.

If a leader is going to be successful, she or he must tell a story that followers will find meaningful. The Star Wars scenario (melodrama) provides this meaning. Witness the success of political leaders who build election campaigns on the melodramatic narrative.

Melodrama has become an essential element in Western news reporting–there is the war on drugs, struggles among competing political powers, between religious groups, between unions and management, and, in government, among political parties or leaders competing for leadership. Wherever we look in the news a melodramatic format is taken, since, as Osler showed in his report to the La Marsh Commission, this perspective meets Canadian journalists' definition of what is newsworthy.[84]

People, it is believed, wish to read about conflict or violence. Journalists, like members of the general public, interpret the world in melodramatic terms. Scandinavian studies of journalistic accounts of the

Gulf War indicate that it was predominantly reported as melodrama with Western leaders as the "good guys" and Saddam Hussein as the most "evil" leader since Adolf Hitler. In fact, in more than one case, Hussein's moustache was altered in photographs to the same size as that worn by Hitler. Nordstrom shows this same photograph on the cover of *Time* and later on *The New Republic.*

What is the effect of constant repetitions of this vision of the world in media content? Which family beliefs and perspectives teach this melodramatic structure of the world in which the viewer lives? Since melodramatic content appeals to the emotions and is often violent, how does melodrama affect perceptions of violence in society and the propriety of aggressive behaviour towards others?

Deborah Tannen provides an interesting answer to these questions in her book, *The Argument Culture: Stopping America's War of Words.*[85] Dr. Tannen demonstrates that the melodramatic structure of culture leads to savage attacks on opponents, negative political advertising, and an increase of violence within all social structures. Professor Tannen approaches these questions from the perspective of a linguist but her conclusions are the same as those we are presenting in this article. North American culture, based on argumentation, creates two sides that constantly denigrate each other. This is agonism or "programmed contentiousness," a "ritualized opposition" in which two sides are formed and only one side can win the struggle between good and evil. The constant presentation of melodrama in media content can lead only to a violent society in which children learn to be abusive to one another.

Another question to be addressed from this dimension of personhood concerns the ways in which the media may displace or replace family and primary group influence. Rosenstock-Huessy raises an interesting question in his book, *Out of Revolution,* when he points out that sometime during the nineteenth century the textbook (a mass medium in its own right) replaced parents and grandparents as an authoritative source of knowledge about the world.[86] What is the role of textbooks in establishing stable interpretations of the self, others, and the world in which we live?

Subjective Speech: The Self as Person (I)

As we communicate with our parents, grandparents and so on, we begin to develop a story repertoire of our own that leads to the development of our self-concept.[87] Beliefs and stories concerning the world, the self, others, authorities, and taste preferences are developed and internalized. Each of us is unique in the way we internalize reality. Here individual differences, perceptual processes, and cognitive growth become important; reality and speech are subjective. Our experience with the media at this level is also subjective and personal.

The theoretical perspective with which to examine relationships to media content at this level is with the use of the construct "interpretative repertoire" and "story" (i.e., narrative or learned scripts). Here the individual is the unit of observation. What is the role of media content in helping the individual to form an interpretative repertoire? What experiences within the family with media help to internalize stories for the child? What media usage within the family structure helps the child to gain competence with various media genre? What stories learned from childhood do the media reinforce and expand? How does the individual project from one's own story to link it with media texts? What is the role of parable (the linkage of one story with another to bring about understanding)?[89] Do the media reinforce, complement, explain, replace, or contradict interpersonal sources?

Is it the viewing of violent TV content or the subjective "liking" of violent content that reinforces aggressive behaviour? Research indicates that it is the "liking," not the "viewing," of such content that is predictive of aggression in adolescents.[90] Therefore, the cognitive factor or "interpretative, repertoire" is more important as a mitigating factor linking violent media content with aggressive behaviour.

One way to assess this cognitive component is to utilize story analysis. As we listen to people telling their stories that contain their understanding of themselves, the family, the world in which they live, other groups within the world, and so on, their interpretative narratives will become clear. If we are going to understand the narrative structures that support viewers' lives, we must listen to them using partially structured interviews. Qualitative research methodologies are necessary to begin to understand the ethnography of the audience.

What media stories are accepted as true or reflective of the world as the viewer understands it? As researchers, we must break away from the speaker-hearer paradigm that has structured so much of media research to the present time. Instead of understanding the viewer as an unconnected, passive bystander, we must listen to what he or she tells us as a participant in a complex environment of life. We must break away from the cultural elitism of critical studies in which "researchers alone could determine the 'true' meanings of texts, and an over emphasis on hegemony—that the media are all powerful and thus the audience is homogeneous in its reception of the same meanings."[91]

As we grow, we develop a large repertoire of stories that we are able to link with one another. The media present us with other stories that we either link with existing stories we possess or reject because they are too foreign to those stories we already possess. The media may present "the official story" that the power forces in the social structure would like people to accept. We know little of how audience members accept or reject "official" media stories. Researchers must listen to people as they describe their understandings of media content. The researcher is not the only determinant of meaning for media texts.

Tate, working with adult viewers in Saskatoon, found that only those with authoritarian beliefs shared the mean world syndrome. Those with authoritarian stories and those alienated from others (those who scored high on an anomie scale) were the ones who believed the world was evil and that things were getting worse instead of better.

To discover how viewers actually interpret television dramatic narratives, Tate[92] showed a Canadian police drama (*Sidestreet*) and a police drama from the United States (*S.W.A.T.*) to adults in Saskatoon and Rosetown, Saskatchewan. The viewers were then interviewed individually or in focus groups about the two programs. They were quick to point out the stereotypes found in the U.S. program.

The U.S. program was filled with gender, racial, and social stereotypes while the Canadian program was "more true to life." In the U.S. program, the police worked on only one case, but in the Canadian program, the police were busy with a large number of cases. Consequently, they were not able to give complete attention to the event that was central to the program.

Respondents discussed the pattern of police dramas in the United States. The general pattern is one of about seven minutes of violence at the beginning of the program. This is followed by a typical melodramatic play with a few minutes of violence just before the halfway point of the program. At the end of the program, there are 10 to 12 minutes of physical violence in which the evil side is captured or defeated. The program ends with an epilogue in which

everyone is happy with the resolution of the story. People need closure to the stories of life. The U.S. drama provided this closure.[93]

Violence in U.S. police programs is usually physical violence with some verbal violence. The Canadian program contained little physical violence but quite a lot of verbal and psychological violence that extended throughout the entire television program. These respondents said that they found themselves relaxed after viewing the American program. It was stereotypical, predictable, and not believable.

The Canadian program, however, with its psychological violence that continued throughout the entire program, left them tired and worn out, even stressful. It was more realistic than its U.S. counterpart, causing them to think about the issues raised in the narrative of the program. For these reasons Canadian viewers preferred the U.S. crime drama to the Canadian one.

Narrative Speech: The Relational Self (We)

As we grow, we develop relationships with significant friends, loved ones, and mentors. This is the realm of interpersonal communication and is understood by examining the narratives of relationship development. Here media usage and effects interact with the development of relationships outside of primary groups. What is the effect of a developing significant relationship on changing patterns of media usage? If A is a sports enthusiast and B dislikes sports, does A stop watching *Monday Night Football* or *Hockey Night in Canada* because B cannot stand them? If one partner disapproves of violent media content, does the other stop viewing such content?

Morley[94] conducted interviews with 18 lower-middle-class families in South London about how they viewed television. Morley took as his basic premise that one should consider the basic unit of consumption of television to be the family/household rather than the individual viewer. This is precisely what we are arguing in this section of our paradigm. Here the unit of study is not the individual viewer but the relationship/family/household of which the viewer is a member. This is necessary to understand the dynamics of decision making in television consumption. If this factor is ignored one cannot understand how decisions about viewing "choices" are made involving questions of power, responsibility, and control within the relationship or family.

First, Morley found gender differences in the definition of the home. For men the home is primarily defined as a place for leisure as compared to the industrial time spent working outside the home. The home was "defined for women as a sphere for work, whether or not they also work outside the home." This means simply that for men television viewing at home is a leisure activity while for women it is more a social event. As Morley points out, this evades the biological definition of differences in gender viewing. It is the differential placement within the relationship and home environment and not biological factors that cause men to be whole-hearted television viewers while women may view guiltily or feel that they need to be doing something else while viewing. It is necessary to come to understand how the "structure of domestic power relations works to constitute these differences."

One of the key factors in family viewing is who controls the remote control of the television while the family is viewing television. This is an indication of the structure of power within the family. In the majority of the families interviewed, the remote control was in the possession of the father while he was viewing television either alone or with other members of the family. This was a consistent factor in those homes with remote-control television sets except when the male was unemployed while the wife was working. In those cases, it was more common for the man to be expected to let other members of the family control program selection. The remote control may well be the modern symbol of power in relationships and family structures.

Morley found that styles of viewing differed, with men stating a clear preference for "viewing attentively, in silence, without interruption." The women interviewed saw viewing as a social occasion with ongoing conversation, "and usually the performance of at least one other domestic activity (ironing, and so forth) at the same time." Several women expressed the conviction that simply to watch without doing anything else would be a waste of time. Women complained that their husbands were always on them to shut up or be silent during the television program. Men did not want to miss anything.

Morley also found clear differences in program preferences. Men preferred documentaries, factual programs such as news or current affairs, and showed a dislike for fictional programming. Women preferred the fictional drama programs and, once in a while, a real "weepy." Men were less likely to discuss television programs with their friends than were women. The only exception to this is where men say they discuss sports programs with their friends. Men were more likely to plan viewing time, consulting the newspaper schedules, television guides, and setting the VCR to record programs they might be missing because they are viewing other programs. Women tended to show a lack of understanding of the technology of the video recorder.

Morley affirms that these findings hold for this group of television viewers of this social class. Further research should be conducted to assess television consumption of other social classes and groups. However, it is clear from Morley's research that we need to understand the "phenomenology of domestic television viewing—that is, the significance of various modes of physical and social organization of the domestic environment as the context in which television viewing is conducted. There is more to watching television than what is on the screen—and that 'more' is, centrally, the domestic context in which viewing is conducted."[95] We would broaden this to state that it is necessary to consider the relational context in which viewing is conducted. This approach will keep us from making broad gender distinctions that are linked to relational structures and not biological determinism.

Objective Speech: The Known Self (He, She, They)

As we enter the world of work, we become known for our activities and accomplishments. Here we enter the world of social activity, group membership, and work organization, so that media usage may be governed by group membership, economic or social conditions, and work expectations. Within the political system, groups gather to manipulate the media in order to get their social message across to a wider audience. These groups may well use violent terrorist activities to catch media attention in order to reach the power structures of a wider society. Other groups may manipulate the media in order to bring pressure to bear on political decision-makers with strikes, protests, and modest violent activities that journalists consider newsworthy.

At this level, one would also consider the audience-as-a-collectivity perspective.[96] Violent TV content draws an audience to the persuasive advertising power of the medium. While violent programming is generally expensive to produce, it may be more or less profitable for advertisers. Shortly after the La Marsh Report was released in 1976, the J. Walter Thompson Advertising Agency presented Canadian advertisers with a multimedia presentation concerning violent media content. The message of this presentation was that, while violent content attracts viewers in the U.S., Canadian viewers were less accepting of it. Polls conducted for the agency indicated that Canadian viewers were more apt to turn off the TV, and less willing to purchase products advertised or associated with violent content. The message was clear to Canadian advertisers, even if it has not reached U.S. sponsors.

Finally, the question of content production in the mass media must also be raised. How do production, artistic, creative, performance, and economic groups in the industry interact with one another to produce violent media content? At the close of her book *Prime-Time Television: Content and Control*,[97] Muriel Cantor affirms that content should never be studied without considering carefully the social context in which it is created. We need more studies of how the various groups involved in the creation and presentation of media content interact with one another.

The audience also has a role in this dimension of media control, not only because of the ability of groups within the audience to accept or reject content, but also because creative and programming groups in media institutions are sensitive to changing audience definitions of reality. Groups petition, picket, and boycott to have objectionable programming removed from the TV schedule. Other groups organize to keep programs on the air after they have been cancelled by network executives, as in the case of *Star Trek*. Yet, the interaction between these various groups—creative, production, performance, business, advertising, and audience—is poorly understood. Until we examine these conflicting pressures and activities in detail, we will not understand completely the effect of violent content in the mass media.

Summary

We have surveyed the various approaches taken by scholars examining the complex question of the relationship between the mass media and violence. The mass society paradigm argues that the audience is passive and moulded by the mass media into a shapeless, unthinking herd, where members live "meaningless, empty, and passionless" lives.[98] Television, especially, has become a substitute for real experience. As one author using this perspective has affirmed, "television is destructive because the ideas, images, and symbols transmitted through the television screen govern the audience."[99] Similarly George Gerbner has argued that television has become the new religion of our age. As the new religion, it is destructive to social stability and groups.[100]

Cultivation theorists believe that the media, especially TV, endow the mass audience with a common symbolic environment with which to interpret all reality. The violent content of this environment leads people to live in fear, anxiety, and alienation from one another.

Scholars of mass communication who take a psychological approach understand the relationship between the audience and the media as one of reinforcement and selective interpretation. Examining the processes related to media practice and the perceptual practices of media consumers, they argue for a learning theory approach of imitation, precipitated by media and environmental cues. These stimulus-response theories view the audience as generally controlled by both societal and media behavioural cues. The catharsis hypothesis argues that identification with characters in violent TV drama drains from the viewer frustrations and psychological tensions. The stimulating effects theory has shown that viewing violent content increases the frustration and tension already in viewers, an effect heightened by cues within the media content.

Observational learning theory argues that people learn aggressive behaviour from violent media content. While social or family norms suppress these aggressive behaviours, environmental cues similar to those in the media content will overcome the restraint of norms and cause the individual to act aggressively.

Other scholars in the field of mass communication follow the synthesis of Joseph Klapper and Jonathan Freedman by arguing for a limited effects model of mass media influence. They have shown that the media reinforce existing beliefs, attitudes, values, and behaviour patterns that the individual has acquired from the family, church, school, and community. This perspective accepts the audience member as a cognitive individual shaped by societal and media forces. The media are, however, relegated to a reinforcing role, supporting the other institutions of society.

Uses and gratifications theorists, on the other hand, conceive of the audience as actively using the media and shaping a response to it. One must first understand how the individual uses the media before one can begin to understand the effect the media has on the individual. Thus, the relationship between violent media content and behavioural effects is more complex than previous theorists have understood.

In examining these perspectives, we have reviewed the problem of reductionism. We have argued, along with DeFleur and Ball-Rokeach, Cantor, Fouts, and many other scholars, for a more complex, multidimensional approach to the problem. We have attempted to present a holistic model of personhood with which to organize and examine more fully the relationship between violence and the mass media. This model is inevitably more complex due to its multidimensional nature than the uni-dimensional models employed traditionally in the field of mass communication.

The question of the causal role of the media is not a simple one. The paradox that confronts all researchers is that one cannot empirically know with absolute certainty (i.e., show specific cause-effect relationships) because there are so many different variables that must be taken into account. Without using qualitative research techniques that allow media consumers to set their own parameters and categories, all that can be presented is a sketch of the complex relationships and interdependence existing between the person, the mass media, institutions in society, and violence. The mass media may, or may not, be able to act independently of other institutions in society. At the same time, media users are inextricably interdependent on other people, the media, and the structures of society. To attempt to understand these relationships fully, a broad theoretical and methodological approach, utilizing both qualitative and quantitative methodologies, will be necessary—something that remains to be fully developed in the future.

Notes

1. This incident happened in Jonesboro, Arkansas, on 24 March 1998. Ambrose Evans-Pritchard, "The child killers: An isolated act of psychopathetic violence would be easier for Americans to accept. But it was not. This was the third deadly playground attack in less than six months," *The Daily Telegram* and *Associated Press*, 27 March 1998.

2. The murder of Jamie Bulger is believed to be linked to the film *Child's Play 3*. It is reported that the father of one of the two boys who kidnapped and murdered Jamie had rented the video some weeks before Jamie was murdered. There is no evidence that the two boys watched it. There are clear parallels between the film, in which a doll dressed in child's clothes is killed on a railway line after being covered with blue paint, and the incident: Jamie Bulger's body was found on a railway line, covered with blue paint. See the report issued by The National Society for the Prevention of Cruelty to Children (NSPCC) in the United Kingdom, 2 September 1997, and Sarah Hall, "Parents Advised to vet TV Viewing for the Young," *The Guardian* (3 September 1997). In response to moral and public outcry to the James Bulger murder, the Gulbenkian Foundation set up a commission to investigate why people become violent. For a discussion of the report findings that "media violence is not a major factor in the development of violent attitudes and actions," refer to *Children and Violence* (Gulbenkian Foundation, 1995). For comparable examples from the United States, see Victoria Sherrow, *Violence and the Media: The Question of Cause and Effect*, (Brookfield, Conn: The Millbrook Press, 1996). Sherrow discusses the Jamie Bulger case on page 58.

3. Jenn Goddu, "It is happening" in Canada, *Canadian Press, The Hamilton Spectator*, 26 March 1998, D1. Jim Wilkes, "School yard fight ends in tragedy," *The Toronto Star*, 24 April 1998, F1 and 2.

4. The description of this imaginary trial is based on the Ronnie Zemora trial held in Miami, Florida, in 1977. For representative television and news footage on the trial see the videotape *Mass Media* (Audiovisual Services, Michigan State University, East Lansing, Mich. 48824).

5. David Berlo, "The Context for Communication," G. Hanneman and W. McEwen, editors, *Communication and Behaviour* (Don Mills, Ont.: Addison-Wesley, 1975), pp.3-20.

6. Lynn Schafer Gross, *The New Television Technologies*, 3rd ed. (Dubuque, Iowa: Wm. C. Brown, 1990); Frederick Williams, *The New Communications*, 2nd ed. (Belmont, Calif.: Wadsworth, 1989); Eugene D. Tate, "Rethinking the Technologies of Mass Communication," *Journal of Comparative Sociology and Religion* (1985) 12: 38-62.

7. Earle Beattie, "Magazines and Violence," Royal Commission on Violence in the Communications Industry, *Violence in Print and Music*, Vol. 4 (Toronto: Queen's Printer for Ontario, 1976), pp.161-221; Wilfred Kesterton, *A History of Journalism in Canada* (Toronto: McClelland & Stewart, 1967); Garth S. Jowett, Penny Reath, and Monica Schouten, "The Control of Mass Entertainment Media in Canada, the United States and Great Britain: Historical Surveys," Royal Commission Report, *Violence in Print and Music*, Vol. 4, pp.1-104.

8. Christopher H. Sterling and John M. Kitross, *Stay Tuned: A Concise History of American Broadcasting*, 2nd ed. (Belmont, Calif.: Wadsworth, 1989); T.J. Allard, *Straight Up: Private Broadcasting in Canada 1918-1958* (Ottawa: Canadian Communications Foundation, 1979).

9. Herbert Blumer, *Movies and Conduct* (New York: Macmillan, 1933); Herbert Blumer and Philip M. Hauser, *Movies, Delinquency and Crime* (New York: Macmillan, 1933); W. W. Charters, *Motion Pictures and Youth* (New York: Macmillan, 1933).

10. Les Daniels, *Comix: A History of Comic Books in America* (London: Wildwood House, 1971), chapter 5; Amy Kiste Nyberg, *Seal of Approval: The History of the Comics Code* (Jackson: University of Mississippi Press, 1998); William W. Savage, Jr., *Comic Books and America: 1845-1954* (Norman: University of Oklahoma Press, 1990). For more recent developments see Associated Press, "New Comic Book: No Laughing Matter," *Stars and Stripes* (20 September 1993), p.5.

11. Karl French, *Screen Violence* (London: Bloomsbury, 1996); Annette Hill, *Shocking Entertainment: Viewer Response to Violent Media* (Luton: University of Luton Press, 1997); William Paul, *Laughing Screaming: Modern Hollywood Horror and Comedy* (New York: Columbia University Press, 1994); Mike Quarles, *Down and Dirty: Hollywood's Exploitation Filmmakers and Their Movies* (London: McFarland, 1993); Mark Seltzer, *Serial Killers: Death and Life in America's Wound Culture* (London: Routledge, 1998); Antonio Bruschini and Antonio Tentori, *Profonde tenebre: il cinema thrilling italiano, 1962-1982* (Bologna: Granata Press, 1992).

12. U.S. Surgeon General's Scientific Advisory Committee on Television and Social Behaviour, *Television and Social Behaviour* (Washington: U.S. Government Printing Office, 1972), Vols. 1-5; George Comstock, *Television in America* (Beverly Hills, Calif.: Sage, 1980), p.109.

13. Royal Commission on Violence in the Communications Industry, *Report* (Toronto: Queen's Printer for Ontario, 1976), Vols. 1-7, and *Approaches, Conclusions and Recommendations* (Toronto: Queen's Printer for Ontario, 1976), Vol. l, p.26.

14. Eugene Tate, "The Ontario Royal Commission on Violence in the Communications Industry: Twenty years later," *British Journal of Canadian Studies* (1998) 13 (1): 148-163.

15. Canadian Radio-television and Telecommunications Commission, "Voluntary Code Regarding Violence in Television Programming," Public Notice CRTC 1993-149 (Ottawa: 1993).

16. Leonard Bloom and Philip Selznick, *Sociology* (Evanston: Row, Peterson, 1958), p.38.

17. Paul F. Lazarsfeld and Robert K. Merton, "Mass Communication, Popular Taste and Organized Social Action," Wilbur S Schramm and Donald Roberts, editors, *The Process and Effects of Mass Communication* (Urbana: University of Illinois Press, 1971), p.557.

18. Eugene D. Tate, "Viewers' Perceptions of Selected Television Programs," Royal Commission on Violence in the Communications Industry, *Vulnerability to Media Effects*, Vol. 6 (Toronto: Queen's Printer for Ontario, 1976), pp.293-94.

19. Harold D. Lasswell, "The Structure and Function of Communication in Society," Lyman Bryson, editor, *The Communication of Ideas* (New York: Institute for Religious and Social Studies, 1948), p.37.

20. James Fletcher, "Developments in Mass Communication Programming and Technology," in Eugene D. Tate, editor, "Violence and the Media," *Peace Research Review* (2000) 15 (4 & 5): 19-36.

21. Marshall McLuhan, *The Gutenburg Galaxy: The Making of Typographic Man* (Toronto: University of Toronto Press, 1962); Marshall McLuhan, *Understanding Media* (New York: McGraw-Hill, 1964). For a discussion of McLuhan's theoretical perspective see Bruce Gronbeck, "McLuhan as Rhetorical Theorist," *Journal of Communication* (1981) 31: 117-28; and Paul Jones, "The technology is not the cultural form? Raymond Williams's sociological critique of Marshall McLuhan," *The Canadian Journal of Communication* (1998) 23 (4): 423-454. Ruth Katz and Elihu Katz, "McLuhan: Where did he come from, where did he disappear," *Canadian Journal of Communication.* (1998) 23 (3): 307-319. See also Stephen Littlejohn, *Communication Theory* (Belmont, Calif.: Wadsworth, 1980), pp.26-70.

22. Harold A. Innis, *The Bias of Communication* (Toronto: University of Toronto Press, 1951), and *Empire and Communications* (Toronto: University of Toronto Press, 1950, 1972). See also William J. Buxton, "Harold Innis' Excavation of Modernity: The Newspaper Industry, Communications, and the Decline of Public Life," *Canadian Journal of Communication* (1998) 23: 321-339.

23. Jacques Ellul, *Propaganda: The Formation of Men's Attitudes* (New York: Knopf, 1968). For a brief summary see Clifford G. Christians and Michael R. Reals, "Jacques Ellul's Contributions to Critical Media Theory," *Journal of Communication* (1979) 29: 83-93.

24. Marie Winn, *The Plug-in Drug* (New York: Viking Press, 1977); Jerry Mander, *Four Arguments for the Elimination of Television* (New York: Morrow Quill, 1978).

25. George Gerbner and Larry Gross, "The Violent Face of Television and Its Lessons," Edward Palmer and Aimee Dorr, editors, *Children and the Faces of Television: Teaching, Violence, Selling* (New York: Academic Press, 1980). See also George Gerbner et al., "The Mainstreaming of America: Violence Profile No. 11," *Journal of Communication* (1980) 30: 10-29. Gerbner has likened television to the new religion in American life in that it sets the norms and taboos of modern society. Scott Stossel, "The Man Who Counts Killings," *Atlantic Monthly*, May 1997.

26. Herbert I. Schiller, *Mass Communication and the American Empire* (New York: Augustus M. Kelley, 1969); Herbert I. Schiller, *The Mind Managers* (Boston: Beacon Press, 1973).

27. Hal Himmelstein, *Television Myth and the American Mind* (New York: Preager, 1984).

28. Tannis MacBeth (Williams) et al., "Windows on the World: Canadian Versus U.S. Television Voices," *Canadian Journal of Communication* (1990) 15(1): 19-44.

29. Anthony Doob and Glenn E. MacDonald, "The News Media and Perceptions of Violence," Royal Commission on Violence in the Communications Industry, *Learning from the Media*, Vol. 5 (Toronto: Queen's Printer for Ontario, 1976), pp.71-226.

30. Tate, "Viewers' Perceptions," pp.283-401.

31. J.M. Wober, "Television violence and paranoid perceptions: The view from Great Britain," *Public Opinion Quarterly* (1978) 42: 314-321. See also J.M. Wober and B. Gunter, "Television and personal threat: Fact or artifact?: A British survey," *British Journal of Social Psychology* (1982) 21: 239-247; B. Gunter and J.M. Wober. *Violence on Television: What the Viewers Think* (London: Libbey, 1988); B. Gunter and Jill McAleer, *Children and Television* (London: Routledge, 1997).

32. André Gosselin, Jacques deGuise, and Guy Paquette, "Violence on Canadian television and some of its cognitive effects," *Canadian Journal of Communication* (1997) 22: 145-169.

33. Raymond A. Bauer, "The Audience," in Ithiel de Sola Pool and Wilbur Schramm, editors, *Handbook of Communication*; Bauer, "The Communicator and Audience," in Lewis A. Dexter and David Manning White, editors, *People, Society and Mass Communications* (New York: The Free Press, 1964), pp.125-40.

34. Seymour Feshbach, "The Stimulating Versus Cathartic Effects of a Vicarious Aggressive Experience," *Journal of Abnormal and Social Psychology* (1961) 63: 381-85.

35. Seymour Feshbach and Robert Singer, *Television and Aggression* (San Francisco: Jossev-Bass, 1971).

36. Percy Tannenbaum, editor, *The Entertainment Functions of Television* (Hillsdale, NJ.: Lawrence Erlbaum, 1980) pp.107-31.

37. Leonard Berkowitz, *Aggression: A Social Psychological Analysis* (New York: McGraw-Hill, 1962).

38. Research indicates that people of a lower social class spend more time viewing television than people of a higher social class. Similarly, as people's educational level goes up, the amount of time spent viewing television goes down. See Tate, "Viewers' Perceptions," p.305.

39. Berkowitz, *Aggression*; Leonard Berkowitz and Russell Geen, "Stimulus Qualities of the Target of Aggression: A Further Study," *Journal of Personality and Social Psychology* (1976) 5:(3): 364-68.

40. Tannenbaum, *Entertainment Functions.*

41. Albert Bandura and Richard Walters, *Social Learning and Personality* (Englewood Cliffs, NJ.: Prentice-Hall, 1963); Albert Bandura, *Social Learning Theory* (Englewood Cliffs, NJ: Prentice-Hall, 1977); Albert Bandura, "Psychological Mechanisms of Aggression," R.G. Geen and C.I. Donnerstein, editors, *Aggression: Theoretical and Empirical Reviews*, Vol. 1 (New York: Academic Press, 1983), pp.1-40; R. M. Liebert and J. Sprafkin, *The Early Window: Effects of Television on Children*, 3rd ed. (New York: Pergamon Press, 1988); and L. Friedrich-Cofer and A.C. Huston, "Television Violence and Aggression: The Debate Continues," *Psychological Bulletin* (1986) 100: 364-71. For an example of the type of research conducted with this theoretical approach see Wendy L. Josephson, "Television Violence and Children's Aggression: Testing the Priming, Social Script, and Disinhibition Predictions," *Journal of Personality and Social Psychology* (1987) 53, no. 5: 882-90; and Michael A. Milburn, *Persuasion and Politics: The Social Psychology of Public Opinion* (Pacific Coast, Calif: Brooks/Cole Publishing Co., 1991).

42. DeFleur and Ball-Rokeach discuss this simply as reinforcement theory. See Melvin L. DeFleur and Sandra Ball-Rokeach, *Theories of Mass Communication*, 4th ed. (New York: Longman, 1982), pp.205-7.

43. Joseph Klapper, *The Effects of Mass Communication* (New York: The Free Press, 1960). Jonathan Freedman, "Effect of television violence on aggressiveness," *Psychological Bulletin* (1984) 96: 227-46; and Jonathan Freedman, "Television Violence and Aggression: A rejoinder," *Psychological Bulletin* (1986) 100: 372-78.

44. Tsiyona Peled and Elihu Katz, "Media Functions in Wartime: The Israel Home Front in October 1973," Jay G. Blumler and Elihu Katz, editors, *The Uses of Mass Communications* (Beverly Hills, Calif.: Sage Publications, 1974), pp.49-69; Bradley S. Greenberg, "Gratifications of Television Viewing and Their Correlates for British Children," Blumler and Katz, *The Uses of Mass Communications*, pp.71-92.

45. Gerald R. Miller discusses three perspectives on communication: (1) the action perspective, which understands that the source encodes a message that is sent through a channel to a receiver. All receivers are considered to be equal. Meanings exist in words; (2) the interaction perspective, which understands that there is a necessity for feedback but communication is still essentially source to receiver; (3) the transactional perspective, in which communication is understood as a shared event with both participants encoding and/or decoding simultaneously and change occurring in both communicators. There is an interdependence of participants that is missing in the other two perspectives. See Cassandra Book, editor, *Human Communication* (New York: St. Martin's Press, 1980).

46. Eugene D. Tate, "A Revised Catharsis Hypothesis: Activation Theory and Uses and Gratifications of Television," an unpublished paper presented to Founding Session, Canadian Communication Association, Saskatoon, Saskatchewan, 1979.

47. Tate, "Viewers' Perceptions," p.312.

48. Donald W. Fiske and Salvatore R. Maddi, *Functions of Varied Experience* (Homewood, Ill.: Dorsev Press, 1961); Salvatore R. Maddi, *Personality Theories: A Comparative Analysis* (Homewood, Ill.: Dorsey Press, 1972).

49. Fletcher, "Developments in Mass Communication."

50. Rick Houghton-Larsen, "Patterns of Media Usage Related to Gratifications Sought," *Canadian Journal of Communication* (1982) 8, no. 4: 42-55.

51. Gregory T. Fouts; "Effects of Television on Children: Developmental Approach," Royal Commission on Violence in the Communications Industry, *Vulnerability*, Vol 6, p.84.

52. James Lemert, *Does Mass Communication Change Public Opinion After All? A New Approach to Effects Analysis* (Chicago: Nelson-Hall. 1981).

53. Fouts, "Effects of Television," p.7.

54. Susan B. Shimanoff, *Communications Rules: Theory and Research* (Beverly Hills, Calif.: Sage, 1980); Donald Cushman and G. Whiting, "An Approach to Communication Theory: Toward Consensus on Rules," *Journal of Communication* (1972) 22: 217-38.

55. Fouts, "Effects of Television."

56. David Gauntlett, *Moving Experiences: Understanding Television's Influences and Effects* (London: John Libbey, 1995).

57. David Gauntlett, *Video Critical: Children, the Environment and Media Power* (Luton: University of Luton Press, 1996).

58. Martin Barker, "Looking at the dangerous media," *Times Higher Education Supplement*, 22 August 1998. Martin Barker and Julian Petley, *Ill Effects: The Mass Media/Violence Debate* (London: Routledge, 1997).

59. Johan Galtung, "Cultural violence," *Journal of Peace Research* (1990) 27 (3): 291-305.

60. Hannah Bradley, editor, *Defining Violence: Understanding the Causes and Effects of Violence* (Aldershot: Avebury, 1996).

61. Johan Galtung, "Cultural violence," *op. cit.*

62. Eugene D. Tate and Kathleen McConnell, "Communication and Cultural Violence: The Role of Communication in the Legitimation Of Violence," *Peace Research Reviews* (2000) 15 (4 & 5): 53-87; Eugene D. Tate and Kathleen McConnell,"Violence in the Media and American Society: Movement from Social Scientific Reductionism to Identification of the Roots of Violence," *Peace Research Reviews* (2000) 15 (4 & 5): 88-116.

63. Sonia M. Livingstone, *Making Sense of Television: The Psychology of Audience Interpretation* (Oxford: Butterworth-Hermann Ltd., 1995); Sonia M. Livingstone and Peter Hunt *Talk on Television: Audience Participation and Public Debate* (London: Routledge, 1994). David Morley in James Hay, Lawrence Grossberg, and Ellen Wartella *The Audience and its Landscape* (Oxford: Westview Press, 1996).

64. Angela McRobbie, *Postmodernism and Popular Culture* (London: Routledge, 1994).

65. Jonathan Kellerman. *Savage Spawn: Reflections on Violent Children* (New York: Ballantine Publishing Group, 1999).

66. Shaun Moores, *Interpreting Audiences: The Ethnography of Audiences* (London: Sage Publications, 1993); Shaun Moores, *Satellite Television and Everyday Life: Articulating Technology* (Luton: John Libbey Media, 1996). See also David Gauntlett, *Video Critical: Children, the Environment and Media Power* (Luton: University of Luton Press, 1996).

67. Robert Coles, "The Inner and Outer World," *The Mind's Fate: A Psychiatrist Looks at His Profession* (Boston: Little Brown and Co., 1995), p.351.

68. Robert Coles, "The Inner and Outer World," pp.359-60.

69. Eugene D. Tate, "The Ontario Royal Commission on Violence in the Communications Industry: Twenty Years Later," *British Journal of Canadian Studies* (1998) 13: 148-163.

70. Eugene D. Tate and Stuart H. Surlin, "Agreement with Opinionated TV Characters Across Cultures," *Journalism Quarterly* (1976) 53: 199-203, 210; Stuart H Surlin and Eugene D. Tate, "All in the Family: Is Archie Funny?" *Journal of Communication* (1976) 26(4): 61-68.

71. Douglas Baer and James Winter, "U.S. Media Imperialism in a Canadian Community: The Inculcation of Anti-Governrment Sentiment," *Canadian Journal of Communication* (1983) 10(1): 51-86.

72. Richard E. Goranson, "Television Violence Effects: Issues and Evidence," Royal Commission on Violence in the Communications Industry, *Learning from the Media*, Vol. 5, pp.1-30; J. Phillipe Rushton, "Television and Pro-social Behaviour," in Royal Commission on Violence in the Communications Industry, *Learning from the Media*, Vol. 5, pp.31-35.

73. See especially the continuing program of content analysis of media content carried on by Tannis MacBeth et al., "Windows on the World," Tannis MacBeth (Williams), editor, *The Impact of Television: A Natural Experiment in Three Communities* (New York: Academic Press, 1987). For a summary of this research, see her article in this volume (Chapter 14).

74. See Eugene Tate, *The Search for Canadian Identity(ies): The Importance of Stories for Defining Identity*, 60th Canada House Lecture (London: Canadian High Commission, 1998), as well as Lawrence Martin, "Continental Union," in *Annals of American Association of Political and Social Science* (March 1995) no. 538: 131-142. See also, George Grant, *Lament for a Nation: The Defeat of Canadian Nationalism* (Ottawa: Carleton University Press, 1989). Peter C. Emberley, editor, *By Loving Our Own: George Grant and the Legacy of Lament for a Nation* (Ottawa: Carleton University Press, 1990); Mel Hurtig, "One Last Chance: The Legacy of Lament for a Nation," in Peter C. Emberley, editor, *By Loving Our Own: George Grant and the Legacy of Lament for a Nation* (Ottawa: Carleton University Press, 1990).

75. *Special Senate Committee On the Mass Media*, Report (Ottawa: Queen's Printer, 1970); *Task Force on Broadcasting*, Report (Ottawa: Supply and Services, 1986).

76. See Eugene D. Tate, "Eugen Rosenstock-Huessy Revolutionizing Communication Theory," M. Darrol Bryant and Hans R. Huessy, editors, *Eugen Rosenstock-Huessy: Studies in His Life and Thought* (Queenston, Ont.: Edwin Mellen Press, 1986), pp.89-107; Eugene D. Tate and Kathleen McConnell, "Restoring Speech and 'Time' to Communication Theory: Contributions of Franz Rosenzweig and Eugen Rosenstock-Huessy," *Resources in Education*, ref. ED290194 (1988); Kathleen McConnell and Eugene D. Tate, "'Glasnost': Restoring Health to Academic Discussion: Eugen Rosenstock-Huessy and V.N. Volosinov," unpublished paper presented to *Respondeo ergo sum* a conference to celebrate the 100th Anniversary of the birth of Eugen Rosenstock-Huessy, August 1989.

77. See especially the work of Eugen Rosenstock-Huessy, Franz Rosenzweig, Martin Buber, and Mikhail Bakhtin. Harold Stahmer, *Speak That I May See Thee (New York: Harper and Row, 1967)*.

78. Grant Noble, *Children in Front of the Small Screen* (London: Constable, 1975).

79. James W. Carey, editor, *Media, Myths and Narratives: Television and the Press* (Beverly Hills, Calif.: Sage Publications, 1988); Willard D. Rowland Jr., and Bruce Watkins, editors, *Interpreting Television: Current Research Perspectives* (Beverly Hills, Calif.: Sage Publications, 1984); Johan Galtung, "Cultural Violence," *Journal of Peace Research* (1990) 27: 291-305; Eugene D. Tate and Kathleen McConnell, "Communication and Cultural Violence: Legitimating the Role of Violence in Society," *Peace Research Reviews* (2000) 15 (4 & 5): 88-110.

80. Fletcher, "Developments in Mass Communication."

81. Laura Stempel Mumford, *Love and Ideology in the Afternoon: Soap Opera, Women, and Television Genre* (Bloomington, Indiana: Indiana University Press, 1995), pp.7-8; Lisa A. Lewis, editor, *The Adoring Audience: Fan Culture and Popular Media* (London: Routledge, 1992); Andrea L. Press, *Women Watching Television: Gender, Class and Generation in the American Television Experience* (Philadelphia: University of Pennsylvania Press, 1991); Lynn Spigel and Denise Mann, editors, *Private Screenings: Television and the Female Consumer* (Minneapolis: University of Minnesota Press, 1992).

82. Eugene D. Tate, *The Search for Canadian Identity(ies): The Importance of Stories for Defining Identity*, 60th Canada House Lecture (London: Canadian High Commission, 1998); Susan Engel, *The Stories Children Tell: Making Sense of the Narratives of Childhood* (Oxford: W. H. Freeman and Company, 1995); Mark Turner, *The Literary Mind* (Oxford: Oxford University Press, 1996); George Lakoff, *Women, Fire and Dangerous Things: What Categories Reveal about the Mind* (Chicago: University of Chicago Press, 1987); Jerome Bruner, *Acts of Meaning* (Cambridge: Harvard University Press, 1990); Roger C. Schank, *Tell Me a Story: A New Look at Real and Artificial Memory* (Toronto: Collier Macmillan Canada, 1990).

83. Howard Gardner, *Leading Minds: An Anatomy of Leadership* (London: Harper Collins Publishers, 1995); Joseph Campbell, *The Hero of a Thousand Faces* (New York: Meridian Books, 1970).

84. Andrew M. Osler, "A Descriptive Study of Perceptions and Attitudes among Journalists in Ontario," *The Media Industries: From Here to Where?* (Toronto: Queen's Printer for Ontario, 1976), Vol. 7, pp.8-46; Andrew M Osler, *News: The Evolution of Journalism in Canada.* (Toronto: Copp Clark Pitman Ltd. 1993). For reporting on the Gulf War see "The Gulf War in the Media," *The Nordicom Review of Nordic Mass Communication Research* (1992), no. 2, especially Gert Z. Nordstrom, "The Outbreak of War and Pictures in Swedish Mass Media": 69-82.

85. Deborah Tannen, *The Argument Culture: Stopping America's War of Words* (New York: Ballantine Books, 1998). See also Deborah Tannen, "Agonism in the Academy: Surviving Higher Learning's Argument Culture," *The Chronicle of Education*, 31 March 2000; Eugen Rosenstock-Huessy, "The Four Diseases of Speech," *Speech and Reality* (Norwich, Vermont: Argo Press, 1970).

86. Eugen Rosenstock-Huessy, *Out of Revolution: Autobiography of Western Man* (Norwich, Vt.: Argo Books, 1969), p.689.

87. Milton Rokeach, *Beliefs, Attitudes and Values* (San Francisco: Jossey-Bass, 1970).

88. Jonathan Potter and Margaret Wetherell, *Discourse and Social Psychology: Beyond Attitudes and Behaviour* (London: Sage, 1987).

89. Mark Turner, *The Literary Mind*, has a specific definition of parable: "Parable begins with narrative imagining—the understanding of a complex of objects, events, and actors as organized by our knowledge of story. It then combines story with projection: one story is projected onto another. The essence of parable is its intricate combining of two of our basic forms of knowledge:–story and projection" (p.5).

90. Kim B. Walker and Donald D. Morley, "Attitudes and Parental Factors as Intervening Variables in the Television Violence-Aggression Relation," *Communication Research Reports* (1991) 8: 41-47. For concerns

about the violent content of video games and their effect on the developing mind see, for example, "Too Violent for Kids," *Time* (27 September 1993), pp.52-53.

91. Sonia Livingstone and Peter Hunt, *Talk on Television*, p.11. See also Lynne Joyrich, "All That Television Allows: TV Melodrama, Postmodernism, and Consumer Culture," in Lynn Spigel and Denise Mann, editors, *Private Screenings*, pp.227-251. Virginia Nightengale, *Studying Audiences* (London: Routledge, 1996).

92. Eugene D. Tate, "Viewers' Perceptions."

93. Research on rumours conducted over the years indicate that all people seek to bring closure to a story by fitting it into an environment they know and give it some form of ending. Laura Stempel Mumfort has suggested that narrative form lacks closure and that closure is masculine. Spigel has shown how the traditional form of closure for Hollywood writers is marriage. In Hollywood films closure is most often brought about by the marriage of the couple around whom the story revolves. See Lynn Spigel and Denise Mann, *Private Screenings*, pp.217-225. See also Sandy Flitterman-Lelvis, "All's Well That Doesn't End–Soap Opera and the Marriage Motif," in Lynn Spigel and Denise Mann, *Private Screenings*.

94. David Morley, "The Gendered Framework of Family Viewing," in Shaun Moores, *Interpreting Audiences: The Ethnography of Audiences* (London: Sage Publications, 1993), pp.173-185.

95. David Morley, page 185. See also Robert P. Hawkins, John M. Wiemann, and Suzanne Pingree, *Advancing Communication Science: Merging Mass and Interpersonal Processes* (London: Sage, 1988); Birgitta Hoijer, Kjell Nowak, and Sven Ross, "Reception of Television as a Cognitive and Cultural Process (REKK), *The Nordicom Review of Nordic Mass Communication Research* (1992), no. 1: 1-14.

96. Dallas W. Smythe, *Dependency Road: Communications, Capitalism, Consciousness and Canada* (Norwood, N.J.: Ablex, 1981); Dallas Smythe, *Counterclockwise: Perspectives on Communication* (Oxford: Westview Press, 1994).

97. Muriel G. Cantor, *Prime-time Television: Content and Control* (Beverly Hills, Calif.: Sage, 1980).

98. Ellul, *Propaganda*, p.378.

99. Cantor, *Prime-time Television*, p.105.

100. Scott Stossel, "The Man Who Counts Killings," *Atlantic Monthly* (May 1997).

20

Pornography in the Mass Media and the Panic over Sex Crimes in Canada

Augustine Brannigan and Kelly Hardwick

In the last five decades, few topics in the social and legal sciences have received more scrutiny than pornography, its consequences, and its censorship under the laws concerning obscenity. This interest is understandable. There have been perceptible changes in the nature of both sexual conduct in real life and sexual representation in the media.

For instance, the Internet has provided a new avenue for the open distribution of pornography. With the introduction and rapid expansion of the Internet, "cyberporn" or computer generated (i.e., simulated) pornography has also exploded. This explosion has created a level of concern and interest in phenomena associated with pornography that was not present even 15 years ago. As of 1997, there were an estimated 40-80 million users of the Internet.[1] Today, estimates are closer to 500 million users and the numbers continue to rise.

What distinguishes the Internet from other media is the ease with which users can obtain pornographic material. Arguably, it is the ease of access and the fear of dire consequences that generates most of the concern over cyberporn. However, the mainstream media have exploited public fears in what has been dubbed the "cyberporn scare"[2] as well as the controversial Rimm Report.[3] The Rimm Report, by Carnegie Mellon University undergraduate engineering student Marty Rimm, described the prevalence of paraphillic images in a survey of over 900,000 pictures downloaded by 8.5 million net users in a four-month period in 1995. It generated a heated debate because of its questionable methods and conclusions.[4]

In the twentieth century, moral panics over sexuality were quite common. Although birth-control technology is thought to have contributed to the "sexual revolution" of the 1960s, Pitirim Sorokin's *The American Sex Revolution*[5] predated widespread use of the pill by a decade, and catalogued what Sorokin believed to be the social plagues that accompanied the change in sexual mores: "sexual addiction,"

soaring divorce rates, delinquency, and "spiritual, moral and mental anarchy." Even prior to the 1960s, the average age at marriage had been declining throughout the century, and over time, there was a much greater tolerance of teenage sexuality.[6] Sorokin's book appeared three years after the advent of *Playboy*, which capitalized on the promotion of male sexual recreation divorced from family and traditional ascetic religious values.

Competition in both erotic entertainment and in mass advertising rolled back the frontiers of sexual modesty in the public culture, as *Penthouse*, *Playboy*, and *Hustler* competed openly for market share, and, like opinion leaders in the fashion industry, attempted to define more permissive standards of sexual aesthetics.[7] Increasingly explicit photography replaced lascivious prose; the jurisprudence moved from *Lady Chatterley's Lover* and *The Story of O* to *Deep Throat* and *Debbie Does Dallas*. By 1985 pornography had become a $7 billion business in the U.S.[8] In the age of cyberspace, a single Internet company, Sex.com, is estimated to be grossing $US100 million dollars per year.[9]

Traditional conservative sectors of society, the evangelical churches and their morality leaders, had maintained opposition to explicit sexual fiction throughout the century, whether in text or pictures, reinforcing their investment in puritanical self-restraint. Over the past three decades, school boards have been enjoined to censor the works of writers such as J.D. Salinger and Margaret Laurence, which treat sexuality with uncommon frankness.[10] Similarly, "genteel society" had objected to the publication of Mark Twain's *Adventures of Huckleberry Finn* in 1885, and the book was banned from the Concord Library in Massachusetts as "trash suitable only for the ghetto," a step that contributed enormously to its sales, and which led its author to thank the library board for the publicity.[11]

In the 1970s, a new perspective emerged. Liberal feminists began to view pornography, particularly violent pornography and "slasher" films, not as a positive fictional counterpart to the sexual revolution of the 1960s, but as a backlash against women's struggle for social emancipation and as a form of discrimination that promoted and reinforced inequality.[12] Erotica, by contrast, was viewed as a positive celebration of sexuality, something to be encouraged; but violent pornography was said to contain deeper misogynistic messages. This analysis was part of the wider "phallic critique" of predatory male sexuality that was explored by feminists in studies of unreported rape, date rape, rape within marriage, sexual harassment, childhood sexual abuse, and teenage prostitution.[13] In the 1980s, evangelicals supported feminists in advancing the Minneapolis anti-pornography by-laws, combining traditional and progressive social elements in the pursuit of censorship.[14] Some feminists, particularly socialists, were alarmed that the control of female sexuality would fall under the traditional patriarchal law, making alternative sexual lifestyles, including lesbian relationships, vulnerable to traditional morality.[15]

Aside from political developments such as these, there were other important dimensions to the public debate. In contrast to obscene Victorian publications, which were characteristically an underground phenomenon,[16] contemporary "pornography" and explicit rock videos, motion pictures, videos, and men's magazines are mass culture products available openly, not to mention the "ease" of consumption provided via a click or two of a mouse in the privacy of one's room. It is instructive that the "obscenity" of the 1930s, which consisted of advertising information about and access to contraceptive devices, was not the subject of mass hysteria. There was little public concern because fertility-control information and birth control devices were not generally available as over-the-counter products. Indeed, the social history of obscenity in this period shows prosecutions under obscenity law only on those infrequent occasions when pharmacists and social activists (as well as their commercial counterparts) tried to publicize these matters.[17]

In the mid-1980s, the Meese Commission in the U.S. appeared more concerned with *Penthouse* and *Playboy*, the most popular sex magazines, than with anything available on an under-the-counter basis. Indeed, the concern with the high-profile market appears to have motivated the campaign of intimidation of the 7-Eleven convenience-store chain in a letter circulated under the letterhead of the U.S. Attorney General by the executive director of the Meese inquiry. This letter advised Southland Corporation, franchiser of 7-Eleven stores, to discontinue sales of these magazines or be cited by the U.S. government as a distributor of harmful publications. *Penthouse* and *Playboy* lawyers succeeded in getting a court order requiring the government to rescind the letter, but the stores in both Canada and the U.S. "voluntarily" decided to drop the magazines, a result the earlier boycotts had failed to achieve.[18] The subsequent rise of the Internet changed the situation entirely. By 1994, there were an estimated 450,000 pornographic images, text, and sound files on the Internet and these files had been "hit" approximately 6 million times.[19] The use of the Internet has been increasing at a rate similar to the advent of television in the 1950s. In 1998 in Canada, almost one-third of all persons over the age of 18 utilized the Internet. While the largest proportion of information available on the "Net" is, in a word, "clean," its use as a medium to exchange and consume pornographic material is bound to increase proportionately as computers become as abundant as televisions.

Developments in computer technology have proven to be invaluable for the production and consumption of pornography. What makes the computer and the Internet so attractive to producers and consumers of pornographic material? Perhaps the key reason for their attractiveness is the perceived anonymity associated with this new medium. In the past, producers needed to own complicated and expensive equipment to process their own film or run the risk of being turned in or reported to the authorities. With the development of home computer and video technologies, the "product" can be produced with little or no risk of detection. And with the rise of digital technology, which allows producers to upload material directly onto the Internet, the risk of detection is lowered even further. "The declining costs of computing and the vast communication networks that encompass the Internet have provided users worldwide with information at their fingertips. The perceived anonymity while using these resources opens the door to pornography and other obscene communications."[20] The Internet has, in sum, markedly reduced the costs and risks associated with producing, advertising, distributing, and also acquiring pornographic materials (especially for consumers living outside large urban areas).

One particular area of the pornographic trade that has been significantly impacted by computer technology and the development of the Internet with its appealing anonymity is child pornography. Skoog and Murray inform us that, by the late 1980s, law enforcement efforts focussing on the importation and distribution of child pornography had cut the flow of kiddie porn down to a trickle.[21] However, the use of the Internet and high-tech equipment such as scanners and digital cameras has resulted in an alarming expansion of the child pornography industry during the last decade. By 1997, Skoog and Murray estimated that there were approximately one million sexually explicit images of children on the Internet.

While *pornographic material is not likely a direct cause of third-person harm*, it may still be harmful by perpetuating victimization and exploitation, especially when children are targeted in its production. With the advent of the Internet, there has been an explosion of the availability of child pornography. And pedophiles go on line with the "intent of enticing children into sexual banter or actual sexual contact."[22] Before computers and the Internet, while producers and distributors of child pornography enjoyed some degree of anonymity, the Internet now makes detection very difficult and kiddie porn readily accessible. Anonymity and ease of access, along with the proliferation of related technologies, is making the computer the tool of choice for pedophiles. With the development of virtual software, the "boom" in child pornography is very difficult to check.

Given the mass-market basis of the pornography phenomenon, the past two decades have witnessed several important inquiries into the impact of pornography on attitudes and conduct in Canada, Britain, the U.S., and Australia. Before we turn to these inquiries, it might be instructive to examine an earlier chapter in the history of obscenity.

Comics Are the Theory, Delinquency Is the Practice

There are some parallels between the current anti-pornography climate and the situation in Canada, the U.S., England, and Australia in the late 1940s and early 1950s regarding offensive literature. Canada's existing Criminal Code section dealing with obscene publications, like that of many Australian and U.S. states, contains a provision making it unlawful to publish or sell a crime comic. Section 163 reads:

Everyone commits an offence who ...

1(b) makes, prints, publishes, distributes, sells or has in his possession for the purposes of publication, distribution or circulation a crime comic....

(7) In this section, "crime comic" means a magazine, periodical, or book that exclusively or substantially comprises mat-

ter depicting pictorially the commission of crimes, real or fictitious; or events connected with crimes, real or fictitious, whether occurring before or after the commission of the crime.

The Canadian law was passed by Parliament in 1949 following a vigorous period of lobbying by interest groups who claimed that comics were causing juvenile delinquency. At trials of offending producers, distributors, or vendors, the *mens rea* ("guilty mind") requirement was suspended from the burden of prosecution, and the Crown was not required to show that the comics were actually harmful, with Parliament taking the responsibility for holding that this was the case. In the House of Commons, E. Davie Fulton attributed murders, suicides, and robberies committed by young offenders to the reading of crime and horror comics. Public officials pointed knowingly to the fact that comics were found in the possession of young people charged with serious offences. In popular psychiatric writing, homosexual and lesbian inclinations were blamed on Batman and Robin on the one hand, and Wonder Woman on the other.[23]

Experts had raised alarms regarding earlier media impacts on young persons. *The Public Health Journal,* published in Toronto, undertook a campaign in 1917 against the "lurid posters" advertising motion pictures that were thought to promote "lascivious conduct." In 1923, the same editorial board expressed alarm over children's magazines such as *Snappy Stories* and *Saucy Stories,* which described the exploits of Nick Carter, Jesse James, and Dead Eye Dick.

This filth purveying medium ... is filled with stories of a dangerous character, most of them relating incidents, which not only have to do with sex, but which are told in such a way and from such an angle as to make any sensible reader conclude that the only safe method by which one can dispose of such muck, is to ban it from the mails altogether. One's determination will not be lessened in the least by the information that these magazines are commonly snapped up with avidity by young school girls. A fine school for moral training they provide![24]

Although the new comic books, which appeared in 1938 and grew to tremendous popularity in the 1940s and 1950s, did replace this relatively innocuous literature, the belief that galvanized legislative and judicial opinion against the comics was that the new subject matter gave ideas to young people that they were imitating, and hence that comics amounted to a threat to public safety. Though the same charge had been made regarding criminogenic motion pictures in the 1930s,[25] the conclusion gained currency among leading law-and-order figures such as J. Edgar Hoover and Elliott Ness only when it was translated into a public-safety problem. J.J. Hayes Doone headed a Canadian Senate committee looking into "salacious literature" in 1952. He claimed, "It has become increasingly evident, even from an economic and safety point of view, that drastic action is called for. No less an authority than Hoover, head of the FBI, advises that filthy literature is the great moron maker and is casting criminals faster than his country can build prisons to house them."[26] Legislative changes to the obscenity law were undertaken in many European and common-law countries to control the comics. In addition, the comic industry instituted its own code to control the language, themes, and morality of comic stories. In 1955 Abraham Kaplan referred to the new literature as the "pornography of violence," an expression we have heard much of in the current debate.[27] Then, as now, a moral problem over an unorthodox literature was translated into a question of public safety: pornography and comics are the theory; rape and delinquency are the practice.

To be sure, the comics were different, as was most popular writing in the 1920s and 1930s. They reflected the alienation of both the urban working class on the one hand and the despair of the western farmer on the other. This was the era of the "hardboiled" heroes and tough-guy detectives such as Philip Marlowe and Sam Spade, the era of Steinbeck and social realism in fiction. The popular entertainment of the 1930s—novels from Hammett and Hemingway to Cain and Chandler, as well as the Bogart motion pictures—explored crime, violence, sex, political corruption, and social alienation, depicting them in a *noire* graphic style unprecedented in the history of murder fiction.[28] Also, the vernacular realism of the Hemingway and Hammett narratives, with their crisp, direct style, gave the crime novel tremendous appeal among working-class readers.[29]

The new genre, appearing with its own book format and with its own narrative conventions ("Kapow!"), was an extension of this literary innovation to younger and less-educated readers and was an immediate commercial success in an industry racked by falling prices throughout the Great Depression. Like the lurid paperback novels, the crime comics, as well as the adventure, jungle, western, war, and horror comics, depicted, though in a more fantastic idiom, the same "mature" adult themes: crimes, violence, and females with cleavage. American comics were distributed internationally, and with the help of the American armed forces, were introduced wherever Americans were based during the Second World

War. However, when the comics were outlawed in Canada in 1949, juvenile delinquency was actually on the decline after a mid-war epidemic in 1942–a situation caused by a combination of wartime vigilance and a baby boom arising from the immigration and economic prosperity of the late 1920s.[30]

The putative link between the literature and the delinquency of children seems to have supplied a rationale for politicians, social workers, and the general public as to why delinquency had become so problematic in everyday life. Given the breadth of censorship created by the 1949 changes to the obscenity law, there was a period in the early 1950s when the Hardy Boys novels were seized by Canadian customs as objectionable literature, an irony considering the original author of the series lived in Ontario. In the U.S., the Kefauver Committee hearings explored the contribution of comics and television to delinquency, but no direct links between media and crime were established. However, the need for scientific investigations of such links was acknowledged and subsequently funded, and the comic industry, with one exception, adopted a code of self-regulation to curb excesses in comic stories. William Gaines, publisher of *Tales from the Crypt, Crime Suspense Stories,* and *Shock Suspense Stories,* refused to comply. He opted to publish a periodical without any self-restraint. *Mad Magazine* was the result.

Contemporary Inquiries into Obscenity and Pornography

Public inquiries into obscenity tend to oscillate between two models—the political/moralistic versus the rational/scientific. In the former, politicians sample public opinion and popular morality regarding sexual fiction and entertainment. In the latter, experts are preoccupied with the effects of pornography, measured scientifically. The 1979 British Inquiry into Obscenity and Film Censorship was chaired by Bernard Williams, the noted British philosopher, and reflected the rationalist model. Its mandate was "to review the laws concerning obscenity, indecency and violence … and to make recommendations."[31] It reiterated the conclusion of the 1970 U.S. Presidential Commission on Obscenity and Pornography, chaired by William B. Lockhart, dean and professor of Law and president of the Association of American Law Schools. Lockhart's mandate was to study "the effects of [pornographic] materials, particularly on youth, and their relationship to crime and other anti social conduct."[32] These rationalistic inquiries were created by liberal administrations only to report subsequently to conservative ones more concerned with popular political agendas, the former to Prime Minister Thatcher, the latter to President Nixon. In both cases, they concluded that, however morally objectionable, there was no empirical evidence of negative attitudinal or behavioural consequences resulting from exposure to explicit sexual entertainment.

In contrast, the appointment of the 1986 Meese Commission in the U.S. followed the political/moralistic approach. The chair of the commission was a Virginia prosecutor with a reputation for campaigning against massage parlours, adult bookstores, prostitutes, and X-rated videos.[33] The Meese Commission reversed Lockhart's and Williams's earlier conclusions, bringing the scientific "facts" into line with the politics of decency. Meese concluded that, depending on the nature of the materials, the evidence suggested that pornography could incite violence against women and engender misogynist attitudes. As with the 1970 report, a minority dissented from these conclusions. The commission's conclusions also drew considerable criticism from academics for misusing and misinterpreting the evidence,[34] including criticism from some of the original researchers who were alarmed by the "gap" between the commission's findings and the scientific facts.[35]

Unlike the 1970 presidential commission with its $US2 million budget (in 1970 dollars), and its volumes of new research, the Meese Commission had a $US400,000 budget, 12 months of inquiry, and no funds for new research in order to discover, in the words of the mandate, "the nature, extent and impact on society of pornography" and to recommend "more effective ways in which the spread of pornography could be contained." Following publication of the 2,000-page report in 1986, C. Everett Koop, the U.S. Surgeon General, seeking to add his medical opinion to the Meese diagnosis of the third-party harm, sponsored a seminar to canvass the "public health effects" of pornography.[36] This resolved an inconsistency that plagued the earlier Nixon administration when the presidential inquiry reported positively on pornography while the Surgeon General reported negatively on the effects of TV, prompting psychologist Leonard Berkowitz to observe in an oft-cited piece in *Psychology Today*,[37] "We Can't Have It Both Ways." Even so, the evidence of harm seemed to go in every possible direction as it came under examination internationally.

In Canada in 1985, a special select committee reported on its study of the effects of pornography and prostitution on Canadian society. The committee, headed by Vancouver lawyer Paul Fraser, canvassed the same literature that was examined by Meese in the U.S. and published some 18 volumes of accompanying working papers. Regarding the evidence of harm, the committee reported that "the research is so inadequate and chaotic that no consistent body of information has been established."[38] The Fraser Committee recommended that controls should be premised on human-rights considerations, not on the basis of third-party harms.

The committee proposed a three-tier hierarchy of offensive material. In the top level was placed visual pornography (such as "snuff" films and, possibly, sadomasochistic films) that caused physical harm to persons in the film's production; in its second level appeared sexually violent pornography as well as portrayals of bestiality, incest, or necrophilia. The penalties for manufacturing and distributing or selling these two commodities involved a maximum period of incarceration for five years. In the lowest tier were placed other explicit visual depictions of sexual activities including "vaginal, oral or anal intercourse, masturbation, lewd touching of the breasts, or the genital parts of the body, or the lewd exhibition of the genitals." The Fraser Committee proposed to make it unlawful to display these sorts of materials publicly, but not to outlaw sale or possession of them. Close inspection of the Fraser proposals seems pointless: they found no favour with successive justice ministers. What is noteworthy about them is that they sidestepped a framework based on protection of society from third-party harm. In place of such a utilitarian strategy, the philosophy employed was more human-rights sensitive: depictions of sexuality were to be regulated simply on the basis that the activities at issue were an affront to human life and dignity. Ergo, explicit sexual activities, including certain "perversions," were available for private consumption; the axe fell on sexual violence, bestiality, incest, and necrophilia. Although ignored by Parliament, this line of reasoning has found some favour in the courts as a result of the arrival of the Charter of Rights and Freedoms.

Evidence of Harm

When we identify harm in association with pornography, there are several rather different considerations. Linda Marchiano reports that she was forced at gunpoint by her boyfriend pimp to make *Deep Throat*, as well as other films, and that in fact her participation was coerced.[39] The Meese Commission heard similar evidence from others who said they were victimized by their participation in the filming of pornographic films, sometimes as adults, sometimes as children.[40] Others reported that they were forced to engage in perversions depicted in the pornography read by their spouses. The ultimate victimization is the "snuff film," in which a person is actually murdered; none of the national inquiries documented the existence of such films. At the other end of the continuum, a more common harm concerns the attack on sensibilities. The Law Reform Commission of Canada[41] suggested that private viewing of pornography ought to be permitted but that what troubled most people was its public display in neighbourhood stores. Offence here is given simply by the presence of pornography in areas open to public commerce. Whether it is explicit, violent, degrading, or positively erotic seems irrelevant. It goes without saying that the Parliament of Canada lacks jurisdiction over the great preponderance of websites in the world, and that therefore its views, whether legislated or not, are without much effect.

The ideological harm raises even thornier issues. Alan Soble suggests that sexual fantasies, being fictional, are "non-propositional" about the place of real women in everyday life, i.e., they are not intended as a general commentary about the status of women.[42] By contrast, Andrea Dworkin points out that the sexual submissiveness and objectification of women, the violence against them, and the humiliating sexual roles they are required to play are quite intentional and recurrent features of pornographic fantasies and are highly offensive, not just for the small number of prostitutes working as porno "stars" but for all women.[43] Dworkin goes on to suggest that in the current relations between the sexes, heterosexual intercourse is itself a degrading act, an act of power, not an act of intimacy. Obviously, the ideological elements of pornography are highly contested; we are not compelled to follow either Soble or Dworkin. In the case of Soble, we know from other contexts, such as anti-Semitic jokes and cartoons in which racism is cloaked in humour, that fantasies may be highly "propositional." In the case of Dworkin, most people, particularly heterosexuals, will find her propositions too all-inclusive in the other direction.

The dominant area of harm on which social scientists have focussed concerns the effects of pornography on the *attitudes* of consumers and their subsequent *conduct* with other third parties. Robin Morgan's proposition that pornography is the theory, rape is the practice, suggests that male readers

undergo a change in their sensibilities towards women that makes them more callous in their attitudes and more likely to become sexually aggressive in their conduct. Generally, there are three sources of evidence that social scientists have examined to explore this linkage. First, there have been attempts by criminological analysis to link aggregate patterns of pornography consumption with variations in the aggregate distributions of rape and sexual assault. If persons who read pornography experience an erosion of inhibition that makes some of them sexually aggressive, such patterns may be discernible in changes in the aggregate patterns of rape. Some analyses are longitudinal, tracking changes in sexual victimization over time as pornography consumption changes.[44] Some are cross-sectional, comparing the rates of victimization in different jurisdictions to determine how highly they correlate with variations in pornography consumption.[45] This sort of link is occasionally explored in the press. For example, on January 31, 1989, 16 hours before his execution in Florida, Ted Bundy "confessed" that he had become a serial rapist and murderer as a result of becoming "addicted" to violent pornography when young.

What does the evidence show? Studies from Denmark, contrary to expectations, suggest that there was no increase in sexual violence following the period of de-censorship that resulted in a proliferation of pornography. Although the conclusions were attacked by Bachy and Court, among others, in an effort to discredit them, and although a number of false allegations were made about the analysis (e.g., that the decline arose from inclusion of categories that were ultimately decriminalized, and so forth), the Williams Inquiry put such matters to rest.[46] The latest reports from Denmark, West Germany, and Sweden, all of which experienced relaxed censorship, indicate that the rate of rape has been declining, not increasing, in all these jurisdictions.[47] Given that these societies are all aging rapidly, the changing age profile of the population would seem to be a confounding factor.

Evidence from the U.S. has been of a cross-sectional character. Baron and Straus initially reported a correlation between states with high pornography-magazine consumption and high rates of forcible rape.[48] Later they indicated that when they controlled for "macho attitudes," the relationship became null, suggesting that the attitudes were causing both sexual aggressiveness and interest in pornographic entertainment.[49] Scott, in a similar study, tried to determine which magazine was most strongly correlated with rape, and particularly whether violent pornography was better correlated than explicit pornography. The correlation was stronger for *Playboy* than for *Penthouse* and *Hustler,* leading him to conclude that the relationship was artifactual, as Baron and Straus had concluded in 1986.[50]

A cross-cultural study of violent pornography by Abramson and Hayashi[51] in Japan suggested that the prevalence of sexual cruelty in Japanese fiction seems inconsequential for real life, for Japan appears to experience one of the lowest levels of sexual aggression among the industrialized countries. As noted by the Williams Inquiry, the rate of rape in Britain during the 1970s, when liberalization of pornography was clearly evident, was much lower and more stable than that of Singapore, whose government practiced vigorous censorship.[52] The longitudinal, cross-sectional, and cross-cultural data do not on the whole suggest convincing evidence of a pornography-rape link. Also, many such studies use only those convicted of sexual aggression as subjects for their investigations (i.e., no control or comparison group). The number or proportion of persons who utilize pornography and then commit sexual assault compared to those who do not utilize pornography yet still commit sex crimes is unknown.[53] Further, to date, no evidence exists as to the number or proportion of persons who utilize pornography but never commit any sexually aggressive acts.

The second major sort of evidence concerning the link is provided by retrospective clinical studies of pornography exposure among populations convicted of sexually aggressive acts. Police and news reporters like to describe assailants as "using" pornography as if it were a drug. Psychologist James C. Dobson suggested to Bundy during his 11th-hour confession that reading pornography created a sexual frenzy, a kind of libidinal automatism, though Bundy denied this.

To what extent does pornographic arousal play a role in the etiology of sexual aggression? This question was examined by the 1970 commission in the U.S., although no positive findings were reported.[54] Regardless, the reliability of this type of evidence is open to question on several counts. Do populations of incarcerated rapists accurately represent the population of real-world rapists? (They could just be the offenders who fail and get caught.) The same question applies to the use of official statistics by criminologists on rape and sexual assault. Certainly there are grounds for thinking that sexual assault is seriously

underreported, although how much is a matter of dispute.[55] If only a portion of the assailants find their way into both the official records and clinical settings, do they reliably represent the larger population? Criminologists speculate that apprehension is influenced by such extra-legal factors as the class and IQ of the offender, as well as characteristics of the victim.[56] In fact, variations in pornography exposure may be related to these differences.[57]

Another issue from the clinical studies relates to the meaning of such a link. Some accounts suggest that sexually aggressive males read and view pornography to put themselves in a high state of arousal prior to stalking their victims.[58] In this scenario, the pornography seems of less importance than the rape motive since any number of textual or visual materials might be employed in a similar fashion.[59] Also, such a link begs the question of the time ordering between pornography exposure and the inclination to rape over the offender's career. Did the pornography foster and cultivate an existing tendency, or did it create it *de novo?*

A final issue in the clinical studies is the possibility of false linkages arising from the invocation of pornography as an excuse or justification for conduct that deflects guilt from the assailant. Some speculate this may have been Bundy's motive. The clinical evidence is suggestive, though, like the criminological notions, not definitive.

The third sort of evidence derives from laboratory experiments in which subjects are exposed to pornographic materials, following which changes are measured in attitudes and conduct. The advantage of the lab approach is that it can control for the direction of effect. Causal inferences can be made with more confidence. By contrast, the criminological evidence is correlational and open to the ecological fallacy (in which correlation is confused with cause). On the first count, it begs the question of whether sexual aggressiveness causes, results from, or is simply coincident with an interest in pornography. On the second count, it cannot determine whether those people in the ecological unit who are sexually aggressive are the same people who are reading the pornography. The lab circumvents these issues with random assignment to treatment and control groups. The self-report bias from clinical studies is similarly circumvented by the use of experimental measures. The lab studies have also shown considerable finesse in differentiating the impact of sexually explicit versus aggressive themes in pornographic and other materials.

However, for obvious ethical reasons, the lab studies cannot actually promote sexual aggression or engender misogynistic attitudes,[60] notwithstanding the report of some researchers who have discovered that the effects of exposure to pornography on attitudes were "non transitory."[61] Proxies must be used, and the construct validity of the studies necessarily suffers as a result. Typically, subjects are aroused or angered through provocation, then exposed to various sorts of stimuli, including different types of sexually explicit, violent, or degrading materials, and finally are provided with an opportunity to retaliate against their initial aggressor. The three phases of the experiment are orchestrated to the subjects as unrelated. Aggressive pornography elevates the levels of aggression on a bogus learning task in which male subjects "teach" their provocateur, a woman, using fake electric shocks.[62] This is the substitute for sexual aggression. Similar results occur when subjects and targets are the same gender, and when the intervening stimulus is aversive noise, physical exercise, or graphic films of eye operations,[63] raising questions about whether the effect is due to autonomic arousal as opposed to social learning.

Aside from changes in conduct, attitude shifts indicative of enhanced callousness towards women have been reported after exposure to sexually explicit X-rated but non-violent films,[64] R-rated "slasher" films,[65] sexually suggestive but non-explicit age-restricted feature-length films,[66] short, sexually suggestive audiotapes,[67] and photographs from *Playboy* and *Penthouse*.[68] These studies raise obvious questions: How can attitudes so basic and entrenched as one's view of the other gender change so dramatically, no matter how little the "input"? The media-effects literature seems to imply that our human nature is only as good as our last movie!

Critics have explored numerous matters. In studies of incited aggression, is the outcome an artifact of prior arousal?[69] Can we generalize from tasks that are socially legitimate (the bogus "learning test" in which "aggression" is encouraged by an authority figure) to unsolicited acts of aggression in real life? The experimental designs use populations of university students from narrow sectors of society who may have no interest whatever in the materials employed, who may react adversely because of this, and who are in any case exposed to it only briefly. Also, the designs seem to give the subjects none of the alternatives to aggression that might characterize everyday life. As a consequence, although the experimental approach may be methodologically powerful, its implementation is fraught with questions that make extrapolation precarious. As though these methodological issues were not serious enough, there is another problem that has to do with the failures to replicate what were thought to be the robust effects of media exposure. Fisher and Barak[70] report a failure to replicate the incitation-to-violence experiments using Donnerstein's original stimulus films. Such studies seem to have become less fashionable, probably because they are subject to such ambiguous interpretation. Linz, Krafka, and Padgett, Brislin, Slutz, and Neal failed to replicate the sorts of attitude shifts reported by Zillmann and Bryant.[71] Linz reports surprising inconsistencies concerning which sorts of stimuli produce which sorts of effect, and there is a growing rift in the research community over whether the worrisome stimuli are explicit or violent, all of which raises "more questions than answers" about the research.[72]

The 1970 U.S. presidential commission paid little attention to experimental studies; only a handful were available at the time. Although such work was becoming better known in the late 1970s, the Williams Inquiry dismissed it categorically since it conflated fantasy and reality.[73] For Williams, the criminological evidence was central. In the Meese Commission the tables were turned; the criminological evidence was occluded in favour of the lab. At the seminar on "Pornography and Public Health" sponsored by the U.S. Surgeon General, the criminological evidence was ignored completely.[74] The Canadian and Australian inquiries examined both sorts of evidence, experimental and criminological. The Australians failed to reach a consensus about their validity and reliability. The Canadians found the scientific link unconvincing.

In the U.S., the legacy of Meese was a more vigorous prosecution of pornography under the existing laws. In Canada, the recommendations of the Fraser Committee to re-vamp the Canadian obscenity law found no favour with successive governments. But if governments have shown reluctance to modernize the law, the courts have not, and the social scientific evidence of harm has been important in encouraging such change.

Recent Evolution of Obscenity in Canadian Common Law

Since the passage of the Charter of Rights and Freedoms in 1982, Canadian obscenity cases have evolved in some startling new philosophical directions. The law of obscenity forbids "the undue exploitation of sex ... or sex in connection with crime, horror, cruelty or violence." What is "due" and "undue" exploitation is a matter of "the community standards of tolerance." The standards must be national, not regional; they must be objective, not the judge's opinion; and they must refer not to what one would care to see oneself but to what one would allow others to view. This definition allows changes to occur over time, reflecting the evolution of changing sexual mores. However, many argue that the flexibility of the law makes it difficult for people to know at any point in time where they stand with respect to it. The current law is like a regulation for speeding that forbids drivers from going "too fast" but does not specify the limit. In this context, the introduction of scientific evidence was thought to take some of the uncertainty out of the standard.

The social science evidence of the harmfulness of pornography was first systematically introduced during a 1984 obscenity trial in Calgary: *R. v. Wagner.*[75] The Crown witness reported that recent work in experimental psychology had established, first, that discrete, socially harmful consequences could be traced to sexually explicit materials that linked sex with violence, especially violence directed against women; second, that sexually explicit materials that were degrading or dehumanizing, that depicted women as "deprived of unique human character or identity" also had been linked to negative attitudinal consequences; and, third, that explicit erotica that depicted "positive and affectionate human sexual interaction, between consenting individuals participating on the basis of equality," had no negative consequences. The harmfulness of the first two categories was described in the written decision by the Honourable Mr. Justice Shannon in *R. v. Wagner* as follows:

> Both sexually violent pornography and degrading and dehumanizing pornography convey the message that women enjoy abusive and anti-social behaviour. Men who are repeatedly exposed to such films become more sexually aggressive in their relations with women and tolerant of such behaviour in others. This leads to increased callousness towards women on a personal level and less receptiveness to their legitimate claims for equality and respect.

The films at issue, on the whole, were not sexually violent, did not involve children or animals, and were not offensive by virtue of linking sexuality to crime, horror, cruelty, or violence, as provided for in the Canadian Criminal Code. Justice Shannon introduced a new standard based on experimental findings from the "media effects" literature about film exposure outcomes that by-passed traditional moral considerations. On the basis of the evidence, he argued that "the contemporary Canadian community

will not tolerate either of the first two classes" of materials (sexually violent and sexually degrading), but "will tolerate erotica no matter how explicit it may be." The distinction between the erotic and the pornographic, which Fraser adopted from feminist critiques of sexual entertainment, and which successive governments were reluctant to introduce, arrived in Canada through the common law. Ironically, Fraser's classification system would not have found fault with the majority of the films at issue since Fraser defined "degrading" more narrowly than the trial judge. Ironically, in the year of the trial, the federal inquiry chaired by Paul Fraser dismissed the effects literature that formed the basis for the decision in *Wagner.*

How consequential has this decision been? By itself, it was initially quite parochial. Coming from a trial judge it was not binding on other judges in the same jurisdiction. The decision of the Alberta Court of Appeal to refuse leave to hear the case, and the decision of the Supreme Court to do likewise, fell short of upholding the legal reasoning. However, *Wagner* subsequently has become a landmark case. The philosophy of Canadian courts regarding harm in the area of obscenity, in fact, preceded *Wagner* and can be traced to *Doug Rankine* (1983)[76] and *Ramsingh* (1984),[77] each of which identified degradation and dehumanization as central elements offensive to community standards. The distinction between explicit and degrading material was developing in law somewhat in advance of the expert evidence. What is of note is that these decisions stressed the problem of harm as a relevant criterion in making a determination of obscenity, despite an earlier authority that expressly denied the need to prove harm in order to register a conviction.[78] *Wagner* and the other "harm criterion" cases were subsequently cited favourably by the B.C. Court of Appeal in *R. v. Red Hot Video*[79] and *Towne Cinema Theatres v. The Queen,*[80] and *Doug Rankine* and *Ramsingh* were followed at trial in *Video World Ltd.*[81]

Although *Wagner* was not considered by the Supreme Court on its merits, this Calgary trial decision proved to be the theoretical foundation for the most recent conclusions of the Supreme Court in the case of *R. v. Butler* (1992). Butler, the operator of the Avenue Video Boutique in Winnipeg, was charged under the Criminal Code for offering to rent hardcore videos. He invoked the Charter protection of freedom of expression. Although all his products had been classified for public distribution by provincial censorship boards, he was nonetheless liable to charges under the federal law. Indeed, the Supreme Court found that the limits on his freedom of expression created by s. 163, the obscenity section of the Criminal Code, were permissible within section 1 of the Charter. It held that the guarantee of Charter rights can be withheld if this is a reasonable limit prescribed by law and "demonstrably justified" in a free and democratic society. The justification for suspending freedom of speech in the case of pornography arose from the charge that such materials had harmful side effects.

The court invoked the distinctions between three types of materials originally articulated in *Wagner:* explicit sex combined with violence, explicit sex without violence but which subjects people to treatment that is degrading or dehumanizing, and explicit sex without violence that is neither degrading nor dehumanizing. The first two types of materials were thought to exceed community standards of tolerance since they were capable of causing harm. According to the Supreme Court, harm means "that it predisposes persons to act in an anti-social manner as, for example, the physical or mental mistreatment of women by men. Anti-social conduct for this purpose is conduct which society formally recognizes as incompatible with its proper functioning." The court furthermore argued in a highly controversial section of the decision that it was not necessary that harm actually be proven, and noted that the social science evidence was deeply contested. It felt that the widely shared *belief* in harmfulness was sufficient cause for the suppression of such material.

The Supreme Court decision followed the thrust and language of the position laid out in the brief of a feminist group, the Legal Education Action Fund (LEAF), given intervenor status during the appeal. However, it would be a mistake to infer that the perspective of LEAF is widely shared by other Canadian feminists. In a piece titled, "If pornography is the theory, is inequality the practice?", Thelma McCormack delivered a scathing condemnation of the *Butler* decision. Where the Supreme Court, LEAF, and Fraser answer "yes" to her question, on the other side "the large group of scholars–economists, political scientists, sociologists, psychologists and anthropologists who study equality and inequality ... find this notion bizarre:"[82] inequality and violence against women are not caused by pornography. McCormack, who directed York University's Centre for Feminist Research before her retirement, argued that choosing between free speech and other feminist ideals is a false dichotomy, since the ability

of women to explore their sexuality requires unencumbered speech, even if some people find that speech disturbing. McCormack's earlier critique of the media-effects literature was suppressed by the Toronto Women's Task Force on Pornography, which originally commissioned it. She found that the evidence of harmfulness was scientifically unsound.[83]

In McCormack's view, "the enemy of gender equality is the stereotype of the traditional woman, not the one-dimensional lust-driven nymphomaniac of pornography." It is the traditional stereotypes that dominate the mass media that keep women in submissive roles and occupations. McCormack's views are similar to those raised by Wendy Kaminer in her critique of "feminists against the first amendment." Feminists in the U.S. who have made common cause with the Christian right in promoting censorship in effect turn the protection of feminist aspirations over to the patriarchal state.[84] Critics of this alliance argue that in the long run, such actions will erode feminism. Indeed, one of the first charges laid in the aftermath of *Butler* involved lesbian materials seized in a feminist bookstore in Toronto.

Commenting on the *Butler* decision, noted philosopher Ronald Dworkin joined the chorus of anti-censorship feminists. Where the Canadian court justified the suppression of free speech to end "the proliferation of materials which seriously offend the values fundamental to our society," Dworkin wrote: "That is an amazing statement. It is the central defining premise of freedom of speech that the offensiveness of ideas, or the challenge they offer to traditional ideas, cannot be a valid reason for censorship. Once that premise is abandoned, it is difficult to see what free speech means."[84]

After publication of the *Butler* decision, complaints were made by members of LEAF to Calgary vice detectives about the availability of materials in the city that were forbidden by the new ruling. LEAF recruited some two dozen volunteers from its membership, mostly female law students at the University of Calgary, who rented hundreds of videos with financial support from the police service and screened the materials for evidence of violence and/or degrading or dehumanizing portrayals of sex. This resulted in the largest single seizure of pornographic videos in the city's history.[86] This raid raises some obvious questions. Should a vigilante group administer the Criminal Code? Should the police have tried to educate the merchants about the nature of the *Butler* decision–as opposed to charging them? Has the law become so technical that it takes a law degree to apply it? If the materials are harmful, how can the police ethically justify exposing students to them? If they are not, what was the point of the raid? Merchants who subsequently pleaded not guilty were acquitted on a verdict of "officially induced error." Having obtained a classification license from a provincial attorney general, they could not be found guilty for trading in what criminal courts deemed to be obscene. The *Butler* decision seems to have had little import, attracting the scorn of many feminists[87] while failing to curb the spread of hardcore pornography. In the meanwhile, the Internet has shifted the field of controversy to children.

In 1993, Parliament expanded the law of obscenity to make it a crime to either make, distribute, or possess child pornography. Child pornography was defined as any *visual* representation depicting a minor, i.e., a person under the age of 18 years, engaging in a sexual activity or having as a dominant characteristic the depiction of the child's sexual organs or anal region, or any *written* material advocating sexual activity with a minor. The law provided for penalties that could result in incarceration for up to 10 years in the case of making and distributing, or up to five years for simple possession. In addition, the Crown has discretion to proceed on any of these provisions by way of summary conviction (which provides for a maximum penalty by way of fine of up to $2,000 and/or a sentence of up to six months in jail). The law was passed without any challenge or questions from the opposition even though the language of the bill appeared to create a strict liability offense, something unusual in criminal law that normally requires established proof of *mens rea* or "guilty mind." Early lower court cases have established that the law applies to Internet cases and creates liabilities for service providers who post pornographic materials on their sites, or who provide communication bulletin boards that permit subscribers to post child pornography. It is less clear what the liability is of service providers who support e-mail, the attachments to which may be contrary to the obscenity law.[88] Though the law provides for defenses based on public good, artistic merit and/or educational, scientific, or medical purposes, in 1995 Toronto artist Eli Langer and the Mercer Union Gallery were charged under the act following the seizure of a series of paintings and sketches depicting the fear and trauma of childhood victims of pedophilia. Although the public outcry led the Ontario Attorney General to drop the charges against Langer per se, and to proceed "in rem," i.e., a forfeiture procedure against the

paintings themselves, the subsequent trial (and ultimate acquittal) cost Langer tens of thousands of dollars.

A British Columbia case involving John Robin Sharpe was brought before courts after a seizure of materials by customs officials and following a raid at his house in 1995. Sharpe was charged with two counts of possession of child pornography, and two counts of possession for the purpose of sale or distribution. Sharpe argued that criminalizing mere possession of visual materials of child pornography and of written materials advocating pedophilia was a violation of his Charter freedoms of conscience (protected by s. 2a), as well as his freedom of thought, belief, opinion, and expression (protected by s. 2b). In 1998, the Supreme Court of British Columbia struck down the possession aspect of the law but upheld the power of Parliament to criminalize written materials advocating pedophilia, even materials written by the person charged. The matter is currently under appeal before the Supreme Court of Canada.

Conclusions: The Larger Context

Where does this leave us now that we have entered the new millennium? The scientific evidence of harm is very uneven, as *Butler* acknowledges. We should not forget that social science evidence is rarely definitive. However, it is not irrelevant. By assembling the various approaches to the question of pornography effects, we expect to discover some convergence of evidence that would allow more confidence to be placed in the independent disciplinary approaches. What we have found in this review is a convergence of sorts–competing approaches that suggest that the case for negative, unintended effects is a long way from being established. The criminological evidence does not bear out a link between pornography consumption and sexual aggressiveness. The clinical cases do suggest a link, though not the sort that had been presupposed, i.e., that normal males become rapists as a result of what they read; rather, the "link" appears to be that serial rapists sometimes use pornography to excite themselves in advance of their attacks. Further, the experimental work is subject to increasing criticism, including that of feminists.[89] However, this conclusion about a lack of convergence should not be misinterpreted. There are some major provisos in interpreting the larger picture we are painting here. First, we would not want to conclude that human beings learn nothing from their environments, and by extension that TV saturation has no impact on culture; that advertising has no impact on our consumption habits; and, more importantly, that mass media contribute nothing to gender socialization or to the status of women. Rather, we are suggesting that the systematic attempt to link a narrow aspect of the popular culture–explicit and sometimes violent pornography viewed by a minority of society–to the most heinous acts of sexual aggression constitutes an extremely ambitious proposition, although one that entails rather simplistic conceptions of human nature and morality.

This does not mean that the media are an unimportant source of learning and social influence. Indeed, they are a ubiquitous source of conflicting values and attitudes, and *probably* a major contributor to the reinforcement of gender ideologies, teaching men and women normative views about heterosexuality, family relations, and appropriate economic and social roles. The ideological components of mass media may have traditionally functioned to reproduce as a "natural fact of life" the dominant role of males and the submissive role of females, whether in commercials[90] or James Bond movies.[91] Pornography may represent the end of the continuum of such representations. Yet, in the middle range (which constitutes our normal fare of media exposure), the most pervasive media–computers and the Internet, TV, magazines, and motion pictures, in both dramas and commercials that reinforce versions of masculinity and femininity that many believe reproduce gender stratification and the unequal exercise of social power in their consumers–are the least likely to be restrained by the Criminal Code.[92] This is the case even if equality is constitutionally guaranteed, and even though normal broadcasting and publishing would appear to be more potent and universal sources of socialization for both men and women. It would seem more plausible to consider the pornographic in the same light as the earlier crime comics–as a scapegoat, which in this case exemplifies all the sexist tendencies of our culture–than as an important cause of sexist attitudes and sexual aggression in our societies. Sexism predates pornography, and gender emancipation requires stronger medicine than censorship: indeed, it may require freedom from censorship.[93] Regrettably, Canada appears to be going in the opposite direction. But given the lack of jurisdiction of Canadian politicians and judges over most of the content of the Internet, it probably does not much matter.

Notes

1. Douglas M. Skoog and Jane L. Murray, *Innocence Exploited: Child Pornography in the Electronic Age* (Ottawa: The Canadian Police College, 2000).
2. See <http://hotwired.lycos.com/special/pornscare>.
3. See <http://trfn.pgh.pa.us/guest/mrtext.html>.
4. See <http://ecommerce.vanderbilt.edu/cyberporn.debate.html>.
5. Pirim Sorokin, *The American Sex Revolution* (Boston: P. Sargent, 1955).
6. James Gilbert, *A Cycle of Outrage: America's Reaction to the Juvenile Delinquent in the 1950s* (New York: Oxford University Press, 1986), pp.20–22.
7. Russell Miller, *Bunny: The Real Story of Playboy* (London: Corgi, 1985).
8. Attorney General's Commission on Pornography, *Final Report* (Washington, D.C.: Department of Justice, 1986).
9. Craig Bicknell, 1999, "The Sordid Saga of Sex.com" <http://www.wired.com/news/business/0,1367,19140,00.html>.
10. H.G. Florence, "Controlling Ideas," *Society* 24, no. 5 (1987): 19–21.
11. A.L. Vogelback, "The Publication and Reception of 'Huckleberry Finn' in America," *American Literature* 11 (1939): 260–72.
12. A. Dworkin, *Pornography: Man Possessing Women* (New York: Perigree, 1981); L. Lederer, *Take Back the Night* (New York: Morrow, 1980); S. Griffin, *Pornography and Silence* (New York: Harper & Row, 1981).
13. D. Russell, *Politics of Rape* (New York: Stein & Day, 1975); D. Russell, *Rape in Marriage* (New York: Collier Books, 1983); D. Russell, *Sexual Exploitation: Rape, Child Sexual Abuse and Workplace Harassment* (Beverly Hills, Calif.: Sage, 1984); D. Russell, *The Secret Trauma: Incest in the Lives of Girls and Women* (New York: Basic Books, 1986).
14. R. West, "The Feminist Conservative Anti-Pornography Alliance and the 1986 Attorney General's Commission on Pornography Report," *American Bar Foundation Research Journal* 4 (1987): 681–711.
15. L. Duggan, N. Hunter, and C.S. Vance, "False Promises: Feminist Antipornography Legislation in the U.S.," in V. Burstyn, ed., *Women against Censorship* (Vancouver and Toronto: Douglas & McIntyre, 1985), pp.130–51.
16. Steven Marcus, *The Other Victorians: A Study of Sexuality and Pornography in Mid-Nineteenth Century* England (London: Corgi Books, 1969).
17. See *R. v. Palmer,* 68 C.C.C. 20 (1937).
18. P. Nobile and E. Nadler, *United States of America vs Sex* (New York: Minotaur Press, 1986).
19. Douglas M. Skoog and Jane L. Murray, *Innocence Exploited: Child Pornography in the Electronic Age* (Ottawa: The Canadian Police College, 2000).
20. Ibid.
21. Ibid., p.16.
22. Ibid., p.17.
23. F. Wertham, *Seduction of the Innocent* (New York: Holt, 1954).
24. Editorial, "It's Time to Act," *Public Health Journal* 14 (June 1923): 289–90.
25. H. Blumer, *Movies and Conduct* (New York: Macmillan, 1933); H. Blumer and P. Hauser, *Movies, Delinquency and Crime* (New York: Macmillan, 1933).
26. Canada, Senate, Special Parliamentary Committee on Salacious and Indecent Literature, *Hansard* (1952), p.157.
27. A. Kaplan, "Obscenity as an Aesthetic Category," *Law and Social Problems* 20 (1955): 544–59.
28. E. Mandel, *Delightful Murder* (London: Pluto Books, 1984).
29. K. Worpole, *Dockers and Detectives: Popular Reading, Popular Writing* (London: Monthly Press, 1983).
30. A. Brannigan, "Mystification of the Innocents: Delinquency in Canada 1931–1949," *Criminal Justice History* 7 (1986): 111–44.
31. Committee on Obscenity and Film Censorship, *Report* (London: HMSO, 1979).
32. United States Commission on Pornography and Obscenity, *Report* (Washington, D.C.: GPO, 1970).
33. Nobile and Nadler, *United States vs Sex.*
34. S. Lab, "Pornography and Aggression: A Response to the U.S. Attorney General's Commission," *Criminal Justice Abstracts* 19 (1987): 301–21.
35. D. Linz, S.D. Penrod, and E. Donnerstein, "The Attorney General's Commission: The Gaps between Findings and Facts," *American Bar Foundation Research Journal* 4 (1987): 713–36.
36. E.P. Mulvey and J.L. Haugaard, *Pornography and Public Health* (Washington, D.C.: U.S. Department of Health and Human Services, 1986).
37. L. Berkowitz, "Sex and Violence–We Can't Have It Both Ways," *Psychology Today* (December 1971): pp.14, 18, 20, 22, 23.

38. Special Committee on Pornography and Prostitution, *Report* (Ottawa: Supply and Services, 1985), p.99.

39. Miller, *Bunny*, p.198; Linda Marchiano (a.k.a. Linda Lovelace), *Ordeal* (New York: Citadel, 1980).

40. Commission on Pornography, *Final Report*, pp.767ff.

41. Law Reform Commission of Canada, *Limits of the Law Obscenity: A Test Case* (Ottawa: Supply and Services, 1975).

42. Alan Soble, "Pornography: Defamation and Endorsement of Degradation," *Social Theory and Practice* 11, no. 1 (1985): 61–87.

43. A. Dworkin, *Testimony to the U.S. Attorney General's Commission on Pornography* (Washington, D.C.: Department of Justice, 1985); A. Dworkin, *Intercourse* (New York: Free Press, 1987); A. Dworkin, "Pornography: A vicious expression of male power, dominance," *London Free Press* (28 April 1993), p.B9.

44. B. Kutchinsky, "The Effect of Easy Availability of Pornography on the Incidence of Sex Crimes: The Danish Experience," *Journal of Social Issues* 29 (1973): 163–79; J. Court, "Pornography and Sex Crimes: A Reevaluation in Light of Trends around the World," *International Journal of Criminology and Penology* 5 (1977): 129–57; J. Court, "Sex and Violence: The Ripple Effect," N. Malamuth and E. Donnerstein, eds., *Pornography and Sexual Aggression* (Orlando: Academic Press, 1984), pp.143–72.

45. L. Baron and M.A. Straus, "Sexual Stratification, Pornography, and Rape in the United States," Malamuth and Donnerstein, *Pornography*, pp.186–209; L. Baron and M.A. Strauss, "Rape and Its Relation to Social Disorganization, Pornography and Sexual Inequality in the United States," a paper presented to the International Congress on Rape, Tel Aviv, June 1986; J. Scott, "Rape Rates and the Circulation Rates of Adult Magazines," *Journal of Sex Research* 24 (1988): 241–50.

46. Committee on Obscenity, *Report.*

47. B. Kutchinsky, "Pornography and Sexual Violence: The Criminological Evidence from Aggregate Data in Several Countries," *International Journal of Law and Psychiatry* 14, no. 1 (1991).

48. Baron and Straus, "Sexual Stratification."

49. Baron and Straus, "Rape and its Relation to Social Disorganization."

50. Scott, "Rape Rates."

51. P.R. Abramson and H. Hayashi, "Pornography in Japan: Cross Cultural and Theoretical Considerations," Malamuth and Donnerstein, *Pornography*, pp.173–85.

52. Committee on Obscenity, *Report.*

53. Douglas M. Skoog and Jane L. Murray, *Innocence Exploited: Child Pornography in the Electronic Age* (Ottawa: The Canadian Police College, 2000).

54. M.J. Goldstein, H.S. Kant, and J.J. Hartman, *Pornography and Sexual Deviance* (Berkeley, Calif.: University of California Press, 1974).

55. D. Russell, "The Prevalence and Incidence of Forcible Rape and Attempted Rape of Females," *Victimology: An International Journal* 7 (1982): 81–93; A. Brannigan and A. Kapardis, "The Controversy over Pornography and Sex Crimes: The Criminological Evidence and Beyond," *Australian and New Zealand Journal of Criminology* 19 (1986): 259– 84; M.J. Hindeland and B.L. Davis, "Forcible Rape in the United States: A Statistical Profile," D. Chappell et al., eds., *Forcible Rape* (New York: Columbia University Press, 1977), pp.87–114.

56. J.Q. Wilson and R.J. Hernstein, *Crime and Human Nature* (New York: Simon & Schuster, 1985).

57. R. Langevin, "Pornography and Sexual Offenses," *Annals of Sex Research* 1, no. 3 (1988): 335–62.

58. W.L. Marshall, "The Use of Sexually Explicit Stimuli by Rapists, Child Molesters, and Nonoffenders," *Journal of Sex Research* 25 (1988): 267–88.

59. N. Polsky, "On the Sociology of Pornography," N. Polsky, *Hustlers, Beats and Others* (Chicago: University of Chicago Press, 1986): pp.182–200.

60. C.W. Sherif, "Comment on Ethical Issues in Malamuth, Heim and Feshbach," *Journal of Personality and Social Psychology* 38 (1980): 408–12.

61. D. Zillmann and W.J. Bryant, "Effects of Massive Exposure to Pornography," Malamuth and Donnerstein, *Pornography*, p.136.

62. Malamuth and Donnerstein, *Pornography*, pp.53ff.

63. D. Zillmann, *Connections Between Sex and Aggression* (Hillsdale, N.J.: Erlbaum, 1984).

64. D. Zillmann and W.J. Bryant, "Pornography, Sexual Callousness and the Trivialization of Rape," *Journal of Communication* 34 (1982): 10–21; Zillman and Bryant, "Effects of Massive Exposure."

65. D. Linz, "Sexual Violence in the Media: Effects on Male Viewers and Implications for Society" (doctoral dissertation, University of Wisconsin, Madison, 1985).

66. N. Malamuth and J. Check, "The Effects of Mass Media Exposure on Acceptance of Violence against Women: A Field Experiment," *Journal of Research in Personality* 15 (1981): 436–46.

67. N. Malamuth and J. Check, "Sexual Arousal to Rape and Consenting Depictions," *Journal of Abnormal Psychology* 89 (1980): 763–66.

68. N. Malamuth, I. Reisin, and B. Spinner, "Exposure to Pornography and Reactions to Rape," a paper presented to the 87th Annual Convention of the American Psychological Association, New York, 1979.

69. S. Gray, "Exposure to Pornography and Aggression against Women: The Case of the Angry Male," *Social Problems* 29 (1982): 387–98; Lab, "Pornography and Aggression."

70. W. Fisher and B.A. Barak, "Erotica, Pornography and Behavior: More Questions than Answers from Experimental Evidence," *International Journal of Law and Psychiatry* 14, no. 1 (1991).

71. Linz, *Sexual Violence;* C.L. Krafka, "Sexually Explicit, Sexually Violent and Violent Media: Effects of Multiple Naturalistic Exposures and Debriefing on Female Viewers" (doctoral dissertation, Department of Psychology, University of Wisconsin, Madison, 1985); V.R. Padgett, J. Brislin Slutz, and J.A. Neal, "Pornography, Erotica and Attitudes towards Women: The Effects of Repeated Exposure," *Journal of Sex Research* 26, no. 4 (1989): 479–91.

72. D. Linz, "Exposure to Sexually Explicit Materials and Attitudes towards Rape: A Comparison of Study Findings," *Journal of Sex Research* 26 (1989): 50–84. Also see Fisher and Barak, "Erotica, Pornography and Behavior."

73. Committee on Obscenity, *Report*, p.66.

74. Mulvey and Haugaard, *Pornography and Public Health.*

75. *R. v. Wagner* (A.Q.B.), 43 C.R. (3d) 301, 1985, quoted at p.315.

76. *R. v. Doug Rankine*, 36 C.R. (3d) 154, 1983.

77. *R. v. Ramsingh*, 14. C.C.C. (3d) 230, 1984.

78. *Prairie Schooner*, 1 C.C.C. (2d) 25, 1970.

79. *R. v. Red Hot Video*, 45 C.R. (3d) 36, (B.C.C.A.) 1985.

80. *Towne Cinema Theatres v. R.*, 45 C.R. (3d) 3, (S.C.C.) 1985.

81. *Video World Ltd.* 32 Man. R., (2d) 41, 1985.

82. Thelma McCormack, "If pornography is the theory, is inequality the practice?" *Philosophy of the Social Sciences* 23, no. 3 (1993): 298–326.

83. Thelma McCormack, "Making Sense of the Research on Pornography," Varda Burstyn, ed., *Women against Censorship* (Vancouver and Toronto: Douglas & McIntyre 1985), pp.181–205.

84. Wendy Kaminer, "Feminists against the First Amendment," *Atlantic Monthly* (November 1992), pp.111–18. Also see "Feminism and Censorship," *CBC Radio Ideas Transcripts* (12 October 1993).

85. Ronald Dworkin, "The Coming Battles over Free Speech," *New York Review of Books* (11 June 1992), pp.55–64.

86. Ron Collins, "Video Sting: Police Seize Hundreds of 'Porn' Films," *Calgary Herald* (21 May 1993), p.A1.

87. Brenda Cossman, Shannon Bell, Lise Gotel, and Becki L. Ross, 1997, *Bad Attitude/s on Trial: Pornography, Feminism and the Butler Decision*, Toronto: University of Toronto Press.

88. See <http://strategis.ic.gc.ca/pics/it/0503118e.pdf>.

89. Gray, "Exposure to Pornography." It is also noteworthy that the only females on the Meese Commission board of inquiry dissented from the main conclusions offered by the majority precisely because they found the evidence of harm unconvincing.

90. Task Force on Sex Role Stereotyping in the Broadcast Media, *Images of Women* (Ottawa: Supply and Services, 1982).

91. T. Bennett, *James Bond* (London: Macmillan, 1988).

92. *Report on Self-Regulation by the Broadcasting and Advertising Industries for the Elimination of Sex Role Stereotyping in the Broadcast Media* (Ottawa: Supply and Services, 1987).

93. Burstyn, *Women against Censorship.*

21

Couched in Compromise: Media-Minority Relations in a Multicultural Society

Augie Fleras

Canadians have always endorsed diversity in principle, if not always in practice, as a legitimate and integral component of Canada's much vaunted "mosaic."[1]

With its potential to bolster both national and minority interests, diversity is no longer routinely dismissed as an anomaly, to be shunted aside in the neverending quest for national unity through the denial of differences. Emphasis instead is on forging a cohesive and prosperous multicultural society that engages with diversity without eroding either the interconnectedness of the parts or distinctiveness of the constituent units in the process. Central to Canada's multiculturalism commitments is the concept of *institutional inclusiveness*. Its varied interpretations and diverse applications notwithstanding, institutional inclusiveness requires a commitment to improving minority access and involvement through institutional responsiveness to minority needs and concerns.

To be sure, the mainstreaming of diversity has not been without controversy or contradiction. In challenging "the way things are done around here," the politics of institutional inclusiveness have transformed the dynamics of official multiculturalism in ways that have simultaneously consolidated and yet compromised Canada's reputation as a multicultural pacesetter for living together with differences. Nevertheless, the politics of inclusiveness have proven to be a more formidable challenge than originally anticipated in the re-making of a Canada both safe *for* diversity, yet safe *from* diversity as well.

International accolades for multicultural initiatives gloss over certain discrepancies between official rhetoric and institutional reality. Criticism has proliferated in recent years, with many pouncing on official multiculturalism as little more than "undertheorized romanticism" in defence of a monocultural status quo.[2] Moreover, despite statutory obligations under the *Multiculturalism Act* of 1988, not all institutions have contributed equally to the attainment of a multicultural Canadian society.[3] Some institutions appear to be lacking in commitment to multicultural inclusiveness beyond the minimum necessary to stay one step ahead of the law, such as compliance with the *Employment Equity Act* of 1986/1996.[4] Others may comply, but only in response to public criticism of institutional foot dragging. Still others acknowledge the usefulness of mainstreaming minority women and men, yet have found the implementation process to be riddled with a slew of cultural landmines and systemic biases. Insofar as official multiculturalism revolves around the transformation of cultural differences into discourses about social equality, mainstream institutions have come under pressure to be more inclusive of Canada's multicultural diversity.[5]

Few institutions, with the possible exception of urban policing, have attracted as much criticism as the mainstream media over failure to be demonstrably inclusive. As repeatedly observed in the literature and research, media treatment of Canada's aboriginal peoples, people of colour, and immigrants and refugees is mixed at best, deplorable at worst.[6] Media representations of minorities have a complex and unhappy history, with minority images continuing to reflect how a "white supremacist" society sees itself and its domination over minority women and men. Minorities have been victimized by disproportionately negative coverage in TV programming, newscasts, films, and advertising. Miscasting of minorities has assumed a variety of guises, including those of peoples (a) trivialized as irrelevant or inferior, (b) demonized as a social menace and a threat to society, (c) scapegoated as having or creating social problems, (d) ridiculed for being too different or not different enough, (e) refracted through the prism of Eurocentric fears and fantasies, and (f) subjected to double standards that damn minorities regardless of what they did or did not do.

Past indictments of media-minority relations may no longer be applicable, however. Minority women and men have emerged as a central focus of media attention, with increasingly positive portrayals, in part because of the creation of a profitable market for the commodification of diversity.[7] Minorities are reaping the benefits of media that acknowledge the value of inclusiveness–if only in pursuit of an enhanced bottom line rather than out of any commitment to social justice. The emergence of ethnic and aboriginal media have also eroded the exclusionist power of mainstream media by providing minorities with the tools to construct images consistent with lived-in realities. But while improvements in the representation of media-minority relations should not go unnoticed, critics tend to underestimate the systemic barriers to institutional inclusiveness.

Put bluntly, the mainstream media do not see themselves as ameliorative agencies for promoting progressive change or minority inclusiveness, despite public expectations for such a social responsibility. Rather, the mainstream media exist essentially as a business whose animating logic is amorally simple: to make money by connecting desired audiences to advertisers by way of improved ratings. Such a bottom-line mentality would appear inconsistent with minority demands for balanced and contextual representations, and it is precisely this anomaly in the representational basis of media-minority relations that makes it doubly important to determine the "what," "why," "who," and "how" behind minority miscasting. In that media representations of minority women and men reflect a pattern of ambivalence between the contradictory discourses of acceptance and rejection, the representational basis of media-minority relations tends to be "couched in compromise," with progressive images counterposed with the regressive, and without denying the simultaneity of each.

Mainstream Media Content

The mainstream media have been singled out as being noticeably negligent in engaging constructively with Canada's multicultural diversity. Accused of acting irresponsibly towards minorities in a society where multicultural principles prevail but do not always translate into practice, such media miscasting must be deplored in light of Canada's multicultural commitment, especially since the mainstream media are often the primary point of contact in shaping the process of living together. In acknowledging media as "machineries of meaning" for conveying powerful yet coded messages about what is acceptable or not,[8] the contention here is that

- the mainstream media continue to distort the representations of media-minority relations by rendering minorities invisible, as stereotypes, problem people, and ornaments;

- media miscasting of minorities is not something out of the ordinary–a kind of discriminatory departure from an otherwise inclusive organizational norm–but systemic and institutionalized within the very nature of contemporary mainstream media;

- critics underestimate the interplay of deeply entrenched and often conflicting institutional values, distinctive agendas, organizational priorities, operational procedures, and corporate commitments–all of which combine to complicate the challenge of engaging diversity in a way that meets widespread approval.

It is precisely around these debates over the politics of media inclusiveness, with its promise of payoff yet continued compromise of minority interests, that the representational dynamics of media-minority relations can be explored by diverse strategies for "multiculturalizing" the media. To assist in this, a social problem perspective can be employed, with the following questions providing an analytical framework:

- Is there a problem in the representational basis of media-minority relations? Who says so, why, and on what grounds? How is the problem expressed with respect to the crafting of minority images by way of newscasts, TV programming, advertising, and film?

- Who and what is responsible for the disjuncture between multicultural commitments and media realities? Is a racist discourse integral to media functioning or does it reflect a kind of 'few bad apples' syndrome? Are prevailing images the result of conscious choice or inadvertent consequences, thus reflecting the organization of power within media institutions?[9]

- Why does the problem of media miscasting continue to persist despite increased awareness of Canada's multicultural commitments, with corresponding pressure to reform? How insurmountable are the barriers towards institutional media inclusiveness? To what extent is the miscasting bias a case of the systemic and the institutionalized rather than the personal and the intentional?

- What exactly constitutes multicultural and inclusive media? What has been accomplished to date in terms of "multiculturalizing" the media? Do solutions lie in working within the system or exploring avenues that fall outside the operational agenda of mainstream media?

Inasmuch as responses to these questions are inseparable from the politics of minority miscasting in a multicultural Canada, the challenges of media institutional inclusiveness cannot be lightly dismissed. The miscasting of minority women and men results in "them" being rendered invisible, stereotyped, "problematized," and "ornamentalized"–in effect "otherizing" minorities as people removed in time and place. Of particular note are moves towards both internal reform through mainstreaming diversity and the expansion of an indigenous and ethnic media. Inasmuch as media minority images remain couched in compromise, reflecting both progress and regression as well as confusion and contestation, redress of past abuses holds out the possibility of optimism alloyed with caution in forging an inclusive and multicultural media.

Surveying the Multicultural Landscape

Canada represents one of several democratic societies that have taken advantage of diversity as a basis for securing national identity and society building. Yet multicultural societies such as Canada's confront a paradox in grappling with the question of how to make society safe "for" diversity, yet also safe "from" diversity.[10] Too much diversity may de-stabilize a society to the point of dismemberment; too little diversity may foster a one-size-fits-all mentality that stifles as it standardizes. Official multiculturalism was initially introduced for a variety of political and economic purposes related to state functions, conflict management, commercial advancement, and electoral survival. Recourse to official multiculturalism invokes a redefinition of minority-majority relations in the same way that assimilation discourses once offered a *de facto* framework for securing race and ethnic relations. A combination of demographic and political upheavals in recent years has culminated in a rethinking of the government's multicultural agenda.[11] A shift towards the principles of diversity, respect, and equality has also had the effect of reconfiguring Canadian society in ways scarcely conceivable even a generation ago, thus reinforcing the perception of official multiculturalism as a bold if somewhat flawed political experiment in social engineering.

Popular definitions of multiculturalism tend to dwell on the celebration of differences as differences, as valuable in their own right or as challenging for cultural space. By contrast, official multiculturalism can be defined as a "tool" for promoting an inclusive society by *proactively engaging with diversity as different yet equal.*[12] With its emphasis on society building through inclusiveness, official multiculturalism is concerned not only with minority women and men but, more importantly, with challenging the mainstream to move over and make space through removal of discriminatory barriers. Still other analysts prefer a political definition: Multiculturalism provides a political framework and official policy for securing the full and equitable participation of all Canadians by doing what is necessary, workable, and fair. It also consists of an explicit doctrine, along with a corresponding set of policies and practices, for advancing the related goals of cultural differences, social equality, and national unity.[13] This multidimensional view of multiculturalism in turn raises the question of whether Canada is in fact a multicultural society at all. Responses will vary depending on how multiculturalism is defined and the different levels of meaning that are employed, including: multiculturalism as (a) empirical fact of what is, (b) an ideology with a corresponding array of ideas and ideals, (c) explicit government policy and programs, (d) a set of practices for promoting political and minority interests; and (e) a critical discourse that invites challenge and resistance.[14] Failure to separate these different levels of meaning is not simply an exercise in sloppy thinking, but a recipe for disaster when people talk past each other. Table 1 provides a brief overview.

Dimensions of Multiculturalism

As fact, multiculturalism makes an empirical statement about what is. Employed in the descriptive sense of the term, few would dispute the notion of Canada as a multicultural society. Canada is home to approximately 5 million foreign-born Canadians from 170 different countries who speak over 100 different languages. Nearly 50 percent of Canada's population of about 30 million report having some non-British or non-French ancestry. Included in this total are visible minorities (people of colour) who account for 11.2 percent of the population. (The term *visible minority* refers to an official government category of native- and foreign-born, non-white, non-Caucasoid individuals, including: Blacks, Chinese, Japanese, Koreans, Filipinos, Indo-Pakistanis, West Asians and

TABLE 1: Levels of Meanings of Multiculturalism

As Fact	As Ideology	As Policy	As Practice	As Critical Discourse
Descriptive statement of what is	Prescriptive statement of what ought to be	Explicit government initiatives for fostering social equality, cultural diversity, and national interests	Putting multiculturalism into practice at different levels: (a) political, (b) commercial, and (c) minority women and men	Challenge the prevailing distribution of power and privilege

Arabs, Southeast Asians, Latin Americans, and Pacific Islanders.) Of the 3.2 million visible minority persons in Canada, most of whom live in the major urban centres of Toronto, Vancouver, and Montreal, those of Chinese origins are the most populous with a total of 860,000 persons or 26.9 percent of the visible minority population, followed by South Asian with 671,000 or 21.0 percent, and black with 574,000 or 17.9 percent. Assuming the continuity of current immigration patterns with nearly three-quarters of new Canadians coming from non-European sources, Canada will indeed remain demographically multicultural.

Unlike its descriptive counterpart, multiculturalism as an ideology embraces a prescriptive ("normative") statement of what ought to be. As a set of ideas and ideals, multiculturalism prescribes a preferred course of thought with respect to how a society should be organized and evaluated. This prescriptive state of affairs is modelled after liberal pluralist virtues of freedom, tolerance, respect for individual differences, with a belief that what we have in common as rights-bearing and morally equal individuals supersedes membership in a particular group. As Prime Minister Pierre Elliot Trudeau explained in 1971, "if national unity is to mean anything in the deeply personal sense, it must be anchored on confidence in one's own identity as a precondition for respecting others."

To say that Canada is officially multicultural in terms of policy is stating the obvious. From its inauspicious inception in 1971 when it barely garnered a paragraph in Canada's national newspaper *The Globe and Mail*, official multiculturalism has evolved to the point where it constitutes a formidable component of Canada's government agenda, having profoundly altered how Canadians think about themselves.[15] Policy considerations are central to Canada's official multiculturalism. By capitalizing on a mix of idealism and self-interest, successive governments have embraced multicultural strategies for "controlling" immigration, "managing" ethnic relations, "engaging" differences, and "integrating" ethnocultural minorities into the mainstream. Two policy levels can be discerned. At one level, multiculturalism provides a broader policy framework that justifies the design and implementation of diversity-driven programs without fear of inciting public concern over the possibility of creeping socialism or cultural apartheid. At another level, multiculturalism consists of specific government initiatives for transforming multicultural ideals into official programs that engage diversity without forfeiting national unity. Only the means for engaging diversity have evolved in response to demographic upheavals and political developments, with cultural solutions giving way to structural reforms and, more recently, the promotion of shared citizenship and belonging and full participation through institutional inclusiveness.[16] For the sake of simplicity these shifts can be partitioned into three mutually connected but analytically separate stages, including folkloric, equity, and civic multiculturalism—keeping in mind that overlap and duplication are the rule rather than exception when dealing with ideal-typical categories.

Canada's official multiculturalism embraces a commitment to consensus by way of "conformity" and "containment." Multiculturalism originated around the quest for integrative society-building functions; it continues to persist for precisely the same reasons, namely, the "containment" of ethnicity by modifying the rules of engagement and entitlement. In that sense, official multiculturalism is not about celebrating diversity or promoting ethnic groups, but about constructing a society in which people can live together with their differences. In contrast with consensus multiculturalism, the kind of critical multiculturalism that is flourishing in the United States challenges the prevailing distribution of power and privilege in society.[17] Critical multiculturalism addresses the issue of group differences and how power relations function to secure inequities and structure identities. A critical multiculturalism seeks to empower minorities by eroding the monocultural firmament of society, politicizes differences as a catalyst for minority empowerment and entitlement, and embraces an affinity for differences, an openness to change, and acceptance of social fragmentation. To the degree that Canada's consensus multiculturalism is about de-politicizing differences, thus making society safe from diversity rather than vice versa, its contrast with the more insurgent multiculturalisms in the United States could not be more forcibly articulated.

Multiculturalism as practice is its use in programs by both political and ethnic sectors to promote their respective goals and ambitions. Politicians and bureaucrats look upon multiculturalism as a resource with economic or political potential to be exploited for practical gain at national or international levels. Multiculturalism is thought to enhance Canada's sales image and competitive edge in a global economy, helping, for instance, to tap into the lucrative Asian market with its potential to harness trade contracts, establish international linkages and mutually profitable points of contact, and penetrate export markets.

Institutional Inclusiveness: "Walking Up a Down Escalator"

Nowhere are the politics of putting official multiculturalism into practice more sharply animated than in debates over institutional inclusiveness[18] in work organizations. Historically, workplaces have tended to marginalize disadvantaged groups such as women, visible minorities, aboriginal peoples, and people with disabilities. But the historically disadvantaged are demanding full and equal participation through removal of discriminatory barriers and creation of more inclusive workplaces. Five dimensions are discernible:

- The workforce should be representative–proportional to that of the regional labour force, not only to entry-level jobs but to all levels of management, access to training, and entitlement to rewards.
- Rules and operations should not deny or exclude anyone from the job recruitment, selection, training, and promotion.
- Institutions must foster a working climate conducive to the health and productivity of all workers. At minimum, such a climate cannot tolerate harassment of any form; at best, minorities are accepted as indispensable in the effective functioning and creative growth of the workplace.
- Service is community based and culturally sensitive. Such a commitment requires both a varied workforce and a commitment to a partnership relation with the community at large.
- Meaningful relations with all community members must be established to ensure productive lines of communication, with full community involvement in the decision-making process.

Numerous barriers exist that interfere with the process of institutional inclusiveness. Stumbling blocks include such aspects as hierarchy, bureaucratic rigidity, and unresponsive corporate and occupational subcultures. Some workers may resist any appeal to move over and make space without an understanding of what is going on, why, and how changes will affect them. This should come as no surprise; after all, few individuals are inclined to relinquish power or privilege without a struggle. The dimension of hierarchy will also inhibit inclusive adjustments. Those in higher echelons may be highly supportive of institutional change for a variety of reasons ranging from genuine concern to economic expediency, but with an eye predominantly towards public relations in between. Publicly articulated positions for reform may be long on platitudes yet prove short on practice or implementation. Bureaucracies by definition are instruments of rational control, and thus efforts to introduce workplace change at this level may be akin to "walking up a down escalator."

Sought for in the mainstream media, the concept of institutional inclusiveness proves an elusive ideal. Mainstream media have taken steps to be inclusive by improving depictions of minority women and men. Yet the representational basis of media-minority relations remains couched in compromise, with advances in some areas but stagnation in others. At the core of this impasse are debates over the nature and magnitude of institutional inclusiveness: Is inclusiveness best achieved by (a) removing discriminatory barriers, (b) augmenting minority personnel and improving workplace practices, (c) creating parallel modules within existing structures, or (d) establishing separate institutions that reflect minority realities? Does institutional inclusiveness involve treating everyone as if they were the same or treating everyone differently, depending on the circumstances? Put another way, are the goals of inclusiveness best attained by denying differences as a basis for defining who gets what, or by taking disadvantages into account as a basis for equal treatment and full participation? Inasmuch as answers to these questions remain inconclusive or clichéd while proposed solutions rarely produce any consensus, the representational politics of media-minority relations will continue to be as contested as ever.

Miscasting Minorities

Canada's mainstream media have been accused of harbouring a love-hate relationship with minority women and men. On one side, the media rely on minorities as content for narratives, for an angle in spicing up a story, as catalysts for driving plot lines or boosting main characters, or for imparting a dash of colour to an otherwise pallid cultural package. On the other side, minorities are subject to media "hate" by virtue of their status as the "other." Repeated visual and verbal references to minorities as irrelevant, inferior, dangerous, or unmarketable have reinforced their marginality in the mainstream media. Four recurrent themes appear to have characterized media (mis)casting of minority women and men, namely minorities as invisible, as stereotypes, as problem people, and as ornaments.[19] Such themes appear across all media, including newscasts, TV programming, advertising, and filmmaking, although each medium may differ from the others in the balance of these four elements.

1. Minorities as Invisible

Numerous studies have shown what many regard as obvious. Canada's multicultural diversity is poorly reflected in virtually all sectors of the popular media.[20] Visible minorities tend to be invisible through underrepresentation in areas that count, but overrepresented in areas that don't. Newscasts ignore minority women and men unless crime or conflict is involved; advertising has long relied on the maxim that "white sells," and TV programming has yet to provide a full complement of roles for minorities to emulate. Consider, for example, the portrayal of minorities in Canadian television advertising. An informal survey by Henry Mietkiewicz,[21] the *Toronto Star* media critic, confirms the cliché that the more things change, the more they stay the same. Considering 1,787 television commercials broadcast over 114 hours of programming on Canadian and American channels in February of 1999, 30.8 percent of the commercials employed minority actors, however

briefly, while only 10.4 percent of the ads provided more than a token appearance of at least 3 seconds of screen time to a minority character. Such low visibility may set into motion self-fulfilling prophecies: white content attracts white consumers who in turn encourage more white-based coverage in a self-perpetuating manner. Visible minorities comprised 11.2 percent of Canada's population in 1996, but constitute 15.8 percent of the population of Ontario and 31.6 percent of Toronto's population.[22]

Even substantial presentation in the media may be misleading if minority women and men are slotted into a relatively small number of programs such as children's programming or reduced to victim and/or assailant roles in reality-based programming. Nor is there much sign of improvement: In 1989, Robert MacGregor acknowledged the invisibility of visible minority women in Canada's national newsmagazine (*Maclean's*) when measured by the quantity and quality of their appearances over a 30-year span.[23] A follow-up study indicated that women of colour continue to be couched in compromise by virtue of mixed messages that concede improvements in quantity but not quality.[24] Or consider the plight of African-Americans on television. Of the 26 new shows scheduled by the four major U.S. networks in 1999, not a single one featured a minority lead, despite the fact that demographics indicate that black American viewers watch up to 70 hours of TV per week.[25] Programs that feature an entirely black cast are common enough, but most comedy TV sitcoms continue to ignore mixed casts except outside of the workplace. As a result there is a dearth of dramatic shows built around black protagonists, possibly in the belief that there is no sizable demographic audience for such programming.[26] Not surprisingly, black casting in prime-time sitcoms remains stuck around the clownish or demeaning.[27] Finally, even audiences appear to be racially segregated in terms of programming preferences, reflecting a lack of crossover appeal for films and TV programs.[28]

However extensive the process of rendering minorities invisible is, it would be inaccurate to accuse mainstream media of ignoring minorities. A "shallows and rapids" treatment is a more accurate appraisal. That is, under normal circumstances, minorities are ignored or rendered irrelevant by the mainstream press ("shallows"). Alternatively, coverage is guided by the context of crisis or calamity, involving natural catastrophes, wars, and colourful insurgents ("rapids"). Mainstream news media appear to prefer visuals of emaciated children and rotting cattle carcasses, according to Susan Moeller, author of *Compassion Fatigue: How the Media Cover War, Famine, and Death.* She concludes that many aid agencies are often only too happy to provide graphic footage. When the crisis subsides or the story gets stale, media interest is suspended–until the next eye-popping debacle. This cycle may simply reflect media preoccupation with audience ratings and advertising revenues. When asked to account for media whitewashing, veteran TV news producer Aaron Spelling did not mince words: "Our industry is not about black or white. Its about money ... the only color that matters in TV is green" (cited in the *National Post,* 26 July 1999, B7).

2. *Stereotyping Minorities*

Minorities have long complained of stereotyping by the mainstream media. Historically, people of colour were portrayed in a manner that conformed to prevailing prejudices. Liberties taken with minority depictions in consumer advertising were especially flagrant. In an industry geared towards image and appeal, advertisers insisted that their products be sanitized and bleached of colour for fear of lost revenue. People of colour were rarely depicted in the advertising of beauty care and personal hygiene products, so entrenched was the image of whiteness as the preferred standard of beauty.[29] Blacks in prime-time TV shows are portrayed as superhero/athletes or sex-obsessed buffoons when not typecast in secondary roles such as hipsters or outlaws.[30] And the news business continues to stereotype: In a study by Francis Henry, chair of Diversity at Ryerson University's School of Journalism, involving 2,622 articles in the *Toronto Star, Globe and Mail,* and *Toronto Sun,* both Vietnamese and Blacks (and especially Jamaicans) were typecast as criminals by way of a racist discourse that overreported problems but underreported successes except as entertainers or athletes. A similar conclusion was drawn in another study involving 8,000 stories in the *Star* and the *Sun* between 1997 and 1998 by Scot Wortley, a University of Toronto criminologist.[31]

In recent years, Muslims appear to have replaced other disadvantaged minorities as the worst victims of media stereotyping. Both the news and entertainment media foster disparaging images of Muslims as backward or fanatic, ruthless or greedy. Muslims are typecast beyond the pale of rational politics and civilized values because of religious fanaticism and seeming disregard for the value of human life and freedom.[32] According to a six-month study by the

Media Watch group of the Canadian Islamic Congress, Muslims have been typecast as sleazy bullies or tyrannical patriarchs. Films including *The Seige* and *True Lies* neatly feed into this stereotyping, with their typecasting of Muslims as warlike and dangerous, while conflating religion with terrorism.[33] In the process, an entire people and civilization are vilified by the actions of those who act outside the boundaries of normalcy as defined by the Muslim world. And since most Canadians rarely encounter Muslims in daily life, what little they do know may be derived at face value from these mainstream media messages.[34]

Consider as well how mainstream media have historically stereotyped Canada's aboriginal peoples. The image of aboriginal peoples as the "other" has been refracted through the prism of a Eurocentric lens, spanning the spectrum from their elevation as "noble savages" and "quixotic romantics" to their debasement as "villains" or "victims," with the stigma of "problem people" or "menacing subversives" sandwiched in between.[35] Images of tribalism and the quixotic continue to resonate, with a spicy mixture of meanings, from backwardness to spiritual mysticism to acting as guardians of the physical environment.[36] Most portrayals embrace a boilerplate mythic image of an imaginary warrior who prowled The Great Plains between 1825 and 1880.[37] The so-called "Indian Identity Kit"[38] was constructed around the following items, few of which were even indigenous to aboriginal peoples prior to European settlement, namely, (a) wig with hair parted in the middle into hanging plaits; (b) feathered war bonnet; (c) headband (a white invention to keep actor's wig from slipping off); (d) buckskin leggings; (e) moccasins; (f) painted skin teepee; and (g) a tomahawk and bow and arrows. This "one size fits all" image has been applied to all first peoples, regardless of whether they were Cree or Salish or Ojibwa or Blackfoot. These images can be further broken down into a series of recurrent stereotypes, in effect reinforcing a "seen one Indian, seen 'em all" mentality.

Collectively, these images have defined aboriginal peoples as a primitive people, both remote in time and removed in place, while what few assets they possessed were derived from colonization and interaction with whites. Collective resistance to colonization is rarely depicted, although individual acts of protest may be valorized, in effect de-politicizing aboriginal contributions to Canada while neutering their stature as first peoples. The net effect of this symbolic "emasculation" has ensured an image of aboriginal peoples as "safe, exotic, and somewhere else" as Philip Hayward writes with respect to music industry co-optation of aboriginal artists, and it is precisely these stereotypes that compromise the aspirations of aboriginal peoples in Canada.[39]

3. Problematizing Minorities

Minority women and men are frequently singled out by the media as social problems, that is, as having problems or creating problems in need of political attention or costly solutions. As problem people, they are taken to task by the media for making demands that may imperil Canada's unity or national prosperity. Recurrent images define aboriginal peoples as:

- a threat to Canada's territorial integrity or national interests (as in the debate over the Nisga'a self-government as an unconstitutional infringement on existing political jurisdictions);

- a risk to Canada's social order (as in violence between aboriginal peoples and lobster fishers at Burnt Church, New Brunswick);

- an economic liability (as in the costs associated with massive land claims settlements, restitution for righting historical wrongs such as in the case of residential schools, or recent proposals to constitutionally entrench inherent self-governing rights);

- a thorn in the side of the criminal justice system (ranging from the wrongful imprisonment of Donald Marshall to police shootings of aboriginal people including the killing of Dudley George at Ipperwash Ontario);

- unscrupulous manipulators who are not averse to breaking the law (as in cigarette smuggling or swindling their own people while hiding behind the smokescreen of aboriginal rights and entitlements).

Time and again aboriginal people come across as "troublesome constituents" whose demands for self-determination and the right to inherent self-government are contrary to Canada's liberal-democratic tradition. Aboriginal activism tends to be framed as a departure from established norms regardless of the context or urgency, while protestors are frequently labelled as dangerous or irrational.

Non-aboriginal minorities are also problematized by the media. People of colour, both foreign and native-born, are subject to negative reporting that dwells on costs, threats, and inconveniencies. As individuals or as groups, minority women and men appear in a dazzling array of trouble spots: hassling policing, stumping immigration authorities, cheating on welfare, or battling among themselves at community or family levels. Media reporting of refugees pounces on illegal entries and the associated costs of processing and integration into Canadian society. Immigrants are routinely cast as potential troublemakers who steal jobs from Canadians, cheat on the welfare system, manipulate educational opportunities without making a corresponding commitment to Canada, engage in illegal activities such as drug distribution, consumption, or smuggling, and imperil Canada's unity and identity by refusing to discard their cultural baggage. This negativity may be coded in different ways, from content to positioning and layout of the story, length of article and size of type, content of headlines and kickers (phrases immediately after the headline), use of newspeak or inflammatory language, coded speech that reinforces negative messages, use of quotes, statistics, and racial origins.[40]

4. Ornamentalizing Minorities

Mainstream media tend to portray minority women and men as ornamental features of society. Rarely do they appear as average, normal, tax-paying Canadians with a broad range of opinions that go beyond their race or community. Rather, minority women and men tend to be trivialized ("miniaturized") as tokens in sorting out who gets what in society. This ornamentalizing effect is achieved by casting minorities in roles that are meant only to amuse or embellish. Moreover, while all people of colour are rendered vulnerable to misrepresentation by race and ethnicity, minority women are subject to additional media mistreatment because of gender: gender is superimposed on ethnicity, class, and race, to create overlapping and mutually intersecting lines of exclusion that relegate aboriginal women, women of colour, and immigrant women to the status of decorative props. Minorities are coupled with the exotic and sensual, invoked as congenial hosts for faraway destinations, enlisted as superstar boosters for athletics and sporting goods, or ghettoized in marketing segments related to rap or hip hop. For example, travel brochures tend to portray minority women and men as background equivalents to the flora and fauna of the locale–a soothing visual backdrop that reinforces a deference to whiteness while further dehumanizing minority women and men.[41]

Recasting the Relation: "Two Steps Forward..."

There is little doubt that Canada's mainstream media once resonated with indifference or hostility towards minority men and women. Minorities were diminished and disparaged by both the quantity and quality of images that had the effect of rendering minorities invisible, or stereotyping, problematizing, and ornamentalizing them. It is obvious however that media have become more inclusive of minority women and men since the days when soap ads portrayed black children being scrubbed in a tub with the slogan: "If you can get this skin clean, think what our products can do for your white complexion."[42]

Both demographic shifts and shifts in intellectual fashion have ignited a broader commitment to the worth and authenticity of diversity as refreshingly different–in contrast to the past when differences were routinely dismissed as inferiority or irrelevancy. Advertising, such as that for Benetton, is increasingly supportive of diversity as something to be positively marketed, while the industry in general is increasingly more responsive to diversity.[43] Similarly, TV programming is more inclined to portray minorities in a positive light by acknowledging people of colour across a broad socioeconomic spectrum. Such a shift would (a) increase interracial familiarity, (b) shatter stereotypes, (c) fortify the comfort zone, and (d) expand the number of minority role models.[44] Similarly, shows such as North of 60 have expanded a multicultural mindset towards aboriginal peoples. According to Linda Wortley in her article on "The Mountie and the Nurse" (1999), positive aboriginal shows provide: (a) a view of aboriginal peoples as individuals living in a community where problems are explored and solutions negotiated rather than passive players in sensationalized stories; (b) insights into the sources of social and personal problems, thus putting issues into context rather than the overwhelmingly negative coverage of the past; (c) affirmation of the continuity in culture and its dynamics–rooted in history but not stuck in the past; and (d) a glimpse into the lives of enterprising aboriginal people. The lack of humour and perpetual crisis mentality in the series is seen by some however, as a serious distortion and a significant disservice.[45]

Even newscasting is making an effort to avert blatant racism, for example, by reducing the number of disparaging references to minorities through "race tagging" of crime stories where race is immaterial in tracking suspects. Finally, films are leading the charge by challenging conventional stereotypes of whites and non-whites. Audience resistance towards interracial romance is gradually eroding under the onslaught of mixed-couple casting on TV or film, suggesting a seismic shift in the gender/race "wars" since the days of Guess Who's Coming to Dinner or Father Knows Best.[46] Similarly the portrayal of aboriginal peoples following the epic Dances with Wolves (1990) has improved, with much greater emphasis on the courage or durability of indigenous people in contrast to the rapacious greed of white settler-colonization.

Despite these changes, there is much to the adage that the more things change, the more they stay the same. Improvements in some areas are undermined by stagnation in others. Appearances are deceiving: improvement in the quantity of minority representations is not the same as quality in representations, prompting Robert Stam to pose the following questions:

> How much space do they occupy in the shot? Are they seen in close-ups or only in distant long shots? How often do they appear compared with the Euro-Canadian characters and for how long? Are they active, desiring characters or only decorative props? How do character positionings communicate social difference or differences in status? How do body language, posture, facial expression communicate social hierarchies, arrogance, servility, resentment, pride? Which community is sentimentalized? Is there an aesthetic segregation whereby one group is haloed and the other made the villain?[47]

Newscasting remains a medium of the negative, with minority men and women continuing to be framed as people who have problems or create problems. Formats have, however, been re-vamped in a way that integrates minorities as acceptable or normal. TV programming is no less ambivalent. Talk of inclusiveness is one thing, but the failure by the four major US networks in 1999 to include minority main characters does not bode well for television. A survey of 1998 movie and television roles in the US by the Screen Actors Guild revealed a drop in the number of parts for minority women and men–the first decline since the annual study began in 1992.[48] Visibility may not be the same as power but invisibility is definitely disempowering, most notably in TV series such as Mad About You, set in New York City, but without any minority presence. Both advertising and TV programming may be exploring new dimensions yet neither is averse to capitalizing on minority stereotypes to connect with audiences.

Portrayal of minorities as the "other" typically entails a cultural Catch-22: they are criticized for being too different yet may be chided for not being different enough; they are taken to task for aspiring to be the same yet vilified when they falter or refuse; and they are expected to pick up the slack in making a contribution to society yet are criticized as too pushy if too successful.[49] Paradoxically, while the mainstream media are critical of other institutions for not living up to their multicultural obligations, they appear reluctant to criticize those standards and practices that contribute to aboriginal miscasting and media racism.[50] Or, as Brian Maracle[51] puts it, mainstream media are so steeped in Eurocentric values (including liberal pluralism and universalism) that even perception of this bias may be elusive without constant reminders to that effect. The fact that media bias exists is not the problem; after all, all social constructions reflect the values, agendas, and priorities of those who create them. Rather problems arise from refusal to admit this bias while claiming to be neutral, fair, and objective.

Accounting for the Miscasting

Why, then, in such a seemingly progressive society such as Canada's have the media faltered in positively engaging diversity? Neglect of minorities in the media may occur for a variety of reasons, spanning the spectrum from hard-boiled business decisions that reflect market forces, to a lack of cultural awareness and deep-seated prejudice among media personnel, to a bias so systemic that it escapes detection or scrutiny but reflects the organization of power within media institutions. Does media mistreatment of minorities imply the presence of personal prejudice or overt discrimination? Is it a case of unwittingly cramming minority realities into Eurocentric categories as a convenience for description or evaluation?[52] Or does it reflect a preference to act out of self-interest by pandering to the dictates of the marketplace? Is it a case of precluding minority input into media outputs, considering that minorities are rarely part of a white boys' network as writers, producers, and directors, but relegated to questionable coverage by outsider perspectives?

Four factors are foremost in preventing media institutional inclusiveness.

1. Institutional (Commercial) Imperatives

Mainstream private media are commercial enterprises with a responsibility to their shareholders. Their goal is to foster those images and representations that generate revenue by maximizing the linkage between audience and advertisers. The commercial media do not see themselves as agents of social change whose primary goal is to criticize, challenge, resist, or reform, even if they may have a social responsibility to do so. Nor do the media exist to inform or to entertain. As a rule, they are not interested in solving social problems or in promulgating progressive social change unless consumer goods are directly involved. Mainstream media are, first and foremost, business ventures whose devotion to the bottom line revolves around generating advertising revenues by attracting the largest possible audience. This preoccupation with audience ratings and advertising revenues is pivotal in shaping the quality and quantity of media representations.[53]

Neither is there any consensus on how to depict diversity: should differences be highlighted to draw attention to disadvantages; or is it best to ignore differences in hopes of conveying a message of commonality "under the skin"? Responses vary. To one side are those who believe race should not be an issue if everyone is the same and is to be treated accordingly. To the other are those who believe that ignoring race is irresponsible because peoples' differences matter in real life, whether we like it or not. Paradoxically, the problem may not lie in applying different standards, but in casting everyone the same, since the consequences of a one-size-fits-all casting have a different impact when the starting blocks are staggered and the playing field is uneven. Stereotyping of a minority is different than stereotyping of a majority; after all, minorities carry a cultural weight in society that renders them more vulnerable to typecasting.[54] This inconsistency crosses racial boundaries: just as the mainstream divides into different publics, so too are minorities divided over proposals for improving media representation. Some prefer minorities to be depicted in high-status images, thus providing role models; others want to be portrayed as an ordinary part of the mainstream, thus reflecting the realities of ordinary minority women and men. An endorsement of cultural separateness as a preferred representational basis is counteracted by the principle of integration as the preferred route.[55] J. Fred MacDonald[56] expresses the conundrum at the heart of media minority representations:

> Should blacks be shown only as middle class and assimilated, as are most whites, or is this a denial of racial authenticity? Should blacks be portrayed in terms of the urban underclass, especially when such imagery might appear crude or unaccomplished? Should the folk images of rural blacks ... be propagated now as authentic, or should they be buried as anachronistic and self-defeating?

Given these contradictory stances, media cautiousness is understandable. In a business renowned for its conservatism and caution, moving too quickly can backfire commercially. Nonetheless, such indecision may be interpreted by minority women and men as waffling discrimination in defence of the status quo.

2. Institutional Dynamics: Systemic Stereotyping

There is little doubt that media-minority relations were historically tainted by the stain of blatant prejudice, open discrimination, and racialized discourses. Media miscasting of minorities reflected and reinforced this dislike of others, together with a belief that conformity rather than diversity should serve as basis for reward, recognition, and relationships. Covert or polite displays continue to persist, often manifest as prejudice, ethnocentrism (belief in cultural superiority), or Eurocentrism (filtering reality through the Western "gaze"). Media "whitewashing" should come as no surprise. According to Paul Farli, a *Washington Post* columnist,[57] middle-aged white males comprise about 98 percent of all TV writers and producers in Hollywood, with the result that minority realities are refracted through the prism of whiteness as natural and normal.

Institutional dynamics are sharply animated by those patterned images known as stereotypes. To be sure, stereotypes are an indispensable component in processing everyday information. In a world of bewildering complexity, stereotypes reduce reality into manageable proportions as a basis for defining situations. Stereotypes become a problem only when serving to justify behaviour that denies or excludes others on the basis of preconceived (and/or irrelevant) characteristics. Media stereotyping of minority women and men is not necessarily a perceptual problem involving individual prejudice by a misinformed industry. Rather, media stereotyping is intrinsic to the operational dynamic of an industry constructed around simplifying information for audiences to consume by tapping into a collective portfolio of popular and unconscious images, both print and visual, each of which imposes a readily identifiable frame or narrative spin. Because of limitations of time and space, mainstream media are rarely in a position to develop complex or complicated interpretations of reality that capture the spectrum of human emotion, conflict, or contradiction. Distortions through simplification are inevitable, thanks to the boxed-in constraints of a 26-inch screen

and a sanitized 22-minute time slot for character development and plot resolution.

Over time, stereotypes solidify into definitive statements about "reality" and, while not "real" in the conventional sense, they become real in their social consequences. Although personal stereotypes reflect individual preferences and dislikes, institutional stereotypes persist without the element of consciousness or intention. These stereotypes are systemic in that they are intrinsic to normal institutional operations, rules, and rewards.

3. Institutional Logic: Systemic Bias

There is another type of institutional bias, both impersonal and unconscious, yet no less invidious or destructive. Its unobtrusiveness makes it that much more difficult to detect, let alone to isolate and combat. Systemic bias refers to this type of subtle yet powerful form of institutional discrimination entrenched within the structure (rules, organization), function (norms, goals), and process (procedures). Systemic bias can be defined as the unintended yet adverse consequences that result from evenly and equally applying seemingly neutral rules to unequal situations, but with dissimilar effects for the historically disadvantaged. With systemic bias, in other words, it is not the intent or motive that counts, but rather the context and the consequences, since identical treatment in unequal contexts may freeze the inequities.

The charge of systemic racism is applicable to contemporary media. Journalists and editors are not free of bias, according to Henry and Tator,[58] despite oft-quoted claims to objectivity or neutrality. Racism continues in the mainstream news media because of language and images reflecting racialized assumptions and beliefs that continue to reinforce negative stereotypes or to construct minority women and men as social problems and outsiders that undermine Canadian society.

4. Institutional Values: Discourses in Defense of Ideology

Few would dispute the ability of the media to shape the way people relate to the world. A media-dominated society tends to elevate electronic and print media to a privileged status as purveyors of right or wrong, acceptable or unacceptable. Mainstream media fix the premises of discourse by circumscribing the parameters of acceptability or desirability, at times by suppressing information at odds with powerful interests and at times through the perpetuation of stereotypes and ethnocentric value judgments. The elite agenda-setting media play key roles in legitimizing dominant values and practices that favour corporate and state monied interests.[59]

The news media are also ideological in that they themselves are replete with ideological assumptions that influence the framing of news stories for sign-posting a preferred way of reading the event.[60] Incidents and issues are routinely framed around conflict formats or conferred a racial or gender "spin" in hopes of playing up an angle (e.g., "gender wars"). Yet this "framing" experience is anything but neutral; the interests of those who own or control the media are advanced while others are crushed or ignored. For example, the very nature of modern media tends to distort minority messages, many of which are far too subtle, complex, or spiritual to fit into the gross guidelines of a conflict driven and image-obsessed mainstream media.[61] The constructed character of the media is rarely conveyed to audiences, many of whom are often unaware of the production process behind the apparent naturalness of media products.[62] Not only are the media constructed through human agency, they also construct realities by naturalizing our perception of the world as necessary and normal rather than conventional and constructed. In short, the mainstream media may be interpreted as discourses in defence of ideology insofar as they (a) represent dominant interests as universal and progressive rather than particular and parochial; (b) deny the existence of contradictions such as those related to capitalist production and distribution; (c) naturalize the present (with its prevailing distribution of power and privilege) as common sense; and (d) secure consensus and control through consent rather than coercion.[63]

Enlightened Propaganda: Thought Control in Democratic Societies

The concept of enlightened propaganda may be helpful in expanding the notion of the media as agents in the defense of a dominant ideology. A distinction is in order. Conventional propaganda can be defined as a systematic process of persuasion in which symbolic communication is manipulated in an organized and deliberate fashion to achieve desired goals by modifying peoples' attitudes or behaviour.[64] By contrast, enlightened propaganda contains the idea of consequence or effect but without explicit intention. That is, it is a given that the organization and distribution of information has the effect (or consequence) of promoting one point of view to the exclusion of others but it need not be a deliberate act. In taking this perspective, enlightened propaganda is not equated with blatant brainwashing or crude displays of totalitarian censorship. Nor is enlightened propaganda equivalent to deliberate thought control. Mainstream media are not propaganda per se; nor do they set out to be propagandistic but may have that effect by creating messages that emphasize one point of view as natural and superior and other perspectives as inferior or irrelevant. Furthermore, enlightened propaganda is not necessarily something deliberately inserted into the media, but natural and normal, in the same way that media miscasting is not something out of the ordinary in doing media business, but consistent with what might be expected of a system of persuasion.[65] As a discursive framework, enlightened propaganda is inherent in media rules and intrinsic to daily operations, in the same way that systemic discrimination reflects the negative but unintended consequences of even-handed rules and well-intentioned procedures.[66]

However unintentional the consequences, the effects of granting a privileged position to the media are anything but inconsequential, resulting in the exclusion of alternate points of view, a reduction in dissent and disagreement, the creation of consensus and compliance with dominant ideologies, and the restriction of free debate. Insofar as minorities are routinely portrayed as problem people (both by having problems and/or making problems), mainstream news media reinforce the notion of enlightened propaganda. To the extent that minority women and men are blamed for their problems rather than focussing attention on social structures, mainstream media indeed constitute a discourse in defence of enlightened propaganda. In other words, the media do not set out to contain or control, but the systemic bias within media messages have a containing or controlling effect on audiences by drawing negative attention to minorities. The net result is the same in both cases: a one-sided interpretation of reality that normalizes even while it marginalizes.

The media thus represent a contested site, a kind of ideological battleground where different interests struggle for control over media agendas. It is precisely the openings in this area of the "in between" that are pivotal in exploring the politics of media inclusiveness. To date, moves to redefine the representational basis of media-minority relations have focussed on institutional inclusiveness through mainstreaming minority women and men or, alternatively, through the establishment of separate media institutions that reflect, reinforce, and advance minority interests and aspirations. Yet proposed changes are likely to be met with increasingly stiff resistance. After all, the mainstream media as institutional structures and culture bearers embody a complex and multifaceted assemblage of logic, values, imperatives, symbols, and norms that, collectively, serve to sustain media miscasting of minority women and men. Nonetheless, the basis for renewal and reform appears to be in place and already in progress.

Mainstreaming Diversity

Mainstream media are powerful agencies with the capacity to dominate and control. In some cases, the exercise of power is blatant; in others, media power is sustained by an aura of impartiality, objectivity, and balance—yet no less powerful in its impact. An ability to frame issues and set agendas in ways that bolster the status quo reinforces the notion of media as thought control in democratic societies.

Media institutions have embarked on an exploration of the possibility of effective internal reforms in a way that ensures a level playing field and equal starting blocks. Reform is premised on the assumption that media structures and values are fundamentally sound, only requiring cosmetic changes to ensure equitable treatment. Proposed changes include the incorporation of minority perspectives into the media process, multicultural programming, removal of discriminatory barriers, balanced and impartial newscasts, and sensitivity and anti-racist training for journalists and decision-makers.[67] The point is not simply to increase or improve the portrayals of minority women and men. Rather the focus is on sharing power so that minority representations reflect, reinforce, and advance minority concerns and ambitions. Yet a conflict of interest is inevitable unless changes are seen as bolstering the bottom line of a typical commercially driven, conservatively oriented media institution.

Some progress is evident in delineating a more positive and realistic portrayal of minority women and men. Reforms within the CBC include sensitivity training for program and production staff, language guidelines to reduce race and role stereotypes, and the monitoring of on-air representation of racial minorities. Abusive representations of individuals on the basis of race, ethnicity, age, gender, religion, or disability are no longer openly tolerated. The *Broadcasting Act* of 1991 firmly endorsed the concept of "cultural expression" by expanding airtime for ethnic communities. As well, the CRTC has made it known that broadcasters will be evaluated on the basis of employment-equity hiring when applying for a renewal of licences. These initiatives are consistent with the premise that positive minority depictions will follow when minorities share power and make decisions. Such initiatives are also consistent with the provisions of the *Multiculturalism Act*, with its expectations that all government departments and Crown agencies improve minority access, equity, and representation. In addition, the *Employment Equity Act* of 1986 requires annual progress reports on minority hiring and equity goals from federally regulated agencies such as the CBC. To date, formal sanctions for non-compliance are largely symbolic.

The concept of mainstreaming is critical to securing institutional inclusiveness. Under a mainstreaming diversity approach, minority women and men are hired and promoted at all levels in the media industry. Such inclusiveness makes good business sense in view of the increasing economic clout of minority-group members. Equally critical is the notion of ensuring that minorities have a say in the kinds of images that appear in newscasts, advertising, or dramatic TV programming. In Southern Ontario, the multicultural channel CFMT delivers a much-needed service. Serving 18 cultural groups in 15 languages, CFMT has proven its worth, not only in producing 23 hours of original programming per week, but also because 60 percent of the programming is non-French and non-English.[68] Vision TV also hosts about 30 programs, largely about different religious faiths and practices. Inroads are also evident in the private sector where multicultural issues since 1984 have been addressed by Toronto's CITY-TV through two large blocks of non-English, non-French programming. On-air programming such as the critically acclaimed but now cancelled series, *North of 60*, and *The Rez*, are also pushing the frontier of acceptance. In advertising, minorities are appearing more frequently across a broader range of products and services. Companies that utilize diversity are now perceived as sophisticated and cosmopolitan compared with their all-white counterparts who come across as staid and outdated. Demographics may be pushing these changes. When people of colour comprise over 30 percent of the populations in Vancouver and Toronto, the media have little choice except to improve the quantity and quality of representation.

One of the more successful stories is the creation in 1999 of an indigenous medium called the Aboriginal Peoples Television Network (APTV). The rationale behind APTV, the world's first national public television network for aboriginal peoples, was clearly defensible, given the miscasting of aboriginal peoples on the screen. Much of the programming will be based initially on content from Television Northern Canada, an aboriginal network that has been broadcasting in the north since 1991 as a cultural response to the intrusion of southern television signals in the 1970s. In time, however, it is expected to provide a full range of services.

The emancipatory potential of local media has altered our perception of traditional mass media.[69] Commodity-driven mass media tend to obliterate identity in an avalanche of American-style programming, yet local productions may assist in locating or consolidating a collective affiliation. But even these efforts will fail unless indigenous peoples can gain local ownership over programming and a sense of community commitment and involvement. That appears to be the case with TVNorthern Ontario and the Indigenous Broadcasting Corporation (IBC). Local programming has elicited high levels of interest in TV and radio programs; the popularity of shows related to language learning, skills acquisition, and northern exposure to regional organizations also indicates a bright future. To be sure, cutbacks in funding have led to uncertainty and increased reliance on the government with its potential to compromise the integrity of indigenous cultures. For example, the federal government cut the IBC budget by 36 percent between 1990 and 1995 ($2.6 million to $1.6 million) even though 65 percent of its operating budget is dependent on federal funds.[70] The Northern Native Broadcasting Access Program has seen its budget slashed from a high of $13.2 million in 1989 to around $9 million by the mid-1990s. Nevertheless, despite contradictions that both advantage yet disadvantage media coverage of aboriginal peoples, evidence suggests that there will be no turning back—even with cutbacks—as Canada's indigenous people re-establish their rightful place in the Canadian communications network.

Conclusion: Adjusting the Mindset

Canada is undergoing a period of profound upheaval at the demographic, social, and political levels simultaneously. Time-honoured rules and conventional practices are eroding under the onslaught of new social and technological realities. This transformation is proving more convulsive than many would have liked. Vested interests balk at discarding the conventional for fear of dismantling prevailing patterns of power and privilege.

Nowhere is this struggle more politicized than in media representations of minority women and men. The world we inhabit is pervaded and transformed by media images in securing a cultural frame of reference about what is acceptable and desirable. The proliferation of media images makes it impossible to distinguish fantasy from reality, as Angus and Jhally[71] explain, especially since the "real" is so thoroughly "media-ted" that any separation of the two is futile except for analytic purposes. Mainstream media images are central in the construction of social identity for both minorities and the general population, with the result that control of knowledge and its dissemination through media representations is fundamental to the exercise of power in society. These images not only assist in the identification and construction of ourselves as social beings; they also serve as "windows" that provide insight into patterns of power and privilege in society.

With images as powerful as they are, minority women and men are under pressure to reclaim control over the representational basis of media-minority relations. They are demanding control over images and representations as one way of escaping those "psychic prisons" that deny or exclude.[72] Knowledge can be empowerment, and reclaiming control can provide an offset to the privileged discourses that serve to control or contain. Control over representations will remain rooted in power insofar as all representations are socially constructed and shaped by those who construct and consume them.[73] For the moment, the representational basis of media-minority relations will remain riddled with ambiguity and couched in compromise.

Notes

[1.] Augie Fleras and Jean Leonard Elliott, *Unequal Relations. An Introduction to Race, Ethnic and Aboriginal Dynamics* (Scarborough: Prentice Hall, 1999); Will Kymlicka, *Finding Our Way: Rethinking Ethnocultural Relations in Canada* (Toronto: OUP, 1998).

[2.] Jim Harvey, "An Undertheorised Romanticism: An Australian Perspective," *Multicultural Teaching* 11 (3): 5-7; Sunera Thobani, "Multiculturalism: The Politics of Containment"; Adie Nelson and Augie Fleras, eds., *Social Problems in Canada. A Reader* (Scarborough: Prentice Hall, 1995), pp.213-216. See also Neil Bissoondath, "A Question of Belonging: Multiculturalism and Citizenship," William Kaplan, ed., *Belonging: The Meaning and Future of Canadian Citizenship* (Kingston/Montreal: McGill-Queen's University Press, 1993), pp.367-87.

[3.] Frances Henry, Carol Tator, Winston Mathis, and Tim Rees, *The Colour of Democracy*, 2d ed. (Toronto: Harcourt, 2000).

[4.] Brian Cryderman, Augie Fleras, and Chris O'Toole, *Policing, Race, and Ethnicity: A Guidebook for the Policing Services*, 3rd ed. (Markham: Butterworths, 1998).

[5.] Adie Nelson and Augie Fleras, *Social Problems in Canada: Conditions and Consequences*, 2d ed. (Scarborough: Prentice Hall, 1998).

[6.] Augie Fleras, "Walking away From the Camera," John W. Berry and Jean Laponce, eds., *Ethnicity and Culture in Canada, The Research Landscape* (Toronto: University of Toronto Press, 1994), pp.340-384; Frances Henry and Carol Tator, *Racist Discourse in Canada's English Print Media* (Toronto: Canadian Race Relations Foundations, 2000).

[7.] Henry Giroux, *Channel Surfing. Race Talk and the Destruction of Today's Youth* (Toronto: Canadian Scholars Press, 1997).

8. U. Hannerz, *Cultural Complexity: Studies in Social Meaning* (New York: Columbia University, 1992), p.26.

9. A. Jakubowicz et al., *Racism, Ethnicity, and the Media* (Sydney: Allen & Unwin, 1994).

10. Arthur Schlesinger, Jr., *The Disuniting of America: Reflections on a Multicultural Society* (New York: W.W. Norton, 1992); Ellie Vasta and Stephen Castle, *The Teeth are Smiling: The Persistance of Racism in Multicultural Australia* (Sydney: Allen & Unwin, 1996); Augie Fleras and Paul Spoonley, *Recalling Aotearoa: Indigenous Politics and Ethnic Relations in New Zealand* (Melbourne: OUP, 1999).

11. Annual Report, *Multiculturalism. Respect, Equality, Diversity.* Report on the Operations of the Canadian Multiculturalism Act, 1998-1999 (Ottawa: Canadian Heritage, Multiculturalism, 2000).

12. Augie Fleras, "Working through Differences. The Politics of Posts and Isms in New Zealand," *New Zealand Sociology* 13 (1): 62-96.

13. Seymour V. Wilson, "Canada's Evolving Multicultural Policy," C.E.S. Frank et al., eds., *Canada's Century: Governance in a Maturing Society* (Montreal/Kingston: McGill-Queens University Press, 1995).

14. Evelyn Kallen, "Multiculturalism: Ideology, Policy, and Reality," *Journal of Canadian Studies* 17 (1982): 51-63; Fleras and Elliott, *Unequal Relations.*

15. Kenneth McRoberts, *Misconceiving Canada: The Struggle for National Unity* (Toronto: OUP, 1997).

16. Annual Report, *Multiculturalism.*

17. David Theo Goldberg, *Multiculturalism: A Critical Reader* (Cambridge MA: Blackwell, 1994).

18. Augie Fleras, *Social Problems in Canada: Constructions, Conditions, and Challenges* (Scarborough: Pearson Education, 2001).

19. Fleras and Elliott, *Unequal Relations.*

20. Fleras, "Walking away from the Camera."

21. Henry Mietkiewicz, "Colour Coded Casting," *Toronto Star* (1 March 1999).

22. Figures from the United States appear more promising in terms of quantity and quality. Nevertheless, a recent report for the Screen Actors Guild conducted by George Gerbner of Temple University has reconfirmed that, Blacks notwithstanding, minorities such as Hispanics, Asians, and Native Americans continue to be underrepresented compared to their numbers in real life (cited in the *Toronto Star*, 23 Dec. 1998).

23. Robert MacGregor, "The Distorted Mirror: Images of Visible Minority Women in Canadian Print Advertising," *Atlantis* 15 (1) (1989): 137-43.

24. Jean Lock Kunz and Augie Fleras, "Women of Colour in Mainstream Advertising. Distorted Mirror or Looking Glass?" *Atlantis* 22 (2) (1998): pp.27-38.

25. John Allemang, "Sitcom Stereotypes Nothing to Laugh At," *The Globe and Mail* (26 January 1999).

26. Fred J. MacDonald, *Black and White TV: African-Americans in Television Since 1948* (Chicago: Nelson-Hall, 1992).

27. John Haslett Cuff, "'Cos' and Effect: A Mixed Message," *The Globe and Mail* (30 April 1992).

28. Leonard Steinhorn and Barbara Diggs-Brown, *By the Color of Our Skin: The Illusion of Integration and the Reality of Race* (New York: Dutton Publishers, 1999).

29. Geraldine Bledsloe, "The Media: The Minorities Still Fighting for Their Share," *Rhythm and Business Magazine* (March/April 1989): 14-18.

30. Sharlene Azam, "Festival Brings Black Reality to Silver Screen," *Toronto Star* (26 April 2000); Gary Granzberg, "Portrayal of Visible Minorities by Manitoba Television: A Summary of Findings," *Currents* 5 (1989): 25.

31. Cited in Haroon Siddiqui, "Damming Indictment of Racism in the Media," *Toronto Star* (26 September 1999).

32. Canadian Islamic Congress, "Anti-Islam in the Media. A Six Month Case Study of Five Top Canadian Newspapers" (Waterloo, Ont., 1999).

33. F. Kutty and B. Youseff, "Hollywoods View of Arabs and Muslims," *Toronto Star* (21 September 1998); Sharon Waxman, "Muslim Fury as the Seige Hits Screen," *Washington Post,* cited in the *NZ Sunday Star-Times* (15 November 1998); M. Almasry, "Framing Islam," *Kitchener-Waterloo Record* (16 December 1999).

34. M. Ali, "Canadian Comedy Sketch Reinforced 'Terrorist' Stereotypes of Muslims," *Silhouette* (a McMaster University Publication) (3 February 2000).

35. Martin Blythe, *Naming the Other: Images of the Maori in New Zealand Film and Television* (Metuchen, NJ: Scarecrow Press, 1994); Melanie Wall, "Stereotypical Constructions of the Maori 'Race' in the Media," *New Zealand Geographer* 53 (2) (1997): 40-45. Fleras and Spoonley, *Recalling Aotearoa.*

36. Jakubowicz et al., *Racism, Ethnicity and the Media.*

37. Daniel Frances, *The Imaginary Indian: The Image of the Indian in Canadian Culture* (Vancouver: Arsunal Pulp Press, 1992).

38. Pierre Berton, *Hollywood's Canada* (Toronto: McClelland and Stewart, 1975).

39. Maurice Switzer, "Indians are Not Red, They are Invisible," *Media* (spring 1997): 21-22.

40. Henry and Tator, *Racist Discourse.* Also Robert A. Hackett, "Coups, Earthquakes, and Hostages? Foreign News on Canadian Television," Marc Grenier, ed., *Critical Studies of Canadian Mass Media* (Toronto: Butterworths, 1992), pp.313-28.

41. Michael Hoeschmann, cited in Barbara Turnbull, "Lecturer Takes on Racism and the Media," *Toronto Star* (18 March 1999).

42. Liz Jones, "Waking up to the Colour of Money," *Style* (27 August 1995): 10-12.

43. Leonard Steinhorn and Barbara Diggs-Brown, *By the Color of Our Skin: The Illusion of Integration and the Reality of Race* (New York: Dutton Publishers, 1999).

44. Ibid.

45. Valerie Alia, *Un/Covering the North: News, Media, and Aboriginal People* (Vancouver: UBC Press, 2000)."

46. Leonard Steinhorn and Barbara Diggs-Brown, *By the Color of Our Skin: The Illusion of Integration and the Reality of Race* (New York: Dutton Publishers, 1999).

47. Robert Stam, "From Stereotype to Discourse: Some Methodological Reflections on Racism in the Media," *Cineaction* 32 (29 October 1993).

48. Spotlight, "Minority Roles in U.S. Moves, TV dip in 1998," *Toronto Star* (4 May 1999).

49. Robert Stam, "From Stereotype to Discourse"; and Deborah Root, "Blood, Vengeance and the Anxious Liberal: Natives and Non-Natives in Recent Movies," *Cineaction* 32 (29 October 1993).

50. Henry and Tator, *Racist Discourse.*

51. Brian Maracle, "One More Whining Indian Tilting at Windmills," J. Littleton, ed., *Clash of Identities* (Scarborough: Prentice Hall 1996).

52. Robert Stam and Ella Shohat, "Contested Histories: Eurocentrism, Multiculturalism and the Media," David T. Goldberg, ed., *Multculturalism: A Critical Reader* (Cambridge MA: Blackwell, 1994), pp.296-324.

53. Herman Gray, *Watching Race: Television and the Struggle for Blackness* (Minneapolis: University of Minnesota Press, 1995).

54. Canadian Islamic Congress, "Anti-Islam in the Media."

55. Canadian Advertising Foundation, *Visible Minorities in Advertising: Focus Groups/CEO Survey Results/National Consumer Survey,* Research Report for Race Relations Advisory Council on Advertising (Toronto: 1992).

56. MacDonald, *Black and White TV*; also b. hooks, *Black Looks: Race and Representation* (Boston: South End Press, 1992); Jannette L. Dates and William Barlow, *Split Images: African-Americans in the Mass Media* (Washington: Howard University Press, 1990).

57. Paul Farli, "TV 'Ghetto' has Last Laugh on Blacks," *Guardian Weekly* (29 January 1995).

58. Henry and Tator, *Racist Discourse.*

59. Edward Herman and Noam Chomsky, *Manufacturing Consent: The Political Economy of the Mass Media* (New York: Pantheon Books, 1988).

60. David Taras, *The Newsmakers* (Toronto: Nelson, 1991); James Winter, *Democracy's Oxygen: How Corporations Control the News* (Montreal: Black Rose Books, 1997).

61. Jerry Mander, *In the Absence of the Sacred: The Failure of Technology and the Survival of the Indian* (San Francisco: Sierra Books, 1991).

62. N. Abercrombie, *Television and Society* (London: Polity Press, 1995)

63. Michael Apple, *Cultural Politics and Education* (Buckingham: Open University Press, 1996).

64. Terry Qualter, "Propaganda in Canadian Society," Benjamin D. Singer, ed., *Communications in Canadian Society,* 3rd ed. (Scarborough, Ont.: Nelson Canada, 1991), pp. 200–12; J. Garth and V. O'Donnell, *Propaganda and Persuasion,* 3rd ed. (Thousand Oaks, CA: Sage, 2000).

65. Jacques Ellul, *Propaganda* (New York: Knopf, 1965).

66. Fleras and Elliott, *Unequal Relations.*

67. Herman and Chomsky, *Manufacturing Consent.*

68. Greg Quill, "CFMT. The World in Miniature," *Toronto Star* (19 May 1996).

69. Michael Meadows, "Northern Exposure: Indigenous Television Developments in Northern Canada," *Media International Australia* (1995) 78: 109-118. Michael Meadows, "The Media and the Mohawk Uprising at Oka," unpublished manuscript.

70. Brian Bergman, "TV That Protects the North from the South," *Macleans* 21 January 1996. Gerald Hannon, "Snow on Your TV," *The Globe and Mail* (2 March 1999).

71. I. Angus and S. Jhally, *Cultural Politics in Contemporary America* (NY: Routledge, 1989).

72. Stephen Riggins, ed., *Ethnic Minority Media. An International Perspective* (Newbury Park, CA: Sage, 1992); Charles Husband, ed., *A Richer Vision: The Development of Ethnic Minority Media in Western Democracies* (Paris: Unesco, 1994).

73. Gill Bottomley, Marie de Lepervanche, and Jeannie Martin, *Intersexions: Gender/Race/Culture/Ethnicity* (Sydney: Allen & Unwin, 1991); John Beverley, *Subalternity and Representation* (Raleigh NC: Duke University Press, 1999).

Index